Mental Health
Law and Practice

MENTAL HEALTH LAW AND PRACTICE
CIVIL AND CRIMINAL ASPECTS

DARIUS WHELAN

B.C.L., LL.M. (N.U.I.), Ph.D. (Dub.), Barrister-at-Law
Lecturer in Law, University College Cork

ROUND HALL

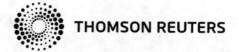

THOMSON REUTERS

Published in 2009 by
Thomson Reuters (Professional) Ireland Limited
(Registered in Ireland, Company No. 80867.
Registered Office and address for service:
43 Fitzwilliam Place, Dublin 2)
trading as Round Hall

Typeset by
Carrigboy Typesetting Services

Printed in England
by MPG Books, Bodmin, Cornwall.

ISBN 978-1-85800-510-2

A catalogue record for this book
is available from the British Library

To Anne Marie

FOREWORD

It has been said, with some justification, that mental health has been the poor relation of the Health Services over the years. Equally, it could be said that it is the poor relation in the protection of human rights, both in the field of legislation and in court decisions. This is probably a result of a number of factors, but undoubtedly among these is the fact that many suffering from mental illness are not able or competent to complain of abuse or wrongful detention, coupled with the fact that for many years social stigma attached to mental illness which meant that it was not talked about, but was quietly swept under the carpet and hidden away. Sadly much of this stigma still exists.

From the middle of the last century, the rights of mentally ill patients and the obligations of the medical profession and of the State to such patients was governed by the Mental Treatment Act 1945. Several attempts were made to challenge the constitutionality of portions of this Act, but they came to nothing. There were some amendments to the Act, but they did little to improve the lot of a mentally ill patient. It was not until the mid-1990s when two cases were taken against the State under the European Convention on Human Rights and pressure was brought by the European Commission of Human Rights that the legislature finally took action. The Mental Health Act 2001 was passed, which radically changed the legal requirements for involuntary admission of patients to mental hospitals and also provided a system of oversight and regulation of such patients similar to that which had been in force in the United Kingdom for many years. The appalling fact is that for some five years this legislation remained on the statute books without being in force and it was not until 2006 that the Minister for Health and Children made an Order bringing the substantial protections for patients contained in that Act into law. At about the same time the Oireachtas passed the Criminal Law (Insanity) Act, which had existed in the form of a Bill since 2002, and which dealt with patients detained in the Central Mental Hospital through the criminal law system as a separate category.

As a result of these Acts the rights of mentally ill patients, and indeed the obligations of psychiatric hospitals, changed dramatically almost overnight. Systems of regulation were put in place overseen by independent tribunals, patients who were involuntarily detained had legal advisors allocated to them, an up to date statutory test of fitness to plead was introduced, and a defence of diminished responsibility in murder cases became possible. Sudden legal changes such as these almost invariably lead to some initial confusion and differences of interpretation, many of which ultimately have to be clarified by the courts. Since 2006 a number of cases have come before the courts dealing with the application of both Acts to specific circumstances. For a busy psychiatrist or legal practitioner it can be difficult and time-consuming to research these decisions and a comprehensive and up-to-date account of them is of great importance.

This book fills that need. It is both comprehensive and up-to-date. More than that, it explains the new statutory provisions and the recent court interpretations of them in a lucid and readable form using extracts from judgments to illustrate the points rather than merely giving references to the decisions which the reader would have to research for himself. It is a book which should be a constant source of reference and information for both medical and legal practitioners. An important feature is that it also gives much practical advice as to the day to day operation of the Acts and advises medical practitioners as to the duty of care imposed on them by common law in relation to psychiatric patients, particularly when questions of consent arise.

One further category of persons will also benefit greatly. Members of Mental Health Tribunals under the 2001 Act and myself as Chairperson and my colleagues on the Mental Health (Criminal Law) Review Board have had to try to administer many of the provisions of both Acts with little guidance other than the, sometimes far from perfect, wording of the Acts themselves. This work is a source which both advises on the legal implications of our functions and should help us to avoid the undoubted pitfalls in applying the legislation. For this we will be grateful to Dr Whelan.

The book is also a reminder, if such be needed, that mentally ill patients are human beings, with the same basic rights and who are entitled to the same protections and remedies for abuse of those rights, as everybody else. For making this clear Dr Whelan is also to be congratulated.

Mr Justice Brian McCracken
Chairperson
Mental Health (Criminal Law) Review Board
October 2009

PREFACE

This book examines civil and criminal aspects of mental health law in Ireland, concentrating on the Mental Health Act 2001, the Criminal Law (Insanity) Act 2006 and the Scheme of the Mental Capacity Bill 2008. As there have now been more than 30 judgments concerning the recent legislation, it was decided to refer only briefly to the law which applied prior to the commencement of the new Acts. The aim has been to keep the book of manageable length, and concentrate on analysing the current law as much as possible. Parts 2 and 3 of the book concern civil aspects and criminal aspects respectively, but it should be noted that there is some overlap. For example, many of the legal provisions concerning treatment for a mental disorder in Chapter 10 apply to patients detained under the criminal legislation as well as to those detained under the Mental Health Act 2001, and cross-references between different chapters have been inserted as much as possible. I have endeavoured to state the law as of September 10, 2009. It has been possible at editorial stage to include some material on version 2 of the rules and codes of practice on ECT, seclusion and restraint, which were issued in October 2009.

I am grateful to the numerous Irish academics and practitioners who have written extensively in the area of mental health law and whose work is cited in footnotes throughout. Special acknowledgement in this regard is due to the books written by Patricia Casey, Tom Cooney, Ciarán Craven, Mary Donnelly, Harry Kennedy, Mary Keys, Finbarr McAuley, Paul McCutcheon, Tom O'Malley, Anne-Marie O'Neill and Orla O'Neill.

I wish to thank Mr Justice Brian McCracken for his thoughtful foreword, and Liam Fitzgerald of the Mental Health (Criminal Law) Review Board, for his help in arranging this. Many colleagues at U.C.C. were of assistance in various ways and I thank all of them, particularly Mary Donnelly, who volunteered her time for discussion of a number of chapters. David Gwynn Morgan collaborated with me on an earlier paper concerning Mental Health Tribunals, elements of which have been incorporated into this book. I also benefited from discussions with and support from Shane Kilcommins, Ursula Kilkelly, Maeve McDonagh, John Mee, Catherine O'Sullivan and Fidelma White. The research environment at U.C.C. is excellent and I am grateful for the sabbatical leave which enabled me to make substantial progress on this book. The law library staff—Helen Mulcahy, David Maguire and Mary Foley—were always helpful and facilitating. Maria Murphy provided invaluable research assistance.

For supply of information and/or fruitful discussion, I wish to thank Bríd Clarke, Gerry Cunningham and Rosemary Smyth of the Mental Health Commission, Noel Doherty of the Wards of Court office, Kerida Naidoo, Gerard Murphy, Niall Nolan, Michael Lynn, William Binchy, Áine Hynes, Mark Felton,

Hilda-Clare O'Shea, Finbarr Phelan, Maria Dillon, Roddy Tyrrell, Joan Doran, Keith Walsh, John Neville, Dara Robinson, Peter Connolly, Mairead Quigley, the Mental Health Lawyers Association, John Redican, Kris Gledhill, Anselm Eldergill, Phil Fennell, Suzanne Doyle, Louise Kennefick, Martin Lawlor, Pat O'Dea and Siobhán Barry. The team at Round Hall—Catherine Dolan, Frieda Donohue, Aisling Hanrahan and Kristiina Kojamo—were professional and committed to high standards.

My deepest personal thanks are due to Anne Marie Mullally, to whom this book is dedicated and who provided extraordinary support and encouragement. I am almost deeply indebted to the other members of the Whelan and Mullally families (too numerous to mention) and our children, Alice, Hugh and Cathal.

DARIUS WHELAN
November 6, 2009

CONTENTS

TABLE OF CASES

IRELAND

ENGLAND

NORTHERN IRELAND

SCOTLAND

UNITED STATES

CANADA

AUSTRALIA

EUROPEAN COURT OF JUSTICE

EUROPEAN COURT OF HUMAN RIGHTS

EUROPEAN COMMISSION OF HUMAN RIGHTS

HUMAN RIGHTS COMMITTEE

TABLE OF LEGISLATION

THE IRISH CONSTITUTION

IRISH STATUTES

IRISH STATUTORY INSTRUMENTS

PRE-UNION IRISH STATUTES

BRITISH PUBLIC STATUTES

UNITED KINGDOM STATUTORY INSTRUMENTS

EUROPEAN UNION DIRECTIVES

EUROPEAN CONVENTION ON HUMAN RIGHTS

CANADIAN STATUTES

AUSTRALIAN STATUTES

PART 1
GENERAL MATTERS

CHAPTER 1

PRINCIPLES OF MENTAL HEALTH LAW

CONSTITUTIONAL AND HUMAN RIGHTS IN MENTAL HEALTH LAW

1–01 Constitutional and human rights obviously take precedence over legislation and common law. It is therefore important to consider possible constitutional or human rights issues which may arise with each aspect of mental health law which is discussed. From a practical point of view, it is more straightforward to raise issues concerning the 1937 Constitution or the European Convention on Human Rights 1950 than to refer to other human rights instruments. All activities in the State are subject to the Constitution and courts must have regard to the Constitution in their decision-making. The European Convention on Human Rights Act 2003[1] permits arguments about the European Convention on Human Rights (ECHR) to be made in all courts (although a declaration of incompatibility may only be sought in the High Court[2]). In addition, all organs of the State[3] must perform their functions in a manner compatible with the State's obligations under the Convention provisions.[4] If a person disagrees with the interpretation of the ECHR by the Irish courts, they may continue on to Strasbourg for a definitive interpretation. They must have exhausted national remedies first (see further paras 2–02 to 2–04 below.)

Constitutional Rights

1–02 The list of constitutional rights which potentially affect the area of mental health is long, stretching from equality to freedom of expression and on to the right to a fair trial. In order to focus discussion, it is helpful to concentrate on the following rights: Liberty, Bodily Integrity and Autonomy.

---

[1] See Ursula Kilkelly (ed.), *ECHR and Irish Law*, 2nd edn (Bristol: Jordan, 2008); Paul Anthony McDermott & Mark William Murphy, "No revolution: the impact of the ECHR Act 2003 on Irish criminal law" (2008) 30 D.U.L.J. 1; Úna Ní Raifeartaigh, "The ECHR and the Criminal Justice System" (2007) 2 *Judicial Studies Institute Journal* 18; Donncha O'Connell, Siobhan Cummiskey and Emer Meeneghan with Paul O'Connell, *ECHR Act 2003: A Preliminary Assessment of Impact* (Dublin: Law Society and Dublin Solicitors Bar Association, 2006).

[2] The Attorney General and the Human Rights Commission must be notified before a court decides whether to make a declaration of incompatibility—s.6 of 2003 Act.

[3] "Organ of the State" includes a tribunal or any other body which is established by law or through which any of the legislative, executive or judicial powers of the State are exercised—s.1(1) of 2003 Act.

[4] European Convention on Human Rights Act 2003, s.3.

Liberty

1–03 Article 40.4.1° of the Constitution provides:

> No person shall be deprived of his personal liberty save in accordance with law.

While "law" was originally interpreted as meaning any ordinary legislation,[5] it was later interpreted very differently. In *King v Attorney General*, Henchy J. said that "save in accordance with law" meant, "without stooping to methods which ignore the fundamental norms of the legal order postulated by the Constitution."[6] The net effect of Art.40.4.1° is that there is a presumption that somebody should be at liberty and the courts will closely examine the legality of any deprivation of liberty.

The applicant in *Re Philip Clarke*[7] argued that s.165 of the Mental Treatment Act 1945 (concerning detention by a garda) was unconstitutional due to the absence of any judicial intervention or determination between the taking into custody of the person alleged to be of unsound mind and his or her subsequent detention under a reception order. He relied on various articles of the Constitution, including the right to liberty.[8] The Supreme Court held that s.165 was not unconstitutional, as it was designed for the protection of the citizen and the promotion of the common good. O'Byrne J. said that the legislation was "of a paternal character, clearly intended for the care and custody of persons suspected to be suffering from mental infirmity and for the safety and well-being of the public generally."[9] (See further paras 1–55 to 1–62 below).

1–04 It is notable that there were no further constitutional challenges to the 1945 Act between 1950 and 1995. No person detained under the 1945 Act argued, for example, that the Act was unconstitutional because it failed to provide for periodic review, by a tribunal or court, of the continuing justification for detention. The lack of challenges may have been due to the general lack of legal representation by patients. Those patients who did have representation tended to take civil actions for damages instead.[10]

1–05 In 1995, a strong High Court decision was issued by Costello P., declaring that s.207 of the 1945 Act (which governed transfers from an ordinary mental hospital to the Central Mental Hospital) was unconstitutional, as it interfered

---

[5] See for example *R. (O'Connell) v Military Governor of Hare Park Camp* [1924] 2 I.R. 104; Majority in *State (Ryan) v Lennon* [1935] I.R. 170.

[6] [1981] I.R. 233 at 257.

[7] [1950] I.R. 235.

[8] The right to liberty in Art.40.4 was cited in legal argument in the Supreme Court (see [1950] I.R. 235 at 242–4.)

[9] [1950] I.R. 235 at 247.

[10] See the various cases taken under s.260 of the 1945 Act, referred to at para.2–52 below.

[11] *R.T. v Director of Central Mental Hospital* [1995] 2 I.R. 65. For a full account of s.207 of the

with a person's constitutional right to liberty.[11] Section 207 was defective because there were no procedures for patients to review the Inspector of Mental Hospital's opinion,[12] to procure their re-transfer or liberty, or to review their continued detention. Costello P. concluded that the section not only fell far short of internationally accepted standards but was unconstitutional. The State had failed to adequately protect the right to liberty of temporary patients, who had "a right to liberty, at most, eighteen months after the reception order which restricted their liberty was made."[13] The President of the High Court said that the State was obviously searching for an ideal solution to the problems with mental health legislation, but this "prolonged search for excellence … has had most serious consequences for the applicant."[14] Quoting Voltaire, the President said, "the best is the enemy of the good".[15]

Having found that s.207 was unconstitutional, Costello P. was obliged by Art.40.4.3 of the Constitution to refer the question of the validity of the section up to the Supreme Court by way of case stated. However, by the time the case reached the Supreme Court, the patient had already been transferred back from the Cental Mental Hospital to an ordinary mental hospital. The case stated lapsed, which meant that s.207 still remained on the statute books until its repeal came into effect in 2006.[16] The State did not transfer back all the other patients who were detained in the Central Mental Hospital under s.207.[17] By transferring one patient back to an ordinary mental hospital, the State succeeded in postponing much-needed reforms in transfer procedures.[18]

1–06 The most significant constitutional case concerning the 1945 Act was *Croke v Smith (No.2)*, decided in 1995–1996.[19] In the High Court, Budd J. found

---

    1945 Act and the *R.T.* case, see Darius Whelan, "Criminal charges against mental patients" (1995) 5 Ir. Crim.L.J. 67.

[12] Under s.207(2) of the Mental Treatment Act, 1945, as amended, the Minister for Health and Children ordered the Inspector of Mental Hospitals to visit the person and report on their condition. After this, the Minister made the decision whether to make the transfer to the Central Mental Hospital.

[13] [1995] 2 I.R. 65 at 80.

[14] [1995] 2 I.R. 65 at 81.

[15] Voltaire, "La Bégueule" in *Contes en Vers et en Prose II* (1772, reprinted by Classiques Garnier, Paris 1993), p.339; based on an old Italian proverb. This quote is given in French by Budd J. in *Croke v Smith (No.2)*, High Court, July 27 and 31, 1995 at p.128.

[16] Section 207 of the 1945 Act was repealed by s.6 of the Mental Health Act 2001, which came into force on November 1, 2006.

[17] In November 1997, 11 patients were still being held in the CMH under s.207—Department of Health, *Report of the Inspector of Mental Hospitals 1997*, p.18. By November 2004 the number had fallen to five: Mental Health Commission, *Annual Report 2004, including the Report of the Inspector of Mental Health Services* (Dublin, 2005), p.499.

[18] Similarly, the State avoided many legal problems by releasing the applicant in *State (Toohey) v Governor Central Mental Hospital*, Supreme Court, March 28, 1968.

[19] *Croke v Smith* (No.2) Budd J. July 27 and 31, 1995; Supreme Court, July 31, 1996: [1998] 1 I.R. 101.

that one of the core sections of the Act, s.172, was an unconstitutional interference with the right to liberty. However, this judgment was overruled by the Supreme Court.

Croke brought an application under Art.40.4 of the Constitution, challenging his detention and the constitutionality of s.172 of the 1945 Act on two main grounds—firstly, that there was no provision for a judicial intervention and process when a patient was being detained and secondly, that the detention was indefinite and there was no independent review procedure. Budd J. delivered a detailed judgment on these points: *Croke v Smith (No.2).*[20] Budd J. had no difficulty in finding that Croke had locus standi to challenge the constitutionality of his detention.[21] Budd J. also considered the role of the ECHR and the general principles of international law, concluding that while these were influential guidelines, they could not be used as a touchstone with regard to constitutionality. The judge referred to United States cases such as *Addington v Texas,*[22] *O'Connor v Donaldson*[23] and *Jackson v Indiana*[24] to illustrate how seriously the courts in that jurisdiction had taken the need for a judicial process before citizens could be detained in mental hospitals.

Having been referred to *Re Philip Clarke,*[25] he acknowledged that he was bound by the decision of the Supreme Court but said that the decision solely concerned s.165 of the 1945 Act, which was not at issue in this case. Also, there had been changes since that case:

> "The certainties implicit in the judgment in Clarke's case in 1949 may be diluted by now with increasing knowledge about the psyche, changing patterns of behaviour, conflicts between psychiatrists as to the nature of mental illness and awareness of the abuses of psychiatric treatment in other countries."[26]

1–07 Budd J. relied heavily on the judgment of Costello P. in *R.T. v Director of Central Mental Hospital* and eventually concluded that s.172 of the 1945 Act was an unconstitutional interference with the patient's right to liberty, as there were no adequate safeguards to protect the patient against an error in the section's operation, there was no formal review procedure in respect of the opinion of the resident medical superintendent and of the Inspector of Mental Hospitals and there was no automatic review of long-term detention of a patient

---

[20] High Court, July 27 and 31, 1995.
[21] The State had argued that Croke did not have locus standi because there was no argument in his application suggesting that he was a suitable person to be discharged from a mental hospital and he had not availed of the existing procedures for review of his situation, such as the making of representations to the President of the High Court or the Inspector of Mental Hospitals. A lengthy list of safeguards of mental patients' interests is provided in Budd J.'s judgment at pp.92–96.
[22] 441 U.S. 418 (1979).
[23] 422 U.S. 563 (1975).
[24] 406 U.S. 715 (1972).
[25] [1950] I.R. 235.
[26] *Croke v Smith (No.2)*, Budd J., High Court, July 27 and 31, 1995, p.124.

such as Croke. As he had decided the issue of constitutionality of s.172 on this ground, he opted to "exercise reticence" and did not express a view on the other ground put forward, namely that other sections of the Act were unconstitutional due to the lack of judicial or quasi-judicial intervention prior to the reception and detention of a patient. He then made a case stated to the Supreme Court, as required by Art.40.4.3.

This judgment treated the issue of detention of mental patients with the seriousness it deserved and Budd J.'s conclusion that s.172 of the 1945 Act was unconstitutional could have had far-reaching implications for mental health law. It might even have spurred the Government into enacting a new Mental Health Act.

1–08 But the potential contained in Budd J.'s judgment was extinguished by the judgment of the Supreme Court, delivered in 1996. The court pointed out that s.172 of the 1945 Act enjoyed a presumption of constitutionality and that it must be presumed that people who issue decisions under the Act will act in accordance with constitutional justice. The court twice reproduced the Supreme Court's view in *Re Philip Clarke*[27] that the 1945 Act "is of a paternal character, clearly intended for the care and custody of persons suspected of suffering from mental infirmity and for the safety and well-being of the public generally."[28] The Supreme Court was obviously not impressed by Budd J.'s view that "the certainties implicit in the judgment in Clarke's case in 1949 may be diluted by now."[29] While the Supreme Court quoted from Costello P.'s judgment in *R.T. v Director of Central Mental Hospital*,[30] it did not believe that the lack of automatic review of a patient's detention interfered with the patient's personal rights or right to liberty.[31] In fact, the Supreme Court stated that many of the sections of the 1945 Act vindicated and protected citizens' rights.[32]

1–09 The Supreme Court rejected the argument that periodic judicial or quasi-judicial intervention was required after the patient's detention, relying heavily on the judgment of O'Flaherty J. in *Keady v An Garda Síochána*.[33] In that case, O'Flaherty J. quoted Kenny J.'s list of the characteristic features of the

[27] [1950] I.R. 235 at 247.
[28] In the Supreme Court judgment in *Croke (No.2)*, this extract appears in [1998] 1 I.R. 101 at p.112 and p.132 of the report.
[29] *Croke v Smith (No.2)*, Budd J., High Court, July 27 and 31, 1995, p.124.
[30] See Supreme Court, [1998] 1 I.R. 101, at pp.117–118 and p.123—the court "must be particularly astute when depriving or continuing to deprive a citizen suffering from mental disorder of his/her liberty."
[31] The court adds, "If, however, it were to be shown in some future case, that there had been a systematic failure in the existing safeguards, and that the absence of such a system of automatic review was a factor in such failure, that might cause this court to hold that a person affected by such failure was being deprived of his constitutional rights." ([1998] 1 I.R. 101 at 131).
[32] For example—[1998] 1 I.R. 101 at 114–5 and 119–120.
[33] [1992] 2 I.R. 197.
[34] [1965] I.R. 217.

administration of justice in *McDonald v Bord na gCon (No.2)*[34] and emphasised that there must be a *contest between parties*. The tribunal of inquiry involved in the *Keady* case "was not a contest between parties; it was, as its name says, an inquiry."[35] Hamilton C.J. in *Croke (No.2)* stated that the resident medical superintendent and the Minister for Health, in exercising the powers conferred on them by the 1945 Act,[36] were obliged to enquire into the mental health of the patient and the necessity for their detention under care and treatment. The court believed that "the nature of this inquiry is not '*a contest between parties*' and does not involve a dispute or controversy as to the exercise of legal rights or a violation of the law. It is simply an inquiry."[37] No judicial intervention was necessary. Automatic review by an independent review board as provided for in the Health (Mental Services) Act 1981 "may be desirable"[38] but the failure to provide for such review did not render the 1945 Act constitutionally flawed. The resident medical superintendent was obliged regularly and constantly to review a patient in order to ensure that they had not recovered and was a proper person to be detained. In so doing, the resident medical superintendent must act in accordance with the principles of constitutional justice. "There is no suggestion that such a review is not carried out."[39] The Supreme Court made no reference to the ECHR, the *Winterwerp* case,[40] the Green Paper and White Paper on Mental Health,[41] or the *O'Reilly* case before the European Commission on Human Rights.[42]

1–10 The *Croke* decision effectively overruled the reasoning of Costello P. in *R.T.* to the effect that there should be adequate safeguards in the 1945 Act to prevent against abuse and error. Hamilton C.J. relied on the fact that medical professionals would periodically review the detention of patients as adequate protection of their constitutional right to liberty, thus adopting the approach that medical decision-making would be assumed to be correct and did not require review by external bodies. He referred uncritically to other sections in the legislation which appeared to provide avenues for complaint by patients, without any regard to the possibility that these sections might be of little use in practice. The decision was a major setback for the rights of patients detained under the 1945 Act. It would be another 10 years before automatic periodic review of

---

[35]   [1992] 2 I.R. 197 at 211.
[36]   E.g. the power of discharge in s.218 and s.220; the Minister's power of discharge under s.222. The court also appears to be referring to the role of the resident medical superintendent in *detaining* the patient as well. The two issues of detention and review after detention are not clearly separated in the judgment.
[37]   [1998] 1 I.R. 101 at 129.
[38]   [1998] 1 I.R. 101 at 131.
[39]   [1998] 1 I.R. 101 at 132.
[40]   *Winterwerp v Netherlands*, Series A, No. 33, judgment October 24, 1979, (1979–80) 2 E.H.R.R. 387. See para.1–23 below.
[41]   Department of Health, *Green Paper on Mental Health* (Dublin: Stationery Office, 1992); Department of Health, *A New Mental Health Act: White Paper* (Dublin: Stationery Office, 1995).
[42]   Application No. 24196/94, *O'Reilly v Ireland* (1996) D.R. 84–A p.72 and Friendly settlement of December 3, 1996. See para.4–22 below.

detention was required by law, whereas if the court had decided differently the Oireachtas would have been obliged to introduce the legislation immediately.

The manner of application of the presumption of constitutionality in *Croke* has been queried, since, "if not carefully employed, it might serve to gloss substantive defects in the statute itself."[43] Hogan has characterised the decision as an example of "result-oriented jurisprudence".[44] It was recently relied on to justify the detention without independent review of a patient with an infectious form of tuberculosis.[45]

1–11 One final curious point about the *Croke (No.2)* case is that on two occasions the court makes substantive errors in quoting from the applicable legislation. Generally, the court is careful to include amendments to the 1945 Act stated in the main body of the Mental Treatment Act 1961 but at the time the judgment was delivered it appears to have ignored s.42 of the 1961 Act and its second schedule. In the unreported version of the judgment at pp.46–47, the court quotes the entire of s.238 of the 1945 Act,[46] even though that section was repealed in 1961.[47] Similarly, at pp.27–28 of the unreported version, the court fails to note that s.208(4) of the 1945 Act[48] was repealed in 1961. The court's use of the section and subsection involved contributes, if only slightly, to the court's view that there are so many safeguards built in to the mental treatment legislation that patients' constitutional rights are protected. Both of these Amendments were noted in the Index of Statutes available at the time of the *Croke (No.2)* decision. In the official report of the case, these defects have been remedied.[49] On a less serious note, the Supreme Court also fails to note the various adaptations of sections of the mental treatment legislation brought about by the Mental Treatment Acts (Adaptation) Order 1971.[50]

---

[43] Gerard Hogan & Gerry Whyte, *J.M. Kelly: The Irish Constitution*, 4th edn (Dublin: Butterworths, 2003), p.858.

[44] Gerard Hogan, "A good and kindly man devoted to public duty", *Irish Times*, December 1, 2000.

[45] *V.T.S. v Health Service Executive, Mercy Hospital and Others* [2009] I.E.H.C. 106; High Court, Edwards J., February 11, 2009.

[46] Section 238 provided that where the Inspector of Mental Hospitals visited any mental institution, they should give special attention to the state of mind of any patient detained therein, the propriety of whose detention they doubted or had been requested by the patient themselves or any other person to examine.

[47] Budd J. in the High Court at p.58 noted the repeal of s.208(4).

[48] Section 208(4) stated that where a person was removed from a mental institution under s.208, a report should be given to the Minister within three days.

[49] [1998] 1 I.R. 101 at 127 (substitution of s.237 as amended for s.238) and 119 (s.208(4) omitted).

[50] S.I. No. 108 of 1971. For example, at p.119 the Supreme Court quotes s.208(1) of the 1945 Act without the adaptations made by the 1971 Statutory Instrument. On a further minor issue, the Supreme Court also refers a number of times to the involvement of hospital visiting committees in the mental health system, even though visiting committees were abolished by the Health Act 1970. While s.3 and s.81 of the 1970 Act removed most references to visiting committees from the 1945 Act, references in s.237 and s.266 were not removed. Thus, the court quotes s.237 and s.266 accurately.

1–12 Mr Croke took his case to Europe and received an undisclosed sum of money in friendly settlement as compensation from the Irish Government.[51] By the time of the settlement, the Government had published its new Mental Health Bill (which would later become the Mental Health Act 2001) and this was acknowledged as part of the terms of the settlement.

1–13 In *S.M. v Mental Health Commission*,[52] McMahon J., referring to detention under the Mental Health Act 2001, stated that it must be remembered that what is at stake is the liberty of the individual and while it is true that no constitutional right is absolute, and a person may be deprived of their liberty "in accordance with the law", such statutory provisions which attempt to detain a person or restrict their liberty must be narrowly construed.[53] He also stated that the approach to an interpretation of a section of the 2001 Act should be that which is most favourable to the patient while yet achieving the object of the Act.[54]

1–14 In the context of bail applications, the Supreme Court has on two occasions categorically stated that the likelihood of commission of future offences while on bail is not admissible as a ground to refuse bail.[55] It has also been held that preventative detention is not permissible after a trial has taken place.[56] In the context of mental health, it was held in *Application of Gallagher (No.2)*[57] that preventative detention would be unconstitutional. Laffoy J. said:

> "[T]o construe s. 2, sub-s. 2 of the Act of 1883 as permitting detention while a person is dangerous but not mentally ill would be to construe it as permitting deprivation of liberty for the purpose of preventing possible future criminal activity or deviant behaviour, in other words, preventive detention, which is a construction which is impermissible under the Constitution *(The People (Attorney General) v. O'Callaghan* [1966] I.R. 501 and *Ryan v. Director of Public Prosecutions* [1989] I.R. 399) and cannot have been intended by the Supreme Court."[58]

---

[51] *Croke v Ireland*, European Court of Human Rights (Fourth Section), Application Number 33267/96, Admissibility Decision, June 15, 1999 and Judgment (Striking out), December 21, 2000; [1999] 1 M.H.L.R. 118.

[52] [2008] I.E.H.C. 441; [2009] 2 I.L.R.M. 127; McMahon J., High Court, October 31, 2008.

[53] [2009] 2 I.L.R.M. 127 at 139.

[54] [2009] 2 I.L.R.M. 127 at 139.

[55] *People (Attorney General) v O'Callaghan* [1966] I.R. 501; *Ryan v DPP* [1989] I.R. 399.

[56] *People (DPP) v Jackson*, Court of Criminal Appeal, April 26, 1993; *People (DPP) v Bambrick* [1996] 1 I.R. 265; *People (DPP) v M.C.*, Central Criminal Court, Flood J., June 16, 1995 (see para.19–18 below).

[57] [1996] 3 I.R. 10.

[58] [1996] 3 I.R. 10 at 34.

Bodily Integrity

1–15 The right to bodily integrity was established as an unenumerated right in *Ryan v Attorney General*.[59] There has also been brief reference to a "right to health" in *Heeney v Dublin Corporation*.[60]

In *State (C.) v Frawley*, there was psychiatric evidence that the applicant had a personality trait disturbance of a sociopathic type. Finlay P. said that when the Executive imprisons an individual in pursuance of a lawful warrant of a court, then it seemed to him to be a logical extension of the principle laid down in the *Ryan* case[61] on bodily integrity that it may not, without justification or necessity, expose the health of that person to risk or danger.[62] (See further para.12–09 below). The case established the principle that freedom from torture and inhumane or degrading treatment or punishment could be raised as part of an argument concerning bodily integrity, although on the facts Finlay P. found that the applicant's constitutional rights had not been breached.

1–16 Hamilton C.J. stated in *Re A Ward of Court (No.2)*[63] that the loss by an individual of their mental capacity does not result in any diminution of their personal rights recognised by the Constitution, including the right to life, the right to bodily integrity, the right to privacy, including self-determination, and the right to refuse medical care or treatment. The ward was entitled to have all these rights respected, defended, vindicated and protected from unjust attack and they are in no way lessened or diminished by reason of her incapacity. The ward had unenumerated rights to privacy, self-determination and bodily integrity, which meant that if she were mentally competent she could refuse to consent to further treatment. See further para.10–11 below.

1–17 As the state has a duty to respect and vindicate persons' rights to bodily integrity, it would appear to follow that it has a duty to care for patients who are in need of care. This has not been explicitly based on the constitutional right to bodily integrity in the case law, but it might be a factor in a future case. The courts are normally content to refer to the duty of care in tort as justifying actions taken to protect the health or safety of patients. For example, in *M.McN. v Health Service Executive*,[64] Peart J. found that the fact that a psychiatric unit was locked, even for voluntary patients, was reasonable because the patients could not look after themselves unaided. The Health Service Executive owed a duty of care to the patients. He continued:

---

[59] [1965] I.R. 294.
[60] [1998] I.E.S.C. 26; Supreme Court, *ex tempore*, August 17, 1998 per O'Flaherty J. at para.16.
[61] *Ryan v Attorney General* [1965] I.R. 294.
[62] [1976] I.R. 365 at 372.
[63] [1996] 2 I.R. 79 at 126.
[64] [2009] I.E.H.C. 236; High Court, Peart J., May 15, 2009. See also *C.C. v Clinical Director of St. Patrick's Hospital (No.1)* [2009] I.E.H.C. 13 (below, paras 4–38 to 4–41), where McMahon J. referred to possible breach of duty which might attract liability under the neighbour principle.

"Also, it would be grossly negligent for the hospital, following the required revocation of the admission/renewal order, to immediately bring these vulnerable patients to the front door of the hospital, lead them down the steps and to pavement and say to them 'we no longer have any legal basis for keeping you in hospital, so off you go—home or wherever you can'. How could such an appalling vista be within the contemplation of an Act such as this which has at its heart the best interests of vulnerable patients?"[65]

1–18 The right to bodily integrity is specifically referred to in s.4(3) of the Mental Health Act 2001. This subsection states that, in making a decision under the 2001 Act concerning the care or treatment of a person (including a decision to make an admission order in relation to a person), due regard shall be given to the need to respect the right of the person to dignity, bodily integrity, privacy and autonomy.

Autonomy

1–19 The unenumerated right to autonomy or self-determination was first recognised in *Re A Ward of Court (No.2)*[66] and later referred to in *North Western Health Board v H.W. and C.W.*[67] and *J.M. v Board of Management of St Vincent's Hospital.*[68] It has recently been confirmed by Laffoy J. in *Fitzpatrick & Ryan v F.K. & Attorney General (No.2).*[69] These cases are discussed below at paras 10–11 to 10–19. Donnelly has noted that there has been little analysis in the case law of how rights such as autonomy, life, dignity, equality and privacy are envisaged to operate and how they interact with each other. On the specific matter of the right of autonomy, there has been little exploration of what the right means and how it should be protected.[70]

Autonomy is referred to in s.4(3) of the Mental Health Act 2001 as one of the rights which applies when making decisions under the Act. Significant issues arise in seeking to balance the best interests principle in s.4(1) with the patient's right to autonomy in s.4(3)—see further para.1–62 below.

ECHR Rights

1–20 The main Articles of the ECHR which are relevant to mental health law are arts 5, 6, 3 and 8. Case law concerning these articles will be referred to throughout this book. In this chapter, a brief overview of the main cases is

---

[65] [2009] I.E.H.C. 236; High Court, Peart J., May 15, 2009, p.37. See further paras 5–38 to 5–40 below.
[66] [1996] 2 I.R. 79.
[67] [2001] 3 I.R. 622.
[68] [2003] 1 I.R. 321.
[69] [2008] I.E.H.C. 104; High Court, Laffoy J., April 25, 2008.
[70] Mary Donnelly, "The Right of Autonomy in Irish Law" (2008) 14 (2) *Medico-Legal Journal of Ireland* 34 at 35.

provided. Extensive literature is available on the role of the ECHR in mental health law.[71]

1–21 The ECHR had a major influence on how the Mental Health Act 2001 and Criminal Law (Insanity) Act 2006 were drafted and it also impacted on amendments made during the Oireachtas debates concerning the legislation. For example, the original version of the Criminal Law (Insanity) Bill 2002 allowed a prison to be classified as a "designated centre" for the purposes of the Bill but this possibility was removed due to concerns about its compatibility with the ECHR.

1–22 It should also be noted that, when arguments are being presented to a court, the normal practice is to make ECHR arguments in parallel with arguments concerning constitutional rights. Practitioners often argue that a particular set of facts breached both constitutional rights and ECHR rights.

Article 5—The Right to Liberty and Security

1–23 Article 5(1) states that everyone has the right to liberty and security of the person and that no one shall be deprived of their liberty save in certain listed circumstances and in accordance with a procedure prescribed by law. The list of circumstances includes art.5(1)(e), "the lawful detention of persons for prevention of the spread of infectious diseases, of persons of unsound mind, alcoholics or drug addicts or vagrants". The case law concerning the meaning of art.5(1) includes, for example, *Winterwerp v The Netherlands*[72] in which it was held that, except in emergency cases, the decision to detain a "person of unsound mind" must be supported by objective medical expertise, the mental disorder must be serious enough to warrant compulsory confinement and the validity of confinement must be based on the persistence of the disorder.[73] These have come to be known as the "Winterwerp Principles". In *Aerts v Belgium*[74] it was held that there must be some relationship between the ground of permitted deprivation of liberty and the place and conditions of detention. The court stated

---

[71] Peter Bartlett, Oliver Lewis and Oliver Thorold, *Mental Disability and the European Convention on Human Rights* (Leiden: Martinus Nijhoff, 2006); Brenda Hale, "The Human Rights Act and Mental Health Law: Has it Helped?" (2007) J. Mental Health L. 7; Philip Fennell, "The Third Way in Mental Health Policy: Negative Rights, Positive Rights, and the Convention" (1999) 26 *Journal of Law and Society* 103. Lawrence Gostin, "Human Rights of Persons With Mental Disabilities: The European Convention of Human Rights" (2000) 23 Int. J. L. & Psychiatry 125; Pauline Prior, "Mentally disordered offenders and the European Court of Human Rights" (2007) 30 *International Journal of Law and Psychiatry* 546; Mental Disability Advocacy Centre, *Summaries of Mental Disability Cases Decided by the European Court of Human Rights* (2007).

[72] (1979–80) 2 E.H.R.R. 387.

[73] (1979–80) 2 E.H.R.R. 387, para.39.

[74] (1998) 29 E.H.R.R. 50.

that in principle the detention of a person as a mental patient will only be lawful if effected in a hospital, clinic or other appropriate institution.[75]

1–24 Article 5(2) states that everyone who is arrested shall be informed promptly, in a language which they understand, of the reasons for their arrest and of any charge against them. In *Van der Leer v The Netherlands*[76] it was held that art.5(2) applies to a detention of a person of unsound mind, in spite of the reference to "arrest".[77] The court stated that it was not unmindful of the criminal law connotation of the words used in art.5(2). However, it agreed with the Commission that they should be interpreted "autonomously", in particular in accordance with the aim and purpose of art.5, which are to protect everyone from arbitrary deprivations of liberty.

1–25 Article 5(4) provides that everyone who is deprived of their liberty by arrest or detention shall be entitled to take proceedings by which the lawfulness of their detention shall be decided speedily by a court and their release ordered if the detention is not lawful. The "court" need not be defined as a court in national law provided it is independent of the executive, independent of the parties to the case and has a judicial character. In Ireland, the Mental Health Tribunal would qualify as a "court" for the purposes of art.5(4). The European Court of Human Rights held in *X. v United Kingdom*[78] that a review by way of habeas corpus procedure was not sufficient for a continuing confinement. As art.5(4) refers to a patient's right to take proceedings by which the lawfulness of detention may be decided "speedily", the Strasbourg court has found breaches of the Convention where there have been delays of 24 days,[79] 5 weeks,[80] 8 weeks[81] and 5 months.[82] In *Rakevich v Russia*[83] it was held that the detainee's access to the court should not depend on the good will of the detaining authority.

---

[75] (1998) 29 E.H.R.R. 50, para. 46.

[76] (1990) 12 E.H.R.R. 567.

[77] (1990) 12 E.H.R.R. 567, para.27.

[78] *X. v United Kingdom*, Application No.7215/75, judgment November 5, 1981 (1981) 4 E.H.R.R. 188.

[79] *L.R. v France*, Application No.33395/96, judgment June 27, 2002, available only in French.

[80] *Laidin v France*, Application No.43191/98, judgment November 5, 2002, available only in French.

[81] *E. v Norway* (1994) 17 E.H.R.R. 30. Eight weeks elapsed between the application for judicial review to the Oslo City Court and the eventual decision. The delay was caused partly by the fact that the application was made during court vacation, and partly by the judge taking three weeks to issue the decision. No compensation was awarded to Mr E.

[82] *Van der Leer v The Netherlands* (1990) 12 E.H.R.R. 567. There was a five-month delay between an application for release and a decision to release the patient. The court stated that it was irrelevant that the patient absconded and that she was granted probationary leave during this period.

[83] [2004] M.H.L.R. 37.

1–26 Article 5(5) states that everyone who has been the victim of arrest or detention in contravention of the provisions of art.5 shall have an enforceable right to compensation. In the English case of *K.B.*,[84] damages of between £750 and £4,000 were awarded to seven patients for delays in their hearings coming before tribunals. The damages were based on the patients' loss of liberty, frustration, distress and damage to mental health.

Article 6—Right to a Fair Trial

1–27 Article 6(1) states that in the determination of their civil rights and obligations or of any criminal charge against them, everyone is entitled to a fair and public hearing within a reasonable time by an independent and impartial tribunal established by law. According to art.6(2), everyone charged with a criminal offence shall be presumed innocent until proved guilty according to law. Article 6(3) contains a number of other fair trial rights for those charged with criminal offences, including a person's right to be informed promptly, in a language which they understand, and in detail, of the nature and cause of the accusation against them; to have adequate time and facilities for the preparation of their defence; to defend themselves in person or through legal assistance of their own choosing or, if they do not have sufficient means to pay for legal assistance, to be given it free when the interests of justice so require; and to examine or have examined witnesses against them.

1–28 The court has held that the procedural guarantees under art.5(1) and (4) are broadly similar to those under art.6(1) of the Convention. In a civil case which does not involve detention, a person with mental disorder may apply art.6(1), as the case involves their civil rights and obligations. It was held that art.6(1) was breached in *Shtukaturov v Russia*[85], where the applicant had been declared legally incapable by a court on the application of his mother. He was not present or represented at the hearing, which lasted 10 minutes. The decision deprived the applicant of his capacity to act independently in almost all areas of life: he was no longer able to sell or buy any property on his own, to work, to travel, to choose his place of residence, to join associations, to marry, etc. See further para.13–19 below.

1–29 There have also been a number of cases concerning the burden of proof in criminal proceedings. In *H. v U.K.*,[86] the Commission found that the burden of proof in insanity cases did not breach the presumption of innocence in

---

[84] *R v MHRT ex parte K.B.* [2003] E.W.H.C. Admin. 193; [2004] Q.B. 936.
[85] [2008] M.H.L.R. 238.
[86] Application No. 15023/89, European Commission of Human Rights (1990).
[87] Application No. 20858/92, European Commission of Human Rights, May 5 1993. See also *R. v Lambert, Ali & Jordan* [2002] Q.B. 1112.
[88] Application No.62960/00; [2003] M.H.L.R. 292. See also *R. v H. (Fitness to Plead)* [2003] U.K.H.L. 1; [2003] 1 W.L.R. 411; [2003] 1 M.H.L.R. 209.

art.6(2). Similarly, the burden of proof in diminished responsibility cases was upheld in *Robinson v UK*.[87] It has also been held in *Antoine v UK*[88] that a "trial of the facts" in fitness to plead cases does not engage art.6 as it is not a determination of a criminal charge.[89]

Article 3—Prohibition of Torture

1–30 Article 3 states that no one shall be subjected to torture or inhuman or degrading treatment or punishment. The behaviour complained of must reach a minimum level of severity to engage Art.3.[90] While intention to degrade is relevant to the threshold, it is not determinative; ill treatment may breach art.3 even if there is no intent to do so.[91]

1–31 In *Herczegfalvy v Austria*[92] the court considered that the position of inferiority and powerlessness which is typical of patients confined in psychiatric hospitals calls for increased vigilance in reviewing whether the Convention has been complied with. The court added that the established principles of medicine are in principle decisive in such cases; as a general rule, a measure which is a therapeutic necessity cannot be regarded as inhuman or degrading. The court must nevertheless satisfy itself that the medical necessity has been convincingly shown to exist.[93] The court found that art.3 had not been breached, even though the applicant's treatment included being force-fed, handcuffed to a bed and forcibly injected.

1–32 In the English case of *R. (Wilkinson) v Broadmoor Special Hospital Authority*[94] it was held that the requirement in *Herczegfalvy* that the medical necessity be "convincingly shown" to exist required a proper hearing on the merits, thus changing the question for the court from one of procedure to one of substance.[95] On the facts, the patient's later application to the Strasbourg Court was found to be inadmissible.[96]

---

[89]   However, the court did consider the applicability of art.5(1) to the detention of the applicant after the trial of the facts and found that he had been detained following proceedings which offered the strong procedural guarantees of a fair, public and adversarial hearing before an independent tribunal and with full legal representation.

[90]   Peter Bartlett, Oliver Lewis and Oliver Thorold, *Mental Disability and the European Convention on Human Rights* (Leiden: Martinus Nijhoff, 2006), p.77.

[91]   *Peers v Greece* (2001) 33 E.H.R.R. 51, para.74; *Price v U.K.* (2001) 34 E.H.R.R. 1285, para.30; Peter Bartlett, Oliver Lewis & Oliver Thorold, *Mental Disability and the European Convention on Human Rights* (2006), p.78.

[92]   (1992) 15 E.H.R.R. 437.

[93]   (1992) 15 E.H.R.R. 437 at para.82.

[94]   [2002] 1 W.L.R. 419; [2001] E.W.C.A. Civ. 1545.

[95]   Peter Bartlett & Raph Sandland, *Mental Health Law: Policy and Practice*, 3rd edn (Oxford: Oxford University Press, 2007), pp.309–312.

[96]   *Wilkinson v. United Kingdom* [2006] M.H.L.R. 144.

Article 8—Right to Respect for Private and Family Life

1–33 Article 8(1) states that everyone has the right to respect for their private and family life, their home and correspondence. Article 8(2) permits interference by a public authority with the exercise of this right if it is in accordance with law and is necessary in a democratic society in the interests of national security, public safety or the economic well-being of the country, for the prevention of disorder or crime, for the protection of health or morals, or for the protection of the rights and freedoms of others.

"Private life" includes a person's physical and psychological integrity and therefore a compulsory medical intervention, even if it is of minor importance, constitutes an interference with this right.[97] Such intervention must therefore at the very least be in accordance with law, which means that it is either authorised by statute or by common law. The law must be accessible and sufficiently precise so as to allow an individual to regulate his or her conduct. Detainees are in a particularly vulnerable position and must be protected against arbitrary interferences with their privacy.[98]

1–34 The Strasbourg Court said in *Pretty v United Kingdom*[99] that the notion of personal autonomy is an important principle underlying the interpretation of the guarantees in art.8.[100] In *Storck v Germany*,[101] the treatment given to the applicant was not lawful under domestic law and so the court did not have to consider whether it was medically necessary.[102] The court did not need to determine whether the applicant's treatment had been *lege artis*,[103] as, irrespective of this, it had been carried out against her will and already therefore constituted an interference with her right to respect for private life.[104] See further para.10–23 below.

1–35 In *Shtukaturov v Russia*[105] the court noted that the interference with the applicant's private life in incapacitation proceedings was very serious. As a result of his incapacitation, the applicant became fully dependant on his official guardian in almost all areas of life. The court stated that, "the existence of a mental disorder, even a serious one, cannot be the sole reason to justify full incapacitation."[106] By analogy with the cases concerning deprivation of liberty,

---

[97] *Y.F. v Turkey* (2004) 39 E.H.R.R. 34, para.33; *Storck v Germany* (2006) 43 E.H.R.R. 6, para.143.

[98] *Y.F. v Turkey* (2004) 39 E.H.R.R. 34, para.43.

[99] *Pretty v United Kingdom* (2002) 35 E.H.R.R. 1.

[100] *Pretty v United Kingdom* (2002) 35 E.H.R.R. 1., para.61.

[101] (2006) 43 E.H.R.R. 6.

[102] Brenda Hale, "The Human Rights Act and Mental Health Law: Has it Helped?" (2007) J. Mental Health L. 7 at 16.

[103] According to the law of the art (medicine).

[104] (2006) 43 E.H.R.R. 6, para.144.

[105] [2008] M.H.L.R. 238.

[106] [2008] M.H.L.R. 238, para.94.

in order to justify full incapacitation, the mental disorder must be "of a kind or degree" warranting such a measure.[107] However, the questions to the doctors, as formulated by the judge, did not concern "the kind and degree" of the applicant's mental illness. As a result, the medical report did not analyse the degree of the applicant's incapacity in sufficient detail. The national law did not leave the judge another choice. The Russian Civil Code distinguished between full capacity and full incapacity, but it did not provide for any "borderline" situation other than for drug or alcohol addicts. The court referred in this respect to the principles formulated by Recommendation No R (99) 4 of the Committee of Ministers of the Council of Europe.[108] Although these principles have no force of law for the court, the court stated that they may define a common European standard in this area.[109] Contrary to these principles, Russian legislation did not provide for a "tailor-made response". As a result, in the circumstances the applicant's rights under art.8 were limited more than strictly necessary. The court concluded that the interference with the applicant's private life was disproportionate to the legitimate aim pursued. There was, therefore, a breach of art.8 of the Convention on account of the applicant's full incapacitation.

Other Human Rights Documents

1–36 Other human rights documents may be relevant in more indirect fashions than the Constitution or the ECHR. For example, the European Court of Human Rights has referred to a Committee of Ministers Recommendation[110] in the *Shtukaturov* case,[111] discussed below at para.13–19, stating that although these principles have no force of law for the court, they may define a common European standard in the area.[112] In the recent case of *Glor v Switzerland*[113] the court made explicit reference to the UN Convention on the Rights of Persons with Disabilities[114] as the basis for the existence of a European and universal consensus on the need to protect persons with disabilities from discriminatory treatment.[115] If the Strasbourg Court refers to a human rights document in interpreting the scope of ECHR rights, this may have an effect on how Irish courts interpret the ECHR.

---

[107] The court cited *Winterwerp v Netherlands* (1979–80) 2 E.H.R.R. 387.
[108] Committee of Ministers, *Principles concerning the legal protection of incapable adults*, Recommendation No R(99)4 (Council of Europe, 1999).
[109] [2008] M.H.L.R. 238, para.95.
[110] Committee of Ministers, *Principles concerning the legal protection of incapable adults*, Recommendation No R(99)4 (Council of Europe, 1999).
[111] [2008] M.H.L.R. 238.
[112] [2008] M.H.L.R. 238, para.95.
[113] Application No. 13444/04, Judgment April 30, 2009, only available in French.
[114] Convention on the Rights of Persons with Disabilities, 2006 [A/RES/61/106].
[115] The case is summarised in Mental Disability Advocacy Center, "Three disability 'firsts' in a European Court of Human Rights case (June 2, 2009)"; 'Human Rights court finds disability discrimination', *Irish Times*, May 18, 2009.

1–37 Occasionally, Irish courts have referred to human rights documents other than the ECHR in mental health cases. For example, Costello P. said in the *R.T.* case that, in considering safeguards against abuse and error in depriving people of their liberty, regard should be had to the standards set by the Recommendations and Conventions of International Organisations of which this country is a member.[116] In *Croke v Smith (No.2)*, Budd J., speaking prior to the European Convention on Human Right Act 2003, said that courts can look to the European Convention and the United Nations principles[117] as being influential guidelines with regard to matters of public policy, but such Conventions may not be used as a touchstone with regard to constitutionality.[118]

1–38 Due to the dualist nature of the Irish legal system, reflected in Art.29.6 of the Constitution,[119] international documents which have not been incorporated into domestic law are not binding in Ireland. However, many international agreements create obligations and enforcement mechanisms at international level. Prior to the 2003 Act,[120] the ECHR was enforceable by means of action before the Strasbourg Court. Similarly, if the State ratifies the Convention on the Rights of Persons with Disabilities,[121] it may also ratify the Optional Protocol which would allow complaints by individuals or groups to the Committee on the Rights of Persons with Disabilities that the State has breached one of its obligations under the Convention. There are other treaties which allow individual complaints by individuals or groups but these have not yet been used in Ireland concerning mental health issues.[122]

1–39 Other treaties include requirements of periodic reporting by state parties. For example, the International Covenant on Civil and Political Rights (ICCPR) requires state parties to submit a report to the Human Rights Committee on a periodic basis. The report describes measures taken to promote the rights recognised in the ICCPR, as well as progress made in the enjoyment of those rights. The Committee studies these reports and puts questions to representatives of the state concerned. The Committee adopts comments and recommendations on each periodic report and provides them to the General Assembly.

1–40 In formulating new legislation and implementing existing legislation, the State should ideally have regard to international human rights principles and

---

[116] *R.T. v Director of the Central Mental Hospital* [1995] 2 I.R. 65 at 79.
[117] United Nations, *Principles for the protection of persons with mental illness and the improvement of mental health care*, adopted by General Assembly resolution 46/119 of 17 December 1991 [Known as the MI Principles].
[118] *Croke v Smith (No.2)*, High Court, Budd J., July 27 and 31, 1995.
[119] Article 29.6 states, "No international agreement shall be part of the domestic law of the State save as may be determined by the Oireachtas."
[120] European Convention on Human Rights Act 2003.
[121] Convention on the Rights of Persons with Disabilities, 2006 [A/RES/61/106].
[122] For example, the International Covenant on Civil and Political Rights (ICCPR) includes a right

there are some references to such documents in the Green and White Papers on Mental Health.[123] Independent statutory bodies appear to refer to human rights principles more frequently than the State itself. The Mental Health Commission makes numerous references to international human rights principles in its documents.[124] The Human Rights Commission[125] and Ombudsman for Children[126] also frequently cite such documents. The independent Expert Group on Mental Health Policy placed a strong emphasis on human rights.[127]

1–41 Another method of human rights enforcement is through the means of visits by international committees. The chief example of relevance to mental health is the European Committee for the Prevention of Torture (CPT), established under the European Convention for the Prevention of Torture.[128] The CPT has visited Ireland on four occasions[129] and has included residential institutions for people with mental disorders and intellectual disabilities in its reports.

1–42 As with the ECHR, most international instruments focus mainly on negative rights rather than positive rights. However, human rights groups are beginning to campaign for more recognition of positive rights in mental health, e.g. the right to the highest attainable standard of health, based on art.2 of the International Covenant on Economic, Social and Cultural Rights.[130] The UN

of individual complaint. An example of a complaint brought against Ireland is *Joseph Kavanagh v Ireland*, Communication No. 819/1998, CCPR/C/71/D/819/1998.

[123] Department of Health, *Green Paper on Mental Health* (Dublin, 1992), Chapter 17; Department of Health, *A New Mental Health Act: White Paper* (Dublin, 1995), Chapter 1 and Appendix 2.

[124] For example, see Mental Health Commission, *Rules Governing the Use of Seclusion and Mechanical Means of Bodily Restraint* (R-S69(2)/02/2006, 2006), citing Principle 11 of the UN Principles for the Protection of Persons with Mental Illness & the Improvement of Mental Health Care (1991); Mental Health Commission, *Mental Health Legal Aid Scheme* (2005) citing, inter alia, UN Universal Declaration of Human Rights, International Covenants on Civil and Political Rights and on Economic, Social and Cultural Rights, and UN Principles for the Protection of Persons with Mental Illness and for the Improvement of Mental Health Care.

[125] For example, see Irish Human Rights Commission, *Observations on the Scheme of the Mental Capacity Bill 2008*.

[126] *Report of the Ombudsman for Children to the UN Committee on the Rights of the Child on the occasion of the examination of Ireland's Second Report to the Committee* (2006), citing the UN Convention on the Rights of the Child. Mental health issues are discussed at pp.28–9 of the report.

[127] Expert Group on Mental Health Policy, *A Vision for Change* (Dublin, 2006). The Group stated at p.15 that one of the primary values underpinning the report was "Citizenship: The individual is at the centre of the mental health system. The human rights of individuals with mental health problems must be respected at all times." It provided further details on human rights in Annex 1 at pp.233–4.

[128] European Convention for the Prevention of Torture and Inhuman or Degrading Treatment or Punishment, Council of Europe, Strasbourg, November 26, 1987.

[129] The visits took place in 1993, 1998, 2002 and 2006.

[130] Carl O'Brien, "Psychiatric care breaks law, claims Amnesty", *Irish Times*, June 16, 2009; Amnesty International, *Strategic Report: Mental Health and Human Rights* (Dublin, 2009).

Human Rights Council has appointed Mr Anand Grover as Special Rapporteur on the Right to Health, and he spoke at a conference in Dublin in May 2009.[131]

PRINCIPLES APPLIED BY THE COURTS

1–43 As the case law on the Mental Health Act 2001 has developed over the past three years (from 2006 to 2009), the courts have frequently referred to the best interests principle, the paternal nature of the Act and purposive inter-pretation. These concepts are sometimes inappropriately conflated, as if they were somehow interchangeable. However, it is important that their distinct meanings be clarified.

The Best Interests Principle

1–44 Section 4 of the Mental Health Act 2001 provides as follows:

(1) In making a decision under this Act concerning the care or treatment of a person (including a decision to make an admission order in relation to a person), the best interests of the person shall be the principal consider-ation with due regard being given to the interests of other persons who may be at risk of serious harm if the decision is not made.

(2) Where it is proposed to make a recommendation or an admission order in respect of a person, or to administer treatment to a person under this Act, the person shall, so far as is reasonably practicable, be notified of the proposal and be entitled to make representations in relation to it and before deciding the matter due consideration shall be given to any representations duly made under this subsection.

(3) In making a decision under this Act concerning the care or treatment of a person (including a decision to make an admission order in relation to a person) due regard shall be given to the need to respect the right of the person to dignity, bodily integrity, privacy and autonomy.

1–45 The best interests of the person are referred to as "the principal consideration". In addition, it is useful to note the reference to "autonomy" in s.4(3). Difficult issues may arise when seeking to act in the patient's best interests *and* respect their autonomy at the same time. The principles in s.4 do not apply to every activity which takes place under the 2001 Act, as they refer primarily to decisions concerning care or treatment, or the making of an admission order.[132] For example, the principles in s.4 do not apply to a legal

---

[131]   Kitty Holland, 'Call for action to improve mental health services', *Irish Times*, May 19, 2009. The conference was organised by the Irish Mental Health Coalition; see *http://www.avisionofrights.ie* [Accessed September 18, 2009].

[132]   Section 4(2) refers also to the making of a recommendation.

representative making a decision as to how to represent a patient before a Mental Health Tribunal.[133]

Eldergill has argued that, reading s.4 in light of the general scheme of the Act, the patient's best interests are not always first. For example, if a patient constitutes a serious risk to others and satisfies the legal criteria for detention then this becomes the principal consideration and the patient's interests become secondary.[134]

1–46 These principles were not in the original Mental Health Bill 1999 and were introduced as an amendment during the legislative process, partly influenced by the statement of principles in s.24 of the Child Care Act 1991.[135] There is no definition of the best interests principle and this has led to difficulties in its interpretation.

There are a number of sources which might have been consulted in seeking to provide a statutory definition of the best interests principle. For example, the Powers of Attorney Act 1996 had provided a list of factors to be taken into account in deciding what was in the donor's best interests under that Act.[136] There had been some references to the best interests principle in Irish cases, e.g. *Re A Ward of Court (No.2)*.[137] There were also a number of cases in England considering the meaning of best interests at common law. For example, the meaning of best interests was reviewed by the House of Lords in *Airedale NHS Trust v Bland*.[138] In *Re M.B. (an adult: medical treatment)*[139] it was stated that

---

[133] See further paras 7–49 to 7–52 below.

[134] Anselm Eldergill, "The Best Is the Enemy of the Good: The Mental Health Act 2001" (2008) J. Mental Health L. 21 at 24. Eldergill also states that it is clear that an "order for admission" may only be made if the patient satisfies the statutory criteria for detention. He says, "This therefore is the principal consideration and, insofar as distinct, at best the patient's best interests can only be a secondary consideration."

[135] See Mary Keys, *Mental Health Act 2001* (Dublin: Round Hall, 2002), p.17.

[136] Powers of Attorney Act 1996 s.6(7): (a) Any personal care decision made by an attorney on behalf of a donor shall be made in the donor's best interests. (b) In deciding what is in a donor's best interests regard shall be had to the following: (i) so far as ascertainable, the past and present wishes and feelings of the donor and the factors which the donor would consider if he or she were able to do so; (ii) the need to permit and encourage the donor to participate, or to improve the donor's ability to participate, as fully as possible in any decision affecting the donor; (iii) so far as it is practicable and appropriate to consult any of the persons mentioned below, their views as to the donor's wishes and feelings and as to what would be in the donor's best interests: (I) any person named by the donor as someone to be consulted on those matters; (II) anyone (whether the donor's spouse, a relative, friend or other person) engaged in caring for the donor or interested in the donor's welfare; (iv) whether the purpose for which any decision is required can be as effectively achieved in a manner less restrictive of the donor's freedom of action.

[137] [1996] 2 I.R. 79. See Mary Donnelly, "Decision Making for Mentally Incompetent People: The Empty Formula of Best Interests" (2001) 20 *Medicine and Law* 405.

[138] [1993] A.C. 789. See for example Lord Goff at 859–875.

[139] [1997] E.W.C.A. Civ. 3093; [1997] 2 F.L.R. 426.

best interests are not limited to best medical interests.[140] Examples of non-medical factors which may be considered include financial considerations, religious views and public policy.[141] The Law Commission of England and Wales issued its report on Mental Incapacity in 1995.[142]

1–47 Since the 2001 Act was passed, there have been a number of other relevant developments. The Law Reform Commission has issued a series of publications which include consideration of the meaning of "best interests".[143] The Department of Justice has produced the Scheme of a Mental Capacity Bill which includes a proposed statutory definition of best interests for the purposes of the Bill.[144] And in England and Wales, the Mental Capacity Act 2005 was passed.[145]

1–48 The following extract from Head 3 of the Scheme of the Mental Capacity Bill 2008 is an example of how a detailed definition of best interests might be formulated:

> In determining for the purposes of this Act what is in a person's best interests, the person making the determination, including the court exercising jurisdiction under the Act, must consider all the relevant circumstances and in particular the following—
> (i) he or she must consider—
>   (a) whether it is likely that the person will at some time have capacity in relation to the matter in question, and
>   (b) if it appears likely that he or she will, when that is likely to be;
> (ii) he or she must, so far as reasonably practicable, permit and encourage the person to participate, or to improve his or her ability to participate, as fully as possible in any act done for him or her and any decision affecting him or her;
> (iii) he or she must consider as far as is reasonably ascertainable—
>   (a) the person's past and present wishes and feelings (and, in particular, any relevant written statement made by him or her when he or she had capacity),
>   (b) the beliefs and values that would be likely to influence his or her decision if he or she had capacity, and
>   (c) the other factors he or she would be likely to consider if he or she were able to do so;

---

[140] [1997] 2 F.L.R. 426 at 439 (Butler-Sloss L.J.)

[141] See *In Re W. (E.E.M.)* [1971] Ch. 123 and discussion in Peter Bartlett and Ralph Sandland, *Mental Health Law: Policy and Practice*, 3rd edn (Oxford: Oxford University Press, 2007), pp.534–8.

[142] Law Commission, *Mental Incapacity*, L.C. No.231 (London: H.M.S.O., 1995)

[143] Law Reform Commission, *Consultation Paper on Law and the Elderly* (CP23–2003); Law Reform Commission, *Consultation Paper on Vulnerable Adults and the Law: Capacity* (CP 37–2005); Law Reform Commission, *Report on Vulnerable Adults and the Law* (Report 83, 2006).

[144] Department of Justice, Equality and Law Reform, *Scheme of Mental Capacity Bill 2008*, Head 3.

[145] Section 4 of the 2005 Act provides a detailed definition of the best interests principle. See

(iv) he or she must take into account, if it is practicable and appropriate to consult, the views of
   (a) anyone named by the person as someone to be consulted on the matter in question or on matters of that kind,
   (b) anyone engaged in caring for the person or interested in his or her welfare,
   (c) any donee of an enduring power of attorney granted by the person, and
   (d) any personal guardian appointed for the person by the court,

as to what would be in the person's best interests, and in particular, as to the matters mentioned in the previous paragraph.

1–49 Returning to the 2001 Act, it must be interpreted as it stands without reference to possible future clarification in amending legislation. The courts are entitled to have regard to case law in other jurisdictions on the meaning of best interests. They should also consider how the 2001 Act was introduced as a radical reform of mental health law. It is such a major departure from the thinking of the 1945 Act that its introduction should be regarded as heralding a new era in mental health law. It introduced criteria for admission which were more narrowly drawn than the vague wording of the 1945 Act. It emphasised patients' rights to autonomy, bodily integrity and privacy. It would seem to be axiomatic, therefore, that the best interests principle was intended to reflect a new approach to mental health law.

1–50 In interpreting the best interests principle in s.4 of the 2001 Act, the courts have provided mixed signals. Some judgments have emphasised how the best interests principle enhances the rights of patients under the 2001 Act. Others have, surprisingly, interpreted the principle as merely a restatement of paternalism as expressed in case law prior to the 2001 Act.

The ambiguity in the judgments is illustrated by *J.H. v Lawlor, Clinical Director of Jonathan Swift Clinic, St. James's Hospital*,[146] in which Peart J. stated that s.4 introduced a "patient centred focus" but, on the other hand, the Act was paternalistic:

> "This provision [s.4] highlights the patient centred focus of the Act's purpose. The Act proceeds to set forth a scheme whereby at all stages the constitutional rights of the patient are to be respected and protected. There are time limits and other safeguards built into the scheme, as well as requirements that the patient at all times has access to legal advice, notice and information regarding all matters pertaining to orders made to detain him/her, so that in a meaningful

generally Richard Jones, *Mental Capacity Act Manual*, 3rd edn (London: Sweet & Maxwell, 2008); Peter Bartlett, *Blackstone's Guide to the Mental Capacity Act 2005*, 2nd edn (Oxford University Press, 2008); Mary Donnelly, "Best Interests, Patient Participation and The Mental Capacity Act 2005" (2009) 17 Med. L. Rev. 1.

[146] [2007] I.E.H.C. 225; [2008] 1 I.R. 476; High Court, Peart J., June 25, 2007.

way his/her detention and the reasons for it must be properly, promptly and independently reviewed by a tribunal hearing at which he/she may be legally represented. The scheme in this regard has been appropriately described as paternalistic in nature. Its purpose is to protect the rights of the patient as well as to care for the patient. The paternalistic nature of the Act is clear also from the definition of "mental disorder" contained in s. 3 of the Act.

It must never be overlooked that persons detained under the provisions are detained so that they may receive care and treatment which they need and will not otherwise receive. Nevertheless the patient retains his/her constitutional rights, subject to necessary and appropriate restrictions to, *inter alia*, the right to liberty which are necessitated or permitted by the Act itself."[147]

1–51 O'Neill J. said in *W.Q. v Mental Health Commission*[148]: "In my opinion the best interests of a person suffering from a mental disorder are secured by a faithful observance of and compliance with the statutory safeguards put into the 2001 Act by the Oireachtas."[149] This statement was approved by MacMenamin J. in the *J.B. (No.2)* case.[150]

O'Neill J. also said in *M.R. v Byrne and Flynn*[151] that: "s. 4 of the Act ... in my opinion gives statutory expression to the kind of paternalistic approach mandated in the case of *Philip Clarke*[152] and approved in the case of *Croke v. Smith*[153] and also ... *Gooden v. St. Otteran's Hospital.*"[154]

1–52 Peart J. has stated in *P.McG v Medical Director of the Mater Hospital.*[155] that the protections put in place by the 2001 Act, "are detailed and specific and it is of the utmost importance that they be observed to the letter, and that no unnecessary shortcuts creep into the way in which the Act is operated." He continued:

"It cannot have been the intention of the Oireachtas when it enacted this piece of legislation that its provisions would have to be acted upon in such a literal way that the best interests of the patient would take second place."[156]

1–53 In *E.H. v Clinical Director of St. Vincent's Hospital*[157] Kearns J. stated in the Supreme Court, "There can be no doubt but that the Mental Health Act, 2001

---

[147] [2008] 1 I.R. 476 at 487.
[148] [2007] I.E.H.C. 154; [2007] 3 I.R. 755; O'Neill J., High Court, May 15, 2007.
[149] [2007] 3 I.R. 755 at 768.
[150] *J.B. v Director of Central Mental Hospital (No.2)* [2007] I.E.H.C. 201; [2007] 4 I.R. 778; High Court, MacMenamin J., June 15, 2007.
[151] [2007] I.E.H.C. 73; [2007] 3 I.R. 211; O'Neill J., High Court, March 2, 2007.
[152] [1950] I.R. 235.
[153] [1998] 1 I.R. 101.
[154] [2005] 3 I.R. 617.
[155] [2007] I.E.H.C. 401; [2008] 2 I.R. 332; High Court, Peart J., November 29, 2007.
[156] [2008] 2 I.R. 332 at 339.
[157] [2009] I.E.S.C. 46; [2009] 2 I.L.R.M. 149; Supreme Court, May 28, 2009.

was designed with the best interests of persons with mental disorder in mind."[158] He also said the fact that s.17(1)(b) of the 2001 Act provides for the assignment by the Commission of a legal representative for a patient following the making of an admission order or a renewal order should not give rise to an assumption that a legal challenge to that patient's detention is warranted unless the best interests of the patient so demand.[159]

1–54 The Mental Health Commission has concluded that clarification of the best interests principle is necessary:

> "As stated in the external commentary the fact that the 2001 Act does not define 'best interests' is unfortunate as different approaches can be taken. This issue will also feature within future capacity legislation and will need a compatible approach. The preparation of a code of practice for the Act will provide an opportunity to discuss how best to approach 'best interests' when applying procedures arising from the provisions of the Act."[160]

Paternalism

1–55 The Oxford English Dictionary defines paternalism as, "the policy or practice of restricting the freedoms and responsibilities of subordinates or dependants in what is considered or claimed to be their best interests."[161] The negative connotations are obvious, with the reference to freedoms being restricted. While "best interests" are referred to, it is with a view to restricting freedoms rather than recognising rights.

1–56 The legal concept of paternalism has both positive and negative implications:

> "There are numerous perceptions of what the term 'paternalism' actually incorporates. In its classical sense, it refers to the parent-child relationship, a concept that contributes to negative connotations of the term 'paternalism'. The concept of 'legal paternalism' originates from Hart's *Law, Liberty and Morality*[162] in which legal paternalism is distinguished from the enforcement of morals. Legal paternalism has since become the subject of widespread debate since it influences and affects the way the law is enforced. Paternalistic legislation can have both positive and negative implications and effects."[163]

---

[158]   [2009] 2 I.L.R.M. 149 at 155.

[159]   [2009] 2 I.L.R.M. 149 at 165. See further paras 5–32 to 5–37 below.

[160]   Mental Health Commission, *Report on the Operation of Part 2 of the Mental Health Act 2001* (2008), p.86.

[161]   Oxford English Dictionary online, March 2008 Draft Revision.

[162]   H.L.A. Hart, *Law, Liberty and Morality* (Oxford University Press, 1963), at pp.30–34, 38.

[163]   Eileen King, "Paternalism and the Law: Taking a Closer Look" (2004) 4 U.C.D.L.R. 134 at 135.

A positive, benign example of paternalism would be the legal requirement to wear a seat-belt, for one's own safety as well as that of others. Negative aspects include the implication that adults are treated as children and that "superior" people decide what "inferior" people need. There may also be undue interference with autonomy, even where there is no risk of harm to others.[164]

1–57 The Law Reform Commission has noted that there is a move away from what may be termed "benign paternalism":

> "Benign paternalism treats adults who are deemed to lack capacity as similar to children in the sense of the parent deciding what is best for them because they know best. The force of paternalism is undermined by a growing recognition that all adults, including those living with a disability, have a right to autonomy and self-determination."[165]

This movement is linked with the move from a medical model of disability to a social model.[166] The social model has now been embraced at United Nations level in the Convention on the Rights of Persons with Disabilities.[167]

The Commission also noted in 2005 that the rise in importance of autonomy and self-determination is difficult to reconcile with the paternalism which has traditionally guided medical practitioners. In certain circumstances the ethical principles of autonomy and beneficence may conflict. The Commission states that while medical practitioners will have a natural interest in ensuring a person's well-being from the point of view of best medical practice, case law in this area emphasises that a person should not be found to lack competence simply because they do not want to take their doctor's advice or because their choice appears objectively irrational.[168]

1–58 Donnelly has argued that the problem is not with paternalism or best interests per se but with the need to modernise them to adapt to changing standards:

> "The Commission is correct in noting that the best interests standard is paternalistic and that it has traditionally been applied in an 'unsubstantiated' manner. In this context, it is important to remember that, when a person lacks capacity, paternalism is not, of itself, inappropriate. ... It is a fundamental aspect of the right of autonomy or self-determination that the individual has the necessary capacity. The difficulty is not with paternalism as such but with

---

[164] See generally Eileen King, "Paternalism and the Law: Taking a Closer Look" (2004) 4 U.C.D.L.R. 134.

[165] Law Reform Commission, *Consultation Paper on Vulnerable Adults and the Law: Capacity* (CP 37, 2005), para.1.21.

[166] See Commission on the Status of People with Disabilities, *A Strategy for Equality: Report of the Commission on the Status of People with Disabilities* (1996).

[167] Convention on the Rights of Persons with Disabilities, 2006 [A/RES/61/106].

[168] *Consultation Paper on Vulnerable Adults and the Law: Capacity*, para.7.20.

paternalism operated in an inappropriate way which fails to protect the rights of the person lacking capacity. As the MCA[169] shows, it is possible to adapt the best interests standard to reflect modern understandings regarding participation and to include an appropriate role for the right of autonomy of the previously capable person who now lacks capacity."[170]

1–59 The Irish courts have not yet engaged with these debates in case law on the 2001 Act. On a number of occasions, they have imported the concept of paternalism which was used in older case law and applied it unquestioningly to the 2001 Act. More worryingly, they have equated best interests in s.4 with paternalism, which appears to be a move backwards rather than forwards.

1–60 In *Re Philip Clarke*, speaking of the Mental Treatment Act 1945, O'Byrne J. said: "The impugned legislation is of a paternal character, clearly intended for the care and custody of persons suspected to be suffering from mental infirmity and for the safety and well-being of the public generally."[171] In *Croke v Smith (No.2)*, Budd J. in the High Court said that, "the certainties implicit in the judgment in Clarke's case in 1949 may be diluted by now".[172] However, Budd J.'s view was overruled in the Supreme Court, where Hamilton C.J. twice quoted O'Byrne J.'s statement from *Re Philip Clarke*.[173]

McGuinness J. again approved of the *Re Philip Clarke* approach in *Gooden v St. Otteran's Hospital*:

> "This passage [in *Re Philip Clarke*] has been generally accepted as expressing the nature and purpose of the Act of 1945. The Act provides for the detention of persons who are mentally ill, both for their own sake and for the sake of the common good."[174]

Hardiman J. in the same case referred to, "the essentially paternal character of the legislation in question here, as outlined in *In Re Philip Clarke*."[175]

Interestingly, in the *R.T.* case,[176] Costello P. makes no reference to *Re Philip Clarke* or to paternalism as a principle. Instead, he emphasises the constitutional right to liberty and the failure of the 1945 Act to conform with international human rights standards. He also makes a brief reference to best interests at the end of his decision.[177]

---

169 Mental Capacity Act 2005 (England and Wales).
170 Mary Donnelly, "Legislating for Incapacity: Developing a Rights-Based Framework" (2008) 30 *Dublin University Law Journal* 395 at 424.
171 [1950] I.R. 235 at 247.
172 *Croke v Smith (No.2)*, High Court, Budd J., July 27 and 31, 1995, p.124.
173 [1998] 1 I.R. 101 at 112, 113 and 132.
174 [2005] 3 I.R. 617 at 634.
175 [2005] 3 I.R. 617 at 639.
176 *R.T. v Director of the Central Mental Hospital* [1995] 2 I.R. 65.
177 [1995] 2 I.R. 65 at 82.

1–61 The post-2006 case law has in general imported the paternalism of *Re Philip Clarke* without question. O'Neill J. said in *M.R. v Byrne and Flynn*[178] that "S.4 of the Act … in my opinion gives statutory expression to the kind of paternalistic approach mandated in the case of *Philip Clarke*[179] and approved in the case of *Croke v. Smith*[180] and also … *Gooden v. St. Otteran's Hospital*."[181] In *J.H. v. Lawlor, Clinical Director of Jonathan Swift Clinic, St. James's Hospital*,[182] Peart J. stated that s.4 introduced a "patient centred focus" but, on the other hand, the Act was paternalistic (see para.1–50 above).

In the Supreme Court in the *E.H.* case, Kearns J. stated that any interpretation of the term "voluntary patient" in the 2001 Act "must be informed by the overall scheme and paternalistic intent of the legislation as exemplified in particular by the provisions of sections 4 and 29 of the Act".[183] He then approved of the judgment of McGuinness J. in the *Gooden* case. He continued: "I do not see why any different approach should be adopted in relation to the Mental Health Act, 2001, nor, having regard to the Convention, do I believe that any different approach is mandated or required by Article 5 of the European Convention of Human Rights."[184]

1–62 Gledhill notes that by taking a paternalistic approach, the courts are effectively reducing the importance of autonomy:

> "[I]f paternalism is a guiding principle,[185] then someone's best interests are those that are designated in their 'objective' best interests (i.e. what supposedly reasonable people would describe as being what should happen); but if the guiding principle is that of autonomy, namely the right of people to make their own choices, then someone's best interests are governed by the question of what they would decide to do if they had the ability to make the choice (with the proposition that someone whose mental disorder clouds the ability to make a choice has to have some form of substitute decision maker, who will make a true choice). The latter approach rests on the basis that the differences between humans and what individuals value are such that there can be no 'objective' best interests and so the only proper approach is one of substitute decision-making designed to secure what the patient would have decided had that been a possibility."[186]

---

[178] [2007] I.E.H.C. 73; [2007] 3 I.R. 211 at 224; O'Neill J., High Court, March 2, 2007.
[179] [1950] I.R. 235.
[180] [1998] 1 I.R. 101.
[181] [2005] 3 I.R. 617.
[182] [2007] I.E.H.C. 225; [2008] 1 I.R. 476; High Court, Peart J., June 25, 2007.
[183] *E.H. v Clinical Director of St. Vincent's Hospital* [2009] I.E.S.C. 46; [2009] 2 I.L.R.M. 149 at 161.
[184] *E.H. v Clinical Director of St. Vincent's Hospital* [2009] I.E.S.C. 46; [2009] 2 I.L.R.M. 149 at 162.
[185] In the following paragraph, Gledhill notes that the courts have taken the paternalistic interpretation approach.
[186] Kris Gledhill, "Report on the Compliance of the Mental Health Act 2001 with International

Eldergill is strongly of the view that the 2001 Act was not supposed to be paternalistic:

> "Although no judge would likely argue otherwise, it must be emphasised that the main purpose of the 2001 legislation was patently not just to repeat the paternal character of the Act of 1945; nor was it intended simply to ensure the care and custody of people suffering from mental disorder. The 1945 Act promoted and secured those objectives. It did not, however, adequately protect citizens against unjustified infringements of liberty. The purpose of the 2001 Act was to address these deficiencies. It does so by prescribing more rigorous detention criteria, by a system of tribunal reviews, by second-opinion procedures, and through an independent Commission. This is as it should be. Those we describe as 'patients' are individuals, no more and no less than any other individual; individuals who suffer, who will certain ends for themselves and their loved ones, who wish to develop, and be happy and fulfilled. They are members of the public—citizens—people whose needs and interests the Government exists to serve; brothers, sisters, mothers, fathers. If this is accepted, the main purpose of the Act may be said to be to seek to ensure that members of the public are not unnecessarily detained, and also that they are protected from those members of the public who must necessarily be detained".[187]

Craven has reviewed the case law on best interests and paternalism and concluded that "there are clear and potent indications of a paternalistic approach emerging from the application of the best interests provisions of the legislation. The distance travelled from *Philip Clarke*, on one view, might not be considered very great".[188]

Nolan has emphasised the importance of the case law which holds that paternalism should not be used to rewrite the legislation:

> "Flowing from these cases I believe is an evolving jurisprudence which, while still recognising the appropriate canon of construction as a paternal one, has necessarily highlighted that there are limits on how far it can be taken. It should not be used to re-write the legislation. The Superior Courts are necessarily vigilant to ensure that the separation of powers, which lies at the core of this State's democratic model, is not in any way imperilled. No amount of well-intentioned action, it has been determined, can make lawful what is patently, on the face of the Act, unlawful. Underwriting therefore the term *best*

Human Rights Law" in Mental Health Commission, *Report on the Operation of Part 2 of the Mental Health Act 2001* (2008), pp.9–28 at 18–19.

[187] Anselm Eldergill, "The Best Is the Enemy of the Good: The Mental Health Act 2001" (2008) J. Mental Health L. 21 at 23–4.

[188] Ciarán Craven, "Signs of paternalist approach to the mentally ill persist", *Irish Times*, July 27, 2009.

interests is the fact that respect for the rule of law, as well a patient's best *legal* interests, must form part of any assessment of best practice in relation to a particular issue arising on the operation of the Act."[189]

Purposive Interpretation

1–63 At common law, the courts must first interpret a statute literally. If the literal interpretation leads to an absurdity, the literal meaning of the words may be modified to avoid the absurdity. The courts may also have regard to the purpose of the statute, or the "mischief" which it was enacted to resolve. The Law Reform Commission summed up the position in 1999 as follows: "it is most accurate to state that there is no single rule of literal or purposive interpretation, but that a principally literal approach is modified by a purposive approach, with an examination of the Act's purpose becoming more important if the Act is ambiguous or absurd."[190]

1–64 The courts have sometimes justified a purposive interpretation by reference to the "paternal" nature of an Act. Thus, in *Gooden v St Otteran's Hospital*, Hardiman J. said:

> "I believe however that in construing the statutory provisions applicable in this case in the way that we have, the court has gone as far as it possibly could without rewriting or supplementing the statutory provisions. The court must always be reluctant to appear to be doing either of these things having regard to the requirements of the separation of powers. I do not know that I would have been prepared to go as far as we have in this direction were it not for the essentially paternal character of the legislation in question here, as outlined in *In Re Philip Clarke* [1950] I.R. 235. The nature of the legislation, perhaps, renders less complicated the application of a purposive construction than would be the case with a statute affecting the right to personal freedom in another context. The overall purpose of the legislation is more easily discerned and, where the medical evidence is unchallenged, the conflicts involved are less acute than in other detention cases. I do not regard the present decision as one which would necessarily be helpful in the construction of any statutory power to detain in any other context."[191]

1–65 The rules of statutory interpretation have now been codified and reformed in the Interpretation Act 2005.[192] The Act adopts a "moderately purposive"

---

[189] Niall Nolan, "Case Law on the Mental Health Act 2001: Part 1" (2009) 14(1) *Bar Review* 13 at 15. See also Part 2, (2009) 14 *Bar Review* 42.

[190] Law Reform Commission, *Consultation Paper on Statutory Drafting and Interpretation: Plain Language and the Law* (CP 14, 1999), para.1.002.

[191] (2001) [2005] 3 I.R. 617, at pp.639–640.

[192] See generally David Dodd, *Statutory Interpretation in Ireland* (Haywards Heath: Tottel, 2008); Brian Hunt, "Interpretation Act 2005" (2005) Irish Current Law Statutes Annotated.

approach, as had been recommended by the Law Reform Commission.[193] Section 5 of the Act provides that, in construing a provision of any Act (other than a provision that relates to the imposition of a penal or other sanction) that is obscure or ambiguous, or that on a literal interpretation would be absurd or would fail to reflect the plain intention of the Oireachtas, the provision shall be given a construction that reflects the plain intention of the Oireachtas where that intention can be ascertained from the Act as a whole.

1–66 In *J.D. v Director of Central Mental Hospital*,[194] Finlay Geoghegan J. reviewed the principles of construction employed in the *Gooden* case and said that the starting point of the court must be to construe the 1945 Act in accordance with "the ordinary meaning of the words used, the meaning sometimes referred to as the literal meaning."[195] Counsel had not referred to any intention of the legislature in the 1945 Act to which it could be said such a construction was contrary, nor indeed to any absurd result. Therefore, she was satisfied that she should construe s.189(1)(a)(ii) of the 1945 Act as requiring any extension made under that section to be made, firstly, by an endorsement on the order but also that such endorsement on the order extend the period for a specified period.

1–67 In *Han v President of the Circuit Court*,[196] discussed below at para.7–76, Charleton J. said that, "primacy, though not total supremacy, has to be given to the actual and literal words of any statute".[197] He went on to say that a section of an Act cannot be seen in isolation from the entire text. In deciding whether words are precise and unambiguous, regard must be had to the whole of the enactment. It would be wrong for the literal rule to isolate a particular expression from the rest of the statute in which it is contained. He believed that that would offend the common law canons of construction and modern statute law.[198] Having quoted s.5 of the Interpretation Act 2005, and reviewed the sections of the Mental Health Act 2001 at issue in the case, he said that he was obliged to give grammatical and ordinary sense to the use of the present tense in s.19 of the 2001 Act, and to the choice given to the Circuit Court of either affirming an admission or renewal order or revoking it. He said: "Grammatical sense can only be modified so as to avoid an absurdity and even there, the modification can go no further than is necessary in that regard: *Grey v. Pearson* (1857) 6 H.L.Cas. 61 at 106 *per* Lord Wensleydale."[199]

---

[193]　Law Reform Commission, *Report on Statutory Drafting and Interpretation: Plain Language and the Law* (LRC 61, 2000).
[194]　[2007] I.E.H.C. 100; High Court, Finlay Geoghegan J., ex tempore, March 20, 2007.
[195]　[2007] I.E.H.C. 100; High Court, Finlay Geoghegan J., ex tempore, March 20, 2007, p.7.
[196]　[2008] I.E.H.C. 160; High Court, Charleton J., May 30, 2008.
[197]　[2008] I.E.H.C. 160; High Court, Charleton J., May 30, 2008, para.13.
[198]　[2008] I.E.H.C. 160; High Court, Charleton J., May 30, 2008, para.15.
[199]　[2008] I.E.H.C. 160; High Court, Charleton J., May 30, 2008, para.19.

1–68 McMahon J. was of the view in *S.M. v Mental Health Commission*[200] that the purposive approach "may be given greater latitude in mental health legislation because of its paternal nature, but it cannot be resorted to willy-nilly by the courts to thwart the clear meaning of the legislator."[201] He said that it was also important to recall that in *Gooden* the court was prepared to act because the matter in dispute had not been provided for in the legislation and the court was prepared to give effect to the purpose of the Act in that situation.[202] He continued:

> "I have little difficulty in accepting the appropriateness of using the purposive interpretive technique, perhaps more generously in the context of legislation which is paternal in nature, but where the rights and protection of the patient are specifically dealt with in the legislation itself, the occasions where this paternal approach comes into play are limited. The first obligation of the court in such a situation is to interpret the section and give effect to the plain meaning of the provision when it is clear. The paternalistic approach in not intended to rewrite the legislation."[203]

As was noted earlier (para.1–13) McMahon J. also emphasised the relevance of the right to liberty and the need to construe restrictions on liberty narrowly. McMahon J. said that he had no difficulty in accepting as a general principle that the courts, in considering the Mental Health Acts, should where possible adopt a purposive or teleological approach to the legislation and should in appropriate cases do so bearing in mind the paternal nature of the legislation itself. However, he said there is no room for the purposive approach to interpretation where a particular section is clear and unambiguous. The literal approach is the first and proper rule of interpretation when one has to construe the meaning of an Act. It is only when the literal rule leads to an ambiguity or an absurdity that other canons of interpretation are called in to assist. In his opinion, the meaning of s.15(2) and (3) of the 2001 Act is clear and unambiguous.[204]

1–69 Peart J. said in *J.H. v Lawlor, Clinical Director of Jonathan Swift Clinic, St. James's Hospital*[205] that he had no doubt that a purposive approach to the interpretation of the Act, consistent with its paternalistic and protective nature, must be adopted when reviewing the lawfulness of a patient's detention thereunder. That was not the same as stating that when errors are made they may always be overlooked if the interests of the patient so require, due regard having been also had to the interests of other persons who may be at risk of serious

---

[200]   [2008] I.E.H.C. 441; [2009] 2 I.L.R.M. 127; McMahon J., High Court, October 31, 2008.
[201]   [2009] 2 I.L.R.M. 127 at 132.
[202]   [2009] 2 I.L.R.M. 127 at 132.
[203]   [2009] 2 I.L.R.M. 127 at 133.
[204]   [2009] 2 I.L.R.M. 127 at 141.
[205]   [2007] I.E.H.C. 225; [2008] 1 I.R. 476; High Court, Peart J., June 25, 2007.

harm if they were to be released.[206] He later quoted s.5 of the 2005 Act and said: "I am also of the view that the purposive interpretation which I have adopted to reflect the intention of the Oireachtas is consistent with the requirement contained in s. 5(1) of the Interpretation Act 2005."[207]

1–70 On a number of occasions, the courts have also stated that the procedures laid down in the 2001 Act must be followed correctly, although this is occasionally tempered by statements that minor deviations from procedure may be permissible.

Peart J. stated in *P.McG. v Medical Director of the Mater Hospital*[208] that there should not be a "slack approach" to the observance of the requirements of this legislation and this would be an undesirable situation to arise in relation to legislation whose very purpose is to put in place a regime of statutory procedures for the protection of vulnerable persons against involuntary unlawful detention.[209] He noted that the protections put in place by the 2001 Act "are detailed and specific and it is of the utmost importance that they be observed to the letter, and that no unnecessary shortcuts creep into the way in which the Act is operated."[210] However, the legislation should not be interpreted in such a literal way that the best interests of the patient would take second place.[211] He said that, "there may be situations where some deviation from the provisions of the Act will not undermine" the protections provided for patients by the 2001 Act.[212]

1–71 The same judge said in *A.M. v Kennedy*[213]: "The greatest care must be taken to ensure that procedures are properly followed, and it ill-serves those whose liberty is involved to say that the formalities laid down by statute do not matter and need not be scrupulously observed."[214] He also said that to pretend that nothing wrong occurred "is to deny the right to liberty other than in due course of law, and that is a slippery slope down which I cannot bring myself to venture."[215]

1–72 At Supreme Court level, Hardiman J. said in *M.D. v Clinical Director of St Brendan's Hospital & Anor*[216]: "The Act … is intended to constitute a regime

---

[206]   [2008] 1 I.R. 476 at 486–7.
[207]   [2008] 1 I.R. 476 at 490.
[208]   [2007] I.E.H.C. 401; [2008] 2 I.R. 332; High Court, Peart J., November 29, 2007.
[209]   [2008] 2 I.R. 332 at 338.
[210]   [2008] 2 I.R. 332 at 338.
[211]   [2008] 2 I.R. 332 at 339.
[212]   [2008] 2 I.R. 332 at 339.
[213]   [2007] I.E.H.C. 136; [2007] 4 I.R. 667; High Court, Peart J., April 24, 2007.
[214]   [2007] 4 I.R. 667 at 676.
[215]   [2007] 4 I.R. 667 at 677.
[216]   [2007] I.E.S.C. 37; [2008] 1 I.R. 632; Supreme Court, July 27, 2007.

of protection for persons who are involuntarily detained because they are suffering from a mental disorder. That purpose will not, in my view, be achieved unless the Act is complied with."[217]

1–73 It must be noted that the courts have been willing to permit procedural irregularities quite frequently, as will be seen in later chapters. This has led to a high degree of unpredictability in case law. Depending on the issue which arises, and depending on the judge who hears the case, if there has been a breach of procedure the court may choose either to regard the breach as so fundamental that it cannot be permitted, or adopt a purposive interpretation and hold that the breach of procedure did not nullify the lawfulness of what occurred.

1–74 Matters are further complicated by the fact that Mental Health Tribunals are given the express power in s.18 of the 2001 Act to waive procedural irregularities, which has led to conflicting case law, discussed below at paras 9–24 to 9–38.

---

[217] [2008] 1 I.R. 632.

CHAPTER 2

REMEDIES AND INSTITUTIONS

REMEDIES

2–01 A variety of remedies are available for breaches of mental health law, each with their own advantages and disadvantages. In this chapter, the features of each remedy will be described and assessed. The chapter must be read in light of subsequent chapters where the substantive details of case law on points which have been litigated are discussed.

Exhaustion of Domestic Remedies

2–02 The focus in this chapter is on national remedies. Once national remedies have been exhausted, consideration may be given to a remedy at international level, most likely an application to the European Court of Human Rights. It is important to fully exhaust national remedies first, as illustrated by previous case law. In *O'D. v Ireland*,[1] the European Commission of Human Rights declared the application inadmissible because the applicant had failed to challenge the constitutionality of s.260 of the Mental Treatment Act 1945 in the Irish courts. The Commission rejected the applicant's argument that it was sufficient that he had argued in the High Court that s.260 was to be interpreted in accordance with the constitutional right of access to the courts, and that it was not the wording of the section itself, but the circumstances and manner in which that section was actually applied to the applicant, which were primarily at issue.

2–03 A different result applied in different circumstances in *O'Reilly v Ireland*.[2] Ireland had argued that the applicant should have challenged the constitutionality of s.184 of the 1945 Act in the Irish courts and sought damages for breach of her constitutional rights. The Commission rejected this argument on a number of grounds: There was a conflict between the parties as to the limitation period applicable to an action in damages against the State; the Government did not provide any case law indicating or establishing the liability of the State to pay

---

[1] Application No.10296/83, *O'D. v Ireland*, Commission Decisions of May 14, 1984 and December 3, 1986. For the proceedings in Ireland, see *O'Dowd v North Western Health Board* [1983] I.L.R.M. 186.

[2] *O'Reilly v Ireland*, European Commission of Human Rights, Application number 24196/94, Admissibility Decision, January 22, 1996 and Report of the Commission on Friendly Settlement, December 3, 1996.

damages pursuant to a finding of unconstitutionality of a legislative provision enacted years beforehand; the Commission was cognisant of the reasonableness of the applicant's decision to pursue the leave proceedings as regards Doctor A and of her decision to have, what was for her, an unexpected interpretation of the word "examine" in s.184(4) of the 1945 Act confirmed by the Supreme Court; the Commission noted the relative novelty in claiming damages from the State in such circumstances and finally, commencing the constitutional and damages actions would involve commencing complex proceedings almost five years after the applicant's detention. However, the Commission found that the applicant had not exhausted domestic remedies regarding her point made regarding denial of access to a lawyer, and thus declared that part of her claim inadmissible.

2–04 In *Croke v Ireland*,[3] the Strasbourg Court had little difficulty in finding that the applicant had exhausted domestic remedies, as he had challenged the constitutionality of the 1945 Act in the Irish courts.

Judicial Review

2–05 As many decisions concerning people with mental disorders are made by public bodies, those decisions may be challenged by way of judicial review.[4] For example, a person might seek judicial review of a decision of a Mental Health Tribunal or a decision of the Mental Health (Criminal Law) Review Board. There has been a small number of judgments handed down in Judicial Review proceedings concerning mental health in the last few years. For example, the proceedings in *S.M. v Mental Health Commission*[5] took the form of judicial review proceedings against the Mental Health Commission, the Mental Health Tribunal and the Clinical Director of St. Patrick's Hospital, Dublin. The Attorney General and the Human Rights Commission were notice parties. *E.J.W. v Watters and Mental Health Commission*[6] was a judicial review application for the grant of a declaration that refusal to grant access to medical records was in breach of the applicant's constitutional right and/or in breach of her rights under the European Convention on Human Rights (ECHR).

2–06 In *J.B. v Mental Health (Criminal Law) Review Board & Others*[7] the respondents were the Mental Health (Criminal Law) Review Board, the Minister for Justice, Equality and Law Reform, Ireland and the Attorney General. The

---

[3] Application Number 33267/96, Admissibility Decision, European Court of Human Rights (Fourth Section), June 15, 1999; [1999] M.H.L.R. 118.

[4] See generally Gerard Hogan & David Gwynn Morgan, *Administrative Law in Ireland*, 3rd edn (Dublin: Round Hall, 1998); Hilary Delany, *Judicial Review of Administrative Action*, 2nd edn (Dublin: Round Hall, 2009).

[5] [2008] I.E.H.C. 441; [2009] 2 I.L.R.M. 127; McMahon J., High Court, October 31, 2008. See further paras 6–20 to 6–29 below.

[6] Unapproved, High Court, Peart J., November 25, 2008. See para.7–55 below.

[7] [2008] I.E.H.C. 303; High Court, Hanna J., July 25, 2008. See paras 18–31 to 18–33 below.

Central Mental Hospital was a notice party. A number of declarations were sought, e.g. a declaration that the applicant was entitled to be discharged subject to conditions and a declaration that the failure of the Review Board to conditionally discharge the applicant was ultra vires the provisions of the Criminal Law (Insanity) Act 2006. The applicant also sought a declaration pursuant to s.5 of the European Convention on Human Rights Act 2003 that s.13 of the Act of 2006 was incompatible with art.5 of the ECHR.

2–07 The application in *Han v President of the Circuit Court*[8] was brought against the President of the Circuit Court, with various notice parties added.[9] It is not entirely clear what form of order was being sought, but the applicant was essentially challenging the decision of the President of the Circuit Court to strike out his appeal. The application in *T.S. v Mental Health Tribunal*[10] was brought against the Mental Health Tribunal. The court ordered that Ireland, the Attorney General, the Minister for Health and Children and the Mental Health Commission be added as respondents. The applicant sought various orders, including a declaration that s.19(4) of the 2001 Act was repugnant to the Constitution and incompatible with art.5(4) of the ECHR.

2–08 The respondent in *E.F. v Clinical Director of St. Ita's Hospital*[11] was the Clinical Director of the hospital, and there were no notice parties. The applicant sought various declarations, e.g. that the Clinical Director acted ultra vires the powers conferred on him by the Mental Health Act 2001 in arranging for the applicant to be physically restrained and removed to the hospital by person not members of the hospital's staff and a declaration that the manner in which the removal of the applicant was effected occurred without reasonable care on the part of the respondent nor otherwise in accordance with law and in breach of the applicant's constitutional rights and ECHR rights.

2–09 While s.73 of the Mental Health Act 2001 requires leave of the High Court to be sought before "civil proceedings" are brought concerning an act purporting to be done in pursuance of the Act, this requirement does not appear to apply to judicial review proceedings. In *Ex Parte Waldron*, Ackner J. reasoned as follows:

> "In my judgment the words of section 139[12] do not provide the clear and explicit words that are necessary to exclude the jurisdiction of the court to grant the remedy of certiorari. On the contrary, the words 'civil proceedings,'

---

[8] [2008] I.E.H.C. 160; High Court, Charleton J., May 30, 2008. See para.7–76 below.
[9] The notice parties were four medical professionals, the Mental Health Commission and the Mental Health Tribunal.
[10] High Court, unapproved, O'Keeffe J., October 24, 2008. See below, para.7–77.
[11] [2009] I.E.H.C. 253; High Court, O'Keeffe J., May 21, 2009. See paras 4–42 below.
[12] Section 139 of the Mental Health Act 1983 [England & Wales], the equivalent of s.73 of the Mental Health Act 2001.

unless specially defined, are apt only to cover civil suits involving claims in private law proceedings. The words are not apt to include proceedings for judicial review".[13]

2–10 In *Blehein v Minister for Health & Children and Others*[14] counsel for the State appears to have stated that s.260 of the Mental Treatment Act 1945, the previous version of s.73 of the 2001 Act, did not apply to judicial review.[15]

2–11 An application for judicial review would ordinarily be brought by the person who was the patient or otherwise being treated for a mental disorder. However, it might also be brought by a hospital or clinic, or family members of patients if they were adversely affected by the decision in question.

2–12 It may even be possible for a representative group to bring judicial review proceedings. The case of *Irish Penal Reform Trust Ltd v Governor of Mountjoy Prison*[16] was initiated by way of a plenary summons[17] rather than an application for judicial review but the finding in the case might be relied upon to support future judicial review applications. Gilligan J. held in the High Court that the Irish Penal Reform Trust Ltd (IPRT) had locus standi to seek declaratory relief concerning conditions in prisons, as the company was alleging systematic deficiencies in the manner in which inmates with psychiatric difficulties are treated and that prisoners with psychiatric illness are not in a position to assert adequately their constitutional rights, particularly as regards systematic deficiencies. Gilligan J. found that the case was analogous with *S.P.U.C. v Coogan*[18] in that the IPRT is a bona fide organisation with an interest in common to that of the prisoners. He also highlighted the special situation concerning persons with psychiatric conditions:

> "I am of the view that while it is arguable that an adult prisoner is fully competent to assert his constitutional rights, this may be an over-simplistic

---

[13] *Ex Parte Waldron* [1986] Q.B. 824 at 845. This case is also reported as *R. Hallstrom, ex parte W. (No.1)* [1985] 3 All E.R. 775.

[14] [2004] I.E.H.C. 374; [2004] 3 I.R. 610.

[15] "Counsel for the defendants emphasised that the presumption of constitutionality applied. It was not a prohibition but a curtailment of access to the courts confined to civil proceedings and did not apply to judicial review or habeas corpus." [2004] 3 I.R. 610 at 616 (Carroll J.) The Supreme Court decision at [2008] I.E.S.C. 40; [2008] 2 I.L.R.M. 401 does not refer to this issue.

[16] [2005] I.E.H.C. 305; High Court, Gilligan J., 2 September 2005.

[17] The plaintiffs sued the defendants for various declaratory reliefs upon the basis that the defendants have failed in their constitutional obligation to provide adequate psychiatric treatment and/or facilities and/or services for prisoners in Mountjoy Men's Prison and Mountjoy Women's Prison and further a declaration that the treatment of named plaintiffs in Mountjoy Prison was a breach of their constitutional rights.

[18] [1989] I.R. 734. Gilligan J. also relied on *R. v Pollution Inspectorate, ex p Greenpeace (No. 2)* [1994] 4 All E.R. 239.

analysis of the facts. It is almost indisputable that prisoners with psychiatric problems are amongst the most vulnerable and disadvantaged members of society. Indeed, many prisoners are ignorant of their rights and might fear retribution if they challenge the prison authorities. Furthermore, prisoners might not be aware of the fact that they have a constitutional right to receive a better standard of treatment. This puts this particular category of persons in an extremely disadvantaged position and their willingness and ability to adequately assert their constitutional rights may suffer as a result.

The I.P.R.T., being a human rights organisation established to campaign for the rights of people in prison and the progressive reform of the Irish penal policy, has a certain expertise and the financial ability necessary to mount an effective challenge to alleged systematic failings in the Irish prison system. I am of the opinion that the claim can be more effectively litigated by the I.P.R.T. who is in a position to identify and analyse systematic failings in the system.

Thus, while a psychiatrically ill prisoner may be theoretically capable of asserting his own constitutional rights, I am not satisfied that they are in a position to adequately assert same. This is especially so since the I.P.R.T. is on hand and willing to effectively litigate this claim on their behalf. Accordingly, a relaxation of the locus standi principles in the present case would appear to accord with the general principle as laid down in *Cahill v. Sutton*."[19]

In 2008, the Supreme Court said that it did not consider that the issue of locus standi could properly be determined in isolation as a preliminary issue and therefore it set aside the order and judgment of the High Court. Murray C.J. said that it would be a matter for the High Court to give such directions as it saw fit concerning the case management of the matter.[20]

2–13 If a judicial review application is successful, it may lead to a declaration that the applicant is in unlawful custody and to their release from detention. However, in the *S.M.* case,[21] McMahon J. put a stay of four weeks on his order releasing the applicant from detention. He stated that this should give the relevant parties sufficient time to comply with the provisions of the legislation before determining what, in the opinion of the relevant authorities, including the applicant's treating psychiatrist, was the appropriate order in these circumstances.[22] This seems an unjustifiably lengthy period of time to postpone the release of a patient who is in unlawful custody. It is in marked contrast to the postponements which are made in applications under art.40 (see below paras 2–42 to 2–44).

---

[19]   *Cahill v Sutton* [1980] I.R. 269. The long quotation above is from [2005] I.E.H.C. 305, p.14.
[20]   *Irish Penal Reform Trust Ltd v Governor of Mountjoy Prison*, Supreme Court, ex tempore, April 2, 2008.
[21]   *S.M. v Mental Health Commission and Others* [2008] I.E.H.C. 441; [2009] 2 I.L.R.M. 127; High Court, McMahon J., October 31, 2008.
[22]   [2009] 2 I.L.R.M. 127 at 147.

2–14 The grounds for judicial review are mainly procedural ones, e.g. that the defendant acted ultra vires its statutory powers, breached the rule against bias, breached the principle of *audi alteram partem* or failed to give adequate reasons for its decision.[23] It is possible to argue that the decision was unreasonable or irrational but the courts have restricted this in various ways. The courts seek to maintain the distinction between review of the legality of the decision and review of the merits, although this is a difficult line to draw. In England and Wales, the courts may apply a test of "*Wednesbury* unreasonableness" or even a "Super-Wednesbury" test in cases involving human rights.[24] However, in Ireland, the main authorities are the *Stardust* and *O'Keeffe* cases.[25] Henchy J. stated in *State (Keegan) v Stardust Victims' Compensation Tribunal*[26] that the test of unreasonableness or irrationality in judicial review lay in considering whether the impugned decision "plainly and unambiguously flies in the face of fundamental reason and common sense".[27] Finlay C.J. stated in *O'Keeffe v An Bord Pleanála*[28] that to satisfy a court that a decision-making authority had acted irrationally, it would be necessary to establish that the authority "had before it no relevant material which would support its decision".[29] Delany has commented that there has been a degree of inconsistency in the manner in which the courts have approached the question of whether a decision-maker can be said to have acted irrationally or unreasonably.[30] It is unclear whether the Irish courts apply a higher standard of review if constitutional or human rights are in issue. In *Z. v Minister for Justice, Equality and Law Reform*[31] McGuinness J. stated that further consideration of this question must await fuller argument in a future case.[32] There have also been some obiter comments in *A.O. v Minister for Justice, Equality and Law Reform*[33] to the effect that the test of reasonableness may need to be modified where constitutional rights are at stake.[34] Uncertainty still prevails in this context.[35]

---

[23] See further paras 8–09 to 8–25 below.

[24] In *Associated Provincial Picture Houses Ltd v Wednesbury Corporation* [1948] 1 K.B. 223 it was held that a decision maker cannot make a decision which is so unreasonable that no other decision maker in a similar situation could make it. In *R. v Ministry of Defence, ex parte Smith* [1996] Q.B. 517 it was held that in cases involving human rights the courts should carry out a "heightened scrutiny" of the policy or decision in question. See Peter Bartlett and Ralph Sandland, *Mental Health Law: Policy and Practice*, 3rd edn (Oxford: Oxford University Press, 2007), pp.193–196.

[25] See Hilary Delany, *Judicial Review of Administrative Action*, 2nd edn (Dublin: Round Hall, 2009), pp.103–121.

[26] [1986] I.R. 642.

[27] [1986] I.R. 642 at 658.

[28] [1993] 1 I.R. 39.

[29] [1993] 1 I.R. 39 at 72.

[30] Hilary Delany, *Judicial Review of Administrative Action*, 2nd edn (Dublin: Round Hall, 2009), p.105.

[31] [2002] 2 I.R. 135.

[32] [2002] 2 I.R. 135 at 158.

[33] [2003] 1 I.R. 1.

[34] [2003] 1 I.R. at 203 (Fennelly J.) and 126–7 (McGuinness J.)

[35] Hilary Delany, *Judicial Review of Administrative Action*, 2nd edn (Dublin: Round Hall, 2009), p.116.

2–15 It can be argued under art.5(4) of the ECHR that if there is no review by a tribunal on the merits available, then if a court is dealing with a judicial review application, it must look at the merits of whether the person continues to require detention, as well as considering the procedural issues. In *R. (Wilkinson) v Responsible Medical Officer Broadmoor Hospital*[36] it was held that in cases concerning forcible treatment of detained patients, the court must engage in full scrutiny on the merits of whether the patient is incapable of consenting to treatment and whether the forcible treatment breaches any of the patient's substantive rights.[37]

2–16 The breadth of judicial review proceedings has important implications for the Mental Health Tribunals and the Mental Health (Criminal Law) Review Board. If the Irish courts hold that judicial review will not consider the merits of whether the person's detention should be continued, then patients may argue that they are entitled to apply for a review by a tribunal more frequently than is currently permitted under the 2001 Act or 2006 Act. Patients would rely on *Rakevich v Russia*,[38] in which it was held that the detainee's access to the court or tribunal should not depend on the good will of the detaining authority. A similar argument was made in England in *R. (Rayner) v Secretary of State for the Home Department*.[39] The argument did not succeed because it was held that the existence of a strong system of judicial review and the possibility of a habeas corpus application meant that the *Rakevich* line of case law did not apply in England. However, the same reasoning might not apply in Ireland. One extra factor to bear in mind in Ireland is the availability of an appeal to the Circuit Court from a Mental Health Tribunal decision.[40] Any civil patient seeking to challenge their continued detention on the merits should ensure that they have availed of the Circuit Court appeal mechanism, where possible, before seeking judicial review.

2–17 It is unclear to what extent the requirement in art.5(4) that a decision be made "speedily" by a court applies to judicial review proceedings. Given that patients detained under the 2001 and 2006 Acts in Ireland now either have a review within 21 days of their detention or are detained in the first place by a judge,[41] if patients bring judicial review proceedings there may not be as much urgency required under the ECHR as there would be regarding a review of initial

---

[36] [2001] E.W.C.A. Civ. 1545; [2002] 1 W.L.R. 419.
[37] See further Peter Bartlett and Ralph Sandland, *Mental Health Law: Policy and Practice*, 3rd edn (Oxford: Oxford University Press, 2007), pp.309–312.
[38] [2004] M.H.L.R. 37.
[39] [2008] E.W.C.A. Civ. 176; [2009] 1 W.L.R. 310. See further para.7–38 below.
[40] Mental Health Act 2001, s.19. The appeal may only be brought on the grounds that the patient is no longer suffering from a mental disorder. See further paras 7–71 to 7–76 below.
[41] It has been held in *Rocha v Portugal*, November 15, 1996, (2001) 32 E.H.R.R. 16, that where a court initially orders detention, judicial review is incorporated in that decision and the right to further judicial review arises later.

detention. However, if there is an unreasonable delay, this may breach the ECHR. For example, in *Reid v U.K.*[42] the Strasbourg Court held that there should not be undue delays at appeal stages. The applicant had originally applied for release on April 8, 1994 and the House of Lords gave judgment on December 3, 1998, nearly 3 years and 10 months later. The court noted that the hearing of the application for release involved the preparation and hearing of considerable psychiatric evidence and complex issues of domestic law arose on which the courts showed some diversity of opinion. The applicant himself was also responsible for some delay in the pursuit of his appeals. Even taking those delays into account, however, there was a delay of three months and eight days between the application to the Outer House of the Court of Session and the decision rejecting his appeal; of nine months and 10 days between the lifting by the Inner House of the adjournment and its judgment; and of seven months and three days between the setting down of the case for hearing by the House of Lords and the delivery of its judgment.[43] The fact that the Scottish system provided a four-tier system of review did not justify depriving the applicant of his rights under art.5(4). The State must organise its judicial system in such a way as to enable its courts to comply with the requirements of that provision. While one year per instance might be a rough rule of thumb in art.6(1) cases, art.5(4), concerning issues of liberty required particular expedition.[44] The fact that the applicant could reapply to the Sheriff for release each year did not remedy any delay in bringing the application for release to the required speedy conclusion. Since no exceptional grounds justified the delay in determining the applicant's application for release, there was a violation of art.5(4).[45] In the *Rayner* case it was held that art.5(4) required reasonable dispatch have regard to all the material circumstances.[46]

2–18 There have been wide variations in the amount of time taken to resolve judicial review applications in Ireland, which might raise questions concerning compliance with art.5(4). For example, the application in *E.F. v Clinical Director of St. Ita's Hospital*[47] concerned events which occurred on April 24, 2007, where leave to apply for Judicial Review was granted on July 2, 2007 but judgment was not delivered until May 21, 2009. The applicant appears to have been discharged from detention at some stage before judgment was delivered, but the date of discharge is not stated. In *S.M. v Mental Health Commission*[48] the applicant's detention appears to have been most recently renewed on May 21, 2008 and

---

[42] (2003) 37 E.H.R.R. 9.
[43] (2003) 37 E.H.R.R. 9, para.76.
[44] (2003) 37 E.H.R.R. 9, paras 77–78.
[45] (2003) 37 E.H.R.R. 9, paras 79–80.
[46] *R. (Rayner) v Secretary of State for Justice* [2009] 1 W.L.R. 310, para.24 (per Keene L.J.), approving of *R. (C.) v London South and West Region Mental Health Review Tribunal* [2002] 1 W.L.R. 176, para.42.
[47] [2009] I.E.H.C. 253; High Court, O'Keeffe J., May 21, 2009.
[48] [2008] I.E.H.C. 441; [2009] 2 I.L.R.M. 127; McMahon J., High Court, October 31, 2008.

judgment was delivered on October 31, 2008. Leave to apply for judicial review was granted on November 19, 2007 in *J.B. v Mental Health (Criminal Law) Review Board & Others*[49] and judgment was delivered on July 25, 2008.

2–19 If the applicant is challenging their detention but has been discharged before the case is resolved, the respondents may argue that the case has become moot. One possible response to such an argument is that there is a real possibility that in the future the applicant would have to institute proceedings on the same or a similar point and that therefore, the applicant has a real interest in having the matter determined. Such reasoning succeeded in *E.F. v Clinical Director of St. Ita's Hospital*,[50] where O'Keeffe J. said that he did not believe that the applicant's case was moot and he believed that a decision could or would be for her benefit should circumstances arise in the future.[51] In this regard, he applied the decision of the Supreme Court in *O'Brien v the Personal Injuries Assessment Board*.[52] The question of mootness is also addressed in the *Han* case.[53] Mootness arguments by respondents appear to be more likely to succeed in applications under Art.40.

2–20 It is interesting to note that in England and Wales there appears to have been a move away from habeas corpus applications to judicial review applications in recent years. This movement is, of course, affected by the different constitutional background in England. However, useful analysis is provided in the case law of the relative features of the two remedies. In *B. v Barking Havering and Brentwood Community Healthcare NHS Trust*[54] Lord Woolf MR said he would discourage applications for habeas corpus unless it was clear that no other relief would be required.[55] Bartlett and Sandland have noted that "habeas corpus has always been a remedy of last resort."[56] They also note that the Human Rights Act 1998 may mark the virtual extinction of habeas corpus applications in mental health law.[57]

Application under Article 40/Habeas Corpus

2–21 Upon complaint being made by or on behalf of any person to the High Court alleging that such person is being unlawfully detained, the court must

---

[49] [2008] I.E.H.C. 303; High Court, Hanna J., July 25, 2008.
[50] [2009] I.E.H.C. 253; High Court, O'Keeffe J., May 21, 2009.
[51] [2009] I.E.H.C. 253; High Court, O'Keeffe J., May 21, 2009, para.40.
[52] [2006] I.E.S.C. 62; [2007] 1 I.R. 328.
[53] *Han v President of the Circuit Court* [2008] I.E.H.C. 160; High Court, Charleton J., May 30, 2008, paras 20–22.
[54] [1998] E.W.C.A. Civ. 1347; [1999] 1 F.L.R. 106.
[55] [1999] 1 F.L.R. 106 at 116.
[56] Peter Bartlett and Ralph Sandland, *Mental Health Law: Policy and Practice*, 3rd edn (Oxford: Oxford University Press, 2007), p.189.
[57] Peter Bartlett and Ralph Sandland, *Mental Health Law: Policy and Practice*, 3rd edn (Oxford: Oxford University Press, 2007), p.189.

forthwith enquire into the complaint under Art.40.4 of the Constitution.[58] This procedure is known either as an application under Art.40 or a habeas corpus application.[59] The High Court must order the release of such person from such detention unless satisfied that he or she is being detained in accordance with the law.

While s.73 of the Mental Health Act 2001 requires leave of the High Court to be sought before "civil proceedings" are brought concerning an act purporting to be done in pursuance of the Act, this requirement does not appear to apply to applications under Art.40. See the reasoning of Ackner L.J. concerning the meaning of "civil proceedings" in *Ex Parte Waldron*[60] (para.2–09 above). In *Blehein v Minister for Health & Children and Others*[61] counsel for the State appears to have stated that s.260 of the Mental Treatment Act 1945, the previous version of s.73 of the 2001 Act, did not apply to applications under Art.40.[62]

Case Law prior to November 2006

2–22 Applications under Art.40 were not brought very often prior to 2006.[63] Keys has argued that many factors might be at play in the apparent low rate of use of the habeas corpus procedure, including the lack of information about rights, or the lack of a "rights culture" in psychiatric hospitals.[64]

In *State (C.) v Frawley*,[65] the possibility of challenging conditions of detention was raised. The applicant, who was detained in Mountjoy prison, argued that his constitutional right to bodily integrity was breached due to his solitary confinement and handcuffing. There was psychiatric evidence that he had a personality trait disturbance of a sociopathic type. Finlay P. said that when the Executive imprisons an individual in pursuance of a lawful warrant of a court,

---

[58] See generally Kevin Costello, *The Law of Habeas Corpus in Ireland* (Dublin: Four Courts Press, 2006); Gerard Hogan & Gerry Whyte, *J.M. Kelly: The Irish Constitution*, 4th edn (Dublin: Butterworths, 2003), pp.1677–1706.

[59] For discussion of the technical differences between an application under Art.40 and a habeas corpus application, see Kevin Costello, *The Law of Habeas Corpus in Ireland* (Dublin: Four Courts Press, 2006), pp.105–110. Costello is of the view that the notion that the Habeas Corpus Act of 1782 (21 & 22 Geo. III, c.11) could still act as a source of habeas corpus law is probably misconceived.

[60] *Ex Parte Waldron* [1986] Q.B. 824 at 845. This case is also reported as *R. Hallstrom, ex parte W. (No.1)* [1985] 3 All E.R. 775.

[61] [2004] I.E.H.C. 374; [2004] 3 I.R. 610.

[62] "Counsel for the defendants emphasised that the presumption of constitutionality applied. It was not a prohibition but a curtailment of access to the courts confined to civil proceedings and did not apply to judicial review or habeas corpus." [2004] 3 I.R. 610 at 616 (Carroll J.) The Supreme Court decision at [2008] I.E.S.C. 40; [2008] 2 I.L.R.M. 401 does not refer to this issue.

[63] One example of a successful application is *Re Brady,* reported in 'Woman claims brothers '"tricked" her into hospital', *Irish Times*, February 16, 1990. See also Jill Nesbitt, 'Parties in unlawful detention case discuss further action', *Irish Times*, February 17, 1990.

[64] Mary Keys, "Challenging the Lawfulness of Psychiatric Detention under Habeas Corpus in Ireland" (2002) 24 D.U.L.J. 26 at 35.

[65] [1976] I.R. 365. See further para.12–09 below.

then it seemed to him to be a logical extension of the principle laid down in the *Ryan* case[66] on bodily integrity that it may not, without justification or necessity, expose the health of that person to risk or danger.[67] He also said that freedom from torture and inhuman or degrading treatment or punishment could be raised as part of an argument concerning bodily integrity. On the facts, he found that the conditions of the applicant's detention were justified and his application for release failed.

O'Higgins C.J. emphasised in *State (McDonagh) v Frawley* that, for an application to succeed, there must be such a default of fundamental requirements that the detention may be said to be wanting in due process of law:

> "The stipulation in Article 40, s. 4, subs-s. 1 of the Constitution that a citizen may not be deprived of his liberty save 'in accordance with law' does not mean that a convicted person must be released on habeas corpus merely because some defect or illegality attaches to his detention. The phrase seems to mean that there must be such a default of fundamental requirements that the detention may be said to be wanting in due process of law. For habeas corpus, therefore, it is insufficient for the prisoner to show that there has been a legal error or impropriety, or even that jurisdiction has been inadvertently exceeded."[68]

2–23 The European Court of Human Rights held in *X. v United Kingdom*[69] in 1981 that a review by way of habeas corpus procedure was not sufficient for a continuing confinement of a patient. The English High Court had declined to determine whether the evidence supported the conclusion that the applicant's mental disorder was of a type which warranted detention. The Strasbourg Court stated that in this case an appropriate procedure was required, allowing a court to examine whether the patient's mental disorder still persisted and whether the Home Secretary was entitled to think that a continuation of the compulsory confinement was necessary in the interests of public safety.[70] But the court also stated that art.5(4) did not guarantee "a right to judicial control of such scope as to empower the court, on all aspects of the case, to substitute its own discretion for that of the decision-making authority".[71]

2–24 In the High Court in *Croke v Smith (No.2)*, Budd J. noted the difficulties for patients with habeas corpus:

---

[66] *Ryan v Attorney General* [1965] I.R. 294 (the water fluoridation case which established the right to bodily integrity as an unspecified constitutional right).
[67] [1976] I.R. 365 at 372.
[68] [1978] I.R. 131 at 136.
[69] *X. v United Kingdom*, Application No.7215/75, judgment 5 November 1981 (1981) 4 E.H.R.R. 188.
[70] (1981) 4 E.H.R.R. 188 at 209.
[71] (1981) 4 E.H.R.R. 188 at 209.

"I have already adverted to the right of the patient or someone acting on the patient's behalf to apply to the High Court for an Order of Habeas Corpus both under common law and under the provisions of Article 40.4.2 of the Constitution. This initiates an inquiry as to the lawfulness of the patient's detention and is undoubtedly a speedy and efficacious remedy. However, the situation of a mental patient who is illiterate, harmless and without kith or kin to initiate such an inquiry on his behalf by way of habeas corpus perhaps poses the problem in a stark form. Such a patient may not be aware of his or her rights to seek habeas corpus and may be incapable of the necessary written or verbal communication to trigger such an inquiry."[72]

The Supreme Court held that the Mental Treatment Act 1945 was not in breach of the applicant's constitutional rights. Hamilton C.J. reviewed the role of the courts in hearing applications under Art.40.4 in cases of this kind:

"By virtue of the provisions of Article 40.4.2 of the Constitution complaint may be made to the High Court by, or on behalf of, a patient detained pursuant to the provisions of the Mental Treatment Act 1945, as amended, alleging that he is being unlawfully detained and once such a complaint is made the High Court is obliged to conduct an inquiry into the lawfulness of the applicant's detention.

The onus is on the person in whose custody the applicant is to justify the detention and the High Court must be satisfied that such detention is in accordance with law before permitting the continued detention of the applicant.

Upon the hearing of the application the High Court must be satisfied that:—
(1) the person detained is a person of unsound mind and in need of care and treatment;
(2) that the procedures outlined in the Act have been complied with;
(3) the person detained has not recovered; and
(4) the person detained is not being unnecessarily deprived of his liberty.
Unless it is satisfied with regard to each of the foregoing, the High Court must order the discharge or release of the person detained."[73]

2–25 Costello has commented that a power of review of such depth is difficult to reconcile with the established principle that a court, in discharging judicial review, is supposed to abstain from reviewing the merits of an administrative order. He states that the decision suggests that, "an unusually interventionist standard of review may be required in the case of non-appealable, administrative detention where the consequences of an erroneous finding of fact upon the individual's rights are so significant as to engage the exceptional protective jurisdiction".[74]

[72] *Croke v Smith (No.2)*, High Court, Budd J., July 27 and 31, 1995, p.46.
[73] [1998] 1 I.R. 101 at 124–5.
[74] Kevin Costello, *The Law of Habeas Corpus in Ireland* (Dublin: Four Courts Press, 2006), p.54.

2–26 Kelly J. referred to the procedure under Art.40.4 as a "great remedy"[75] in *Application of Gallagher (No.2)* but also emphasised that it should not be used in circumstances where the complaints made should more properly be addressed by some other inquiry or procedure, for example judicial review.[76] Geoghegan J. warned that the court must avoid combining judicial review with the task in hand, which was an Art.40 enquiry.[77] Laffoy J. stated that Gallagher was "constrained" to advance certain arguments because of the nature of an Art.40 application.[78] She later imposed an interesting limitation on the procedure: "Fourthly, the gravity of the irregularity, breach or default falls to be considered and whether it can be appropriately redressed by a less radical remedy than immediate release."[79]

2–27 In *Orton v St. John of God Hospital*[80] the application under Art.40 failed on procedural points but it is notable that Finnegan P. stated that he had "the benefit of the medical report from [his] own Medical Visitor". This report confirmed the two medical opinions obtained for the purposes of the detention of the applicant. Finnegan P. said that on the basis of the Medical Visitor's Report it was desirable and indeed essential that he should receive treatment. Presumably the Medical Visitor's report was obtained by using the power of the President of the High Court in s.241 of the Mental Treatment Act 1945.[81]

2–28 *L.K. v Clinical Director of Lakeview Unit, Naas General Hospital*[82] was decided in May-July 2006 and concerned the Mental Treatment Act 1945. Clarke J. noted that an issue had arisen as to the scope of the substantive hearing which should be afforded a party on foot of an inquiry under Art.40.4.2 seeking to question the validity of that person's detention under the Acts. It was agreed by both counsel, and he agreed, that the passages from the judgment of Hamilton C.J. in *Croke v Smith (No.2)* were clear authority for the proposition that such an inquiry included a substantive inquiry into whether the mental health and other circumstances of the applicant concerned justified their detention. In those circumstances an inquiry under Art.40.4.2 in relation to a person detained under the provisions of the Acts may well be more extensive than a normal inquiry under the jurisdiction exercised under that Article.[83] Clarke J. said that the court is not normally concerned with the substance of the reason for custody in the

---

75   [1996] 3 I.R. 10 at 47.
76   [1996] 3 I.R. 10, p.47
77   [1996] 3 I.R. 10, p.16.
78   [1996] 3 I.R. 10, p.35.
79   [1996] 3 I.R. 10, p.36.
80   [2004] I.E.H.C. 361; High Court, Finnegan P., November 15, 2004.
81   Kevin Costello, *The Law of Habeas Corpus in Ireland* (Dublin: Four Courts Press, 2006), p.228, fn.3.
82   Two judgments were issued, both reported at [2007] 2 I.R. 465. The first was [2006] I.E.H.C. 196; High Court, Clarke J., May 17, 2006 and the second was High Court, Clarke J., July 6, 2006.
83   [2007] 2 I.R. 465 at 482.

first place, but it was clear from *Croke v Smith (No. 2)* that the court was required, on a hearing such as this, to consider the substantive merits of the detention.[84] He referred to art.5(4) of the ECHR and said: "It is, however, clear that the type of inquiry identified in *Croke v. Smith (No. 2)* arising under Article 40.4.2 goes even further than the requirements necessary to satisfy article 5(4) of the Convention."[85]

Clarke J. also stated that the jurisdiction of the High Court in applications under Art.40 might change once the 2001 Act was commenced:

> "Finally I should add that the somewhat extensive jurisdiction to review, identified in *Croke v. Smith (No. 2)* [1998] 1 I.R. 101 seems to me to be necessitated by the requirements of the Constitution and might well also have arisen by virtue of the necessity of compliance, where possible, with the Convention. However it does not necessarily follow that that extensive jurisdiction would be required in the event that the full provisions of the Mental Health Act 2001 concerning mental health tribunals are implemented. In those circumstances the question remains open as to whether it would be necessary, or indeed appropriate, for the court to entertain a full substantive review on foot of an inquiry under Article 40.4.2. That is an issue which may need to be addressed if and when the relevant provisions of the Act of 2001 are commenced."[86]

Case Law since November 2006

2–29 The general tendency in case law since November 2006[87] has been for the courts to restrict the scope of applications under Art.40 as a remedy. In *J.H. v Lawlor, Clinical Director of Jonathan Swift Clinic, St. James's Hospital*[88] Peart J. quoted from the judgment of O'Higgins C.J. in *State (McDonagh) v Frawley*[89] (above, para.2–22) and said: "I see no reason why such reasoning should not extend to an application by a person whose detention is under the Mental Health Act 2001 whose purpose is to protect and care for a person rather than to punish, and where those protections have been afforded without dilution."[90]

2–30 Kearns J. also used the same quote from *State (McDonagh) v Frawley* in *E.H. v Clinical Director of St. Vincent's Hospital*.[91] He said that Art.40.4 should not be used to challenge "mere technical defects":

---

[84] [2007] 2 I.R. 465 at 482.
[85] [2007] 2 I.R. 465 at 483.
[86] [2007] 2 I.R. 465 at 484.
[87] The majority of sections of the Mental Health Act 2001 came into force on November 1, 2006—Mental Health Act 2001 (Commencement) Order 2006, S.I. No. 411 of 2006.
[88] [2007] I.E.H.C. 225; [2008] 1 I.R. 476; High Court, Peart J., June 25, 2007.
[89] [1978] I.R. 131.
[90] [2008] 1 I.R. 476 at 490.
[91] [2009] I.E.S.C. 46; [2009] 2 I.L.R.M. 149; Supreme Court, May 28, 2009.

"These proceedings were initiated and maintained on purely technical and unmeritorious grounds. It is difficult to see in what way they advanced the interests of the applicant who patently is in need of psychiatric care. The fact that s.17(1)(b) of the Act of 2001 provides for the assignment by the Commission of a legal representative for a patient following the making of an admission order or a renewal order should not give rise to an assumption that a legal challenge to that patient's detention is warranted unless the best interests of the patient so demand. Mere technical defects, without more, in a patient's detention should not give rise to a rush to court, notably where any such defect can or has been cured—as in the present case. Only in cases where there had been a gross abuse of power or default of fundamental requirements would a defect in an earlier period of detention justify release from a later one."[92]

2–31 The Supreme Court has also held on three occasions that a "domino effect" does not apply. If there is an unlawfulness at an earlier stage of detention it may be "cured" by a subsequent lawful detention. Hardiman J. said in *R.L. v Clinical Director of St. Brendan's Hospital & Ors*[93]:

"But the question, the legal question has to be isolated. This is, does that breach of s.13 or to put it even more widely, let us assume that the other two breaches alleged by Mr. Finlay are established, do those breaches of s.13 operate to prevent the making of an admission order under s.14 and if it did that, would it logically also prevent the making of further orders under the Act?

The Court can simply see no reason whatever to believe that an irregularity or a direct breach of s.13 would render what is on the face of it a lawful detention on foot of an admission order invalid."[94]

Hardiman J. said that this was not a case which called for protection under Art.40 of the Constitution, fortunately. The scheme of Art.40 is that the court orders the person detaining to certify. The Clinical Director certified relying on the admission order and when these things are done the court must order the release of such person from detention unless satisfied that they are being detained in accordance with law. The court was satisfied that the patient was being detained in accordance with law and therefore the court would decline to order her release.[95] He noted that the applicant certainly had rights in the event of her being able to establish breaches of s.13 of the 2001 Act. But in the court's

---

[92] [2009] 2 I.L.R.M. 149 at 165.

[93] Supreme Court (*ex tempore*), February 15, 2008.

[94] Supreme Court (*ex tempore*), February 15, 2008, pp.5–6. See also Feeney J. in the High Court— [2008] I.E.H.C. 11; [2008] 3 I.R. 296 at 301—"if complaint is to be made in relation to a suggested breach of s.13 it is a matter to be taken under O.84 of the Rules of the Superior Courts 1986 as a matter to be pursued by means of judicial review."

[95] Supreme Court (*ex tempore*), February 15, 2008, pp.7–8.

view this was something which had happened and in legal terms was spent, so that it would appear that L.'s remedy in relation to any breach of the law was a right to compensation.[96] See further paras 4–36 to 4–37 below.

2–32 In *S.C.* Hardiman J. quoted his own views in *R.L.* and continued:

> "Now in this case a very similar position applies. We are quite satisfied that Dr. McAuley's certification of the 19th February, 2009 grounds the detention of the applicant in St. Brigid's Hospital. We do not feel called upon by authority or otherwise to apply to this case the sort of reasoning that would be applied if it were a criminal detention and to investigate whether previous matters which might have a causal relationship to the present detention are invalid."[97]

2–33 In *E.H.*, Kearns J. said he could see "no justification whatsoever for the bringing or maintenance of this appeal following the rulings delivered by this Court in both the *R.L.* case and the *[S.C.]* case which effectively put paid to any suggestion that a domino effect or theory of infection applied to cases of this nature".[98] The Supreme Court therefore held that the case was moot (compare the courts' statements on mootness in judicial review cases, para.2–19 above).

2–34 Charleton J. said in *T.O'D. v Kennedy* that if, at a time when the High Court considers an application for habeas corpus, a period of unlawful detention has been cured validly by a decision of the mental health tribunal under s.18(1), the remedy is no longer available.[99]

2–35 Clarke J. said in *J.H. v Russell* that in general habeas corpus cannot be used to challenge treatment:

> "I am prepared to accept, for the purposes of argument in this case, that the conditions in which a person may be detained as a mental health patient might, in theory, fall so far short of acceptable conditions as to render unlawful a detention which might otherwise be regarded as lawful. I am also prepared to accept, for the purposes of argument in this case, that amongst the relevant conditions that might, theoretically, render such detention unlawful would be the treatment (or perhaps more accurately the lack thereof) being afforded to the person concerned in all the circumstances of the case. However, by a parity of reasoning with the jurisprudence of the courts in respect of persons who are detained within the criminal justice process, it does not seem to me that

---

[96] Supreme Court (*ex tempore*), February 15, 2008, p.9.
[97] *S.C. v Clinical Director of St. Brigid's Hospital*, Supreme Court, March 13, 2009, Judgment not available, quoted in *E.H. v Clinical Director of St. Vincent's Hospital* [2009] 2 I.L.R.M. 149 at 164.
[98] *E.H. v Clinical Director of St. Vincent's Hospital* [2009] 2 I.L.R.M. 149 at 164.
[99] [2007] I.E.H.C. 129; [2007] 3 I.R. 689 at 705.

anything other than a complete failure to provide appropriate conditions or appropriate treatment could render what would otherwise be a lawful detention, unlawful."[100]

2–36 Decisions on applications under Art.40 tend, in general, to be delivered quite quickly. If there were any delay in the delivery of the decision, it might be argued that art.5(4) of the ECHR was breached (see para.1–25 above.)

2–37 As was noted above (para.2–20), in England and Wales there has recently been a movement away from habeas corpus as a remedy in mental health cases.

Release of Patient

2–38 The High Court must order the release of the applicant from detention unless satisfied that he or she is being detained in accordance with the law.[101] However, if the High Court has found that the person is being detained in accordance with a law but that the law is unconstitutional, Art.40.4.3 states that the High Court must refer the question of the validity of the law to the Supreme Court by way of case stated. The High Court may release the person on bail until the Supreme Court has determined the case stated.[102] This unusual provision effectively requires a compulsory review by the Supreme Court of a High Court decision in these circumstances. If the patient has been released by the time the Supreme Court hears the case stated, the Supreme Court may decide not to proceed with the case, as it no longer concerns a live issue. This was what occurred in *R.T. v Director of the Central Mental Hospital*.[103] Costello P. found that s.207 of the Mental Treatment Act 1945 was unconstitutional. In the light of the medical evidence, he said that he did not think he could admit T. to bail. He also commented that whatever view the Supreme Court would take of the section, the end result was likely to be T.'s retransfer to St. Brendan's and the making of a new reception order. Therefore, it should be explained to T. that his best interests might be served by availing of an immediate transfer to St. Brendan's.[104]

After the High Court decision, T. was transferred back to St. Brendan's Hospital, meaning he had been released from the Central Mental Hospital, which was the aim of his challenge. On November 3, 1995, the State applied to the Supreme Court for a decision as to whether the Case Stated should now go ahead. Counsel for the State said that the law would be changed in the future. The Supreme Court asked that Costello P.'s view be sought on the matter.

---

[100] *J.H. v Russell* [2007] I.E.H.C. 7, paras 7.4–7.5; [2007] 4 I.R. 242 at 261; Clarke J., High Court, February 6, 2007.
[101] Article 40.4.2 of the Constitution.
[102] Article 40.4.3 of the Constitution.
[103] [1995] 2 I.R. 65.
[104] [1995] 2 I.R. 65 at 82.

Costello P. stated that in view of the changed facts he withdrew the Case Stated. This meant that the Case Stated lapsed.[105] R.T. was awarded his costs against the State.[106] As a result, s.207 remained on the statute book.

2–39 In many cases, applicants will not argue that they are detained under a law which is unconstitutional, and Art.40.4.3 will not apply. While the Constitution appears to require that the person be released if their detention is unlawful, other considerations may mean that the court does not order immediate release. Costello notes that there are cases where the strict text in Art.40.4.2 has been regarded as accessible to qualification in the interests of competing constitutional concerns.[107]

2–40 At common law, there was a reluctance to order release of a patient who might be dangerous. In *Re Shuttleworth*,[108] Lord Denman C.J. stated:

> "If the Court thought that a party, unlawfully received or retained, was a lunatic, we should still be betraying the common duties of members of society if we directed a discharge. But we have no power to set aside the order, only to discharge. And should we, as Judges or individuals, be justified in setting such a party at large? It is answered, that there may be a fresh custody. But why so? Is it not better, if she be dangerous, that she should remain in custody till the Great Seal or the commissioners act? Therefore, being satisfied in my own mind that there would be danger in setting her at large, I am bound by the most general principles to abstain from so doing: and I should be abusing the name of liberty if I were to take off a restraint for which those who are most interested in the party ought to be most thankful."[109]

In *R. (Fetherstone) v Riall and Riall*[110] the court refused to release a person detained as a "dangerous lunatic"; instead Lefroy C.J. said that the court would "let the matter stand over until the state of the man's mind be ascertained by the examination of two medical men, one to be named by the applicant's counsel, and the other to be named by the Crown."[111] In the much more recent case of *Re Briscoe*[112] the court found detention to be unlawful but did not order the applicant's release, instead adjourning the case for two days. Tucker J. said that if there was no representation to the contrary from the respondent hospital by

---

[105] "This is unfortunate as the Supreme Court could have delivered a definitive judgment on this controversial section"—Jarlath Spellman, "A Lawyer's Comment on the White Paper on a New Mental Health Act" (1995) 1 M.L.J.I. 86 at 89, fn.12.
[106] Information provided by Ms Muireann Ó Briain, S.C., counsel for R.T.
[107] Kevin Costello, *The Law of Habeas Corpus in Ireland* (Dublin: Four Courts Press, 2006), p.101.
[108] (1846) 9 Q.B.D. 651; 115 E.R. 1423.
[109] (1846) 9 Q.B.D. 651 at 662.
[110] (1860) 11 I.C.L.R. 279.
[111] (1860) 11 I.C.L.R. 279 at 287.
[112] [1998] E.W.H.C. Admin. 771; [1998] C.O.D. 402.

that time he would direct that the applicant be released from hospital.

The common law on this point is summarised in textbooks by Hoggett[113] and Sharpe.[114] Costello surmises that the *Shuttleworth* and *Riall* approach might apply in Ireland, "It is at least possible that the same exceptional jurisdiction might exist under the Constitution."[115]

2–41 In *Croke v Smith (No.1)*[116] Flood J. stated that in certain circumstances a bona fide absence of appropriate certification might exist concerning the patient in that case. He said that in the event of legal proceedings based on such lacuna, "the somewhat archaic but nonetheless rational common sense expressed in *Re Shuttleworth* may well be apt".[117] However, he did not need to apply this reasoning in the case, as he found that the patient's detention was lawful. On appeal, the Supreme Court found the detention to be unlawful and ordered the patient's release. Blayney J. stated that if the applicant's present mental condition was such as to warrant the making of a new application for a reception order under the 1945 Act, then it would appear that if his parents were not willing to make such application, urgent consideration should be given to an application being made by the appropriate officers of the Health Board so that a reception order might be made if the chief medical officer saw fit. He said: "It is important that the people concerned with this matter should clearly understand that this decision and any order consequent upon it which may be made by the court does not in any way impede such a course of conduct."[118]

2–42 Since most sections of the Mental Health Act 2001 came into force in 2006, if the High Court has found that the patient's detention was unlawful, it has generally ordered the patient's release but put a stay on the release to facilitate a fresh application under the 2001 Act to be made for the patient's detention. This is sometimes referred to as a "staggered release".

This did not occur in *Q. v Governor of St. Patrick's Hospital*,[119] the first case where a patient's detention under the 2001 Act was found to be unlawful, where O'Higgins J. ordered the patient's immediate release.

More detailed consideration was given to the question of whether the patient should be released immediately in *J.H. v Russell*.[120] Clarke J. noted that in *N. v Health Service Executive (the "Baby Ann" case)*[121] Murray C.J. had stated that a successful application pursuant to Art.40.4 concerning an unlawful detention

---

[113]　Brenda Hoggett, *Mental Health Law*, 4th edn (London: Sweet and Maxwell, 1996), pp.78–9.

[114]　Robert J Sharpe, *The Law of Habeas Corpus*, 2nd edn (Oxford: Clarendon Press, 1989), p.157.

[115]　Kevin Costello, *The Law of Habeas Corpus in Ireland* (Dublin: Four Courts Press, 2006), p.232.

[116]　[1994] 3 I.R. 525.

[117]　[1994] 3 I.R. 525 at 537.

[118]　[1994] 3 I.R. 525 at 545.

[119]　High Court, O'Higgins J., *ex tempore*, December 21, 2006.

[120]　[2007] I.E.H.C. 7; [2007] 4 I.R. 242; Clarke J., High Court, February 6, 2007.

[121]　[2006] I.E.S.C. 60; [2006] 4 I.R. 374.

would normally lead to an order for the release of the person concerned from the unlawful detention concerned with no further order being necessary. However, the court took into account the fact that there were special circumstances, namely on the facts of that case the welfare of an infant of tender years, to be taken into account when determining the manner in which effect might be given to the order of the court pursuant to Art.40.4. Murray C.J. had stated: "In my view the court has jurisdiction, in the circumstances of a case such as this, involving as it does a minor of very tender age, to make ancillary or interim orders concerning the immediate custody of such infant which are necessary in order to protect her rights and welfare pending effect being given to the substantive order of the court."[122] In coming to that view, Murray C.J. had placed reliance on the decision of the Supreme Court in *D.G. v Eastern Health Board*[123] where a minor was ordered to be detained in St. Patrick's Institution in order to provide for his welfare, having regard to a severe personality disorder, in special circumstances where there was no other suitable facility within the State for his detention and notwithstanding the fact that St. Patrick's Institution was not designed for holding persons in his circumstances. Clarke J. stated in *J.H. v Russell* that while both of those cases were concerned with under age persons, he saw no reason in principle why that jurisprudence should not equally apply, in an appropriate case, to persons under a mental disability.[124] The underlying logic of the approach of the Supreme Court in both those cases was that the normal rule (i.e. immediate release) might not be appropriate in all circumstances involving persons whose detention was, at least in significant part, designed for their own good. A similar situation arose in the case of involuntary patients. Clarke J. continued:

> "I am therefore satisfied that the court has a jurisdiction to make an ancillary order of the type identified by the Supreme Court in *N. v. Health Service Executive* as to how best to give effect to the decision of the court. I was, therefore, persuaded that, in all the circumstances of this case, it was appropriate to put in place arrangements that would facilitate appropriate procedures being put in place to seek to invoke the new process set out in the Act of 2001 for the purposes of seeking a fresh detention order in respect of the applicant under the provisions of that Act. In coming to that view, I was principally motivated by the fact that no argument was addressed to the court, nor was there any evidence before the court, which sought to contradict the contention that the applicant was in need of treatment in an institution. Obviously very different considerations would apply in circumstances where a court was persuaded that there was a difficulty with the conclusions reached concerning the mental status of the patient concerned. There was no such difficulty in this case."[125]

---

[122] [2006] 4 I.R. 374 at 470.
[123] [1997] 3 I.R. 511.
[124] [2007] 4 I.R. 242 at 263.
[125] [2007] 4 I.R. 242 at 263.

Clarke J. therefore directed the release of the applicant at 6 pm on January 8, 2007 (being 6 pm on the day when he made the order concerned, the order having being made at 11 am). It was made clear to the parties that the purpose of directing the release of the applicant some six to seven hours after he had issued a brief ruling in the case (indicating the form of order which he intended to make) was to facilitate the authorities in Cavan General Hospital to put in place a regime which would allow for a fresh application for detention to be made in accordance with the process set out in the 2001 Act.[126]

2–43 In *M. v Director of Central Mental Hospital*,[127] Hanna J. applied a staggered release for a seven-day period in a case concerning detention under the Mental Treatment Act 1945. He stated that this was a place where the law and medicine meet. In ordinary circumstances an order directing the release of a person under Art.40 has immediate effect but in a rare instance, such as the current application, a balance had to be struck between the applicant's right to immediate freedom and his physical well-being. If the applicant was simply released it would have had a catastrophic effect on his life. The order releasing the applicant would not be effective for a period of seven days, during which the orderly transfer to St. Vincent's Hospital could be effected. Counsel for the respondents requested a stay on the order for leave to appeal. Hanna J. said that this was not available in an Art.40 case and he refused the application.

2–44 The practice of staggered release was widely used in cases decided in 2007 and 2008 in which detention under the 2001 Act was found to be unlawful. However, in December 2008, in *S.C. v Clinical Director of Jonathan Swift Clinic, St. James's Hospital*,[128] the Supreme Court refused to place a stay on release where there was no evidence that the patient was dangerous. On December 4, the applicant complained to the High Court (Bermingham J.) that she was being unlawfully detained in a "mental institution". When those who were detaining her came before the court to explain her detention, they did not challenge her assertion that it was unlawful. The trial judge was asked to order the applicant's release but to put a stay on that order for 24 hours. This was done over the objections of counsel for the applicant. The following day, the applicant appealed to the Supreme Court against the stay on the order for her release. Counsel for the detaining authorities stated that the purpose of the stay was to afford them some time during which they might arrange for the applicant to be lawfully detained. Speaking for the Supreme Court, Hardiman J. reasoned as follows:

> "It is important to note that neither in this Court nor in the High Court was it disputed that this lady had full capacity to institute the proceedings and to

---

[126] [2007] 4 I.R. 242 at 263–4.
[127] High Court, Hanna J., April 13, 2007 (counsel's note of *ex tempore* judgment).
[128] Supreme Court, *ex tempore*, December 5, 2008.

instruct her lawyers. It was also said that, while the application for a stay was made on the basis of medical evidence, there was no evidence or even suggestion that the applicant is a danger to herself or to any other person. There was evidence that, in the opinion of a doctor whose name we have not been given the applicant needed treatment and needed to take medication.

We do not consider it necessary, in those circumstances, to decide whether or not there may ever be a stay on an order for release from psychiatric detention. It is sufficient to say firstly that the *Trimbole decision*[129] suggests strongly that such release must be immediate and, secondly, that evidence which goes only as far as the medical evidence of which we have been informed could not conceivably form the basis for a continuation of a detention admitted to be unlawful.

In those circumstances we will simply make an order for the release of the moving party."[130]

It is difficult to assess the implications of this judgment, as details regarding the medical evidence tendered are sketchy. On one construction, the judgment is simply reiterating the decision of Clarke J. in *J.H. v Russell*.[131] In that case, no argument was addressed to the court, nor was there any evidence before the court, which sought to contradict the contention that the applicant was in need of treatment in an institution. Clarke J. stated that very different considerations would apply in circumstances where a court was persuaded that there was a difficulty with the conclusions reached concerning the mental status of the patient concerned. The *S.C. v Clinical Director of Jonathan Swift Clinic* case may be seen as applying that reasoning in a situation where the patient was contesting the medical evidence that she continued to require treatment.

However, it is also arguable that the *S.C.* decision sets the bar higher than it had been set in previous cases in two respects. Firstly, it appears to indicate that the patient does not need to produce medical evidence to contradict the evidence of the detaining authorities; instead, it may be sufficient for the patient to argue that they do not agree that they continue to require detention, assuming they have capacity to instruct their lawyers to make that argument. Secondly, the case may mean that, if the patient has sufficient capacity to instruct their lawyers, the staggered release procedure may only be used if the patient is dangerous to themselves or others. It may no longer be sufficient for the patient to satisfy the need for care and treatment criterion in s.3 of the 2001 Act, though the courts may require that the patient satisfy the risk of serious harm criterion.

---

[129] Counsel had referred to *Trimbole v Governor of Mountjoy Prison* [1985] I.R. 550 and in particular a passage from the judgment of Finlay C.J. at p.567 to the effect that when a person's release is ordered by the High Court under Art.40, that person is in law released from custody. The Court refused to grant a stay on such an Order in order to make the authorities' appeal effective, considering that such a course would be inconsistent with the Constitution.

[130] Supreme Court, *ex tempore*, December 5, 2008, pp.3–4.

[131] [2007] I.E.H.C. 7; [2007] 4 I.R. 242; Clarke J., High Court, February 6, 2007.

Anonymity

2–45 In *M.D. v Clinical Director of St Brendan's Hospital & Anor.*,[132] the court was requested on both sides of the case to take such steps as were possible to prevent the publication of the applicant's name or of any detail which might identify him. This was requested on the basis that he was, undisputedly, a person under a disability. Hardiman J. said that the court did not consider that it had, in these proceedings, any power to make an order in that regard. However the court agreed to, and did, request any representatives of the media who might be present not to publish his name and said that it would not itself do so.[133]

Section 27 of the Civil Law (Miscellaneous Provisions) Act 2008 now provides that where in any civil proceedings a relevant person[134] has a medical condition,[135] an application may be made to the court by any party for an order prohibiting the publication or broadcast of any matter relating to the proceedings which would, or would be likely to, identify the relevant person as a person having that condition. The court shall grant the order under this section only if it is satisfied that the relevant person has a medical condition, his or her identification as a person with that condition would be likely to cause undue stress to him or her, and the order would not be prejudicial to the interests of justice. This section appears to be modelled on s.181 of the Criminal Justice Act 2006, which allows anonymity for witnesses in criminal cases who have a medical condition.

Role of Lawyer in bringing Applications under Art.40

2–46 The courts have occasionally commented on the appropriateness of the application under Art.40 being brought. In *P.McG. v Medical Director of the Mater Hospital*,[136] Peart J. said that it was not for the solicitor appointed to represent the interests of the patient to ignore the failure to observe the provisions of the 2001 Act on the basis that she may not have believed that this court was likely to order his release. However, he also said that that was not to say that there could never be a case which the High Court would consider ought never to have been made. He stated that the court must always retain the discretion to consider that the defect alleged is of such a trivial and insubstantial nature as to have always been bound to fail.[137]

Kearns J. stated in *E.H. v Clinical Director of St. Vincent's Hospital*[138] that the fact that s.17(1)(b) of the Act of 2001 provides for the assignment by the

---

[132]   [2007] I.E.S.C. 37; [2008] 1 I.R. 632; Supreme Court, July 27, 2007.
[133]   [2008] 1 I.R. 632 at 641.
[134]   A relevant person means a party to the proceedings or a person called or proposed to be called to give evidence in the proceedings—s. 27(11)(b), Civil Law (Miscellaneous Provisions) Act 2008.
[135]   The Act does not define "medical condition".
[136]   [2007] I.E.H.C. 401; [2008] 2 I.R. 332; High Court, Peart J., November 29, 2007.
[137]   [2008] 2 I.R. 332 at 338.
[138]   [2009] I.E.S.C. 46; [2009] 2 I.L.R.M. 149; Supreme Court, May 28, 2009.

Commission of a legal representative for a patient following the making of an admission order or a renewal order should not give rise to an assumption that a legal challenge to that patient's detention is warranted unless the best interests of the patient so demand. Mere technical defects, without more, in a patient's detention should not give rise to a rush to court, notably where any such defect can or has been cured.[139]

It is to be hoped that this paragraph in *E.H.* was intended merely to advise legal representatives to exercise restraint concerning applications under Art.40 in circumstances where there is settled law to the effect that the application will fail.[140] It is notable that in *E.H.* Kearns J. was strongly of the view that the case was a moot[141] and this may have influenced the language which he used in the paragraph concerning mere technical defects not giving rise to a rush to court. However, there is a risk that the paragraph will deter legal representatives from bringing applications under Art.40 even when there is a strong case to be made. The reference in the paragraph to "best interests of the patient" will also cause difficulties, as the statutory best interests principle does not normally apply to decisions made by a legal representative (see paras 7–49 to 7–52 below) and the legal representative will find it difficult to reconcile their ethical duty to represent the client with the best interests principle.[142]

Negligence

2–47 The relevance of the tort of negligence to mental health law will be considered below in Chapter 11. Patients are owed a duty of care by any medical professionals treating them and patients may sue for breach of the duty of care. For example, in *Armstrong v Eastern Health Board*[143] an action in negligence succeeded where it was found that the psychiatrist's assessment was based on insufficient information.

The leave of the High Court under s.73 of the 2001 Act must be sought for actions in negligence and other torts in respect of an act purporting to have been done in pursuance of the Act.[144]

Other Torts

2–48 If a person is detained without lawful justification, this may be actionable as the tort of false imprisonment.[145] False imprisonment has been defined as "the

---

[139] [2009] 2 I.L.R.M. 149 at 165.
[140] In *E.H.* itself the question of whether there was settled law to this effect is debatable.
[141] [2009] 2 I.L.R.M. 149 at 164.
[142] See generally Michael Lynn, Discussion Paper for Mental Health Lawyers Association, July 2009.
[143] High Court, Egan J., October 5, 1990.
[144] See further paras 2–51 to 2–57 below.
[145] See generally Bryan McMahon & William Binchy, *Law of Torts*, 3rd edn (Dublin: Butterworths,

unlawful imposition of constraint on another's freedom of movement from a particular place".[146] The confinement must be total, and there must be no safe means of escape of which the plaintiff could reasonably be aware.[147]

In *Meering v Grahame-White Aviation Co. Ltd*,[148] Atkin L.J. drew a distinction between restraint upon the plaintiff's liberty which is conditional upon their seeking to exercise their freedom (which would not amount to false imprisonment), and an actual restraint upon their liberty, as where the defendant decided to restrain the plaintiff within a room and placed a police officer outside the door to stop them leaving (which would amount to false imprisonment).[149] Lord Goff approved of this distinction in the *Bournewood* case[150] (see further paras 5–26 to 5–28 below). However, the European Court of Human Rights has adopted a broader definition of deprivation of liberty in *H.L. v United Kingdom*.[151]

2–49 Assault and battery are aspects of the tort of trespass to the person. Assault is where a person is caused immediately to apprehend a contact with the person. Battery is directly and intentionally (or possibly negligently) causing some physical contact with the person of another without consent.[152] On the question of the law concerning consent, see Chapter 10 below.

2–50 Torts other than negligence may be tried with a jury.[153] Difficulties may arise where the action concerns a combination, e.g. of battery and negligence.[154] In the *Manweiler* case, a jury trial was held concerning an action for battery, false imprisonment, negligence and breach of constitutional rights.[155] High Court leave is required before instituting any civil proceedings in respect of an act purporting to have been done in pursuance of the Act.[156]

Leave of High Court Requirement for Civil Proceedings

2–51 Section 260 of Mental Treatment Act 1945 required the leave of the High Court before civil proceedings could be commenced in respect of an act

---

2000), pp.626–632; Eoin Quill, *Torts in Ireland*, 2nd edn (Dublin: Gill and Macmillan, 2004), pp.184–186.

[146] *Collins v Wilcock* [1984] 1 W.L.R. 1172 at 1177 (Robert Goff L.J.).

[147] Eoin Quill, *Torts in Ireland*, 2nd edn (Dublin, Gill and Macmillan, 2004), p.184.

[148] (1919) 122 L.T. 44.

[149] (1919) 122 L.T. 44 at 54–55.

[150] *R. v Bournewood Community and Mental Health NHS Trust, ex parte L.* [1998] U.K.H.L. 24; [1999] 1 A.C. 458 at 486.

[151] (2005) 40 E.H.R.R. 32. See further paras 5–28 to 5–29 below.

[152] See generally Eoin Quill, *Torts in Ireland*, 2nd edn (Dublin, Gill and Macmillan, 2004), pp.181–4.

[153] Courts Act 1988, s.1.

[154] See *Sheridan v Kelly* [2006] I.E.S.C. 26, [2006] 1 I.R. 314 and *M.O'C. v The K.L.H.* [2006] I.E.H.C. 199; [2007] 1 I.R. 802.

[155] See para.11–14 below.

[156] See further paras 2–51 to 2–57 below.

purporting to have been done in pursuance of the Act. Such leave could not be granted unless the High Court was satisfied that there were substantial grounds for contending that the person against whom the proceedings were to be brought acted in bad faith or without reasonable care.[157] Where proceedings were, by leave granted in pursuance of s.260, instituted in respect of an act purporting to have been done in pursuance of this Act, the court could not determine the proceedings in favour of the plaintiff unless it was satisfied that the defendant acted in bad faith or without reasonable care.[158]

Section 260 was based on s.15 of the Mental Treatment Act 1930 (England and Wales), which in turn had been based on s.330 of the Lunacy Act 1890.[159] The current English and Welsh provision is s.139 of the Mental Health Act 1983, as amended.

2–52 There were a number of cases decided between 1980 and 2002 in which the courts considered whether to grant leave to institute proceedings under s.260.[160] In most of these cases, leave to institute proceedings was not granted. Where leave was granted, it was either because a time limit had been breached,[161] a doctor did not appear to have examined the plaintiff at all, or a relative who applied for a recommendation for admission had failed to notify the plaintiff of the nature of the medical certificate and the plaintiff's right to a second medical examination.[162]

---

[157] Mental Treatment Act 1945, s.260(1).

[158] Mental Treatment Act 1945, s.260(3).

[159] See Joseph & Anne Jaconelli, "Tort Liability under the Mental Health Act 1983" (1998) J. Soc. Welf. & Fam. L. 151. English case law on the 1930 Act includes *Richardson v London County Council* [1957] 1 W.L.R. 751.

[160] See generally Anne Marie O'Neill, *Irish Mental Health Law* (Dublin: First Law, 2005), pp.348–353; Jarlath Spellman, "Section 260 of the Mental Treatment Act 1945 Reviewed" (1998) 4 M.L.J.I. 20. Cases concerning applications under s.260 include *O'Dowd v North Western Health Board*, High Court, Costello J., December 8, 1980 (no judgment available); Supreme Court, [1983] I.L.R.M. 186; *Murphy v Greene* [1990] 2 I.R. 566; [1991] I.L.R.M. 404; *O'Reilly v Moroney and Mid-Western Health Board,* High Court, [1992] 2 I.R. 145; Supreme Court, November 16, 1993; *Melly v Moran and North Western Health Board* [1997] I.E.H.C. 101; McGuinness J., High Court, June 19, 1997; Supreme Court, May 28, 1998; *Kiernan v Harris* [1998] I.E.H.C. 71; High Court, O'Higgins J., May 12, 1998; *Blehein v Murphy and Others* [1999] I.E.H.C. 183; High Court, Geoghegan J., July 2, 1999; *Blehein v St John of God Hospital* [2000] I.E.H.C. 133; High Court, O'Sullivan J., July 6, 2000; *Blehein v Murphy* [2000] I.E.S.C. 1; [2000] 2 I.R. 231; [2000] 2 I.L.R.M. 481; *Blehein v Murphy (No.2)* [2000] I.E.S.C. 65; [2000] 3 I.R. 359; *Blehein v St. John of God Hospital* [2001] I.E.S.C. 73; Supreme Court, July 31, 2001; *Blehein v St John of God Hospital* [2002] I.E.S.C. 43; Supreme Court, May 31, 2002; *Lehany v Loftus and the Western Health Board* [2001] I.E.H.C. 108; High Court, Ó Caoimh J., July 20, 2001; *Dervan v Moran & Cahill*, High Court, Kelly J., June 25, 2002.

[161] *Bailey v Gallagher* [1996] 2 I.L.R.M. 433 (more than seven days elapsed between the doctor's examination of the plaintiff and the plaintiff being detained); *Melly v Moran and North Western Health Board*, Supreme Court, May 28, 1998 (more than 24 hours elapsed between examination by doctor and his completion of recommendation for admission).

[162] The latter two circumstances applied in *Kiernan v Harris* [1998] I.E.H.C. 71; High Court, O'Higgins J., May 12, 1998.

2–53 Costello J. said in *O'Dowd* in 1980 that s.260 must be interpreted in light of the constitutional right of access to the courts:

> "I accept Mrs. Robinson's contention that I must interpret the Section [i.e. s.260] in light of the guarantee given in the Constitution to citizens of access to the courts under Article 40.3. It is in this light that I must consider the wording of Section 260. An action should be allowed to be commenced without prejudicing in any way the right of an individual to litigate before the courts."[163]

However, the Supreme Court did not address the constitutional dimension in its decision and, by a majority of two to one, overturned Costello J.'s decision on the facts. O'Higgins C.J. stated that one of the reasons for this curtailment is to prevent a person from mounting a vexatious or frivolous action or one based on imagined complaints.[164] When Mr O'Dowd took his case to Strasbourg, it was declared inadmissible because he had failed to challenge the constitutionality of s.260 in the Irish courts and thus he had failed to exhaust his domestic remedies.[165]

2–54 In 1985, the European Court of Human Rights held in *Ashingdane v United Kingdom*[166] that the then English equivalent of s.260 (s.141 of the Mental Health Act 1959) did not transgress a patient's right to fair trial under art.6(1). The court stated that the right of access to the courts is not absolute but may be subject to limitations; these are permitted by implication since the right of access by its very nature calls for regulation by the State, regulation which may vary in time and place according to the needs and resources of the community and of individuals. The court said that in laying down such regulation, the Contracting States enjoy a certain margin of appreciation. Whilst the final decision as to observance of the Convention's requirements rested with the court, it was no part of the court's function to substitute for the assessment of the national authorities any other assessment of what might be the best policy in this field.[167] Nonetheless, the limitations applied must not restrict or reduce the access left to the individual in such a way or to such an extent that the very essence of the right is impaired. The court also stated that a limitation will not be compatible with art.6(1) if it does not pursue a legitimate aim and if there is not a reasonable relationship of proportionality between the means employed and the aim sought to be achieved.[168]

---

[163] *O'Dowd v North Western Health Board*, High Court, Costello J., December 8, 1980 (no judgment available), quoted in Application No.10296/83, *O'D. v Ireland*, European Commission on Human Rights Decisions of May 14, 1984 and December 3, 1986.

[164] [1983] I.L.R.M. 186 at 190.

[165] Application No.10296/83, *O'D. v Ireland*, European Commission on Human Rights Decisions of May 14, 1984 and December 3, 1986.

[166] (1985) 7 E.H.R.R. 528.

[167] (1985) 7 E.H.R.R. 528, para.57.

[168] (1985) 7 E.H.R.R. 528, para.57.

Gostin has described the *Ashingdane* case as "remarkable" and queries its implications as follows:

> "The Court's decision implies that because a person's claim may fail, for that reason he can be barred from access to a court to determine the merits. The very essence of Article 6, however, is that citizens have rights of access to the judicial system to pursue their claims; if they are meritless, the domestic courts are free to dismiss them after hearing the evidence."[169]

The reasoning in *Ashingdane* has recently been applied in *Seal v Chief Constable of South Wales*.[170]

2–55 Section 260 was eventually found to be unconstitutional in *Blehein v Minister for Health & Children*.[171] In the High Court, Carroll J. focussed on the requirement in s.260 that the applicant for leave show bad faith or lack of reasonable care. She did not believe that the requirement of substantial grounds was problematic, referring for example to In *Re Illegal Immigrants (Trafficking) Bill*.[172] But s.260 was unconstitutional for the following reasons:

> "In my opinion, the limitation of access to the courts on two specified grounds constitutes an impermissible interference by the legislature in the judicial domain contrary to Article 6 of the Constitution providing for the separation of powers and Article 34 providing for the administration of justice in the courts."[173]

She also said that the presumption of constitutionality did not apply as the defect was apparent on the face of the section.[174]

The Supreme Court agreed with Carroll J., in a judgment issued more than three years after her decision.[175] Denham J. said that the court was satisfied that the High Court was correct and would affirm its decision for the reasons given by Carroll J. She said that at issue in the case was the liberty of the plaintiff, an important constitutional right. While the aim of the Act of 1945 was legitimate, the limitation on the right of the plaintiff should not be overbroad, should be proportionate and should be necessary to secure the legitimate aim.[176] Denham J. stated that s.260 failed the test of proportionality:

---

[169] Lawrence Gostin, "Human Rights of Persons With Mental Disabilities: The European Convention of Human Rights" (2000) 23 Int. J. L. & Psychiatry 125 at 156.

[170] [2007] U.K.H.L. 31; [2007] 1 W.L.R. 1910.

[171] High Court, Carroll J., December 7, 2004; [2004] I.E.H.C. 374; [2004] 3 I.R. 610; Supreme Court, July 10, 2008, [2008] I.E.S.C. 40; [2008] 2 I.L.R.M. 401.

[172] [2000] 2 I.R. 360.

[173] [2004] 3 I.R. 610 at 616.

[174] She cited *Loftus v Attorney General* [1979] I.R. 221 on this point.

[175] [2008] I.E.S.C. 40; [2008] 2 I.L.R.M. 401. The High Court decision was on December 7, 2004; the Supreme Court judgment was delivered on July 10, 2008.

[176] Denham J. quoted *Heaney v Ireland* [1994] 3 I.R. 593 at 607; [1994] 2 I.L.R.M. 420 at 431 on this point.

"In this case the objective of the Act of 1945, as set out above, is legitimate. It is important. But it is not of sufficient importance to override the constitutional right of liberty and the constitutional right of access to the courts, in the terms of the section, for the reasons given by the High Court. The terms of the section do not pass a proportionality test, for while being rationally connected to the objective, it is arbitrary (in referring to only two possible grounds of application) and hence unfair. It therefore does not impair the rights involved as little as possible, and so the effect on rights is not proportionate to the object to be achieved."[177]

2–56 Section 260 of the 1945 Act was repealed by the 2001 Act[178] but was still relevant to Mr Blehein, as he was challenging actions which had taken place while the 1945 Act was in force.[179]

2–57 Section 73 of the Mental Health Act 2001 replaces s.260 and rewords it slightly. The main change is that rather than a requirement of "substantial grounds" the new section requires "reasonable grounds". In addition, the burden of proof has shifted. While s.260 stated that leave *could not be granted unless* the court was satisfied that there were substantial grounds for contending certain matters, s.73 of the 2001 Act states that leave *shall not be refused unless* the court is satisfied either (a) that the proceedings are frivolous and vexatious or (b) that there are no reasonable grounds for contending that the defendant acted in bad faith or without reasonable care.[180]

A test case will need to be brought to establish whether s.73 is unconstitutional. It is possible that the courts might find that the new wording is more proportionate than the wording in s.260. In any future challenge, the focus will probably be on the shift in the burden of proof. The difference between reasonable grounds and substantial grounds may not be of much consequence as regards constitutionality, as both the High Court and Supreme Court in *Blehein* found that the "substantial grounds" part of s.260 did not breach constitutional rights.

It must also be remembered that it appears that s.73, like s.260 before it, does not apply to judicial review proceedings,[181] applications under Art.40, and plenary summonses seeking to have statutory provisions declared unconstitutional and damages for breach of constitutional rights.[182] Section 73 also does not apply to voluntary patients, unless they are challenging an act purporting to have been done in pursuance of the 2001 Act.

---

[177] [2008] I.E.S.C. 40, para.18.
[178] Mental Health Act 2001, s.6 and Schedule.
[179] For a subsequent ruling on another aspect of his case, see *Blehein v Minister for Health and Others* [2009] I.E.H.C. 182; High Court, Laffoy J., March 16, 2009.
[180] Mental Health Act 2001, s.73(1).
[181] See *Ex Parte Waldron* [1986] Q.B. 824 at 845; above para.2–09.
[182] *Blehein v Minister for Health and Others* [2009] I.E.H.C. 182; High Court, Laffoy J., March 16, 2009.

Criminal Charges

2–58 It is possible that some actions which take place concerning patients in psychiatric centres might lead to criminal charges. For example, if a member of staff assaulted a patient, this might lead to charges under the Non-Fatal Offences against the Person Act 1997.[183] Patients might also be charged with assault of other patients, or assaults of staff.

2–59 The Mental Health Act 2001 includes a number of criminal offences. A person who, for the purposes of or in relation to an application for a recommendation, makes any statement which is to his or her knowledge false or misleading in any material particular, is guilty of an offence.[184] It is an offence to breach the requirement that where following the refusal of an application any further such application is made in respect of the same person, the applicant so far as he or she is aware of the facts relating to the previous application and its refusal, shall state those facts to the doctor to whom the further application is made.[185] A person who obstructs or interferes or fails to co-operate with an independent psychiatrist appointed under s.17 of the 2001 Act in the performance of his or her functions shall be guilty of an offence.[186]

Various offences concerning Mental Health Tribunals are contained in s.49 of the 2001 Act, e.g. if a person gives false evidence before a tribunal in such circumstances that, if he or she had given the evidence before a court, he or she would be guilty of perjury, he or she shall be guilty of that offence.[187] It is an offence to obstruct or interfere with the Inspector of Mental Health Services, or to fail to supply him or her information.[188] It is an offence to "carry on a centre" unless the centre is registered as an approved centre and the person is the registered proprietor thereof.[189] Where, in relation to an approved centre, there is a contravention of a condition of registration, the registered proprietor shall be guilty of an offence.[190] Where, in relation to a centre, there is a failure or refusal to comply with a provision of the Approved Centre Regulations,[191] the registered proprietor shall be guilty of an offence.[192] A person who fails or

---

[183] See for example "Nurse jailed for attack on patient who later died", *Irish Times*, June 24, 2006; "Jailed ex-nurse wins appeal", *Irish Independent*, March 28, 2007; "Suspended term for assaults on patients", *Irish Times*, December 19, 2006; Eithne Donnellan and Sonya McLean, "Sentence later for nurse who poisoned patient", *Irish Times*, December 5, 2006; "Jury finds nurse guilty of three charges", *Irish Times*, October 30, 2006.
[184] Mental Health Act 2001, s.9(6).
[185] Mental Health Act 2001, s.11.
[186] Mental Health Act 2001, s.17(4).
[187] Mental Health Act 2001, s.49(5).
[188] Mental Health Act 2001, s.53. See also s.66(5).
[189] Mental Health Act 2001, s.63.
[190] Mental Health Act 2001, s.64(13).
[191] Mental Health Act 2001 (Approved Centres) Regulations 2006, S.I. No. 551 of 2006.
[192] Mental Health Act 2001, s.66(3)(a).

refuses to comply with a provision of the Approved Centre Regulations shall be guilty of an offence.[193] It is also an offence to breach the Commission's rules regarding seclusion and mechanical restraint.[194]

2–60 Summary offences under the 2001 Act may be prosecuted by the Mental Health Commission.[195] Offences under Pt 2 may only be prosecuted summarily with a maximum fine of €1,904 or imprisonment up to 12 months or both.[196] Similar penalties are specified in various other sections.[197] However, breaches of Pt 5 concerning approved centres may also be prosecuted on indictment with a maximum penalty of a fine of €63,486 or imprisonment for up to two years or both.[198]

The Criminal Law (Insanity) Act 2006 creates various offences concerning the Mental Health (Criminal Law) Review Board, e.g. if a person gives false evidence before the Review Board in such circumstances that, if he or she had given the evidence before a court, he or she would be guilty of perjury, he or she shall be guilty of that offence.[199]

Other Remedies

2–61 A claim for damages for breach of constitutional rights may be initiated by way of plenary summons. In appropriate cases, a person may also wish to seek a declaration that a statutory provision is unconstitutional or that it is incompatible with the ECHR. The Attorney General must be notified of claims of unconstitutionality. Both the Attorney General and the Human Rights Commission must be notified of applications for declarations of incompatibility.[200]

2–62 Any patient may write to the President of the High Court seeking a review of their detention. The President may by order require and authorise the Inspector of Mental Hospitals to visit and examine any person detained at any place "as a person of unsound mind" and to report to the President of the High Court on the condition of such person.[201] This power appears to have been used in the *Orton* case (above, para.2–27). In *Croke v Smith (No.2)*, Hamilton C.J. stated that the President of the High Court, upon receipt of a complaint from a

---

[193] Mental Health Act 2001, s.66(3)(b).
[194] Mental Health Act 2001, s.69(3).
[195] Mental Health Act 2001, s.74(1).
[196] Mental Health Act 2001, s.30.
[197] For example, s.49 (tribunals), s.53 (Inspector) and s.69 (seclusion and mechanical restraint).
[198] Mental Health Act 2001, s.68.
[199] Criminal Law (Insanity) Act 2006, s.12(5).
[200] European Convention on Human Rights Act 2003, s.6.
[201] Mental Treatment Act 1945, s.241. This section was not repealed by the 2001 Act. See also s.276: Where the President of the High Court is of opinion that the assistance of counsel is necessary for the conduct of any visit or investigation under this Act, he may by order appoint a barrister-at-law of not less than six years' standing to assist in such visit.

person of unsound mind, not only has jurisdiction but also a duty to intervene on their behalf and cause an inquiry to be made into the lawfulness of such a person's detention and to direct their release if they have recovered or are otherwise being unlawfully detained.[202]

2–63 If patients wish to make representations about their treatment, letters of complaint should be written to the clinical director of the relevant centre and to the Health Service Executive (HSE). The HSE has appointed complaints officers for responding to complaints, many of whom are named on the HSE website (*http://www.hse.ie*).

2–64 As was stated above, international remedies may be available, e.g. at the European Court of Human Rights or the UN Human Rights Committee, but domestic remedies must first be exhausted. Letters may also be written to the Irish Human Rights Commission or the Council of Europe Commissioner for Human Rights.

2–65 In appropriate cases, a complaint to the Mental Health Commission, the Ombudsman or the Ombudsman for Children might be considered. Exercise of rights under data protection legislation or freedom of information legislation may be considered.[203] It may also be worthwhile to notify lobby groups such as the Free Legal Advice Centres, the Irish Council for Civil Liberties or Amnesty International's Irish branch. There are also a range of advocacy services and representative bodies concerning mental health issues.[204]

2–66 Complaints regarding medical staff may be made to the Medical Council and those regarding nurses may be made to An Bord Altranais. Complaints regarding solicitors and barristers may be made to the Law Society[205] and the Bar Council. See also the Legal Services Ombudsman Act 2009.

INSTITUTIONS

The Mental Health Commission

2–67 The Mental Health Commission was established by s.32 of the Mental Health Act 2001, its principal functions (under s.33) being to promote, encourage and foster the establishment and maintenance of high standards and good practices in the delivery of mental health services and to take all reasonable steps to protect the interests of persons detained in approved centres under the Act.

---

[202] [1998] 1 I.R. 101 at 125.
[203] Data Protection Acts 1988–2003; Freedom of Information Acts 1997–2003.
[204] See for example listings on website of Mental Health Commission (*http://www.mhcirl.ie*) or Irish Mental Health Coalition (*http://www.imhc.ie*).
[205] The Law Society also has an Independent Adjudicator.

2–68 There are 13 members of the Commission, all appointed by the Minister for Health and Children. There are detailed requirements concerning member-ship of the Commission. Three members shall represent voluntary bodies, three shall be doctors (of which two shall be consultant psychiatrists), two shall be nurses and the others must be a psychologist, a social worker, a lawyer, an employee of the HSE and a representative of the interest of the general public.[206] The Commission also has a chairperson, a chief executive and staff.

2–69 The Commission makes rules and codes of practice governing issues such as seclusion and restraint, electro-convulsive therapy, and admission of children to approved centres. The Commission does *not* make the regulations governing standards in approved centres; these are made by the Minister for Health and Children after consultation with the Commission.[207]

The Commission prescribes the forms which are used for the various statutory processes laid down in the 2001 Act, e.g. involuntary admission to approved centres, decisions of Mental Health Tribunals and authorisation of medicine for longer than three months.

2–70 The Commission appoints the Inspector of Mental Health Services and Assistant Inspectors, the members of Mental Health Tribunals, the independent psychiatrists who are appointed under s.17 of the 2001 Act and the legal representatives for patients detained under the 2001 Act. It establishes and runs the legal aid scheme under the 2001 Act.[208] It also maintains the register of approved centres. It may establish an Inquiry under s.55, and two Inquiry reports have been issued.[209]

The Commission issues an annual report describing its activities, organises training and conferences, provides information on the 2001 Act, commissions research reports and maintains a website at *http://www.mhcirl.ie*. It may also prosecute offences under the 2001 Act.

2–71 The Commission has no functions under the Criminal Law (Insanity) Act 2006, except for a minor function regarding new "designated centres".[210] It is unfortunate that the opportunity was not taken in drafting the 2006 Act to provide for more integration between the 2001 and 2006 Acts. For example, the Commission could have been given powers in relation to appointment of members of the Mental Health (Criminal Law) Review Board.

---

[206] Mental Health Act 2001, s.35.
[207] Mental Health Act 2001, s.66.
[208] Mental Health Act 2001, s.33(3).
[209] Mental Health Commission, *Report of the Committee of Inquiry into Current Care and Treatment Practices in the Central Mental Hospital* (2006); Mental Health Commission, *Report of the Committee of Inquiry to review care and treatment practices in St. Michael's Unit, South Tipperary General Hospital, Clonmel and St. Luke's Hospital, Clonmel, including the quality and planning of care and the use of restraint and seclusion and to report to the Mental Health Commission* (2009).
[210] Criminal Law (Insanity) Act 2006, s.3(2).

The Mental Health (Criminal Law) Review Board

2–72 The Mental Health (Criminal Law) Review Board was established under s.11 of the Criminal Law (Insanity) Act 2006. Its composition and functions will be dealt with in detail in Chapter 18.

The members of the Review Board are appointed directly by the Minister for Justice, Equality and Law Reform. There are currently three members: Mr Justice Brian McCracken, Dr Michael Mulcahy, Consultant Psychiatrist, and Mr Tim Dalton, Former Secretary General of the Department of Justice, Equality & Law Reform.

The Commission issues an annual report on its activities and maintains a website at *http://www.mhclrb.ie*.

The Inspector of Mental Health Services

2–73 The office of Inspector of Mental Health Services is established by s.50 of the 2001 Act. The Commission shall from time to time appoint a consultant psychiatrist to be the Inspector. The Inspector must visit and inspect every approved centre at least once in each year and visit and inspect any other premises where mental health services are being provided as they think appropriate. The Inspector must also carry out an annual review of mental health services in the State and furnish a report to the Commission on the quality of care and treatment given to persons in receipt of mental health services, what they have ascertained pursuant to any inspections carried out by them of approved centres or other premises where mental health services are being provided, and the degree and extent of compliance by approved centres with any code of practice prepared by the Commission.[211]

2–74 The Inspector has extensive powers to facilitate their functions, e.g. to require any person in an approved centre or other premises to furnish them with information and to examine and take copies of any record or other document made available to them or found on the premises.[212] When making an inspection under s.51, the Inspector shall (a) see every resident whom they have been requested to examine by the resident themselves or by any other person, (b) see every patient the propriety of whose detention they have reason to doubt, (c) ascertain whether or not due regard is being had to the 2001 Act and the provisions made thereunder, and (d) ascertain whether any regulations made under s.66, any rules made under ss 59 and 69 and the provisions of Pt 4 are being complied with.[213]

The Commission may appoint Assistant Inspectors of Mental Health Services[214] and may also request the Inspector, or other persons, to carry out an inquiry under s.55.

[211] Mental Health Act 2001, s.51.
[212] Mental Health Act 2001, s.51(2).
[213] Mental Health Act 2001, s.52.

2–75 There were serious problems with the inspection regime as laid down in the Mental Treatment Act 1945. Boland has highlighted a number of issues, e.g. there was a practice of giving several days' notice to the institutions about to be inspected, and the Inspector felt obliged to give the responsible authorities every opportunity to consult on the report before its publication.[215] Once the Inspector had written their version of the annual report, they sent it to the Department of Health who "edited" it and returned it to the Inspector for approval. It was then sent to the various health boards for their comments and when these were received the Inspector amended their report. The reports of the Inspector were not published for several years. Those reports which were published often contained serious criticisms of the conditions in hospitals, but there was no method of enforcement of the reports.

2–76 The Health (Mental Services) Act 1981 (which was never commenced) would have abolished the post of Inspector of Mental Hospitals and replaced it with inspections by "a designated medical officer of the Minister".[216] These reports would not be laid before the Oireachtas.

2–77 The new inspectorate established by the 2001 Act is independently appointed by the Mental Health Commission and shares offices with the Commission. There were seven assistant inspectors at the end of 2008.[217] There is now a possible enforcement mechanism as the Commission may attach conditions to the registration of an approved centre, or even remove a centre from the register (see further Chapter 12).

2–78 In keeping with best international practice, one-third of inspections are unannounced. Centres may be chosen for unannounced inspections on a random basis, or where possible concerns exist.[218] In 2008, the Inspectorate changed its practice and started publishing its reports of inspections of approved centres on the Mental Health Commission website in an effort to make them available as early as possible, rather than waiting until the annual report is published each year.

Other Institutions

The Minister for Health and Children

2–79 The Minister for Health and Children[219] appoints the members of the Mental Health Commission according to the criteria in s.35 of the 2001 Act. The

---

[214]   Mental Health Act 2001, s.54.
[215]   Faye Boland, "Improving Conditions in Irish Psychiatric Hospitals?" (2001) 7 M.L.J.I. 14.
[216]   Health (Mental Services) Act 1981, s.36.
[217]   Mental Health Commission, *Annual Report 2008*, Book 1, pp.15–16.
[218]   Mental Health Commission, *Annual Report 2008*, Book 1, p.58.
[219]   Note that the Minister frequently delegates functions concerning mental health to a Minister of State.

Minister has various other functions under the 2001 Act, e.g. the Minister provides grants of money to the Commission, the Commission must send its annual report to the Minister and must account to the Minister for expenditure. In the performance of his or her duties under s.47 (concerning accounts and audit), the Chief Executive of the Commission shall not question or express an opinion on the merits of any policy of the Government or a Minister of the Government or on the merits of the objectives of such a policy.[220] The Minister makes the Regulations governing approved centres, following consultation with the Commission.[221]

The Minister for Health and Children is responsible for introducing any changes in the Mental Health Act which are made. There have already been two minor amendments to the Act in 2008 and 2009.[222] At a policy level, the Minister for Health and Children appointed the expert group which produced the *Vision for Change* report in 2006.[223]

The Minister for Justice, Equality and Law Reform

2–80 The Minister for Justice, Equality and Law Reform appoints the members of the Mental Health (Criminal Law) Review Board.[224] The structure and functions of the Review Board will be considered in Chapter 18. The procedure of the Review Board regarding reviews must be consented to by the Minister.[225] The Minister has various other functions under the 2006 Act, e.g. they must consent to a temporary release of a patient.[226]

The Scheme of the Mental Capacity Bill 2008 was produced by the Department of Justice, Equality and Law Reform. It might be wondered whether perhaps this Bill would more appropriately emanate from the Department of Health and Children. However, as the Bill is a general law reform measure resulting from Law Reform Commission reports, it comes under the "law reform" function of the Department. In addition, the Department of Justice is responsible for the Courts Service, where the current wards of court office is located.

The Health Service Executive

2–81 The HSE is responsible for managing and delivering health and personal social services in the State. It has a crucial role in delivery of mental health services and implementation of the *Vision for Change* policy. The HSE handles individual complaints regarding services. It has a Mental Health Expert Advisory Group.

---

[220] Mental Health Act 2001, s.47(7).
[221] Mental Health Act 2001, s.66.
[222] Mental Health Act 2008 and s.63 Health (Miscellaneous Provisions) Act 2009.
[223] Expert Group on Mental Health Policy, *A Vision for Change* (Dublin, 2006).
[224] Criminal Law (Insanity) Act 2006, Sch.1.
[225] Criminal Law (Insanity) Act 2006, s.12(6).
[226] Criminal Law (Insanity) Act 2006, s.14(1).

The independent monitoring group on implementation of Vision for Change comments on an annual basis on the delays in implementing *Vision for Change*. In its latest report, issued in 2009, it states that it acknowledges the commitment and dedication of the staff of the HSE to the development of mental health services. However, the Monitoring Group considers that the recommendations of *A Vision for Change* cannot be implemented effectively without a National Mental Health Service Directorate.[227]

---

[227]   *Third Annual Report of the Independent Monitoring Group for A Vision for Change—the Report of the Expert Group on Mental Health Policy* (2009), p.18.

PART 2
CIVIL ASPECTS

CHAPTER 3

LEGAL CRITERIA FOR INVOLUNTARY CIVIL ADMISSION

INTRODUCTION

3–01 One of the most fundamental issues in mental health law is the definition of which types of mental disorders will justify involuntary detention. One of the defects of the Mental Treatment Act 1945 was that it failed to define clearly the criteria for detention. The 1945 Act permitted people to be detained on two main alternative grounds: that they were "suffering from a mental illness"[1] or a "person of unsound mind".[2] However, no definition was provided of "mental illness" or "person of unsound mind". The Health (Mental Services) Act 1981, which was never commenced, did not contain a definition of mental disorder as such, but required the medical practitioner to certify that he or she was satisfied (i) that the person was suffering from mental disorder of such a degree that detention and treatment in a psychiatric centre were necessary in the interest of the person's health or safety or for the protection of other persons or property, and (ii) that the person was not prepared to accept or is not suitable for treatment otherwise than as a detained patient.[3]

3–02 The Mental Health Act 2001 provides a much more comprehensive statement of the criteria for detention. This definition is mainly of importance regarding involuntary civil admissions. However, it is also relevant in cases under the Criminal Law (Insanity) Act 2006, as that Act states that a person may be detained if they have a "mental disorder within the meaning of the Act of 2001".[4]

3–03 According to s.3 of the 2001 Act, "mental disorder" means mental illness, severe dementia or significant intellectual disability, where:

> (a) because of the illness, disability or dementia, there is a serious likelihood of the person concerned causing immediate and serious harm to himself or herself or to other persons, or

---

[1] Section 184(4)(a)(i) Mental Treatment Act 1945.
[2] Section 171(1)(a) and s.178(2)(c) Mental Treatment Act 1945.
[3] Section 19(5)(b) Health (Mental Services) Act 1981.
[4] See further, paras 15–55 to 15–59 and 17–25 to 17–27 below.

(*b*) (i) because of the severity of the illness, disability or dementia, the judgment of the person concerned is so impaired that failure to admit the person to an approved centre would be likely to lead to a serious deterioration in his or her condition or would prevent the administration of appropriate treatment that could be given only by such admission, and

(ii) the reception, detention and treatment of the person concerned in an approved centre would be likely to benefit or alleviate the condition of that person to a material extent.

"Treatment" includes the administration of physical, psychological and other remedies relating to the care and rehabilitation of a patient under medical supervision, intended for the purposes of ameliorating a mental disorder.[5]

3–04 According to s.3(2), "mental illness" means a state of mind of a person which affects the person's thinking, perception, emotion or judgment and which seriously impairs the mental function of the person to the extent that he or she requires care or medical treatment in his or her own interest or in the interest of other persons. "Severe dementia" means a deterioration of the brain of a person which significantly impairs the intellectual function of the person, thereby affecting thought, comprehension and memory and which includes severe psychiatric or behavioural symptoms such as physical aggression. "Significant intellectual disability" means a state of arrested or incomplete development of mind of a person which includes significant impairment of intelligence and social functioning and abnormally aggressive or seriously irresponsible conduct on the part of the person.

   Section 8 provides that a person may not be involuntarily admitted to an approved centre by reason only of the fact that the person (a) is suffering from a personality disorder, (b) is socially deviant, or (c) is addicted to drugs or intoxicants.

3–05 The effect of these provisions is that a person may be involuntarily admitted on one of two alternative grounds: (a) the "harm ground",[6] where there is a serious likelihood of the person causing immediate and serious harm to themselves or to other persons or (b) the "need for treatment" ground.[7] It is important to note that the "need for treatment" ground requires a number of different elements. Since most patients are detained due to a mental illness, the definition of a mental illness can be combined with the "need for treatment" ground as follows. All three of the following points would need to be satisfied[8]:

---

[5] Section 2(1) Mental Health Act 2001.
[6] This ground could also be referred to loosely as a "police power" ground.
[7] This ground may be classified loosely as a *parens patriae* ground.
[8] The first point is a paraphrase of the definition of "mental illness"; the second and third points are derived from s.3(1)(b).

1. The person's mental function is seriously impaired to the extent that they require care or medical treatment in their own interest or in the interest of other persons,
2. The person's judgement is so impaired that failure to admit them would be likely to lead to a serious deterioration in their condition or would prevent the administration of appropriate treatment that could be given only by such admission,[9] and
3. The reception, detention and treatment of the person would be likely to benefit or alleviate their condition to a material extent.

In the case of a person detained due to severe dementia or significant intellectual disability, the first point above would be substituted by the relevant definition as quoted earlier.

3–06 While the Act states that a person may be detained on one of the two alternative grounds, a person might, of course, satisfy both grounds at once, i.e. the person might satisfy the harm ground and the need for treatment ground at the same time.[10] As a result of comments made by O'Neill J. in *M.R. v Byrne and Flynn*,[11] discussed below at paras 3–15 to 3–16, the current versions of the various statutory forms specifically permit it to be certified that a person either satisfies s.3(1)(a) or s.3(1)(b) or *both* (a) and (b).

POLICIES REFLECTED IN THE CRITERIA

3–07 The Oireachtas has chosen to include both a "harm ground" and a "need for treatment" ground. Practice in other jurisdictions varies, with some countries only including the harm ground, often referred to as the "danger" ground. For example, Salize and Dressing[12] found that although the laws of all EU member states stipulate a confirmed mental disorder as a major condition for detention, additional criteria are heterogeneous. Threatened or actual danger to oneself or to others is the most common additional criterion across the EU, but is not a prerequisite in Italy, Spain or Sweden. Among countries stipulating the need for

---

[9] This point may even be split into two separate points—see the analysis of O'Neill J. in *M.R. v Byrne and Flynn* [2007] 3 I.R. 211 at 223.

[10] See also Harry Kennedy, *The Annotated Mental Health Acts* (Dublin: Blackhall, 2007), p.68: "Section 3(1)(a) and Section 3(1)(b)(i) of this Act are linked by an 'or' clause which makes them mutually exclusive. The wording has simply been copied from the UN Principles without modification. However it is submitted that many patients present to mental health services that fulfil both criteria, while many others who present because of a crisis, meeting the first criterion, soon prove to meet the second criterion. To prevent the certifying doctor from certifying on both grounds obliges the certifying doctor to give an incomplete account of the true situation."

[11] [2007] I.E.H.C. 73; [2007] 3 I.R. 211.

[12] Hans-Joachim Salize & Harald Dressing, "Epidemiology of involuntary placement of mentally ill people across the European Union" (2004) 184 *British Journal of Psychiatry* 163.

treatment (the second most common criterion), Denmark, Finland, Greece, Ireland, Portugal and the UK consider the danger criterion to be sufficient on its own. In addition, some countries emphasise a lack of insight by the patient. No significant correlation could be identified with compulsory admission quotas or rates when comparing countries applying the "danger" or "need for treatment" criterion.

Procedural Regulations for compulsory admission in European Union member states
(Source: Salize and Dressing, 2004[13])

Country	Essential legal criteria for detention (additional to mental disorder)
Austria	Danger
Belgium	Danger
Denmark	Danger or need for treatment
Finland	Danger or need for treatment
France[14]	Danger
Germany	Danger
Greece	Danger or need for treatment
Ireland	Danger or need for treatment
Italy	Need for treatment
Luxembourg	Danger
The Netherlands	Danger
Portugal	Danger or need for treatment
Spain	Need for treatment
Sweden	Need for treatment
United Kingdom	Danger or need for treatment

3–08 The World Health Organisation (WHO) states that the "need for treatment" criterion solicits a great deal of controversy and that there are a number of organisations and individuals, including users of mental health services and user groups, who object to this criterion. The Organisation continues:

---

[13] Salize & Dressing, "Epidemiology of involuntary placement of mentally ill people across the European Union" (2004) 184 *British Journal of Psychiatry* 163. This table is an adapted version of Table 3, 184 Brit. J. Psych. 163 at 166.

[14] According to the *Hospitalisation d'Office* (HO) procedure.

"This principle usually includes the concurrent presence of a number of factors. First, the illness must be 'severe' (issue of definition); secondly, it must be proved that there is 'impaired judgement' (issue of capacity); and thirdly, there must be reasonable grounds to suspect that failure to admit the person will lead to serious deterioration in his/her condition or prevent administering appropriate treatment (prediction of treatment issue)."[15]

3–09 Another significant policy choice is the emphasis on narrowing the criteria in order to prevent over-detention. For example, the definition of mental illness requires *serious* impairment of mental function, the "harm ground" requires a *serious* likelihood of *immediate and serious* harm and the need for treatment ground refers to a *serious* deterioration in the person's condition if not admitted.

The definitions of severe dementia and significant intellectual disability are narrowly drawn. However, some have questioned whether it is ever appropriate to detain people under a civil Act for these conditions.[16] The exclusion of personality disorders, addictions to drugs or intoxicants and social deviance also serve to narrow the scope of involuntary detention. In particular, the specific exclusion of personality disorders is in marked contrast to the specific inclusion of psychopathic disorder in England's Mental Health Act 1983.[17] While the specific reference to psychopathic disorder was removed in 2007, people with personality disorders continue to be covered by England's mental health legislation.[18]

When O'Donoghue and Moran surveyed psychiatrists, they found that 78 per cent agreed that patients should not be admitted involuntarily solely on the grounds that they are suffering from a personality disorder. However, 58 per cent felt that there was a risk in such patients not being involuntarily admitted in situations in which it is clinically necessary. In addition, 56 per cent felt that there was a similar risk in patients with a diagnosis of substance misuse.[19] The authors state that this, "uncovers an intriguing insight into the complex area of risk and responsibility"[20] and that the finding suggests that consultant psychiatrists,

---

[15] Melvyn Freeman & Soumitra Pathare, *WHO Resource Book on Mental Health, Human Rights and Legislation* (Geneva: World Health Organization, 2005), p.49.

[16] See Edel Therese Quirke, "Older People in Irish Mental Health Law" in Eoin O'Dell (ed.), *Older People in Modern Ireland: Essays on Law and Policy* (Dublin: FirstLaw, 2006), 268 at 278–280.

[17] Mental Health Act 1983, s.1(3). See discussion in Brenda Hoggett, *Mental Health Law*, 4th edn (London: Sweet and Maxwell, 1996), pp.34–37.

[18] Explanatory Notes on the Mental Health Act 2007 prepared by the Department of Health and the Ministry of Justice, para.17; cited in Richard Jones, *Mental Health Act Manual*, 11th edn (London: Thomson Sweet and Maxwell, 2008), pp.17–18.

[19] Brian O'Donoghue and Paul Moran, "Consultant psychiatrists' experiences and attitudes following the introduction of the Mental Health Act 2001: a national survey" (2009) 26 *Irish Journal of Psychological Medicine* 23. The survey also found that prior to the 2001 Act, 16 per cent of consultant psychiatrists admitted patients involuntarily solely on the grounds that they were suffering from a personality disorder and 21 per cent admitted patients involuntarily solely on the grounds of substance misuse.

[20] O'Donoghue and Moran, "Consultant psychiatrists' experiences and attitudes following the

being aware of the long-term risk of patients with a diagnosis of a personality disorder and addiction, also recognise that involuntary admissions are not the solution. They state that the 2001 Act may also resolve the dilemma whereby consultant psychiatrists come under pressure from relatives/friends to admit a patient involuntarily for the above indications. The authors hypothesise that there may be higher rates of patients being admitted with ICD-10[21] diagnosis of psychiatric illness of an acute nature, such as "adjustment disorders" or "brief depressive episode".[22]

HUMAN RIGHTS ISSUES

3–10 At United Nations level, the Mental Illness Principles[23] specifically include both the harm ground and the need for treatment ground by stating that a person may be involuntarily admitted if the person has a mental illness and it is considered:

(a) That, because of that mental illness, there is a serious likelihood of immediate or imminent harm to that person or to other persons; or

(b) That, in the case of a person whose mental illness is severe and whose judgement is impaired, failure to admit or retain that person is likely to lead to a serious deterioration in his or her condition or will prevent the giving of appropriate treatment that can only be given by admission to a mental health facility in accordance with the principle of the least restrictive alternative.[24]

The Principles also state that a determination that a person has a mental illness shall be made in accordance with internationally accepted medical standards.[25]

3–11 Article 5(1)(e) of the European Convention on Human Rights (ECHR) permits the detention of persons of unsound mind.[26] The European Court of

---

introduction of the Mental Health Act 2001: a national survey" (2009) 26 *Irish Journal of Psychological Medicine* 23 at 26.

[21] World Health Organisation, *International Classification of Mental and Behavioural Disorders* (ICD-10) (1992).

[22] O'Donoghue and Moran, "Consultant psychiatrists' experiences and attitudes following the introduction of the Mental Health Act 2001: a national survey" (2009) 26 *Irish Journal of Psychological Medicine* 23 at 26.

[23] United Nations, *Principles for the protection of persons with mental illness and the improvement of mental health care*, adopted by General Assembly resolution 46/119 of December 17, 1991.

[24] United Nations, *Principles for the protection of persons with mental illness and the improvement of mental health care*, adopted by General Assembly resolution 46/119 of December 17, 1991, Principle 16.

[25] United Nations, *Principles for the protection of persons with mental illness and the improvement of mental health care*, adopted by General Assembly resolution 46/119 of December 17, 1991, Principle 4(1).

[26] Of course, the term "person of unsound mind" is derogatory and would not now be used in such a Convention.

Human Rights has stated in the *Winterwerp* case[27] that the person must be reliably shown to have a "true mental disorder", established by objective medical expertise, that is "of a kind or degree warranting compulsory confinement."[28] These are known as the Winterwerp Principles. The court stated that the term "person of unsound mind" is not one that can be given a definitive interpretation: it is a term whose meaning is continually evolving as research in psychiatry progresses, an increasing flexibility in treatment is developing and society's attitudes to mental illness change, in particular so that a greater understanding of the problems of mental patients is becoming more widespread.[29] The court noted that art.5(1)(e) obviously cannot be taken as permitting the detention of a person simply because his or her views or behaviour deviate from the norms prevailing in a particular society. To hold otherwise would not be reconcilable with the text of art.5(1), which sets out an exhaustive list of exceptions calling for a narrow interpretation. Neither would it be in conformity with the object and purpose of art.5(1), namely, to ensure that no one should be dispossessed of their liberty in an arbitrary fashion. Moreover, it would disregard the importance of the right to liberty in a democratic society.[30] Similarly, a report for the Northern Ireland Human Rights Commission noted that the main human rights concern associated with the definition of "mental disorder" is that if the definition is too broad and does not have specific exclusions it could allow the detention of people on the basis of moral, social, political or cultural judgments rather than mental health and safety necessity.[31]

It has also been held in *Litwa v Poland*[32] that detention must be a proportionate response to the patient's circumstances:

> "The Court reiterates that a necessary element of the 'lawfulness' of the detention within the meaning of Article 5(1)(e) is the absence of arbitrariness. The detention of an individual is such a serious measure that it is only justified where other, less severe measures have been considered and found to be insufficient to safeguard the individual or public interest which might require that the person concerned be detained. That means that it does not suffice that the deprivation of liberty is executed in conformity with national law but it must also be necessary in the circumstances."[33]

In *Guzzardi v Italy*, the court noted that persons of unsound mind could be detained both due to dangerousness and in their own interests.[34] These grounds

---

[27] *Winterwerp v The Netherlands* (1979–80) 2 E.H.R.R. 387.
[28] (1979-80) 2 E.H.R.R. 387, para.39.
[29] (1979-80) 2 E.H.R.R. 387, para.37.
[30] (1979-80) 2 E.H.R.R. 387, para.37.
[31] Gavin Davidson, Maura McCallion and Michael Potter, *Connecting Mental Health and Human Rights* (Northern Ireland Human Rights Commission, 2003), p.20.
[32] (2001) 33 E.H.R.R. 53.
[33] (2001) 33 E.H.R.R. 53, para.78.
[34] "In addition to vagrants, sub-paragraph (e) refers to persons of unsound mind, alcoholics and

were referred to as "medical and social grounds" in *Litwa v Poland*.[35] In an admissibility decision in *Koniarska v UK*[36] the court reiterated these points and stated that they could form the basis for detention of a person with psychopathic disorder where there was a danger of her injuring herself or other persons. The court did not require that the condition be "treatable".[37] In *Reid v UK*,[38] it was held that there was no requirement imposed by art.5(1)(e) that detention in a mental hospital be conditional on the illness or condition being of a nature or degree amenable to medical treatment.[39] The applicant in that case had anti-social personality or psychopathic disorder. Most of the psychiatric reports stated that his condition was not treatable, but the court stated that treatability was not required for detention.[40]

The *Koniarska* and *Reid* decisions would not have direct application in Irish civil law due to the explicit exclusion of personality disorders in s.8 of the 2001 Act. However, as these cases show that the European Court does not require treatability for detention, this means, for example, that once a person has a "true mental disorder", they may be detained under the "harm ground" even if their condition is not treatable.

3–12 The United Nations Convention on the Rights of Persons with Disabilities (CRPD)[41] includes an important provision in art.14 stating that the existence of a disability shall in no case justify a deprivation of liberty.[42] Ireland signed this Convention in 2007 and the Government intends to ratify the Convention.[43] The Office of the High Commissioner for Human Rights has stated that as a result of art.14, unlawful detention encompasses situations where the deprivation of liberty is grounded in the combination between a mental or intellectual disability and other elements such as dangerousness, or care and treatment.[44] The Office

drug addicts. The reason why the Convention allows the latter individuals, all of whom are socially maladjusted, to be deprived of their liberty is not only that they have to be considered as occasionally dangerous for public safety but also that their own interests may necessitate their detention". (*Guzzardi v Italy* (1980) 3 E.H.R.R. 333, para.98.)

35   *Litwa v Poland* (2001) 33 E.H.R.R. 53, para.60.
36   (2000) 30 E.H.R.R. C.D.139, Application No. 33670/96, December 10, 2000.
37   The court specifically noted that the applicant could not be detained under the domestic mental health legislation as her psychopathic disorder could not be treated, before stating that under the Convention, there could be said to be both medical and social reasons for her detention.
38   (2003) 37 E.H.R.R. 9.
39   (2003) 37 E.H.R.R. 9, para.51.
40   See also the litigation at domestic level: *Reid v Secretary of State for Scotland* [1999] 2 A.C. 512; *Anderson & Others v Scottish Ministers* [2001] U.K.P.C. D5; [2003] 2 A.C. 602. See Phil Fennell, "Detention of Untreatable Psychopaths and Article 5 of the European Convention on Human Rights" (2002) 10 Med. L. Rev. 92.
41   Convention on the Rights of Persons with Disabilities, 2006 [A/RES/61/106].
42   Convention on the Rights of Persons with Disabilities, 2006 [A/RES/61/106], art.14(1)(b).
43   659 *Dáil Debates*, July 8, 2008, Written Answer 23518/08.
44   *Thematic Study by the Office of the United Nations High Commissioner for Human Rights on enhancing awareness and understanding of the Convention on the Rights of Persons with Disabilities* (A/HRC/10/48, January 26, 2009), p.15.

states that legislation authorising the institutionalisation of persons with disabilities on the grounds of their disability without their free and informed consent must be abolished and this must include the repeal of provisions authorising institution-alisation of persons with disabilities for their care and treatment without their free and informed consent, as well as provisions authorising the preventive detention of persons with disabilities on grounds such as the likelihood of them posing a danger to themselves or others, in all cases in which such grounds of care, treatment and public security are linked in legislation to an apparent or diagnosed mental illness. However, the Office notes that this should not be interpreted to say that persons with disabilities cannot be lawfully subject to detention for care and treatment or to preventive detention, but that the legal grounds upon which restriction of liberty is determined must be de-linked from the disability and neutrally defined so as to apply to all persons on an equal basis.[45] When the United Kingdom ratified the UN Convention in June 2009, it did not repeal its mental health legislation and only entered four relatively minor reservations to the Convention.[46] However, Australia made a declaration of its understanding that the Convention allows for compulsory assistance or treatment of persons, including measures taken for the treatment of mental disability, where such treatment is necessary, as a last resort and subject to safeguards.[47]

INTERPRETATION BY THE IRISH COURTS

3–13 As the vast majority of cases which have come before the Irish courts have concerned procedural matters, the courts have only rarely had occasion to interpret the meaning of the criteria for involuntary admission in the Act.

However, in *M.R. v Byrne and Flynn*[48] O'Neill J. analysed the meaning of the statutory criteria for involuntary admission, as it was relevant to the issues raised before him. The patient had originally been detained under the Mental Treatment Act 1945. On June 21, 2006, a temporary chargeable patient reception order for six months was made. This order was affirmed by a Mental Health Tribunal, referring to the need for treatment ground in s.3(1)(b) of the 2001 Act on December 21, 2006. On December 21, 2006 the psychiatrist made a renewal order, referring to s.3(1)(a), the risk of harm criterion. This renewal order was affirmed by the MHT on January 9, 2007, referring to the need for treatment ground in s.3(1)(b).

[45] *Thematic Study by the Office of the United Nations High Commissioner for Human Rights on enhancing awareness and understanding of the Convention on the Rights of Persons with Disabilities* (A/HRC/10/48, January 26, 2009), p.16.
[46] See information at *http://www.odi.gov.uk/working/un-convention/* [Accessed September 19, 2009].
[47] Australia, Declaration on Ratification of Convention on the Rights of Persons with Disabilities (2008), available at *http://www.un.org/disabilities/default.asp?id=475*. [Accessed September 19, 2009]
[48] [2007] I.E.H.C. 73; [2007] 3 I.R. 211.

In making the renewal order, the psychiatrist was of the opinion that both s.3(1)(a) and s.3(1)(b) applied, and he had ticked the box opposite s.3(1)(a) on Form 7 because he felt in the first instance it was appropriate and secondly, because in his view the form did not provide for or allow both boxes to be ticked, i.e. the boxes opposite s.3(1)(a) and s.3(1)(b).[49]

The patient argued that the renewal order purported to have been made by the psychiatrist was invalid in that there was no proper basis for the certification that because of illness, disability or dementia there was a serious likelihood of her causing immediate and serious harm to herself or other persons. It was also argued that the reasons advanced by the tribunal for concluding that the patient continued to suffer from mental disorder could not support a decision that she continued to suffer from mental disorder as defined in s.3 of the 2001 Act.

3–14 In analysing the criteria for admission, O'Neill J. said that he was merely setting out the legal framework of the operation of the statutory provisions. He emphasised that on a daily basis these provisions will have to be operated by clinical experts who within the broad framework set out have to make clinical judgments and it was not intended in this judgment to interfere in the proper realm of clinical judgment or to cut down or limit the proper scope of clinical judgment.[50]

O'Neill J. referred to the harm criterion and the need for treatment criterion in s.3(1)(a) and (b). He said that he was quite satisfied that these two bases are not alternative to each other and it would be probable in his view that in a great many cases of severe mental illness there would be a substantial overlap between the two.[51] Thus, it would be very likely that in a great many cases in which a person could be considered to fall within the categorisation in s.3(1)(a) that they would also be likely to fall within s.3(1)(b). To a much lesser extent, it was probable that persons who were primarily to be considered as falling within s.3(1)(b), would also be likely to have s.3(1)(a) applied to them.[52]

Strictly speaking, it may be more appropriate to state that the two bases are presented as alternatives in the Act but this does not preclude the possibility that in certain cases both alternatives may be present. Otherwise, the statement that the two bases "are not alternative to each other" may become a source of confusion.

O'Neill J. stated that the threshold for detention under the harm criterion in s.3(1)(a) is set high, as there must be a serious likelihood of the person concerned causing *immediate and serious* harm to themselves or to other persons.[53] In the course of argument in the case it had become common case that

---

[49] [2007] 3 I.R. 211 at 228.
[50] [2007] 3 I.R. 211 at 224.
[51] [2007] 3 I.R. 211 at 222.
[52] [2007] 3 I.R. 211 at 222.
[53] [2007] 3 I.R. 211 at 222.

the standard of "serious likelihood" was said to be higher than the ordinary standard of proof in civil actions, namely balance of probability, but somewhat short of certainty. He continued:

> "In my view what the Act envisages here is a standard of proof of a high level of probability. This is beyond the normal standard of proof in civil actions of 'more likely to be true', but it falls short of the standard of proof that is required in a criminal prosecution namely beyond a reasonable doubt and what is required is proof to a standard of a high level of likelihood as distinct from simply being more likely to be true."[54]

He said that the harm apprehended must in the first instance be "immediate". This presented obvious difficulties of construction in the context of mental illness because of the unpredictability of when the person concerned may cause harm either to themselves or others. In his view the critical factor which must be given dominant weight in this regard is the propensity or tendency of the person concerned to do harm to themselves or others. If the clinicians dealing with a person concerned are satisfied to the standard of proof set out above that that propensity or tendency is there then, having regard to the unpredictability of when the harm would be likely to occur, the likelihood of the harm occurring would have to be regarded as "immediate".[55]

3–15 O'Neill J. said that the word "harm" is a very general expression and thus physical and mental injury are included. As regards seriousness of harm, a different standard might apply, depending upon whether the harm was inflicted on the person themselves or on others. Clearly, the infliction of any physical injury on another could only be regarded as "serious" harm, whereas the infliction of a minor physical injury on the person themselves could be regarded as not "serious". Where the likely end result of the person's behaviours was merely trivial injury, it should not normally be regarded as constituting "serious" harm.[56]

Eldergill has commented that objection may be made to the meaning given by O'Neill J. to the word "immediate". In his view:

> "Some people who have been diagnosed as having a significant mental disorder certainly do have a propensity or tendency to seriously harm themselves or others. However, it is a long step from there to a finding that there is a serious likelihood of this occurring immediately. That judgment depends not just on the existence of a propensity or tendency to cause serious harm but on a whole range of other factors such as the person's current mental state, the risk factors, their present situation, the level of security and

---

[54] [2007] 3 I.R. 211 at 222.
[55] [2007] 3 I.R. 211 at 222–3.
[56] [2007] 3 I.R. 211 at 223.

supervision, their compliance with treatment, etc. If they are presently stable, the immediate risk may well be quite low, as in the case of many conditionally discharged restricted patients."[57]

As regards the need for treatment criterion in s.3(1)(b), O'Neill J. analysed this as follows:

"In my view it is appropriate to take the two parts of this subsection together namely (b)(i) and (ii). Between them they establish three essential elements which must be present before 'mental disorder' under this provision is established.
These are as follows:—
   (1) the severity of the illness, disability or dementia must result in the judgment of the person concerned being impaired to the extent that failure to admit the person to an approved centre is likely to
   (2) lead to a serious deterioration in his or her condition or prevent the administration of appropriate treatment that can be given only on such admission and
   (3) that the reception, detention and treatment of the person in an approved centre would be likely to benefit or alleviate the condition of that person to a material extent.
These elements in s. 3(1)(b)(i) and (ii) are in my view clear and self explanatory. It is perhaps worth drawing attention to the fact that in 3(1)(b)(i) there are alternative provisions, namely that the failure to admit to an approved centre would be likely to lead to a serious deterioration in the condition of the person or that the failure to admit into an approved centre would prevent the administration of appropriate treatment that could be given only by such admission."[58]

3–16 O'Neill J. then went on to apply his analysis of the statutory criteria to the issues before him in the case. Much of what he said was specific to the facts in that case. He rejected the argument that the patient's detention was not lawful because the psychiatrist had renewed her detention with reference to s.3(1)(a), based on serious likelihood of harm, but the tribunal had on two occasions affirmed her detention with reference to s.3(1)(b), the need for treatment criterion. This was because he had found that in many cases of severe mental illness there was overlap between s.3(1)(a) and (b)[59] and that the condition of this applicant or any other applicant, perhaps in response to treatment, could change.[60] He analysed the tribunal's decision in great detail and concluded that its decision was entirely consistent with the evidence before it, all of the

---

57   Anselm Eldergill, "The Best Is the Enemy of the Good: The Mental Health Act 2001" (2008) J. Mental Health L. 21 at 28.
58   [2007] 3 I.R. 211 at 223–4.
59   [2007] 3 I.R. 211 at 222.
60   [2007] 3 I.R. 211 at 225.

elements as provided for in s.3(1)(b) for a finding of "mental disorder" were considered and a determination made in respect of each of these essential elements, and the record of the tribunal recorded all of this.[61]

GUIDANCE FROM MENTAL HEALTH COMMISSION

3–17 The Mental Health Commission has produced reference guides[62] to provide all those whose work may bring them into contact with persons suffering from a mental illness or a mental disorder with a clear and practical understanding of the major objectives and requirements of the Mental Health Act 2001.

As regards the criteria for involuntary admission, the reference guides primarily reproduce the relevant provisions of the Act. However, they provide some additional guidance on the meaning of "severe dementia" and "significant intellectual disability."

Regarding severe dementia, the reference guide states that, "to fulfil the criteria for involuntary admission, the person must also present with severe psychiatric or behavioural symptoms such as aggressive behaviour. The symptoms could also include delusions or hallucinations—the 2001 Act does not limit the symptoms to aggressive behaviour."[63]

On the topic of "significant intellectual disability", the reference guide states that to establish a mental disorder through a finding of significant intellectual disability, in accordance with the 2001 Act, a state of arrested or incomplete development of the mind must include significant impairment of intelligence, significant impairment of social functioning and abnormally aggressive or seriously irresponsible conduct. The Commission notes that all of the above criteria must be established separately.[64] The Commission states that psychometric testing is required. The person's I.Q. level is not conclusive but should be below 69. The assessment should have taken place within the past five years, or as best practice dictates.

3–18 According to the reference guide, the assessment of "abnormally aggressive or seriously irresponsible conduct" can be seen to have both observational (i.e. the actual behaviour) and judgement (i.e. the abnormality and/or seriousness) components. To meet the criteria for each, abnormally aggressive and seriously irresponsible conduct should result in actual damage and/or real distress (in some cases to the self), and should occur either recently or persistently or with excessive severity.[65] The guide also advises that if conduct has ceased then the

---

[61] [2007] 3 I.R. 211 at 230.
[62] Mental Health Commission, *Reference Guide: Mental Health Act 2001—Part One (Adults)* (2006) and *Reference Guide: Mental Health Act 2001—Part Two (Children)* (2006).
[63] *Reference Guide Part One*, section 1.3, p.5.
[64] *Reference Guide Part One*, section 1.3, p.6.
[65] *Reference Guide Part One,* section 1.3, p.7.

person should no longer be regarded as having a significant intellectual disability under the Act.

Section 8 provides that a person may not be involuntarily admitted to an approved centre by reason only of the fact that the person (a) is suffering from a personality disorder, (b) is socially deviant, or (c) is addicted to drugs or intoxicants. The reference guide quotes the definition in ICD-10 of Personality disorders:

> "Personality disorders are described in the International Classification of Mental and Behavioural Disorders (ICD-10)[66] as 'deeply ingrained and enduring behaviour patterns, manifesting themselves as inflexible responses to a broad range of personal and social situations'; they represent either extreme or significant deviations from the way an average individual in a given culture perceives, thinks, feels and particularly relates to others and are 'developmental conditions, which appear in childhood or adolescence and continue into adulthood'."[67]

The guide states that "socially deviant" is a term that refers to any behaviour that does not conform to social norms.[68] What is perceived as deviant behaviour is subject to change, as it is culturally determined and depends on the values and beliefs of society. Different cultures have different perceptions of social order, therefore making what may be perceived as deviant behaviour in one culture wholly acceptable in another.[69] Difficulty in adapting to moral, social, political, or other values, in itself, should not be considered a mental disorder.[70] Nonconformity with moral, social, cultural or political values, or religious beliefs prevailing in a person's community shall never be a determining factor in diagnosing mental illness.[71]

STATISTICAL INFORMATION

3–19 Detailed statistics regarding admissions to psychiatric centres are available from two main sources, the Mental Health Commission and the Health Research Board. The figures from the two bodies differ in some respects due to differences

---

[66] World Health Organisation, *International Classification of Mental and Behavioural Disorders* (ICD-10) (1992).
[67] *Reference Guide Part One*, section 1.3, p.8.
[68] The Commission cites Anthony Giddens, *Sociology*, 4th edn (Cambridge: Polity Press, 2001).
[69] *Reference Guide Part One*, section 1.3, p.9.
[70] The Commission cites *Council of Europe Recommendation No. R(83)2 of the Committee of Ministers to Member States concerning the legal protection of persons suffering from mental disorders placed as involuntary patients* (1983).
[71] The Commission cites the *UN Principles for the Protection of Persons with Mental Illness and the Improvement of Mental Health Care* (1991), Principle 4.3.

in their respective roles. Some of the most notable points for the purposes of this book are as follows.

The numbers of residents in psychiatric centres, recorded in periodic censuses, have dramatically declined over the years. In 1958, there were 21,000 "asylum" residents for the 26 counties, 0.7 per cent of the population or 700 per 100,000.[72] The numbers of residents declined steadily. The 1971 figure was 16,661, there were 13,984 in 1981, 8,207 in 1991 and 4,321 in 2001.[73] In 2007 there were 3,314 persons on the registers of approved centres for adults, giving a rate of 103.4 per 100,000 of the 2006 Census population.[74] The proportion of non-voluntary residents declined from 78 per cent in 1963 to 17 per cent in 2001.[75] In 2007, 10.1 per cent of residents were involuntary, 2.1 per cent were wards of court and 2.4 per cent were subject to a court order, all of whom were in the Central Mental Hospital.[76]

Statistics on admissions are gathered more frequently than numbers of residents. There are naturally more admissions than there are residents, as a particular hospital bed may be occupied by a number of different patients in the course of a year. In 1965, there were 15,440 admissions, in 1975 there were 25,892, the number peaked at 29,392 in 1986 and had fallen to 23,736 in 2002.[77] In 2008, there were 20,752 admissions.[78]

3–20 Prior to the Mental Treatment Act 1945, it was not possible for a patient to be admitted to a public hospital on a voluntary basis. Since the "voluntary" categorisation was introduced, the percentage of involuntary admissions has declined steadily. In 1971, 17.6 per cent of admissions were non-voluntary but by 2002 this had fallen to 11.4 per cent.[79] On one calculation, in 2007, only 8.5 per cent of admissions were non-voluntary and the remaining 91.5 per cent were voluntary.[80] However, this figure does not include 623 patients who were re-

---

[72] Dermot Walsh & Antoinette Daly, *Mental Illness in Ireland 1750–2002: Reflections on the Rise and Fall of Institutional Care* (Dublin: Health Research Board, 2004), p.33.

[73] Walsh & Daly, *Mental Illness in Ireland 1750–2002: Reflections on the Rise and Fall of Institutional Care* (Dublin: Health Research Board, 2004), p.69. See also Mental Health Commission, *Annual Report 2006*, Book 1, p.48.

[74] Mental Health Commission, *Annual Report 2007*, Book 1, p.55.

[75] Walsh & Daly, *Mental Illness in Ireland 1750–2002: Reflections on the Rise and Fall of Institutional Care* (Dublin: Health Research Board, 2004), p.76.

[76] Mental Health Commission, *Annual Report 2007*, Book 1, p.58.

[77] Walsh & Daly, *Mental Illness in Ireland 1750–2002: Reflections on the Rise and Fall of Institutional Care* (Dublin: Health Research Board, 2004), p.102.

[78] Antoinette Daly, *National Psychiatric In-Patient Reporting System Preliminary National Bulletin Ireland 2008* (Health Research Board, 2009), p.1.

[79] Walsh & Daly, *Mental Illness in Ireland 1750–2002: Reflections on the Rise and Fall of Institutional Care* (Dublin: Health Research Board, 2004), p.109.

[80] There were 20,769 admissions in 2007 of which 19,013 (91.5 per cent) were voluntary and 1,756 (8.5 per cent) were non-voluntary—Antoinette Daly, Dermot Walsh & Ros Moran, *H.R.B. Statistics Series 5: Activities of Irish Psychiatric Units and Hospitals 2007* (Health Research Board, 2008), Table 2.7, p.46. The preliminary HRB bulletin for 2008 records 20,752

graded from voluntary to involuntary status in 2007,[81] which would make the percentage of involuntary admissions and re-gradings combined roughly 11.5 per cent.[82]

In recent years, the number of re-gradings from voluntary to involuntary status has been included in the figures and the most recent trends are as follows:

Year	Involuntary admissions (Form 6)	Re-gradings from voluntary to involuntary status (Form 13)	Total
2005[83]	2,289	541	2,830
2006[84]	2,170	Not available	
2007[85]	1,503	623	2,126
2008[86]	1,420	584	2,004

It is clear that the number of involuntary admissions and re-gradings has fallen since the 2001 Act came into force. There was a decrease of 25 per cent in overall involuntary admission activity from 2005 to 2007, and a further 6 per cent decrease from 2007 to 2008.[87] The decrease is 29 per cent from 2005 to 2008.[88]

3–21 Most patients admitted involuntarily are diagnosed with schizophrenia, schizotypal and delusional disorders, mania or depressive disorders. In 2008, only four episodes of involuntary admission were classified as "intellectual

admissions of which 8 per cent were involuntary—Daly, *National Psychiatric In-Patient Reporting System Preliminary National Bulletin Ireland 2008*, p.1.

[81] Mental Health Commission, *Annual Report 2007*, Table 9, Book 1, p.36.

[82] The non-voluntary admissions and re-gradings combined would total 2,379 of 20,769 admissions. However, note the differences between Health Research Board and Mental Health Commission figures. The H.R.B. records 1,756 involuntary admissions, whereas the Mental Health Commission records 1,503. For an explanation of these discrepancies see Daly, Walsh & Moran, *H.R.B. Statistics Series 5: Activities of Irish Psychiatric Units and Hospitals 2007* (Health Research Board, 2008), p.14, fn.1, "Data contained in this report does not include data on Admission Orders to detain Voluntary Patients whereas M.H.C. figures do. In addition, this report does not include data for all centres approved by the Mental Health Commission (MHC) in accordance with the provisions of the Mental Health Act 2001 (Department of Health and Children 2001)."

[83] Mental Health Commission, *Annual Report 2005*, Book 1, p.46.

[84] *Activities of Irish Psychiatric Hospitals and Units 2006* (Health Research Board), p.43.

[85] Mental Health Commission, *Annual Report 2007*, Table 9, Book 1, p.36.

[86] Mental Health Commission, *Annual Report 2008*, Book 1, p.38.

[87] *Annual Report 2008*, p.39. This is a decrease of 704 from 2,830 to 2,126.

[88] A decrease of 826 from 2,830 to 2,004.

disability" at close of episode.[89] A small number of patients were classified as having alcoholic disorders (29), other drug disorders (34) or personality and behavioural disorders (18).[90] As the Commission noted in its 2007 report, a person may not be involuntarily admitted by reason only of the fact that the person is (a) suffering from a personality disorder, (b) is socially deviant, or (c) is addicted to drugs or intoxicants. On the other hand, involuntary admissions are coded by diagnostic grouping at close of episode and this may differ from the patient's diagnosis on admission.[91] The Health Research Board has also recorded non-voluntary admissions in these categories.[92]

---

[89] *Annual Report 2008*, Book 1, p.43.

[90] *Annual Report 2008*, Book 1, p.43.

[91] *Annual Report 2007*, Book 1, p.39.

[92] Antoinette Daly, Dermot Walsh & Ros Moran, *H.R.B. Statistics Series 5: Activities of Irish Psychiatric Units and Hospitals 2007* (Health Research Board, 2008), p.30, "Under the Mental Health Act 2001 persons with a diagnosis of alcoholic disorders or personality disorder cannot be involuntarily admitted without an accompanying mental disorder. However, it should be noted that there were 77 non-voluntary (all) admissions for alcoholic disorders and of these, only 19 were recorded as having a secondary diagnosis. In addition, there were 35 non-voluntary (all) admissions for personality disorders and of these, only 7 were recorded as having a secondary diagnosis."

CHAPTER 4

ADMISSION UNDER THE MENTAL HEALTH ACT 2001

INTRODUCTION

4–01 There are a number of methods of involuntary admission, both initial admissions and renewals of such admissions, provided for in the Mental Health Act 2001. This chapter will focus mainly on involuntary admissions, as well as the procedures for discharges and transfers. Chapter 5 will consider the law concerning voluntary patients and the procedure for "re-grading" a voluntary patient as an involuntary patient. Renewal orders will be discussed in Chapter 6.

4–02 In addition to the statutory requirements, the Mental Health Commission has produced a code of practice on admission, transfer and discharge in 2009.[1]

TIME LIMITS

4–03 When time limits are stated in the legislation, these must be interpreted in accordance with the Interpretation Act 2005.[2] This includes the important rule that where a period of time is expressed to begin on or be reckoned from a particular day, that day shall be deemed to be included in the period.[3] So, for example, the Mental Health Act 2001 states that a recommendation remains in force for seven days from the date of its making and then expires.[4] This does not mean that a recommendation remains in force for seven 24-hour periods. Instead, it remains in force up to midnight at the end of a seven-day period, which includes the day of its making. For example, if a recommendation is made at 2.40pm on a Tuesday, it expires at midnight on the following Monday.

---

[1] Mental Health Commission, *Code of Practice on Admission, Transfer and Discharge to and from an Approved Centre* (2009). See also Mental Health Commission, *Knowledge Review: Code of Practice on Admission, Transfer and Discharge to and from an Approved Centre* (2007).

[2] The 2005 Act supersedes the Interpretation Act 1937 and the Interpretation (Amendment) Act 1993.

[3] Section 18(h), Interpretation Act 2005. See consideration of previous similar section of Interpretation Act 1937 in *D.P.P. v Curtin*, Circuit Court, Moran J., April 23, 2004, *Irish Times*, April 24, 2004. See also David Dodd, *Statutory Interpretation in Ireland* (Sussex: Tottel, 2008), pp.271–2.

[4] Section 10(5), Mental Health Act 2001.

Similarly, a decision of a Mental Health Tribunal (MHT) must be made not later than 21 days after the making of an admission order or renewal order.[5] This means that the decision must be made by midnight at the end of a 21-day period which includes the day the admission order or renewal order was made. The calculation of this time limit may lead to some confusion, as is illustrated by an apparent miscalculation by the High Court in one case.[6]

4–04 The Mental Health Commission has produced a document explaining the various time limits in operation.[7] However, this document must now be read in light of the changes regarding renewal orders which were made as a result of the decision in *S.M. v Mental Health Commission*.[8] In light of the numerous issues which have arisen regarding time limits in the 2001 Act, it may now be better to reword the Act so that the time limits operate in a more logical and streamlined manner.[9]

INVOLUNTARY ADMISSION OF AN ADULT

4–05 This procedure is sometimes referred to as involuntary admission from the community, to distinguish it from a re-grading case (see Chapter 5 below), where the person is already being treated in an approved centre on a voluntary basis. It may also be referred to as an "assisted admission" if the clinical director becomes involved in arranging the removal of the person to the approved centre (see paras 4–31 to 4–46 below).

There are four stages in this admission:

1. Application for Recommendation
2. Recommendation for Admission
3. Removal to Approved Centre
4. Admission Order

Application for Recommendation

4–06 Where it is proposed to have a person (other than a child) involuntarily admitted to an approved centre, an application may be made to a registered medical practitioner[10] under s.9. Three parties are involved here:

---

[5]   Section 18(2), Mental Health Act 2001.
[6]   In *A.M.C. v St. Luke's Hospital, Clonmel* [2007] I.E.H.C. 65; [2007] 2 I.R. 814 a 21-day renewal order was made on December 4, 2006. Peart J. stated at p.818 that the 21-day period would have expired on December 25, 2006.
[7]   *Duration of Involuntary Admission and Renewal Orders* (2007).
[8]   [2008] I.E.H.C. 441; [2009] 2 I.L.R.M. 127; McMahon J., High Court, October 31, 2008.
[9]   See further Darius Whelan, "Legacy of Unresolved Legal Issues on Mental Health", *Irish Times*, November 4, 2008.
[10] A "registered medical practitioner" means a person whose name is entered in the General

- The person who applies for admission (the applicant)
- The person it is proposed to admit (the proposed patient)
- The registered medical practitioner to whom the application is made (the doctor)

The applicant must have observed the proposed patient "not more than 48 hours before the date of the making of the application."[11] It is noteworthy that the Act refers to 48 hours "before *the date of* the making", rather than "48 hours before the making".[12] To take an example, the observation by the applicant could take place at 1.10pm on January 1 and the application could be made *at any time* on January 3, for example at 6.20pm

4–07 There is no definition of "observed" in the Act but Dunne J. suggested in *S.C. v Clinical Director, St Brigid's Hospital*[13] that the observation should be more than fleeting:

> "I am aware of the fact that the applicant in this was under an obligation to sign on at Drogheda Garda station on Monday, Wednesday and Friday as a condition of the bail which had been granted to him, but there is no suggestion that any incident occurred during the signing on which might have provoked an application under s.9 and indeed there is no suggestion that that process provided any appropriate or necessary period of observation."[14]

4–08 The application may be made by any of the following people listed in s.9(1), unless they are disqualified under s.9(2):

- the proposed patient's spouse or relative
- an authorised officer of the Health Service Executive (HSE)
- a member of An Garda Síochána
- an authorised person[15]
- subject to the provisions of s.9(2), any other person

A "spouse" does not include a spouse of a proposed patient who is living separately and apart from the proposed patient or in respect of whom an

Register of Medical Practitioners (s.2(1)). The Register may be consulted online at *http://www.medicalcouncil.ie/registration/check.asp* [Accessed September 20, 2009].

[11] Section 9(4) of the Mental Health Act 2001.

[12] By way of contrast, s.10(2) refers to an examination being carried out "within 24 hours of" receipt of an application, rather than within 24 hours of *the date of* receipt of the application.

[13] [2009] I.E.H.C. 100; High Court, Dunne J., February 26, 2009.

[14] [2009] I.E.H.C. 100, p.8.

[15] The reference to "an authorised person (but without prejudice to any capacity that the authorised person has to make such an application by virtue of paragraph (a), (b) or (c) of subsection (1))" was inserted by s.63 of the Health (Miscellaneous Provisions) Act 2009. At time of writing, the commencement date is not known. The main purpose of the amendments made by the 2009 Act is to permit independent contractors to take part in the assisted admissions procedure. See further paras 4–45 to 4–46 below.

application or order has been made under the Domestic Violence Act 1996.[16] Boland and Laing have argued that it is very important to exclude separating spouses from applying for recommendations for admission.[17] In *F.W. v Dept. of Psychiatry James Connolly Memorial Hospital*[18] an application had originally been made by the proposed patient's husband but once it was discovered that the proposed patient had previously initiated proceedings under the Domestic Violence Act against her husband, the psychiatrist revoked the admission order. Hedigan J. noted that the psychiatrist considered the application under the Domestic Violence Act to be a consequence of the proposed patient's paranoid delusions.[19] Other aspects of this case are considered below at paras 4–117 to 4–119.

The "spouse" category covers a husband and wife, or a man or woman who is cohabiting with a proposed patient of the opposite sex for three years.[20] This obviously precludes a gay or lesbian partner although, of course, such a partner might apply under the "any other person" category. The Civil Partnership Bill 2009 proposes to add "or civil partner" to all references to spouse in the 2001 Act.[21] "Relative", in relation to the proposed patient, means a parent, grandparent, brother, sister, uncle, aunt, niece, nephew or child of the proposed patient or of the proposed patient's spouse, whether of the whole blood, of the half blood or by affinity.[22]

4–09 An "authorised officer" means an officer of the HSE:

    (i) who is of a prescribed rank or grade, *and*
    (ii) who is authorised by the chief executive officer to exercise the powers conferred on authorised officers by section 9.[23]

The prescribed grades are: Local Health Manager, General Manager, Grade VIII, Psychiatric Nurse, Occupational Therapist, Psychologist or Social Worker.[24]

The reference to a member of An Garda Síochána could legally include a reference to a reserve member, as a reserve member has, while on duty, the same powers, immunities, privileges and duties as a person appointed to the rank of garda.[25] However, the Garda Commissioner may determine the range of powers

---

[16] Section 9(8) of the Mental Health Act 2001.
[17] Faye Boland & Judith M. Laing, "Out of Sight and Out of Mind? A Feminist Perspective on Civil Commitment in Britain and Ireland" (1999/00) 4 *Contemporary Issues in Law* 257.
[18] [2008] I.E.H.C. 283; Hedigan J., High Court, August 18, 2008.
[19] [2008] I.E.H.C. 283; Hedigan J., High Court, August 18, 2008, p.2.
[20] Section 2(1) of the Mental Health Act 2001.
[21] Civil Partnership Bill 2009, s.95.
[22] Section 2(1) of the Mental Health Act 2001.
[23] Section 9(8) of the Mental Health Act 2001. The original Act referred to an officer "of a health board", but this was amended by s.75 and sch.7 of the Health Act 2004 to refer to an officer of "the Health Service Executive." See also s.77 of the 2004 Act regarding certificates of delegation of functions.
[24] Mental Health Act 2001 (Authorised Officer) Regulations 2006, S.I. No. 550 of 2006.
[25] Section 15(3) of the Garda Síochána Act 2005.

and duties of reserve members[26] and, at present, powers under the Mental Health Act 2001 do not appear to be part of the list of powers.[27]

If an application is made under the "any other person" category, it must contain a statement of the reasons why it is so made, of the connection of the applicant with the proposed patient and of the circumstances in which the application is made.[28]

4–10 A number of categories of people are disqualified from making an application in respect of a proposed patient by s.9(2). Therefore, the applicant must not be:

- a person under 18 years of age;
- a HSE authorised officer or a Garda who is a relative of the proposed patient or of the proposed patient's spouse[29];
- a member of the staff of the approved centre concerned[30];
- a person with an interest in any payments to be made in respect of the proposed patient's care in the approved centre concerned;
- any doctor who provides a regular medical service at the approved centre concerned; or
- the spouse, parent, grandparent, brother, sister, uncle or aunt of any of the above persons.

4–11 Applications must be made in a form specified by the Mental Health Commission.[31] The Commission has specified separate forms for different categories of applicant:

- Form 1: Application by a Spouse or Relative
- Form 2: Application by a HSE Authorised Officer
- Form 3: Application by a Garda
- Form 4: Application by a Member of the Public

4–12 Each form includes a space in which the applicant gives the name and address of the approved centre to which the applicant is applying for the proposed patient to be admitted. The Act does not require that the applicant specify a particular approved centre and perhaps this is more a matter for the

---

[26] Section 15(5) of the Garda Síochána Act 2005.

[27] See *Establishment of a Garda Síochána Reserve*, Department of Justice, Equality and Law Reform information leaflet, May 2006, p.11.

[28] Section 9(5) of the Mental Health Act 2001.

[29] The same definitions of "spouse" and "relative" as given earlier apply.

[30] The full wording is: "a member of the governing body, or the staff, or the person in charge, of the approved centre concerned." Note also s.9(7), as amended, which states that the reference to a member of the governing body of the approved centre concerned does not include a reference to a member of the Board of the HSE.

[31] Section 9(3) of the Mental Health Act 2001.

doctor than the applicant. It is unclear what would happen if the applicant did not specify an approved centre (by leaving the answer to this question blank) or if the applicant specified one centre and the doctor, in their recommendation, specified a different centre.

4–13 The applicant must disclose any previous application for a recommendation, of which they are aware, which was refused in respect of the same proposed patient.[32] The Act states that in these circumstances, "the applicant, so far as he or she is aware of the facts relating to the previous application and its refusal, shall state those facts" to the doctor to whom the current application is made. Forms 1 to 4 each contain a space in which this information is to be recorded. Each form asks the applicant to state, if known, the name of the doctor who refused the previous application, the date of refusal and the circumstances of the refusal. It is an offence not to comply with the requirements regarding disclosure.[33]

4–14 The requirement to disclose previous refusals appears to extend only to *applications for recommendations* which were refused. This is because the relevant section refers to previous refusals of "applications" rather than "recommendations".[34] For example, in January 2009 Jane applies to Dr Murphy for a recommendation for admission in respect of Tony. Dr Murphy makes the recommendation for admission, but when Tony is brought to the approved centre, Dr Sullivan, the consultant psychiatrist, refuses to make an admission order. In June 2009, if Jane applies to another doctor, Dr Redmond, for a recommendation for admission in respect of Tony, Jane does not need to disclose the fact that Tony was not admitted in January, as this was not a refusal of an application for a recommendation. Even if Jane wanted to disclose that Tony was not admitted on that occasion, she should not use the part of the Form which refers to previous refusals, as this would not be an accurate response to the question on the Form.

4–15 It is an offence for a person, for the purposes of or in relation to an application, to make any statement which is to his or her knowledge false or misleading.[35]

4–16 There is no statutory limit on the amount of time which may elapse between the making of the application and its receipt by the doctor. In addition, none of the statutory forms record the time that the application form was

---

[32] Section 11(1) of the Mental Health Act 2001.
[33] Section 11(2) of the Mental Health Act 2001. The maximum penalty on summary conviction is a fine of €1,904.61, 12 months' imprisonment, or both: s.30.
[34] Section 11(1) of the Mental Health Act 2001. See also the definition of "application" in s.2(1).
[35] Section 9(6) of the Mental Health Act 2001. The maximum penalty on summary conviction is a fine of €1,904.61, 12 months' imprisonment, or both: s.30.

received by the doctor. So Karen might fill in an application form at 6.20pm on January 3, but not bring it along to the doctor until 8.00pm on January 8.

4–17 Analysis of types of applicant in 2008 was as follows[36]:

Form Number	Type	Number	%
1	Spouse/Relative	908	63.9%
2	Authorised Officer	65	4.6%
3	Garda Síochána	324	22.8%
4	Any other Person	123	8.7%
TOTAL		1,420	100%

Comparison of the 2007 figures for type of applicant with the 2008 figures showed that the number of applicants by spouse/relative had fallen from 69 per cent to 63.9 per cent, the authorised officer category had fallen from 7 per cent to 4.6 per cent, applications by Gardaí had risen from 15 per cent to 22.8 per cent and the category of any other person remained almost the same.[37] The Commission chairman, Dr Edmond O'Dea, expressed concern in 2007 over "the increase in the proportion of applications initiated by the gardaí" and said, "the development of the authorised officer system is an urgent priority".[38] A Joint Working Group of the Mental Health Commission and An Garda Síochána issued a report in 2009.[39]

The 2007 report contains an analysis of the "any other applicant" category.[40]

	Number	%
Health/care staff	45	34%
Prison staff	10	8%
Garda	3	2%
Friend	12	9%
Partner	2	1%
Business/professional	6	5%
Relative	6	5%
Not stated on the form	47	36%
Total	131	100%

---

[36] Mental Health Commission, *Annual Report 2008*, Book 1, Table 9, p.43.

[37] The 2007 figures are available in Mental Health Commission, *Annual Report 2007*, Book 1, Table 10, p.37.

[38] Mary Regan, "Gardaí take mentally ill patients into care", *Irish Examiner*, November 9, 2007. See also Mental Health Commission, *Report on the Operation of Part 2 of the Mental Health Act 2001* (2008), p.80.

[39] Mental Health Commission and An Garda Síochána, *Report of Joint Working Group on Mental Health Services and the Police* (2009).

[40] Mental Health Commission, *Annual Report 2007*, Book 1, Table 12, p.37.

Previous research on applicants for involuntary admissions in 2002 showed 76 per cent were performed by a relative, 7 per cent by a health board official, 9 per cent by members of the Garda, and 5 per cent by others.[41]

Recommendation for Admission

4–18 Section 10 of the 2001 Act lays down the requirements for making a recommendation for admission. Before the doctor can make a recommendation, the doctor must carry out an "examination" of the patient within 24 hours of *receipt* of the application. There is no specific time limit between the examination and the making of the recommendation.[42]

If the doctor refers to the application form, this states the exact date and time the application was *made*; however, none of the forms record the time that the application form was *received* by the doctor. It would be good practice where possible to record the time of receipt elsewhere on the file. In addition, a lawyer representing a patient would be well advised to look for the time of receipt on the file, or to seek oral evidence on this point from the applicant and the doctor.

4–19 It is unclear whether the examination of the patient must take place before or after the receipt of the form. In *M.McN. v Health Service Executive*,[43] the doctor had examined the proposed patient at 2pm on December 17, 2008, and the application by the proposed patient's husband for a recommendation had been completed at 9.45am on December 18, 2008. The solicitor had intended bringing this matter to the attention of the Tribunal at the review hearing, but on January 6, 2009, before the review hearing, the solicitor received a letter from the Mental Health Commission stating that the involuntary admission and treatment of the applicant had ended and that the arrangements for the review hearing had "for the time-being been discontinued". Peart J. stated, "I do not have to decide whether in fact [s.10 of the 2001 Act] means that the examination must take place within 24 hours following that receipt or within the previous 24 hours."[44] He said that even if the provision is to be construed as meaning the former, that failure to comply with the provision in s.10 was, in any event, a matter which the Tribunal would have had power to consider overlooking on the review, in accordance with the provisions of s.18(1)(a)(ii), if it was satisfied that the failure did not affect the substance of the order and did not cause an injustice. However, he said, "I express no view on the matter".[45]

---

[41] Dermot Walsh, Arthur O'Reilly, Brid Clarke, Rosalyn Moran, Donna Tedstone Doherty, *Pathways to Involuntary Admission to Irish Psychiatric Hospitals in 2002* (Health Research Board and Mental Health Commission, 2004).

[42] Anne Marie O'Neill, *Irish Mental Health Law* (Dublin : First Law, 2005), p.135.

[43] [2009] I.E.H.C. 236; High Court, Peart J., May 15, 2009.

[44] [2009] I.E.H.C. 236; High Court, Peart J., May 15, 2009, p.4

[45] [2009] I.E.H.C. 236; High Court, Peart J., May 15, 2009, p.4.

4–20 The doctor must inform the proposed patient of the purpose of the examination unless in their view the provision of such information might be prejudicial to the proposed patient's mental health, well-being or emotional condition.[46]

The Meaning of an "Examination"

4–21 An "examination" means a personal examination carried out by the doctor of the process and content of thought, the mood and the behaviour of the proposed patient.[47] The doctor must also have regard to the principles in s.4, i.e. best interests of the proposed patient, entitlement of the proposed patient to make representations and rights to dignity, bodily integrity, privacy and autonomy.

4–22 The Mental Treatment Act 1945 required that the doctor have "visited and examined" the patient and that the admitting psychiatrist "examine" the patient. There was no definition of "visit" or "examine". In *O'Dowd v North Western Health Board*[48] the majority of the Supreme Court held that the examination (at admission stage by the psychiatrist) was adequate but Henchy J., dissenting, took the opposite view using very strong language.

It was held in *O'Reilly v Moroney & Mid-Western Health Board*[49] by a majority of two to one that observation from 12 to 15 yards away was sufficient examination for the purposes of the Act. Ms O'Reilly later received a friendly settlement of her claim before the European Commission on Human Rights.[50] In *Melly v Moran*,[51] where it was argued that a visit and examination had taken place by telephone,[52] the Supreme Court held that there had been a *prima facie* want of reasonable care. O'Flaherty J. appeared to approve of the following argument by the plaintiff's counsel: "Leaving aside whether an examination can take place without the doctor and the patient being in the same location (in other

---

[46] Section 10(2) of the Mental Health Act 2001.

[47] Section 2(1) of the Mental Health Act 2001. See also discussion of examination in Richard Jones, *Mental Health Act Manual*, 11th edn (London: Thomson Sweet and Maxwell, 2008), p.90, including discussion of *Routley v Worthing Health Authority*, unreported, Court of Appeal, July 14, 1983.

[48] [1983] I.L.R.M. 186.

[49] High Court [1992] 2 I.R. 145; Supreme Court, unreported, November 16, 1993.

[50] *O'Reilly v Ireland*, European Commission of Human Rights, Application number 24196/94, Admissibility Decision, January 22, 1996 and Report of the Commission on Friendly Settlement, December 3, 1996.

[51] *Melly v Moran and North Western Health Board* [1997] I.E.H.C. 101; McGuinness J., High Court, 19 June 1997; Supreme Court, May 28, 1998

[52] There had been an examination in the doctor's surgery on April 8, 1994 but the problem was that the application for recommendation and the recommendation for admission were not completed until April 11. Section 163 of the 1945 Act, as amended, required that the patient be visited and examined within 24 hours before or after receipt of the application. Counsel for the defendants argued that the visit and examination had taken place over three days, including the phone calls which occurred.

words, assuming, without deciding, that telephone conversations might pass muster as a form of 'examination'), nevertheless there certainly was not within 24 hours any visitation of the patient by the doctor."[53]

4–23 There is no European Convention on Human Rights (ECHR) case directly in point on the meaning of an "examination". There is some material of relevance in *Varbanov v Bulgaria*,[54] in which the court stated as follows:

> "The Court considers that no deprivation of liberty of a person considered as being of unsound mind may be deemed in conformity with Article 5 § 1(e) of the Convention if it has been ordered without seeking the opinion of a medical expert. Any other approach falls short of the required protection against arbitrariness, inherent in Article 5 of the Convention. The particular form and procedure in this respect may vary depending on the circumstances. It may be acceptable, in urgent cases or where a person is arrested because of his violent behaviour, that such an opinion be obtained immediately after the arrest. In all other cases a prior consultation should be necessary. Where no other possibility exists, for instance due to a refusal of the person concerned to appear for an examination, at least an assessment by a medical expert on the basis of the file must be required, failing which it cannot be maintained that a person has reliably been shown to be of unsound mind (cf. the *X v the United Kingdom* judgment of 5 November 1981, Series A no. 46). Furthermore, the medical assessment must be based on the actual state of mental health of the person concerned and not solely on past events. A medical opinion cannot be seen as sufficient to justify deprivation of liberty if a significant period of time has elapsed."[55]

4–24 In *M.Z. v Khattak and Tallaght Hospital Board*[56] the doctor, Dr W., had arrived at a Garda station to carry out an examination, having been called there by the Gardaí. When Dr W. arrived at the station the sergeant introduced him to the applicant at a location outside the rear of the Garda Station where the applicant, the sergeant and Dr W. smoked cigarettes. Dr W. chatted to the applicant at this location for a period of about 10 minutes. Dr W. stated that as a result of what he called his "chat" with the applicant he was satisfied that he should be in hospital since he was not taking his medication, was elated and paranoid. Dr W. stated that he could not recall exactly what they spoke about, but confirmed that he did not carry out what is called a mental state examination as such. He was not aware, and did not ask, what particular medication the applicant was on. Dr W. stated also that he was unaware of what particular "examination" was required to be carried out in accordance with the provisions

---

[53] Supreme Court, May 28, 1998, pp.8–9.
[54] Application no. 31365/96; [2000] M.H.L.R. 263.
[55] [2000] M.H.L.R. 263, para.47.
[56] [2008] I.E.H.C. 262; High Court, Peart J., July 28, 2008.

of the Act, having been referred by counsel to the definition of an 'examination' contained in s.2 of the Act.[57]

Peart J. said that he listened to Dr W.'s evidence as to the manner in which he conducted his examination of the applicant "with some disquiet."[58] It seemed to him to be a too informal manner in which to conduct such an examination, a consequence of which can be that the person is to be detained involuntarily at an approved centre. Peart J. said that there was no question but that Dr W. is a registered medical practitioner, and thus a qualified person to have examined the applicant for the purpose of the s.10 recommendation. He continued:

> "It also could not be gainsaid that the examination carried out for the purpose of an application under s.9 or indeed under s.10 is not to be equated with the later examination to be carried out by a consultant psychiatrist under s. 14 of the Act within 24 hours of any admission of the patient, even though the definition of 'examination' covers an examination in relation to a recommendation. It must, I would have thought, be an examination which is less detailed and thorough, and therefore of shorter duration than one carried out by a consultant psychiatrist following admission, in particular since there is no requirement under the Act that the registered medical practitioner have any particular psychiatric qualification or other expertise."[59]

Even though Peart J. had reservations about the appropriateness of such an examination taking place in such an informal way, nevertheless one could not discount completely the probability that Dr W.'s 30 years' experience as a general practitioner and his later experience of examining patients in a Garda station, enabled him to reach the necessary conclusions, for the purpose of making this recommendation, quite rapidly both from observation and conversation with the person, armed as he was, and was entitled to be, with necessary background information provided to him by the applicant's brother and the Garda sergeant at the time.[60]

4–25 It is unclear what will happen if the patient does not consent to the examination by the doctor. Eldergill raises this point as follows:

> "What if the named person refuses to be examined during the 24 hour period? The doctor is under a duty to examine the individual within 24 hours, but the named individual is under no duty to co-operate or to attend for examination. Nor is there any statutory power, equivalent to section 135 MHA 1983,[61]

---

[57] [2008] I.E.H.C. 262; High Court, Peart J., July 28, 2008, p.7.
[58] [2008] I.E.H.C. 262; High Court, Peart J., July 28, 2008, p.14.
[59] [2008] I.E.H.C. 262; High Court, Peart J., July 28, 2008, p.16.
[60] [2008] I.E.H.C. 262; High Court, Peart J., July 28, 2008, p.16.
[61] Mental Health Act 1983 (England and Wales), s.135.

which authorises a person's removal from private premises for the purposes of examining and assessing them."[62]

The question of consent to examinations will be considered further below at paras 10–04 to 10–06.

Procedure Following Examination

4–26 If the doctor is satisfied, following the examination, that the proposed patient is suffering from a mental disorder within the meaning of the Act, they shall make a recommendation that the person be admitted to a specified approved centre, other than the Central Mental Hospital (CMH).[63] The use of the word "shall" indicates that a doctor is obliged to make a recommendation on receipt of an application, if the examination shows that mental disorder within the meaning of the Act is present.

4–27 The doctor must make the recommendation in a form specified by the Mental Health Commission. The relevant form is Form 5, Recommendation for Involuntary Admission of an Adult.[64] The form requires the doctor to state the exact date and time when the examination of the proposed patient took place, and that this was within 24 hours of receipt of the application. The date that the application was made is specified, but not the date and time of its receipt by the doctor. The date and time of the making of the recommendation for admission are specified at the foot of the form. The doctor must answer either "yes" or "no" for the statement "I have informed the above named person of the purpose of the examination". If the answer is "no", then they must confirm that such information has been withheld "because the provision of such information *would* be prejudicial to the person's mental health or well-being or emotional condition." (In the Act the words "*might* be prejudicial" are used.) The doctor must tick a box to indicate what type of mental disorder the patient has, i.e. whether s.3(1)(a) (the harm ground) or s.3(1)(b) (the need for treatment ground), or both, apply. The full wording of the relevant subsections is provided. At item 8, the doctor must state the grounds on which their opinion is based by filling in a box labelled "Give clinical description of the person's mental condition."

4–28 Certain doctors are, by virtue of s.10(3), disqualified from making a recommendation:

- A doctor who has an interest in any payments to be made in respect of the proposed patient's care in the approved centre

---

[62] Anselm Eldergill, "The Best Is the Enemy of the Good: The Mental Health Act 2001" (2008) J. Mental Health L. 21 at 31.
[63] Section 10(1) of the Mental Health Act 2001.
[64] The current version at the time of writing is the version issued in December 2007.

- A doctor who is a member of the staff of the approved centre
- A doctor who is a spouse or relative of the proposed patient
- A doctor who is the applicant

The same definitions of "spouse" and "relative" apply as described under the Application for Recommendation stage above, except that the exclusion of a separated spouse, etc. does not apply.[65]

4–29 The doctor must send the recommendation to the clinical director of the approved centre concerned, and must give a copy of the recommendation to the applicant.[66] The copy may either be given to the applicant, or sent to them by post or electronically.[67] There is no requirement that a copy be given to the proposed patient.

4–30 A recommendation remains in force for seven days from the date of its making and then expires.[68] This does not mean that a recommendation remains in force for seven 24-hour periods. Instead, it remains in force up to midnight at the end of a seven-day period, which includes the day of its making.[69] For example, if a recommendation is made at 2.40pm on a Tuesday, it expires at midnight on the following Monday.

Charleton J. provides the following description of the sequence of events in *Han v President of the Circuit Court*[70]:

> "On the 7th June, the applicant's brother requested his involuntary admission to a mental hospital. A recommendation was made by a consultant psychiatrist in a particular hospital that he should be detained. This operated to confine him to the hospital for a period of seven days. On the 9th June an involuntary admission order was signed by a consultant psychiatrist in the hospital."[71]

This may contain a typographical error, as a recommendation for admission does not operate to confine a person to a hospital for seven days. It remains in force

---

[65] The exclusion of separated spouses and those in respect of whom an application or order has been made under the Domestic Violence Act 1996 applies to Applications for Recommendation only. It is not necessary to cover this issue in the case of disqualification of doctors from making recommendations for admission, as it is more straightforward to simply disqualify all doctors who are spouses, whether separated or not.

[66] Section 10(4) of the Mental Health Act 2001.

[67] See definition of "give" in s.2(1) of the Mental Health Act 2001.

[68] Section 10(5) of the Mental Health Act 2001.

[69] Section 18(h) of the Interpretation Act 2005. See consideration of previous similar section of Interpretation Act 1937 in *DPP v Curtin*, Circuit Court, Moran J., April 23, 2004, *Irish Times*, April 24, 2004.

[70] *Han v President of the Circuit Court* [2008] I.E.H.C. 160; High Court, Charleton J., May 30, 2008.

[71] *Han v President of the Circuit Court* [2008] I.E.H.C. 160; High Court, Charleton J., May 30, 2008, para.2.

for seven days, but when the person is brought to the approved centre they can only be detained for 24 hours, under s.14(2), before an involuntary admission order is made.

Removal to Approved Centre

4–31 Once a recommendation for admission has been made, the applicant must arrange for the removal of the proposed patient to the approved centre.[72] If the applicant is unable to arrange the removal, the doctor who made the recommendation can request that the clinical director of the approved centre (or a psychiatrist acting on his or her behalf) arrange for the removal by members of the approved centre's staff or by authorised persons.[73] The reference to "authorised persons" was inserted in 2009 to allow for participation of independent contractors in the removals process (see further paras 4–45 to 4–46 below).

The members of staff or authorised persons have no specific statutory powers of restraint in connection with the removal. If the clinical director becomes involved in arranging the removal of the person to the centre, then this is often referred to as an "assisted admission".

4–32 If the clinical director (or psychiatrist acting on their behalf) and the doctor who made the recommendation are of opinion that there is a serious likelihood of the proposed patient causing immediate and serious harm to themselves or to others, the director (or psychiatrist) may, if necessary, request the Garda Síochána to assist the members of the approved centre's staff in the removal of the proposed patient to the centre. The Gardaí must comply with such a request.[74] The Gardaí have the following powers:

- They may enter, if need be by force, any dwelling or other premises where they have reasonable cause to believe that the proposed patient may be, and
- They may take all reasonable measures necessary for the removal of the proposed patient to the approved centre including, where necessary, the detention or restraint of the proposed patient.[75]

These powers are granted to the Gardaí only, not to the members of the approved centre's staff or to authorised persons. Eldergill suggests that there may be a drafting omission here,[76] but it was probably intentional that the Gardaí would only be involved if the harm ground applied.

[72] Section 13(1) of the Mental Health Act 2001.
[73] Section 13(2) of the Mental Health Act 2001, as amended by s.63 of the Health (Miscellaneous Provisions) Act 2009.
[74] Section 13(3) of the Mental Health Act 2001.
[75] Section 13(4) of the Mental Health Act 2001.
[76] "There is, it seems, a drafting omission here. The criteria for compulsory admission are (a) that there is a serious likelihood of the person causing immediate and serious harm to themselves

4–33 In 2007 there were 575 instances of removal of a person to approved centres; 413 of these provided by HSE staff and 162 carried out by an independent contractor.[77] In 2008 there were 604 assisted admissions; 42 per cent or 250 of those assisted admissions were provided by the external agency and all the assisted admissions in the Dublin-mid-Leinster region were provided by the external agency.[78]

4–34 In *M.Z. v Khattak and Tallaght Hospital Board*,[79] the patient's brother had made the application for recommendation but the Gardaí had arranged removal to the hospital. Peart J. was satisfied that the patient's removal to the hospital was in compliance with s.13, as the patient's brother was present in the Garda Station while all this was happening. The fact that he himself did not lift the phone and himself request the ambulance was of no material significance.[80]

4–35 There have been three major cases on removals to approved centres: *R.L. v Clinical Director of St. Brendan's Hospital & Ors.*,[81] *C.C. v Clinical Director of St. Patrick's Hospital (No.1)*[82] and *E.F. v Clinical Director of St. Ita's Hospital*.[83]

R.L. v Clinical Director of St. Brendan's Hospital and Others

4–36 The main issue which arose in *R.L. v Clinical Director of St. Brendan's Hospital & Ors.*,[84] an application under Art.40 of the Constitution, was whether a patient's detention was rendered unlawful by her removal to an approved centre by contractors who were not members of the staff of the approved centre. At the time of the case, s.13(2) required that removal of the person to the approved centre be "by members of the staff of the approved centre." In the case of Ms L., it was suggested that no members of staff of the approved centre had been involved and that private contractors were used instead.[85] In the High

---

or others, or (b) that failure to admit the person would be likely to lead to a serious deterioration of their condition, etc. As drafted, it is only if a person requires admission on the first of these grounds that the Garda can be required to assist and may enter premises without a warrant. If the recommendation has been given on the other ground, the Garda have no such powers. The named person may therefore prefer to remain indoors until the medical recommendation has expired."—Eldergill, "The Best Is the Enemy of the Good: The Mental Health Act 2001" (2008) J. Mental Health L. 21, p.32.

[77] Mental Health Commission, *Report on the Operation of Part 2 of the Mental Health Act 2001* (2008), p.52.

[78] Áine Brady. Minister of State, *Seanad Debates*, July 2, 2009.

[79] [2008] I.E.H.C. 262; High Court, Peart J., July 28, 2008.

[80] [2008] I.E.H.C. 262; High Court, Peart J., July 28, 2008, p.13.

[81] [2008] I.E.H.C. 11; [2008] 3 I.R. 296; High Court, Feeney J., January 17, 2008; Supreme Court (ex tempore), February 15, 2008.

[82] [2009] I.E.H.C. 13; High Court, McMahon J., January 20, 2009.

[83] [2009] I.E.H.C. 253; High Court, O'Keeffe J., May 21, 2009.

[84] [2008] I.E.H.C. 11; [2008] 3 I.R. 296; High Court, Feeney J., January 17, 2008; Supreme Court (*ex tempore*), February 15, 2008.

[85] See Supreme Court decision at pp.3–4.

Court, Feeney J. said that even if non-compliance with s.13 was established, that did not vitiate or relate to a valid Admission Order made under s.14.[86] This view was significantly reinforced having regard to s.18 where it is indicated that the question of whether the provisions of ss.9, 10 12, 14, 15 and 16 have been complied with is a matter which requires consideration by the tribunal, but that is not so in relation to s.13. When one looked at the scheme of the Act, that was not surprising because s.13 relates to the manner in which somebody is brought to the institution and received and not detained.[87] He said, "removal or means of removal is not and cannot be read as a *sine qua non* to an Admission Order. An Admission Order is a separate and stand-alone matter."[88] He continued:

> "In this instance any wrong which might potentially have been done to this Applicant is cured by the complete and proper implementation of the provisions in relation to an admission order and, as the Court has already indicated, it is the admission order which is the order which in the first instance results in the detention of this particular applicant. There has been no breach of fundamental requirements causing a wanting in due process of law."[89]

4–37 The judgment in the Supreme Court appeal was delivered by Hardiman J.[90] He agreed that there was, on the face of it, a breach of s.13(2).[91] He said that the requirement in s.13(2) that the removal be by members of the staff at the centre seemed an extraordinary one given that the need for a removal under the section might arise suddenly and might arise in circumstances much more acute than those exhibited in this case. It would seem ludicrous, he said, to provide by statute for a position that if no nurses or other staff members were available, it could not happen at all.[92] He recommended that those responsible for the legislation in this area consult with the hospital staff and achieve a situation in which the statutory requirements are in some way realistic.

While it was not a "light matter that a statute has been breached", Hardiman J. said that the legal question had to be isolated: did that breach of s.13 operate to prevent the making of an admission order under s.14? He found that "the Court can simply see no reason whatever to believe that an irregularity or a direct breach of s.13 would render what is on the face of it a lawful detention on foot of an admission order invalid."[93] He added the following comments:

---

[86] [2008] 3 I.R. 296 at 299.
[87] [2008] 3 I.R. 296 at 299.
[88] [2008] 3 I.R. 296 at 299.
[89] [2008] 3 I.R. 296 at 302.
[90] *R.L. v Clinical Director of St. Brendan's Hospital & Ors.*, Supreme Court, *ex tempore*, February 15, 2008.
[91] *R.L. v Clinical Director of St. Brendan's Hospital & Ors.*, Supreme Court, p.4.
[92] *R.L. v Clinical Director of St. Brendan's Hospital & Ors.*, Supreme Court, pp.4–5.
[93] *R.L. v Clinical Director of St. Brendan's Hospital & Ors.*, Supreme Court, ex tempore, February 15, 2008, pp.5–6.

"That is not to say that we excuse or draw a veil over the alleged breaches of s.13. On the contrary, we will say that these breaches, if they occurred, are serious matters and that a person in the position of a Clinical Director may be in a very difficult position ... Now that is a serious matter which requires discussions with those responsible for the legislation. But of course we must say that even if the provisions of s.13 are impractical, those affected by it must comply with it and Mr. Finlay's client certainly has rights in the event of her being able to establish these breaches. But this is in our view something which has happened and in legal terms anyway is spent so that it would appear that L.'s rights in relation to any breach of the law is a right to compensation. We say that, simply so that it is not thought, and we do not wish it to be thought, that the Court is in any way excusing any breaches of s.13 that may have occurred."[94]

C.C. v Clinical Director of St. Patrick's Hospital (No.1)

4-38 In *C.C. v Clinical Director of St. Patrick's Hospital (No.1)*[95] the applicant appears to have been taken into custody by Gardaí while out walking near her home with her son. The Gardaí brought her to St. Patrick's Hospital, and produced a recommendation from a G.P. and an application for a recommendation by the patient's husband. The remaining parts of the admission process were followed as usual. The Gardaí did not have power to bring Ms C. to the hospital, as they had not been requested by any members of the hospital staff to become involved. At the later tribunal hearing, the patient's legal representative raised the question of non-compliance with s.13 but the tribunal ruled that an apparent breach of s.13 during the admission procedure did not render the admission order void. It was then argued in Art.40 proceedings that the patient's continued detention was unlawful.

4-39 To a large extent, the main issue in this case had already been resolved in the *R.L.* case,[96] discussed above, and which McMahon J. quoted with approval in the instant case. In fact, as McMahon J. pointed out, in the *C.C.* case, the act complained of was not carried out by the hospital authorities but rather by a third party and when the admission order was made, the clinical director had no knowledge or suspicion regarding the removal of the patient to the centre and at all times acted in a bona fide manner. He said it could additionally be advanced that the actions of the Gardaí complained of were in any event not the acts of the hospital authorities or of persons for whom they were vicariously liable.[97] It was not surprising, therefore, that McMahon J. applied similar reasoning to that

---

[94] *R.L. v Clinical Director of St. Brendan's Hospital & Ors.*, Supreme Court, pp.8–9.
[95] [2009] I.E.H.C. 13; High Court, McMahon J., January 20, 2009
[96] *R.L. v Clinical Director of St. Brendan's Hospital & Ors.* [2008] I.E.H.C. 11; [2008] 3 I.R. 296; High Court, Feeney J., January 17, 2008; Supreme Court (ex tempore), February 15, 2008
[97] [2009] I.E.H.C. 13, p.15.
[98] [2009] I.E.H.C. 13, p.10.

used in the *R.L.* case and held that the patient's continued detention was lawful. His reasoning includes the following passage:

> "It is my view therefore that the admission order was valid and that its continuance or survival is to be assessed, not by the possibility of some historical frailty causally unconnected with the director's determination, but on its own terms and in its own context, in this instance the context of the Mental Health Act 2001. Its legitimacy and its validity is determined not by something totally unconnected (i.e. the garda's actions) but by reference to its own legal basis in the Act."[98]

4–40 McMahon J. emphasised that he was not holding that there can never be a situation where persons in authority under the 2001 Act have an obligation to fully investigate allegations of improper arrival to the designated centre and to release the person if necessary, observing appropriate safeguards in the circumstances. In relation to their obligations on the person's arrival at the hospital, he said that the authorities may well have to assess the circumstances and even perhaps the history of the presentation, if the particular circumstances involved their own actions or if they are on notice of peculiar and suspicious circumstances surrounding the conduct of others when the patient is first presented at the centre.[99] If, for some reason, the patient needs to be released, McMahon J. said that to release them from unlawful detention without first considering the personal circumstances, including the time and the location of the release, is a breach of duty to such a person which may attract liability under the neighbour principle at common law if foreseeable damage ensues.[100]

4–41 McMahon J. analysed the role of the tribunal in this case, holding that the tribunal did not have the power to release the patient if s.13 were breached, but the patient could apply to the clinical director for release, or make an application under Art.40 (see further para.9–17 below). As regards *Storck v Germany*,[101] he acknowledged the positive obligation on the State to protect the applicant's liberty, but he said that this does not mean that any part of the State's apparatus must intervene to secure the release. The State had a mechanism which, if addressed, would have been obliged to consider such a request immediately. He found that the protections under the Mental Health Act 2001, moreover, were continuous and adequate in this regard.[102]

E.F. v Clinical Director of St. Ita's Hospital

4–42 *E.F. v Clinical Director of St. Ita's Hospital*[103] was a judicial review concerning the use of independent contractors to effect a removal to an approved

---

[99] [2009] I.E.H.C. 13, p.17.
[100] [2009] I.E.H.C. 13, p.18.
[101] *Storck v Germany* (2006) 43 E.H.R.R. 6. See para.10–23 below.
[102] [2009] I.E.H.C. 13, p.27.
[103] [2009] I.E.H.C. 253; High Court, O'Keeffe J., May 21, 2009.

centre under s.13. The patient's counsel stated that the case was not made that the patient's detention was unlawful.[104] Instead, various declarations were sought, e.g. that the applicant was removed to St. Ita's Hospital otherwise than in accordance with the provisions of the Mental Health Act 2001 and in particular s.13(2) and that the hospital's clinical director acted ultra vires those powers conferred on him by the Act in arranging for the applicant to be physically restrained and removed to St. Ita's by persons not members of the hospital's staff. The applicant was not constrained by the limitations of an application under Art.40 as a remedy, which had applied in the *R.L.* case, for example. The removal to hospital took place on April 24, 2007 but judgment in the judicial review was not issued until May 21, 2009,[105] which demonstrates that it takes much longer to process a judicial review case than an application under Art.40. By the time the judgment was delivered, Ms F. had already been discharged from detention. However, O'Keeffe J. did not believe that her case was moot, as he believed that a decision could or would be for her benefit should circumstances arise in the future.[106]

Ms F. had been detained on the evening of April 24, having just left a restaurant in Howth. She said that she was most unhappy at the nature of her removal to St. Ita's Hospital. She gave evidence at the tribunal hearing that she was "bundled" and "man-handled" into a car and that she was bruised as a result. She stated that the individuals responsible did not identify themselves and she did not know who they were. She stated that it was never explained to her where she was being taken and why. Her solicitor commented that the experience appeared to have been very traumatic for her. She was then taken to St. Ita's and admitted under the 2001 Act. She had unsuccessfully challenged the removal process at the subsequent tribunal hearing. It was established that the removal to the approved centre was effected by a company called Nationwide Health Solutions Ltd (NHS), based in Naas, Co. Kildare. This company had been contracted by the HSE to provide an assisted admissions service. The HSE had entered into this contract as an interim arrangement, as there were ongoing issues with the use of hospital staff in admissions, partly as a result of injuries which had occurred in the past. The personnel involved in the assisted admission of Ms F. included four people supplied by NHS; three of those were registered psychiatric nurses with appropriate experience and the fourth was the driver of the vehicle used to transport the patient. The team leader was a psychiatric nurse.

---

[104]   [2009] I.E.H.C. 253, para.12.

[105]   The judicial review application was made on July 2, 2007 and the respondent argued that it had not been brought promptly. However, it had taken some time for Ms F's solicitor to receive sufficient information about the use of independent contractors in the removal, in order to prepare the application for judicial review. O'Keeffe J. stated at para.29 that "the Applicant did act promptly in bringing this application, once she had been provided by the Respondent and the Health Service Executive with the information she requested."

[106]   [2009] I.E.H.C. 253, para.40. In this regard, he stated that he applied the decision of the Supreme Court in *O'Brien v. the Personal Injuries Assessment Board* [2007] 1 I.R. 328.

The consultant psychiatrist at St. Ita's made the decision that an assisted admission was necessary. The assisted admission was then organised by the Assistant Director of Nursing, who contacted NHS by fax.

4–43 The applicant argued that the removal had not been effected by "members of the staff of the approved centre", as was required by s.13(2) as it was at the time. Counsel referred to Part 5 of the Mental Health Act 2001 (Approved Centres) Regulations 2006,[107] which prescribed requirements as to the staffing, including requirements as to the suitability of members of staff of centres. It was submitted that if the respondent did not know the identity of the persons who were engaged in the assisted removal of the applicant, it was difficult to say that there was conformity with such Regulations. The judgment of Hardiman J. in *R.L.* was quoted,[108] in which he had stated that there was, on the face of it, a breach of s.13(2).

The respondent submitted that the three psychiatric nurses and the driver were "staff" within the meaning of s.13(2). In an affidavit, the HSE's National Planning Specialist Mental Health had stated that he believed that the HSE discharges its statutory duty to provide health and related social services to the community by providing those services directly, or by funding the provision of those services. St. Ita's Hospital had a broad range of health personnel involved working there. There were persons who were employed full time by the HSE to work there. There were part-time employees who worked there and at other separate locations and unconnected places of work, and there were also independent contractual personnel who provided a range of services on a periodic basis in the hospital complex and also in the external catchment area of the hospital. He believed that the term "staff" in St. Ita's Hospital in the context of an assisted admission to that hospital meant a person under the continuous command and control of that hospital in relation to the work or service they are doing for the hospital. Throughout assisted removal to hospital there was a senior Health HSE official in continuous command and control of this removal, and the operational decisions and instructions were continuously given by this individual, from the commencement to the completion of the process.

Counsel for the respondent submitted that the word "staff" in s.13(2) is a broad term, i.e. a word or a phrase in an enactment which in its application to certain factual situations is vague and therefore ambiguous. As with any form of statutory ambiguity, the meaning of the term is to be applied in relation to the particular facts, as determined by reference to the interpretative criteria. The concept "of staff" in s.13(2) would take account of the nature of the services provided, the nature of the employment of the personnel involved in the provision of those services and the statutory context in which those services are sought to be provided.

---

[107] S.I. No. 551 of 2006.
[108] *R.L. v Clinical Director of St. Brendan's Hospital & Ors.*, Supreme Court (ex tempore), February 15, 2008.

4–44 O'Keeffe J. granted a declaration as requested in the case.[109] He said that
the term "members of the staff of the approved centre" is not defined in the Act.
It was to be concluded that the Oireachtas deliberately determined that no
definition should be given to the term. It was a question of fact in each case as
to whether or not a particular person is a member of the staff of St. Ita's
Hospital. No written contract had been exhibited between the HSE and/or St.
Ita's Hospital of the one part, and NHS of the other part. Certain relevant terms
of the relationship were set out in the affidavits. NHS retained responsibility for
the care and well-being of the patient until the patient had been assessed. The
engagement of NHS was the engagement of an independent contractual provider
in the external catchment area of the hospital. It appeared that the identity or
qualification of the personnel engaged or assisted (other than the team leader)
were unknown in advance to the respondent and indeed it took some time before
their identities were revealed to the applicant in these proceedings. The vehicle
used to convey the applicant and its driver and other personnel was supplied by
NHS. There was no nexus or known contract between the psychiatric nurses
involved in the assisted admission, who were provided by NHS (and were part
of its staff), and the approved centre, namely St. Ita's Hospital.[110] In O'Keeffe
J.'s opinion, the meaning of who is a "member of staff" is confined to an
individual. A corporate entity such as NHS could not be a member of staff. In
effect, St. Ita's Hospital was outsourcing this service to a third party. The nurses
and staff provided by NHS were at all material times staff of that entity and were
not staff of St. Ita's Hospital. This appeared to be contemplated from the HSE
documentation.[111] He also said:

> "Furthermore, adopting the ordinary canons of interpretation to this word
> 'staff' as used in the legislation, it would be straining the ordinary meaning of
> the word 'staff' to conclude that based on the information supplied by Dr
> Blennerhassett and Mr Leahy, persons engaged in bringing the applicant to St.
> Ita's were at all material times staff of St. Ita's Hospital".[112]

Amendment Regarding "Authorised Persons"

4–45 Section 63 of the Health (Miscellaneous Provisions) Act 2009 was enacted
as a result of the *E.F.* case. It inserts a new s.71A in the Mental Health Act 2001.
The purpose of the amendment was to enable independent contractors to
participate in removals or bringing back of patients to approved centres.

Section 71A provides that the registered proprietor of an approved centre may
enter into an arrangement with a person for the purposes of arranging for
persons who are members of the staff of that person to provide services relating

[109]   The exact nature of the declaration is not stated.
[110]   [2009] I.E.H.C. 253, paras 30–35.
[111]   [2009] I.E.H.C. 253, paras 36–38.
[112]   [2009] I.E.H.C. 253, para.39.
[113]   Section 71A(1).

to (a) the removal pursuant to s.13 of persons to that centre, (b) the bringing back pursuant to s.27 of patients to that centre, or both.[113] The clinical director may then authorise, in writing and for a period not exceeding 12 months, such and so many persons who are members of the staff of that person to provide the services which are the subject of that arrangement.[114] The staff so authorised are referred to as "authorised persons".[115]

The 2009 Act makes consequential amendments to s.13 regarding removals and s.27 regarding bringing back of patients. It also amends s.9 to allow an authorised person to make an application for a recommendation.

4–46 Finally, the 2009 amendments seek to avoid retrospective challenges to detentions where independent contractors were used. Section 71A(3) states that where, before the date of commencement of the section,[116] a person was removed to an approved centre pursuant to and in accordance with s.13 except in so far as the removal was carried out (whether in whole or in part) by a relevant person,[117] such removal shall, to the extent that it was carried out by the relevant person, be deemed to be and to always have been carried out by a member of the staff of that centre, save for the purposes of any proceedings commenced before such date. Section 71A(4) makes the same provisions regarding relevant persons who carried out a bringing back of a patient.

Admission Order

4–47 When the clinical director of the approved centre receives a recommendation for admission, a consultant psychiatrist on the staff of the centre must carry out an examination of the proposed patient as soon as may be.[118]

4–48 The clinical director of the approved centre must receive the recommendation for admission. There is no specific statutory provision permitting the recommendation for admission to be received by anybody else.[119] There is a general section in the 2001 Act about clinical directors, s.71, but this does not permit delegation by them of their functions. The Health Act 2004, which set up

---

[114] Section 71A(2).
[115] Section 2 of the Mental Health Act 2001, as amended by s.63 of the Health (Miscellaneous Provisions) Act 2009.
[116] At the time of writing, the date of commencement is not known.
[117] "Relevant person" means a person who carried out (whether in whole or in part) a removal or bringing back of a patient pursuant to an arrangement entered into by the registered proprietor of the centre.
[118] Section 14(1) of the Mental Health Act 2001.
[119] Similarly, see Kevin Costello, *The Law of Habeas Corpus in Ireland* (Dublin: Four Courts Press, 2006), p.229: "The sole officer authorised to receive a recommendation is the director of the approved centre, and the function of receiving a recommendation may not (by contrast with the delegation procedure instituted by the Mental Treatment Act 1953) be delegated to any other officer."

the HSE, contains provisions concerning delegation by the chief executive officer,[120] but not by a clinical director. The case of *In Re Donnelly*[121] demonstrates that courts may interpret requirements of this kind in a literal fashion. The legislation as it was at the time required that a temporary private reception order be made to the "person in charge" of the institution, and that the person in charge could then make the reception order.[122] As the order in this case had not been made by the person in charge, Davitt P. held that it was made without any statutory authority and was legally void and of no effect. The detention of the person thereunder was, therefore, illegal. An amending piece of legislation was later passed, stating that a power of a person in charge could be exercised by any officer of the institution authorised in that behalf by the person in charge.[123]

It could be argued that the clinical director has received the recommendation for admission if it has been placed in their post tray for collection, but a court might not be willing to interpret the requirement in this manner. Alternatively, the approved centre staff could fax a copy of the recommendation to the clinical director and they could confirm by phone that they have received the copy.

Even if it were found that the statutory requirement that the clinical director receive the recommendation had been breached, a court might hold that this did not invalidate the admission order, as the Act is clear that the admission order may be made by any consultant psychiatrist on the approved centre's staff. Here, the legislation is very different from the provision considered in the *Donnelly* case, which required that the application be made to the person in charge and that the person in charge then make the reception order.

4–49 In the case of *P.McG. v Medical Director of the Mater Hospital*[124] it was held that a patient's detention was lawful, even though a requirement in s.22 of the 2001 Act that the clinical director "arrange" transfer out of the approved centre had not been complied with. Peart J. said that, "there may be situations where some deviation from the provisions of the Act will not undermine" the protections provided for patients by the 2001 Act.[125] However, it may be argued that s.22, the section being considered in that case, was not central to the admission and renewal order process, and that the courts might be stricter in their consideration of such central requirements.

4–50 As regards the meaning of "as soon as may be" in s.14(1), reference may be made to *M.Z. v Khattak and Tallaght Hospital Board*.[126] In that case, the

120   Section 19 of the Health Act 2004.
121   [1954] I.R. 124. Also reported as *Re J.* (1954) 88 I.L.T.R. 120. The decision was made on December 1, 1953.
122   Section 185 of the Mental Treatment Act 1945.
123   Section 3 of the Mental Treatment Act 1953. This Act was passed on December 18, 1953.
124   [2007] I.E.H.C. 401; [2008] 2 I.R. 332; Peart J., High Court, 29 November 2007. See para.4–108 below.
125   [2007] I.E.H.C. 401.
126   [2008] I.E.H.C. 262; High Court, Peart J., July 28, 2008.

recommendation for admission was made at 10.10am at Mountjoy Garda station. M.Z. was taken to Tallaght Hospital by ambulance and a junior registrar saw him at about 12.00 noon. The registrar contacted the consultant psychiatrist, Dr Khattak, by telephone at about 12.30pm after he had completed an assessment of the applicant, which would have taken about half an hour. Dr Khattak told the registrar that the applicant should be admitted. It was some seven and a half hours later that Dr Khattak actually saw the applicant himself at the hospital. He was the HSE sector consultant on call, and therefore was not present at the hospital at the time that the applicant was admitted. In any event, he stated that it is, "no harm to let some time pass before seeing a patient at the hospital as it allows the patient to settle."[127] He stated that being the consultant on call, he would have had calls to take in relation to other patients, even though it had not been necessary for him to actually attend other patients at another hospital or otherwise. Dr Khattak signed an Admission Order at 7.30pm

Peart J. said that there was little doubt on the evidence from Dr Khattak himself that there was nothing occurring while he was acting as consultant psychiatrist on call on the date in question which was of such a pressing nature that he could not have arrived at Tallaght Hospital sooner than he did.[128] Peart J. said:

> "The phrase 'as soon as may be' is difficult to precisely interpret. It is conceptually different to a word such as 'forthwith', or even 'as soon as possible' or 'as soon as practicable'. It seems to permit of some more latitude than any of these. Mr Craven referred to the judgment of Geoghegan J. in *McCarthy v Garda Siochána Complaints Tribunal*[129] where some consideration was made of the meaning to be given to the phrase 'as soon as may be' and similar phrases in various statutory provisions. The learned judge concluded that 'as soon as may be means as soon as may be reasonably [practicable] in all the circumstances'."[130]

In the 2001 Act, there was clearly an imperative that following a patient's admission to an approved centre as an involuntary patient, they must be examined quickly; but Peart J. said that it must be borne in mind also that s.14(2)[131] of the Act itself at least contemplates that such an examination may not occur for up to 24 hours following admission. That was not to say that in all cases this must be taken as permitting of a 24-hour delay, but in the present case a delay of seven and a half hours, "no matter what the reason or the lack of it",

---

127 [2008] I.E.H.C. 262; High Court, Peart J., July 28, 2008, p.8.
128 [2008] I.E.H.C. 262; High Court, Peart J., July 28, 2008, p.17.
129 [2002] 2 I.L.R.M. 341
130 [2008] I.E.H.C. 262, p.17, quoting [2002] 2 I.L.R.M. 341 at 362. In the original *McCarthy* judgment, the word "practicable" is used. In the *M.Z.* judgment, this is accidentally quoted as "possible".
131 In the judgment at p.17, Peart J. refers to s.10(2) but he appears to mean s.14(2)—[2008] I.E.H.C. 262, p.17.

did not seem to offend against the concept of "as soon as may be reasonably [practicable] in all the circumstances".[132] It did not mandate that Dr Khattak should immediately drop whatever he was doing while acting as consultant on call, and attend immediately or forthwith upon being told of the applicant's arrival at Tallaght Hospital. Peart J. concluded that it was no basis for a finding of unlawfulness of detention.[133]

4–51 Temporary detention for up to 24 hours, pending examination of the proposed patient, is authorised by s.14(2). A consultant psychiatrist, a medical practitioner or a registered nurse on the approved centre's staff is entitled to take charge of the proposed patient and detain him or her for a period not exceeding 24 hours for the purpose of carrying out an examination under s.14(1). If an admission order is made or refused during that period, the power of temporary detention comes to an end.[134]

4–52 After the proposed patient arrives at the approved centre, a short period of time may elapse while a decision is made as to whether to detain them temporarily under s.14(2). Therefore, the 24-hour period does not necessarily run from the time that the proposed patient arrives at the centre. In *L.K. v Clinical Director of Lakeview Unit, Naas General Hospital and the HSE, South Western Area*,[135] Clarke J. held that it was implicit in the 1945 Act that a short period may elapse between the person's arrival at the institution and a decision being made by the appropriate official to receive and detain the person. He said it was only after a decision to receive and detain had in fact been taken that the statutory period of temporary detention starts to run.[136] In that case, the relevant short period was 20 minutes.

There is now a space on Form 6 to record the time when the proposed patient arrived in the centre,[137] whereas this was not recorded on the original version of the Form.

4–53 The Mental Health Commission has provided a useful Clinical Practice Form for the purposes of temporary detention under s.14(2).[138] This is described as a Clinical Practice Form rather than a statutory form as the Act does not require that the temporary detention be made in a form specified by the Commission. The Form records the date and time the proposed patient was detained from and the date and time the period of detention ended. The name of

---

[132] [2008] I.E.H.C. 262, p.17.
[133] [2008] I.E.H.C. 262, p.17.
[134] Section 14(2) of the Mental Health Act 2001.
[135] [2007] 2 I.R. 465; [2007] 2 I.L.R.M. 69; Clarke J., High Court, July 6, 2006.
[136] [2007] 2 I.R. 465 at 480. At the time, the statutory period of temporary detention was 12 hours, under s.5 of the Mental Treatment Act 1953.
[137] Item 5, Form 6, version of March 2009.
[138] Mental Health Commission, *Clinical Practice Form: Mental Health Act Section 14(2): Detention of a Person (Adult) for the Purpose of Carrying out an Examination.*

the staff member detaining the person must be given, and their designation (i.e. consultant psychiatrist, other registered doctor or registered nurse.) The form asks whether Risk Assessment was used and if so, that details be given. The form also asks whether the person was informed they were being detained under s.14(2), and if not, that details be recorded. It must be stated whether an Admission Order was completed following the period of detention. Finally, the staff member signs a declaration that it has been necessary, in the best interest of the person, to detain them. The date and time of signature must be given.

4–54 If the proposed patient agrees to stay in the approved centre as a voluntary patient, pending examination by the consultant psychiatrist, there is no special procedure which needs to be followed, but this should be recorded clearly on the file. However, the application and recommendation for admission will lapse. If the consultant psychiatrist then examines the patient and believes that the patient should be admitted for a longer period, this should be done by means of a voluntary admission rather than by completion of Form 6. If the voluntary patient indicates a wish to leave at any stage, the re-grading procedure might be used (see Chapter 5).

4–55 As was stated earlier, a consultant psychiatrist on the centre's staff must carry out an examination of the person "as soon as may be".[139] An examination means a personal examination carried out by the psychiatrist of the process and content of thought, the mood and the behaviour of the proposed patient.[140] Following the examination, the psychiatrist must either make an admission order, or refuse to make one. The admission order must ("shall") be made if the psychiatrist is satisfied that the proposed patient "is suffering from a mental disorder".[141] The admission order must be made on the form specified by the Commission. It appears that the psychiatrist is obliged to make the admission order if the criteria are fulfilled, as the word "shall" is used. The Act does not require the psychiatrist to provide information in writing to the patient in advance of making the admission order. While seven items of information must be provided under s.16(2) (discussed below), the information need only be supplied within 24 hours of the admission order. It is unfortunate that the proposed patient does not need to be informed of the possibility of voluntary admission until after the Admission Order is made. However, it is possible that some psychiatrists will provide the information notice to the patient at the time that the possibility of admission is being discussed, and that therefore the proposed patient may become aware of the possibility of voluntary admission at an earlier stage.

---

[139] Section 14(1) of the Mental Health Act 2001.
[140] Section 2(1) of the Mental Health Act 2001.
[141] Section 14(1) of the Mental Health Act 2001.

4–56 Where it is proposed to make an Admission Order, the proposed patient must, "so far as is reasonably practicable", be notified of the proposal and be entitled to make representations in relation to it and before deciding the matter, due consideration must be given to any representations made.[142]

4–57 A psychiatrist is disqualified from making an Admission Order if they are a spouse or relative of the proposed patient, or if they are the applicant.[143] The definitions of "spouse" and "relative" are the same as for the recommendation for admission.

4–58 Form 6 is the statutory form which must be used for the Admission Order.[144] The psychiatrist must tick a box to indicate what type of mental disorder the patient has, i.e. whether s.3(1)(a) (the harm ground) or s.3(1)(b) (the need for treatment ground), or both, apply. The full wording of the relevant subsections is provided. At item 8, the psychiatrist must state the grounds on which their opinion is based by filling in a box labelled "Give clinical description of the person's mental condition." The form asks for the date and time of various other events:

- the proposed patient's arrival in the approved centre
- the psychiatrist's examination of the proposed patient
- the psychiatrist's signature of the order

It appears that the time of the psychiatrist's signature of the order is taken to be the time of making the order. The psychiatrist must also certify that they are not disqualified under s.14(3) and that they shall, within 24 hours of making the order, provide a written information notice to the patient under s.16(2) and send a copy of the admission order to the Mental Health Commission.

The form does not ask the psychiatrist to specify a period of detention; instead at item 9 the psychiatrist states, "I make an admission order for the reception, detention and treatment of the above named person for a period of 21 days from the date of the making of this order". This is because the Admission Order lasts 21 days[145] not "up to" 21 days. The period of 21 days may be extended by the MHT in certain circumstances for two periods of up to 14 days each.[146] The Admission Order might, of course, be revoked (under s.28, using Form 14) within the 21-day period.

4–59 The 21-day period is not 21 periods of 24 hours each. Instead, the Admission Order lasts up to midnight at the end of a 21-day period, which

---

[142] Section 4(2) of the Mental Health Act 2001.
[143] Section 14(3) of the Mental Health Act 2001.
[144] At the time of writing, the current version is the version issued in March 2009.
[145] Section 15(1) of the Mental Health Act 2001.
[146] The Mental Health Tribunal (MHT) may only extend Admission Orders, not Renewal Orders. See para.7–35 below and discussion of *J.B. (No.3)* case at para.7–36.

includes the day of its making.[147] For example, if an Admission Order is made at 9.15am on Wednesday, January 5, it expires at midnight on Tuesday, January 25.

4–60 Where the consultant psychiatrist makes the Admission Order, he or she must, not later than 24 hours thereafter, do two things as required by s.16:

- send a copy of the Admission Order, the application and the recommendation to the Mental Health Commission[148]
- give notice in writing of the making of the Admission Order, the application and the recommendation to the patient[149]

In *M.Z. v Khattak and Tallaght Hospital Board*[150] the Admission Order was made at 7.30pm on Saturday, July 5, 2008, but the copy of the order was not sent to the Commission until Monday, July 7, 2008 at around 4.30pm Peart J. held that this did not invalidate the patient's detention. While there had been a breach of a technical requirement in this regard, it had "not affected any right of the applicant in any fundamental way or at all."[151]

It is notable that the patient need not be given a copy of the Admission Order, which includes more detailed information than the information notice which must be provided under s.16.

Information Notice to Patient (s.16)

4–61 Article 5(2) of the ECHR states that everyone who is arrested shall be informed promptly, in a language which they understand, of the reasons for their arrest and of any charge against them. In *Van der Leer v The Netherlands*[152] it was held that art.5(2) applies to a detention of a person of unsound mind, in spite of the reference to "arrest".[153] The court stated that it was not unmindful of the criminal law connotation of the words used in art.5(2). However, it agreed with the Commission that they should be interpreted "autonomously", in particular in accordance with the aim and purpose of art.5, which are to protect everyone from arbitrary deprivations of liberty.

---

[147] Section 18(h) of the Interpretation Act 2005. See consideration of previous similar section of Interpretation Act 1937 in *DPP v Curtin*, Circuit Court, Moran J., April 23, 2004, *Irish Times*, April 24, 2004.
[148] Section 16(1)(a) of the Mental Health Act 2001. This paragraph refers to a copy of the Admission Order, but s.16(3) states that in s.16, references to an Admission Order shall include references to the relevant recommendation and the relevant application.
[149] Section 16(1)(b).
[150] [2008] I.E.H.C. 262; High Court, Peart J., July 28, 2008.
[151] [2008] I.E.H.C. 262; High Court, Peart J., July 28, 2008, p.18.
[152] (1990) 12 E.H.R.R. 567.
[153] (1990) 12 E.H.R.R. 567, para.27.

4–62 Section 16 of the 2001 Act requires that the psychiatrist who makes an Admission or Renewal Order must, within 24 hours, give notice in writing of the making of the order to the patient. The notice must include a statement in writing of seven pieces of information, to the effect that the patient:

- is being detained pursuant to s.14 (Admission Order) or s.15 (Renewal Order) as the case may be,
- is entitled to legal representation,
- will be given a general description of the proposed treatment[154] to be administered to them during the period of their detention,
- is entitled to communicate with the Inspector of Mental Health Services,
- will have their detention reviewed by a Mental Health Tribunal (MHT),
- is entitled to appeal to the Circuit Court against a decision of a tribunal if they are the subject of a renewal order, and
- may be admitted to the approved centre as a voluntary patient[155] if they indicate a wish to be so admitted.[156]

4–63 While the patient is informed that they are entitled to legal representation, in practice it will be a number of days before a legal representative will be appointed for them by the Mental Health Commission. The patient is informed that they "may" be admitted as a voluntary patient. The timing of this information is strange, because an Admission Order will normally already have been made before the information is given (although it is permissible to give the information notice beforehand.) In addition, copies of the documentation may already be on their way to the Commission. The information notice may mislead patients to some extent, as it gives the impression that there is a "right" to be admitted as a voluntary patient if they wish. However, the actual legal position is that if the psychiatrist is satisfied that the criteria for an Admission Order apply, the psychiatrist "shall" make the order.[157] This legal obligation may override the patient's desire to be admitted as a voluntary patient. If the psychiatrist agrees with the patient's wish to be admitted as a voluntary patient, and if the Admission Order has already been made, the psychiatrist must revoke it (under s.28) and only then may the patient be re-graded as a voluntary patient.

4–64 There appears to be a drafting error in s.16(2)(f), which states that the patient must be informed of the entitlement to appeal to the Circuit Court against a tribunal decision under s.18 "if he or she is the subject of a renewal order."

---

[154] "Treatment" includes the administration of physical, psychological and other remedies relating to the care and rehabilitation of a patient under medical supervision, intended for the purposes of ameliorating a mental disorder. (s.2(1) of the Mental Health Act 2001).

[155] A voluntary patient is a person receiving care and treatment in an approved centre, who is not the subject of an Admission Order or a Renewal Order (s.2(1) of the Mental Health Act 2001).

[156] Section 16(2) of the Mental Health Act 2001.

[157] Section 14(1) of the Mental Health Act 2001.

The correct position is that the patient is entitled to appeal to the Circuit Court against any tribunal decision to affirm any order made in respect of them, both as regards Admission Orders and Renewal Orders.[158]

4–65 The Mental Health Commission has provided a useful "Patient Notification" form, which may be used for the purposes of compliance with s.16(2).[159] The seven items of information are given, as in the Act. The exact date on which the period of detention under the Admission Order or Renewal Order will end is stated. In the case of a Renewal Order, the date of its coming into effect is also given. The psychiatrist must tick a box to indicate whether the patient is being detained under an Admission Order or a Renewal Order. The drafting error regarding appeals to the Circuit Court is corrected.[160] The psychiatrist signs the Form.[161] While the form states that the patient may communicate with the Inspector of Mental Health Services, it does not provide contact details for the Inspector. The Form also includes a space for a general description of the proposed treatment to be administered to the patient during the period of detention. This is not required by the Act, which allows this information to be given later (the words "will be given" are used.) The psychiatrist gives the date and time of signature of the form.

In the Notes on the back of the form, the psychiatrist is instructed to ensure that all fields are completed. The patient must be given a comprehensive verbal explanation of the information in the written notification. The original written notification must be given to the patient, and a copy must be retained on the patient's clinical file. All further discussions with the patient in relation to the Patient Notification should be recorded in the patient's clinical file.

4–66 There is no further statutory requirement to provide more detailed information to the patient about the Mental Health Act 2001. It is likely that many patients will require further detail on the Act, and provision of a leaflet on the main features of the Act would help them to know more about what was happening. The Act could usefully be amended to require that such a leaflet be given to each patient.[162]

---

[158] Section 19 of the Mental Health Act 2001.

[159] Mental Health Commission, *Patient Notification of the Making of an Admission Order or a Certificate and Renewal Order.* At the time of writing, the current version is the version issued in February 2009.

[160] The notice states, "You are entitled to appeal to the Circuit Court against the decision of a Mental Health Tribunal under Section 18 of the Mental Health Act 2001 (Admission Order or a Certificate and Renewal Order)."

[161] In earlier versions of the form, the patient's signature was also required but this has now been removed.

[162] See, for example, the requirement in the Terms of Employment (Information) Act, 1994 (S.3 (6)) Order 1997, S.I. No. 4 of 1997, to provide all employees under the age of 18 with a copy the prescribed abstract of the Protection of Young Persons (Employment) Act 1996.

4–67 The same information notice must be given to the patient within 24 hours of each Renewal Order. In *M.D. v Clinical Director of St. Brendan's Hospital*[163] a Renewal Order was made on May 10, 2007 and the s.16 information notice may have been given to the patient,[164] but no box had been ticked to indicate whether he was being detained under an Admission Order or a Renewal Order. It is not stated whether the patient had signed the information notice, as was suggested by the form at the time.[165] In the High Court, Peart J. stated that he had been informed that the failure to tick the relevant box was simply an error or oversight. He said he did not believe that this oversight resulted in any unlawfulness of detention. It would be preferable if such oversights did not occur in documents whose very purpose was to inform the patient of the basis of their detention, but nonetheless it was easily rectified and would not justify the court in ordering the release of the applicant from the detention, which was clearly in his best interests at the time.[166]

4–68 While the Supreme Court rejected M.D.'s appeal, Hardiman J. took the opportunity to emphasise that the s.16 information notice was of great importance. He said that no explanation had ever been given for the failure to tick the relevant box on the form, but it was a serious one, a breach of the statute, and something which caused considerable avoidable suspicion.[167] He stressed that the patient had an absolute right to be informed whether he was being detained under an Admission Order or a Renewal Order. If the doctor herself was uncertain as to the power she was considering exercising, that was a matter which would cast doubt on the question of whether she should proceed to make an order at all.[168] The obligation to notify the patient of the statutory basis of his detention was mandatory and not a matter for the discretion of the doctor. The information must relate to the detention of the patient at the time he or she is served with the notice and not at any earlier or later time.[169] However, Hardiman J. did not consider that the doctor's omission in this regard could possibly operate to deprive a tribunal of the powers necessary to carry out its statutory obligations under s.18 of the Act. So to hold would be to compound the confusion which had arisen and to deprive the patient of his entitlement to a review of the s.14 detention.[170]

---

[163]   [2007] I.E.H.C. 183; Peart J., High Court, May 24, 2007 and [2007] I.E.S.C. 37; Supreme Court, July 27, 2007; [2008] 1 I.R. 632.
[164]   In the High Court, Peart J. stated at 636, 638 and 640 that the applicant had been given the information notice. However, in the Supreme Court, Hardiman J. stated at 645 that the applicant argued that the Renewal Order had been made "without his knowledge". This may mean that the argument was that the patient had not received the s.16 information notice at all.
[165]   This is not a statutory requirement, but in the first version of the form, a space for the patient's signature appeared on the Patient Notification Form.
[166]   [2008] 1 I.R. 632 at 640.
[167]   [2008] 1 I.R. 632 at 643.
[168]   [2008] 1 I.R. 632 at 648.
[169]   [2008] 1 I.R. 632 at 648.
[170]   [2008] 1 I.R. 632 at 649.

Hardiman J. went on to state that the MHT should not have certified that s.16 had been complied with when it manifestly had not.[171] He noted that, at the subsequent MHT hearing on May 29, the psychiatrist purported to amend her order of May 10 by indicating that the power she had then been exercising was that conferred by s.15 of the 2001 Act.[172] He said that this could not be regarded as a satisfactory amendment: there was an obligation on the doctor to give notice of the making of her order to the patient and to the Mental Health Commission within 24 hours of its making. An amendment made 19 days after the original order was purportedly made could hardly be regarded as meeting such a requirement.[173]

Finally, Hardiman J. suggested that the Patient Notification Form might need to be reconsidered on the basis of experience in operating the Act and further consideration. He noted that the form did not appear to provide for the possibility that the Renewal Order might not become the basis for detention for some time into the future.[174] He seemed to be suggesting that the Patient Notification Form could include an extra item: the date when the Renewal Order will come into effect. As will be discussed later (see paras 6–16 to 6–19 below), a Renewal Order does not come into effect until the admission order expires. The new version of the form has duly been amended to include a reference to the date when the Renewal Order comes into effect. The form does not note that this date might be extended by a MHT under s.18(4).[175]

POWER OF A GARDA TO TAKE A PERSON INTO CUSTODY

4–69 A Garda may become involved in the involuntary admission process in two ways: They may act as an applicant for a recommendation for admission under s.9 (see para.4–08 above) or they may take a person into custody under s.12 of the 2001 Act. If a choice is being made between s.9 and s.12, it should be noted that s.9 may only be used where the applicant has observed the person not more than 48 hours before the date of making the application.[176]

4–70 Where a Garda has reasonable grounds for believing that a person has a mental disorder (within the meaning of the Act) and that because of the mental disorder there is a serious likelihood of the person causing immediate and serious harm to themselves or to other persons, the Garda may exercise the

---

[171] See further the discussion of the *M.D.* case at paras 6–16 to 6–19 below.
[172] It is not entirely clear whether the psychiatrist was purporting to amend "her order" (i.e. the Renewal Order itself) or the Patient Notification Form. Earlier, Hardiman J. stated that a Renewal Order using Form 7 was made on May 10. Form 7 applies only to renewals and therefore would not need to be amended to show that it was a renewal.
[173] [2008] 1 I.R. 632 at 648.
[174] [2008] 1 I.R. 632 at 650.
[175] See discussion of s.18(4) at paras 7–30 to 7–36 below.
[176] Mental Health Act 2001, s.9(4).

powers granted by s.12. The prerequisites for use of the section need to be examined carefully: the Garda must have reasonable grounds for believing that the person has a mental disorder *and* that the person is likely to cause "immediate and serious" harm to themselves or others.

The powers which the Garda has under s.12 may be exercised either alone or with any other Gardaí. The relevant powers are:

- to take the person into custody, and
- to enter if need be by force any dwelling or other premises or any other place if they have reasonable grounds for believing that the person is to be found there.[177]

As these powers are only conferred on Gardaí, they can only be exercised by them, and not by anybody accompanying them, e.g. psychiatric nurses or doctors.

Where a Garda takes the person into custody, he or she or any other Garda must make an application forthwith to a doctor for a recommendation.[178]

4–71 The Act refers to the Garda taking the person "into custody." Presumably, in many cases the person will be brought to a Garda station. The 1945 Act specifically referred to the person being brought to a Garda station,[179] but the new section allows more flexibility by referring only to "custody". In England and Wales, the 1983 legislation referred to the person being brought to a "place of safety". The English legislation has now been amended so that a person may be transferred from one place of safety to another before an assessment has been carried out.[180]

4–72 Form 3 is the form which must be used for making the application. This is the same form which is used for an application by a Garda under s.9, and at the beginning of the form the Garda is asked to indicate whether this is an application under s.9 or s.12. It is arguable that a separate statutory form should have been specified for applications under s.12, as there are significant differences in the statutory requirements. Form 3 asks for the time of last observation of the proposed patient and notes that the Garda making the application must have observed the proposed patient within 48 hours before the date of making the application. However, this is not a statutory requirement regarding an application made under s.12. The Garda making the application need not necessarily have ever observed the proposed patient, as the matter may

---

[177]   Section 12(1) of the Mental Health Act 2001.
[178]   Section 12(2).
[179]   Section 165 of the Mental Treatment Act 1945.
[180]   Section 44 of the Mental Health Act 2007 (E. & W.). See also Home Office Circular 007/2008, "The Use Of Police Stations As Places Of Safety Under Section 136 Of The Mental Health Act 1983".

have been referred on to them by the Garda who took the proposed patient into custody. Form 3 also notes certain disqualifications from making the application, but these do not apply to applications under s.12. It also requires information on previous refused applications and this information is required for an application under s.12.[181]

4–73 The Act clearly states that the provisions of ss.10 and 11[182] shall apply to an application under s.12 as they do to an application under s.9 with any necessary modifications.[183] The absence of a reference to s.9 at the beginning of this subsection means that the requirements of s.9 do not apply to an application under s.12.

4–74 Once the Garda has made the recommendation for admission, they may give it to a doctor and from then on the procedure to be followed is as specified in paras 4–18 to 4–68 above, i.e. the doctor may make a recommendation for admission, the patient may be removed to an approved centre and an Admission Order may be made at the centre.

4–75 The equivalent section of the previous legislation was s.165 of the Mental Treatment Act 1945. In *E.P. v Medical Director of St. Vincent's Hospital and the Attorney General*,[184] the applicant was taken into custody by Gardaí under s.165 of the 1945 Act, in circumstances where the Gardaí were of opinion that he was of unsound mind and a threat to other people or himself. He was then detained under a Reception Order purportedly under s.184 of the 1945 Act. As the court was not satisfied that the applicant was informed (as required by s.165) of the basis of his detention, O'Higgins J. held that, at the time when the examination leading to and decisions concerning the making of an order under s.184 were conducted and made, the applicant was in unlawful custody, and an order for his release was made.

While a full written judgment is not available for this case, it may have turned on a close reading of ss.165 and 184 of the 1945 Act, together with s.5 of the Mental Treatment Act 1953. The combined effect of these sections was that if a Garda detained the person and then applied for a temporary reception order, the Garda was required to inform the person of the nature of the medical certificate which had been made by a doctor and their right to a second medical examination.

---

[181] The requirement to disclose previous applications is stated in s.11 of the Mental Health Act 2001 and s.12(3) states that the provisions of s.11 apply to an application under s.12.

[182] Section 10 lays down the requirements regarding the making of the recommendation for involuntary admission; s.11 requires disclosure of previous applications for involuntary admission.

[183] Section 12(3).

[184] O'Higgins J., High Court, March 15, 2004, ex tempore, summarised in *L.K. v Clinical Director of Lakeview Unit, Naas General Hospital and the HSE, South Western Area* [2007] 2 I.R. 465; [2007] 2 I.L.R.M. 69.

Eight months later, Finnegan P. reached a different conclusion in *Orton v St. John of God Hospital*.[185] Very few details of the facts are contained in the judgment. It appears that the applicant was in Donnybrook Garda station and was informed by the Sergeant attending to the matter in relation to the certificate under s.184 of the 1945 Act as follows: "This entitles me to arrest you under the Mental Health Act." The applicant argued that there was a non-compliance with s.5(3)(i) of the Mental Treatment Act 1953 in that he was not informed of the nature of the medical certificate. Finnegan P. stated that in the circumstances of this case this represented a sufficient compliance with the section. The applicant had previously been detained as a temporary chargeable patient, and in these circumstances he was satisfied that this was a sufficient notification of the effect of the certificate.[186]

4–76 In some situations where a Garda has dealings with a person who might require detention under s.12, the Garda may also believe that the person may have committed a criminal offence. In such situations, Gardaí may have to decide whether a criminal charge should be brought, or whether the person should be diverted from the criminal justice system into the civil mental health system. Important questions of policy arise at this stage, and these will be discussed further at paras 19–01 to 19–08 below.

4–77 Section 12 may also become important at other stages of the criminal process. For example, if a person has been charged with a criminal offence and is awaiting trial, the courts do not have the power to remand them in custody to hospital. However, the courts may facilitate the person's admission to a psychiatric centre by granting bail which is conditional on the person permitting themselves to be taken to a centre, and allowing themselves to be admitted based on application by a Garda under s.9 or s.12.[187]

4–78 In *M.Z. v Khattak and Tallaght Hospital Board*[188] the applicant had been taken into custody by Gardaí under s.12, but the application for recommendation had been made by the applicant's brother, who attended at the Garda station. It was argued that this was in breach of s.12(2), which requires that if a Garda takes a person into custody, a member of the Garda "shall" make an application for a recommendation. Peart J. rejected this argument, referring to the fact that the applicant's brother was entitled to apply for a recommendation under s.9. The fact that the process had commenced under s.12 did not preclude matters from proceeding further under s.9. The application for a recommendation under s.9 was to be regarded as the commencement of a fresh procedure under s.9.[189]

---

185   [2004] I.E.H.C. 361; High Court, Finnegan P., 15 November 2004.
186   The applicant also made an argument, which was rejected, concerning the requirement that he be notified of his right to request a second medical examination.
187   See further paras 17–37 to 17–38 below.
188   [2008] I.E.H.C. 262; High Court, Peart J., July 28, 2008.
189   [2008] I.E.H.C. 262; High Court, Peart J., July 28, 2008, p.12.

Peart J. said that "in an ideal world" it would have been desirable that the applicant should have been informed immediately prior to the time when his brother signed the application for a s.9 recommendation, that he was no longer in custody pursuant to s.12 of the Act, and in that sense released and no longer detained under that provision.[190] Even though this had not been done, and an unusual sequence of events had occurred, Peart J. was satisfied that the detention was not unlawful.

4–79 In *F.W. v Dept. of Psychiatry James Connolly Memorial Hospital*,[191] considered below at paras 4–117 to 4–119, it was argued that the removal of F.W. by the Gardaí to hospital on the recommendation of a doctor was not valid because the Gardaí's initial belief under s.12(1) of the 2001 Act was not an independent judgment, as it had been made entirely at the behest of the psychiatrist. Hedigan J. considered that taking the applicant into custody at the hospital was in accordance with law.[192]

4–80 A number of points concerning the powers of Gardaí under s.12 were considered by Dunne J. in *S.C. v Clinical Director, St Brigid's Hospital, Ardee, Co Louth*.[193] On February 5, 2009, the applicant drove his vehicle the wrong way down a one way street and then drove straight into a shop. He was taken into custody and brought to a Garda station. His father applied to a G.P. for a recommendation for admission to an approved centre, he was brought to the approved centre but the psychiatrist did not make an Admission Order. The psychiatrist later stated that he had very serious concerns in relation to Mr C.'s mental state at that time. However, he was also aware that Mr C. was engaged in the criminal process at that time. The psychiatrist had previously worked in the Central Mental Hospital (CMH) and he was aware of the CMH's involvement in the criminal legal system and with individuals within that system who may be suffering from psychiatric difficulties. He believed that the most appropriate manner in which Mr C. should be dealt with was to receive the forensic psychiatric services available within that system, and in those circumstances he did not form a view as to whether Mr C. was or was not suffering from a mental disorder within the meaning of the 2001 Act at that time.[194] Dunne J. said that whilst she had no doubt as to the good intentions of the psychiatrist in this regard, it was, in her view, unwise to deal with the applicant in that way.[195]

The applicant was remanded to Cloverhill prison and was later granted bail and required to sign on at Drogheda Garda station on Mondays, Wednesdays and Fridays. While at Cloverhill, a psychiatrist examined him and on February

---

[190]   [2008] I.E.H.C. 262; High Court, Peart J., July 28, 2008, p.12.
[191]   [2008] I.E.H.C. 283; High Court, Hedigan J., August 18, 2008.
[192]   [2008] I.E.H.C. 283; High Court, Hedigan J., August 18, 2008, p.7.
[193]   [2009] I.E.H.C. 100; High Court, Dunne J., February 26, 2009.
[194]   [2009] I.E.H.C. 100; High Court, Dunne J., February 26, 2009, p.13.
[195]   [2009] I.E.H.C. 100; High Court, Dunne J., February 26, 2009, pp.13–14.

13 that psychiatrist wrote to the Gardaí stating that Mr C. required admission to an approved centre as a matter of urgency. The psychiatrist stated that he was concerned that Mr C. posed a significant risk to the general public and specifically to his father as a result of his psychotic symptoms, and that it would be helpful if it were possible for a member of the Gardaí to act as applicant for admission to hospital, given the immediate risks identified and the dangerousness of his recent offence.[196] The psychiatrist at the hospital also wrote to the Gardaí on February 17 stating that he had exhausted all avenues with Mr C.'s family and had been unable to organise an admission. There were serious concerns about the risks Mr C. posed to his family and to the public. He sought the assistance of the Gardaí to secure Mr C's admission.

On February 19, a number of members of the Gardaí arrived at the family home of the applicant and took him into custody pursuant to s.12 of 2001 Act. He was brought to Drogheda Garda station. An application was made by a Garda Inspector pursuant to s.12 for a recommendation for involuntary admission, and he was admitted to the hospital. In the Admission Order, the psychiatrist certified that Mr C. had a mental disorder under the "need for treatment" ground in s.3 rather than the "risk of harm" ground. It was the detention on February 19 which was challenged in the court proceedings.

It was argued that the taking into custody carried out by the members of the Gardaí under s.12 was a deliberate and conscious violation of the applicant's constitutional rights. This argument was based essentially on the contention that the Gardaí could not have had reasonable grounds for believing that there was a serious likelihood of the applicant causing immediate harm to himself or other persons. That contention was based on the events leading up to the taking into custody on February 19, 2009. One of the matters relied on was that the psychiatrist on February 6 did not see fit to detain the applicant. On this point, Dunne J. noted the evidence of the psychiatrist as to why he acted as he did and commented that in her view it was unwise to deal with the applicant in this way.[197] She said that the issue was whether the Gardaí had reasonable grounds to carry out the taking into custody under s.12 and in her view the answer to that question was in the affirmative. The Gardaí acted on the basis of the information contained in the letters of February 13 and 17. The letters both referred to the serious risk posed by the applicant as a result of his mental state. The fact that the psychiatrist on his examination on February 19 did not tick the box at para.8(a) of the Admission Order relating to serious likelihood of the person concerned causing immediate and serious harm did not mean that the Gardai did not have reasonable grounds to act under s.12.[198]

4–81 Dunne J. agreed with the submission that, "there must be a temporal link between the event or events giving rise to reasonable grounds under s.12 and the

[196]   [2009] I.E.H.C. 100; High Court, Dunne J., February 26, 2009, p.3.
[197]   [2009] I.E.H.C. 100; High Court, Dunne J., February 26, 2009, pp.13–14.
[198]   [2009] I.E.H.C. 100; High Court, Dunne J., February 26, 2009, pp.14–15.

exercise of the power of arrest under that section".[199] However, this was not a case in which the psychiatrist had no involvement with the matter after February 6, albeit that he did not personally examine the applicant between February 6 and 19. Various steps occurred between those dates and it was clear that the two psychiatrists in their discussions had serious concerns and those serious concerns led them both to write to the Gardaí. The Gardaí then acted promptly on foot of the correspondence from the two psychiatrists. She said that had the Gardaí failed to act on foot of the letters, serious criticism would have been made of the Gardaí if any harm had come to the applicant, any member of his family or any member of the public.[200]

Dunne J. held that the taking into custody under s.12 had been a "valid arrest". She also noted that it would not have been possible for the Gardaí to use s.9 of the 2001 Act, as they had not observed the applicant sufficiently, not more than 48 hours before the date of the application, as is required by s.9(4). She added, obiter, that as a general proposition, a breach of the provisions of s.12 of the 2001 Act would not affect the subsequent process by which someone may be detained.[201]

4–82 A judgment in an appeal in this case was issued by the Supreme Court on March 13, 2009.[202] The result of that appeal is not definitively known, as the judgment is not available. However, it appears that the court dismissed the appeal, judging by the tenor of the quotation from the case which is available. Having quoted from the *R.L.* case,[203] Hardiman J. stated:

> "Now in this case a very similar position applies. We are quite satisfied that Dr. McAuley's certification of the 19th February, 2009 grounds the detention of the applicant in St. Brigid's Hospital. We do not feel called upon by authority or otherwise to apply to this case the sort of reasoning that would be applied if it were a criminal detention and to investigate whether previous matters which might have a causal relationship to the present detention are invalid."[204]

---

[199] [2009] I.E.H.C. 100; High Court, Dunne J., February 26, 2009, p.15.

[200] [2009] I.E.H.C. 100; High Court, Dunne J., February 26, 2009, p.15.

[201] [2009] I.E.H.C. 100; High Court, Dunne J., February 26, 2009, p.15, citing *C.C. v Clinical Director of St. Patrick's Hospital (No.1)* [2009] I.E.H.C. 13; High Court, McMahon J., January 20, 2009 and *R.L. v Clinical Director of St. Brendan's Hospital & Ors.* [2008] I.E.H.C. 11; [2008] 3 I.R. 296 and Supreme Court (ex tempore), February 15, 2008.

[202] *S.C. v. Clinical Director of St. Brigid's Hospital*, Supreme Court, March 13, 2009, no written judgment available, quoted in *E.H. v Clinical Director of St. Vincent's Hospital* [2009] 2 I.L.R.M. 149 at 163–4.

[203] *R.L. v Clinical Director of St. Brendan's Hospital & Ors.*, Supreme Court (*ex tempore*), February 15, 2008.

[204] *S.C. v. Clinical Director of St. Brigid's Hospital*, Supreme Court, March 13, 2009, no written judgment available, p.6, quoted in *E.H. v Clinical Director of St. Vincent's Hospital* [2009] 2 I.L.R.M. 149 at 164.

INVOLUNTARY ADMISSION OF A CHILD

4–83 Section 25 of the Mental Health Act 2001 prescribes the procedure for involuntary admission of children to approved centres. A "child" means a person under the age of 18, other than a person who is or has been married.[205] As originally enacted, the section referred throughout to "a health board" but those references were later changed to "the Health Service Executive", or HSE.[206]

4–84 Where it appears to the HSE that a child is suffering from a mental disorder and the child requires treatment which they are unlikely to receive unless an order authorising the child's detention in an approved centre is made, the HSE may make an application to the District Court for an order authorising the child's detention.[207] The application is made to the District Court in the district court district where the child resides or is found. An application may be made ex parte, if the court is satisfied that the urgency of the matter so requires.[208] Rules of court are prescribed in the District Court (Mental Health) Rules 2007.[209]

4–85 Normally, the child must have been examined by a consultant psychiatrist who is not a relative of the child before the application is made, and a report of the results of the examination must be furnished to the court.[210] However, an application may be made without such prior examination and report if the child's parents, or either of them, or a person acting in *loco parentis*, refuses to consent to the child's examination, or if the parents or person acting in *loco parentis* cannot be found.[211] In such a case, the court may direct that the HSE arrange the child's examination if it is satisfied that there is reasonable cause to believe that the child is suffering from a mental disorder.[212]

Between the making of the application and its determination, the court may give such directions as it sees fit as to the child's care and custody pending such determination.[213]

Having considered the psychiatric report and any other evidence, if the court is satisfied that the child is suffering from a mental disorder, the court must make an order that the child be admitted and detained for treatment in a specified approved centre for a period not exceeding 21 days.[214]

---

[205] Section 2(1) of the Mental Health Act 2001.
[206] Health Act 2004, s.75 and sch.7, pt 12.
[207] Section 25(1) of the Mental Health Act 2001.
[208] Section 25(7).
[209] S.I. No. 97 of 2007.
[210] Section 25(2).
[211] Section 25(3).
[212] Section 25(4) and s.25(5).
[213] Section 25(8).
[214] Section 25(6).

4–86 There is no statutory requirement that the child be given a written information notice.[215] But children are covered by (less tangible) rights to be notified of proposals and to make representations in s.4(2) of the 2001 Act, and the right to be heard in art.12 of the Convention on the Rights of the Child.[216]

4–87 The HSE may apply to the court for a first extension of detention of up to three months and second and subsequent extensions of up to six months each.[217] A new psychiatric report must be produced before an extension order may be made by the court.[218]

While the child is detained under the 2001 Act, psycho-surgery or electro-convulsive therapy may not be performed on or administered to the child without the court's approval.[219]

4–88 The provisions of certain sections[220] of the Child Care Act 1991 apply to proceedings to detain a child under s.25 of the Mental Health Act 2001.[221] These sections concern issues such as the effect of appeals from orders, variation or discharge of orders, the welfare of the child to be paramount, the power of the court to join the child as a party, appointment of a guardian *ad litem* for the child, power to procure reports on children, jurisdiction, hearing of proceedings, power to proceed in the absence of the child, prohibition on publication or broadcast of certain matters, presumption and determination of age, rules of court, failure or refusal to deliver up the child, warrant to search for and deliver up the child, access to children in care, and applications for directions.

The most significant of these sections is s.24 of the Child Care Act 1991, which states that the court, having regard to the rights and duties of parents, whether under the Constitution or otherwise, shall:

(a) regard the welfare of the child as the first and paramount consideration, and

(b) in so far as is practicable, give due consideration, having regard to his or her age and understanding, to the wishes of the child.

Useful sources are available which may be consulted for further details of the relevant provisions of the Child Care Act.[222]

---

[215] Section 16(2), governing the standard information which must be given to a patient on the making of an Admission or Renewal order, applies only to adult patients.

[216] The UN Convention on the Rights of the Child is not part of Ireland's domestic law, but the Mental Health Commission considers that due consideration should be given to the Convention, as appropriate—*Reference Guide: Children*, section 2.1.

[217] Section 25(9) and (10).

[218] Section 25(11).

[219] Section 25(12) and (13).

[220] Sections 21, 22, 24 to 35, 37 and 47 of the Child Care Act 1991.

[221] Section 25(14) of the Mental Health Act 2001.

[222] See Ursula Kilkelly, *Children's Rights in Ireland: Law, Policy and Practice* (Sussex: Tottel,

4–89 The courts are involved from the outset in an involuntary detention of a child, and this contrasts with the procedure concerning adults, where the initial detention is by a psychiatrist, subject to review by an MHT. From a legal point of view, a decision by a court is regarded as more protective of the child's rights than a decision by a psychiatrist which is later reviewed by a tribunal. It is reminiscent of some earlier mental health laws, whereby detentions were ordered by judges or peace commissioners.[223] During the first review of the operation of the Act, concern was expressed in some submissions that the detention of a child under s.25 and any extension of the period of detention is not subject to a review by an MHT. However, the Department of Health pointed out that both the detention under s.25 and the extension of the period of the detention require an order of the District Court. In addition, the provisions of the Child Care Act 1991, which includes the appointment of a guardian *ad litem* if required, apply to proceedings under s.25. The review document stated that the Minister was of the view that the protections provided for in legislation ensured that the child's best interests were protected.[224]

4–90 There were eight involuntary admissions of children in 2008. Six of these were to adult units and two were to child units. There were 392 admissions of children in total in 2008, which means that the vast majority of admissions were on a voluntary basis.[225]

4–91 The Mental Health Commission has produced a 30-page statutory Code of Practice on the admission of children under the Mental Health Act 2001.[226] An Addendum was published in 2009.[227] In the Preamble, the Commission states that the provision of age-appropriate approved centres for children and adolescents must be addressed as a matter of urgency. It considers that the admission of children to units in approved centres providing care and treatment to adults is undesirable, but that in situations where there is no available alternative, such admissions may be necessary. The Commission also notes that the admission of 16- and 17-year-olds, pursuant to the Mental Treatment Act 1945, was to adult mental health in-patient units/hospitals. It states that in the absence of appropriate facilities, it is unlikely that this situation will change in

---

2008); Paul Ward, *The Child Care Acts*, 2nd edn (Dublin: Thomson Round Hall, 2005) and Geoffrey Shannon, *Child Law* (Dublin: Thomson Round Hall, 2005)

[223] See for example s.10 of the Lunacy (Ireland) Act 1867, which covered a "dangerous lunatic" or "dangerous idiot" who had a criminal purpose, and required the committal order to be made by two Justices of the Peace, later adapted to one District Justice or two Peace Commissioners; *State (Power) v Jones and Murray* [1944] I.R. 68.

[224] Department of Health and Children, *Review of the Operation of the Mental Health Act 2001: Findings and Conclusions* (May 2007), p.20.

[225] Mental Health Commission, *Annual Report 2008*, Book 1, p.31.

[226] Mental Health Commission, *Code of Practice Relating to Admission of Children Under the Mental Health Act 2001*, COP–S33(3)/01/2006.

[227] Mental Health Commission, *Code of Practice Relating to Admission of Children Under the Mental Health Act 2001 Addendum* (2009).

the immediate future. It is important, therefore, to ensure that appropriate interim arrangements are put in place to ensure the protection and safety of such children.

4–92 The code states that it must be read taking into account that the best interests of the child shall be the principal and overarching consideration.[228] It goes on to refer to the principles in s.4 of the Mental Health Act 2001, i.e. best interests, notification of proposals and dignity/privacy etc. The code advises that all of these principles apply to children as well as adults. The code contains guidance on issues such as voluntary admission, involuntary admission, treatment and leave. Some important features of the code are as follows:

- It is a matter for the treating psychiatrist to satisfy themselves as to whether it is practicable and in the child's best interests to notify him or her of the proposal to administer treatment in accordance with s.4(2).[229]
- All children receiving treatment pursuant to the Act should be involved, consistent with their identified needs and wishes, in the planning, implementation and evaluation of their care and treatment. Provision of information should be in a form and language that the child can understand. Interpretation services should be made available as required.[230]
- The Addendum states that no child under 16 years is to be admitted to an adult unit in an approved centre from July 1, 2009; no child under 17 years is to be admitted from December 1, 2010; and no child under 18 years is to be admitted from December 1, 2011.[231] If, in exceptional circumstances, the admission of a child to an adult unit in an approved centre occurs in contravention of the above, the approved centre is obliged to submit a detailed report to the Mental Health Commission outlining why the admission has taken place.[232]
- Special guidance is provided for situations where a child is admitted to an approved centre for adults, e.g. age-appropriate facilities and a programme of activities appropriate to age and ability should be provided; staff having contact with the child should have undergone Garda Síochána/police vetting; the approved centre should have a policy requiring each child to be individually risk assessed.[233]
- If a child is to receive voluntary in-patient treatment, consent of one or both parents must be obtained.[234] See further paras 10–54 to 10–61 below.

[228] *Code of Practice re Admission of Children*, para.1.12.
[229] *Code of Practice re Admission of Children*, para.1.14.
[230] *Code of Practice re Admission of Children*, para.1.15.
[231] *Code of Practice re Admission of Children Addendum* (2009), p.3.
[232] This report must be in the form specified by the Mental Health Commission as per Section B of the Notification to the Mental Health Commission of the admission of a child to an adult unit in an approved centre, p.7 of Addendum.
[233] *Code of Practice re Admission of Children*, para.2.5.
[234] *Code of Practice re Admission of Children*, para.2.8.

- It is difficult to reconcile the Mental Health Act with s.23 of the Non-Fatal Offences against the Person Act 1997.[235] See further paras 10–54 to 10–61 below. The more extensive and/or far-reaching the intervention proposed, the more cautious the treating professional should be in relying exclusively on a child's consent. Such caution would be particularly indicated where the parent(s) of the child is/are opposed to the intervention.[236] Where there is disagreement as between child and parent(s), particularly in respect of some significant aspect of treatment, it is open to the professional involved to decline to give that treatment or to seek guidance from the High Court as to how to proceed.[237]

- If the parents wish to remove a child who is being treated on a voluntary basis from an approved centre, the staff may invoke s.23(2) of the Mental Health Act 2001[238] to detain the child, and then apply to the District Court for an order authorising involuntary admission under s.25. The code provides details of procedures to be followed in such cases.[239] The relevant clinical practice form should be completed.[240]

- The code refers[241] to a section of the Reference Guide[242] which advises that in considering an involuntary admission of a child, the following principles should be considered:
  - (i) The least restrictive form of care should be used initially
  - (ii) The involuntary admission and treatment should be for the minimum period in line with best interests of the child
  - (iii) Consideration of the child's view should extend in line with age and maturity

- In light of the seriousness of an application for involuntary admission to an approved centre of a child, in particular for those under 16 years of age, the Commission recommends that, in as far as is practicable, the HSE should arrange for a report for the District Court to be made by a *child and adolescent* consultant psychiatrist.[243]

- The code summarises the sections of the Child Care Act which apply to proceedings under the Mental Health Act.[244]

---

[235] Section 23 of the Non-Fatal Offences Against the Person Act 1997 provides that the consent of a minor who has attained the age of 16 years to any surgical, medical or dental treatment shall be as effective as it would be if he or she were of full age.

[236] *Code of Practice re Admission of Children*, para.2.12.

[237] *Code of Practice re Admission of Children*, para.2.13.

[238] See paras 5–54 to 5–55 below.

[239] *Code of Practice re Admission of Children*, paras 2.15–2.20.

[240] Mental Health Commission, *Clinical Practice Form: Mental Health Act Section 23(2) and 23(3): Power to Detain Voluntary Patient (Child) in an Approved Centre.*

[241] *Code of Practice re Admission of Children*, para.2.21.

[242] *Reference Guide–Children*, section 4.2.3.

[243] *Code of Practice re Admission of Children*, para.2.25.

[244] *Code of Practice re Admission of Children*, para.2.32.

- The Commission's legal advice is that it would appear that s.56[245] of the Mental Health Act 2001 only applies to adults and not to children.[246]
- Parental consent is required before a child can be treated while admitted as a voluntary patient. The three key components of consent—provision of adequate information, decisional capacity and voluntarism—should apply.[247]
- Irrespective of whether a 16- or 17-year-old is capable, as a matter of law or fact, of providing an effective consent to treatment, their views as to their treatment should be sought as a matter of course.[248]
- Due to the problem with the drafting of s.61 of the Mental Health Act 2001 regarding administration of medicine to children,[249] the Commission advises that both the approval of the consultant psychiatrist responsible for the care and treatment of the child and authorisation from another consultant psychiatrist are sought.[250]
- The Commission should be notified of all children admitted to (or discharged from) approved centres for adults within 72 hours of admission (or discharge) by using the associated forms.[251]

4–93 If a child is being treated at an approved centre, whether on an involuntary or voluntary basis, then the Approved Centres Regulations[252] must be followed. These include the requirement of an individual care plan and, in the case of a child, provision of appropriate educational services.

EXTENSION OF INVOLUNTARY ADMISSION OF A CHILD

4–94 The first involuntary admission order for a child lasts for up to 21 days.[253] While the first order is in force, the HSE may apply for an extension, and the court may order an extension of up to three months.[254] Subsequent extensions may last up to six months each.[255]

---

[245] Section 56 defines "consent" as consent obtained freely in circumstances where the responsible consultant psychiatrist is satisfied that the patient is capable of understanding the nature, purpose and likely effects of the proposed treatment and where the patient has been given adequate information, in a form and language that they can understand.

[246] *Code of Practice re Admission of Children*, para.3.1.

[247] *Code of Practice re Admission of Children*, para.3.2.

[248] *Code of Practice re Admission of Children*, para.3.3.

[249] See further para.10–40 below.

[250] *Code of Practice re Admission of Children*, para.3.5.

[251] *Code of Practice re Admission of Children*, para.2.5(m), as amended by Addendum in 2009. The Form for Admission is: *Notification to the Mental Health Commission of the admission of a child to an approved centre for adults: Clinical Practice Form*, revised July 2009.

[252] Mental Health Act 2001 (Approved Centres) Regulations 2006, S.I. No. 551 of 2006

[253] Section 25(6) of the Mental Health Act 2001.

[254] Section 25(9).

[255] Section 25(10).

In the case of all extensions, the child must be examined by a consultant psychiatrist who is not a relative of the child and the psychiatrist's report must be furnished to the court. The court must consider the report and may only extend the child's detention if it is satisfied that the child is still suffering from a mental disorder.[256]

TRANSITIONAL PROVISIONS REGARDING PATIENTS WHO STOOD DETAINED IN 2006

4–95 Section 72(1) of the 2001 Act provides that where immediately before November 1, 2006, a person stood detained under s.171, 178, 184 or 185 of the 1945 Act, he or she shall be regarded for the purposes of the Act as having been involuntarily admitted under Part 2 of the 2001 Act to the institution in which they were so detained. In the case of temporary patients, their detention shall be regarded as authorised until the expiration of the period during which they may be detained pursuant to the 1945 Act. In the case of "persons of unsound mind", their detention shall be regarded as authorised for a period not exceeding six months after November 1, 2006.[257] The detention of a person referred to above shall be referred to a tribunal by the Commission before the expiration of the period referred to above, as may be appropriate, and the tribunal shall review the detention as if it had been authorised by a Renewal Order under s.15(2).[258]

4–96 In *J.H. v Russell*,[259] Peart J. stated that an important issue was the meaning of the provision which refers (in s.72(1)) to a person who "stood detained" under any one of the relevant sections. The question which arose was as to whether a person who might not have been validly detained at the time of the commencement of the relevant provisions of the 2001 Act (by reference to the compliance with the provisions of the 1945 Act) could have the validity of their detention rendered good by virtue of going through the review process of the 2001 Act.[260] He was satisfied that where s.72 refers to "persons detained", that reference is to persons validly detained. He continued:

> "I am satisfied that a necessary pre-condition for the invocation of s.72 is a
> valid s. 184 detention order (or, in an appropriate case an order under one of
> the other sections of the 1945 Act expressly referred to in s. 72). In the absence
> of clear wording to the contrary, it does not seem to me to be appropriate to

---

[256]   Section 25(11).
[257]   Mental Health Act 2001, s.72(2)–(3). November 1, 2006 is the date of commencement of Part
        2 of the Mental Health Act 2001—Mental Health Act 2001 (Commencement) Order 2006, S.I.
        No.411 of 2006.
[258]   Section 72(4).
[259]   [2007] I.E.H.C. 7; [2007] 4 I.R. 242; Clarke J., High Court, February 6, 2007.
[260]   [2007] 4 I.R. 242 at 255.

construe s.72 as curing a prior invalid detention. It would, in my judgment, require very clear wording indeed for a court to interpret a statutory provision as rendering lawful an involuntary detention which was otherwise unlawful. There is no such wording present in the instant case and it therefore seems to me that the proper construction of s. 72 requires that there be in place a valid detention order under (on the facts of this case) s. 184 prior to the provisions of s. 72 kicking in."[261]

Having found that the patient was not validly detained as of November 1, 2006, Peart J. therefore granted the application under Art.40.[262]

4–97 In *R.W. v Clinical Director of St. John of Gods Hospital*[263] the High Court was asked to consider whether, if a "transitional" patient's detention were affirmed by an MHT four weeks before the expiry of his detention, it was necessary to hold a further review of this affirmation within 21 days.[264] Normally, the timing of MHT hearings is not related to the date of an MHT hearing but instead to the date of the relevant Admission Order or Renewal Order. However, the applicant's counsel referred to s.72(4), which states that in "transitional" cases, the tribunal "shall review the detention as if it had been authorised by a renewal order under section 15(2)." It was argued that it followed that the MHT order "had a shelf-life of only 21 days"[265] as provided by s.15(2) of the Act, and a review ought to have taken place within those 21 days.

Peart J. rejected this argument, stating that it was based on a misunderstanding of the provisions of s.72. He stressed that s.72(2) provides that the detention of a person who immediately before the commencement of the 2001 Act stood detained under s.184 of the 1945 Act shall be regarded as authorised until the expiration of the period during which they may be detained pursuant to s.184. He said that s.72 of the 2001 Act must be seen as making specific provision for such a case where it was necessary to carry over the detention ordered under s.184 into the new scheme without the necessity to bring his detention temporarily to an end and re-commence the process of detaining him under the 2001 Act. That was why these so-called "transitional provisions" were included in the new Act. In his view "they must be seen as operating in a sense independently of any order actually made under section 14 (or s.15 in the case of a renewal thereof), even though some of the provisions of sections 15 et seq. will be applied."[266]

---

261 [2007] 4 I.R. 242 at 256–7.
262 See further paras 5–07 to 5–08 below.
263 [2007] I.E.H.C. 184; Peart J., High Court, May 22, 2007.
264 The applicant was originally detained on October 25, 2005 under s.184 of the 1945 Act. His detention was extended on April 25, 2006 and on October 25, 2006, and was due to expire on April 25, 2007. The MHT hearing under s.72(4) of the 2001 Act took place on March 27, 2007 and affirmed the detention. A Renewal Order was made under s.15 of the 2001 Act on April 23, 2007 and was affirmed by the MHT on May 10, 2007.
265 [2007] I.E.H.C. 184, p.6.
266 [2007] I.E.H.C. 184, p.7.

4–98 While s.72(4) states that the MHT reviews the detention "as if it had been authorised by a renewal order under section 15(2)", that did not mean that it was such a Renewal Order. Peart J. said:

> "It [section 72(4)] means what it says, namely that the Tribunal must conduct its review in the same manner as if it was such a renewal. In other words it must afford the applicant the same rights, and conduct itself in the same way, as it would in the case of a renewal order made under section 15(2). ... [T]he invocation of the procedures of section 15 et seq. does not convert the order detaining the applicant into an admission order made on the 27th March 2007, requiring to be reviewed not later than twenty one days thereafter. That would fly in the face of section 72(2)."[267]

PATIENT ABSENCES (WITH AND WITHOUT LEAVE)

4–99 The Responsible Consultant Psychiatrist (RCP) may grant permission in writing to the patient[268] to be absent from the approved centre for such period as they may specify in the permission, this period being less than the unexpired period provided for in the relevant Admission Order, the relevant Renewal Order or the relevant order concerning a child under s.25, as the case may be.[269] The permission may be made subject to such conditions as the RCP considers appropriate and so specifies.

Where a patient is absent from an approved centre pursuant to such permission, the consultant psychiatrist may, if they are of opinion that it is in the interests of the patient to do so, withdraw the permission and direct the patient in writing to return to the approved centre.

4–100 There is no statutory form laid down for the granting of leave to patients. From 2005 to 2007, the Mental Health Commission's annual census form recorded whether a patient was on leave at the date of the census[270] but these figures did not appear in the annual reports. The annual census was discontinued in 2008.

During the review of the operation of the Act, it was suggested that the requirement to direct a patient in writing to return to the approved centre was unworkable, as the psychiatrist might not have the current address for the patient. The Minister stated that it was his view that the psychiatrist would be

---

[267] [2007] I.E.H.C. 184, p.8.
[268] The reference to "patient" here includes a child in respect of whom an order under s.25 is in force (s.26(3) of the Mental Health Act 2001.)
[269] Section 26 of the Mental Health Act 2001.
[270] Mental Health Commission, *Annual Report 2005*, p.137, item 11; *Annual Report 2006*, p.76, item 11; *Annual Report 2007*, Book 1, p.68, item 11. The end of year return form used in 2004 did not request this information–see *Annual Report 2004*, pp.102–106.

expected to satisfy themselves, prior to granting absence with leave, as to where the patient will reside and how the patient can be contacted.[271]

4–101 In England and Wales, patients are frequently granted leave of absence and a number of court judgments have been delivered on the topic. For example, in *B. v Barking, Havering and Brentwood Community Healthcare NHS Trust*[272] the patient was allowed to be absent from the hospital on a number of days each week, and was merely assessed rather than treated on her days in hospital. When her detention was renewed, she sought judicial review on the basis that the statutory conditions for detention no longer applied. The Court of Appeal upheld the renewal of her detention, as the legislation permitted treatment partly as an in-patient and partly as an out-patient. This decision meant that the decision in the previous case of *R v Hallstrom, ex parte W.*[273] was confined to certain narrowly defined situations.[274]

4–102 Withdrawal of permission to be absent (or "recall" of the patient) may give rise to ECHR issues, as it is arguable that the requirement of "objective medical expertise" applies.[275]

4–103 Absences *without* leave are dealt with in s.27. The section applies where an involuntary patient[276]:

    (a) leaves an approved centre without permission under s.26,
    (b) fails to return to the centre in accordance with any direction given under s.26 or on the expiration of the period for which absence or leave was permitted under that section, or
    (c) fails, in the opinion of the RCP, to comply with any condition specified in s.26.[277]

---

[271] Department of Health and Children, *Review of the Operation of the Mental Health Act 2001: Findings and Conclusions* (May 2007), p.21.

[272] [1998] E.W.C.A. Civ. 1347; [1999] 1 F.L.R. 106.

[273] [1986] Q.B. 1090; [1986] 2 All E.R. 306.

[274] It appears that *R. v Hallstrom, ex parte W.* now means that renewal of authority to detain is only unlawful where there is no intention of hospitalising a patient on leave and the only reason for extension of detention is to permit continued treatment in the community, sometimes referred to as the "long leash"—See Anselm Eldergill, "Casenote on Barker v Barking Havering and Brentwood Community Healthcare NHS Trust" (1999) 1 *Journal of Mental Health Law* 68; discussion in Peter Bartlett & Ralph Sandland, *Mental Health Law: Policy and Practice*, 3rd edn (Oxford: Oxford University Press, 2007), pp.354–357.

[275] See Bartlett and Sandland, *Mental Health Law: Policy and Practice*, p.358; referring to *K. v UK* (1998) 40 B.M.L.R. 20.

[276] This includes a child in respect of whom an order under s.25 is in force—s.27(3).

[277] There are no conditions specified in s.26. The reference should instead refer to conditions specified *in accordance with* s.26, i.e. conditions specified in writing to the patient when they were granted leave to be absent. The *Reference Guide: Adults* interprets s.27 in this fashion—section 2.5, p.1.

In any of these situations, the clinical director of the approved centre may arrange for members of the centre's staff or authorised persons to bring the patient back to the centre.[278] The reference to authorised persons was inserted in 2009 to enable independent contractors to participate in the process (see further paras 4–45 to 4–46 above). If they are unable to do so and the clinical director is of the opinion that there is a serious likelihood of the patient[279] causing immediate and serious harm to themselves or others, the clinical director or a consultant psychiatrist acting on their behalf may, if necessary, request the Gardaí to assist in such bringing back of the patient to the centre and the Gardaí must comply with any such request. For the purposes of the section, a Garda may:

    (a) enter if need be by force any dwelling or other premises where they have reasonable cause to believe that the patient may be, and

    (b) take all reasonable measures necessary for the return of the patient to the approved centre including, where necessary, the detention or restraint of the patient.[280]

4–104 In the review of operation of the Act, clarification was requested as to the time and geographical criteria for defining absence without leave. The Minister stated that he did not consider this a matter appropriate to legislation. Responses to absences without leave would vary and must take into account the individual circumstances of each instance. The Minister considered that it would be helpful for the HSE and the Mental Health Commission to develop guidance on this matter.[281]

Eldergill notes that the Act does not make any provision at all for extending a patient's liability to detention where they are absent without leave at the time when renewal is due. He states:

> "All the Act states is that the patient's consultant must examine them during the week before the renewal order is made and certify that the patient continues to suffer from mental disorder. On the face of it therefore, if the patient is absent for the whole of the renewal week, so that no examination can take place, the order simply expires at the end of that period."[282]

---

[278] Section 27(1), as amended by s.63 of the Health (Miscellaneous Provisions) Act 2009.
[279] The word "patient" was substituted for "person" by an amendment made by s.63 of the Health (Miscellaneous Provisions) Act 2009.
[280] Section 27(2), as amended by s.63 of the 2009 Act.
[281] *Review of the Operation of the Mental Health Act 2001*, p.21.
[282] Anselm Eldergill, "The Best is the Enemy of the Good: The Mental Health Act 2001" (2008) J. Mental Health L. 21 at 36.

PATIENT TRANSFERS (CIVIL)

4–105 There are a number of different types of transfers of detained patients provided for in the Mental Health Act 2001. Section 20 deals with transfers between approved centres at the request of the patient or the person who applied for the recommendation for admission. Section 21 deals with a transfer between approved centres on the initiative of the clinical director. Section 22 provides for a transfer from an approved centre for treatment to a hospital or other place. Transfers from approved centres to the Central Mental Hospital must be authorised by a Mental Health Tribunal under s.21(2) and these transfers will be considered at paras 7–66 to 7–69 below.

4–106 Section 20 states that where a patient or the person who applied for a recommendation under which a patient is detained in an approved centre applies to the clinical director of the centre for a transfer of the patient to another approved centre, the clinical director may, if he or she so thinks fit, arrange for the transfer of the patient to the centre with the consent of the clinical director of the second-mentioned approved centre. The Commission must be notified in writing of the transfer, and this is done by means of Form 10.

4–107 Section 21(1) states that where the clinical director of an approved centre is of the opinion that it would be for the benefit of a patient detained in that centre, or that it is necessary for the purpose of obtaining special treatment for such patient, that they should be transferred to another approved centre (other than the CMH), the clinical director may arrange for the transfer of the patient to the other centre with the consent of the clinical director of that centre. The Commission must be notified in writing and Form 10 is again used for this purpose. Section 21(4) states that the detention of a patient in another approved centre under the section shall be deemed for the purposes of the Act to be detention in the centre from which they were transferred.

In *B. v Clinical Director of Our Lady's Hospital Navan*[283] the applicant was admitted to St Patrick's Hospital, Dublin, as a voluntary patient on September 28, 2007. On October 2, 2007 her status was changed from voluntary to involuntary, and she was transferred to Our Lady's Hospital, Navan, Co. Meath on October 10, 2007. On October 22, 2007, an MHT affirmed the admission order and on the same date a three-month renewal order was made in Our Lady's Hospital, signed by a psychiatrist from that hospital. The applicant's counsel argued that the renewal order should have stated that she was being detained in St. Patrick's Hospital (the hospital from which she had been transferred), and that it should have been made by a psychiatrist from that hospital rather than Our Lady's Hospital. Counsel referred to s.21(4) of the 2001 Act, which states that the patient's detention in another approved centre shall be deemed to be detention in the centre from which they were transferred.

---

[283] [2007] I.E.H.C. 403; Sheehan J., ex tempore, 5 November 2007.

Sheehan J. said that, "on the face of it, [this] was one way of reading the section."[284] However, he noted that if this interpretation were correct, the patient's treatment would have to be interrupted by returning her to St. Patrick's Hospital until the necessary orders were made to transfer her back to Our Lady's Hospital. Counsel for the MHT and Mental Health Commission argued that s.21(4) was an enabling provision which enabled a Renewal Order to relate back to the first hospital, in circumstances where that would make sense. Counsel argued that s.21(4) was intended to provide flexibility and was not intended to be some sort of additional mandatory hurdle. He took the example of someone admitted to hospital while on holiday in Donegal and then transferred back to their local hospital in Cork. He submitted that it would be absurd to say that all the Renewal Orders extending that person's detention would have to be done on the basis that the person was deemed to be a patient in the Donegal hospital when they were going to remain in Cork until they were well again, and that there was not the slightest chance that they would return to Donegal.[285]

Sheehan J. said that he was mindful of the guidelines contained in the Supreme Court judgment of *Gooden v St. Otteran's Hospital*[286] and, bearing in mind the submissions of the respondents, he held with the respondents on this ground. In other words, he held that the applicant's detention was lawful. He said that he was bearing in mind in particular counsel's submission that what the Act was contemplating was that these temporary transfers would be applicable only for as long as the basic order was in place.[287]

4–108 Section 22(1) states that a clinical director of an approved centre may arrange for the transfer of a patient detained in that centre for treatment to a hospital or other place and for their detention there for that purpose. A patient removed under this section to a hospital or other place may be kept there as long as is necessary for the purpose of their treatment and shall then be taken back to the approved centre from which they were transferred.[288] The detention of a patient in a hospital or other place under this section shall be deemed for the purposes of this Act to be detention in the centre from which they were transferred.[289] There is no requirement in the Act to notify the Commission in writing of a transfer under s.22 and Form 10 does not apply to such a transfer.

A failure to comply with s.22 was in issue in *P.McG. v Medical Director of the Mater Hospital*.[290] The applicant had been admitted to an approved centre (St Aloysius's Ward at the Mater Hospital) but was then transferred to another part of the hospital, a medical ward, which was not an approved centre, due to a deteriorating physical condition. The psychiatrist noted on the file a request

---

[284]   [2007] I.E.H.C. 403, para.9.
[285]   [2007] I.E.H.C. 403, para.10.
[286]   [2005] I.R. 617.
[287]   [2007] I.E.H.C. 403, para.11.
[288]   Mental Health Act 2001, s.22(2).
[289]   Mental Health Act 2001, s.22(3).
[290]   [2007] I.E.H.C. 401; [2008] 2 I.R. 332; Peart J., High Court, November 29, 2007.

that the patient be transferred to the medical ward, but he did not speak to the clinical director of the approved centre about the matter. When the case came before an MHT, the patient's solicitor argued that s.22(1) had not been complied with because the transfer must be arranged by the clinical director. However, the MHT affirmed the patient's detention, noting that it was concerned that s.22 had not been complied with. The MHT could not discharge the patient due to non-compliance with s.22, as this is not one of the procedural sections within its jurisdiction.[291]

In the subsequent Art.40 proceedings, Peart J. noted that the protections put in place by the 2001 Act, "are detailed and specific and it is of the utmost importance that they be observed to the letter, and that no unnecessary shortcuts creep into the way in which the Act is operated."[292] However, the legislation should not be interpreted in such a literal way that the best interests of the patient would take second place.[293] Section 22 only required that the clinical director "arrange" the transfer, not that they "authorise" it. In an emergency situation, the clinical director might not be able to be contacted. The circumstances in this case were "completely bona fide" and the patient's detention was not unlawful. It would have been better practice if the clinical director made the arrangements, or was at least aware that this was being done, but it may well simply have been an oversight in this case.[294] Peart J. warned that in other circumstances the courts might not be so tolerant of such an oversight:

> "If there had been any evidence that the transfer had not been required for medical reasons, and was done for some other reason such as lack of space in St. Aloysius's ward, then the Court's view would have to be entirely different since such a transfer would have implications for the fundamental right of the applicant to be detained only in an approved centre."[295]

DISCHARGE OF PATIENTS OR RE-GRADING FROM INVOLUNTARY TO VOLUNTARY STATUS

4–109 If an admission or renewal order expires without being renewed, or if the MHT revokes the order, then the patient is no longer involuntarily detained. In the case of a revocation by the MHT, s.18 of the 2001 Act requires that the MHT "direct that the patient be discharged from the approved centre."[296] The patient might, of course, choose to remain in the centre on a voluntary basis.

---

[291] Peart J. stated that the tribunal was correct in its view that any lack of compliance with s.22 was not something which was within its jurisdiction to examine and make findings in relation to—[2008] 2 I.R. 332 at 338.
[292] [2008] 2 I.R. 332 at 338.
[293] [2008] 2 I.R. 332 at 339.
[294] [2008] 2 I.R. 332 at 339.
[295] [2008] 2 I.R. 332 at 339–40.
[296] Mental Health Act 2001, s.18(1)(b).

4–110 In many cases, the decision to end the involuntary detention will be made by the responsible psychiatrist under s.28. Where the RCP becomes of opinion that the patient is no longer suffering from a mental disorder, he or she must revoke the relevant Admission Order or Renewal Order and discharge the patient.[297] Again, the patient might decide to stay on in the centre on a voluntary basis. In deciding whether and when to discharge a patient, the psychiatrist must have regard to the need to ensure:

(a) that the patient is not inappropriately discharged, and
(b) that the patient is detained pursuant to an admission order or a renewal order only for as long as is reasonably necessary for their proper care and treatment.[298]

4–111 In *S.M. v Mental Health Commission*,[299] McMahon J. said that the obligation to discharge under s.28 is clearly an ongoing obligation for the treating psychiatrist, and is an independent obligation which rests on the treating psychiatrist irrespective of whether the patient is classified as a voluntary or involuntary patient: when the treating psychiatrist forms the opinion that the patient no longer suffers from a mental illness, they must revoke any orders authorising detention.[300] McMahon J. also stated that by placing the best interests of the patient (s.4) at the centre of the decision-making process and by imposing a statutory obligation on the treating consultant to revoke detention orders when the patient no longer suffers from a mental illness (s.28), the 2001 Act ensures that due respect will be given to the patient's rights including their right to dignity and bodily integrity.[301]

McMahon J. also considered the relationship between renewals (s.15) and discharge (s.28):

> "From the scheme and history of the Act it is clear that the purpose of s. 15 is to protect the involuntary patient and to give him/ her public assurance that an external monitoring mechanism exists to ensure that the involuntary patient is being properly cared for and treated. It is proper, as several counsel have suggested, to consider s.28 in this context. Section 28 gives the treating consultant psychiatrist power at any time to release the patient when he/she concludes that the patient is no longer suffering from a mental illness. It is clearly a power which, when it operates, trumps the existing admission or renewal orders. It operates without reference to, and is independent of, section 15. It is important to note, however, that it is a section that only operates for the benefit of the patient: it grants the treating psychiatrist the power to revoke

---

[297]   Mental Health Act 2001, s.28(1).
[298]   Section 28(2).
[299]   [2008] I.E.H.C. 441; [2009] 2 I.L.R.M. 127; McMahon J., High Court, October 31, 2008.
[300]   [2009] 2 I.L.R.M. 127 at 131.
[301]   [2009] 2 I.L.R.M. 127 at 131–2.

existing renewal orders and discharge the patient. In contrast s.15 is concerned with orders which authorise the detention of the patient."[302]

4–112 The first version of Form 14, which is used for revocation of the involuntary admission or renewal order, included a note that it was to be used "upon discharge or re-grading to voluntary status of all patients who have been subject to an in involuntary admission order." This indicated the Mental Health Commission's view that s.28 covers both a complete discharge (where the patient leaves the approved centre) and a change from involuntary to voluntary status, where the patient does not leave the centre. This view is supported by s.29, which states that nothing in the Act prevents a person from being admitted voluntarily to an approved centre for treatment without any admission order rendering them liable to be detained under the Act, or from remaining in an approved centre after they have ceased to be so liable to be detained. A similar interpretation applies in England and Wales, where the term "discharge" is considered to mean discharge from detention, not discharge from hospital.[303]

4–113 McCarthy J. said of s.18 in *P.G. v Branigan*[304] that he did not think that discharged could mean anything in the context other than released.[305] The first version of Form 14 had given the psychiatrist the option of ticking a box stating that the patient "has chosen to remain in the approved centre on a voluntary basis." Perhaps as a result of the *P.G. v Branigan* case, the latest version of Form 14 (issued in March 2009) does not include the reference to re-grading to voluntary status. However, this does not preclude a re-admission of the patient on a voluntary basis. Incidentally, in May 2009, Peart J. noted that the previous version of Form 14 might need to be re-worded to remove the reference to "chosen to remain" to allow for cases where the patient does not have capacity to choose to remain.[306]

4–114 In *M.McN. v Health Service Executive*[307], Peart J. takes a different approach from that of McCarthy J. in *P.G.* and distinguishes between discharge from the admission or renewal order and discharge from the approved centre:

> "One could also make a distinction between a discharge from involuntary detention under the admission order/ renewal order, and an actual discharge from the approved centre. The Act does not define what is meant by

---

[302] [2009] 2 I.L.R.M. 127 at 139.
[303] Section 23 of the Mental Health Act 1983 (England and Wales); Richard Jones, *Mental Health Act Manual*, 11th edn (London: Thomson Sweet and Maxwell, 2008), p.158.
[304] [2008] I.E.H.C. 450; High Court, McCarthy J., December 12, 2008.
[305] [2008] I.E.H.C. 450, p.7.
[306] *M.McN. v Health Service Executive* [2009] I.E.H.C. 236; High Court, Peart J., May 15, 2009, p.40. Peart J. suggested that Form 14 could be re-worded to state that the patient "remains in the approved centre as a voluntary patient."
[307] [2009] I.E.H.C. 236; High Court, Peart J., May 15, 2009.

'discharge'. But the provisions of s.29 of the Act support the idea that a person, whose detention under an admission order/renewal order, may remain at the approved centre after he or she has ceased to be subject to an involuntary detention order. That section does not state in any way that consent in that regard is required. It facilitates the situation in which these applicants are, by giving the approved centre the ability to continue to care and treat the patient where it would be inappropriate to release him or her onto the street, where to do so would place the patient at risk if not accompanied by a responsible family member."[308]

Earlier in the same judgment, Peart J. notes that while s.28(1) requires that the order be revoked if the opinion is that the patient is no longer suffering from a mental disorder and that the patient be discharged, the provisions of s.28(2) are also relevant. He says that, "the revocation of the order and the discharge of the patient are two distinct matters, even if one follows upon the other."[309] Section 28(2) requires the consultant psychiatrist, following the revocation of the Admission/Renewal order, to have regard, inter alia, to the need to ensure "(a) that the patient is not inappropriately discharged." Peart J. continues:

"The section does not provide that before making a revocation order the psychiatrist must have regard to the need not to inappropriately discharge the patient. The appropriateness of a discharge is not a condition precedent to the revocation of the order. The order must be revoked if the patient no longer suffers from a mental disorder as defined. It seems to me to make complete sense that following the revocation order, a consultant psychiatrist must retain the capacity to ensure that a patient is not thereupon discharged from the hospital into a situation of, say, danger, to himself or others. As I have said, this follows from the ongoing duty of care owed to a particularly vulnerable person."[310]

4–115 Where the RCP discharges the patient under s.28, they must give to the patient and their legal representative a notice to the effect that they:

(a) are being discharged pursuant to s.28, and
(b) are entitled to have their detention reviewed by a tribunal or, where such review has commenced, completed, if they so indicate by notice in writing addressed to the Commission within 14 days of the date of discharge.

This notice is incorporated into Form 14, a copy of which must be given to the patient. A copy of the form must also be sent to the Commission and, where appropriate, the HSE and housing authority.[311] The Commission has also noted

---

[308] [2009] I.E.H.C. 236; High Court, Peart J., May 15, 2009, p.41.
[309] [2009] I.E.H.C. 236; High Court, Peart J., May 15, 2009, p.41.
[310] [2009] I.E.H.C. 236; High Court, Peart J., May 15, 2009, p.41.
[311] Section 28(4).

that it is good practice to send a copy of the form to the person's registered medical practitioner.[312]

4–116 A number of Admission and Renewal orders are revoked shortly before MHT hearings are due to take place, an issue which will be discussed at para.7–13 below.

The Minister of State for Mental Health has expressed concern at the high number of revocations before tribunal hearings, and suggested that, if MHT hearings were held at an earlier stage in the 21-day period, the number of orders revoked before the MHT hearing would be likely to fall. He also noted that, "[i]t is of course appropriate that admission orders are revoked when the patent is no longer suffering from a mental disorder."[313]

Discharge due to Defect in Admission Order

4–117 If a fundamental defect in an Admission Order is discovered after the patient has been detained, the psychiatrist may decide to revoke the order and request that the patient remain in the approved centre as a voluntary patient. If the patient does not wish to remain as a voluntary patient, and the psychiatrist believes that the patient is a risk of harm to themselves or others, the psychiatrist might choose to inform the Gardaí of this, with a view to initiating the procedure under s.12 of the 2001 Act. This is what occurred in *F.W. v Dept. of Psychiatry James Connolly Memorial Hospital*.[314] An application for a recommendation had originally been made by the proposed patient's husband but once it was discovered that the proposed patient had previously initiated proceedings under the Domestic Violence Act against her husband, the psychiatrist revoked the Admission Order. The psychiatrist tried to persuade F.W. to remain. F.W. used her mobile phone to leave a voice message for her solicitor. Despite being advised by the psychiatrist that she was free to leave, she did not do so. She subsequently received a text message from her solicitor, advising her to leave the hospital. She approached staff at 11.00pm and told them that she had received this message. At 11.30pm she left the hospital, but was met outside by the Gardaí, with whom she went to the Garda station. The Garda presence was as a result of the psychiatrist earlier notifying the Gardaí of the situation.

At the Garda station she was examined by a doctor. He had previously spoken with the psychiatrist and taken a medical history from her of the applicant. He talked with F.W. for about 45 minutes. He formed the view on the basis of the history he had taken at his interview that she needed to be admitted in order to keep her safe from herself. As a result of this doctor's certification, the applicant was delivered back to the hospital at 1.10am and was there assessed, admitted and detained.

---

[312] *Reference Guide: Adults*, section 2.5, p.2.
[313] *Review of the Operation of the Mental Health Act 2001*, p.22.
[314] [2008] I.E.H.C. 283; High Court, Hedigan J., August 18, 2008.

One of the arguments made was that F.W. had never been released in reality from an admitted unlawful detention. Hedigan J. said that the hospital was not responsible for the fact that her admission had been invalidly made and, in fact, had discovered this fact itself. The hospital had then acted promptly to obtain legal advice to clarify the situation and had notified the applicant that she was free to go. Rather than allow F.W. to depart into the night with no arrangements made to ensure her safety or continuing care, the psychiatrist contacted the Gardaí with a view to having them act under s.12 of the Mental Health Act. They delayed her departure until the Gardaí could come and when she left the hospital, she was immediately taken into custody by them under s.12(1)(a). The applicant was told at 8pm she was free to leave but she did not do so. When she did finally decide to leave she was allowed to do so but not until she had been delayed by staff insisting she talk to the psychiatrist first. There was no evidence that she was restrained in any physical way. She was delayed for about 40 minutes, although she could have ignored all requests to talk to the psychiatrist and could have just walked out. The 40-minute delay period was used to alert the Gardaí, who dispatched a car to the hospital. In Hedigan J.'s view, F.W. was free to leave from 8pm The fact that she was told there would likely be a recommital process did not invalidate her release.[315]

4–118 Hedigan J. considered the action of the psychiatrist and her staff to be "highly creditable in the circumstances."[316] Dealing with a very difficult situation, their predominant interest was the care and safety of the applicant. Their action ensured as best they could that when the applicant did leave their care, she did not depart into the night with no arrangements to ensure her safety and well-being. The actions of the psychiatrist and her staff and those of the Gardaí may well have prevented a tragic outcome to the day's events.[317]

It was also argued that the removal of F.W. by the Gardaí to the hospital on the recommendation of the doctor was not valid because the Gardaí's initial belief under s.12(1) of the 2001 Act was not an independent judgment and neither was the recommendation made by the doctor. It was argued that both had been made entirely at the behest of the psychiatrist. Hedigan J. said that the fact that the approved centre itself is precluded under s.9(2)(c) of the 2001 Act from making an application for involuntary admission to their own centre, does not preclude them from being an informant.[318] In certain circumstances, notably present in this case, they may well be the very body with the greatest respon-sibility to do so. Because they act on information of great weight does not mean that the belief of the Gardaí is ipso facto not an independent one. No other evidence or submission being made against the belief of the Gardaí in this case,

[315]   [2008] I.E.H.C. 283; High Court, Hedigan J., August 18, 2008, p.5.
[316]   [2008] I.E.H.C. 283; High Court, Hedigan J., August 18, 2008, p.5.
[317]   [2008] I.E.H.C. 283; High Court, Hedigan J., August 18, 2008, pp.5–6.
[318]   [2008] I.E.H.C. 283; High Court, Hedigan J., August 18, 2008, pp.6–7.

he considered their taking the applicant into custody at the hospital was in accordance with law.[319]

4–119 Regarding the role of the doctor who examined F.W. at the Garda station, it was clear that he did, in fact, make contact by telephone with the psychiatrist earlier in the evening when he was first alerted to the possibility that he would be called to the Garda station for a s.12 investigation. It was, in Hedigan J.'s judgment, perfectly correct and proper for him to do so; indeed, he would have thought it something he was bound to do where possible.[320] The fact that he accepted the psychiatrist's view of the applicant's mental state was hardly surprising but did not show a failure to exercise an independent judgment. He interviewed F.W. for 45 minutes and showed considerable compassion and sympathy for her situation. There was no evidence that the doctor failed to exercise an independent judgment and in this regard his recommendation was properly made.[321]

---

[319]   [2008] I.E.H.C. 283; High Court, Hedigan J., August 18, 2008, p.7.
[320]   [2008] I.E.H.C. 283; High Court, Hedigan J., August 18, 2008, p.7.
[321]   [2008] I.E.H.C. 283; High Court, Hedigan J., August 18, 2008, p.7.

CHAPTER 5

VOLUNTARY PATIENTS

INTRODUCTION

5–01 Voluntary admissions represent the vast majority of admissions to psychiatric centres. On one calculation, in 2007 91.5 per cent of patients were admitted on a voluntary basis.[1] However, this figure does not include 623 patients who were re-graded from voluntary to involuntary status in 2007,[2] which would make the percentage of involuntary admissions and re-gradings combined roughly 11.5 per cent and the voluntary admissions roughly 88.5 per cent.[3] In the 2007 Mental Health Commission census, 84.8 per cent of residents of approved centres had been admitted on a voluntary basis.[4] The percentage of residents with voluntary status is lower than the percentage of admissions on a voluntary basis. The census records the numbers of residents (3,314) on one particular night, whereas the number of admissions (20,769) is recorded over the full 365 days of the year.

5–02 Even though most patients have voluntary status, there is very little by way of direct reference in the Mental Health Act 2001 to voluntary patients. However, as will be seen below, the various requirements concerning approved centres apply to all residents, whether voluntary or involuntary.

---

[1] There were 20,769 admissions in 2007 of which 19,013 (91.5 per cent) were voluntary and 1,756 (8.5 per cent) were non-voluntary—Antoinette Daly, Dermot Walsh & Ros Moran, *H.R.B. Statistics Series 5: Activities of Irish Psychiatric Units and Hospitals 2007* (Health Research Board, 2008), Table 2.7, p.46. The preliminary HRB bulletin for 2008 records 20,752 admissions, of which 8% were involuntary—Daly, *National Psychiatric In-Patient Reporting System Preliminary National Bulletin Ireland 2008*, p.1.

[2] Mental Health Commission, *Annual Report 2007*, Table 9, Book 1, p.36.

[3] The non-voluntary admissions and re-gradings combined would total 2,379 of 20,769 admissions. However, note the differences between Health Research Board (HRB) and Mental Health Commission figures. The HRB records 1,756 involuntary admissions, whereas the Mental Health Commission records 1,503. For an explanation of these discrepancies see Daly, Walsh & Moran, *H.R.B. Statistics Series 5: Activities of Irish Psychiatric Units and Hospitals 2007* (Health Research Board, 2008), p.14, fn.1: "Data contained in this report does not include data on Admission Orders to detain Voluntary Patients whereas MHC figures do. In addition, this report does not include data for all centres approved by the Mental Health Commission (MHC) in accordance with the provisions of the Mental Health Act 2001 (Department of Health and Children 2001)."

[4] Mental Health Commission, *Annual Report 2007*, p.58.

5–03 A central issue in discussion of voluntary patients is the question of de facto detention, which may occur in a number of ways. The "voluntary" patient may wish to leave the centre but may not insist on this for fear of being re-graded to involuntary status. Alternatively, the patient may not have capacity to express a wish either way and simply comply with residence and treatment in the approved centre. A final complication is that the doors of many wards are locked, even for voluntary patients. In the Tipperary inquiry report, it was found that most long-stay wards were locked and some staff referred to "parole" for residents, although few were detained. No policy governed the locking of wards and the necessity was not reviewed. Residents' choices, freedoms and opportunities were restricted more than was necessary for their care and treatment and, as a result, their lives were "impoverished".[5]

5–04 Principle 15 of the UN's Mental Illness Principles[6] states that every patient not admitted involuntarily shall have the right to leave the mental health facility at any time unless the criteria for their retention as an involuntary patient, as set forth in Principle 16, apply, and they shall be informed of that right. In order to comply with this principle, ideally any patient admitted on a voluntary basis should be given a document stating that they have the right to leave at any time unless it is determined that they have a mental disorder within the meaning of s.3 of the 2001 Act. As this does not happen in practice, it is arguable that legislation is required to comply fully with the Principles.[7] It may be argued that in some situations, informing a person that they have a right to leave (unless they come within s.3) will confuse them, upset them or interfere with their care plan but, through consultation with service users and professional bodies, these issues could be addressed.

VOLUNTARY ADMISSION UNDER THE MENTAL TREATMENT ACT 1945

5–05 Under the Mental Treatment Act 1945, the expression "voluntary patient" meant "a person who acting by himself or, in the case of a person less than sixteen years of age, by his parent or guardian, submits himself voluntarily for treatment for illness of a mental or kindred nature".[8] Where a voluntary patient became mentally incapable of expressing themselves as willing or not willing

---

[5] Mental Health Commission, *Report of the Committee of Inquiry to review care and treatment practices in St. Michael's Unit, South Tipperary General Hospital, Clonmel and St. Luke's Hospital, Clonmel, including the quality and planning of care and the use of restraint and seclusion and to report to the Mental Health Commission* (2009), p.7.

[6] United Nations, *Principles for the protection of persons with mental illness and the improvement of mental health care*, adopted by General Assembly resolution 46/119 of 17 December 1991 [Known as the MI Principles].

[7] As an interim measure, a Mental Health Commission code of practice on the issue could be developed.

[8] Mental Treatment Act 1945, s.3.

to remain in the institution, they had to be discharged within 28 days unless a Reception Order, i.e. an order for involuntary admission, was obtained.[9]

5–06 In the case of an adult (i.e. a person over 16), the person was required to complete a statutory form, if a public patient, or apply in writing, if private, to be admitted.[10] Children under 16 could be admitted on the application of a parent or guardian, following a recommendation from a doctor.[11] Where a child who was being treated as a voluntary patient ceased to have a parent or guardian or the parent or guardian was incapable of performing or refused or neglected to perform their duties as such, the person in charge of the institution was required to send to the Minister a report on the circumstances of the case and to carry out all such directions as the Minister might think fit to give consequent upon such report.[12] An offence was committed by any person who, otherwise than in accordance with the provisions of the 1945 Act, received and detained, or undertook for payment the care and control of, a person who was, or was alleged to be, of unsound mind.[13]

5–07 In *J.H. v Russell*[14] Clarke J. held that, if the relevant period where a patient was, apparently, a voluntary patient under the 1945 Act, was not in substance properly voluntary, this rendered their detention unlawful. Mr H. had been detained on an involuntary basis for two years (March 2003 to March 2005), followed by apparently voluntary status for six months (March to September 2005) and then, finally, further involuntary detention from September 2005 to January 2007. Clarke J. outlines the circumstances as follows:

> "In early March, 2005 it is clear that Mr. H. was approaching the expiry of the maximum two year detention period permitted under the 1945 Act for temporary patients. In those circumstances it would appear that Mr. H. was informed that it would be necessary that he be certified to be a person of unsound mind and transferred to St. Davnet's, Co. Monaghan or to the Central Mental Hospital. It is clear that Mr. H. was unhappy with that prospect and in those circumstances signed a document which, on its face, allowed him to continue in Cavan General as a voluntary patient. It appears to be accepted that notwithstanding the fact that Mr. H. was a voluntary patient he was,

---

[9]   Section 195 of 1945 Act.
[10] For public patients, see s.190 of the Mental Treatment Act 1945 as amended and adapted by s.19 of the Mental Treatment 1961 and Mental Treatment Acts (Adaptation) Order 1971, S.I. No.108 of 1971 and see Form 8 of Mental Treatment Regulations 1961 (S.I. No. 461 of 1961.) For private patients see s.191 of 1945 Act as amended by s.20 of 1961 Act.
[11] Sections 190–191 of 1945 Act as amended by ss.19–20 of 1961 Act and adapted by Adaptation Order 1971. Interestingly, the requirement of a recommendation from a doctor had originally applied to both adults and children, and it was only by the amendments in 1961 that this was limited to children.
[12] Section 196 of 1945 Act.
[13] Section 250 of 1945 Act.
[14] [2007] I.E.H.C. 7; [2007] 4 I.R. 242.

nonetheless, subject to restrictions. Furthermore it appears that some of those, in whose charge Mr. H. was, had concerns as to whether he had truly become a voluntary patient."[15]

It was suggested that the period of apparent voluntary detention was not genuine in that Mr H. was subjected to an identical regime concerning control (some of it not, apparently, in accordance with his wishes) when he was formally detained under detention orders and when he was, apparently, a voluntary patient. It was also questioned as to whether Mr H. was truly a consensual patient during the relevant period. Some of those in whose charge Mr H. was placed questioned, at that time, the validity of his detention on that basis.[16]

In those circumstances, Clarke J. stated that he "was not satisfied that the relevant period during which Mr. H. was, apparently, a voluntary patient, was in substance properly voluntary and [he was] therefore satisfied that he was inappropriately detained."[17] Clarke J. was mindful of the fact that the courts have had regard, when looking at the process which may have led to the detention of persons under the Mental Treatment Acts, to the fact that the legislation is designed, at least in significant part, for the protection of the individuals concerned. However, he noted that "the legislation cannot be construed in a way which goes against the clear meaning and intent of the provisions which limit involuntary detention under s. 184 to a maximum of twenty four months."[18] While he fully understood the pressures which may have led those in charge of Mr H. to attempt to devise means of ensuring his continued treatment (which they clearly considered desirable), notwithstanding the defective legislation within which they were operating, he was nonetheless satisfied that his detention was unlawful.

5–08 The unlawfulness of this supposedly voluntary period of detention was a major factor[19] in Clarke J.'s eventual decision to release Mr H. from custody, although he did make the order in a form which allowed the hospital to re-invoke the provisions of the 2001 Act and detain Mr H. again before he was released. It is interesting that no argument appears to have been made that the restrictions on H. were justified by the common law doctrine of necessity. Perhaps the legal teams decided that there was no point in making such arguments given the decision in the *Bournewood* case at European Court of Human Rights level, which had been issued in 2004 and will be discussed below at paras 5–28 to 5–29.

In this case, Clarke J. held that, under the 1945 Act, if a patient was in "voluntary" detention which was not genuinely voluntary, their detention was

---

[15] [2007] I.E.H.C. 7 at para.2.7.
[16] [2007] I.E.H.C. 7 at para.6.4.
[17] [2007] I.E.H.C. 7 at para.6.4.
[18] [2007] I.E.H.C. 7 at para.6.5.
[19] The other factor was that the applicant had been detained under the "temporary patient" provisions of the 1945 Act even though he was not likely to recover within six months.

unlawful. The requirement of genuine voluntariness did not apply for a number of reasons: Mr H. had signed the voluntary patient form because he did not wish to be transferred to another hospital, he was subjected to the same control as if he were involuntary (some of it apparently against his wishes) and he was not "truly a consensual patient". Clarke J. does not engage in a textual analysis of the 1945 Act and it appears that he is relying on the ordinary meaning of the word "voluntary" in the Act.

5–09 If a voluntary patient admitted under the 1945 Act wished to leave, they, or their parent or guardian, could give notice of their intention to leave. In the case of an adult, this notice had to be of at least 72 hours duration, but no such requirement applied to children.[20] It was held in *Gooden v St. Otteran's Hospital*[21] that, during the 72-hour period, an application for involuntary admission could be made, and that the patient did not have a statutory right to a second opinion.

PROVISIONS OF THE MENTAL HEALTH ACT 2001 CONCERNING
VOLUNTARY PATIENTS

5–10 In general, the 2001 Act does not apply to voluntary patients. The main purpose of the Act, as stated in the Long Title, is to provide for involuntary admission to approved centres. Throughout the Act, references to a "patient" refer to an adult who is admitted on an involuntary basis under the Act.[22]

5–11 Section 2 states that a "voluntary patient" refers to a person receiving care and treatment in an approved centre who is not the subject of an admission order or a renewal order.[23] The word "voluntary" is not defined and, while it might be assumed that the person should have the mental capacity to agree to their treatment, the case of *E.H. v Clinical Director of St. Vincent's Hospital* (below, paras 5–32 to 5–37) holds otherwise.

If the Supreme Court's interpretation of the meaning of "voluntary patient" in the *E.H.* case is correct, then it is arguable that the 2001 Act provides less protection for voluntary patients than the 1945 Act did. As was stated above, the 1945 Act defined a voluntary adult patient as a person who "submits himself voluntarily for treatment" and Clarke J. held in *J.H. v Russell* that the voluntary detention must be genuinely voluntary. By way of contrast, the 2001 Act defines a voluntary patient as a person receiving care and treatment who is not the subject of an Admission or Renewal Order. Implicit in the definition may be a sense that the State is not concerned with whether the person "volunteered" or

---

[20]   Section 194 of 1945 Act.
[21]   [2001] I.E.S.C. 14; [2005] 3 I.R. 617.
[22]   Section 2(1) of the 2001 Act states that "patient" is to be construed in accordance with section 14. Section 14 provides for Admission Orders for persons other than children.
[23]   Section 2(1).

consented to their admission. To unpack this further, it may be that the State was conscious in drafting the Act that there were a number of people in psychiatric institutions, at least at the time of drafting the legislation, who had never submitted voluntarily for their treatment but had become institutionalised. Rather than retaining the previous involuntary/voluntary distinction, the State created a new categorisation of involuntary/everybody else. This allows less scope for querying the basis on which a so-called "voluntary" patient came to be in the centre and continues to be there.

5–12 If the above interpretation is to apply, then it may be queried why the word "voluntary" was used at all. The English and Welsh legislation refers to "informal" admission and this might have been a more appropriate label to apply to people in this category.[24] Eldergill has commented as follows:

> "In most jurisdictions, the term 'voluntary admission' denotes a patient who has capacity to consent, or 'volunteer', to go into hospital. In contrast, 'informal admission' means admission without legal formalities—the underlying idea being that a person may be admitted without the need for a legal order even if they lack capacity to consent to this.
>
> What is the position here? The wording of sections 2 (Interpretation) and 29 (Voluntary admission to approved centres) suggests that in fact 'voluntary admission' means 'informal admission'."[25]

Similarly, in the *Bournewood* case, it was submitted by the Secretary of State for Health that "informal patients" should, strictly speaking, be distinguished from "voluntary patients".[26]

5–13 The use of the word "voluntary" has certainly led to misunderstandings as to the meaning of voluntary status under the 2001 Act. It is likely that many people reading the Act, and associated information and commentary, would assume that the status of voluntary patient applied to people who chose to admit themselves voluntarily and had capacity to do so. As a matter of principle, in any revision of the 2001 Act, the wording should be clarified and the word "voluntary" should be replaced where appropriate. Categorisations and labels are important, and have a real impact on how legislation is operated.

5–14 As a matter of statutory interpretation, should judges have regard to the use of the word "voluntary" to define patients who are not, in fact, voluntary? It is quite common for legislation to define words in a manner which is different

---

[24] See heading of s.131 of the Mental Health Act 1983 (England and Wales); Richard Jones, *Mental Health Act Manual*, 11th edn (London: Thomson Sweet and Maxwell, 2008), p.479 *et seq.*

[25] Anselm Eldergill, "The Best Is the Enemy of the Good: The Mental Health Act 2001" (2008) J. Mental Health L. 21 at 26.

[26] *R. v Bournewood Community and Mental Health NHS Trust, ex parte L.* [1999] 1 A.C. 458 at 483.

from the ordinary meaning of the words. Murnaghan J. said in 1952 in *Mason v Leavy*, "where a statute such as the Rent Restrictions Act, 1946, defines its own terms and makes what has been called its own dictionary, a Court should not depart from the definitions given by the statute and the meanings assigned to the words used in the statute."[27] However, the canons of statutory interpretation have evolved since 1952, and been modified by the Interpretation Act 2005. In addition, we are not dealing here with rent restrictions legislation; this is an Act concerning constitutional and human rights to liberty.

5–15　The first part of s.29 states that nothing in the Act prevents a person from being admitted voluntarily to an approved centre for treatment, without any application, recommendation or admission order being made under the Act. The second part states that nothing in the Act prevents a person from remaining in an approved centre after they have ceased to be so liable to be detained.

　　The first part of s.29 applies to a person who is admitted on a voluntary basis from the start and the second part means that if a person has been detained on an involuntary basis under the Act and the period of their detention has expired without being renewed, they may remain in the centre as a voluntary patient. The word "voluntarily" does not appear in the second part of s.29.

　　The wording of s.29 is quite similar to the equivalent English section on "informal admission".[28] However, the English section refers to a patient being admitted who "requires treatment for mental disorder", whereas the Irish section refers to a person being admitted "for treatment."[29] Either way, reference may be made to the English case of *R. v Kirkless Metropolitan Borough Council, ex parte C.*,[30] in which it was held that the section on informal admission applied to treatment only, not to assessment of a patient. However, the court went on to hold that a patient could be admitted to hospital for assessment at common law, provided he or she consented. As a result, the patient's action to quash the admission failed.[31]

5–16　It is arguable that the reference to "admitted voluntarily" in the first part of s.29 is not covered by the definition of "voluntary patient" in s.2. However, a counter-argument is that, reading the Act as a whole, it would appear that any reference to "voluntary" or "voluntarily" is intended to be covered by the

---

[27]　[1952] I.R. 40 at 47.

[28]　Section 131 of the Mental Health Act 1983 (England and Wales).

[29]　Another difference is that the English section refers to a "patient", which is defined in s.145(1) of the English Act as "a person suffering or appearing to be suffering from mental disorder" whereas the Irish s.29 refers to a "person".

[30]　[1993] 2 F.L.R. 187.

[31]　See discussion of this case in Peter Bartlett & Ralph Sandland, *Mental Health Law: Policy and Practice*, 3rd edn (Oxford: Oxford University Press, 2007) at p.112, where they express doubts as to the self-evidence of such a common law power of admission. The case concerned a child aged 12 who was in care, and consent for voluntary admission had been given by the local authority.

definition of voluntary patient in s.2. In addition, s.20(2) of the Interpretation Act 2005 states that where an Act defines or otherwise interprets a word or expression, other parts of speech and grammatical forms of the word or expression have a corresponding meaning. This is not a complete answer to the issue, as it remains arguable that s.2 defines the *expression* "voluntary patient" (as opposed to the *word* "voluntarily") and the expression "voluntary patient" does not appear in any grammatical form in s.29.

Perhaps the drafters of the 2001 Act intended to keep the concept of voluntary admission as contained in the 1945 Act (but removing the formalities for such admission), while adding on a new concept of informal status (without reference to voluntariness) for those who remained in the centre after their involuntary detention had ended. Rather than defining these concepts separately, a decision was made to use the expression "voluntary patients" to apply to both. Once this was done, this may have had the unintended consequence that the word "voluntary" ceased to have the meaning it had under the 1945 Act.

5–17 Another reference to voluntary patients in the Act is contained in s.16(2), concerning the information notice given to patients who are detained involuntarily. One of the items of information is that the patient must be told that he or she "may be admitted to the approved centre concerned as a voluntary patient if he or she indicates a wish to be so admitted".[32] This appears to indicate that the Oireachtas believed that voluntary status is something which is normally requested by means of indicating a wish to have that status. A counter argument which may be made is that s.16(2) is merely stating that *some* patients might become voluntary patients in this manner, but it does not necessarily apply to all voluntary patients.

5–18 While those sections of the Act dealing with involuntary admission and Mental Health Tribunal (MHT) hearings do not apply to voluntary patients, the following sections *do* apply to them:

- Section 2(1): "Mental health services" means services which provide care and treatment to persons suffering from a mental illness or mental disorder under the clinical direction of a clinical psychiatrist.
- Section 33: The Mental Health Commission must promote and foster high standards in the delivery of mental health services and must prepare codes of practice for the guidance of persons working in the mental health services
- Section 51: The Inspector of Mental Health Services visits every approved centre and any other premises where mental health services are being provided as he or she thinks appropriate
- Part 5 (ss.62–68) concerning approved centres applies to both involuntary and voluntary patients being treated at those centres (referred to as "residents")

---

[32] Mental Health Act 2001, s.16(2)(g).

- Section 69 on bodily restraint and seclusion applies to both involuntary and voluntary patients
- Section 23 applies when an adult voluntary patient indicates that they wish to leave an approved centre, or the parent(s) of a child who is voluntary patient indicate that they wish to remove the child from the centre. This may then lead to invocation of the "re-grading" procedures discussed below.[33]

In addition, the Approved Centre Regulations[34] apply to both involuntary and voluntary residents. The Regulations include the important requirement of an individual care plan for each resident.[35]

5–19 Because Part 4 of the 2001 Act (ss.56–61) regarding consent to treatment only applies to involuntary patients, the voluntary patient is governed by common law rules regarding consent. In addition, medical and nursing staff need to take care *not* to use the procedures in Pt 4 regarding voluntary patients. This means, for example, that if a voluntary patient does not have the capacity to consent to administration of medicine, such medicine may not be administered except under common law rules.

Voluntary patients may participate in clinical trials, as s.70 of the 2001 Act only applies to a person admitted to an approved centre under the 2001 Act.[36]

5–20 The procedure under the 2001 Act regarding "re-grading" of voluntary patients who wish to leave (or children whose parents wish to remove them) is covered below at paras 5–41 to 5–55. Adults may be detained for up to 24 hours, while children may be detained for up to three days. The reason for the difference in timing is because a District Court sitting needs to be arranged in the case of a child.

5–21 If a voluntary patient wishes to institute civil proceedings in respect of their admission or treatment, leave of the High Court will not be required. This is because s.73 only applies to proceedings "in respect of an act purporting to have been done in pursuance of" the Mental Health Act 2001.[37] A voluntary patient is not admitted or treated under the Mental Health Act 2001.[38] English

---

[33] See paras 5–41 to 5–55 below.

[34] Mental Health Act 2001 (Approved Centres) Regulations 2006, S.I. No. 551 of 2006.

[35] See further Chapter 12 below.

[36] Section 70 of the 2001 Act states that notwithstanding s.9(7) of the Control of Clinical Trials Act 1987, a person suffering from a mental disorder who has been admitted to an approved centre under this Act shall not be a participant in a clinical trial. See further paras 10–62 to 10–67 below.

[37] Section 73(1) of 2001 Act.

[38] Contrast the position prior to the 2001 Act, where the voluntary patient was admitted under the Mental Treatment Act 1945 and therefore would have required leave of the High Court for civil proceedings in respect of an act purporting to have been done in pursuance of the 1945 Act.

authorities on this point must be read with caution.[39] Even though a voluntary patient may well be a resident in an approved centre and approved centres are regulated by the 2001 Act, the patient could still bring proceedings without the leave of the High Court regarding most aspects of their treatment, except where there was a direct connection (or a purported direct connection) between the Mental Health Act and the cause of action.

5–22 The code of practice on admission, transfer and discharge states that it is considered good administrative practice to use an admission form for voluntary patients, similar to that used for persons admitting themselves to hospital for medical or surgical procedures, which includes a general consent for admission and treatment. The code states that this does not obviate the need to obtain consent for specific treatment interventions.[40]

VOLUNTARY ADMISSION OF CHILDREN

5–23 If a child is to be admitted and treated on a voluntary basis, the 2001 Act does not state whether it is the child who consents to admission or their parents or guardians. In s.23(2), it is stated that parents or persons acting in *loco parentis* might wish to remove the child who is being treated as a voluntary patient from the approved centre, which implies that parents and persons acting in *loco parentis* would normally make the decision to have the child admitted. The Code of Practice on the admission of children states that if a child is to receive voluntary in-patient treatment, consent of one or both parents must be obtained.[41] The code discusses in detail the difficulty in reconciling the 2001 Act with s.23 of the Non-Fatal Offences against the Person Act 1997 (see further paras 10–54 to 10–61 below).

5–24 In *Nielsen v Denmark*[42] it was held by nine votes to seven that a deprivation of liberty under art.5 had not occurred where a 12-year-old boy was placed in a psychiatric hospital with his mother's consent, but against his own wishes and those of his father. His mother had sole legal guardianship. The boy had been living "underground" with his father for a number of years, as he did

---

[39] See *R v Runighian* [1977] Crim. L.R. 361 (dealings with informal patients are not covered by s.139 Mental Health Act 1983, which requires leave of the court for proceedings to be brought, as such dealings are not conducted "in pursuance of this Act"); however, Peter Bartlett and Ralph Sandland, *Mental Health Law: Policy and Practice*, 3rd edn (Oxford: Oxford University Press, 2007), p.339, comment that this is questionable under English law.

[40] Mental Health Commission, *Code of Practice on Admission, Transfer and Discharge to and from an Approved Centre* (2009), para.22.2.

[41] Mental Health Commission, *Code of Practice Relating to Admission of Children Under the Mental Health Act 2001*, COP–S33(3)/01/2006, para.2.8.

[42] (1989) 11 E.H.R.R. 175.

not wish to live with his mother. The chief physician accepted the request for admission because he found that the applicant was in a neurotic state requiring treatment and that hospitalisation was in the interest of the boy's health.

The court stated that the decision on the question of hospitalisation was taken by the mother in her capacity as holder of parental rights.[43] The care and upbringing of children normally and necessarily require that the parents or an only parent decide where the child must reside and also impose, or authorise others to impose, various restrictions on the child's liberty.[44] The boy was in need of medical treatment for his nervous condition and the treatment administered to him was curative, aiming at securing his recovery from his neurosis. This treatment did not involve medication, but consisted of regular talks and environmental therapy. The restrictions on his freedom of movement and contacts with the outside world were not much different from restrictions which might be imposed on a child in an ordinary hospital. The door of the ward, like all children's wards in the hospital, was locked, but this was to prevent the children exposing themselves to danger or running around and disturbing other patients. In general, conditions in the ward were said to be "as similar as possible to a real home". The duration of his treatment was five-and-a-half months. This may appear to be a rather long time for a boy of 12 years of age, but it did not "exceed the average period of therapy at the ward and, in addition, the restrictions imposed were relaxed as treatment progressed.[45] The restrictions imposed on him were not of a nature or degree similar to the cases of deprivation of liberty specified in art.5(1). In particular, he was not detained as a person of unsound mind so as to bring the case within art.5(1)(e).[46]

The dissenting judges stated that they attached great importance to the fact that the committal lasted over a period of several months and involved the placing in a psychiatric ward of a 12-year-old boy who was not mentally ill. In their view, that constituted a deprivation of liberty within the meaning of art.5.[47] Six of the dissenting judges also would have found a violation of art.5(4) because the boy was detained in a psychiatric hospital over a period of several months, during which period he did not have the right to take proceedings in a court because he was not suffering from a mental disorder, whereas, para-doxically, he would have had such a right if he had, in fact, been mentally ill.

Grosz and others have doubted whether the *Nielsen* case will be followed in future. They also state that in considering any similar issue today, account should

[43]   (1989) 11 E.H.R.R. 175, para.63.
[44]   (1989) 11 E.H.R.R. 175, para.61.
[45]   (1989) 11 E.H.R.R. 175, para.70.
[46]   (1989) 11 E.H.R.R. 175, para.72.
[47]   Joint Dissenting Opinion of Judges Thór Vilhjálmsson, Pettiti, Russo, Spielmann, De Meyer, Carrillo Salcedo and Valticos.

be taken of the Convention on the Rights of the Child 1989.[48] *Nielsen* has been referred to elsewhere as a "somewhat extreme case".[49]

5–25 The International Covenant on Civil and Political Rights (ICCPR) shadow report of 2008 noted that the voluntary admission of a child under the Mental Health Act 2001 appears to be the sole responsibility of parents or persons acting in *loco parentis*. The report stated that this could result in children being admitted to institutions and detained against their will under the Act, despite being competent to make their own decisions.[50]

DE FACTO DETENTION AND THE *BOURNEWOOD* CASE

5–26 Even though a person may be classified as a "voluntary" patient, it may well happen that they feel coerced in some manner, in other words that they are "*de facto* detained." This is a phenomenon which has been widely commented upon and discussed in mental health law.[51] One way in which this may occur is because the patient may not wish to be re-graded as an involuntary patient, and so continues in the voluntary category, even though they would actually prefer to leave the centre. These problems become more acute in the case of a person who lacks capacity to consent to admission as a voluntary patient, who may be referred to as an "incapable compliant patient".[52] The categorisation "the *Bournewood* gap" has recently been applied to some of these patients, due to the *Bournewood* case, which went through the English courts and then on to the European Court of Human Rights.

5–27 The proceedings in the Court of Appeal and the House of Lords are reported as *R. v Bournewood Community and Mental Health NHS Trust, ex parte L.*[53] L. was 48 years old and had autism, could not speak and had learning disabilities. He became agitated from time to time and sometimes injured himself. He was being cared for by foster carers, Mr and Mrs E. He was

---

[48] Stephen Grosz, Jack Beatson & Peter Duffy, *Human Rights: The 1998 Act and the European Convention* (London: Sweet & Maxwell, 2000), p.199.

[49] Peter Bartlett, Oliver Lewis and Oliver Thorold, *Mental Disability and the European Convention on Human Rights* (Leiden: Martinus Nijhoff, 2006), p.132, fn.74.

[50] Free Legal Advice Centres, Irish Council for Civil Liberties and Irish Penal Reform Trust, *Shadow Report to the Third Periodic Report of Ireland under the International Covenant on Civil and Political Rights* (2008), p.53.

[51] See, for example, Peter Bartlett and Ralph Sandland, *Mental Health Law: Policy and Practice*, 3rd edn (Oxford: Oxford University Press, 2007), p.113, and articles cited therein.

[52] Claire Murray, "Safeguarding the Right to Liberty of Incapable Compliant Patients with a Mental Disorder In Ireland" (2007) 14 D.U.L.J. 279.

[53] [1999] 1 A.C. 458 (C.A. and H.L.); [1997] E.W.C.A. Civ. 2879; [1998] U.K.H.L. 24.

admitted to Bournewood Hospital as an informal patient, against the wishes of Mr and Mrs E. He was kept in an unlocked ward, but the staff of the hospital said that if he had tried to leave, they would have detained him under the Mental Health Act 1983. Through his next friend, L. sought various remedies, including judicial review of the decision to detain him, habeas corpus and damages for false imprisonment. At High Court level, it was held that L. was free to leave (until a doctor might take steps to detain him) and therefore was not detained. The Court of Appeal disagreed, holding that L. was not lawfully detained, as he was not capable of consenting to detention and no guardian had been appointed who could consent on his behalf, and awarded nominal damages of £1 for false imprisonment.[54] L. was then formally admitted under the Mental Health Act 1983 and later discharged into the care of Mr and Mrs E.[55]

5–28 At House of Lords level, Lord Goff referred to the potential impact of the Court of Appeal decision, as it would require additional numbers of patients to be formally admitted.[56] He relied heavily on the legislative history of the relevant English section on voluntary patients, and pointed out that this history had not been outlined to the Court of Appeal and the Court of Appeal had not had the benefit of the extra submissions which were made at House of Lords stage. In particular, Lord Goff referred to the Percy Commission report[57] in which it was said that compulsion and detention were quite unnecessary for the great majority of patients in mental hospitals. The Commission believed that it should no longer be assumed that compulsory powers must be used unless the patient can express a positive desire for treatment; instead, this should be replaced by the offer of care, without deprivation of liberty, to all who need it and are not unwilling to receive it. Lord Goff found that patients such as L. could be admitted as informal patients under the relevant English section (s.131) and their care and treatment could be justified on the basis of the common law doctrine of necessity.[58] He found that the tort of false imprisonment had not occurred, given the necessity for L's detention at the time and the fact that the medical staff were acting in L's best interests. He emphasised that the precedents on false imprisonment required that there must *in fact* be a complete deprivation of, or restraint upon, the plaintiff's liberty, and that restraint upon liberty which is conditional upon a person's seeking to exercise their freedom does not amount to false imprisonment.[59]

---

54 The damages were nominal due the principle that a person who is unaware that they have been imprisoned and who has suffered no harm can normally expect to recover nominal damages only—[1999] 1 A.C. 458 at 475.

55 [1999] 1 A.C. 458 at 480.

56 [1999] 1 A.C. 458 at 481–2. Lord Goff referred to submissions made by the Mental Health Commission, the Registered Nursing Home Association and the Secretary of State for Health.

57 *Report of the Royal Commission on the Law Relating to Mental Illness and Mental Deficiency 1954–1957*, chaired by Lord Percy, Cmd. 169 (London: H.M.S.O., 1957).

58 Here, Lord Goff cited *In Re F. (Mental Patient; Sterilisation)* [1990] 2 A.C. 1.

59 Lord Goff referred (at 486) to *Meering v. Grahame-White Aviation Co. Ltd.* (1919) 122 L.T. 44, 54–55.

While all five Law Lords agreed that the appeal should be allowed, and that L.'s detention was lawful, Lords Nolan and Steyn differed from the majority on the point of whether L. was, in fact, detained. Lord Steyn said that the suggestion that L. was free to go was a "fairy tale."[60] While he found that L.'s detention was lawful, he said it was regrettable that patients such as L. would not have adequate protection under legislation, but he took some comfort from the fact that reform of the law was being actively considered.[61]

The decision of the House of Lords has been criticised on various grounds. For example, it has been argued that it is "medico-centric", confirming what the doctors did, rather than patient-centred.[62]

The House of Lords did not make any reference to the European Convention on Human Rights (ECHR), because the Convention did not become part of English domestic law until after the *Bournewood* decision. L. sought redress before the European Court of Human Rights and the Court upheld his claim in *H.L. v United Kingdom*.[63] This case is one of the key European Court of Human Rights cases on mental health law, and has important implications for Irish law.

5–29 The European Court of Human Rights found breaches of both art.5(1) and art.5(4). The court said that it was not bound by the domestic court's legal conclusion as to whether L. was detained. The key factor was that the healthcare professionals treating and managing L. exercised complete and effective control over his care and movements.[64] The court recalled that the right to liberty was too important in a democratic society for a person to lose the benefit of Convention protection for the single reason that they might have given themselves up to be taken into detention, especially when it was not disputed that that person was legally incapable of consenting to, or disagreeing with, the proposed action.[65] It agreed that any suggestion that L. was free to leave was a "fairy tale." It was not determinative whether the ward was locked or not, and the court found that L. was deprived of his liberty.[66] While L. was "of unsound mind", his detention under art.5(1) was not lawful due to the lack of formalised admission procedures. L. was detained on the basis of the common law doctrine of necessity, but there were no limits in terms of time, treatment or care.[67] The court found that the absence of procedural safeguards failed to protect against arbitrary deprivations of liberty on grounds of necessity and therefore violated art.5(1).[68]

---

[60] [1999] 1 A.C. 458 at 495.
[61] [1999] 1 A.C. 458 at 497.
[62] John Hodgson, "Detention, Necessity, Common Law and the European Convention: Some Further Aspects of the Bournewood Case" (1999) J. Mental Health L. 23.
[63] (2005) 40 E.H.R.R. 32.
[64] (2005) 40 E.H.R.R. 32, para.91.
[65] (2005) 40 E.H.R.R. 32, para.91.
[66] (2005) 40 E.H.R.R. 32, para.94.
[67] (2005) 40 E.H.R.R. 32, para.120.
[68] (2005) 40 E.H.R.R. 32, para.124.

As regards art.5(4), which requires that a person be able to take proceedings by which the lawfulness of their detention may be decided, the European Court of Human Rights found that habeas corpus and judicial review were not adequate remedies for this purpose. It had already been held in *X. v UK*[69] that habeas corpus was not adequate, and there was no substantial difference in the circumstances in this case which would cause the *X.* case to be distinguished.[70] The court also found that judicial review was not sufficiently intrusive to constitute an examination of the merits of the relevant medical decisions.[71]

The court had held in previous cases[72] that, where violations established of art.5(1) and art.5(4) are of a procedural nature, the finding of a violation was sufficient just satisfaction as regards non-pecuniary damage.[73] Therefore, the court did not make any award of damages, but did order that costs and expenses be repaid.

5–30 The *H.L./Bournewood* case led to new legislation being passed in England and Wales, as part of the Mental Health Act 2007.[74] Jones has described these reforms as creating a procedure which is "hugely complex, voluminous, badly drafted, overly bureaucratic and difficult to understand, and yet provides mentally handicapped people with minimum safeguards."[75]

Reform of the law is also necessary in Ireland. At present, the only review available to incapable compliant patients is an application under Art.40, which has severe limitations as a remedy. As Murray has pointed out, the effect of this is that "some of the most vulnerable patients in the mental health system in Ireland are *de facto* detained without an adequate review mechanism".[76] The Scheme of a Mental Capacity Bill has been published but it does not address the problem of the *Bournewood* gap.[77] A comprehensive examination is needed of all the ramifications of the *H.L./Bournewood* case for Ireland.

CASE LAW CONCERNING VOLUNTARY PATIENTS UNDER THE 2001 ACT

5–31 There have been two significant cases concerning voluntary patients under the 2001 Act: *E.H. v Clinical Director of St. Vincent's Hospital*[78] and *M.McN. v*

---

[69] (1981) 4 E.H.R.R. 188.

[70] (2005) 40 E.H.R.R. 188, para.137.

[71] (2005) 40 E.H.R.R. 188, para.139.

[72] For example, *Nikolova v Bulgaria* (2001) 31 E.H.R.R. 3.

[73] *H.L. v U.K.* (2005) 40 E.H.R.R. 32, para.148.

[74] See Mental Health Act 2007, s.50, amending the Mental Capacity Act 2005.

[75] Richard Jones, *Mental Health Act Manual*, 11th edn (London: Thomson Sweet and Maxwell, 2008), p.v.

[76] Claire Murray, "Safeguarding the Right to Liberty of Incapable Compliant Patients with a Mental Disorder in Ireland" (2007) 14 D.U.L.J. 279 at 294.

[77] Department of Justice, Equality and Law Reform, *Scheme of Mental Capacity Bill 2008*. See further Chapter 13 below.

[78] [2009] I.E.H.C. 69; High Court, O'Neill J., February 6, 2009; [2009] I.E.S.C. 46; [2009] 2 I.L.R.M. 149; Supreme Court, May 28, 2009.

Health Service Executive.[79] In both cases, the patients were initially admitted on an involuntary basis and then remained in the centre after their involuntary detention ended. This means that their situations were governed by the second part of s.29 rather than the first. The second part of s.29 does not use the word "voluntarily". Arguments might be made in subsequent cases, governed by the first part of s.29, which uses the word "voluntarily", that a different interpretation should apply. These would be cases where the patient was initially admitted on a "voluntary" basis. One possibility might be that a person is admitted on a voluntary basis for a period of time and is then discharged. The person might then seek a declaration that their detention was unlawful due to factors such as restriction of liberty, psychological coercion, lack of genuine consent to residence in the centre, or lack of capacity to consent to voluntary admission. They could also perhaps seek a declaration that their treatment (e.g. medication given) was unlawful, as it was not administered with their genuine consent. This application would probably need to be taken by means of judicial review rather than an application under Art.40, as the patient's time in the centre would have ended.

A more complicated scenario would be where a patient is admitted on a voluntary basis and then seeks to argue while still in the centre that their status is unlawful. If legal proceedings were initiated, it is likely that the centre would either immediately discharge the patient or seek to use the re-grading procedure under ss.23 and 24. The discharge would weaken the patient's case, as it would be taken as evidence that the patient was free to leave if they requested. The re-grading under ss.23–24 would mean that reference could be made by the centre to the meaning of "voluntary patient" in ss.23–24, which is different from the use of the word "voluntarily" in s.29.

E.H. v Clinical Director of St. Vincent's Hospital

5–32 The patient in *E.H. v Clinical Director of St. Vincent's Hospital*[80] was detained in August 2008 but her renewal order was revoked by a tribunal on December 10, 2008, because the wrong date appeared on the order. The psychiatrist chose to treat her as a voluntary patient from then on, being of the opinion that she understood her status and was willing to undertake treatment in the hospital on that basis. There was a difference of psychiatric opinion as to whether or not at that time the applicant was capable of understanding her status as a voluntary patient and whether, in reality, she was free to leave the hospital.[81] On December 22, 2008, in response to an attempt by the applicant to leave the

---

[79] [2009] I.E.H.C. 236; High Court, Peart J., May 15, 2009.
[80] [2009] I.E.H.C. 69; High Court, O'Neill J., February 6, 2009; [2009] 2 I.L.R.M. 149; [2009] I.E.S.C. 46; Supreme Court, May 28, 2009.
[81] [2009] I.E.H.C. 69, pp.10–11.

hospital, the psychiatrist moved to convert her status to that of an involuntary patient by invoking ss.23 and 24 of the 2001 Act. This admission order was affirmed by a tribunal on January 9 and the patient's detention was renewed on January 12, 2009.

5–33 Counsel for the applicant argued that the patient's detention was unlawful. It was argued that she was not a voluntary patient from December 10 to December 22 because she lacked the capacity to become a voluntary patient and at no time during that period was she free to leave the hospital. In the High Court, O'Neill J. found that the detention was lawful, relying on the broad scope of the definition of "voluntary patient" in s.2. Of this definition, he said:

> "No provision of the Constitution, in my view, requires that for the purposes of construing this definition in conformity with the Constitution, that, in effect, the definition is to be narrowed to exclude a detention which, apart from the compliance with the express provisions of the definition in the Act, was otherwise illegal in law. It would seem to me that the definition was cast in the wide terms used in order to provide for the variety of circumstances wherein a person is in an approved centre receiving care and treatment, but not subject to an admission order or a renewal order, including, in my view, the type of situation which has indeed arisen in this case, namely, where a detention pursuant to an admission order or a renewal order breaks down, but where the patient is suffering from a mental disorder and receiving care and treatment."[82]

He said that even if the applicant was illegally detained during the period, that did not stop that situation being brought to an end by the use of ss.23 and 24. This was not to say that the detention during that period was not illegal. For the purposes of this enquiry, he found that it was not necessary for him to determine whether it was or was not or what remedy would be appropriate if it was illegal.[83] Effectively, even though he did not use these words, he held that a "domino effect" did not apply.

5–34 Turning to the European Convention, O'Neill J. considered whether it is necessary to interpret the definition of "voluntary patient" so as to exclude persons whose detention might otherwise be illegal, notwithstanding compliance with the express provisions of the definition. Relying on an extract from *H.L. v U.K.*[84] where it was emphasised that detention must not be arbitrary, he found that the patient's detention at all times during her presence in the approved centre could not be characterised as the deprivation of her liberty in an arbitrary fashion.[85] The protection of the procedural requirements of the 2001 Act, if

---

[82]   [2009] I.E.H.C. 69, p.11.
[83]   [2009] I.E.H.C. 69, p.12.
[84]   (2005) 40 E.H.R.R. 32.
[85]   [2009] I.E.H.C. 69, pp.12–13.

suspended for a short period, was at all times in the contemplation of the psychiatrist who was competent to exercise that responsibility and was charged with the duty of ensuring that the protection of the Act was made available to the patient, when appropriate.[86]

Before considering the Supreme Court's decision in this case, a number of points may be noted about the High Court judgment. It is very significant that O'Neill J. did *not* state that the Act requires that a "voluntary" patient be capable of consenting to their admission. He did not refer to *J.H. v Russell*,[87] where it was held that if the relevant period where a patient was, apparently, a voluntary patient, was not in substance properly voluntary, this renders their detention unlawful. While *J.H. v Russell* concerned the 1945 Act, it would have been useful to compare the meaning of "voluntary patient" in the 1945 Act with its meaning in the 2001 Act. *H.L. v U.K.*[88] could have been discussed in greater detail, for example, the requirement for periodic review in art.5(4) as applied in that case. It is unclear why O'Neill J. suggests that s.23 might have been used on December 10,[89] as it can only be used if the patient indicates a wish to leave. It is significant, however, that O'Neill J. expressly reserved the question of whether the detention from December 10 to 22 was illegal. This, at least, might have allowed scope for further argument on these points in cases where the facts differed from the *E.H.* case.

5–35 The Supreme Court dismissed the appeal on May 28, 2009.[90] By that time, Ms H. was detained on foot of a further Renewal Order made on April 9, 2009. The judgment was delivered by Kearns J., who said that the proceedings "were initiated and maintained on purely technical and unmeritorious grounds."[91] In his view, it was difficult to see in what way they advanced the interests of the applicant, who patently was in need of psychiatric care. He said that mere technical defects, without more, in a patient's detention should not give rise to a rush to court, notably where any such defect can or has been cured—as in the present case. Only in cases where there had been a gross abuse of power or default of fundamental requirements would a defect in an earlier period of detention justify release from a later one.[92] His views here are in contrast with those of Peart J. in *P.McG. v Medical Director of the Mater Hospital*,[93] discussed below at para.7–44.

Kearns J. also said that he had a difficulty in reconciling the assertions of counsel for the applicant as to his client's lack of mental capacity, on the one

86 [2009] I.E.H.C. 69, p.14.
87 [2007] I.E.H.C. 7; [2007] 4 I.R. 242.
88 (2005) 40 E.H.R.R. 32.
89 [2009] I.E.H.C. 69, p.10.
90 *E.H. v Clinical Director of St. Vincent's Hospital* [2009] I.E.S.C. 46; [2009] 2 I.L.R.M. 149; Supreme Court, May 28, 2009.
91 [2009] 2 I.L.R.M. 149 at 165.
92 [2009] 2 I.L.R.M. 149 at 165.
93 [2007] I.E.H.C. 401; [2008] 2 I.R. 332.

hand with the contradictory assertion, and on the other that the applicant was and remained capable of instructing legal advisers. He said, "it is disquieting to say the least that in a matter of such importance and sensitivity that no rational basis beyond mere assertion was advanced for these two apparently irreconcilable propositions."[94]

5–36 Kearns J. considered the meaning of "voluntary patient" as follows:

> "The terminology adopted in s.2 of the Act of 2001 ascribes a very particular meaning to the term 'voluntary patient'. It does not describe such a person as one who freely and voluntarily gives consent to an admission order. Instead the express statutory language defines a 'voluntary patient' as a person receiving care and treatment in an approved centre who is not the subject of an admission order or a renewal order. This definition can not be given an interpretation which is *contra legem*. The furthest Mr. Rogers can go is to argue that the definition must be construed and applied in accordance with the provisions of the Constitution and those provisions of the Convention designed to respect and uphold the individual's right to freedom and personal autonomy."[95]

He said that any interpretation of the term in the Act must be informed by the overall scheme and paternalistic intent of the legislation as exemplified in particular by the provisions of ss.4 and 29 of the Act. The trial judge had ample evidence upon which to find that Ms H. was a voluntary patient within the meaning of the 2001 Act between December 10 and 22, 2008, in circumstances where the psychiatrist, as treating specialist, gave evidence on affidavit to that effect and was not cross-examined about her opinion at that time. Even if Kearns J. had taken a different view of the status of E.H. as of December 22, 2008, the certification of grounds justifying the detention of the applicant in St. Vincent's Hospital was the Renewal Order made on April 9, 2009, an order against which no challenge of any sort had been brought. The Admission Order made on December 23, 2008 pursuant to s.24(3) of the 2001 Act was in all respects valid. He continued:

> "To the extent that the applicant was at any time denied the benefit of certain procedural protections, it is absurd and unreal to suggest that she was removed at any point from the protection of the Act of 2001. Indeed, as noted by O'Neill J., the first named respondent maintained a very high level of supervision of the applicant's condition and was at all times poised to reinstate her status as an involuntary patient when in her judgement it was appropriate to do so. Accordingly, the protection of the procedural requirements of the Act

---

[94] [2009] 2 I.L.R.M. 149 at 161.
[95] [2009] 2 I.L.R.M. 149 at 161.

of 2001, even if suspended for a short period of time, was fully restored to the applicant as a result of the admission order made on 22nd December, 2008."[96]

Regarding *H.L. v U.K.*,[97] Kearns J. had "great difficulty in understanding" how the decision availed the patient's counsel to any degree.[98] The case in question could not possibly bear on the applicant's detention subsequent to December 22, 2008. All of the statutory protections and procedures which counsel contended were absent from December 10, 2008 to December 22, 2008 were fully restored from that time onwards and there was no want of any procedure whereby the rights of the applicant could be asserted.[99]

Finally, Kearns J. found that the "domino effect" did not apply. The *R.L.* case[100] and *S.C.* case[101] had "effectively put paid to any suggestion that a domino effect or theory of infection applied to cases of this nature."[102] Only in cases where there had been a gross abuse of power or default of fundamental requirements would a defect in an earlier period of detention justify release from a later one. This therefore meant that this case was a moot, and had been from December 22, 2008, onwards.

5–37 Given the facts of the *E.H.* case, the Supreme Court found that the short period of detention from December 10 to 22 was not unlawful, as the treating psychiatrist's affidavit stated that Ms H. was a voluntary patient. The court's finding that there cannot be a "domino effect" unless there had been a gross abuse of power or default of fundamental requirements is consistent with previous case law on the nature of applications under art.40. However, the court's finding that a "voluntary patient" need not have capacity to agree to their admission remains questionable. The court expresses no concern or difficulty with the fact that patients may be classified as "voluntary" even though they may not have capacity to consent to their admission on a voluntary basis.

As Kearns J. states, in *H.L. v U.K.*,[103] as a result of the lack of procedural regulation and limits, the hospital's healthcare professionals assumed full control of the liberty and treatment of a vulnerable, incapacitated individual solely on the basis of their own clinical assessments completed as and when they considered fit. The European Court said that the very purpose of procedural safeguards is to protect individuals against any misjudgements and professional

---

[96] [2009] 2 I.L.R.M. 149 at 163.
[97] (2005) 40 E.H.R.R. 32.
[98] [2009] 2 I.L.R.M. 149 at 162.
[99] [2009] 2 I.L.R.M. 149 at 163.
[100] *R.L. v Clinical Director of St. Brendan's Hospital & Ors.*, Supreme Court (ex tempore), February 15, 2008.
[101] *S.C. v Clinical Director of St. Brigid's Hospital*, Supreme Court, March 13, 2009, Judgment not available, quoted in *E.H. v Clinical Director of St. Vincent's Hospital* [2009] 2 I.L.R.M. 149 at 163–4.
[102] [2009] 2 I.L.R.M. 149 at 164.
[103] (2005) 40 E.H.R.R. 32.

lapses and concluded that it had not been demonstrated that the applicant had available to him a procedure which satisfied the requirements of art.5(4) of the ECHR. The Supreme Court's response to this in *E.H.* is to state that *H.L.* could not possibly bear on the applicant's detention subsequent to December 22, 2008. However, this glosses over the fact that from December 10 to 22, those protections were not available.

M.McN. v Health Service Executive

5–38 *M.McN. v Health Service Executive*[104] concerned two patients with severe dementia who had initially been admitted on an involuntary basis to Unit 5B of Mid-Western Regional Hospital, Dooradoyle, Limerick. Their involuntary admission orders were then revoked and their status was changed to voluntary, but they remained in Unit 5B. The medical staff acknowledged that the applicants did not have sufficient mental capacity to make a decision to choose to remain in the centre. The ward was locked at the entrance, and the applicants would only be free to leave if they were accompanied by a family member. If they tried to leave, the re-grading procedure under ss.23 and 24 might be invoked. The applicants argued that they were in unlawful de facto detention.

The judgment includes detailed summaries of the legal submissions on both sides, which covered the *Bournewood* case in great detail, and included references to *J.H. v Russell*[105] and *E.H. v Clinical Director of St. Vincent's Hospital*.[106] Peart J. found that the fact that the unit was locked was reasonable because the patients could not look after themselves unaided. The Health Service Executive (HSE) owed a duty of care to the patients. He continued:

> "Also, it would be grossly negligent for the hospital, following the required revocation of the admission/renewal order, to immediately bring these vulnerable patients to the front door of the hospital, lead them down the steps and to pavement and say to them 'we no longer have any legal basis for keeping you in hospital, so off you go—home or wherever you can'. How could such an appalling vista be within the contemplation of an Act such as this which has at its heart the best interests of vulnerable patients?"[107]

5–39 Peart J. said that this was similar to the locking of doors in a school for the safety of the children. The patients were free to leave, provided they did so with a family member who could look after them. If the patient tried to leave,

---

[104] [2009] I.E.H.C. 236; High Court, Peart J., May 15, 2009.
[105] [2007] I.E.H.C. 7; [2007] 4 I.R. 242.
[106] [2009] I.E.H.C. 69; High Court, O'Neill J., February 6, 2009; [2009] I.E.S.C. 46; Supreme Court, May 28, 2009. Only the High Court decision had been issued at the time of the *M.McN.* judgment.
[107] [2009] I.E.H.C. 236; High Court, Peart J., May 15, 2009, p.37.

such an exit could be prevented by the invocation of powers under s.23, but only if the requirements of that section were met. He said that s.23, "could not be invoked simply as a pragmatic device to prevent a person leaving who cannot do so without posing a danger either to himself or to others."[108] Even if the requirements of s.23 were not met, the hospital could still keep the patient safe within the hospital by reasonable means and s.29, quite apart from any common law duty of care, gave it ample powers in that regard.[109]

He distinguished the *Bournewood* case on its facts as follows:

> "[I]t is necessary to draw a fundamental distinction between the facts of the present case and the case of L. The point at issue in L. was really whether s. 131 empowered the hospital to admit L. as a voluntary patient who could not so consent, or whether by doing so he was 'detained' and unlawfully detained. That is a different situation to the present applicants. There is no dispute about the fact that they were each lawfully made the subject of an Admission Order when first admitted as involuntary patients. Their detention there under these orders, one of which was the subject of a later Renewal Order, was completely in accordance with the clear statutory provisions. The Mental Health Tribunal may have decided that these orders, or either of them, should be revoked, had they not been revoked prior to the hearing, but that is not relevant for present purposes. But, Section 29 was not the basis of their admission, as s. 131 of the English Act had been the case in respect of L. For that reason it is necessary to distinguish L on its facts."[110]

However, Peart J. went on to note that the *Bournewood* case was "of interest" and as he was obliged to have regard to the *H.L. v UK*[111] case he had regard to it, although it was of limited value.

He said that it did not seem to him that there was any statutory requirement that a person must be capable of expressing, and express, a consent to being in an approved centre on a voluntary basis before that person can be categorised as being a "voluntary patient".[112] If a patient was discharged from their admission or renewal order, this did not necessarily mean that they should be discharged from the approved centre. The provisions of s.29 supported the idea that a person, whose detention has been revoked, may remain at the approved centre after they have ceased to be subject to an involuntary detention order. That section did not state in any way that consent in that regard was required. It facilitated the situation in which these applicants were, by giving the approved centre the ability to continue to care and treat the patient where it would be

---

108   [2009] I.E.H.C. 236; High Court, Peart J., May 15, 2009, p.38.
109   [2009] I.E.H.C. 236; High Court, Peart J., May 15, 2009, p.38.
110   [2009] I.E.H.C. 236; High Court, Peart J., May 15, 2009, p.39.
111   (2005) 40 E.H.R.R. 32.
112   *M.McN. v Health Service Executive* [2009] I.E.H.C. 236; High Court, Peart J., May 15, 2009, p.39.

inappropriate to release them on to the street, where to do so would place the patient at risk if not accompanied by a responsible family member.[113]

As a result of the above findings, Peart J. held that the patients were not in unlawful detention and refused the application for their release.

5–40 Peart J.'s conclusion that a "voluntary" patient need not consent to their admission may be queried on the same grounds as were discussed above at paras 5–34 and 5–37 concerning the *E.H.* case. His treatment of the *H.L. v U.K.*[114] case may also be questioned. He distinguishes *H.L.* from the current case on rather thin grounds. In *H.L.*, the patient was admitted as a voluntary patient. In *M.McN.*, the patients were initially admitted on an involuntary basis, their orders were revoked and they then remained on a voluntary basis. Either way, the patients in both cases were classified as voluntary or informal and in *H.L.* the European Court of Human Rights held that such de facto detention breached the ECHR.

RE-GRADING OF A VOLUNTARY ADULT PATIENT AS AN INVOLUNTARY PATIENT

5–41 The re-grading procedure of a voluntary adult patient as an involuntary patient only applies to a patient who is already being treated in an approved centre. It is important that this procedure only be used in such circumstances. If it is proposed to detain a person who is currently not in an approved centre, then the standard procedure for Involuntary Admission of an Adult (see Chapter 4 above), sometimes referred to as admission from the community, applies.

There are two stages to the procedure for re-grading of a voluntary adult patient as an involuntary patient:

1. Temporary Detention under s.23(1)
2. Certificate and Admission Order under s.24

Both stages must take place and it is not possible to proceed to the Certificate and Admission Order stage without Temporary Detention taking place first. This is because the second stage must be based on an examination following a detention pursuant to s.23.[115] The Temporary Detention might only last 10 minutes, but it must have occurred in order to proceed to the second stage.

---

[113] *M.McN. v Health Service Executive* [2009] I.E.H.C. 236; High Court, Peart J., May 15, 2009, p.41.
[114] (2005) 40 E.H.R.R. 32.
[115] Section 24(1) begins, "Where a person … is detained pursuant to section 23 …" an examination may be arranged and it is only "following such an examination" (s.24(2)) that a Certificate and Admission Order may be made.

5–42 The High Court confirmed the necessity for the two stages in *Q. v St. Patrick's Hospital*.[116] Ms Q. was a voluntary patient in St. Patrick's Hospital. She was re-graded under s.24 but s.23 had not been invoked, as she had not indicated an intention to leave. The psychiatrist stated on the statutory form (Form 13) and in evidence that he did not invoke s.23 before s.24. The Mental Health Tribunal (MHT) had relied on s.18(1), which allows a detention to be affirmed if there has been a procedural irregularity which does not affect the substance of the order or does not cause an injustice. However, O'Higgins J. found that while a purposive approach was to be adopted in interpreting the Act, one could not do violence to the section and he found that s.18(1) could not be used in these circumstances. (It may also be noted that a tribunal does not have jurisdiction to consider procedural issues concerning ss.23 and 24; see further para.9–18 below.) He stated, "… it seems to me that that is not merely a procedural defect, that it is a *sine qua non* for the exercise of the jurisdiction in Section 24 because it says 'where a person is detained pursuant to Section 23' and that did not apply." O'Higgins J. continued:

> "In my view I cannot accept the submission that this is merely a procedural matter, this is merely a way of getting the person before the Tribunal analogous to a summons. It is not. … [J]ust because a result would be maybe desirable and maybe the right outcome the law cannot be bent so far by virtue of purposive interpretation as to do violence to the words of the Act itself. Personally from what I have heard it seems a pity that the result might be what it is. I regret if there are practical difficulties, though I am assured there are I am not told they are in any way insurmountable or anything like that, but it seems to me I would be really violating the words of the Act if I came to any other conclusion."[117]

O'Higgins J. found Ms Q.'s detention to be unlawful and ordered her immediate release.

5–43 The Act does not require that every time a voluntary patient indicates a wish to leave, the procedure in ss.23 and 24 must be invoked. It appears that in practice voluntary patients may, for example, state that they would like to go home. Nursing staff may well deal with this request by talking to the patient about their treatment and suggesting that they talk to the doctor later in the day. It is only if the request to leave the centre becomes more serious, or the patient actually takes serious steps towards leaving, that the procedure will be invoked. From a legal point of view, it is important that in any conversations of this nature which take place, the patient is not psychologically coerced into remaining in the centre.

---

[116] High Court, O'Higgins J., *ex tempore*, December 21, 2006; noted in Gerry Cunningham & Orla Keane, "Summary of Article 40.4 Judgments Since the Commencement of the Mental Health Act 2001" (Dublin: Mental Health Commission, 2007).

[117] High Court, O'Higgins J., *ex tempore*, December 21, 2006.

Temporary Detention under s.23(1)

5–44 There are two pre-conditions here:

- The patient is being treated in an approved centre as a voluntary patient, and
- The patient indicates at any time that he or she wishes to leave the approved centre

The phrase "being treated" appears to indicate that it is not necessary for the patient to have been admitted to the centre, or to be resident in the centre. They might, for example, be receiving treatment on an out-patient basis. The definition of "voluntary patient" does not require admission or residence.[118] In practice, however, s.23 is normally only used for a patient who is resident at the centre.

The patient must have indicated that they wish to leave the centre. The use of the word "indicated" is presumably broad enough to cover oral indications and indications by actions. If the patient has never indicated a wish to leave, then the power under s.23 cannot be used. The clinical practice form for this detention, discussed below, does not require confirmation that the patient has indicated that they wish to leave. It would be advisable to record details of the patient's indication of a wish to leave elsewhere on the file.

If these two pre-conditions are satisfied, then if a consultant psychiatrist, another doctor or registered nurse on the staff of the approved centre is of opinion that the person has a mental disorder (within the meaning of the Act), they may detain the patient for a period not exceeding 24 hours.[119]

The 24-hour period is calculated from the time that the patient indicates that he or she wishes to leave the centre. The subsection refers to the patient indicating "at any time" that he or she wishes to leave and then states that the detention is for a period "beginning at the time aforesaid."[120] This requirement may well cause a certain amount of confusion, as it may be assumed that the 24 hours lasts from the time when the relevant staff member decides to detain the patient under s.23(1). However, if the patient indicated a desire to leave at 2.00pm and the clinical practice form detaining the patient was signed at 3.30pm, the 24-hour period would run from 2.00pm.

5–45 Part A of the Mental Health Commission's Clinical Practice Form[121] asks for the time and date that the patient was detained (item 5) and the time and date that the period of detention ended. It asks whether a Risk Assessment was used,

---

[118] Section 2(1): A voluntary patient is a person receiving care and treatment in an approved centre, who is not the subject of an Admission Order or a Renewal Order.

[119] Section 23(1). A shorter period may be prescribed by regulations, but this has not been done.

[120] Section 23(1).

[121] Mental Health Commission, *Clinical Practice Form: Mental Health Act Section 23(1): Power To Prevent Voluntary Patient (Adult) From Leaving An Approved Centre.*

and for details of the assessment if one took place. At item 10, it is noted whether the patient was informed that they were being detained under s.23(1) and if not, why not. The psychiatrist, other doctor or nurse then signs the form, certifying their opinion that the patient has a mental disorder and giving the date and time of signature. Part B of this form is completed after the s.24 examination of the patient has taken place (see below.) It notes whether the person was admitted following the s.24 examination, and if not, whether they stayed in the approved centre as a voluntary patient. Part B is then signed and dated. Part B need not necessarily be completed by the same person who completed Part A, or even by a person with the same qualifications as required for Part A.

While the Clinical Practice Form records the key information which it is desirable to record, and includes a reproduction of s.23(1), it is unfortunate that it does not emphasise for people completing it that the time detention begins should be the time when the patient expressed a desire to leave the approved centre. In addition, there is no requirement to certify that the patient has indicated a desire to leave.

5–46 In *B. v Clinical Director of Our Lady's Hospital Navan*[122] the applicant was admitted to St Patrick's Hospital, Dublin as a voluntary patient on September 28, 2007. On October 2, 2007, her status changed from voluntary to involuntary. At the subsequent tribunal hearing, her solicitor raised the issue of compliance with ss.23 and 24 of the 2001 Act. The Chair of the MHT stated in a subsequent affidavit that the MHT concluded that ss.23 and 24 had been complied with as a result of the following factors (quoted as in the affidavit):

1. The fact that Dr Lucey had signed form 13. This is something he would only have done if he was satisfied that the applicant had indicated that she wished to leave St. Patrick's Hospital.
2. The fact that Section 24.2 (a) certificate and form 13 had been signed by Michael McDonagh, consultant psychiatrist to the effect that the applicant refuses to remain in hospital and requires inpatient care.
3. The fact that the note from Dr Lucey's registrar expressly referred to the risk of the applicant absconding. This note was shown to both Dr Curtin and Mr Walsh. The note forms part of the applicant's records in Our Lady's Hospital, Navan. We would have sight of that note from our inspection of the charge prior to the hearing but we would not have been furnished with a copy of the note otherwise.[123]

The applicant's counsel contended that it was "simply not good enough for the tribunal to rely upon a ticked box as evidence of compliance and in view of the issue being raised, the said tribunal should not have proceeded to its deter-

[122] [2007] I.E.H.C. 403; High Court, Sheehan J., November 5, 2007.
[123] [2007] I.E.H.C. 403, para.6.

mination on this matter without hearing oral evidence on the issue."[124] However, Sheehan J. rejected this argument, stating that the tribunal was entitled to hold that there was corroboration of s.23 compliance in the note of Dr Lucey's registrar, as well as in the certificate of Dr Michael McDonagh and in all the circumstances of this case he held that the tribunal was entitled to be satisfied that s.23 had been complied with.[12]

It is notable that Sheehan J. did not require specific evidence that the applicant indicated a wish to leave the hospital; it was sufficient that the psychiatrists signed the relevant forms and that there was a note to the effect that there was a risk of the applicant absconding (which is not the same as an indication of a desire to leave.)

Incidentally, the tribunal did not have the statutory power to consider compliance with ss.23 and 24, as these are not listed as procedural issues which may be considered under s.18(1)(a). This point is not referred to in the judgment.

Certificate and Admission Order (s.24)

5–47 Section 24 states that where an adult is detained temporarily under s.23, the responsible consultant psychiatrist (RCP), or a consultant psychiatrist acting on their behalf,[126] must either discharge the adult or arrange for them to be examined by a second consultant psychiatrist who is not the adult's spouse or relative.[127] On the meaning of RCP, see paras 6–37 to 6–50 below. There is no need for an examination by the responsible psychiatrist, or the psychiatrist acting on their behalf, before the decision to discharge or refer for a second opinion. As was emphasised earlier, it is not possible to proceed to this stage if there has not been a temporary detention under s.23 first (even if that only lasted 10 minutes.)

An examination means a personal examination of the process and content of thought, the mood and the behaviour of the person concerned.[128] For the purposes of carrying out the examination, the second psychiatrist is entitled to take charge of the person for the period of 24 hours referred to in s.23.[129]

5–48 Following the examination, the second psychiatrist has two options. If the psychiatrist *is not* satisfied that the person has a mental disorder within the meaning of the Act, they will certify that the person should not be detained and

---

[124]   [2007] I.E.H.C. 403, para.7.
[125]   [2007] I.E.H.C. 403, para.8.
[126]   Section 24(6) states that references in s.24 to the RCP include references to a consultant psychiatrist acting on behalf of the RCP.
[127]   Section 24(1) of the Mental Health Act 2001.
[128]   Section 2(1) of the Mental Health Act 2001.
[129]   Section 24(5).

the person will be discharged.[130] The certificate must be made on the relevant statutory form, Form 13.[131] Even though the patient is discharged, they might choose to remain in the approved centre as a voluntary patient, and this is recognised by Part B of the Clinical Practice Form discussed earlier.

The second option is that the psychiatrist *is* satisfied that the patient has a mental disorder, and certifies that because of that disorder they should be detained in the approved centre,[132] again on Form 13. Where the second psychiatrist issues a certificate in these terms, the Responsible Consultant Psychiatrist (RCP), or a consultant psychiatrist acting on their behalf,[133] must make an admission order for the reception, detention and treatment of the person in the approved centre.[134] As the word "shall" is used in the relevant subsection, it is clear that the RCP has no choice in the matter.

There are no statutory disqualifications laid down in s.24 regarding the RCP or psychiatrist acting on their behalf for the purposes of s.24. However, the Mental Health Commission's view is that because s.24(3) refers to an "admission order" and s.14(1) states that an involuntary admission order under s.14 will be referred to in the Act as an "admission order", then the disqualification of a spouse, relative or the applicant in s.14(3) also applies to an admission order under s.24.[135] An argument to the contrary could be made by referring to the restrictive wording of s.14(3), which only applies "for the purposes of this section." In addition, while the Act states that the provisions of ss.15 to 22 shall apply to a person detained under s.24,[136] s.14 is not included in that statement.

5–49 In *C.C. v Clinical Director of St. Patrick's Hospital (No.2)*,[137] considered below at para.7–65, Hedigan J. held that the s.23 and s.24 re-grading procedure may be used in some circumstances, even if the patient was recently discharged by an MHT.

A second point taken in the *C.C. (No.2)* case concerned the alleged lack of independence of the second psychiatrist who certified that the patient had a mental disorder and needed to be detained. This certificate had been signed by a psychiatrist on the staff of the approved centre. The applicant submitted that if the term "another consultant psychiatrist" in s.24 were interpreted to include consultant psychiatrists on the staff of the approved centre in question then the same consultant would be permitted to initiate the s.23 procedure while also providing the second opinion for the purposes of s.24. She argued that such an

---

[130] Section 24(2)(b).
[131] At the time of writing, the current version of the form is the version issued in June 2009.
[132] Section 24(2)(a).
[133] Section 24(6).
[134] Section 24(3).
[135] The Mental Health Commission's view is clear from the requirement in item 17 of Form 13 for the RCP to certify that they are "not a person disqualified from making an admission order (see Section 14(3) replicated overleaf)."
[136] Section 24(4).
[137] [2009] I.E.H.C. 47; High Court, Hedigan J., February 6, 2009.

arrangement would be incompatible with the spirit of the legislation and would defeat the objective of obtaining an independent second opinion. Further and in the alternative, the applicant submitted that the second psychiatrist could not appropriately be classed as "another consultant psychiatrist" because he was also one of the RCPs.

Hedigan J. said that he did not think that the phrase "another consultant psychiatrist who is not a spouse or relative of the applicant" could conceivably be read to involve the highly limiting criterion being suggested by the applicant in this case.[138] Such a requirement would be impractical and dangerous:

> "I am inclined to agree with the submissions made by the respondent to the effect that such a requirement would be extremely impractical, and even dangerous, in many of the more urgent cases which engage the procedure created by sections 23 and 24. Moreover, to oblige the responsible consultant psychiatrist to screen potential assessors on the basis of allegations of objective bias would be an unnecessarily onerous burden and one which might well be inimical to the best interests of the patient in question."[139]

5–50 Once a patient has been admitted under s.24, the provisions of ss.15 to 22 apply to the person as they apply to a person detained under s.14, with any necessary modifications.[140] This means, for example, that the Admission Order lasts 21 days, Renewal Orders may be made, the psychiatrist must give an information notice to the patient, the Admission Order and any Renewal Order will be reviewed by a tribunal, there can be an appeal to the Circuit Court and the patient may be transferred to another approved centre or the Central Mental Hospital (CMH).

Form 13 is used to record the Certificate and Admission Order.[141] Taking the example of an RCP completing the form, the first page requires the RCP to state when they last examined the patient and to certify that they have a mental disorder and tick indicating which subsection of the s.3 definition of mental disorder applies, or if both apply. As was stated earlier, strictly speaking, the RCP need not have examined the patient recently. However, by requiring the RCP to state the date and time of last examination, the form reminds them of the general duty to make a decision based on the current mental state of the patient. At the end of the first page, the RCP states that they are satisfied that the person should be detained in an approved centre. It would be clearer if the RCP also certified that as a result they will arrange for the person to be examined by a second consultant psychiatrist. There is a slight danger that an RCP filling in the form quickly might believe that page one is an Admission Order.

---

[138] [2009] I.E.H.C. 47; High Court, Hedigan J., February 6, 2009, para.46.
[139] [2009] I.E.H.C. 47; High Court, Hedigan J., February 6, 2009, para.47.
[140] Section 24(4).
[141] At time of writing, the current version of the form is the version issused in March 2009.

As temporary detention under s.23 is obligatory before admission under s.24, at item 5 the form requires the date and time of the temporary detention be stated in all cases.

5–51 Page 2 of Form 13 provides space for the Certificate by the second psychiatrist, having examined the patient, either that the patient be detained or discharged. The second psychiatrist must give a clinical description of the reasons for forming the opinion. The second psychiatrist must give the date and time of signing the certificate, but need not state the date and time of the examination of the patient.

If the second psychiatrist has certified that the patient should be detained, the RCP, or consultant psychiatrist acting on their behalf, will make an admission order by completing Part 3 on p.2. The Form requires the RCP to certify that they will, within 24 hours of making the order, give an information notice to the patient, and send a copy of the Admission Order to the Commission. As was discussed earlier, the Commission has provided a Clinical Practice Form which may be used to provide the information notice to the patient.[142]

In signing the Admission Order, the RCP is required to certify that they are not disqualified from making an Admission Order. However, the legislation is not 100 per cent clear on this point (see para.5–48 above).

Finally, if an Admission Order is made using Form 13, a member of staff should go back to the Clinical Practice Form which was used to detain the person on a temporary basis, and complete Part B by stating that the patient was later admitted under s.24.

Cases where the 24-hour period in s.23 has been exceeded

5–52 In *T.O'D. v Kennedy*,[143] discussed below at para.9–27, the patient was classified as voluntary, indicated a desire to leave and was detained for 24 hours under s.23. He should then have been re-graded within the 24-hour period under s.24, but in fact this did not happen until six days after the expiry of the 24-hour period. The tribunal decided to affirm the order under s.18. Again, it may be noted that technically the tribunal did not have jurisdiction to consider compliance with ss.23 and 24. Charleton J. found the detention to be lawful. He specifically held that the purpose of s.18(1) was to enable the tribunal to affirm the lawfulness of a detention which had become flawed due to a failure to comply with relevant time limits.[144]

---

[142] Mental Health Commission, *Patient Notification of the Making of an Admission Order or a Certificate and Renewal Order.*

[143] [2007] I.E.H.C. 129; [2007] 3 I.R. 689; High Court, Charleton J., 25 April 2007.

[144] [2007] 3 I.R. 689 at 705.

5–53 In *J.H. v Lawlor, Clinical Director of Jonathan Swift Clinic, St. James's Hospital*,[145] the patient had initially been admitted on a voluntary basis but three days later the provisions of s.23 of the 2001 Act were invoked by a nurse at 9.20am on April 30, 2007. The first psychiatrist completed the first part of Form 13 at 12.02pm and the second psychiatrist signed the certificate section of the form at 8.04pm The following morning, at 9.40am, the first psychiatrist signed the admission order. It was evident that the 24-hour period of detention had been exceeded by 20 minutes. The admission order was affirmed by a tribunal on June 1, 2007, the tribunal finding that the admission order "was signed within the 24 hour period."

The patient argued that his detention was unlawful because the 24-hour period permitted in s.23 and s.24 had been exceeded by 20 minutes. The patient's counsel relied on statements from Charleton J. in *T.O'D.*[146] to the effect that the time limit in s.23 was a strict one and that he looked in vain for any provision which might allow detention beyond that period. Counsel for the MHT referred to the power of the tribunal to waive procedural irregularities in s.18(1)(a)(ii). Peart J. found, however, that while the tribunal clearly had the power to overlook non-compliance which causes no injustice and does not affect the substance of the order, the tribunal did not as a matter of fact rely in any way upon s.18(1)(a)(ii). He commented that if the tribunal had in fact decided the matter by availing of s.18(1)(a)(ii) of the Act, it would appear to have been entitled to do so.[147]

Peart J. said that a purposive approach to the interpretation of the Act, consistent with its paternalistic and protective nature, must be adopted. That was not the same as stating that when errors are made they may always be overlooked if the interests of the patient so require, due regard having been also had to the interests of other persons who may be at risk of serious harm if they were to be released. But the court was obliged to have regard to the provisions of s.4(1) of the Act which laid down the best interests principle.[148] The court was obliged to have regard to the best interests of the applicant when balancing the nature of the failure to adhere strictly to the procedures and time limits, against the need, in the applicant's own best interests, to be detained for care and treatment. It was therefore not every incident of non-compliance which would render the detention of a person unlawful, particularly where no injustice has occurred, and where no protection which the applicant is entitled to under the statutory scheme had been denied to him.[149]

The purpose of the examination by the second psychiatrist was "to give the patient the protection of a second opinion"[150] before the 24-hour period would

---

[145]   [2007] I.E.H.C. 225; [2008] 1 I.R. 476; High Court, Peart J., June 25, 2007.
[146]   *T.O'D. v Kennedy* [2007] I.E.H.C. 129; [2007] 3 I.R. 689; High Court, Charleton J., April 25, 2007.
[147]   [2008] 1 I.R. 476 at 485.
[148]   [2008] 1 I.R. 476 at 486–7.
[149]   [2008] 1 I.R. 476 at 487.
[150]   [2008] 1 I.R. 476 at 488.

be extended by an admission order for a further 21 days. The certificate of the second psychiatrist was signed at 8.04pm and the applicant's further detention was mandated by the Act, since once that certificate was issued the first psychiatrist was required to make an Admission Order. Peart J. was firmly of the view that the patient had suffered no prejudice:

> "Therefore no prejudice of any kind has been suffered by the applicant by the fact that the mandated admission order was not in fact signed until 9.40 a.m. on the 1st May, 2007. No fundamental right of the applicant has been breached in any way whatsoever. No protection intended by the Act to be afforded to the applicant has been denied to him as a result. The purpose intended by the Oireachtas to be fulfilled by this Act has been in all respects fulfilled by the events which occurred."[151]

Peart J. said that there must inevitably be some "give" permitted as to when the Admission Order is actually signed, since the existence of a certificate mandates the making of the Admission Order. He said that, "[t]o order the release of such a person onto the side of the street because of such slavish adherence to the time scale provided in this section would truly enable form to triumph over substance."[152] He said that his view was consistent with case law concerning other forms of detention such as *The State (McDonagh) v Frawley*[153] and the purposive construction of the Act was consistent with s.5(1) of the Interpretation Act 2005.

Re-grading of a Voluntary Child Patient as an Involuntary Patient

5–54 Where one or both parents[154] of a voluntary child patient, or a person acting in *loco parentis*, indicate that they wish to remove the child from an approved centre, and a consultant psychiatrist, doctor or nurse on the staff of the approved centre is of the opinion that the child is suffering from a mental disorder, the child may be detained and placed in the custody of the HSE.[155] The Mental Health Commission provides a clinical practice form for this purpose.[156]

The HSE must, unless it returns the child to the parent(s), apply for involuntary detention of the child under s.25 at the next sitting of the District Court held in the same district court district. If that sitting is not to be held within three days, a special sitting must be arranged within the three-day period. The HSE retains custody of the child pending the hearing of the application.

---

[151] [2008] 1 I.R. 476 at 488.
[152] [2008] 1 I.R. 476 at 489.
[153] [1978] I.R. 131. See para.2–22 above.
[154] "Parents" includes a surviving parent or adoptive parent(s) (s.2(1)).
[155] Section 23(2) of the Mental Health Act 2001, as amended by s.75 and sch.7 of the Health Act 2004.
[156] Mental Health Commission, *Clinical Practice Form, Mental Health Act Section 23(2) and 23(3), Power to Detain Voluntary Patient (Child) in an Approved Centre*.

The provisions of s.13(4) of the Child Care Act 1991 apply to the making of an application in respect of a child to whom s.23 applies with any necessary modifications.[157] This means that where a judge for the district in which the child resides, or is for the time being, is not immediately available, an order may be made by any judge of the District Court; an application may, if the judge is satisfied that the urgency of the matter so requires, be made ex parte; and an application may, if the judge is satisfied that the urgency of the matter so requires, be heard and an order made thereon elsewhere than at a public sitting of the District Court.[158]

5–55 The Code of Practice on Admission of Children provides details of procedures to be followed in these cases.[159] The relevant clinical practice form should be completed.[160] Having quoted the standard principles of best interests, autonomy, privacy, etc. the Code goes on to state that the principle to be adhered to is that the degree of intervention used should be the minimum necessary to preserve safety for all concerned. It advises that risk should be assessed and appropriate risk management strategies should be in place to reduce the likelihood of harm and deterioration in the voluntary child's well-being. Before preventing the voluntarily admitted child from leaving the approved centre, best efforts should be made to encourage the child and the parent(s) to agree to the child remaining voluntarily at the approved centre for care and treatment. Finally, there is no right under the Act to give any treatment to the child without consent. In the absence of consent, treatment can only be given under the common law doctrine of necessity, or with a Court Order authorising same.[161]

---

[157]   Section 23(4) of the Mental Health Act 2001.
[158]   Section 13(4) of the Child Care Act 1991.
[159]   *Code of Practice re Admission of Children*, paras 2.15–2.20.
[160]   Mental Health Commission, *Clinical Practice Form: Mental Health Act Section 23(2) and 23(3): Power to Detain Voluntary Patient (Child) in an Approved Centre.*
[161]   *Code of Practice re Admission of Children*, para.2.17.

CHAPTER 6

RENEWAL ORDERS

RENEWAL OF AN INVOLUNTARY ADMISSION ORDER OF AN ADULT

6–01 An Admission Order generally remains in force for 21 days from the date of the making of the order and then expires.[1] The 21-day period is not 21 periods of 24 hours each. Instead, the Admission Order lasts up to midnight at the end of a 21-day period, which includes the day of its making.[2] For example, if an Admission Order is made at 9.15am on Wednesday, January 5, it expires at midnight on Tuesday, January 25.

The patient may be discharged within the 21-day period, or re-graded to voluntary status.[3] Otherwise, if it is not renewed or extended[4] within 21 days, the Admission Order expires at the end of the period. Note, however, that in *P.G. v Branigan*[5] McCarthy J. appears to have contemplated that if a review is impossible and "simply cannot be done", it could not mean that the Act could have intended that the order would lapse or be avoided with the consequence that the detention would be unlawful.[6]

6–02 The Responsible Consultant Psychiatrist (RCP) may make a first Renewal Order for a further period not exceeding three months, a second renewal of up to six months and third and subsequent renewals of up to 12 months each.[7] Each Renewal Order triggers a Mental Health Tribunal (MHT) review, which must take place within 21 days of the order being made. While a MHT may extend the duration of an Admission Order for two further periods of 14 days each, it may not extend the duration of a Renewal Order.[8]

6–03 A Mental Health Tribunal (MHT) does not renew Admission Orders or Renewal Orders. Instead, a tribunal reviews each Admission Order and Renewal

---

[1] Section 15(1) of the Mental Health Act 2001.
[2] Section 18(h) of the Interpretation Act 2005. See consideration of previous similar section of Interpretation Act 1937 in *DPP v Curtin*, Circuit Court, Moran J., April 23, 2004, *Irish Times*, April 24, 2004.
[3] See ss.23, 24 and 28 of the Mental Health Act, 2001, Form 13 and Form 14.
[4] Extensions by a Mental Health Tribunal are covered in s.18(4). See paras 7–30 to 7–36 below.
[5] [2008] I.E.H.C. 450; High Court, McCarthy J., December 12, 2008.
[6] [2008] I.E.H.C. 450; High Court, McCarthy J., December 12, 2008, para.16.
[7] Section 15(2) and (3) of the Mental Health Act 2001.
[8] See discussion of extension of admission orders at paras 7–30 to 7–34 below and discussion of *J.B. (No.3)* case at para.7–36 below. The MHT is entitled to extend the period for its decision regarding a Renewal Order, but not to extend the duration of the Renewal Order.

Order and either affirms or revokes it. Even if the tribunal affirms the relevant order, the patient must be discharged or re-graded to voluntary status at the end of the period of admission or renewal, unless a new Renewal Order is made.

To take an example, if an Admission Order is made on Wednesday, January 5 and affirmed by an MHT on Monday, January 24, the patient must be discharged, or choose to remain in the centre on a voluntary basis, at midnight on Tuesday, January 25 unless a Renewal Order is made by the RCP before that time.

6–04 Before making a Renewal Order, the RCP must have examined the patient not more than one week before making the order and must certify in a form specified by the Commission that the patient continues to suffer from a mental disorder.[9] An examination means a personal examination carried out by the psychiatrist of the process and content of thought, the mood and the behaviour of the proposed patient.[10]

6–05 It is essential that a period of renewal be stated, as otherwise the patient will no longer be in lawful detention. This issue arose under the 1945 Act in *J.D. v Director of Central Mental Hospital*.[11] That case involved interpretation of the wording of s.189 of the Mental Treatment Act 1945, as amended, which permitted an extension of detention "for a further period not exceeding six months". On October 14, 2006, the psychiatrist had endorsed the order as follows: "temp. order extended 14/10/06." The patient argued that his continued detention was unlawful, as no period of extension was specified in the endorsement. The respondents submitted that s.189 need not be construed literally, but interpreted in light of the scheme and intention of the Act.[12] Alternatively, they submitted that by reason of the maximum period of six months in s.189 the court should construe the endorsement as including a six-month period because it did not specify any differing period of time. Finlay Geoghegan J. held that the applicant was no longer in lawful detention. The starting point had to be the ordinary meaning of the words of the statute, and there was no reason (in the form of the intention of the legislature) to depart from the ordinary meaning. Regarding the alternative argument, she stated:

> "I do not think on a warrant, which is a warrant the purpose of which is to detain somebody and thereby deprive them of their liberty that there is any basis for so construing an endorsement without any specified period of time."[13]

---

9   Section 15(4) of the Mental Health Act 2001.
10 Section 2(1) of the Mental Health Act 2001.
11 [2007] I.E.H.C. 100, High Court, Finlay Geoghegan J., ex tempore, March 20, 2007.
12 The respondents relied on *Gooden v St. Otteran's Hospital* [2001] I.E.S.C. 14; [2005] 3 I.R. 617.
13 [2007] I.E.H.C. 100, p.8.

6–06 Similarly, it has been held in a case concerning the 1945 Act that if a Renewal Order is stated to run until a particular date, then it expires on that date: *A.M. v Kennedy.*[14] On August 18, 2006 there was an endorsement on Form 6 (under the 1945 Act) which read "extended for a further period of six months from 18/8/06", signed by the consultant. Peart J. held that this did "what it says on the tin"[15] and so it expired on February 18, 2007. The consultant purported to make a Renewal Order on February 19, 2007. Peart J. was not satisfied that on February 19, 2007 the applicant was lawfully detained. The detention order dated February 19, 2007 was one which could not be lawfully made, given the expiration of the previous order on the previous day, and the affirmation of that order by the MHT on February 20, 2007 was of no effect.[16] Peart J. rejected the argument that the renewal would not come into effect until the expiry of the previous period of detention, which would have meant that the renewal would expire on February 24, 2007. His judgment included the following important observations:

> "No purposive statutory interpretation can alter what is stated in the endorsement. The only way in which this Court could hold that the renewal order made on the 18th August 2006 endured until the 24th February 2007 would be to decide that it does not matter what is stated on the form of endorsement, and that the only matter to be considered is the over-riding interest of ensuring that the applicant is detained in his own and others' best interests. Such a manner of approaching the meaning of orders depriving a person of his or her liberty could not in my view be correct, as it would nullify the very purpose of inserting safeguards in the statutory procedures put in place."[17]

As the wording of s.15(2) and (3) of the 2001 Act, including the words "not exceeding" the relevant number of months in each case, is very similar to the wording of s.189 of the 1945 Act, which refers to "not exceeding six months", it is to be assumed that the same consequence would follow if a psychiatrist did not specify the period of renewal by specifying the period of renewal on the form.

---

[14] [2007] I.E.H.C. 136; [2007] 4 I.R. 667; High Court, Peart J., April 24, 2007.

[15] [2007] 4 I.R. 667 at 676; [2007] I.E.H.C. 136, p.10.

[16] The tribunal hearing took place on February 20 as under the transitional section of the 2001 Act, s.72, the first review of a patient detained for six months under the 1945 Act took place before the end of the six-month period. The date of the hearing was calculated on the basis that the six months would expire on February 24, 2007.

[17] [2007] 4 I.R. 667 at 676; [2007] I.E.H.C. 136, p.11.

Form 7

6–07 The relevant form is Form 7—Renewal Order by Responsible Consultant Psychiatrist.[18] Interestingly, this form is not referred to in the Act as a "form specified by the Commission", in contrast to many other forms referred to in the Act.[19] In *S.M. v Mental Health Commission*[20] McMahon J. commented on this point as follows:

> "[I]t is relevant to note that although some sections in the Act require the treating psychiatrist to make the relevant order in question 'in a form specified by the Commission' (see for e.g. s. 14(1)(a)—admission orders; s. 15(5)— certification of continuing mental disorder), s. 15(3) is not, however, one of these and this suggests that the order to be made by the treating psychiatrist under this subsection is hers not only in substance but in form also."[21]

However, the Act states that the patient's detention shall not be extended unless the consultant psychiatrist has not more than one week before the making of the Renewal Order examined the patient and certified in a *form specified by the Commission* that the patient continues to suffer from a mental disorder.[22] So while the Renewal Order itself does not need to be made by means of a form specified by the Commission, the certification of mental disorder does.

6–08 The RCP states the date and time of the examination of the patient and then states that in their opinion the patient should continue to be detained for a period not exceeding either three months (on the first Renewal Order), six months (on the second Renewal Order) or 12 months (on any subsequent Renewal Order).

6–09 The original version of the form did not permit the RCP to state a period less than either of those three periods, e.g. the RCP could not make a first renewal for two months, which would then trigger a MHT hearing at the end of the two months if a further Renewal Order were made. This issue has now been addressed as a result of the *S.M.* decision (see paras 6–20 to 6–36 below.)

6–10 Previous versions of Form 7 did not state when the renewal would come into effect, and it was arguable that it should be amended to include this information for the sake of clarity, as otherwise a person who was unfamiliar with the case law might have assumed that the renewal ran from the date of

---

[18] At the time of writing, the current version is the version issued in February 2009.
[19] For example, an admission order is referred to in s.14(1) as "an order to be known as an involuntary admission order … in a form specified by the Commission" whereas in s.15(2) a renewal order is not referred to in these terms.
[20] [2008] I.E.H.C. 441; [2009] 2 I.L.R.M. 127; High Court, McMahon J., October 31, 2008.
[21] [2009] 2 I.L.R.M. 127 at 147.
[22] Section 15(4) of the Mental Health Act 2001.

making of the order. The latest version of Form 7 (issued in February 2009) now addresses this issue to some extent by stating, for example, in the case of a first renewal that detention is being renewed "for a further period ending on [insert date] (being a period not exceeding 3 months) beginning upon the expiration of the Order on foot of which the reception, detention and treatment of the patient is currently authorised." However, it might be preferable for the Form to state the exact dates on which the current order expires and the new order comes into effect. The Patient Notification Form includes this information.[23]

6–11 The Act does not require the psychiatrist to provide information in writing to the patient in advance of making the Renewal Order. While seven items of information must be provided under s.16(2), discussed at paras 4–61 to 4–68 above, the information need only be supplied within 24 hours of the Renewal Order. It is possible that some psychiatrists will provide the information notice to the patient at the time that the possibility of a Renewal Order is being discussed, and that therefore the proposed patient may become aware of the possibility of a change to voluntary status at an earlier stage.

The patient does not appear to have a statutory entitlement to make representations in relation to a proposed Renewal Order.[24]

6–12 The RCP must tick a box to indicate what type of mental disorder the patient has, i.e. whether s.3(1)(a) (the harm ground) or s.3(1)(b) (the need for treatment ground), or both, apply. The full wording of the relevant subsections is provided. At item 8, the psychiatrist must state the grounds on which their opinion is based by filling in a box labelled "Give clinical description of the person's mental condition." The psychiatrist must certify that they shall within 24 hours of making the order provide a written information notice to the patient under s.16(2) and send a copy of the admission order to the Mental Health Commission. Finally, the psychiatrist signs the form, giving the date and time of signature.

6–13 *A.R. v Clinical Director of St. Brendan's Hospital*[25] concerned a failure on the part of a psychiatrist to tick any of the boxes on the renewal form indicating that the patient continued to suffer from a mental disorder. In the space on the form for a clinical description of the person's mental condition the psychiatrist had stated: "My opinion above is based on the following reasons: He has not yet fully treated psychotic illness and impaired insight: community treatment is likely to be unsuccessful." The tribunal had decided that, while s.15 was not complied with, the failure did not affect the substance of the order or cause an injustice.[26] O'Keeffe J. held that the failure to comply with s.15(4) in

---

[23] Mental Health Commission, *Patient Notification of the making of an admission order or a certificate and renewal order, Mental Health Act 2001 section 16(2)* (Revised February 2009).

[24] Section 4(2) of the Mental Health Act 2001 only applies to a recommendation or an admission order.

[25] [2009] I.E.H.C. 143; High Court, O'Keeffe J., March 24, 2009.

[26] The tribunal had erroneously ticked the box stating that the provisions of ss.9, 10, 14, 15 and

this limited respect did not affect the substance of the order. The Tribunal acted lawfully and was entitled to apply s.18(1)(a)(ii) in the manner it did. For these reasons, he was satisfied that the applicant was detained in accordance with law, and he refused the application for his release.

6–14 The remaining aspects of the procedure for renewal are as described for the admission order in Chapter 4, including the giving of the information notice to the patient, and the sending of the Renewal Order to the Commission.

Reviews of Renewal Orders must take place within 21 days of making of orders

6–15 In the early months of operation of the Act, there was some uncertainty about the time frame for review of a Renewal Order, but this uncertainty was resolved by *A.M.C. v St. Luke's Hospital, Clonmel.*[27] In that case, a Renewal Order was made on December 4, 2006 but the MHT review did not take place until 25 days later, on December 29, 2006. This appeared to breach the requirement that a MHT hearing take place within 21 days. However, C's previous detention period[28] expired on December 8, 2006 and it was argued that the time should be calculated by adding 21 days to December 9, which would allow a MHT hearing on December 29. The written record of the MHT review hearing noted legal advice from the Mental Health Commission in an email that the period of detention in an Admission Order must expire before the "further" period of detention in the Renewal Order commenced.

Clarke J. said that the Mental Health Act 2001 was clear and unambiguous as to when the period of time runs for the purpose of considering when the order must lapse. Section 18(2) stated that a MHT decision must be made not later than 21 days after the making of the Admission Order or Renewal Order concerned. The Renewal Order made on December 4, 2006 need not have been made on that date. However, there was no obstacle to the Renewal Order being made when it was, as people might be planning ahead to the expiration of the 21 days for review. There was nothing absurd in arriving at such a conclusion, and the court was obliged to ascertain the intention of the legislature from the plain and ordinary meaning of the words used in the section. The fact that the final day for review fell on Christmas Day was not sufficient of itself to get over the clear meaning of the words of the section. The Act was unforgiving in that respect and the court could not invent a means of forgiveness from without the terms of the Act.[29] He said he

16, where applicable, had been complied with. However, at the High Court hearing, the evidence was that the tribunal's decision was that s.15 had been breached but this did not affect the substance of the order or cause an injustice.

[27]   [2007] I.E.H.C. 65; [2007] 2 I.R. 814; High Court, Peart J., February 28, 2007.

[28]   This was detention as a temporary involuntary patient under s.184 of the Mental Treatment Act 1945 for a period of six months, which commenced on June 9, 2006.

[29]   [2007] 2 I.R. 814 at 823; [2007] I.E.H.C. 65 at p.11.

had the greatest sympathy for the hardworking personnel in hospitals of this kind. The effect of renewing the order on December 4 was that unless a review was completed by December 25[30] it expired by virtue of s.15(1). Thereafter, the applicant was not held in detention by virtue of any extant order and the review and the affirmation of the expired order on December 29 was of no effect in reviving it.

Renewal Order takes effect once admission order (or previous renewal order) expires

6–16 In *M.D. v Clinical Director of St. Brendan's Hospital*,[31] it was clarified that a Renewal Order takes effect once the Admission Order (or previous Renewal Order) expires. The Admission Order was made on April 26, 2007 and a MHT confirmed the Admission Order on May 15, 2007. Meanwhile, on May 10, 2007, five days before the MHT hearing, a Renewal Order for three months was made. In the letter notifying the applicant's solicitor of the MHT hearing, he was not informed that the Renewal Order had been made on May 10, but he discovered it on the evening of May 14 when he inspected the applicant's file. At the MHT hearing, the solicitor submitted that the MHT did not have jurisdiction to review the Admission Order but the MHT rejected this submission.

In the subsequent court proceedings, the applicant's counsel argued that the Renewal Order could not be made before the MHT review on the Admission Order. He submitted that unless this was so an absurd situation could exist where an Admission Order was made, and was renewed before the review took place, only to find that upon the review of the Admission Order it was revoked, leaving in place the Renewal Order under which the patient could continue to be detained. He submitted that this could never have been and was not the plain intention of the Oireachtas when enacting the legislation. It was also argued that the making of the Renewal Order on May 10, 2007 had deprived the MHT of jurisdiction to review the Admission Order, on the basis that the Renewal Order must take effect from the date on which it is made, and replaces the Admission Order. Alternatively, it was argued that if the Renewal Order took effect upon the expiration of the Admission Order, the applicant was deprived of his opportunity to have the Admission Order revoked upon the review of it.

6–17 The High Court and Supreme Court both rejected these arguments. In the High Court, Peart J. provided the following analysis:

"It seems to me that there is a clear sequencing of events contemplated by the terms of sections 14, 15, 16, 17 and 18 of the Act. Various periods of detention

---

[30] Technically, Clarke J. should have referred to midnight on December 24 here.
[31] [2007] I.E.H.C. 183; High Court, Peart J., May 24, 2007 and [2007] I.E.S.C. 37; Supreme Court, July 27, 2007; [2008] 1 I.R. 632.

and extensions of detention are provided for, and none of these periods can be seen as overlapping. Each new period of detention commences upon the expiry of the previous period. Each period of detention is required to receive a review also, and it does not seem to me to be contrary to anything stated in the sections under scrutiny, or the plain meaning intended by the Oireachtas, to conclude that an order renewing an admission order may for any reason be made a day or some days or at any time in fact before the review of that admission order has been completed, since the renewal order will take effect only at the conclusion of the specified 21 day period following the making of the admission order."[32]

He said that this was, "a sensible interpretation of the section, and one which does not do any violence to the words used by the Oireachtas."[33] If the Admission Order was revoked by the MHT, it was "unreal" to suggest that an order for renewal made prior to that revocation would still entitle the hospital to detain a patient.

6–18 The Supreme Court rejected the applicant's appeal against this decision.[34] Hardiman J. remarked that it was "a remarkable feature of the case" that the letter notifying the applicant's solicitor of the MHT hearing on May 15 did not notify him of the Renewal Order which had been made on May 10.[35] He said that the Admission Order was not spent at the time the MHT sat on May 15. He specifically adopted the reasoning of Peart J. in the High Court to the effect that the Renewal Order takes effect on the expiration of the 21-day duration of the Admission Order. He also adopted the paragraph quoted above about the "clear sequencing of events" contemplated by the Act. The Supreme Court therefore held that the applicant was being detained in accordance with law and in his own interest. However, Hardiman J. expressed concern about certain aspects of the case which will be considered elsewhere: first, the failure to notify the patient of the statutory provision under which he was being detained[36] and secondly, the fact that the MHT certified that s.16 had been complied with when it manifestly had not.[37]

6–19 As noted earlier, Hardiman J. suggested that the Patient Notification Form might need to be reconsidered on the basis of experience in operating the Act and further consideration. He noted that the form did not appear to provide for the possibility that the Renewal Order might not become the basis for detention

---

[32] [2008] 1 I.R. 632 at 639–640.

[33] [2008] 1 I.R. 632 at 639.

[34] Hardiman J. noted that by the time of the Supreme Court hearing, a subsequent MHT on May 29 had reviewed the renewal order of May 10.

[35] [2008] 1 I.R. 632 at 643.

[36] See paras 4–67 to 4–68 above.

[37] See discussion of this aspect of *M.D.* case at para.9–31 below.

for some time into the future.[38] He seemed to be suggesting that the Patient Notification Form could include an extra item: the date when the Renewal Order would come into effect.

The Patient Notification Form has now been revised so that in the case of a Renewal Order it informs the patient:

(a) You are being currently detained on foot of an Order dated (date) for a period ending on (date). ... This is a Certificate and Renewal Order extending the detention pursuant to s.15.

(b) You have been examined by Dr. (name of consultant psychiatrist) on (date) for the purpose of extending your detention for a further period ending on (date). This extension will come into effect on (date) after the expiry of your current Order. This extension has been made pursuant to s.15.[39]

Renewal Order must be for specific time period and failure to indicate exact period renders it void for uncertainty

6–20 *S.M. v Mental Health Commission*[40] was one of the most significant decisions to date regarding the 2001 Act. The applicant had been admitted to St. Patrick's Hospital on 23 occasions, of which 15 were involuntary admissions. Her condition was deteriorating as the interval between admissions had become shorter, and her admissions had increased in frequency. Her psychiatrist was of the view that her ongoing medical needs could only be met by the applicant taking sustained and stabilising medication. Ideally, the more suitable regime for the applicant's care was by way of supported accommodation rather than involuntary admission in St. Patrick's Hospital. The psychiatrist had made persistent, systematic attempts to secure appropriate supported accommodation for the applicant and this approach was ongoing. The dates of the applicant's various Admission and Renewal Orders were not given, but it appears that she was currently on a third renewal of up to 12 months made on May 21, 2008, which, if renewed, would be reviewed by a MHT in May or June of 2009.

6–21 The case took the form of a Judicial Review application, but the exact nature of the order being sought is not stated. Initially, the applicant's counsel made two arguments:

(i) If the Mental Health Tribunal's jurisdiction is limited under s.18 to affirm-ing or revoking the Renewal Order then it fails to provide a sufficient independent review mechanism for the purpose of art.5 of the European

---

[38] [2008] 1 I.R. 632 at 650.

[39] Mental Health Commission, *Patient Notification of the making of an admission order or a certificate and renewal order, Mental Health Act 2001 section 16(2)* (Revised February 2009).

[40] [2008] I.E.H.C. 441; [2009] 2 I.L.R.M. 127; High Court, McMahon J., October 31, 2008.

Convention on Human Rights (ECHR) and accordingly the court should make a declaration that the statutory provision is incompatible with the State's obligations under the Convention provisions.

(ii) In the alternative, s.18 may be read in a manner that is compatible with art.5 of the Convention, and should be so read as to enable the tribunal to *vary* the psychiatrist's order.

These points are not discussed in any detail in the decision, because McMahon J. highlighted another part of counsel's outline submissions. In those submissions, counsel had noted that in the applicant's case, no time limit was fixed on the Renewal Order such that it remained in force for the maximum permitted period of one year. The order was issued in this form despite the fact that it was the psychiatrist's view that the most appropriate regime for the applicant was supervised accommodation and not involuntary admission. The applicant was now the subject of an involuntary Admission Order of such length that she had no right of independent review of her detention until May, or more probably June 2009. No independent assessment of her detention would be carried out during that time. Counsel submitted that the failure to fix a time limit on the Renewal Order might result from the design of the Renewal Order form, Form 7. Its wording required a doctor who was signing the form to make it "for a period not exceeding 12 months" where it is the third successive Renewal Order being made, regardless of the patient's condition, future needs and prognosis. It was submitted that it had no regard to a patient's right of periodic review, the timing of which should be assessed according to the patient's condition. In the applicant's case, it had no regard to the fact that she should be released from hospital and placed in supervised accommodation. It was submitted that the psychiatrist failed to exercise the power vested in her by s.15(3) of the Act, to assess and determine the appropriate maximum length of the Renewal Order and to fix it with regard to the individual circumstances of the applicant, such that the order was unlawful.[41]

6–22 McMahon J. was concerned whether, when the psychiatrist was authorised to make a Renewal Order "for a period not exceeding 12 months", she had power to make the Renewal Order which was stated to be for "a period not exceeding 12 months" without fixing any more definite period. He was concerned with the apparent lack of certainty in such an order. He indicated his concern on the issue and also indicated that it was an issue which was more fundamental, and perhaps less subtle, than the arguments advanced by the applicant's counsel. For this reason, he requested all parties to address it as a preliminary issue before proceeding to the more subtle arguments advanced by the applicant's counsel. The matter was adjourned to enable counsel to prepare submissions.

---

[41] [2009] 2 I.L.R.M. 127 at 134.

6–23 When the matter resumed, counsel for the applicant applied to amend the Statement Required to Ground the Application for Judicial Review by the inclusion of a paragraph seeking a declaration that the Renewal Order was invalid and void by reason of its failure to specify a definite duration. This proposed amendment was opposed by counsel for the respondents but McMahon J. acceded to the application. He said he was granting it bearing in mind the unusual way in which the issue had arisen, being prompted by the court itself, the fact that the liberty of the individual was at stake, since the amendment did not extend the statement of grounds in a significant manner and was made in a timely fashion by counsel for the applicant once the matter was raised by the court.[42] He accepted that it was unusual to grant amendments in judicial review proceedings, but because it was a matter of importance which would resurface again, and because it would be wholly artificial to pretend that there was not a fundamental issue beneath the applicant's initial arguments which needed to be confronted, he formed the view that it was in the interests of all parties to have the issue addressed.[43]

6–24 The first and second respondents, the Mental Health Commission and MHT argued that when the Act referred to a period which "does not exceed 12 months" it meant a period of 12 months. McMahon J. did not accept this argument:

> "Apart from greatly departing from the plain meaning of the language used, this argument excludes the possibility of the consultant psychiatrist who is treating the patient making an order for a period of less than 12 months. This is an extraordinary proposition and would clearly not be in the interests of the patient where, for example, a consultant psychiatrist who was of the opinion that detention for a shorter period (e.g. three weeks to complete a course of medication or therapy) was appropriate would not be permitted to make a renewal order for less than 12 months."[44]

The first and second respondents also argued that because of the law as stated in *A. v The Governor of Arbour Hill Prison*[45], the court should not entertain the application advanced by the applicant. In the *Arbour Hill* case, the applicant had been convicted in 2004 on a plea of guilty of unlawful carnal knowledge contrary to s.1(1) of the Criminal Law (Amendment) Act 1935. The applicant contended that his detention was unlawful on the basis that the Supreme Court declared s.1(1) of the 1935 Act to be unconstitutional in *C.C. v Ireland* in 2006.[46] The Supreme Court held that the applicant was not entitled to be released even

---

[42] [2009] 2 I.L.R.M. 127 at 135.
[43] [2009] 2 I.L.R.M. 127 at 135.
[44] [2009] 2 I.L.R.M. 127 at 135.
[45] [2006] 4 I.R. 88.
[46] *C.C. v. Ireland* [2006] I.E.S.C. 33; [2006] 4 I.R. 1.

though the piece of legislation under which he was earlier found guilty had subsequently been struck down. In the *S.M.* case, McMahon J. said that in the *Arbour Hill* case the court was dealing with an applicant who was claiming that he was a beneficiary of a subsequent Supreme Court decision in *another* case declaring a particular piece of legislation unconstitutional. This was not what was happening here. Apart from the *Arbour Hill* case being concerned with the constitutionality of a statute, the applicant here, S.M., was not seeking to free-ride on the slipstream of another court. He continued:

> "Ours is the first case in which the renewal order which is stated to be for 'a period not exceeding 12 months', has been explicitly challenged and it is challenged in the context of its own facts. The objections which the first and second respondents advance would be more appropriately made if the other 200 involuntary patients, who, it has been suggested, are detained under similar orders, were to advance it later as a result of a decision made in this case. Our case is more analogous to the court's decision in *C.C. v Ireland* itself, the first case which declared the legislation unconstitutional, than with the *Arbour Hill* case which concerned persons subsequently claiming a collateral benefit from the decision in *C.C. v. Ireland*."[47]

6–25 McMahon J. said that the argument advanced under this heading on behalf of the first and second respondents and based on the *Arbour Hill* case really addressed the issue of the consequences of a decision favouring the applicant for others involuntarily detained under similarly worded orders in the past. And in this regard the *Arbour Hill* decision boded well rather than ill for the respondents.[48]

6–26 Turning to what had now become the core issue in the case, McMahon J. found that a Renewal Order made under subss (2) and (3) of s.15 and which does not specify a particular period of time, but merely provides that it is an order for a period "not exceeding 12 months" is not an order permitted under the legislation and is void for uncertainty. An order made in such unspecified terms does not comply with the power given to the consultant psychiatrist under the Act.[49] What was at stake here was the liberty of the individual and while it was true that no constitutional right is absolute, and a person may be deprived of their liberty "in accordance with the law", such statutory provisions which attempt to detain a person or restrict their liberty must be narrowly construed. Further, such a Renewal Order has consequences for the applicant in that while an order is in existence, the applicant is denied the right to be referred to the tribunal and the right to an independent medical examination by a consultant psychiatrist under s.18.[50]

McMahon J. emphasised the need for proportionality:

[47]   [2009] 2 I.L.R.M. 127 at 137.
[48]   [2009] 2 I.L.R.M. 127 at 138.
[49]   [2009] 2 I.L.R.M. 127 at 138.
[50]   [2009] 2 I.L.R.M. 127 at 139.

"Section 15 since it purports to restrict a constitutional right to liberty albeit for the patient's own good and safety and the safety of others, should be interpreted in a proportionate way so that the detention is not for longer periods than are necessary to achieve the object of the legislation. The approach to an interpretation of the section should be that which is most favourable to the patient while yet achieving the object of the Act. To accept the arguments advanced by the respondents, that a renewal order for a period 'not exceeding 12 months' is an order for a fixed period of 12 months, would be to adopt an interpretation which is neither in the patient's interest, nor proportionate in the circumstances. On the contrary, one would be restricting the patient's rights in an unnecessarily wide way. To accept the respondents' interpretation would mean that the patient would have an order for the maximum period allowed in every situation when a shorter period might be warranted. This would in turn deprive the patient of a fresh tribunal hearing and an examination by an independent psychiatrist as well as the possibility of a fresh appeal to a Circuit Court (see [sections] 17 and 19). Such an interpretation is not justified on the wording of the section, does not advance the intention of the section and results in a greater erosion of the patient's right to liberty than is necessary to attain the objects of the section itself or the Act in general. More significantly, however, such an interpretation would prevent the treating psychiatrist from making shorter orders, in the best interests of the patient, where the consultant psychiatrist deems it appropriate to do so."[51]

6–27 McMahon J. approved of the reasoning adopted by Finlay Geoghegan J. in *J.D. v Clinical Director of Central Mental Hospital*,[52] in which she held that an extension of detention under the 1945 Act must be for a specified period. He also relied on Peart J.'s reasoning in *A.M. v Kennedy*[53] where the need for definite periods of detention was emphasised.

McMahon J. noted that the error in this case was prompted by the wording of the form used by the Commission and offered to the treating psychiatrist when complying with her obligations under s.15(3). He said that, "one must not think that the skies will fall as a result of this decision", which did not prevent the psychiatrist from making 12-month detention orders where they deem it appropriate. All it meant was that they must indicate the specific period in the order they make under those provisions. The procedures which the Mental Health Commission adopts and the forms which they use would have to be revisited to comply with this interpretation, but this was a simple administrative matter.[54]

[51] [2009] 2 I.L.R.M. 127 at 139–40.
[52] [2007] I.E.H.C. 100; High Court, Finlay Geoghegan J., *ex tempore*, March 20, 2007.
[53] [2007] I.E.H.C. 136; [2007] 4 I.R. 667.
[54] [2009] 2 I.L.R.M. 127 at 147–8.

6–28 Having found that the applicant's detention was unlawful, McMahon J. referred to the applicant's ongoing mental disorder, which required care and treatment. In the circumstances, he was not prepared to order her immediate release from her detention, as to do so would not be in the interests of the applicant herself or other persons with whom she might come in to contact. He therefore ordered her release with a stay of four weeks, saying that this should give the relevant parties sufficient time to comply with the provisions of the legislation before determining what was the appropriate order in these circumstances.[55]

6–29 The decision in the *S.M.* case was entirely logical and Form 7 should never have been drafted in such a manner that it required the psychiatrist to tick a box renewing the detention for a period not exceeding 3, 6 or 12 months, without permitting detention for a shorter period. This issue had been pointed out at conferences held in 2007 and 2008.[56] Even before the Form was amended, a psychiatrist could theoretically have altered it to detain the patient for a shorter period, but presumably this never occurred. The design of the forms was a matter for the Mental Health Commission, and questions arise as to how such a fundamental issue could arise. One possible explanation is that it was thought that since the psychiatrist could discharge the patient at any time under s.28, the patient's rights were adequately protected during detention. However, McMahon J. rightly dismisses this argument in the judgment as follows:

> "This argument of course suffers from the flaw that s. 28 can only be operated by the consultant psychiatrist who is responsible for the care and treatment of the patient and this is the very exclusivity which s. 15 is designed to address. Section 15 is designed to protect the patient from the risks of unnecessary detention at the hands of the establishment and it can be no consolation to the patient to say to him that as soon as the treating psychiatrist thinks he/she is well he/she is obliged to release him. What the Act is designed to do and what the patient wants is the possibility of more frequent independent reviews by an outside psychiatrist and pointing to s.28 gives no comfort to the patient in this situation. For this reason too it is quite clear that renewal orders for shorter periods (i.e. for less than 12 months), as already noted, give the patient more frequent reviews, examinations and appeals to the Circuit Court."[57]

Another possible explanation is that it was hoped that by restricting Renewal Orders to these longer periods, this would in turn restrict the number (and cost)

---

[55] [2009] 2 I.L.R.M. 127 at 147.

[56] Darius Whelan, "More than a Rubber Stamp? The Role of Mental Health Tribunals", Conference on Law and Mental Health, NUI Galway, November 2007; "Mental Health Tribunals and the Best Interests Principle", Centre for Recovery and Social Inclusion Conference, U.C.C., June 2008; "Mental Health Tribunals: Recent Developments", Mental Health Lawyers Association Conference, Dublin, July 2008.

[57] [2009] 2 I.L.R.M. 127 at 140.

of MHT hearings, although this suggestion has never been made in any reports or reviews produced.

It is unclear why McMahon J. chose to place a stay of four weeks on his order for release of the applicant. Given that her detention was unlawful, the normal practice would be to put a stay of up to 24 hours on the order and four weeks seems unusually lengthy. It might be argued that the fact that this was a judicial review case rather than a habeas corpus application makes a difference but it is difficult to see why. After all, McMahon J. himself emphasised that the right to liberty was at stake.

Mental Health Act 2008 and Revised Form 7

6–30 While the decision in the *S.M.* case was still awaited, the Government decided, on the advice of the Attorney General and the Minister for Health, to close off the potential loophole which might arise if the statutory forms were found to be inappropriate. On October 30, 2008, the Mental Health Act 2008 was introduced, passed by both Houses of the Oireachtas and signed by the President. The Minister stated that she had been advised by the Attorney General that emergency legislation was required to avert a situation where all 209 people who were currently involuntarily detained would be entitled to their freedom if the High Court decision went against the State. At a briefing for journalists, Ms Harney said that the retrospective element of the legislation was unusual but a similar approach had been adopted before, in regard to EU directives, asylum procedures and a case where a judge was wrongly appointed but whose decisions were retrospectively covered by an emergency law. She said all the patients involved have been clinically reviewed in the previous week and 99 per cent had their admissions upheld. Over the next five days, all the cases would be reviewed again and new forms prepared by the Mental Health Commission signed by their psychiatrists.[58]

The Mental Health Act 2008 provided that an unexpired Renewal Order[59] would be deemed to be valid notwithstanding either (a) that the consultant psychiatrist failed to consider that he or she had the discretion to extend the period for a lesser period than the maximum period concerned, or (b) that the order did not specify a period during which the order was to remain in force or a date on which the order was to expire.[60] In addition, every act done or purporting to have been done pursuant to that order would be deemed to be valid and effective and always to have been valid and effective notwithstanding these matters.[61] Subject to s.28 of the 2001 Act, an unexpired Renewal Order would

---

[58] Stephen Collins, 'Emergency mental health law rushed through Dáil', *Irish Times*, October 31, 2008.
[59] Section 1(1) of the 2008 Act provided that an unexpired renewal order meant an order purporting to be a renewal order where the maximum period concerned specified in s.15(2) or (3) of the 2001 Act had not, before October 30, 2008, expired.
[60] Mental Health Act 2008, s.3(1).
[61] Mental Health Act 2008, s.6.

remain in force until either the expiration of five working days following October 30, 2008, a replacement Renewal Order was made or the expiration of the maximum period specified in s.15(2) or (3) of the 2001 Act, whichever occurred first.[62]

6–31 "Replacement Renewal Orders" (RROs) were dealt with in s.4. Where a patient was the subject of an unexpired Renewal Order, the RCP could carry out an examination of the patient after October 30, 2008 but before the expiration of five working days following that date. If the psychiatrist was satisfied that the patient continued to suffer from a mental disorder, they could certify this and make an order replacing the unexpired Renewal Order for a specified period not exceeding the period remaining unexpired of the maximum period specified in s.15(2) or (3) of the 2001 Act.[63] A replacement Renewal Order was in substitution for, and not in addition to, the unexpired Renewal Order which it replaced and took effect as if it were a Renewal Order under s.15(2) or (3) of the 2001 Act.[64]

Where an unexpired Renewal Order had been replaced by a replacement Renewal Order and, before that replacement, a tribunal had completed its review of the detention, then ss.16 to 19 of the 2001 Act would apply to the making of the replacement Renewal Order in the same manner as they applied to the making of a Renewal Order.[65] In other words, a further MHT hearing would take place regarding the replacement Renewal Order.

6–32 The Act also provided that an expired Renewal Order[66] was deemed always to have been valid notwithstanding either (a) that the consultant psychiatrist failed to consider that he or she had the discretion to extend the period for a lesser period than the maximum period concerned, or (b) that the order did not specify a period during which the order was to remain in force or a date on which the order was to expire.[67] Again, every act done or purporting to have been done pursuant to that order would be deemed to be valid and effective and always to have been valid and effective notwithstanding these matters.[68]

McMahon J. added a postscript to his judgment, issued on October 31, 2008, stating that he noted from media reports the enactment of new legislation by the

---

[62] Mental Health Act 2008, s.3(2).
[63] Mental Health Act 2008, s.4(1).
[64] Mental Health Act 2008, s.4(2).
[65] Mental Health Act 2008, s.4(5).
[66] Section 1(1) of the 2008 Act provided that an expired renewal order meant an order purporting to be a renewal order (a) where the maximum period concerned specified in s.15(2) or (3) of the 2001 Act had, before October 30, 2008, expired or (b) which had, before October 30, 2008, been revoked.
[67] Mental Health Act 2008 s.5(1).
[68] Mental Health Act 2008, s.6.

Oireachtas in anticipation of his decision. He said that his decision related to the law as it stood before the recent amendment.[69]

6–33 As part of the implementation of the 2008 Act, the Commission issued RRO forms, which were used during the five working days after October 30, 2008. The Commission received 206 RROs by midnight on November 5, 2008; 11 per cent of these were revoked before the MHT hearing and 12 per cent were revoked at the MHT hearing.[70]

Form 7 was also revised, so that all Renewal Orders made since November 2008 required the psychiatrist to specify the date when the detention will end. The latest version of Form 7 (issued in February 2009) states, for example, in the case of a first renewal that detention is being renewed "for a further period ending on [date] (being a period not exceeding 3 months) beginning upon the expiration of the Order on foot of which the reception, detention and treatment of the patient is currently authorised."

No information is yet available on how lengths of Renewal Orders have changed since the revised form was introduced. It would be expected that renewals for 12 months, for example, should be made less frequently than before.

6–34 The enactment of the Mental Health Act 2008 might have led to a large amount of litigation, as challenges might have been brought to Renewal Orders made prior to the enactment of the 2008 Act. In fact, there was no flurry of litigation and it is likely that practitioners, on examining the *S.M.* case and the 2008 Act, understandably decided that the chances of success were low. In particular, McMahon J. had clearly indicated that the *Arbour Hill* case[71] might be of benefit to the respondents in such cases.[72]

The only case concerning the Mental Health Act 2008 which has led to a written judgment at the time of writing is *P.G. v Branigan*.[73] In this case, the replacement Renewal Order had only lasted 10 days because that was the remaining "unexpired" duration of the previous Renewal Order when it was made.[74] Subsequently, a further Renewal Order for three months was made by the psychiatrist and affirmed by a tribunal. As was pointed out, these circumstances would only rarely arise.

---

[69] [2009] 2 I.L.R.M. 127 at 148.
[70] Mental Health Commission, *Annual Report 2008*, Book 1, pp.45–6.
[71] *A. v Governor of Arbour Hill Prison* [2006] I.E.S.C. 45; [2006] 4 I.R. 88.
[72] [2009] 2 I.L.R.M. 127 at 138.
[73] [2008] I.E.H.C. 450; High Court, McCarthy J., December 12, 2008.
[74] The original Renewal Order was made on August 15, 2008 and would have expired on November 14, 2008. The replacement Renewal Order was made on approximately November 5, 2008 (the precise date is not given in the judgment) and expired on November 14, 2008.

6–35 Under the terms of the 2008 Act, ss.16 to 18 of the 2001 Act applied to the replacement Renewal Order,[75] which meant that normally it would be expected that there would be an MHT hearing concerning that order. However, no such hearing had taken place due to the brevity of the 10-day replacement order. The applicant argued that her detention was unlawful, as she had been deprived of the benefit of a tribunal hearing concerning this 10-day detention. McCarthy J. rejected this argument, chiefly because it would have meant holding an MHT hearing when the period of detention had already expired. Since s.18 of the 2001 Act required a tribunal to consider whether the patient "is suffering" from a mental disorder, a review could not take place after the expiry of the period of detention. McCarthy J. dealt with this issue as follows:

> "Obviously the tribunal is not thereby called upon to decide whether or not, at some time in the past, a person was suffering from a mental disorder and, indeed, it has no power to do so. If the tribunal, on undertaking its review, is concerned with the then existing state of health of a patient, it must surely presuppose that what is in issue, is whether or not by reason of a mental disorder, a detention should be continued and the order of the psychiatrist affirmed. If what is said by the respondents is correct a tribunal conducting a review after the expiry of a relevant period of detention, would be required to consider whether or not, in the past a patient had been suffering (historically) from such mental disorder. It would not be called upon to satisfy itself whether or not, as in the present, the patient was suffering from a mental disorder, notwithstanding the fact that its only jurisdiction is to decide on the existing state of the patient."[76]

McCarthy J. accepted that a different position pertains under s.28(5) of the 2001 Act. That provision permits the commencement of, or continuation of, reviews, even after discharge of a patient, at the option of that patient. He said that the view he had taken was supported by the fact of this provision: it permits the commencement or continuation of a review after the end of the period of detention and then only at the option of the patient. That seems to presuppose that without the exercise of such option by such patient, a review would either not be held or discontinued by virtue of discharge.[77]

6–36 McCarthy J.'s decision is consistent with the wording of the legislation and, in any event, the patient had a review shortly after her 10-day detention expired.[78] While the 2008 Act could have included a provision stating that patients in P.G.'s position would be entitled to a tribunal review even after their

---

[75] Mental Health Act 2008, s.4(5).
[76] [2008] I.E.H.C. 450, para.8.
[77] [2008] I.E.H.C. 450, para. 10.
[78] The 10-day period expired on November 14, 2008 and the patient would have had a tribunal review within 21 days of that date, as it was also the date on which the detention was renewed.

detention under the RRO had expired, this would have created further problems, as if the patient's detention had been renewed in the meantime, the tribunal would still be required to focus on the position as it was some days earlier. If the tribunal decided that the patient was not suffering from a mental disorder some days earlier, the tribunal could not discharge the patient from the new Renewal Order.

MEANING OF "RESPONSIBLE CONSULTANT PSYCHIATRIST"

6–37 A Renewal Order may only be made by the Responsible Consultant Psychiatrist (RCP), who is referred to in the Act as "the consultant psychiatrist responsible for the care and treatment of the patient concerned."[79] References to the RCP also occur in s.17 (independent psychiatrist shall interview RCP); s.18(5) (notification of MHT decision to RCP); s.24 (re-grading of voluntary patient as involuntary patient); ss.26–27 (absence with and without leave); s.28 (discharge); s.49 (tribunals) and ss.58–61 (consent to treatment). The case law considered below has relevance not only to Renewal Orders, but also to the other sections in which references to the RCP are made.

6–38 Four cases have considered the status of the RCP, and in three of these the Central Mental Hospital (CMH) was involved. By way of background to these three cases, it must be noted that under the 1945 Act, patients could be transferred from an ordinary psychiatric hospital to the CMH under s.208 and, if this occurred, the transfer was regarded as temporary and the ordinary hospital remained involved in decisions concerning extensions of temporary detention orders.[80] As was stated in the *J.B. (No.2)* case:

> "When a patient was transferred to the Central Mental Hospital he retained his original doctor and the doctor in the Central Mental Hospital was a specialist dealing with his care in accordance with s.208 of the Mental Treatment Act 1945. This regime ensured continuity of care."[81]

The patient might also be transferred under s.207 of the 1945 Act up to 1995,[82] in which case the ordinary hospital might not necessarily remain involved, as s.207 involved a District Court order, followed by an order of the Minister for Health. Under the 2001 Act, again, a special procedure was introduced for

---

[79] Section 15(2) and s.15(3) of the Mental Health Act 2001. This phrase also appears in s.24, s.26, s.27, s.28, s.49 and ss.56–61.

[80] See summary of 1945 Act provisions in *J.B. v Director of C.M.H. (No.2)* [2007] 4 I.R. 778 at 781–3 and 790. See also *Croke v Smith (No.1)* [1994] 3 I.R. 525.

[81] [2007] 4 I.R. 778 at 790.

[82] Section 207 of the 1945 Act was found to be unconstitutional in *R.T. v Director of Central Mental Hospital* [1995] 2 I.R. 65; [1995] 2 I.L.R.M. 354.

transfers from ordinary approved centres to the CMH.[83] A recommendation for an Admission Order may not be made directly to the CMH.[84] The 2001 Act provides that where a patient is transferred from one approved centre to another, their detention in the other centre is deemed to be detention in the centre from which they were transferred.[85] It is unclear whether this principle applies to a transfer from an approved centre to the CMH.[86]

W.Q. v Mental Health Commission

6–39 In *W.Q. v Mental Health Commission*[87], the applicant had spent 20 years in the CMH up to July 2006, having been transferred to the CMH under s.207 of the 1945 Act in 1986.[88] In or about 2003, Q's case had been referred to the Tipperary Mental Health Services by the CMH because he was from the catchment area for South Tipperary Mental Health Services. A psychiatrist from the Tipperary Services was invited to attend a case conference at the CMH in relation to the applicant in November, 2003. Dr O'Leary, a second psychiatrist from the Tipperary Services was requested to attend at the CMH to review the applicant in May 2006. After this examination, the applicant was discharged from the CMH and transferred to St. Luke's Hospital in Clonmel, Co. Tipperary on July 3, 2006, for six months, under s.184 of the 1945 Act. Dr O'Leary completed a transfer form under s.208 of the 1945 Act, and on foot of this, the applicant was transferred back to the CMH on July 5, 2006. On January 2, 2007, Dr O'Leary attended at the CMH for the purpose of reviewing the applicant in order to consider whether his continued detention was warranted. Dr O'Leary completed Form 7 in accordance with s.15 of the 2001 Act, renewing the applicant's detention for three months from that date. This Renewal Order was affirmed by a MHT, as was a subsequent Renewal Order signed by Dr Mohan of the CMH.

6–40 The above chronology of dates shows that W.Q. was clearly being cared for and treated in the CMH at the time when the Renewal Order was signed in January 2007. He only spent two days in Tipperary, from July 3 to 5, 2006. Because a transfer under s.208 of the 1945 Act from ordinary psychiatric services to the CMH was intended to be temporary in nature, the CMH continued to involve the Tipperary Services in decisions about W.Q.'s future. It is likely that the CMH asked Dr O'Leary to remain involved and make the

---

[83]   See paras 7–66 to 7–69 below.

[84]   A registered medical practitioner makes a recommendation that a person be involuntarily admitted to an approved centre *(other than the CMH)* specified by him or her in the recommendation—s.10(1) Mental Health Act 2001.

[85]   Mental Health Act 2001, s.20(4) and s.21(4).

[86]   See also discussion of transfers from approved centres to the CMH at paras 7–66 to 7–69 below.

[87]   [2007] I.E.H.C. 154; [2007] 3 I.R. 755; High Court, O'Neill J., May 15, 2007.

[88]   The applicant was transferred to the CMH from St. Brendan's Hospital in Dublin by order of the Minister for Health made on September 19, 1986 pursuant to s.207 of the Mental Treatment Act, 1945. The applicant was detained at the CMH pursuant to this order until July 3, 2006.

Renewal Order because under the 1945 Act this would have been the practice for a patient transferred to the CMH under s.208. However, O'Neill J. found that it was not permissible for a Renewal Order to be signed by a psychiatrist from outside the CMH who was not involved in care and treatment, but was brought in for purposes of review. This meant that the Renewal Order was "fatally flawed"[89] and this defect could not be excused by the MHT.[90] According to O'Neill J.:

> "The restriction of this power to the '*Consultant Psychiatrist responsible for the care and treatment of the patient*' is one of the significant safeguards provided by the Oireachtas in this legislation for the benefit of persons suffering from mental disorder within the meaning of s. 3 of the Act of 2001 and in my opinion a failure to comply with this provision vitiates the lawfulness of a detention based upon a Renewal Order signed by someone who lacked the power to make that order."[91]

He said that it was, of course, the case that for reasons of practicality more than one psychiatrist would have to be considered as "responsible for the care and treatment of the patient concerned". This would arise as a matter of necessity where, for example, the psychiatrist primarily responsible for the care and treatment of a person was absent for one reason or another, such as holidays or illness, at a time when it was necessary to make a Renewal Order. In this situation, another psychiatrist who was involved in the care and treatment of the applicant in the approved centre in question could lawfully make a Renewal Order. However, a psychiatrist not attached to the approved centre where the person was detained, and not involved in the care and treatment of the patient concerned but who was brought in for the purposes of review, could not exercise the power of renewal contained in s.15(2) and s.15(3).[92]

While the psychiatrist who signed the Renewal Order did not have the power to do so, this point should have been raised at the MHT hearing which affirmed the order. As no objection along these lines had been made, and the detention had subsequently been renewed, the applicant had lost competence to lay claim to, or place reliance on, this defect to challenge the validity of the subsequent Renewal Order by Dr Mohan of the CMH.[93]

J.B. v Director of Central Mental Hospital (No.2)

6–41 A different result was reached in *J.B. v Director of Central Mental Hospital (No.2)*.[94] The facts differed significantly from the *W.Q.* case. In 2000,

---

89 [2007] 3 I.R. 755 at 766.
90 [2007] 3 I.R. 755 at 768.
91 [2007] 3 I.R. 755 at 765.
92 [2007] 3 I.R. 755 at 765.
93 [2007] 3 I.R. 755 at 771. See further para.9–39 below.
94 [2007] I.E.H.C. 201; [2007] 4 I.R. 778; High Court, MacMenamin J., June 15, 2007.

the applicant was treated by Cluain Mhuire Mental Health Services, a community-based service which also maintained beds at St John of God's Hospital. The applicant was serving prison sentences for some years afterwards, and was transferred from prison to the CMH. From 2002 to 2004, during which time the applicant was a patient in the CMH, Dr Hearne of Cluain Mhuire Services was invited to attend case conferences in relation to the applicant in anticipation that J.B. would continue to require mental health services on his release from prison. From 2004 on, J.B. was involuntarily admitted to St John of God's Hospital, but then immediately transferred to the CMH under s.208 of the 1945 Act.[95] MacMenamin J. outlines in detail Dr Hearne's various contacts and reviews with J.B. over the years. Dr Hearne reviewed J.B.'s condition by attending at the CMH and visiting him on a number of occasions between 2003 and 2005. It appears that Dr Hearne may have signed the Renewal Orders which were made concerning the applicant.[96] His contact with J.B. in 2006 appears to have been in the form of correspondence with the CMH only.[97] It is not clear what form of contact he had with J.B. in 2007, apart from the signing of the Renewal Order on April 24, 2007.

6–42 The applicant's legal team argued that Dr Hearne was not his RCP as defined in the 2001 Act, and therefore should not have signed the renewal order. They argued that Dr Linehan of the CMH was in fact the RCP and this was supported by a number of factors:

- Dr Linehan had drawn up a separate Renewal Order concerning J.B. on May 1, 2007, a week after the one drawn up by Dr Hearne. This was then destroyed following legal advice that the order of April 24 was valid.
- She was described in the independent psychiatrist's report as the RCP.[98]
- She had described herself as the RCP in an affidavit sworn in earlier court proceedings.[99]

It had already been stated in the *W.Q.* case that there might be more than one RCP for a patient. It was also noted that the Act did not require that the RCP be a member of the staff of the centre in which the patient was resident. In resolving this issue, MacMenamin J. emphasised that all the consultant psychiatrists were of the opinion that a responsible psychiatrist is not simply one person but is rather the psychiatrists, not only within the hospital itself, but may include consultant psychiatrists outside the hospital, provided they have a real and

---

[95] The first admission took place on April 28, 2004 for six months and was extended for two periods of six months. The second admission took place on October 18, 2005 for six months, and was extended on April 21, 2006 and October 17, 2006. See further *J.B. v Central Mental Hospital (No.1)* [2007] I.E.H.C. 147; High Court, McGovern J., May 4, 2007.

[96] [2007] 4 I.R. 778 at 785 and 793; [2007] I.E.H.C. 201, para.19 and para.56.

[97] [2007] 4 I.R. 778 at 788; [2007] I.E.H.C. 201, para.32.

[98] [2007] 4 I.R. 778 at 785; [2007] I.E.H.C. 201, para.20.

[99] [2007] 4 I.R. 778 at 785; [2007] I.E.H.C. 201, para.20.

continuing part in the care and treatment of the patient.[100] He referred to s.21(4) of the 2001 Act, which states that if a patient is transferred from one centre to another, the detention in the other centre is to be deemed as detention in the centre from which the patient was transferred. He said that this was "carefully framed so as not to preclude the role of the treating psychiatrist who is not a member of the staff of the approved centre to which the patient is transferred."[101] He does not appear to have any doubt that s.21(4) applies to a transfer to the CMH, although this is a debatable point.[102] He distinguished the *W.Q.* case on the basis that in that case it had been held that the psychiatrist was "not involved in the care and treatment of the patient concerned", whereas in this case Dr Hearne was so involved.[103]

6–43 MacMenamin J. also referred to the definition of "treatment" contained in s.2 of the 2001 Act which "includes the administration of physical, psychological and other remedies relating to the care and rehabilitation of a patient under medical supervision, intended for the purposes of ameliorating a mental disorder."[104] He said that this clearly envisaged the involvement of practitioners of more than one discipline. According to MacMenamin J., s.15(2) of the 2001 Act, when read in conjunction with the definition of treatment, did not preclude the possibility, which clearly existed in this case, of there being more than one consultant psychiatrist responsible for the care and treatment of the patient any more than there might have been more than one consultant psychiatrist involved or responsible for the care and treatment of the patient within the ambit of and employed by the CMH.[105] Having found that Dr Hearne was entitled to sign the Renewal Order, he held that J.B.'s detention was lawful.

6–44 While there were significant differences between the facts in *W.Q.* and *J.B. (No.2)*, MacMenamin J. may perhaps have overstated these in his decision. Looking at the psychiatrist's dealings with J.B. in 2006–2007, for example, it appears that he only had contact in the form of correspondence with the CMH.It is surprising that MacMenamin J. concludes that the psychiatrist's "role was essential to the applicant's case"[106], that he was "directly concerned and engaged in the treatment regime of the applicant"[107] and that there was an "ongoing relationship of doctor and patient."[108] If the restriction of this power of renewal to the "consultant psychiatrist responsible for the care and treatment of the patient" is supposed to be one of the significant safeguards provided by the

---

[100] [2007] 4 I.R. 778 at 790; [2007] I.E.H.C. 201, para.42.
[101] [2007] 4 I.R. 778 at 791; [2007] I.E.H.C. 201, para.51.
[102] See further para.7–66 below.
[103] [2007] 4 I.R. 778 at 792–3; [2007] I.E.H.C. 201, para.53–57.
[104] Mental Health Act 2001, s.2(1).
[105] [2007] 4 I.R. 778 at 793; [2007] I.E.H.C. 201, para.60.
[106] [2007] 4 I.R. 778 at 785; [2007] I.E.H.C. 201, para.18.
[107] [2007] 4 I.R. 778 at 788; [2007] I.E.H.C. 201, para.33.
[108] [2007] 4 I.R. 778 at 793; [2007] I.E.H.C. 201, para.57.

Oireachtas for the benefit of persons with mental disorder,[109] then it is difficult to see how the judge permitted this role to be fulfilled by a psychiatrist who appears to have had very little contact with the patient in the months before the signing of the Renewal Order.

J.H. v Lawlor

6–45 The case of *J.H. v Lawlor, Clinical Director of Jonathan Swift Clinic, St. James's Hospital*[110] did not concern a Renewal Order but instead concerned a re-grading of a patient from voluntary to involuntary status under s.23 and s.24. The phraseology regarding the RCP is slightly different here, as s.24(3) refers to "the consultant psychiatrist responsible for the care and treatment of the person immediately before his or her detention under section 23". Issues can therefore arise as to whether the psychiatrist was the RCP at the time of the earlier detention under s.23.

6–46 The patient in *J.H. v Lawlor* had initially been admitted on a voluntary basis but three days later the provisions of s.23 of the 2001 Act were invoked by a nurse at 9.20am on April 30, 2007. The first psychiatrist, Dr Fitzmaurice, completed the first part of Form 13 at 12.02pm and the second psychiatrist signed the certificate section of the form at 8.04pm The following morning, at 9.40am, Dr Fitzmaurice signed the Admission Order. The 24-hour detention period had been exceeded by 20 minutes, and this part of the decision is considered above at para.5–53.

According to affidavit evidence, at the tribunal hearing, the patient's solicitor asked Dr Fitzmaurice about when he first came into contact with the applicant at the hospital. Dr Fitzmaurice stated that his first contact with the applicant was some time after 11.00am on the morning of April 30, 2007. The solicitor also asked him whether he had been the consultant psychiatrist who was responsible for the applicant during his period of "voluntary detention" between the time of his voluntary admission on April 27, 2007 and the making of the detention order under s.23, and the response was a confirmation that he had not been responsible for the applicant during that period, and that he thought that his colleague, Dr Greene, consultant psychiatrist, would have been the person responsible for the applicant during that period. In a replying affidavit, Dr Fitzmaurice stated that the post of consultant psychiatrist at the clinic had been vacant since the retirement of another psychiatrist and that he held the post of consultant psychiatrist on a *locum* basis. When the applicant was first admitted on April 27 as a voluntary patient, he was admitted under the care of Dr Gargi, who was the *locum* consultant psychiatrist for the last two weeks of April up to 5pm on April

---

[109] O'Neill J. in *W.Q. v Mental Health Commission* [2007] 3 I.R. 755 at 765, quoted with approval by MacMenamin J. in *J.B. (No.2)* at para.61; [2007] 4 I.R. 778 at 794.

[110] [2007] I.E.H.C. 225; [2008] 1 I.R. 476; High Court, Peart J., June 25, 2007.

27. Between that time and 9am on April 30, the *locum* was Dr Greene, and Dr Fitzmaurice took up the *locum* position again at 9am on April 30. On the morning of April 30, at "shortly after 10 a.m.", he came on to the applicant's ward, and he reviewed the applicant's file and case notes, and spoke to nursing staff and the junior doctors on the ward in order to gain some background information about the applicant. After some initial reluctance on the part of the applicant, he eventually agreed to meet and talk to Dr Fitzmaurice, who was then able to carry out an assessment of the applicant.

6–47 Peart J. said it was clear that Dr Fitzmaurice came on duty at 9am on April 30, which was 20 minutes prior to the making of the detention order by the nurse in question. In his view, a reasonable explanation was that Dr Fitzmaurice came on duty at 9am on April 30. From that moment, *which was before the making of the s.23 detention order*, he was in charge of the applicant's case as the *locum* consultant. As such, he was the person referred to in s.24 and whose obligation it was, after the detention order was made at 9.20am, to make a referral to a second consultant psychiatrist for a certificate under s.24(2) of the Act. He was, therefore, also the person referred to in s.24(3) whose obligation it is to make an Admission Order where that second consultant psychiatrist has issued the required certificate under s.24(2) of the Act.[111] Peart J. considered alternative situations which might occur:

> "I would go so far as to state that even if he had not physically arrived at the hospital at 9 a.m., his period of responsibility had nonetheless commenced whereby he became the consultant psychiatrist responsible for the applicant. A realistic and practical view must be taken of such matters. It is possible, for example, that on his way to work at the hospital that morning he may have a puncture which could delay his arrival. Alternatively there may be a traffic congestion which delays his arrival until after 9.20 a.m., even though he was supposed to come on duty at 9 a.m. These things happen in the real world, and I reject the notion that because the consultant concerned may not have been physically present in the hospital, either through that type of delay or otherwise, that he or she loses the status of being the consultant responsible for the patient at a relevant time. Once his shift started he was the person to whom those working under him would refer matters on which they needed advice or consultation."[112]

Since he had decided the point on this basis, he did not need to consider s.24(6), which provides that references in s.24 to the consultant psychiatrist responsible for the care and treatment of the person include references to a consultant psychiatrist acting on behalf of the first-mentioned consultant psychiatrist. But Peart J. commented that this provision certainly would seem to cover a situation

---

[111] [2008] 1 I.R. 476 at 493.
[112] [2008] 1 I.R. 476 at 493.

where the consultant psychiatrist responsible for the patient immediately prior to the making of the s.23 detention order has gone off duty, or is ill, or otherwise absent or unavailable at a time when the Admission Order should be made under s. 24(3) of the Act. In such circumstances, he said, some consultant who takes their place is entitled to make the Admission Order, since they are acting on behalf of the first-mentioned consultant.[113]

M.M. v Clinical Director of the Central Mental Hospital

6–48 The patient in *M.M. v Clinical Director of the Central Mental Hospital*[114] had originally been detained in the Mercy Hospital, Cork, in May 1998 under the 1945 Act, under the care of Dr Cooney, consultant psychiatrist at that hospital. In November 1998, Dr Cooney authorised Mr M.'s transfer to the CMH,[115] and it was Dr Cooney who, since that date, had signed the various orders renewing his detention at the CMH, both under the 1945 Act and the 2001 Act. Both he and the relevant staff at the CMH, together with the applicant himself and his family, considered Dr Cooney to be the consultant psychiatrist who was most familiar with Mr M.'s condition and requirements for treatment and care. Dr Cooney was in regular correspondence with the CMH and attended a number of case conferences at the hospital. Dr Cooney did not give evidence at the tribunal hearing concerning the latest Renewal Order and was not notified that it was due to take place. It was Dr Duffy of the CMH who gave evidence at the tribunal. The independent psychiatrist appointed under s.17 had not consulted Dr Cooney when writing the report. At the tribunal hearing, Mr M.'s solicitor submitted that as Dr Cooney was not on the staff of the CMH, this constituted a fundamental defect in the lawfulness of his detention. This issue was also the subject of detailed evidence at the High Court hearing, much of which concerned the fact that while Dr Cooney was not involved in the day-to-day treatment of Mr M., he had seen him three times in 2007 and was involved in the management of when a possible transfer of Mr M. back to Cork might occur.

There were detailed legal submissions from the parties, citing case law such as *W.Q.*[116], *J.H. v Lawlor*[117] and *J.B. (No.2)*[118] and textbooks by Baroness Hale[119] and Professor Kennedy.[120]

---

113 [2008] 1 I.R. 476 at 494.
114 [2008] I.E.H.C. 44; High Court, Peart J., February 1, 2008; [2008] I.E.S.C. 31; Supreme Court, May 7, 2008.
115 This transfer took place under s.208 of the 1945 Act—[2008] I.E.H.C. 44, p.17.
116 *W.Q. v Mental Health Commission* [2007] I.E.H.C. 154; [2007] 3 I.R. 755.
117 *J.H. v Lawlor, clinical director of Jonathan Swift Clinic, St. James's Hospital, Dublin* [2007] I.E.H.C. 225; [2008] 1 I.R. 476.
118 *J.B. v Director Central Mental Hospital (No.2)* [2007] I.E.H.C. 201; [2007] 4 I.R. 778.
119 Brenda Hoggett, *Mental Health Law*, 4th edn (London: Sweet and Maxwell, 1996).
120 Harry Kennedy, *The Annotated Mental Health Acts* (Dublin: Blackhall, 2007).

6–49 Peart J. noted that, clearly, if Dr Duffy, the psychiatrist in the CMH, had signed the Renewal Order, her capacity to do so as the person in charge of Mr M. at the CMH could not be impugned, given her day-to-day involvement at the hospital. The Oireachtas had chosen not to define the term "the consultant psychiatrist responsible for the care and treatment of the patient concerned." He stated that the term is not confined to a consultant attached to the approved centre in which the patient is detained, but, on the other hand, it refers to "the" consultant.[121] It was important that Dr Duffy herself considered that Dr Cooney was the appropriate person to be considered the responsible consultant psychiatrist. In the absence of any express statutory definition of the phrase in the Act, a measure of discretion could be seen to exist in those involved in the care and treatment of the patient to consider and reach a view on who was the consultant best placed to be considered that person. However, Peart J. noted, "[t]hat is not to say that simply any consultant with a modicum of knowledge about the patient's illness and care and treatment requirements could simply be chosen out of convenience to sign a renewal order."[122] There was a discretion left open by the Act as to who in any particular case could be regarded as the person who is "the consultant psychiatrist responsible", and accordingly it was permissible for a responsible and considered decision to be made by those concerned as to who shall sign a Renewal Order, and it need not be one who is attached to the hospital in which the patient is detained, provided that the person so considered can be objectively seen to be so placed. Each case would need to be considered on its own facts and circumstances, and the primary concern will always have to be whether the best interests of the patient are protected.[123]

Peart J. approved of the reasoning in the *J.B. (No.2)* case.[124] He was not satisfied that the fact that the Mental Health Commission notified the independent psychiatrist that Dr Duffy was the person to be interviewed as the consultant psychiatrist responsible could be determinative of the issue. It might well have been appropriate for that consultant to interview both Dr Cooney and Dr Duffy, but that was "neither here nor there". No fundamental protection to which the applicant was entitled by virtue of the Act had been denied him.[125] Accordingly, the Renewal Order was appropriately signed by Dr Cooney and Mr M.'s detention was not unlawful.

6–50 The Supreme Court dismissed the patient's appeal in a judgment delivered by Geoghegan J.[126] The court said that it agreed with Peart J.'s conclusion that both Dr Cooney and Dr Duffy fell within the meaning of RCP in the Act, "though this approach necessarily entails a court giving an unorthodox though

---

[121] [2008] I.E.H.C. 44, p.19.
[122] [2008] I.E.H.C. 44, p.20.
[123] [2008] I.E.H.C. 44, p.20.
[124] *J.B. v Director Central Mental Hospital (No.2)* [2007] I.E.H.C. 201; [2007] 4 I.R. 778.
[125] [2008] I.E.H.C. 44, p.24.
[126] *M.M. v Clinical Director of the Central Mental Hospital* [2008] I.E.S.C. 31; Supreme Court, May 7, 2008.

purposive interpretation of the definite article before the words 'consultant psychiatrist' in section 15(2) of the 2001 Act."[127] Geoghegan J. was convinced that the absence of a statutory definition of the expression "the consultant psychiatrist responsible for the care and treatment of the patient" is quite deliberate. Given the lack of statutory definition, it was clearly a question of fact to determine whether Dr Cooney fell within the description when he signed the Renewal Order.

Geoghegan J. reviewed the High Court transcripts, in which the psychiatrists clarified the exact nature of their involvement in Mr M's care and treatment. For example, Dr Cooney said, "I certainly regard Dr. Duffy as the psychiatrist who is caring for M. on a day to day basis but I regard her care and the staff's care of M. as being, if you like, on loan from service in Cork, from his home service."[128]

Dr Duffy said that M. was having his care and treatment along a pathway from his local service to the CMH and, ultimately in the future, back again to Cork, and that M. would have more than one treating psychiatrist in his pathway of care.[129]

Geoghegan J. concluded on the facts that both Dr Cooney and Dr Duffy fell within the description "the consultant psychiatrist responsible for the care and treatment of the patient concerned." He approved of MacMenamin J.'s reasoning in *J.B. (No.2)*[130] where he had held that more than one person could come within the definition. The Supreme Court therefore dismissed the appeal and held that the applicant was in lawful custody.

---

[127]   *M.M. v Clinical Director of the Central Mental Hospital* [2008] I.E.S.C. 31; Supreme Court, May 7, 2008. p.5.

[128]   *M.M. v Clinical Director of the Central Mental Hospital* [2008] I.E.S.C. 31; Supreme Court, May 7, 2008. p.9.

[129]   *M.M. v Clinical Director of the Central Mental Hospital* [2008] I.E.S.C. 31; Supreme Court, May 7, 2008. p.11.

[130]   *J.B. v Director Central Mental Hospital (No.2)* [2007] I.E.H.C. 201; [2007] 4 I.R. 778.

CHAPTER 7

MENTAL HEALTH TRIBUNALS

INTRODUCTION

7–01 The Mental Health Tribunal (MHT) system introduced by the Mental Health Act 2001 was one of the main reasons for the enactment of the Act and marked a radical reform of Irish mental health law. While such tribunals had existed in England and Wales for decades, there may have been a view in Ireland that the fact that a patient could apply for review of their detention through an application under Art.40 was sufficient protection of their rights.

7–02 In 1979, the European Court of Human Rights held in the *Winterwerp* case that deprivation of liberty based on mental disorder required a review of lawfulness by a court or tribunal to be available at reasonable intervals.[1] This was followed by the enactment of the Health (Mental Services) Act 1981, which was passed in May 1981.[2]

7–03 The 1981 Act, which was never brought into force, would have established a "psychiatric review board or boards" for each health board area. If a person (other than a close relative) applied for a review of detention, the board could hold a review at its discretion. If a close relative applied, it was mandatory that the board hold a review. The board would have had power to discharge the patient, either unconditionally or subject to conditions concerning their continuing care or supervision.[3] If the board found that the patient should not be discharged, then no further review could be held for at least six months. A patient could appeal a decision of the board to the Minister for Health. In the case of a patient in long-term detention for over two years, a review was required at least every two years, if there was no application for a review. The Minister also had the power to reduce this two-year period to one year by regulations.

The European Court of Human Rights then held in *X. v United Kingdom*[4] in November 1981 that a review by way of habeas corpus procedure was not sufficient for a continuing confinement.[5] At Commission stage in that case, in

---

[1] *Winterwerp v The Netherlands* (1979–80) 2 E.H.R.R. 387.
[2] There is no reference to the *Winterwerp* case or to the European Convention on Human Rights (ECHR) in the Oireachtas debates on the 1980 Bill which became the 1981 Act.
[3] Review could also be held of the conditions applying to a patient who had been discharged conditionally.
[4] *X. v United Kingdom*, Application No.7215/75, Judgment November 5, 1981 (1981) 4 E.H.R.R. 188.
[5] Note, however, that in other contexts the habeas corpus procedure in Northern Ireland has been held to comply with art. 5(4)—see *Brogan v UK* (1989) 11 E.H.R.R. 117 at para.65.

July 1980, it was found that if a patient was required to wait six months before being entitled to apply for a review of detention by a tribunal, this was not "speedy" enough to comply with art.5(4).[6]

It is not entirely clear why the 1981 Act was not commenced. In response to a Parliamentary Question in 1987, the Minister for Health pointed out some defects and limitations in the 1981 Act which had been spotted while regulations were being drafted.[7] The *Green Paper on Mental Health* (1992) noted that the provisions of the 1981 Act, "have been overtaken by developments in international law which require different safeguards against improper detention" and that "the general thrust of the Act has been superseded by developments in the psychiatric services".[8] Raftery has argued that the 1981 Act was not commenced due to "opposition from psychiatrists, who regarded the establishment of independent tribunals (with non-medical members) to review their diagnoses and committal orders as an unwarranted interference in their professional expertise."[9]

7–04 In 1995, Costello P. referred to the delay in enacting new legislation and complained that "the best is the enemy of the good."[10] He found that s.207 of the Mental Treatment Act 1945 was unconstitutional for various reasons including the fact that there was no practical way in which a transferred patient could have their continued detention reviewed.[11] However, the main sections of the 1945 Act remained in force and continued to be used. The White Paper was published in 1995 and confirmed that a new Act was needed to conform with the European Convention.[12] Croke's constitutional challenge to the main sections of the 1945 Act succeeded in the High Court,[13] partly on the basis that the 1945 Act should have provided for an automatic independent review of

---

[6] (1981) 4 E.H.R.R. 188, para.138. The question of speed is not specifically referred to in the court's decision.

[7] (a) A review board could order a conditional discharge or revoke an order for conditional discharge (s.39) but there was no definition of conditional discharge or power to prescribe such a definition. (b) There was no power to make regulations under s.41 regulating the procedures to be adopted by a board reviewing long-stay patients, such as was provided in s.38 where a review was requested. (c) There was no provision for prescribing the form of an extension of a detention order in s.24. (d) A review board could order discharge or continued detention (s.39) but could not make any other order or recommendations, for instance relating to rehabilitation and re-training of a patient with a view to their discharge. (e) While the Act permitted designation and dedesignation of a hospital it did not provide for the dedesignation of part of a hospital, for instance for use as a mental handicap centre—376 *Dáil Debates*, December 17, 1987, Written Answer No.91.

[8] Department of Health, *Green Paper on Mental Health* (Dublin: Stationery Office, 1992), para.16.13.

[9] Mary Raftery, "Psychiatric Profession At It Again", *Irish Times*, May 26, 2005.

[10] *R.T. v Director of Central Mental Hospital* [1995] 2 I.R. 65 at 81.

[11] [1995] 2 I.R. 65 at 80.

[12] Department of Health, *A New Mental Health Act: White Paper* (Dublin: Stationery Office, 1995)

[13] *Croke v Smith (No.2)*, High Court, Budd J., July 27 and 31, 1995.

detention, but the challenge was rejected in the Supreme Court in 1996.[14] There were friendly settlements in *O'Reilly v Ireland*[15] and *Croke v Ireland*,[16] and the Government promised that new legislation was on its way. A Government Bill was finally published in 1999, and was passed as the 2001 Act. The main provisions came into force in November 2006.[17]

The main reason for the five-year delay in implementing the MHT system from 2001 to 2006 appears to have been that consultant psychiatrists were trying to negotiate the appointment of extra consultants to provide cover for those who were attending tribunals.[18]

7–05 While the Mental Health Bill 1999 was being debated in the Oireachtas, it was predicted that there would be roughly 2,000 reviews by MHTs each year.[19] Now that the tribunal system is up and running, it has been confirmed that the level of MHT hearings is running at an average of 175 per month. There were 2,248 MHT hearings in 2007[20] and 2,096 hearings in 2008.[21] Certain Irish solicitors and barristers have developed specialist expertise in Mental Health Law, and there is a Mental Health Lawyers Association. Conferences have been held to discuss the tribunal system.[22]

7–06 The gross fees paid in association with the operation of MHTs during 2007 were approximately €10.685 million. The average fees were €3,103 per notification and €4,753 per hearing in 2007.[23] Preliminary figures for 2008 showed gross fees paid of €9,755,433. A number of unclaimed fees were still outstanding for 2008. Based on the above expenditure, the average cost per notification was €2,922.[24]

[14] [1998] 1 I.R. 101.
[15] *O'Reilly v Ireland*, European Commission of Human Rights, Application number 24196/94, Admissibility Decision, January 22, 1996 and Report of the Commission on Friendly Settlement, December 3, 1996.
[16] *Croke v Ireland* [1999] 1 M.H.L.R. 118; Application Number 33267/96, Admissibility Decision, European Court of Human Rights (Fourth Section), June 15, 1999; Judgment (Striking out), December 21, 2000.
[17] Mental Health Act 2001 (Commencement) Order 2006, S.I. No. 411 of 2006. See also Mental Health Act 2001 (Sections 1 to 5, 7, 31 to 55) (Commencement) Order 2002, S.I. No. 90 of 2002 and Mental Health Act 2001 (Establishment Day) Order 2002, S.I. No. 91 of 2002.
[18] Eithne Donnellan, "'Psychiatrists' Dispute Over Tribunals Finally Resolved", *Irish Times*, January 24, 2006.
[19] An estimate of 2,000 completed reviews per year was made by Minister Mary Hanafin on May 23, 2001—536 *Dáil Debates* 1439.
[20] Mental Health Commission, *Annual Report 2007 Including the Report of the Inspector of Mental Health Services 2007* (Dublin, 2008), Book 1, Part 1, p.41.
[21] Mental Health Commission, *Annual Report 2008 Including the Report of the Inspector of Mental Health Services 2008* (Dublin, 2009), Book 1, Part 1, p.44.
[22] For example, Annual Conference of Mental Health Commission, November 2007. See also Áine Hynes, "The Mental Health Act 2001 in Practice: A Legal Representative's Viewpoint"— UCC CCJHR Seminar, 2007.
[23] Parliamentary Question 28090/08, July 9, 2008.
[24] Parliamentary Questions 11201/09 and 11202/09, March 24, 2009.

7–07 A number of academics have studied the English Mental Health Review Tribunals (MHRTs) in action and made observations which suggest that the tribunal system does not operate strictly in accordance with legal principles.[25] In her 1989 study,[26] Peay found that the decision-making process in tribunals was sometimes back-to-front: the members determined the outcome they preferred and then selected the evidence to accord with that view. She found that decisions of the MHRTs were frequently dictated by the psychiatrist in the hospital—the Responsible Medical Officer (RMO).[27] RMOs were not impressed by the legal criteria for detention and were known to reduce patients' medication before a hearing to demonstrate the need for detention.

Another study by Dolan et al[28] which surveyed the experiences of patients found that only 9 per cent of them accurately understood the powers of MHRTs.[29] The majority of the patients (64 per cent) were happy with their legal representation and 56 per cent believed that the tribunal format was too formal. Ferencz and McGuire[30] observed that tribunal hearings were alienating experiences for patients. Patients were given little opportunity to speak and tribunals were uninterested in the patient's side of the story. They argued that tribunal hearings have a therapeutic quality, and that tribunals need to be more sensitive to these implications.

Richardson and Machin[31] found that the requirements of the Mental Health Act 1983 were discussed before the hearing in only one of 50 cases observed. The questions asked at the hearing demonstrated a clinical rather than a legal focus. Tribunals tended to be aware of, and to comply with, judicial rulings relating to interpretation of their specific powers, but compliance was lower on some other points, e.g. issues of procedural fairness concerning the medical

25 See Darius Whelan, "Mental Health Tribunals: A Significant Medico-Legal Change" (2004) 10 *Medico-Legal Journal of Ireland* 84.

26 Jill Peay, *Tribunals on Trial: A Study of Decision-Making Under the Mental Health Act 1983* (Oxford: Clarendon Press, 1989).

27 In 84 per cent of their decisions, tribunals agreed with the recommendation made by the RMO. See also a similar finding of a high level of agreement in Damian Mohan, Kevin Murray, Penny Steed & Mark A. Mellee, "Mental Health Review Tribunal Decisions in Restricted Hospital Order Cases at One Medium Secure Unit" (1998) 8 Crim. Behav. & Ment. H. 57.

28 Mairead Dolan, Robert Gibb & Placid Coorey, "Mental Health Review Tribunals: A Survey of Special Hospital Patients' Opinions" (1999) 10 J. Forensic Psychiatry 264. This study was conducted at Ashworth Hospital in Liverpool, a "Special Hospital", i.e. a high-security hospital.

29 The authors suggested that information sheets for patients not only inform them of their right to apply to a tribunal, but also set out the powers of the tribunal (Dolan, Gibb & Coorey, "Mental Health Review Tribunals: A Survey of Special Hospital Patients' Opinions" (1999) 10 J. Forensic Psychiatry 264, p.271.)

30 Nicola Ferencz & James McGuire, "Mental Health Review Tribunals in the UK: Applying a Therapeutic Jurisprudence Perspective" (2000) 37(1) *Court Review: The Journal of the American Judges Association* 48, available at *http://aja.ncsc.dni.us/htdocs/publications-courtreview.htm* [Accessed October 20, 2009.] Their study is based on a very small sample—17 patients and 10 tribunal members.

31 Genevra Richardson & David Machin, "Judicial Review and Tribunal Decision-Making: A Study of the Mental Health Review Tribunal" [2000] *Public Law* 494. The authors observed 50 tribunal hearings and conducted 38 interviews with patient representatives, tribunal members and members of tribunal staff.

member of the tribunal.[32] The reasons given by tribunals for their decisions were often inadequate,[33] the reasons did not reflect the issues in the hearing[34] and apparent compliance with the duty to give reasons was relatively easy to achieve.[35] Overall, the influence of judicial review on decision making was patchy at best.[36]

Writing an opinion piece from the perspective of the psychiatric profession, Obomanu and Kennedy[37] pull no punches in their critique of the adversarial tactics employed by lawyers at tribunals. They suggested that four principles should be written into the English Mental Health Bill which was being discussed at the time, including a principle that nothing should be said or done to undermine an existing or future therapeutic relationship. Another principle they suggest is that tribunals should give greater weight to opinions of clinicians who would take responsibility for the care and treatment of the patient following their move to a lower level of security.[38] Their article is in stark contrast to that of Richardson and Machin, and reading the two articles together provides a thought-provoking illustration of the difficult balancing act involved in tribunal decision making.

7–08 The 2001 Act contains the basic rules for the operation of the MHTs. There are no formalised rules of procedure, although the Mental Health Commission has produced procedural guidance and administrative protocols.[39]

Tribunals deal with various categories of case:

---

[32] For example, the medical member did not express a direct clinical opinion at any hearing, even though this was required for fairness, especially where the member's view differs from that of a medical witness. Genevra Richardson and David Machin, "Judicial Review and Tribunal Decision-Making. A Study of the Mental Health Review Tribunal" [2000] *Public Law* 494.

[33] See example given at p.510 of their article, in which there was no indication of the type of disorder which the patient had. Genevra Richardson and David Machin, "Judicial Review and Tribunal Decision-Making. A Study of the Mental Health Review Tribunal" [2000] *Public Law* 494 at 507

[34] For example, in 76 per cent of hearings the emphasis was on risk rather than the presence of a disorder, while in relation to reasons the figure was only 32 per cent. Genevra Richardson and David Machin, "Judicial Review and Tribunal Decision-Making. A Study of the Mental Health Review Tribunal" [2000] *Public Law* 494 at 512.

[35] The authors note that the record provided by the reasons given by the tribunal is partial and provides an inadequate basis on which to judge the legality of a tribunal's decision-making by means of judicial review. Genevra Richardson and David Machin, "Judicial Review and Tribunal Decision-Making. A Study of the Mental Health Review Tribunal" [2000] *Public Law* 494 at 512.

[36] Genevra Richardson & David Machin, "Judical Review and Tribunal Decision-Making. A Study of the Mental Health Review Tribunal" [2000] *Public Law* 494 at 514.

[37] William Obomanu & Harry Kennedy, "Juridogenic Harm: Statutory Principles for the New Mental Health Tribunals" (2001) 25 Psych. Bull. 331.

[38] They state that the opinion of "independent" experts can be less reliable because they are disconnected from responsibility and vulnerable to market pressures. William Obomanu & Harry Kennedy, "Juridogenic Harm: Statutory Principles for the New Mental Health Tribunals" (2001) 25 Psych. Bull. 331 at 332.

[39] Mental Health Commission, *Mental Health Tribunals: Procedural Guidance and Administrative Protocols* (2006).

- Involuntary Admission Orders (s.14; Form 6)
- Re-grading of a patient from voluntary to involuntary status (s.23 and s.24; Form 13)
- Renewal Orders (s.15; Form 7)
- Proposals to transfer to the Central Mental Hospital (CMH) (s.21; Form 11)
- Proposal to perform psychosurgery (s.58; Form 15)
- Transitional provisions for adults (s.72)

MHTs have no role in the following:

- Treatment/medication decisions
- Admission of children (dealt with by the District Court)
- Criminal matters (dealt with by the Mental Health (Criminal Law) Review Board)

7–09 The MHT system involves a number of different personnel, but it is noteworthy that at least three psychiatrists are involved: the Responsible Consultant Psychiatrist (RCP) at the approved centre; the second opinion psychiatrist and the psychiatrist member of the tribunal. It is arguable that the involvement of three psychiatrists serves to reinforce the medical model of civil commitment, and gives undue weight to medical opinion. On the other hand, each psychiatrist performs a very different role and the weight of their involvement is counter-balanced by the involvement of the tribunal chairperson, the lay member and the patient's legal representative.

7–10 Once the Mental Health Commission receives an Admission or Renewal Order, it must refer the matter to a tribunal; assign a legal representative to the patient and direct a second opinion psychiatrist to examine the patient, interview the responsible consultant psychiatrist, and review the records.[40] The second opinion psychiatrist must report within 14 days of the direction. The second opinion psychiatrist must send their report to the Mental Health Commission and a copy to the patient's legal representative.

The MHT must decide to confirm or revoke the order within 21 days of the making of the order.[41] After conducting its review the MHT must either:

> (a) if satisfied that the patient is suffering from a mental disorder, and
>> (i) that the provisions of ss.9, 10, 12, 14, 15 and 16, where applicable, have been complied with, or
>> (ii) if there has been a failure to comply with any such provision, that the failure does not affect the substance of the order and does not cause an injustice,
> affirm the order, or

---

[40] Section 17 of the Mental Health Act 2001.
[41] Section 18 of the Mental Health Act 2001.

(b) if not so satisfied, revoke the order and direct that the patient be discharged from the approved centre concerned.[42]

7–11 In the first full calendar year of their operation, MHTs revoked the Admission Order, Renewal Order or re-grading in 11.5 per cent of cases.[43] In 2008, the MHT revocation rate was also 11.5 per cent.[44] Monthly figures show that the revocation rate was 12.9 per cent in the first six months of 2007 and dropped to 9.7 per cent in the second half of the year.[45] During 2008, the monthly percentages varied from 6 per cent to 15 per cent.[46] Revocation of the order means that the MHT ordered the patient's discharge, even though the RCP in most of these cases presumably remained of opinion that the patient had a mental disorder as defined in the 2001 Act. There has been some media commentary to the effect that this is a high rate of revocation[47] but it is arguably a demonstration that the MHT system is robust and engages in meaningful review of each patient's case. It is difficult to find comparative figures for other jurisdictions, but one example is that in England and Wales in 2004, patients were discharged by tribunals in 11 per cent of cases.[48]

7–12 Decisions to revoke an order at the MHT in 2007 have been analysed by individual file review by the Commission and this showed that decisions could be grouped into the following categories shown in the following table:

---

[42] Section 18(1) of the Mental Health Act 2001.

[43] There were 2,248 MHT hearings in 2007 (*Annual Report 2007*, Book 1, p.41), including 21 proposals to transfer to the CMH, which cannot be "revoked" by the MHT. In 256 (11.5 per cent) of the 2,227 MHT hearings other than those concerning transfers to the CMH, the MHT revoked the order. The figure of 256 appeared in statistics published on the Mental Health Commission website at *http://www.mhcirl.ie* [Acessed September 20, 2009].

[44] Statistics on the Mental Health Commission website record that in 2008 MHTs revoked 241 orders at 2,096 hearings. See also *Annual Report 2008*, Figure 6, Book 1, p.45, showing the percentage of MHT revocations in each month in 2008.

[45] From January to June 2007 there were 1,212 hearings and 156 revocations (12.9 per cent). From July to December 2007 there were 1,036 hearings and 100 revocations (9.7 per cent). The Commission has commented that the initial rise appears to be linked to a number of the transitional cases and decisions in a number of early High Court challenges that clarified procedural aspects of the involuntary admission process—*Annual Report 2007*, p.41.

[46] *Annual Report 2008*, Figure 6, Book 1, p.45.

[47] "12% revocation rate in Mental Health Tribunals", *Irish Medical News*, February 11, 2007.

[48] In 2004 in England there were 1,351 discharges out of a total of 11,897 hearings. The discharges include absolute discharges, delayed discharges, conditional discharges and deferred conditional discharges. These figures come from Freedom of Information requests by Dave Sheppard. The percentage of discharges for 2005 (up to September) was actually higher at 15 per cent, but this was not for a full year.

*Analysis of Decision to Revoke an Order at the
Mental Health Tribunal 2007*

Reason	%
Patient not suffering from mental disorder at time of hearing	60%
Provisions of the Act have not been complied with	39%
Other, e.g. Patients AWOL	1%
Total	**100%**

Source: *Mental Health Commission, 2008*[49]

These figures show that in 60 per cent of cases where the MHT revoked the order, the tribunal's decision was based on the substantive issue of whether the patient had a mental disorder as defined in the Act. In 39 per cent of cases, the revocation was for a procedural reason. The breakdown is somewhat surprising, as it might have been thought, based on Art.40 applications, that the main issues arising at MHTs were procedural points, but in fact the majority of revocations are on the substantive issue instead. In some of the cases where the tribunal revokes the order, it is possible that the tribunal may have asked the patient if they are willing to remain in the hospital on a voluntary basis, as happened in *C.C. (No.2).*[50]

7–13 It is also possible for the RCP to revoke the order before the MHT hearing takes place. In 2007, this occurred in 42 per cent of cases[51] and in 2008 it occurred in 39 per cent of cases.[52] The Minister of State at the Department of Health and Children has expressed his concern about the high level of revoked Admission Orders that do not progress to an MHT.[53] O'Donoghue and Moran reported that 69 per cent of consultant psychiatrists acknowledge that involuntarily admitted patients are being changed to voluntary early to avoid a tribunal, and 21 per cent believe it occurs in over 40 per cent of cases.[54] However, it is also possible that a large number of these revocations simply

---

[49] *Annual Report 2007* (2008), Table 17, p.42. This type of analysis was not included in the 2008 Report.

[50] *C.C. v Clinical Director of St. Patrick's Hospital (No.2)* [2009] I.E.H.C. 47; High Court, Hedigan J., February 6, 2009. See para.7–65 below.

[51] There were 3,422 admissions, renewals or regradings and 1,444 (42 per cent) revocations before hearing by the RCP.

[52] There were 3,328 admissions, renewals or regradings and 1,290 (39 per cent) revocations before hearing by the RCP.

[53] Department of Health and Children, *Review of the Operation of the Mental Health Act 2001: Findings and Conclusions* (2007), p.13.

[54] Brian O'Donoghue and Paul Moran, "Consultant Psychiatrists' Experiences and Attitudes Following the Introduction of the Mental Health Act 2001: a National Survey" (2009) 26 *Irish Journal of Psychological Medicine* 23.

reflect the fact that patients' treatment is progressing well within the 21-day period, so that they can be either discharged or converted to voluntary status.

7–14 Even though tribunal hearings take place in private, it is arguable that selected decisions of MHTs need to be published in order to assist legal representatives for other patients in preparing their cases. In *P.P.A. v Refugee Appeals Tribunal*[55] it was held that applicants for refugee status were entitled to copies of relevant previous decisions of the Refugee Appeals Tribunal in which issues of substantive legal principle were decided. In the Supreme Court, Geoghegan J. reasoned as follows:

> "The kind of fair procedures the Constitution may require in any given instance will always depend on the particular circumstances and, in the case of tribunals, what constitutes fair practice may differ greatly. The refugee appeals are heard by single members of the tribunal taken from a large panel. The chairman of the tribunal assigns a particular member of the tribunal to hear a particular appeal. It is of the nature of refugee cases that the problem for the appellant back in his or her country of origin which is leading him or her to seek refugee status is of a kind generic to that country or the conditions in that country. Thus, as in these appeals, it may be a problem of gross or official discrimination against homosexuals or it may be a problem of enforced female circumcision or it may be a problem of some concrete form of discrimination against a particular tribe. Where there are such problems, it is blindingly obvious, in my view, that fair procedures require some reasonable mechanisms for achieving consistency in both the interpretation and the application of the law in cases like this of a similar category. Yet, if relevant previous decisions are not available to an appellant, he or she has no way of knowing whether there is such consistency. It is not that a member of a tribunal is actually bound by a previous decision, but consistency of decisions based on the same objective facts may, in appropriate circumstances, be a significant element in ensuring that a decision is objectively fair rather than arbitrary."[56]

This reasoning would appear to have direct relevance to MHTs. While the State might well rely on the fact that "what constitutes fair practice may differ greatly", ultimately a court may decide to follow the reasoning above and apply it to the MHTs. In order for this to occur, a test case will need to be brought.

COMPOSITION OF TRIBUNALS

7–15 Members of MHTs are appointed by the Mental Health Commission for up to three years.[57] Each MHT has three members: a lawyer who acts as

---

[55] [2006] I.E.S.C. 53; [2007] 4 I.R. 94; [2007] 1 I.L.R.M. 288.
[56] [2007] 4 I.R. 94 at 105.
[57] Section 48 of the Mental Health Act 2001

chairperson, a consultant psychiatrist and another person.[58] The chairperson must be a practising barrister or solicitor who has had not less than seven years' experience as a practising barrister or solicitor ending immediately before appointment.[59] It is not possible for a judge to act as chairperson. The reference to a consultant psychiatrist[60] includes a person who was employed as a consultant psychiatrist by the HSE or an approved centre not more than seven years before their appointment.[61] In other words, the psychiatrist can be a recently retired psychiatrist or a psychiatrist who has recently left the employment of the HSE or an approved centre. The other person (commonly referred to as the lay member[62]) must *not* be a psychiatrist, a lawyer qualified to act as chairperson, a registered medical practitioner or a registered nurse.[63] There are no other criteria laid down in the Act for appointment of the lay member.[64]

MHT members hold office for up to three years and may be reappointed.[65] Rates of remuneration and expenses are determined by the Commission with the consent of the Ministers for Health and Finance.[66] Members are disqualified if they are adjudged bankrupt or sentenced to imprisonment, and may be removed by the Commission for certain reasons.[67]

The Commission publishes advertisements from time to time seeking new members of tribunal panels. All tribunal members receive initial training and refresher training as required. In 2007, there were 204 MHT members involved in hearing cases—66 chairs, 54 consultant psychiatrist members and 84 other members.[68]

At tribunal sittings, every member has a vote and every question shall be determined by a majority of the vote of the members.[69] In some cases, this may mean that if the chairperson is being "too legalistic" or if the psychiatrist is overly inclined to agree with the diagnosis by the RCP, they can be outvoted by the other two members.

---

[58] This person must *not* be a psychiatrist, a lawyer qualified to act as chairperson, a registered medical practitioner or a registered nurse—s.48(3)(c).

[59] Section 48(3)(b) of the 2001 Act.

[60] Section 2 of the 2001 Act as amended by the Health Act 2004 defines a consultant psychiatrist as one who is employed by the HSE or by an approved centre or a person whose name is entered on the division of psychiatry or the division of child and adolescent psychiatry of the Register of Medical Specialists maintained by the Medical Council in Ireland.

[61] Section 48(12) of the Mental Health Act 2001 as amended by the Health Act 2004.

[62] In Scotland, this member is referred to as the "general member"—Sch. 2, Mental Health (Care and Treatment) (Scotland) Act 2003.

[63] Section 48(3)(c) of the 2001 Act.

[64] In England and Wales, the third member must be a person "with experience in administration … knowledge of social services or such other suitable qualifications and experience as the Lord Chancellor considers suitable"—Mental Health Act 1983, Sch.2, para.1(c).

[65] Section 48(6) and s.48(11) of the 2001 Act.

[66] Section 48(8) of the 2001 Act.

[67] Section 48(10) and s.48(9) of the 2001 Act.

[68] Mental Health Commission, *Report on the Operation of Part 2 of the 2001 Act* (2008), p.57.

[69] Section 48(4) of the 2001 Act.

MHTs perform the role of a "court" under art.5 of the European Convention on Human Rights (ECHR) and it has been held that any body which performs such a role must be independent and impartial.[70] The method of appointment of the MHTs appears to conform with these requirements, assuming any issues regarding impartiality in particular cases are addressed.[71]

It is arguable that the tribunals should have a separate office and/or a president, to emphasise their separate role from the Mental Health Commission. On the other hand, the fact that the tribunals are administratively supported by the Commission helps to streamline matters and ensures that the tribunals aspect of mental health fits in with overall developments in mental health.

THE ROLE OF THE INDEPENDENT PSYCHIATRIST

7–16 A panel of consultant psychiatrists[72] for purposes of independent examination of patients is appointed by the Commission[73] following advertisements from time to time as necessary. These independent psychiatrists are often referred to as "s.17 psychiatrists", as their role is set out in s.17 of the 2001 Act.

Once the Commission has received an Admission or Renewal Order, it must, as soon as possible, direct in writing a member of the panel of consultant psychiatrists to examine the patient, interview the RCP and review the records relating to the patient.[74] On the meaning of the RCP, see paras 6–37 to 6–50 above. Strictly speaking, the "examination" is not defined by s.2, as that definition is restricted to recommendations, Admission Orders or Renewal Orders. However, it is likely that a court would expect the requirements of s.2 to be satisfied, i.e. that it should be a personal examination of the process and content of thought, the mood and the behaviour of the patient. The independent psychiatrist must be admitted to the approved centre to carry out these functions and it is an offence to fail to co-operate with them.[75] The independent psychiatrist's role is "to determine in the interest of the patient whether the patient is suffering from a mental disorder".[76] They must report in writing within 14 days to the MHT and provide a copy to the patient's legal representative.

---

[70] *D.N. v Switzerland*, Application 27154/95, Judgment March 29, 2001 (2003) 37 E.H.R.R. 21, para.42.

[71] See however, Anselm Eldergill, "The Best is the Enemy of the Good: The Mental Health Act 2001: Part 2" (2009) J. Mental Health L.7 at 12.

[72] Section 2 of the 2001 Act as amended by the Health Act 2004 defines a consultant psychiatrist as one who is employed by the HSE or by an approved centre or a person whose name is entered on the division of psychiatry or the division of child and adolescent psychiatry of the Register of Medical Specialists maintained by the Medical Council in Ireland.

[73] Section 33(3)(b) of the 2001 Act.

[74] Section 17(1)(c) of the 2001 Act.

[75] Section 17 of the 2001 Act.

[76] Section 17(1)(c) of the 2001 Act.

7–17 In 2007, there were 48 independent psychiatrists involved in cases which had been referred to MHTs.[77] The Commission assigned 3,338 independent medical examinations to consultant psychiatrists for completion in 2008 in accordance with s.17.[78] It is not clear how many of these actually led to reports being written. Some patients are discharged after only a few days and presumably no report is written in those cases.[79]

The independent psychiatrist's report is a further control which attempts to minimise the possibility of abuse or error in psychiatric detention.

The independent psychiatrist's report may assist the MHT in making its decision whether to continue to affirm or revoke the Admission or Renewal Order. It is an additional factor which may have a bearing on the final outcome. It may assist in ensuring that the burden of proof is not placed on the patient.[80] There are no statistics available on the frequency with which the independent psychiatrist's opinion differs from that of the RCP, but practitioners in the area have suggested that such disagreement is virtually non-existent. It is important to bear in mind that the independent psychiatrist's report is frequently prepared before Day 14 of detention, while the MHT may be sitting on Day 18, for example. This means that the independent psychiatrist's report may already have become dated and of limited relevance to the question of whether the patient has a mental disorder within the meaning of the Act on Day 18.

7–18 There is some case law in criminal cases which suggests that judges may exclude some psychiatric evidence which goes beyond an opinion on whether the person has a mental illness.[81] However, in later cases the courts have been more willing to admit such evidence provided the central role of the jury as fact-finder is not interfered with.[82] While not directly relevant to the role of the independent psychiatrist in civil mental health cases, these cases are a reminder that the psychiatrist's report should focus on the facts of the case and the psychiatrist's expert opinion on the person's mental state as much as possible.

7–19 The Act does not specifically permit the patient to appoint their own psychiatric expert, but presumably if the patient had sufficient means to do so, the MHT would admit evidence from such an expert.[83]

---

[77] *Report on the Operation of Part 2 of the 2001 Act* (2008), p.57.

[78] Mental Health Commission, *Annual Report 2008*, p.44.

[79] For example, in 2007, 17.59 per cent of episodes of involuntary admission lasted 10 days or less (*Annual Report 2007*, Table 14, p.38.)

[80] See further paras 8–32 to 8–34 below.

[81] *R. v Turner* [1975] Q.B. 834 at 841; *People (D.P.P.) v Kehoe* [1992] I.L.R.M. 481 at 484.

[82] *D.P.P. v Abdi* [2005] 1 I.L.R.M. 382; *R. v O'Brien, Hall & Sherwood* [2000] E.W.C.A. Crim. 3; *Murphy v R.* (1989) 167 C.L.R. 94; [1989] 86 A.L.R. 35. See also Gerry Johnstone, "From Experts in Responsibility to Advisers on Punishment: The Role of Psychiatrists in Penal Matters" in Peter Rush et al (eds.), *Criminal Legal Doctrine* (Ashgate, Dartmouth, 1997).

[83] Compare s.76 of the Mental Health Act 1983 (England and Wales), which entitles the patient to seek their own independent medical report.

7–20 In practice, the independent psychiatrist is not called to give oral evidence at the MHT hearing. As was stated earlier, the independent psychiatrist's report may already have become dated and of limited relevance by the time of the hearing. On the other hand, if the MHT bases its decision to some extent on the independent psychiatrist's report, then on first principles of fair procedure it would be expected that the psychiatrist should be available for oral evidence and questioning. If a patient wished to insist on the attendance of the psychiatrist, reference could be made to s.49(6)(d) of the 2001 Act, which states that written statements can be admitted as evidence "with the consent of the patient the subject of the review or his or her legal representative." It would appear to follow that if the patient does not consent to admission of the psychiatrist's written report, then the report cannot be admitted. It might be counter argued that the written report prepared by the independent psychiatrist under s.17 is of a different nature from other written evidence, but a court could still hold that no written evidence can be admitted without the patient's consent. (See also the discussion of confidentiality at paras 11–20 to 11–27 below.)

In administrative law, there are authorities which suggest that in some circumstances admission of a written report may breach fair procedures. In *Kiely v Minister for Social Welfare (No.2)*[84] Mrs Kiely's husband, a blacksmith with CIE, sustained an accident at work which caused severe burns which eventually led to depression. He died of a heart attack a few months later, and Mrs Kiely was claiming death benefit. Her case came before an appeals officer in the Department of Social Welfare. The key issue was whether it was possible for a heart attack to have been caused by depression and thus be connected with her husband's employment. Mrs Kiely's two medical witnesses gave oral evidence that the coronary thrombosis resulted from the accident. However, the appeals officer based his decision mainly on a letter written for the Department three years earlier by a cardiac specialist, who concluded that there was no causal connection between the accident and the death. The cardiac specialist had based his conclusion on a summarised version of Mr Kiely's case history. The appeals officer did not require that expert to give oral evidence or submit himself to cross-examination. The appeals officer rejected Mrs Kiely's application for death benefit.

The Supreme Court quashed the appeals officer's decision on various grounds, including the failure to hear oral evidence from the cardiac specialist. The court held that this created an unfair imbalance in the proceedings and Henchy J. said:

> "Of one thing I feel certain, that natural justice is not observed if the scales of justice are tilted against one side all through the proceedings. *Audi alteram partem* means that both sides must be fairly heard. That is not done if one party is allowed to send in his evidence in writing, free from the truth-eliciting processes of a confrontation which are inherent in an oral hearing, while his

[84] [1977] I.R. 267.

opponent is compelled to run the gauntlet of oral examination and cross-examination. The dispensation of justice, in order to achieve its ends, must be even-handed in form as well as in content. Any lawyer of experience could readily recall cases where injustice would certainly have been done if a party or a witness who had committed his evidence to writing had been allowed to stay away from the hearing, and the opposing party had been confined to controverting him simply by adducing his own evidence. In such cases it would be cold comfort to the party who had been thus unjustly vanquished to be told that the tribunal's conduct was beyond review because it had acted on logically probative evidence and had not stooped to the level of spinning a coin or consulting an astrologer. Where essential facts are in controversy, a hearing which is required to be oral and confrontational for one side but which is allowed to be based on written and, therefore, effectively unquestionable evidence on the other side has neither the semblance nor the substance of a fair hearing. It is contrary to natural justice."[85]

In applying the *Kiely* case to MHT hearings, it must be remembered that there will always be oral evidence from a psychiatrist at the approved centre and so the stark unfairness which had occurred in *Kiely* will not normally apply. However, Henchy J.'s reasoning may well apply in some cases where there are assertions in the independent psychiatrist's report which are being relied upon by the MHT in making its decision, and which are disputed by the patient. Reference may also be made to the more recent case of *The State (Boyle) v General Medical Services (Payment) Board*[86] in which the applicant wished to call an expert who had compiled some economic data which went against him and the request was refused. Keane J. held that this refusal did not constitute a violation of constitutional justice because when the applicant received a copy of the data, he had not raised any specific issue as to its reliability, which required oral evidence to be resolved. Keane J. cited *Russell v Duke of Norfolk*, where it was said that the requirements of natural justice must depend on the circumstances of the case, the nature of the inquiry, the rules under which the tribunal is acting, the subject matter that is being dealt with, and so forth.[87]

It seems quite possible that before a patient could insist that the psychiatrist be called for cross-examination, the patient would need to indicate specific and real grounds of inquiry that they would like to raise with the psychiatrist. On the other hand, the fact that MHT hearings involve the right to liberty may mean that the courts will require stricter adherence to the requirements of fair procedures.

---

[85] [1977] I.R. 267 at 281–2.
[86] [1981] I.L.R.M. 14.
[87] Tucker L.J. in *Russell v Duke of Norfolk* [1949] 1 All E.R. 109 at 118.

Time Limits for MHT Hearings

7–21 Our system of MHT hearings involves automatic reviews within 21 days of each Admission or Renewal Order. The reviews are automatic, even though the Strasbourg Court has never explicitly ruled that this is required. In the *Winterwerp* case[88] it was held that the validity of confinement must be based on the persistence of the disorder.[89] The ECHR also stated that a review of detention must be available "at reasonable intervals."[90] However, as Baroness Hale has noted, "[t]here is no Strasbourg case which implies into article 5(4) the requirement of a judicial review in every case where the patient is unable to make her own application."[91]

The Act requires that a MHT hearing take place "as soon as may be" but not later than 21 days after the Admission Order or Renewal Order. The Minister of State at the Department of Children has noted that the Mental Health Commission believes that it is not cost effective to refer the matter to an MHT as soon as possible.[92] This is because of the high proportion of Admission Orders that are revoked prior to the holding of an MHT review within 21 days, and the fact that fees are payable to MHT members, legal representatives and consultants providing second opinions, when a planned hearing is cancelled due to the revocation of an Admission Order by the RCP. The Minister of State reiterated that the interests of patients were paramount and stated that he was concerned about the high level of revoked Admission Orders that do not progress to an MHT. He was also concerned about the disruption to services which can arise from the late notification of MHT hearings. The Minister stated that MHT hearings should take place at the earliest possible opportunity and that all necessary arrangements should be made to facilitate this. One way of enabling this would be to reduce the 14-day time period allowed for to receive the second consultant's report.[93]

The Mental Health Commission has not publicly acknowledged that its decisions on timing of MHT reviews are affected by cost considerations. Instead, it states that, once notified of an Admission or Renewal Order, it aims to arrange the MHT hearing at the earliest possible opportunity.[94] Hearings for involuntary Admission Orders were monitored by the Commission as to when in the 21-day period of the order the MHT occurred. In March 2007, 41 per cent of these

---

[88] *Winterwerp v The Netherlands* (1979–80) 2 E.H.R.R. 387.

[89] (1979–80) 2 E.H.R.R. 387 at 403 (para.39).

[90] (1979–90) 2 E.H.R.R. 387 at 408 (para.55).

[91] *R. (M.H.) v Secretary of State for Health* [2005] U.K.H.L. 60, para.24; [2006] 1 A.C. 441 at 455. See critical commentary in Peter Bartlett & Ralph Sandland, *Mental Health Law: Policy and Practice*, 3rd edn (Oxford: Oxford University Press, 2007) at pp.573–4.

[92] Department of Health and Children, *Review of the Operation of the Mental Health Act 2001: Findings and Conclusions* (2007), p.13.

[93] Department of Health and Children, *Review of the Operation of the Mental Health Act 2001: Findings and Conclusions* (2007), pp.13–14.

[94] Mental Health Commission, *Annual Report 2007*, Book 1, p.42.

hearings were occurring at or before Day 18 of the order. This increased to 46 per cent for September 2007 and to 66 per cent for December 2007.[95] No detailed breakdown of these figures is provided. It would appear that, either for cost reasons or due to practical considerations, most MHT hearings are taking place in the final few days of the 21-day period for review.

7–22 MHT hearings must take place at the latest within 21 days of each Admission or Renewal Order. This means that the decision must be made by midnight at the end of a 21-day period, which includes the day the Admission Order or Renewal Order was made. The calculation of this time limit may lead to some confusion, as is illustrated by an apparent miscalculation by the High Court in one case.[96] In a hypothetical case where a patient requires long-term treatment, the MHT reviews might take place as follows:

- Admission Order Day 1—MHT review within 21 days (e.g. Day 18)
- First Renewal Order for 3 months made on Day 19—MHT review within 21 days of Day 19
- Second Renewal Order for 6 months—MHT review within 21 days of making of Renewal Order
- Third Renewal Order for 12 months—MHT review within 21 days of making of Renewal Order

The example given above focuses on the question of the timing of the review by the MHT, which is always within 21 days of the making of the Admission or Renewal Order. One of the key consequences of this rule is that within the first 42 days of detention, the patient's case is reviewed twice by MHTs.

Note also *S.M. v Mental Health Commission* (above, paras 6–20 to 6–29), where it was held that a renewal order must be for a stated period, and it is not lawful for it to be "for a period not exceeding 3 months", for example.

7–23 The Mental Health Commission has commented that the review by an MHT of the second detention order, i.e. Renewal Order for up to three months, occurs within a short time interval of the first 21-day review, approximately 19 days in most cases. The Commission states that this can be confusing for the patient if they are very unwell and places a significant amount of administrative work on the approved centre within that time frame.[97]

The Commission has also stated that in response to concerns expressed that 12-month orders are for an overly long period, for which there is only one review in each period, the Commission will monitor the extent of use of these orders, as to date there have been a relatively small number. The Commission

---

[95] Mental Health Commission, Annual Report 2007, Book 1, p.42.
[96] See *A.M.C. v St. Luke's Hospital, Clonmel* [2007] I.E.H.C. 65; [2007] 2 I.R. 814; paras 4–03 and 6–15 above.
[97] Mental Health Commission, *Report on the Operation of Part 2 of the 2001 Act* (2008), p.81.

will further examine if it would be appropriate to recommend that the patient have a right to a further review within the 12-month period of the order, either automatically or by request.[98]

7–24 Care must also be taken to comply with the requirements regarding timing of the making of Renewal Orders, duration of Renewal Orders and possible extensions of time for MHT hearings in limited circumstances.[99] In summary, a Renewal Order may be *made* at any time before the expiry of the previous detention period, but does not *come into effect* until the expiry of that previous period. The MHT may extend the duration of an Admission Order for two further periods of 14 days each, but it may not extend the duration of a Renewal Order.

The Mental Health Commission is not required to remind approved centres of the expiry of detention periods. The approved centre has a duty to ensure that each patient's case is reviewed continually, especially as their period of detention approaches expiry. It is only if a Renewal Order is made that the Mental Health Commission will then set up an MHT hearing to review the renewal. Approved centres must take care to ensure that orders are renewed on time, and put systems in place to avoid orders lapsing without being renewed.

7–25 The strict statutory deadline for an MHT hearing must be observed and a tribunal would act ultra vires if it issued a decision outside the statutory time frame. The patient's detention would become unlawful after the relevant period. There is general case law from England and Strasbourg which emphasises the need for a decision to be made speedily. As art.5(4) refers to a patient's right to take proceedings by which the lawfulness of detention may be decided "speedily", the Strasbourg Court has found breaches of the Convention where there have been delays of 24 days,[100] 5 weeks,[101] 8 weeks[102] and 5 months.[103] In England, there have been delays in tribunal hearings for various reasons, such as increasing case loads, shortages of tribunal members and the low number of staff at the MHRT Secretariat.[104] The English courts have found breaches of the

---

[98] Mental Health Commission, *Report on the Operation of Part 2 of the 2001 Act* (2008), p.88.

[99] See paras 6–15 to 6–19 on timing of making of Renewal Orders; paras 6–20 to 6–36 on duration of Renewal Orders and paras 7–30 to 7–36 on possible extensions of time for MHT hearings.

[100] *L.R. v France*, Application No.33395/96, judgment June 27, 2002, available only in French.

[101] *Laidin v France*, Application 43191/98, judgment November 5, 2002, available only in French.

[102] *E. v Norway* (1994) 17 E.H.R.R. 30. Eight weeks elapsed between the application for judicial review to the Oslo City Court and the eventual decision. The delay was caused partly by the fact that the application was made during court vacation, and partly by the judge taking three weeks to issue the decision. No compensation was awarded to Mr E.

[103] *Van der Leer v The Netherlands* (1990) 12 E.H.R.R. 567. There was a five-month delay between an application for release and a decision to release the patient. The court stated that it was irrelevant that the patient absconded and that she was granted probationary leave during this period.

[104] Peter Bartlett and Ralph Sandland, *Mental Health Law: Policy and Practice*, 3rd edn (Oxford: Oxford University Press, 2007), pp.387–392.

Human Rights Act 1998 in such cases. In the *ex parte C.* case,[105] the Court of Appeal held that an eight-week delay was too long when it was for purely administrative reasons. Lord Phillips M.R. cited Strasbourg case law[106] to the effect that regard would not be had to any alleged constraint of resources, as it is the responsibility of the Contracting State to sufficiently resource its tribunal system so as to enable Convention compliance. This principle has been applied in subsequent cases such as *K.B.*,[107] in which damages of between £750 and £4,000 were awarded to seven patients for the delays in their hearings coming before tribunals. The damages were based on the patients' loss of liberty, frustration, distress and damage to mental health.

While this case law is important for the general principles it states, it will probably not arise directly in Ireland as regards MHT hearings, due to the very tight time limits which apply under the 2001 Act.

7–26 However, it is important to look closely at the case of *L.R. v France*[108] in which it was held that a delay of 24 days between an application for release and actual release was held to be unacceptable. On December 4, 1995, Ms L.R. went to a police station to complain against an unknown person. The police transferred her to a psychiatric infirmary where she was diagnosed as mentally ill on December 5. She was then detained in hospital on December 5 by a decision of the prefect of police. On January 17, 1996, she applied to the prosecutor and on January 22, she applied to the *tribunal de grande instance* for immediate release. On February 22, the tribunal sent a letter to the hospital doctor asking him to inform her that the court would rule on her application soon. Meanwhile, on February 15, she had been released on a trial basis. The case was adjourned on several occasions due to the applicant's absence. The president of the *tribunal de grande instance* finally struck the case out on July 5, 1996, after being informed that the order committing the applicant had been lifted on May 3, 1996. The court found that there had been a breach of art.5(4) as follows:

> "Confining ourselves to considering that the request for immediate release was sent on January 22, 1996 and the applicant was released on trial on the following February 15, the court finds that this delay of 24 days does not conform with the requirement of Art.5 §4 for a decision to be made 'speedily'."[109]

[105]   *R. v MHRT London South & West Region ex parte C.* [2001] E.W.C.A. Civ. 1110; [2002] 1 W.L.R. 176.
[106]   *Bezicheri v Italy* (1989) 12 E.H.R.R. 210.
[107]   *R v MHRT ex parte K.B.* [2003] E.W.H.C. Admin. 193; [2004] Q.B. 936.
[108]   Application No.33395/96, Judgment June 27, 2002, only available in French.
[109]   *L.R. v France*, App. No. 33395/96, judgment June 27, 2002, para.38. French original: "En se limitant à considérer que la demande de sortie immédiate a été déposée le 22 janvier 1996 et que la requérante est sortie à l'essai le 15 février suivant, la Cour constate que ce délai de vingt-quatre jours ne répond pas à l'exigence de « bref délai » posée par l'article 5 §4 de la Convention."

It is difficult to establish how this case may apply to the Mental Health Act 2001. On the facts, it concerned an application for release by the patient, rather than an automatic review as applies in Ireland. The ECHR might well hold that in a jurisdiction where there is a speedy automatic review, the *L.R.* case is not directly applicable. It is noteworthy that Ms R. was actually detained for six weeks (from December 5 to January 17) before she began applying for her release, and without any tribunal review of her detention, and did not challenge this initial six-week period of detention. While there is no case law cited in the *L.R.* decision, reference may be made to the *Winterwerp* case, where six weeks of "emergency" confinement was not held to be unlawful, although the court said that some hesitation may be felt as to the need for such confinement to continue for as long as six weeks.[110]

The *L.R.* decision may have a more direct application in Ireland in the following situations: First, if an MHT extends the time for hearing a review under s.18(2),[111] this may mean that the first review of detention does not take place for up to seven weeks. Even though the request for extension may have been made by the patient, it might be found that the patient's request was affected by factors (such as non-availability of an important witness) which were not the responsibility of the patient. Secondly, a patient might apply for a review to an MHT during one of the renewed periods of detention. The 2001 Act does not allow for applications for reviews between renewals, and so if the patient were refused a review (as is likely) and told that the next review would take place in four months' time, for example, the patient might claim a violation of art.5(4). Thirdly, a patient might apply to the courts under the Art.40 procedure or the judicial review procedure and challenge a delay in deciding their case.[112] Finally, it has been suggested that the language of the *L.R.* case is so emphatic that it means that a period of 14 days for a decision on an application for release is a more appropriate one to ensure compliance with the Convention.[113] If this suggestion proves correct, this would mean that time limits would need to be shortened even further.

MHT MEMBERS HAVE NO POWER TO MAKE DECISIONS PRIOR TO MHT HEARING

7–27 The Act does not explicitly grant any powers to the members of the MHT prior to the hearing. All the powers of the tribunal are granted to "the tribunal"

---

[110] *Winterwerp v Netherlands* (1979–80) 2 E.H.R.R. 387, para.42.

[111] See paras 7–30 to 7–36 below.

[112] See further Chapter 2 above.

[113] Peter Bartlett, Oliver Lewis and Oliver Thorold, *Mental Disability and the European Convention on Human Rights* (Leiden: Martinus Nijhoff, 2006), p.66. The authors also note that the UN Human Rights Committee takes the view that a two-week detention without court review is incompatible with the International Covenant on Civil and Political Rights, citing Human Rights Committee, *Concluding Observations of the Human Rights Committee: Estonia*, March 15, 2003, CCPR/CO/77/EST, para.10.

in s.49 of the 2001 Act, which means that the tribunal must make a collective decision to exercise any of its powers. As there will ordinarily not be any meeting of the three members until the date of the hearing, they cannot exercise any powers prior to the hearing. This means, for example, that the tribunal cannot decide to call a witness prior to the date of the hearing.

7–28 There are some technical issues in the drafting of ss.48 and 49 as regards the procedure prior to the tribunal hearing. While these sections continuously refer to the tribunal exercising powers, some of the powers in question may need to be exercised before the tribunal meets. For example, the tribunal "shall make provision for" notifying the psychiatrist and legal representative of the date, time and place of the relevant sitting of the tribunal.[114] In practice, this notification is made by the Mental Health Commission, presumably acting on behalf of the tribunal. The tribunal may also direct the psychiatrist in writing to arrange for the patient to attend before it.[115] If this power is exercised by the Commission on behalf of the tribunal before the tribunal sits, again this may be slightly anomalous. On the other hand, the Commission appoints the members of the tribunals and must provide staff and facilities for the tribunals.[116]

7–29 On a creative reading of the Act, it might be arguable that the tribunal members can instruct the Commission to exercise one of the tribunal's powers prior to the date of the hearing. This might involve stretching the meaning of the relevant sections too far, but if it were in the best interests of the patient, a court might uphold such a practice. If, for example, the tribunal members received the papers for the case a few days before the hearing, and all three decided that they believed it would be important to hear evidence from the independent consultant psychiatrist at the hearing, they could perhaps instruct the Commission to direct the psychiatrist to attend and give evidence.

It appears that in practice tribunal members do not exercise any powers prior to the hearing. If they wish to call a witness who has not been called to the hearing, they need to meet as a tribunal on the day assigned for hearing, decide to call the witness and then adjourn to allow time for the witness to be called.

By way of contrast, in England and Wales, in the Tribunal Rules which applied until 2008, it was stated that the tribunal chair could, as regards matters preliminary or incidental to an application, at any time up to the hearing of an application by the tribunal, exercise the powers of the tribunal under certain stated rules.[117] These powers included the power to subpoena witnesses (Rule 14), extend time limits (Rule 26), call for further information or reports (Rule 15) and cure irregularities in documents (Rule 28). They also included the power

---

[114]　Mental Health Act 2001, s.49(6)(a).
[115]　Mental Health Act 2001, s.49(2)(a).
[116]　Mental Health Act 2001, s.33(3)(a).
[117]　Mental Health Review Tribunal Rules 1983, S.I. 1983/942, rule 5.

to decide not to disclose a document to the patient if this would adversely affect the health or welfare of the patient or others (Rule 12).[118]

Those English rules have now been replaced by a new version governing the Health, Education and Social Care Chamber of the First-Tier Tribunal.[119] The new rules are not as detailed as the previous version, but it is intended that many of the existing practices will continue. The rules contain general requirements of flexibility of procedures and active case management by the tribunal. They even permit judicial powers to be delegated to the staff of the tribunal.

EXTENSIONS OF TIME FOR MHT DECISIONS

7–30 Section 18(2) of the 2001 Act states that an MHT decision must be made as soon as may be but not later than 21 days after the making of the Admission Order concerned or, as the case may be, the Renewal Order concerned. Section 18(4) then provides as follows:

> The period referred to in subsection (2) may be extended by order by the tribunal concerned (either of its own motion or at the request of the patient concerned) for a further period of 14 days and thereafter may be further extended by it by order for a period of 14 days on the application of the patient if the tribunal is satisfied that it is in the interest of the patient and the relevant admission order, or as the case may be, renewal order shall continue in force until the date of the expiration of the order made under this subsection.

If the two extensions occur, the effect will be that an Admission Order may last up to seven weeks[120] instead of the standard three weeks. This might be open to challenge under the ECHR, where some case law suggests that, at least as regards initial admission, a hearing must be held within 24 days.[121]

7–31 Extensions are ordered using Form 9 issued by the Commission.[122] The form includes a space for the tribunal to record the reasons for the extension. According to the form, the tribunal informs the following persons of its decision and the reasons for its decision: the Commission, the RCP, the patient and their legal representative and any other person who, in the opinion of the tribunal, should be given notice.

---

[118] However, the document would be disclosed to the patient's *representative* if that representative is (a) a barrister or solicitor, (b) a registered medical practitioner, or (c) in the opinion of the tribunal, a suitable person by virtue of his experience or professional qualification.

[119] Tribunal Procedure (First-Tier Tribunal) (Health, Education and Social Care Chamber) Rules 2008, S.I. 2008 No. 2699 (L.16)

[120] This calculation is based on 21 days plus two extensions of 14 days each, making a total of 49 days.

[121] See paras 7–25 to 7–26 above.

[122] At the time of writing, the version of the form is the version issued in November 2007.

7–32 A number of questions arise concerning s.18(4):

- On what basis is such an extension of time to be granted, and is there a difference between the first extension and second extension?
- Can the patient be discharged during an extension of this type?
- Can MHTs extend Renewal Orders as well as Admission Orders?

It is clear that the first extension may be ordered either of the tribunal's own motion or on the patient's application, but the second extension may only be ordered on the patient's application. It appears that in the case of both the first and second extensions the tribunal may only order such extension if it is "satisfied that it is in the interest of the patient". An alternative view would be that the requirement that it be in the patient's interest only applies to the second extension, but this would then mean that the Act laid down no criterion or criteria for such extension.

Each extension must be for a period of 14 days. The tribunal cannot order an extension for a lesser period, e.g. five days. However, the 14-day extension order permits the re-convening of the tribunal at any time during the 14 days.

Presumably the courts would only uphold extensions which are granted for good reason, and not merely for administrative convenience. In *J.B. (No.2)*, an extension had been ordered as the psychiatrist had a family bereavement, and this was implicitly approved by MacMenamin J.[123] Sheehan J. also approved of this in *J.B. (No.3)*, saying that "a crucial witness was absolutely understandably unavailable".[124] It has also been noted in the *E.J.W.* case that an extension might be granted if the legal representative needed extra time to review medical records, in a case where access to the records was not possible prior to the day of the hearing due to the patient's incapacity.[125]

7–33 In *C.C. v Clinical Director of St. Patrick's Hospital (No.1)*,[126] McMahon J. suggested that in some cases, if a patient has raised a preliminary issue and the MHT has ruled against them, the legal representative might avail of an adjournment[127] to seek an immediate meeting with the clinical director, who is the person with powers to release the patient in these circumstances. McMahon J. acknowledged that this was unlikely to have yielded a different result, as the clinical director had already examined the patient and had made a clinical decision that the applicant was suffering from a mental disorder and was capable

[123] *J.B. v Director of Central Mental Hospital (No.2)* [2007] I.E.H.C. 201; High Court, MacMenamin J., June 15, 2007, paras 21 and 45.
[124] *J.B. v Director of Central Mental Hospital (No.3)* [2007] I.E.H.C. 340; [2008] 3 I.R. 61 at 64; High Court, Sheehan J., August 15, 2007.
[125] *E.J.W. v Watters and Mental Health Commission,* unapproved, High Court, Peart J., November 25, 2008. See further para.7–55 below.
[126] [2009] I.E.H.C. 13; High Court, McMahon J., January 20, 2009.
[127] This adjournment might either be offered by the tribunal (as happened in the *C.C.* case) or requested by the legal representative.

of doing harm to herself. But in failing to direct her complaint to the person who had authority over the detention, the applicant could not complain that the tribunal, which did not have authority under the Act, failed to order her release.[128] Later in the judgment, McMahon J. states that if the applicant got no satisfaction from the clinical director then the applicant could have commenced proceedings against the clinical director's refusal under Art.40.4 of the Constitution.[129]

7–34 Before the *S.M.* case, it was unclear whether the patient could be discharged by the responsible consultant psychiatrist during the 14-day extension period. On one view, the tribunal has exclusive jurisdiction concerning the case and has ordered that the Admission Order be extended, meaning that the psychiatrist cannot discharge the patient during that period. On another view, which seems more consistent with the constitutional right to liberty, if the patient recovers during the period, the psychiatrist has a duty to discharge them.[130] This matter now appears to have been resolved by *S.M. v Mental Health Commission*.[131] In that case, McMahon J. stated that s.28 gives the treating consultant psychiatrist power at any time to release the patient when they conclude that the patient is no longer suffering from a mental illness. He said, "It is clearly a power which, when it operates, trumps the existing admission or renewal orders."[132] While he did not specifically state that it would also trump an extension of an order by an MHT, this would seem to logically follow from his statement.

7–35 When the MHT extends time under s.18(4), this may have two effects at once: it extends the time for the MHT decision to be made *and* the actual Admission or Renewal Order "shall continue in force" until the expiration of the MHT's order. These words clarify that the patient does not need to be discharged during the extension. They must be read in light of the following earlier subsections[133]:

> Section 15(1): An admission order remains in force for 21 days from the date of the making of the order and, subject to subsection (2) and section 18(4), shall then expire.

> Section 15(2): The period referred to in s.15(1) may be extended by a renewal order made by the RCP for a further period not exceeding 3 months. (Section 15(3), concerning subsequent renewals, is in similar terms.)

---

[128]   [2009] I.E.H.C. 13, p.22.
[129]   [2009] I.E.H.C. 13, p.27.
[130]   See the wording of s.28(1): "Where the consultant psychiatrist … becomes of opinion that the patient is no longer suffering from a mental disorder, he or she shall by order … revoke the relevant admission order or renewal order, as the case may be, and discharge the patient."
[131]   [2008] I.E.H.C. 441; [2009] 2 I.L.R.M. 127; McMahon J., High Court, October 31, 2008.
[132]   [2009] 2 I.L.R.M. 127 at 139. See further paras 6–20 to 6–29 above.
[133]   These are abbreviated and paraphrased versions of the relevant subsections.

It is clear from s.15(1) and s.15(2) that an Admission Order's expiry may be extended under s.18(4) but this is not the case with a Renewal Order, which expires after the period specified by the RCP, such period not exceeding three months (or 6 or 12 months, as the case may be.)

It might be argued that the reference to a Renewal Order towards the end of s.18(4) is superfluous, but it serves to clarify that the Renewal Order continues in force and the patient is not discharged by the *MHT's extension order*. If, for example, the Renewal Order is a short one of 30 days and has 5 days left to run during the 14-day extension, it will remain in force for those 5 days, and then expire if not renewed by the RCP.

In practice, many Renewal Orders are made for the maximum periods stated in the Act, i.e. three months for a first renewal, etc. In those circumstances, the words about the Renewal Order towards the end of s.18(4) appear not to apply at all, as the reference to the "relevant" Renewal Order means the Renewal Order which is being reviewed by the MHT, not any earlier Renewal Order. If a patient is detained on a three-month renewal, or approximately 12 weeks, then this renewal should be reviewed by a MHT within 21 days of its being made, which period may be extended by a maximum of 28 days. If the three-month Renewal Order were made on January 1, and came into effect on January 2, then no problem could arise about whether the MHT adjournments extend the Renewal Order. The Renewal Order would of necessity be reviewed within seven weeks of January 1, at which time the order would still have five weeks to run.

7–36 The Act could be clearer on this point, though, and a definitive interpretation was required from the courts on the issue. The test case which provided this interpretation was *J.B. v Director of the Central Mental Hospital (No.3)*.[134] As this is an *ex tempore* decision, it does not contain full details of the facts of the case. It appears that the applicant was detained in the CMH under a three-month Renewal Order made on April 24, 2007. The MHT extended the time for its hearing under s.18(4) on two occasions, first because there had been a bereavement which affected the psychiatrist, and secondly because the tribunal wanted to await the outcome of an Art.40 application which had been brought by the patient. The tribunal affirmed the Renewal Order in May 2007. When the three months expired at the end of July, no further Renewal Order was made, and the patient's counsel argued that the patient was no longer lawfully detained. However, the CMH argued that the three-month renewal had been extended by 28 days under s.18(4), which should be added on to the end of the three-month period.

Sheehan J. said that the purpose of s.18(4) is, "to give the Mental Health Tribunal an option to do its work in a meaningful and fair way, and that the purpose of allowing a hearing to be adjourned is essentially to give the Mental Health Tribunal further time when such is required to enable it to do its work properly."[135] In this particular case there was a clear example of that where the

---

[134] [2007] I.E.H.C. 340; [2008] 3 I.R. 61; High Court, Sheehan J., August 15, 2007.
[135] [2008] 3 I.R. 61 at 64.

matter was listed for hearing within the 21-day period, a crucial witness was absolutely understandably unavailable and the matter had to be adjourned. He was of the view that it would be "going too far" if the court were to import into s.18(4) the implication that the adjournment, or further adjournment, allows the court to take the view that the order for renewal is extended in that way. He also noted that an order for renewal was effectively made by a consultant psychiatrist following a consultation and an assessment of the situation and they can only make the order for a period of up to three months and no more.[136]

In the circumstances of this case, a further Renewal Order was not in place at the end of the three-month period because the CMH believed that the period of renewal was automatically extended as a result of the adjournments of the MHT hearing. Sheehan J. held that that interpretation of s.18(4) of the Mental Health Act 2001 was not correct and that the applicant was not detained in accordance with law.[137]

PATIENTS MAY NOT APPLY FOR MHT REVIEWS BETWEEN RENEWAL ORDERS

7–37 In setting up our tribunal system, an important policy decision made was to grant patients automatic reviews of their detention by tribunals, at regular intervals. However, in granting those automatic reviews, the Oireachtas does not appear to have considered the question of whether a patient should be able to apply for a review between automatic reviews. The lack of such a facility appears particularly unjust where the renewal can be for up to 6 months or even 12 months. If the patient believes that they have recovered during a 12-month period of a Renewal Order, for example, they cannot apply for an MHT hearing. This contrasts with the situation in England and Wales, where the patient can choose to apply for a tribunal review at any stage between renewals, provided they only apply once during a period of renewal.[138]

While automatic reviews are desirable, they do not necessarily fully comply with art.5 of the ECHR. In *Rakevich v Russia*[139] Ms Rakevich was taken to a mental hospital on the initiative of an acquaintance, M., because of her behaviour. Two days later, she was diagnosed as suffering from paranoid schizophrenia. On the same day, the hospital applied to a court, as it was required to do by Russian law, for approval of her confinement in the hospital. Six weeks later the court gave its approval. The court held that art.5(4) had been violated as follows:

---

[136] [2008] 3 I.R. 61 at 64.

[137] The court stated that its order would not take effect until 4.00pm the following day, to facilitate a fresh admission of the applicant to St Brendan's Hospital.

[138] Section 66 and s.68 of the Mental Health Act 1983 as amended. See Richard Jones, *Mental Health Act Manual*, 11th edn (London: Thomson Sweet and Maxwell, 2008), pp.346–354.

[139] [2004] M.H.L.R. 37.

"The Law did not permit the applicant to apply to the court herself. Instead, the initiative lay solely with the medical staff. However, Art. 5(4) requires in the first place an independent legal device by which the detainee may appear before a judge who will determine the lawfulness of the detention. When this remedy is available, the detainee's access to the judge should not depend on the good will of the detaining authority. Whilst the legal mechanism contained in sections 33–35 of the Psychiatric Treatment Law, ensuring that a mental patient is brought before a judge automatically, constitutes an important safeguard against arbitrary detention, it would still be deficient if it does not contain the basic guarantee of Art. 5(4). Surplus guarantees do not eliminate the need for fundamental ones.

It does not appear that the Law on Psychiatric Treatment provided the applicant with a direct right of appeal in order to secure her release. Sections 47 and 48 of the Law referred to by the Government recognised a detainee's right to complain about the unlawful actions of medical staff in general, but Art. 5(4) requires a specific remedy to protect the liberty of a detainee."[140]

Similar conclusions were reached in *Gorshkov v Ukraine*[141] and *Kucheruk v Ukraine.*[142] In *Gorshkov*, the court stated, "The Art 5§4 review is not required to be automatic, but should rather be an opportunity for proceedings to be taken by the patient himself or herself."[143]

7–38 The lack of a statutory right in the Mental Health Act 2001 for the patient to apply for reviews outside of the automatic time periods laid down would appear to constitute a breach of art.5(4). If a challenge were brought to the system, reference could be made by the State to the English case of *R. (Rayner) v Secretary of State for the Home Department.*[144] In the *Rayner* case, the Court of Appeal held that the existence of a strong system of judicial review and the possibility of a habeas corpus application meant that the *Rakevich* line of case law did not apply in England. However, the reasoning of the Court of Appeal's decision is not very convincing, and the court appears to have been determined to distinguish *Rakevich*, even on the thinnest of grounds. It has been noted elsewhere that it would perhaps be overly cynical to suggest that the Court of Appeal's judgment relied on a theoretically available direct right of access to the courts which, while convenient as an art.5(4) compliant veneer, is never likely to be of practical use.[145]

---

140 [2004] M.H.L.R. 37, paras 44–45.
141 [2006] M.H.L.R. 32.
142 [2008] M.H.L.R. 1.
143 [2006] M.H.L.R. 32, para.39. The court cited *De Wilde, Ooms and Versyp v Belgium* (1971) 1 E.H.R.R. 373 and *Keus v Netherlands* (1990) 13 E.H.R.R. 700.
144 [2008] E.W.C.A. Civ. 176; [2009] 1 W.L.R. 310.
145 Roger Pezzani & Stephen Simblet, "Section 75(1) of the Mental Health Act 1983 is Compliant with Art. 5(4) of the European Convention on Human Rights … Just" (2008) J. Mental Health L. 88 at 92.

In order to resolve the doubts on this matter, a test application will need to be brought by a patient whose detention has been renewed for a long period, e.g. six months. If the patient wrote to the Mental Health Commission requesting a review and the Commission refused, the patient could then claim that their rights under art.5(4) were being breached. In addition, if the Commission in its reply stated that the next review would take place in (for example) four months time, the patient could claim that this long delay violated the "speediness" principle as required by cases such as *E. v Norway* or *L.R. v France*.[146]

LOCATION OF MHT HEARINGS

7–39 Tribunal hearings are held in the approved centres, normally in a board room or meeting room. The practice is similar in England and Northern Ireland. In Northern Ireland, concern has been expressed that holding the tribunal on the premises of one of the parties to the hearing may create an appearance of bias and/or disadvantage the patient. A report prepared for the Northern Ireland Human Rights Commission has suggested that it may be that the majority of tribunal hearings could be heard at an independent location, which would help to ensure that arts 5 and 6 of the ECHR standards are respected.[147]

THE ROLE OF THE LEGAL REPRESENTATIVE

7–40 Each patient is assigned a legal representative by the Mental Health Commission, as soon as possible after the Commission receives an Admission or Renewal Order, unless the patient proposes to engage their own representative.[148] In the vast majority of cases, the patient will be represented by the legal representative assigned by the Commission. "Legal representative" is defined in s.2 as meaning a barrister or solicitor, therefore a non-lawyer may not act as representative.[149]

7–41 If the patient objects to the lawyer appointed by the Commission, the Act does not provide a statutory right to a replacement, but the Legal Aid Scheme permits the patient to apply to the Commission for a change of legal

---

[146] See above, paras 7–25 to 7–26.

[147] Gavin Davidson, Maura McCallion and Michael Potter, *Connecting Mental Health and Human Rights* (Northern Ireland Human Rights Commission, 2003), pp.42–3.

[148] Mental Health Act 2001, s.17(1)(b). See generally Dara Robinson, "Representing a Client with Mental Disability under the Mental Health Act 2001", Law Society Conference on Mental Health Act 2001, Dublin, May 2005.

[149] Contrast the situation in England and Wales, where the MHRT rules provided that any person may represent the patient—Peter Bartlett and Ralph Sandland, *Mental Health Law: Policy and Practice*, 3rd edn (Oxford: Oxford University Press, 2007), p.381.

representative.[150] If the patient is unwilling to be represented by any lawyer, then the MHT will have to accept this and proceed with the hearing.[151] Note, however, that the Legal Aid Scheme states that in cases where a patient decides to represent themselves before the MHT the Commission shall nevertheless appoint a legal representative for that patient.[152]

7–42 There is no specific statutory provision for legal representation of other persons before the tribunal. If, for example, the HSE engages a barrister to make submissions to the tribunal, the MHT would not be statutorily obliged to permit this. However, a strong case could be made on grounds of general constitutional justice that the MHT should permit such submissions.[153]

7–43 The Mental Health Commission has established a panel of legal representatives, and pays the fees of lawyers who act for patients before the MHTs. The Act does not specifically state that the fees will be paid by the Commission, but states that the Commission must establish a scheme or schemes for the granting by the Commission of legal aid to patients.[154] This scheme must be made with the consent of the Minister for Health and Children and the Minister for Finance. The relevant scheme was made in 2005 and provides that, when the Commission assigns a legal representative to represent a patient, the Commission shall do so without regard to the patient's means or assets and no payment shall be made by the patient either to the Commission or to the legal representative.[155]

7–44 Peart J. noted in *E.J.W. v Watters* that the legal representative is appointed prior to the MHT hearing and thus has a general role of advising the patient, and acts as an advocate on their behalf both at the tribunal review hearing, and where necessary, with or without the assistance of counsel, in any application which may appear necessary by way of application for release under Art.40.4.2 of the Constitution, or judicial review or otherwise.[156] He added that the legal representative is "standing in the shoes of the patient".[157]

---

[150]   Mental Health Legal Aid Scheme, para.7.4(1).
[151]   According to s.49(6)(c), the patient may present their case to the tribunal either in person or through their legal representative.
[152]   Mental Health Legal Aid Scheme, para.4.1(4).
[153]   The English legislation in force until recently was clearer on this point: any party may be represented (Mental Health Tribunal Rules 1983, Rule 10); "party" means the applicant, the patient, the responsible authority, any other person to whom a notice under rule 7 or rule 31(c) is sent or who is added as a party by direction of the tribunal (Mental Health Tribunal Rules 1983, Rule 2).
[154]   Mental Health Act 2001, s.33(3)(c).
[155]   Mental Health Legal Aid Scheme (2005), para.3.1(1)(c).
[156]   *E.J.W. v Watters and Mental Health Commission*, unapproved, High Court, Peart J., November 25, 2008, p.30.
[157]   *E.J.W. v Watters and Mental Health Commission*, unapproved, High Court, Peart J., November 25, 2008, p.22.

In *P.McG.*, Peart J. emphasised that legal representatives have a duty to make applications under Art.40.4.2 where a breach of statutory procedure has occurred:

> "It is not for the solicitor appointed to represent the interests of the patient to ignore the failure to observe the provisions of s. 22 on the basis that she may not have believed that this Court was likely to order his release. That is a matter within the jurisdiction of this Court to decide. To fail to bring the matter to Court for such an inquiry on such a basis would lead to a risk that in some case or cases a patient might remain in unlawful detention without redress, given in particular the vulnerability of many such patients who may not be in a position to themselves instruct their appointed legal representative to apply for an order releasing him or her from detention. ... That is not to say that there could never be a case which the High Court would consider ought never to have been made. The Court must always retain the discretion to consider that the defect alleged is of such a trivial and insubstantial nature as to have always been bound to fail."[158]

7–45 Legal representatives on the panel are normally solicitors, although the Commission may engage barristers if it considers it appropriate to do so.[159] A barrister might not be permitted by the Bar Council to represent a patient without an attending solicitor. The panel is restricted to practising solicitors and barristers who have not less than three years' experience as practising solicitors or barristers ending immediately before application.[160] In 2007, there were 65 legal representatives involved in MHT hearings.[161]

Training is mandatory for all members of the panel.[162] The training requirement acts as a quality control measure and minimises the possibility of a patient being represented by a lawyer who knows very little about the Mental Health Act 2001. Garda vetting is applied to all panel members, and they must also declare any potential conflicts of interest.

7–46 Under the Mental Health Commission's Legal Aid Scheme, a complaints procedure will be put in place.[163] A lawyer must be providing a professional service to remain on the panel, which is reviewed every three years, or as considered necessary by the Commission.[164] Some judicial review applications were filed in 2009 by solicitors whose membership of the panel was not

---

[158] *P.McG. v Medical Director of the Mater Hospital* [2007] I.E.H.C. 401, [2008] 2 I.R. 332 at 338.
[159] Mental Health Legal Aid Scheme (2005), para.7.1(2).
[160] Mental Health Legal Aid Scheme (2005), para.7.2(7).
[161] *Report on the Operation of Part 2 of the 2001 Act* (2008), p.57.
[162] Mental Health Legal Aid Scheme (2005), para.8.1(2).
[163] Mental Health Legal Aid Scheme, para.8.1(2).
[164] Mental Health Legal Aid Scheme, para.7.2(6). See also Terms and Conditions Pursuant to the Mental Health Legal Aid Scheme (2005), clause 15.

renewed.[165] An individual representative may be removed from the panel follow-ing the procedures in the Terms and Conditions of each legal representative.[166]

The assignment of legal representatives is generally done using a rota system. The Commission endeavours to assign the same legal representative to a patient on subsequent occasions unless the patient requests a different legal represen-tative to be assigned, or the legal representative is unavailable.[167] The Terms and Conditions require that the legal representative take instructions from the patient on a number of occasions, and this will normally require a visit to the approved centre.[168]

The standard legal representative's fee for an MHT hearing for review of an Admission Order is €1,340.[169] There are reduced fees if the hearing does not proceed, e.g. €750 if the hearing is cancelled prior to the hearing and all of the necessary preparatory work has been carried out on the case.[170] The fee for an MHT hearing on a Renewal Order is €375. While it is understandable that this fee would be lower than the fee for an Admission Order, as the representative will normally be familiar with the patient's case history, it is questionable whether this reduced fee is adequate for the time which a representative would need to devote to taking instructions and representing the patient at the hearing.[171]

Principles applicable to the Role of the Legal Representative

7–47 The requirement that the patient be assigned a legal representative, paid for by the State, is an important protection of the patient's constitutional and human rights. Case law such as *State (Healy) v Donoghue*,[172] *Stevenson v Landy*[173] and *Kirwan v Minister for Justice*[174] suggests a right to legal aid in certain circumstances.[175]

European case law does not require legal representation in all cases. The ECHR stated in the *Winterwerp* case that the judicial proceedings referred to in

---

[165] Mark Tighe, "Mental Health Lawyers Dropped", *Sunday Times*, August 23, 2009; Ray Managh, "Court Challenge to Mental Health Care Lawyers", *Irish Independent*, August 27, 2009.

[166] Terms and Conditions Pursuant to the Mental Health Legal Aid Scheme (2005), clauses 48–51.

[167] Terms and Conditions Pursuant to the Mental Health Legal Aid Scheme (2005), clause 26.

[168] Terms and Conditions Pursuant to the Mental Health Legal Aid Scheme (2005), clauses 23–24.

[169] Terms and Conditions Pursuant to the Mental Health Legal Aid Scheme (2005), Schedule 1 (as updated).

[170] A fee of €1,071 applies if the hearing is cancelled on the day of the hearing for "Admission or Renewal–new solicitor".

[171] Fees for Junior Counsel and Senior Counsel are not set in the Terms and Conditions but are agreed in advance of a case—see Terms and Conditions Pursuant to the Mental Health Legal Aid Scheme (2005), clause 55.

[172] [1976] I.R. 325.

[173] High Court, Lardner J., February 10, 1993.

[174] [1994] 2 I.R. 417.

[175] See further para.13–07 below.

art.5(4) need not always be attended by the same guarantees as those required under art.6(1) for civil or criminal litigation, but it is essential that the person concerned should have access to a court and the opportunity to be heard either in person or, where necessary, through some form of representation. Special procedural safeguards may prove called for in order to protect the interests of persons who, on account of their mental disabilities, are not fully capable of acting for themselves.[176] The court also said that art.5(4) does not require that persons committed to care under the head of "unsound mind" should themselves take the initiative in obtaining legal representation before having recourse to a court.[177] In *Megyeri v Germany*[178] a violation of art.5(4) was found due to the lack of legal representation for a patient when his detention was being reviewed by a court. The applicant had been detained as a result of criminal proceedings, and his mental illness was so severe that the court had ruled that he was incapable of conducting legal proceedings. It has also been held in *Aerts v Belgium*[179] that a failure to grant legal aid to an applicant who cannot afford to pay for his own lawyer may constitute a violation of art.6(1).[180]

The UN Mental Illness Principles state that the patient shall be entitled to choose and appoint a counsel to represent the patient, including representation in any complaint procedure or appeal. If the patient does not secure such services, a counsel shall be made available without payment by the patient to the extent that the patient lacks sufficient means to pay.[181]

7–48 Automatic assignment of legal representation means that disputes will not arise about whether the patient ought to have been assigned a lawyer due to their mental condition. It is noteworthy that the legal aid scheme requires the State to pay for the legal representative regardless of the patient's means or assets. This means that a patient who is multi-millionaire will not pay for their legal representation. European case law would only require that legal aid be granted to those who cannot afford to pay for their own lawyer.

7–49 As a matter of statutory construction, the "best interests" principle in s.4 of the 2001 Act does not apply to the legal representative, as the principle applies

---

[176] (1979–80) 2 E.H.R.R. 387, para.60.

[177] (1979–80) 2 E.H.R.R. 387, para.66.

[178] (1993) 15 E.H.R.R. 584

[179] (2000) 29 E.H.R.R. 50.

[180] The court stated at para.60 that Mr Aerts could legitimately apply to the Legal Aid Board with a view to an appeal on points of law, since in civil cases Belgian law requires representation by Counsel before the Court of Cassation. It was not for the Legal Aid Board to assess the proposed appeal's prospects of success; it was for the Court of Cassation to determine the issue. By refusing the application on the ground that the appeal did not at that time appear to be well founded, the Legal Aid Board impaired the very essence of Mr Aerts' right to a tribunal and there had accordingly been a breach of art.6(1).

[181] United Nations, *Principles for the protection of persons with mental illness and the improvement of mental health care*, adopted by General Assembly resolution 46/119 of December 17, 1991, Principle 18(1).

"in making a decision under this Act concerning the care or treatment of a person (including a decision to make an admission order in relation to a person)."[182] Legal representatives do not make decisions about care, treatment or admission of patients. Eldergill emphasises the non-application of s.4 to legal representatives and their professional duty to their clients:

> "The legitimate needs and interests of patients, the tribunal and of society in general, are best promoted by ensuring that vulnerable citizens subject to compulsion have available to them a legal advocate, to test the strength of the evidence and to promote *their* case. It would be unethical for a legal representative to do otherwise, not simply in terms of their professional code but more generally."[183]

7–50 A Task Force of the Law Society has issued useful guidelines for solicitors on representing clients before MHTs.[184] The guidelines state that, "the solicitor's role is limited to acting in the client's best interests in *terms of legal representation*" (emphasis added). This appears to imply that solicitors should not be swayed to act in the patient's *medical* best interests.

The guidelines state that it is the patient's views or wishes that should be represented to the tribunal. A solicitor should act in accordance with the patient's instructions, unless the client is incapable of giving clear instructions. In general, the solicitor's role is to act on the patient's instructions, advocating the patient's views and wishes, even if these may be considered by the solicitor to be bizarre or contrary to the patient's best interests. On the other hand, as already stated, the guidelines acknowledge that a solicitor must act in the patient's best interests in terms of legal representation and they state that in deciding what is in the patient's best interests, regard should be had to the following:

- The client should be encouraged to participate as fully as possible in the decision-making process
- The person's known past and present wishes and feelings and the facts that they would consider important
- The views of other people/professionals whom the solicitor decides are appropriate or practicable to consult in the preparation of the case, and

---

[182] Contrast Maria Dillon, "Legal Representation and 'Best interests': Mental Health Act 2001", Conference Paper, Law Society, Dublin, September 2009.

[183] Anselm Eldergill, "The Best Is the Enemy of the Good: The Mental Health Act 2001" (2008) J. Mental Health L. 21 at 25.

[184] Law Society of Ireland Mental Health and Capacity Task Force, "Practice Note: Representation at Mental Health Tribunals: Guidelines for Solicitors" (2008) 102(6) Gaz. L.S.I. 58. See also the earlier version: Law Society of Ireland Mental Health Subcommittee, "Practice Note: Representation at Mental Health Tribunals: Guidelines for Solicitors" (2007) 101(1) Gaz. L.S.I. 49.

- Whether the purpose for which any action or decision with regard to the detention and treatment of the patient was made can be achieved in a manner less restrictive of that person's liberty.[185]

7–51 The Mental Health Commission emphasises in its Procedural Guidelines that MHTs should not be conducted in an adversarial manner.[186] The Commission also states that an inquisitorial approach which seeks to protect each patient's human rights and is governed by best interest principles is viewed by the Commission as the most effective manner in which to conduct an MHT. These instructions are aimed at the members of the tribunals, rather than the legal representatives.

The Commission's Quality Assurance Directions for legal representatives contain numerous references to the best interests principle. As was discussed at paras 1–44 to 1–62 above, the best interests principle can be interpreted in a benign manner to emphasise that the focus must be on the needs of the patient, or in a paternalistic fashion to treat patients like children. Bearing in mind that the best interests principle in s.4 is not actually addressed to legal representatives, it may be queried why it has been emphasised so much in the Quality Assurance Directions. The Directions note that legal representatives are not prevented from taking immediate and decisive action where necessary and that it may be necessary to depart from the Directions from time to time if professional rules or duties so require in the particular circumstances of the case.[187]

7–52 In *E.H. v Clinical Director of St. Vincent's Hospital*[188] Kearns J. stated that the fact that s.17(1)(b) of the 2001 Act provides for the assignment by the Commission of a legal representative for a patient following the making of an Admission Order or a Renewal Order should not give rise to an assumption that a legal challenge to that patient's detention is warranted unless the best interests of the patient so demand.[189] As was stated at para.2–46, it is to be hoped that this statement was intended merely to advise legal representatives to exercise restraint concerning applications under Art.40 in circumstances where there is settled law to the effect that the application will fail. The statement has led to concern amongst legal representatives as to its implications for their role.[190]

---

[185] Law Society of Ireland Mental Health Subcommittee, "Practice Note: Representation at Mental Health Tribunals: Guidelines for Solicitors" (2007) 101(1) Gaz. L.S.I. 49. at 59.

[186] Mental Health Commission, *Mental Health Tribunals: Procedural Guidance and Administrative Protocols* (2006), para.3.5.

[187] Mental Health Commission, *Quality Assurance Directions: Legal Representatives* (2008), p.4.

[188] [2009] 2 I.L.R.M. 149.

[189] [2009] 2 I.L.R.M. 149 at 165. See further paras 5–32 to 5–37.

[190] See further Michael Lynn, Discussion paper for Mental Health Lawyers Association, Dublin, July 2009.

Capacity and Consent Issues

7–53 If patients are "unable or unwilling to communicate their instructions", the legal aid scheme advises the legal representative to listen to the views of the patient and to then articulate those views in the patient's best interest in order to ensure that the patient's views are known to a tribunal when it is considering its decision so that the tribunal can arrive at an informed decision.[191]

The Quality Assurance Directions state that any decision made on behalf of a client who lacks capacity, or has limited capacity and as a result has difficulty giving instructions, must be made in that person's best interest and having regard, where appropriate, to any decisions or opinions they previously expressed (where known). The Directions advise that where there is uncertainty about what the best interests of the client are, the legal representative should follow a structured approach in seeking to ascertain them, and they include guidelines as to the factors to be taken into account.[192] Legal representatives are also advised that a best interests approach to client representation could include the following:

- representing the capable client in accordance with their instructions generally and insofar as that course best protects the autonomy of the patient; and
- representing the incapable client in accordance with any instructions generally and insofar as that course best protects the autonomy of the patient; and by adopting clear principles, for example, the entitlement to be unwise, and a less or more restrictive approach to determining best interests.

7–54 It is obviously vital for the legal representative to have access to the patient's health records, and therefore the legal aid scheme advises that the representative should request the patient to sign a form consenting to the representative having access to the patient's mental health records.[193] The Act does not specifically enable the representative to have access to the records in the absence of the patient's consent, which meant that representatives would have to wait until the day of the hearing to obtain access to the records. It appears that MHTs adopted the practice on the day of the hearing of directing that the representative be provided with access to the records under their general powers in s.49(2)(e).[194]

---

[191] *Mental Health Legal Aid Scheme* (2005), para.7.6(2).
[192] The guidelines state that the legal representative should encourage participation; seek to ascertain any views/opinions expressed by the client prior to the onset of incapacity or limited capacity; find out the client's views, past and present wishes, and any beliefs and values (moral, religious, political); assess whether the client may regain capacity; consult others if appropriate (do not assume close family support); and avoid making assumptions about the best interests on the basis of the client's age, condition or behaviour.
[193] *Mental Health Legal Aid Scheme* (2005), para.4.1(3).
[194] *E.J.W. v Watters and Mental Health Commission*, unapproved, High Court, Peart J., November 25, 2008, pp.3–4.

L.K. v Clinical Director of Lakeview Unit, Naas General Hospital[195] was a case decided prior to the coming into force of the Mental Health Act 2001 concerning a patient who was challenging her detention under Art.40.4.2 of the Constitution and who did not have capacity to consent to the disclosure of her medical records to her lawyers. In May 2006, Clarke J. directed that a consultant psychiatrist, on the nomination of the applicant's solicitor, should have reasonable access to the patient and to all relevant medical records; that such consultant might report to the applicant's solicitor on their views on any of the issues relevant to the case; and that the applicant's solicitor should not disclose the contents of any such report, save to the patient's counsel and for the purposes of discussion of the general conclusions of the report with the patient. In a later judgment in the same case delivered in June 2006,[196] Clarke J. stated that in the absence of special or unusual circumstances, a person acting on behalf of someone detained is entitled to be facilitated with reasonable access both to that person and to that person's medical records for the purposes of facilitating a review by the court of the lawfulness or otherwise of the detention of the person concerned. He said that the order which he previously made in the case, giving access to an appropriate consultant psychiatrist nominated on behalf of the applicant to both the applicant and her medical records would, in most cases, suffice. However, what might be necessary in order to facilitate reasonable access to the court by a person in detention could vary according to the circumstances of the case and the limitation that may reasonably be imposed on such access might also vary.[197]

The *L.K.* case did not necessarily mean that approved centres could, prior to the day of the MHT hearing, provide access to medical records to legal representatives in cases where people who had been detained under the Mental Health Act 2001 lacked capacity to consent to the disclosure of their records. In 2008, the Mental Health Commission noted that there had been a number of submissions to its review on the operation of the Act requesting that the Act be amended to allow a patient's legal representative to review the records relating to the patient at the approved centre, as is the case for the consultant psychiatrists who carry out independent medical examinations under s.17.[198] The Commission therefore recommended that the 2001 Act be amended to allow a patient's legal representative to review the records relating to the patient at the approved centre.[199]

7–55 In late 2008, a test case was brought concerning the situation where a patient does not have the capacity to consent to the disclosure of their medical records: *E.J.W. v Watters and Mental Health Commission*.[200] The patient was

---

[195] [2006] I.E.H.C. 196; [2007] 2 I.R. 465.
[196] Also reported at [2007] 2 I.R. 465.
[197] [2007] 2 I.R. 465 at 484.
[198] Mental Health Commission, *Report on the Operation of Part 2 of the 2001 Act*, p.82.
[199] Mental Health Commission, *Report on the Operation of Part 2 of the 2001 Act*, p.88.
[200] Unapproved, High Court, Peart J., November 25, 2008.

detained in St Senan's Psychiatric Hospital, Enniscorthy on February 22. Her legal representative, Mr Phelan, sought access to her records but the hospital would not grant access, as the patient, who had Alzheimer's disease and lacked the capacity to consent,[201] refused consent. On the day of the MHT hearing, the MHT granted Mr Phelan access to the records and adjourned for 14 days. However, all parties felt that the High Court should determine the issue of access to records, as the issue would arise in other cases.[202] Both the Mental Health Commission and the HSE were in favour of granting access to the records at an early stage in such cases, provided a mechanism could be found for doing so.

Peart J. stated that the provision of a review of the detention by a tribunal is absolutely central to the statutory scheme for the protection of the patient.[203] The information notice under s.16 must tell the patient that they are entitled to legal representation. The Act is silent as to the date on which the right to legal representation is to commence. It followed that the Act therefore intended that the patient should have legal representation from the moment that the Commission appoints the legal representative, and therefore, that the patient's legal representative is acting on behalf of that patient, not simply in relation to the hearing of the review hearing, which could be more than two weeks away, but generally in order to protect the patient's interests, as may be appropriate in any particular case.[204] A legal representative would need access to medical records in advance of the MHT hearing in order to prepare for the examination of medical witnesses. It was important to adopt creative procedures in order to ensure that the patient's right to fair procedures is fully vindicated.[205] The legal representative would also need access to the medical file if an application under Art.40.4.2, or an application for judicial review, were necessary.

Peart J. believed that it could not have been the intention of the Oireachtas that the patient's best interests be protected by the assignment of a legal representative who has no opportunity to obtain adequate information about their client until the very moment at which the tribunal convenes. As he said, "that is to expect the legal representative to perform his/her role while blindfolded."[206] In addition, it disadvantaged such a patient in a way that another patient who has capacity to consent to release of records is not disadvantaged. That would constitute an inequality which would be so unfair as to raise issues of constitutionality, and certainly one which Peart J. could not view as having been the intention of the Oireachtas. He believed that affording prior access to the legal representative is such an obvious and necessary ingredient of the role of

---

[201] There was no dispute between the parties regarding the patient's mental incapacity.
[202] The proceedings took the form of a Judicial Review application for a declaration that refusal to grant access to medical records was in breach of the applicant's constitutional right and/or in breach of her rights under the ECHR.
[203] Unapproved, High Court, Peart J., November 25, 2008, p.26.
[204] Unapproved, High Court, Peart J., November 25, 2008, p.26.
[205] Unapproved, High Court, Peart J., November 25, 2008, p.29.
[206] Unapproved, High Court, Peart J., November 25, 2008, p.30.

the legal representative that it was not considered necessary to make any specific provision in relation to it.[207] The Medical Council's Guidelines[208] allowed disclosure to protect the interests of the patient and Peart J. held that that situation applied here. The legal representative was "standing in the shoes of the patient"[209] and of course was under professional obligation not to disclose the information to any third person.

Peart J. therefore declared, for the sake of clarity, that in a case where a patient does not have the mental capacity to give a written consent, the disclosure by the hospital or treating psychiatrist to the assigned legal representative of the medical records and/or medical file relevant to the reason(s) why the Admission Order or Renewal Order has been made, is "necessary to protect the interests of the patient" and not a contravention of the duty of confidentiality upon members of the medical profession as enunciated in the Medical Council's Guide to Ethical Conduct and Behaviour. Such a finding did not preclude the hospital or treating psychiatrist from reasonably forming a view in a given case that the decision to give such access should await a decision of the tribunal. It would not be appropriate to speculate as to what might reasonably justify such a view but the reason would need to be exceptional in nature given the professional duties and obligations expected of the solicitor assigned by the Commission, such duties being as weighty in nature as those contained in the Guidelines of the Medical Council for members of the medical profession.[210] Earlier in the judgment, Peart J. said that there might, in a given case, be some unusual circumstance which the hospital might consider justified awaiting a direction from the tribunal, such as a countervailing interest arising from some aspect of the records which could impact adversely on third parties, or on the patient if the contents were disclosed to them.[211]

7–56 The 2001 Act should have contained a specific statutory scheme for the release of medical records to legal representatives. While the *E.J.W.* case has improved the situation somewhat, it is no substitute for a proper statutory framework for the resolution of the complex issues of confidentiality which arise in such cases. As was discussed at paras 7–27 to 7–29 above, it is unfortunate that the chairperson of the MHT does not have power to make any rulings prior to the day of the MHT hearing.

---

[207] Unapproved, High Court, Peart J., November 25, 2008, p.31.
[208] Medical Council, *Guide to Ethical Conduct and Behaviour*, 6th edn (2004), para.16.3.
[209] *E.J.W. v Watters and Mental Health Commission*, unapproved, High Court, Peart J., November 25, 2008, p.32.
[210] *E.J.W. v Watters and Mental Health Commission*, unapproved, High Court, Peart J., November 25, 2008, p.33.
[211] *E.J.W. v Watters and Mental Health Commission*, unapproved, High Court, Peart J., November 25, 2008, p.24.

DISCLOSURE OF DOCUMENTATION TO THE PATIENT

7–57 Following the *E.J.W.* case,[212] discussed above at para.7–55, in a case where a patient does not have the mental capacity to give a written consent, the hospital or treating psychiatrist may disclose the medical records and medical file to the legal representative. The hospital or treating psychiatrist may also decide in a given case that the decision to give such access should await a decision of the tribunal.

However, there is a need for clarification of the law concerning disclosure of documentation to the patient generally, both where the patient has capacity to consent and does not have such capacity. In England and Wales, the Mental Health Tribunal Rules contained a provision authorising the tribunal to decide not to disclose documents to the patient, if satisfied that disclosure would adversely affect the health or welfare of the patient or others.[213] In these cases, the documents were nevertheless disclosed to the patient's representative if they were a barrister or solicitor, provided the documents were not disclosed by the barrister or solicitor to the patient.[214]

7–58 A patient's right to privacy under art.8 of the ECHR normally requires that they have access to documents concerning them. But this is qualified by art.8(2), which states that the exercise of this right may be interfered with, inter alia, for the protection of health or morals, or for the protection of the rights and freedoms of others.[215] In considering arguments concerning arts 5 and 6 in the *Winterwerp* case, the European Commission on Human Rights stated that the fact that the applicant was not allowed access to the medical records relating to him was not incompatible with the requirements of a judicial procedure.[216]

Bartlett and Sandland have noted that in England and Wales it is now rarely the case that all documents are not disclosed to patients. In the cases where full disclosure does not take place, the fact that the patient's solicitor or barrister (Authorised Representative) has access to the documents "is a pragmatic solution to a moral problem, which would most probably satisfy Arts. 5 and 6, but it can place the [Authorised Representative] in an impossible position vis-à-vis the patient."[217]

---

[212]   *E.J.W. v Watters and Mental Health Commission*, unapproved, High Court, Peart J., November 25, 2008.

[213]   Mental Health Review Tribunals Rules 1983, S.I. No. 942 of 1983 Rule 12(2).

[214]   Mental Health Review Tribunals Rules 1983, S.I. No. 942 of 1983 Rule 12(3).

[215]   See also Principle 18 of United Nations, Principles for the Protection of Persons with Mental Illness and the Improvement of Mental Health Care, adopted by General Assembly resolution 46/119 of December 17, 1991, which states that full disclosure of documentation is to be made "except in special cases where it is determined that a specific disclosure to the patient would cause serious harm to the patient's health or put at risk the safety of others".

[216]   *Winterwerp v Netherlands*, Application No. 6301/73, European Commission on Human Rights, December 15, 1977, para.101.

[217]   Peter Bartlett and Ralph Sandland, *Mental Health Law: Policy and Practice*, 3rd edn (Oxford: Oxford University Press, 2007), p.384. See also p.581.

The Role of the Responsible Consultant Psychiatrist

7–59 The RCP is interviewed by the independent psychiatrist as part of the process of preparation of the independent psychiatrist's report.[218] On the meaning of "Responsible Consultant Psychiatrist", see paras 6–37 to 6–50 above. The MHT may direct the RCP to arrange for the patient to attend before the tribunal on a date and at a time and place specified in the direction.[219] The MHT's procedures must make provision for notifying the RCP of the date, time and place of the relevant sitting of the tribunal.[220] The Act does not specifically state that the RCP should receive a copy of the independent psychiatrist's report, but it seems that this report is normally sent to them in advance of the hearing.

The RCP normally attends the MHT hearing and is a key witness who will give evidence as to the patient's current mental condition. In giving this evidence, the RCP will state their opinion as to whether the patient satisfies the criteria for "mental disorder" in s.3 and continues to require detention.[221] If the RCP gives evidence to the tribunal, presumably they are generally regarded as a witness who has been called by the tribunal and therefore may be cross-examined by or on behalf of the patient.[222]

The approved centre is not a party to the MHT hearing, as the only party is the patient.[223] The approved centre, and the RCP who is employed by the HSE or the centre, do not have legal representation at the hearing.

Reviews if Order has Already been Revoked

7–60 If a psychiatrist revokes the Admission or Renewal Order before the MHT hearing, they must give notice in writing to the patient and their legal representative that the patient is entitled to have their detention reviewed by a tribunal or, where such review has commenced, completed, if they so indicate by notice in writing to the Commission within 14 days of the discharge.[224] The relevant section, s.28, was considered above at paras 4–109 to 4–116. Form 14 is the relevant form which must be used by the psychiatrist. If such a review is requested, the provisions of ss.17–19 shall apply in relation to the review with any necessary modifications.[225] During 2007, 16 patients requested a review of this type.[226]

---

[218] Mental Health Act 2001, s.17(1)(c).
[219] Mental Health Act 2001, s.49(2)(a).
[220] Mental Health Act 2001, s.49(6)(a).
[221] See earlier discussion at para.7–18 above regarding case law on the role of psychiatric evidence in criminal trials, and the different role of a psychiatrist in civil cases.
[222] Mental Health Act 2001, s.49(6)(f).
[223] See para.8–19 below.
[224] Section 28(3) of the Mental Health Act 2001.
[225] Section 28(5).
[226] Mental Health Commission, *Report on the Operation of Part 2 of the Mental Health Act 2001* (2008), p.85.

The Commission has commented that there may be a number of reasons for the very small number of requests for a review of this type. Patients may not be aware of this right, may not be clear as to the purpose or outcome of such a review or they may be reluctant to revisit the matter of their involuntary admission.[227]

7–61 It is difficult to determine exactly how a tribunal can hold a review of detention in such cases and apply ss.17–19 with "necessary modifications." For example, s.18 states that a tribunal considers whether a patient "is" suffering from a mental disorder, but as the patient's Admission or Renewal Order has been revoked it seems inappropriate to consider their current mental state. It is unclear whether the tribunal has power to consider the patient's mental condition as of the date of admission or renewal instead. In addition, the tribunal's role under s.18 is normally to affirm or revoke an Admission or Renewal Order, but again it is difficult to interpret how this applies when the order has already been revoked. The Mental Health Commission has referred to these difficulties in its review of the operation of Pt 2 of the Act, stating that the fact that the MHT does not have an order to affirm or revoke this would appear to be contrary to what is provided for in s.18.[228] Eldergill is of the view that the tribunal must determine the patient's mental condition as of the day of the hearing and not at the time of admission. He believes that asking a tribunal to affirm that the patient does not have a mental disorder at the time of the hearing does not take matters much further. However, he notes that it carries a risk that the tribunal will find that, in their opinion, the person is mentally disordered, i.e. that the patient does meet the criteria for involuntary admission. Such a decision would put the relevant professionals under pressure to arrange for a new Admission Order.[229]

A different view was held by the former Minister of State for Mental Health. He considered that the intention was that in such reviews the MHT should review the detention of the patient concerned to satisfy itself, insofar as is possible, that the patient was suffering from a mental disorder when the Admission Order or Renewal Order was made. The MHT was also required to satisfy itself that the correct procedure for involuntary admission was complied with and that the patient was not unjustly detained.[230]

7–62 In *Han v President of the Circuit Court*[231] Charleton J. said that the legislative purpose of s.28(5) is unclear. He asked:

---

[227] Mental Health Commission, *Report on the Operation of Part 2 of the Mental Health Act 2001* (2008), p.85.

[228] *Report on the Operation of Part 2 of the Mental Health Act 2001* (2008), p.85.

[229] Anselm Eldergill, "The Best is the Enemy of the Good: The Mental Health Act 2001" (2008) J. Mental Health L. 21 at 37.

[230] Department of Health and Children, *Review of the Operation of the Mental Health Act 2001: Findings and Conclusions* (2007), pp.21–22.

"What is the purpose of such a review? The sole ground for discharging a patient under s. 28 is that 'the patient is no longer suffering from a mental disorder'. A review by a Mental Health Tribunal is concerned with that issue and with whether the relevant procedures under ss. 9, 10, 12, 14, 15 and 16 have been complied with and, if they have not, with whether an admission or renewal order should justly be affirmed notwithstanding a breach of one or more of those sections. It can, therefore, happen that a patient has been detained pursuant to an admission order or renewal order and has become well, but is entitled under s. 28, upon being discharged, to have a review of these issues by the Tribunal. It is clear that such a review is historical since the relevant sections are not only concerned with whether the patient is suffering from a mental disorder but whether the administration sections leading to a patient's detention have been complied with. Since the operation of all of these sections depends on whether or not a patient was, at the time they were used against them, suffering from a mental disorder, one cannot remove that issue from the review before the Mental Health Tribunal insisted on by a patient, notwithstanding his or her discharge, no more than one can remove the technical operation of the relevant detention sections."[232]

His comments were obiter in that case, but they are a strong indication that the courts would hold that an MHT hearing when an order has been revoked concerns the patient's mental condition at the time the order was made.

7–63 In *M.McN. v Health Service Executive*,[233] discussed fully above at paras 5–38 to 5–40, the question arose of how s.28 applies in cases where a patient is mentally incapable of making a decision to request an MHT hearing. Peart J. commented that, "it is true that there can be no tribunal hearing as the revocation has taken place and s.28 implies a degree of mental capacity which is lacking in these cases"[234] and ultimately decided that the applicants' detention was lawful on other grounds.

RE-ADMISSION BY PSYCHIATRISTS SOON AFTER DISCHARGE BY TRIBUNAL

7–64 In some cases, a new admission for treatment might be made soon after the patient's discharge by the tribunal. Such a practice was approved in a 1994 English case, provided the admissions team is acting objectively and bona fide.[235] More recently, the House of Lords has held in the *Von Brandenburg* case

---

[231] [2008] I.E.H.C. 160; High Court, Charleton J., May 30, 2008.
[232] [2008] I.E.H.C. 160; High Court, Charleton J., May 30, 2008, p.17.
[233] High Court, Peart J., May 15, 2009.
[234] High Court, Peart J., May 15, 2009, p.17.
[235] *R v South Western Hospital Managers, ex parte M.* [1993] Q.B. 683. Laws J. said that an approved social worker (A.S.W.), in applying for an Admission Order, is not fettered in any way by a recent tribunal decision.

that the team must have information not known to the tribunal which puts a significantly different complexion on the case as compared with that which was before the tribunal.[236] Lord Bingham gave three hypothetical examples: A social worker might learn of a previous suicide attempt; a patient might cease to take medication; or there might be a significant deterioration in the patient's condition. Bartlett and Sandland have commented that this decision means that, "matters of legal semantics aside, a new fact rule does now operate in England and Wales."[237] In other words, the prior decision of the tribunal may not be departed from unless justified by the existence of some new fact.

7–65 This issue arose in Ireland in *C.C. v Clinical Director of St. Patrick's Hospital (No.2).*[238] The applicant appears to have been taken into custody by Gardaí while out walking near her home with her son. In the first High Court case concerning her detention, discussed above at paras 4–38 to 4–41, McMahon J. held on January 20, 2009 that the patient's continued detention was lawful.[239] While McMahon J.'s judgment was being prepared, a tribunal sat on January 5 to review the patient's detention. During the course of the MHT hearing, the chairperson asked the applicant and her legal representative whether she would be willing to remain in hospital as a voluntary patient for a period of two weeks. She indicated that she would be willing to do so and the tribunal revoked the Renewal Order. Ms C. then became a voluntary patient at the hospital. She seemed generally content with the arrangement. She indicated on occasion that she wished to leave the hospital but was persuaded to remain on a voluntary basis. On January 13, her solicitor wrote to the respondent indicating that the applicant intended to leave the hospital the following day at noon. Over the following two days,[240] she was re-detained using the re-grading procedure in ss. 23 and 24 of the 2001 Act. It was noted that her condition had deteriorated in the previous week.

The patient argued that the MHT's decision to revoke or affirm the Admission or Renewal Order was absolutely binding on all parties. She argued that no other body, judicial or otherwise, has the competence to change or disregard such a decision. She contended that the statutory scheme established by the 2001 Act mandates that there be a system of independent review by the MHT, to which deference ought to be shown by all other relevant bodies. For a s.23 order to be justified, such a short period of time after the tribunal had ordered the applicant's release, she submitted that there would have to be a significant deterioration in

---

[236] *R v East London and the City Mental Health NHS Trust, ex parte Von Brandenburg* [2003] U.K.H.L. 58; [2004] 2 A.C. 280. See Lord Bingham at para.10.

[237] Peter Bartlett and Ralph Sandland, *Mental Health Law: Policy and Practice*, 3rd edn (Oxford: Oxford University Press, 2007), p.429.

[238] [2009] I.E.H.C. 47; High Court, Hedigan J., February 6, 2009.

[239] *C.C. v Clinical Director of St. Patrick's Hospital (No.1)* [2009] I.E.H.C. 13; High Court, McMahon J., January 20, 2009.

[240] On January 14, the 24–hour period of detention was commenced and on January 15, the patient was re-detained under s.24.

her condition such that the tribunal would now be compelled to reach a different conclusion.

Hedigan J. said that he could not accept, in the absence of an express legislative provision, that the Oireachtas intended that a decision of the MHT should in some way be immune from contradiction for an indeterminate period after its issue.[241] A MHT decision was not a bar to bona fide clinical judgments:

> "The finely nuanced and potentially changeable differences that may exist between those patients who meet the criteria for involuntary detention and those who do not, require that the decision of a Mental Health Tribunal should not be regarded as creating a bar for some indeterminate period to *bona fide* clinical judgments by treating consultants. The nature of mental illness demands a certain flexibility, albeit one requiring careful oversight by the courts."[242]

Hedigan J. said that in light of the unusual facts of the case, he would consider it highly desirable that another Tribunal should sit in relation to a person such as the applicant as soon as possible to assuage concerns which naturally arise when apparently conflicting assessments are made.[243]

Transfer of Patient to CMH

7–66 A transfer from an approved centre to the CMH must be authorised by an MHT under s.21(2). The clinical director of the approved centre first notifies the Commission that they are of the opinion that it would be for the benefit of the patient, or that it is necessary for the purpose of obtaining special treatment for the patient, to transfer them to the CMH. Form 11 is completed by the Clinical Director for this purpose. There were 21 proposals to transfer to the CMH in 2007 and 10 in 2008.[244]

The Commission then refers the proposal to an MHT. The tribunal must review the proposal as soon as may be, within 14 days thereafter. The tribunal authorises the transfer if it is satisfied that the transfer is in the best interest of the health of the patient concerned. The provisions of ss.19 and 49 apply to the referral of such a proposal to a tribunal, as they apply to the referral of an Admission Order to a tribunal under s.17 with any necessary modifications.[245] The tribunal's decision is recorded on Form 8, which is the form used for all tribunal decisions.

---

[241] [2009] I.E.H.C. 47, para.43.
[242] [2009] I.E.H.C. 47, para.44.
[243] [2009] I.E.H.C. 47, para.45.
[244] Statistics from Mental Health Commission website. (http.//www.mhcirl.ie/Mental_Health_Tribunals/Involuntary_Admission_Activity/) [Accessed October 20, 2009].
[245] Mental Health Act 2001, s.21(2)(c).

Effect must not be given to the decision before the expiration of the time for the bringing of an appeal to the Circuit Court (i.e. 14 days[246]), or if such an appeal is brought, the determination or withdrawal thereof.[247] The clinical director then completes Form 12, the notice of transfer to the CMH. The detention of a patient in another approved centre (which appears to include the CMH[248]) is deemed for the purposes of this Act to be detention in the centre from which they were transferred.[249]

7–67 Eldergill has commented that the procedure regarding transfers to the CMH is an important protection for patients. But he adds that the "only weakness" is that, once a patient is in the CMH, the tribunal has no similar power to review, direct or recommend the patient's transfer from the CMH to a local approved centre.[250]

If there is an appeal to the Circuit Court, it is not clear how that court will decide the appeal, as a literal reading of s.19(4) would suggest that it may only consider whether the patient is suffering from a mental disorder. However, it is arguable that using the reference to "necessary modifications" in s.21(2)(c), the Circuit Court can instead consider whether the transfer to the CMH was in the patient's best interests.

Some applications under Art.40, considered above in Chapter 6, have concerned patients who were transferred from approved centres to the CMH.[251] The cases have concerned the meaning of the "responsible consultant psychiatrist" in such cases. However, in those cases the patient was originally detained and transferred under the 1945 Act. There has not yet been a written judgment concerning a patient who was transferred to the CMH under the 2001 Act.

7–68 In the 2007 review by the former Minister of State for Mental Health, it was noted that the Act does not require the consent of the clinical director of the CMH for the transfer of a patient to that hospital.[252] Submissions had suggested that the advice of the Clinical Director of the CMH be sought prior to submitting a proposal for the transfer of a patient to the CMH. The Minister pointed out that transfers to the CMH are through the MHT process. Therefore, to require the

---

[246] The period for an appeal is 14 days from the receipt by the patient or by their legal representative of notice under s.18 of the decision concerned—s.19(2).

[247] Mental Health Act 2001, s.21(2)(d).

[248] It is arguable that s.21(4) does not apply to patients transferred to the CMH. However, in *J.B. (No.2)* MacMenamin J. was clearly of the view that it did—[2007] 4 I.R. 778 at 791–2.

[249] Mental Health Act 2001, s.21(4).

[250] Anselm Eldergill, "The Best is the Enemy of the Good: The Mental Health Act 2001" (2008) J. Mental Health L. 21 at 37.

[251] See *J.B. v Director of Central Mental Hospital (No.2)* [2007] I.E.H.C. 201; [2007] 4 I.R. 778, *M.M. v Director of the Central Mental Hospital* [2008] I.E.H.C. 44; High Court, Peart J., February 1, 2008 and [2008] I.E.S.C. 31; Supreme Court, May 7, 2008.

[252] Department of Health and Children, *Review of the Operation of the Mental Health Act 2001: Findings and Conclusions* (2007), p.17.

consent of the Clinical Director of the CMH could theoretically result in an opposite view. The Minister was of the opinion that the MHT could consult with the Clinical Director of the CMH in the course of reviewing the proposal to transfer a patient to the CMH.[253]

This review also noted that the time period required by the Act before a patient may be transferred to the CMH was causing difficulties in the approved centres, as they may not have suitable facilities for the detention of a patient who requires treatment in the CMH pending their transfer. The Minister appreciated the difficulties that were being experienced by local services but considered that these would be alleviated by the development of intensive care rehabilitation units.[254]

7–69 The Commission's Report on the Operation of Pt 2 of the Act stated that there had been criticism arising from cases where a patient's detention in the CMH under the Criminal Law (Insanity) Act 2006 comes to an end and a complex procedure of admission to another approved centre and the instigation of the procedures for a proposal to transfer to the CMH have to occur. The Commission stated that the risks associated with this flaw in the interaction between the 2001 Act and the Criminal Law Insanity Act (2006) are that delivery of the appropriate care to patients could be disrupted.[255] The report recommended that the 2001 and 2006 Acts be reviewed with the aim of providing a seamless transfer from one form of detention to the other, and that the Department of Health and Children and the Department of Justice and Law Reform commence discussions to address the difficulties that arise in continuing a patient's treatment where they move from the jurisdiction of the 2006 Act to the 2001 Act.[256]

PSYCHOSURGERY[257]

7–70 "Psychosurgery" means any surgical operation that destroys brain tissue or the functioning of brain tissue and which is performed for the purposes of ameliorating a mental disorder.[258] It is only very rarely performed, e.g. in England and Wales there were two such operations in 2007–2009.[259] It does not appear to be performed in Ireland, but a patient in a centre in Ireland might be

---

[253] Department of Health and Children, *Review of the Operation of the Mental Health Act 2001: Findings and Conclusions* (2007), p.37.
[254] Department of Health and Children, *Review of the Operation of the Mental Health Act 2001: Findings and Conclusions* (2007), pp.37–38.
[255] Mental Health Commission, *Report on the Operation of Part 2 of the Mental Health Act 2001* (2008), pp.52–3.
[256] Mental Health Commission, *Report on the Operation of Part 2 of the Mental Health Act 2001* (2008), p.89.
[257] See further paras 10–51 to 10–53 below.
[258] Mental Health Act 2001, s.58(6).
[259] Mental Health Act Commission, *Thirteenth Biennial Report 2007–2009*, p.167.

referred abroad for the surgery. There are no statistics on the Mental Health Commission website concerning authorisations of psychosurgery, which suggests that there have been no cases since the commencement of the 2001 Act.

In order for psychosurgery to take place, the patient must give their consent in writing to the psychosurgery and it must be authorised by an MHT.[260] The consultant psychiatrist then notifies the Commission using Form 15, and the Commission refers the matter to a tribunal. The tribunal authorises the psychosurgery if it is satisfied that it is in the best interests of the health of the patient concerned.[261] The provisions of ss.19 and 49 apply to the referral of psychosurgery to a tribunal as they apply to the referral of an Admission or Renewal Order to a tribunal under s.17 with any necessary modifications.[262]

The tribunal will use Form 8 to record its decision. Effect must not be given to the decision before the expiration of the time for the bringing of an appeal to the Circuit Court (i.e. 14 days[263]), or if such an appeal is brought, the determination or withdrawal thereof.[264]

As with decisions concerning transfers to the CMH, it is not clear how the Circuit Court will decide the appeal, as a literal reading of s.19(4) would suggest that it may only consider whether the patient is suffering from a mental disorder. However, it is arguable that using the reference to "necessary modifications" in s.58(4), the Circuit Court can instead consider whether the psychosurgery is in the patient's best interests.

APPEALS TO THE CIRCUIT COURT

7–71 The patient may appeal to the Circuit Court against the decision to affirm an Admission or Renewal Order within 14 days of receipt of notice of a MHT decision.[265] This appeal may only be based on one ground—that the patient argues that he or she is not "suffering from a mental disorder."[266] The burden of proof is on the patient in these appeals:

> On appeal to it under subsection (1), the Circuit Court shall—
> (a) unless it is shown by the patient to the satisfaction of the Court that he or she is not suffering from a mental disorder, by order affirm the order, or
> (b) if it is so shown as aforesaid, by order revoke the order.[267]

---

[260] Mental Health Act 2001, s.58(1).

[261] Section 58(3).

[262] Section 58(4).

[263] The period for an appeal is 14 days from the receipt by the patient or by their legal representative of notice under s.18 of the decision concerned—s.19(2).

[264] Mental Health Act 2001, s.58(5).

[265] Section 19.

[266] Section 19(1). As was noted earlier, the question of whether the patient is "suffering from a mental disorder" involves both a consideration of the patient's diagnosis and the necessity for their detention.

[267] Section 19(4).

A document purporting to be a report of an independent psychiatrist prepared pursuant to s.17 shall be evidence of the matters stated in the document without further proof and shall, unless the contrary is proved, be deemed to be such a document.[268] The court shall exclude from the court all persons except officers of the court, persons directly concerned in the hearing, bona fide representatives of the press and such other persons (if any) as the court may in its discretion permit to remain.[269] No matter likely to lead members of the public to identify a patient who is or has been the subject of proceedings under this section shall be published in a written publication available to the public or be broadcast.[270]

7–72 There may be two drafting errors in s.19. Section 19(10) states that the court may, in any case if satisfied that it is appropriate to do so in the interests of the patient, by order dispense with the prohibitions of s.19(8) in relation to them to such extent as may be specified in the order. It is likely that the reference to s.19(8), the exclusion of all persons other than stated categories from the court, should instead be a reference to s.19(9), concerning publication of the patient's identity. Similarly, s.19(11) creates an offence of making a publication or broadcast in contravention of s.19(8). Again, it is likely that this should instead refer to s.19(9) regarding the patient's identity.

7–73 The relevant rules of court are contained in the Circuit Court Rules (Mental Health) 2007.[271] These rules state that the patient shall be the appellant and the tribunal concerned shall be the respondent. The Circuit Court decision may be appealed to the High Court, but only on a point of law.[272] The Commission may grant legal aid for appeals to the Circuit Court and on to the High Court.[273] For purposes of compliance with the ECHR, it is important that these appeals should be determined "speedily".[274] In *Han v President of the Circuit Court*[275] Charleton J. stated that the Circuit Court should deal with an appeal as promptly as possible. He noted that a tribunal reviewing an order should make a decision within 21 days and continued:

> "To adjourn a live issue as to whether a patient who has been the subject of an admission order or a renewal order is or is not suffering from a mental disorder for a matter of some months appears to go outside the strictures as to time imposed by the Act which are all in favour of a speedy review of these matters. The same comment arises in the context of an appeal on a point of

---

[268] Section 19(14).
[269] Section 19(8).
[270] Section 19(9).
[271] S.I. No.11 of 2007.
[272] Section 19(16).
[273] Mental Health Legal Aid Scheme, paras 4.2–5.3.
[274] See *Reid v U.K.* (2003) 37 E.H.R.R. 9.
[275] [2008] I.E.H.C. 160; High Court, Charleton J., May 30, 2008.

law from the Circuit Court decision to the High Court, under [s.19][276] of the Act."[277]

7–74 There were 39 appeals to the Circuit Court from November 1, 2006 to the end of 2007. The Commission has commented that this is a low uptake, only 2 per cent of episodes in 2007.[278] Ten of these cases came before the court in relation to interlocutory matters or for a full hearing. One of the 10 related to an appeal of a transfer to the CMH. The remainder of the cases were withdrawn due to orders being revoked by the responsible consultant, patients not wishing to proceed or Art.40.4 proceedings. None of the appeals resulted in an order being revoked.[279] The Commission commented that this may need to be explored further given this low uptake, the high percentage of withdrawals and the fact that none of the appeals have resulted in an order being revoked.[280] There were 48 Circuit Court appeals filed during 2008. Some of these cases were withdrawn due to orders being revoked by the responsible consultant or patients not wishing to proceed. In relation to the cases that were heard by the Circuit Court, none resulted in an order being revoked.[281]

7–75 The former Minister of State for Mental Health noted that it had been suggested that there should be greater parity between the two parties in Circuit Court appeals and that the onus of proof should be on the detainer rather than the patient to ensure full compliance with the ECHR.[282] The Minister said that this matter was considered prior to the enactment of the legislation. He continued:

> "The Act is premised on the principle that the decision as to mental disorder is a medical one. It is, therefore, the Mental Health Tribunal which has the function of review and appeal of the decision. An appeal to the Circuit Court is not a full appeal in the ordinary sense but, rather, a new statutory mechanism to challenge the substance of the decision of the Mental Health Tribunal. Legal advice received is that the correct balance in this additional appeal mechanism is provided for in the Act: it gives the individual the means to overturn a decision while at the same time giving due weight to the decision of the Mental Health Tribunal."[283]

---

[276] Charleton J. refers to s.28 here, but it is likely that he intended to refer to s.19.

[277] [2008] I.E.H.C. 160, para.24.

[278] Mental Health Commission, *Report on the Operation of Part 2 of the Mental Health Act 2001* (2008), p.82.

[279] Mental Health Commission, *Report on the Operation of Part 2 of the Mental Health Act 2001* (2008), p.82.

[280] Mental Health Commission, *Report on the Operation of Part 2 of the Mental Health Act 2001* (2008), p.82.

[281] Mental Health Commission, *Annual Report 2008*, Book 1, p.46.

[282] Department of Health and Children, *Review of the Operation of the Mental Health Act 2001: Findings and Conclusions* (2007), p.16.

[283] Department of Health and Children, *Review of the Operation of the Mental Health Act 2001: Findings and Conclusions* (2007), p.16.

The issue of the burden of proof at tribunal stage will be considered below at paras 8–32 to 8–34. European human rights law clearly holds that the burden of proof must be on the detainer at tribunal stage. The European Court of Human Rights has held on a number of occasions that while art.5(4) does not compel the Contracting States to set up a second level of jurisdiction for the examination of applications for release from detention, if a State institutes such a system it must in principle accord to the detainees the same guarantees on appeal as at first instance.[284] This principle was reiterated recently in the mental health case of *Reid v U.K.*[285] in which the court found a violation of art.5(4) due to the delays in hearing appeals. There is therefore strong authority that the burden of proof at appeal stage should not be placed on the patient.

7–76 In *Han v President of the Circuit Court*,[286] Deery J., the President of the Circuit Court, had struck an appeal out from the hearing list because the patient had become well and been discharged. Deery J. considered the matter to be moot. The patient challenged this decision by way of Judicial Review. Charleton J. reviewed the statutory provisions and noted in passing that s.19(14) provides that a report prepared by an independent psychiatrist under s.17 is evidence of the matter stated in the document. He commented that this, however, does not mean that the Circuit Court hearing is an historical analysis of whatever condition that the patient was in when a detention order was made against them. He added, "By way of analogy; it is clear that if a person had a physical disease in the past, that this is a relevant consideration in attempting a diagnosis of a current condition."[287]

Turning to the meaning of the key parts of s.19, Charleton J. said that it was impossible to ignore the express wording, when it states that the issue before the Circuit Court is whether a patient "is not suffering from a mental disorder", a phrase that occurs only in the present tense in s.19(1) and (4)(a). Further, any court in reviewing an order under appeal either quashes or affirms the order, whereas the wording in s.19(4)(b) indicates that the burden of proof that is on the patient is to show that he or she "is not suffering from a mental disorder", and that if this is not shown then the court affirms the order or, if the patient has met the burden of proof, the Circuit Court is required to revoke the order.[288]

Charleton J. said that primacy, though not total supremacy, has to be given to the actual and literal words of any statute. The literal construction did not create

---

[284] See, for example, *Toth v Austria*, December 12, 1991, Series A No. 224, Application No. 11894/85, para.84; *Navarra v France* (1994) 17 E.H.R.R. 594, para.28; *Rutten v the Netherlands* [2001] E.C.H.R. 482, July 24, 2001, Application no. 32605/96, para.53. See also *Delcourt v Belgium* (1979–80) 1 E.H.R.R. 355, para.25, where it was held that appeal courts must comply with art.6.

[285] (2003) 37 E.H.R.R. 9.

[286] [2008] I.E.H.C. 160; High Court, Charleton J., May 30, 2008.

[287] [2008] I.E.H.C. 160; High Court, Charleton J., May 30, 2008, para.9.

[288] [2008] I.E.H.C. 160; High Court, Charleton J., May 30, 2008, para.12.

an absurdity and was not inconsistent with the Act as construed as a whole. A review by an MHT under s.28 concerning a patient whose order had already been revoked was of a different kind. It was clearly historical since the relevant sections are not only concerned with whether the patient is suffering from a mental disorder but whether the administration sections leading to a patient's detention have been complied with.[289] Charleton J. did not agree that just because a discharged patient can insist on the MHT looking at the issues surrounding their detention as a patient, that an appeal must lie in respect of all of those issues to the Circuit Court. Expressly, the Circuit Court on appeal from the MHT, and the High Court on appeal from that on a point of law, can only consider one issue: is the patient suffering from a mental disorder at the time of the hearing? If they are not, the court must order their release from detention under the Act. As to what modification of s.19 is necessary as a result of s.28, the answer to that was that s.19 is limited by its express words to the current condition of the patient and that the power of appeal under s.28, is expressly stated as being to an MHT. The modification necessary is that a patient being discharged can seek to have what happened to them as to detention in a mental hospital reviewed by the MHT. They have no further power to appeal any decision of that tribunal once they are released.[290]

In Charleton J.'s view, the legislative purpose behind s.19 of the 2001 Act is to allow those patients who are still detained, following a hearing before the MHT, to have the condition of their mental health reviewed before a judge of the Circuit Court. It is not to engage in an historical analysis.[291]

Charleton J. also rejected the argument that the President of the Circuit Court was wrong to hold that the issue of Mr Han's mental health was moot. Referring to US case law,[292] Charleton J. said that the test for currency of an issue (as opposed to mootness) was that the issue should be capable of repetition yet evading review. It was possible that the applicant would fall mentally ill again. Should that occur, his rights under the 2001 Act, not to be the subject of an Admission Order or a Renewal Order, were secured by the detailed provisions of the Act, which required that he be independently examined and independently legally advised and that any issue as to whether he is suffering from a mental disorder, or whether the Act has been complied with, or whether a non-compliance may be excused because it does not cause an injustice, is properly to be dealt with by the MHT and not by the Circuit Court. If he fails in a review before the MHT to secure his release and is still detained as a patient when any appeal to the Circuit Court that he may take comes up, he has the further comfort

---

[289]   [2008] I.E.H.C. 160; High Court, Charleton J., May 30, 2008, para.17.

[290]   [2008] I.E.H.C. 160; High Court, Charleton J., May 30, 2008, para.18.

[291]   [2008] I.E.H.C. 160; High Court, Charleton J., May 30, 2008, para.19.

[292]   *Southern Pacific Terminal Co. v Interstate Commerce Co.* 219 U.S. 498 (1911); *Roe v Wade* 410 U.S 113 (1973).

that there will be a review by a judge of that court as to whether he is then continuing to suffer from a mental disorder.[293]

Charleton J. concluded that the Circuit Court has no jurisdiction to decide any appeal from a decision of an MHT affirming an Admission or Renewal Order unless the person is then the subject of an Admission Order or a Renewal Order, and is thus detained in a hospital. The sole issue that can come before the Circuit Court under the Mental Health Act 2001, is whether or not at the time of the hearing the patient is or is not suffering from a mental disorder.[294]

7–77 The burden of proof in appeals to the Circuit Court was considered in *T.S. v Mental Health Tribunal*,[295] an application for judicial review by a patient detained in St. Brigid's Hospital, Ballinasloe. An MHT had affirmed a six-month renewal order in July 2007, and the patient issued a notice of appeal to the Circuit Court. He then sought judicial review against the MHT and other State respondents[296] seeking various orders, including a declaration that s.19(4) of the 2001 Act was repugnant to Art.40.4.1 of the Constitution and incompatible with art.5(4) of the ECHR.[297]

The patient argued that, in an appeal to the Circuit Court, the effect of s.19(4) of the 2001 Act was that the burden of proof was imposed upon him to prove that he was not suffering from a mental disorder. He claimed that the imposition of the burden of proof in accordance with s.19(4) was repugnant to Art.40.4.1 of the Constitution which provides that "no citizen should be deprived of his personal liberty save in accordance with law" and that it was contrary to the principles of natural justice and fair procedures. He relied on *R.T. v Director of the Central Mental Hospital*,[298] in which Costello P. stated that the Oireachtas needed to be particularly astute when depriving persons suffering from mental disorder of their liberty to ensure that legislation should contain adequate safeguards against abuse and error in the interests of those whose welfare the legislation is designed to support. He also quoted *Croke v Smith (No.2)*,[299] in which Hamilton C.J. stated that, in an Art.40 application, the onus is on the person in whose custody the applicant is to justify the detention and the court must be satisfied that such detention is in accordance with law before permitting the continued detention of the applicant. O'Keeffe J. stated that the starting point

---

[293] [2008] I.E.H.C. 160, para.22.
[294] [2008] I.E.H.C. 160, para.23.
[295] High Court, unapproved, O'Keeffe J., October 24, 2008.
[296] The other respondents, added by order of the court, were Ireland, the Attorney General, the Minister for Health and Children and the Mental Health Commission.
[297] The Irish Human Rights Commission was also notified of the proceedings (see p.3 of the judgment).
[298] [1995] 2 I.R. 65.
[299] [1998] 1 I.R. 101.

for the court's consideration was the presumption of constitutionality which the 2001 Act and s.19(4) enjoyed. He found that s.19(4) was not unconstitutional:

> "The applicant failed to demonstrate any basis for arguing that s.19(4) is repugnant to Article 40.4.1. No authority has been shown to justify the appellant's submissions. I agree with the submission of the State respondents, the casting of a burden of proof on an appellant under s.19 is not unconstitutional. I agree that the effect of s.19(4) replicates the general principle applied in appeals, namely that the appellant must prove his or her case."[300]

As regards the European Convention, O'Keeffe J. reviewed the authorities on art.5(4) and the burden of proof, including *Reid v United Kingdom*,[301] *Steel and Morris v United Kingdom*[302] and *R. v MHRT, North & East London, ex parte H.*[303] He also referred to *Ilijkov v Bulgaria*[304] in which the European Court of Human Rights stated that the court examining an appeal against detention must provide guarantees of a judicial procedure, the proceedings must be adversarial and must adequately ensure "equality of arms" between the prosecutor and the detained.[305] O'Keeffe J. distinguished *Reid* and *ex parte H.* (discussed below at paras 8–32 to 8–33) from the present case, on the basis that they concerned the burden of proof at first instance rather than on appeal. In his opinion there was nothing in the case law to suggest that the normal principles applicable in valid procedures before a court which apply, namely that the appellant must prove his or her case, should be disapplied in appeals relating to detention on psychiatric grounds. No case law had been advanced by the applicant to justify this conclusion. O'Keeffe J. accepted the respondents' position that there was no basis for the submission that s.19(4) breached art.5(4) of the ECHR.[306]

O'Keeffe's J's interpretation of the meaning of s.19(4), that it replicates the general principle applied in appeals that the appellant must prove their case, differs from the general interpretation which has been applied to date. Ordinarily, a section which grants a right of appeal merely states that there shall be an appeal to a particular court, and perhaps provides for the possible outcomes of such appeal.[307] Section 19 goes further: in subs.(1), it provides that the patient may appeal on the grounds that they are not suffering from a mental disorder; then in subs.(4), in providing for the outcome of the appeal, it appears to phrase the burden of proof in such a way that it is on the patient. Rather than stating that the court shall affirm the MHT's order if it finds that the patient is

---

[300] *T.S. v Mental Health Tribunal*, High Court, Unapproved, O'Keeffe J., October 24, 2008, p.18.
[301] (2003) 37 E.H.R.R. 9. See para.2–17 above and para.8–33 below.
[302] (2005) 41 E.H.R.R. 22.
[303] [2001] E.W.C.A. Civ. 415; [2002] Q.B. 1. See para.8–32 below.
[304] [2001] E.C.H.R. 489; Application No.33977/96, July 26, 2001.
[305] [2001] E.C.H.R. 489; Application No.33977/96, July 26, 2001, para.103.
[306] *T.S. v Mental Health Tribunal*, High Court, Unapproved, O'Keeffe J., October 24, 2008, p.14.
[307] See, for example, ss.7 and 8 of the Criminal Law (Insanity) Act 2006, discussed at paras 15–60 to 15–62 and 17–42 to 17–43 below.

no longer suffering from a mental disorder (which would be to phrase the question in a neutral manner), s.19(4) clearly states that the court shall affirm the MHT's order *unless* it is shown by the patient to the satisfaction of the court that he or she is not suffering from a mental disorder. If that is not placing the burden on the patient, then it is difficult to see what would constitute such a burden. Section 19(4) does not merely state that the appellant must prove their case, it states that unless the appellant proves their case, the court must dismiss the appeal. In *ex parte H.*, the court did not consider that it could interpret a requirement that a tribunal must act if satisfied that a state of affairs does not exist as meaning that it must act if not satisfied that a state of affairs does exist, because "[t]he two are patently not the same".[308]

As regards art.5(4) of the ECHR, it is true that the precedents on the burden of proof have concerned first instance reviews rather than appeals. O'Keeffe J. notes that the European Court of Human Rights has held that, once an appeal against detention is available, the court must provide guarantees of a judicial procedure, the proceedings must be adversarial and must adequately ensure "equality of arms" between the prosecutor and the detained. It is likely, therefore, that it will eventually be held by the Strasbourg court that the burden of proof cannot be placed on a patient in an appeal. Pending such a decision, an Irish court could quite safely have deduced from the existing caselaw that such a burden of proof at appeal stage is incompatible with art.5(4).[309]

---

[308] *R. v MHRT, North & East London, ex parte H.* [2002] Q.B. 1 at 10, *per* Lord Phillips M.R. See para.8–32 below.
[309] See further para.7–75 above.

CHAPTER 8

MENTAL HEALTH TRIBUNAL HEARINGS

OUTLINE OF MHT HEARING PROCEDURE

8–01 Statutory provisions concerning Mental Health Tribunal (MHT) hearings are mainly laid down in s.49 of the Mental Health Act 2001. Charleton J. has commented that "when one turns to s. 49(2) which, as the side note indicates, defines the powers of such Tribunals, one is disappointed in one's expectation."[1]

Section 49 states that reviews must take the form of tribunal sittings at which submissions and evidence are received.[2] The MHTs have extensive powers to facilitate their work. An MHT may direct the responsible consultant psychiatrist (RCP)[3] for the patient to arrange for the patient to attend before the MHT, direct any witness to attend and/or produce documents or things[4] and give any other reasonable and just directions.[5] Failures to co-operate with a tribunal in various ways, such as refusal to answer questions, are criminal offences.[6]

A tribunal will determine its own procedure and it must enable examination and cross-examination of witnesses, administration of oaths in appropriate cases and admission of written statements with the patient's consent.[7] Sittings must be held in private and the patient will not be required to attend if, in the tribunal's opinion, such attendance might prejudice their health.[8]

The patient is the only party, as s.49 refers to questions being asked by the tribunal on the one hand and the patient or their legal representative on the other.[9] In making their decisions, all members of the MHT have a vote and every question shall be determined by a majority of the votes of the members.[10]

It is not clear why it was decided that the Act would state that MHTs determine their own procedure, as this means that the Commission cannot lay down procedural rules. There is no direct means of ensuring consistency of procedure between tribunals. The Commission has, however, produced Procedural

---

[1] *T.O'D. v Kennedy* [2007] I.E.H.C. 129; [2007] 3 I.R. 689 at 699.
[2] Mental Health Act 2001, s.49(1).
[3] On the meaning of RCP, see paras 6–37 to 6–50 above.
[4] Reasonable witness expenses may be paid by the Commission—s.49(3) of the Mental Health Act 2001.
[5] Mental Health Act 2001, s.49(2).
[6] Section 49(4) and (5).
[7] Section 49(6).
[8] Section 49(9) and (11). See further para.8–05 below.
[9] Section 49(6)(f) and (g).
[10] Section 48(4).

Guidance,[11] which is referred to in training of tribunal members. The Guidance states that the right to a fair hearing is a basic human rights requirement and an MHT must be patently independent in its decision making and free from influence by any party. MHT members must have an open mind and not allow themselves to be influenced by prejudice of any kind. They must treat all participants in the MHT in exactly the same fair and courteous manner.[12] The Guidance advises tribunal members not to show bias towards any particular party, and to adopt a level of formality befitting the gravity of the matters being reviewed. The best interests principle is emphasised and the Mental Health Commission takes the view that under no circumstances should MHTs be conducted in an adversarial manner. An inquisitorial approach which seeks to protect each patient's human rights and is governed by best interest principles is viewed by the Commission as the most effective manner in which to conduct an MHT.[13]

8–02 To put the patient at ease, it is recommended that where it is required that evidence be taken directly from the patient, this be done as early in the hearing as is reasonably possible. Due consideration should be given by the MHT to each patient's mental health, well being or emotional condition when evidence is being heard.[14] All records and documentation should use suitable language that avoids jargon and can be understood by a lay person.[15] Where the patient has difficulty understanding the proceedings due to a sensory or cognitive impairment, time must be taken to communicate as far as possible and in a suitable manner. Where necessary, the Mental Health Commission will arrange suitable communication aids or an interpreter.[16]

The record of proceedings should include details as to majority or unanimous decisions, and the dissenting member, if they request this to be recorded. Tribunal members may make notes during the hearing to assist the record and these shall form part of the MHT file.[17]

Lee reports that legal submissions regarding procedural matters and any motions for adjournments are usually heard at the outset of the hearing.[18] He

---

[11] Mental Health Commission, *Mental Health Tribunals: Procedural Guidance and Administrative Protocols* (2006).

[12] Mental Health Commission, *Mental Health Tribunals: Procedural Guidance and Administrative Protocols* (2006), para.3.1.

[13] Mental Health Commission, *Mental Health Tribunals: Procedural Guidance and Administrative Protocols* (2006), para.3.5.

[14] Mental Health Commission, *Mental Health Tribunals: Procedural Guidance and Administrative Protocols* (2006), para.3.8.

[15] Mental Health Commission, *Mental Health Tribunals: Procedural Guidance and Administrative Protocols* (2006), para.3.11.

[16] Mental Health Commission, *Mental Health Tribunals: Procedural Guidance and Administrative Protocols* (2006), para.3.14.

[17] Mental Health Commission, *Mental Health Tribunals: Procedural Guidance and Administrative Protocols* (2006), para.4.3.

[18] Gary Lee, "Far From the Madding Crowd" (2008) 102(6) Gaz. L.S.I. 40 at 41. Mr Lee is an MHT chairperson.

also states that it has become the practice to hear the evidence of the RCP first, followed by that of the patient and any other person who may be called.[19] Lee states that the tribunal has a relatively short period of time in which to draft the decision and in practice it is usually delivered within an hour or so following the hearing. Once the decision is delivered, the tribunal, in his opinion, is functus officio.[20]

8–03 If the MHT revokes the Admission or Renewal Order and orders that the patient should be discharged, the Commission recommends that appropriate discharge arrangements are put in place. To facilitate discharge planning it is advised that in most circumstances where the MHT decision is to discharge, it will be in the patient's best interests to return to their ward and be discharged from there in accordance with agreed procedures.[21] In some cases where the MHT discharges the patient, he or she will remain in the approved centre on a voluntary basis.[22] In others, the patient may be re-detained if the medical view is that the patient continues to require detention.[23]

8–04 It is unclear whether a patient, when discharged, must be released immediately. McCarthy J. said of s.18 in *P.G. v Branigan*[24] that he did not think that discharged could mean anything in the context other than released.[25] However, in *M.McN. v Health Service Executive*,[26] Peart J. distinguished between discharge from the Admission or Renewal Order and discharge from the approved centre. See further para.4–114 above.

PRESENCE OF THE PATIENT

8–05 Normally, the patient will be present at the hearing.[27] The patient shall not be required to attend the hearing if, in the tribunal's opinion, such attendance might prejudice their health, well-being or emotional condition.[28] This decision must be made by the tribunal, and presumably it will require clear and convincing evidence that the statutory criteria are applicable. In *Van der Leer v*

---

[19] "Far From the Madding Crowd" (2008) 102(6) Gaz. L.S.I. 40, pp.41–42.
[20] "Far From the Madding Crowd" (2008) 102(6) Gaz. L.S.I. 40, p.42.
[21] Mental Health Commission, *Mental Health Tribunals: Procedural Guidance and Administrative Protocols* (2006), para.4.2.
[22] See for example *E.H. v Clinical Director St. Vincent's Hospital* [2009] I.E.H.C. 69, High Court, O'Neill J., February 6, 2009; [2009] I.E.S.C. 46; [2009] 2 I.L.R.M. 149; Supreme Court, May 28, 2009. See discussion in Chapter 5 above.
[23] See further Chapter 5 above.
[24] [2008] I.E.H.C. 450; High Court, McCarthy J., December 12, 2008.
[25] *P.G. v Branigan* [2008] I.E.H.C. 450; High Court, McCarthy J., December 12, 2008, p.7.
[26] [2009] I.E.H.C. 236; High Court, Peart J., May 15, 2009.
[27] Section 49(2)(a) states that the MHT has the power to direct the RCP to arrange for the patient to attend before the tribunal on a date and at a time and place specified in the direction.
[28] Section 49(11).

The Netherlands,[29] it was held that if national law requires the presence of the patient, unless certain conditions apply, then this must be complied with.[30] The 2001 Act does not provide guidance for a case where the patient chooses not to attend, but on first principles it is likely that the MHT should not force a patient to attend if they have chosen not to attend.

If the patient's behaviour interferes substantially with the conduct of the hearing, an adjournment might be appropriate to give time for an improvement in their condition. Ultimately, the hearing might have to continue without the patient if the statutory time limit for review would otherwise be breached. This might be justified on the grounds that it is better in some exceptional situations that there is a hearing concerning the patient's case, with the potential for the tribunal to order the patient's release, even in their absence, than that there be no hearing at all.

WRITTEN RECORD OF PROCEEDINGS AND DECISIONS

8–06 An MHT must make provision for the making of a sufficient record of the proceedings of the tribunal.[31] The Commission provides a form entitled "Record of Mental Health Tribunal Proceedings" for this purpose. This form records names of all relevant persons, whether the patient attended, the start and finish time of the hearing, whether any recesses occurred and details of any submissions and documents received. The form also records whether the patient's notes were made available to the tribunal and notes any irregularities, e.g. disruption to proceedings, missing papers, reports etc. The form asks whether the patient has been verbally informed of the outcome by the tribunal. Finally, a large space is provided for the recording of the tribunal's reasons for its decision.

8–07 If the Tribunal decides to extend the time for its decision under s.18 (e.g. to allow time for a witness to be called), Form 9 must be used. A space is provided for the tribunal to record details of the reasons for the decision to extend by 14 days. The tribunal must inform the Commission, the RCP, the patient and their legal representative and any other person who, in the opinion of the tribunal, should be given notice. On extensions of time, see further paras 7–30 to 7–36 above.

---

[29] (1990) 12 E.H.R.R. 567.

[30] At para. 23, the court stated, "Notwithstanding the requirements of the Mentally Ill Persons Act, the Cantonal Court judge failed to hear Mrs van der Leer before authorising her confinement, although the legal conditions under which such a hearing might be dispensed with were not satisfied. At the very least he should have stated, in his decision, the reasons which led him to depart from the psychiatrist's opinion in this respect. The Government accepted this. There has therefore been a violation of Art. 5(1) in this regard."

[31] Section 49(6)(j).

8–08 Form 8 is used for the decision of the MHT.[32] The form is primarily designed for the most common decisions, i.e. to confirm or revoke an Admission or Renewal Order. But it also must be used in cases where the tribunal authorises a transfer to the Central Mental Hospital (CMH)[33] or authorises psychosurgery.[34] If it is a decision concerning an Admission or Renewal Order, the MHT must indicate whether the patient is suffering from a mental disorder. If the patient is suffering from such a disorder, the MHT then indicates whether the provisions of ss.9, 10, 12, 14, 15 and 16, where applicable, have been complied with or if they have not been complied with, whether the failure affects the substance of the order or causes an injustice. The decision of the tribunal is recorded in a four-line box. The full reasons for the decision are not given on Form 8, but are given in the Record of Proceedings Form instead.

ADMINISTRATIVE LAW APPLICABLE

8–09 MHTs are obviously public bodies, having been established by statute to review the detention of patients, and so their decisions are subject to Judicial Review.[35] The MHTs are classified as quasi-judicial tribunals and therefore they must abide by the standards of natural and constitutional justice. In England and Wales, it has been held by the House of Lords that MHRTs must comply with the rules of natural justice.[36] In Irish law, tribunals are not required to follow the same strict rules of evidence and procedure as a court, provided the procedures actually adopted are not in themselves unfair. As Henchy J. said in the *Kiely* case:

> "Tribunals exercising quasi-judicial functions are frequently allowed to act informally—to receive unsworn evidence, to act on hearsay, to depart from the rules of evidence, to ignore courtroom procedures, and the like—but they may not act in such a way as to imperil a fair hearing or a fair result."[37]

Legality (Ultra Vires)

8–10 Tribunal members must constantly bear in mind the provisions of the Mental Health Act 2001, and not stray beyond the powers bestowed by the legislation. This means that the Tribunal must only consider the questions which

---

[32] At the time of writing, the current version of Form 8 is the version issued in November 2007.
[33] Section 21.
[34] Section 58.
[35] I am grateful to Professor David Gwynn Morgan for his collaboration in preparing an earlier version of the content of this chapter concerning application of administrative law to MHTs.
[36] *Campbell v Secretary of State for the Home Department* [1988] 1 A.C. 120 (holding that in a case concerning a restricted patient, the Home Secretary must be notified of the tribunal hearing).
[37] *Kiely v Minister for Social Welfare (No.2)* [1977] I.R. 267 at 281.

it is legally permitted to consider, e.g. whether the patient has a mental disorder within the meaning of the Act. For example, the Tribunal does not have the power in routine cases (apart from rare psychosurgery cases) to authorise any kind of treatment for the patient, and to do so would be ultra vires. The tribunal must not make an order other than extension for 14 days, or affirmation or revocation of the Admission or Renewal Order. This means that the tribunal cannot make a conditional discharge, defer a discharge or order that a patient be transferred from one centre to another (unless it is a case where a clinical director has applied for the patient to be transferred to the CMH under s.21(2)). Similarly, the tribunal has no power to award any kind of compensation to patients.

Natural Justice and Constitutional Justice

8–11 The constitutional right to liberty requires that rules of constitutional justice be followed strictly to ensure that people are not unnecessarily detained. This is confirmed by the European Convention on Human Rights (ECHR) and Strasbourg case law. As can be seen in the *Winterwerp* case,[38] the right to liberty may well lead to a patient's detention order being quashed if procedures were breached. The right to liberty has also been emphasised in Ireland in cases such as *R.T. v Director of Central Mental Hospital*[39] and was discussed above at paras 1–03 to 1–14.

8–12 A good example of the courts' application of constitutional justice to tribunals is provided by *Kiely v Minister for Social Welfare (No.2).*[40] Mrs Kiely's husband, a blacksmith with CIE, sustained an accident at work which caused severe burns which eventually led to depression. He died of a heart attack a few months later, and Mrs Kiely was claiming death benefit. Her case came before an appeals officer in the Department of Social Welfare. The key issue was whether it was possible for a heart attack to have been caused by depression and thus be connected with her husband's employment. The appeals officer decided to disallow Mrs Kiely's claim.

The High Court quashed the appeals officer's decision on the grounds that he had given the impression that her claim was likely to succeed.[41] In consequence, her solicitor did not persist with his request for an adjournment to enable him to

---

[38] (1979–80) 2 E.H.R.R. 387.

[39] [1995] 2 I.R. 65. For example, Costello P. said at p.79: "So, it seems to me that the constitutional imperative to which I have referred requires the Oireachtas to be particularly astute when depriving persons suffering from mental disorder of their liberty and that it should ensure that such legislation should contain adequate safeguards against abuse and error in the interests of those whose welfare the legislation is designed to support." See generally D. Whelan, "Criminal Charges Against Mental Patients" (1995) 5 Ir. Crim. L.J. 67.

[40] [1977] I.R. 267.

[41] *Kiely v Minister for Social Welfare (No.1)* [1971] I.R. 21.

call a medical witness. The misleading statement by the officer interfered with Mrs Kiely's presentation of her case, through her solicitor, and therefore breached constitutional justice.

A second appeals officer then heard the case and again rejected her application for death benefit. The Supreme Court quashed the appeals officer's decision on grounds which included the following:

1. After the hearing of the appeal but before the notification of the decision, the medical assessor had written a letter to the appeals officer giving new evidence as to why depression would not cause a heart attack, including the bulletin of an international medical association. The Supreme Court held that this evidence had been obtained in breach of the rules of constitutional justice, stating that new evidence should not have been introduced without allowing Mrs Kiely to comment upon it,[42] and that the assessor's function was "to act as a medical dictionary and not as a medical report."[43]

2. The appeals officer based his decision mainly on a written report prepared for the Department by a cardiac specialist, without requiring that expert to give oral evidence or submit himself to cross-examination. The court held that this created an unfair imbalance in the proceedings, as Mrs Kiely's medical witnesses gave oral evidence.

3. The medical assessor, who attended the hearing to give advice to the appeals officer, had intervened unduly in the hearing, cross-examining witnesses and appearing to present the case for the deciding officer. This was an unfair descent by the medical assessor "into the forensic arena."[44]

8–13 In many MHT cases, there will probably not be any "dispute" if the independent psychiatrist takes the view that there are strong grounds for the continued detention of the patient. The patient and his/her legal representative may well agree that the patient remains in need of detention. Tribunals revoke Admission or Renewal Orders in 11.5 per cent of cases[45], suggesting that in a large number of cases there is no real contest between the parties.

If it is what might loosely be called an "uncontested" case, to what extent can the patient and his/her representative waive their strict legal rights? Great care needs to be taken on this point and Tribunals should err on the side of caution. On reading the preparatory documents, it may appear that the case is uncontested, but during the hearing real points of conflict may emerge, and so fair procedures must be followed throughout to allow for this possibility. In addition, due to the patient's mental condition, he/she may not be in a position to waive any legal rights, which again serves as a reason for caution on the part of the Tribunal.

---

[42]   For further case law on the disclosure of relevant material, see Hilary Delany, *Judicial Review of Administrative Action*, 2nd edn (Dublin: Round Hall, 2009), pp.273–7.

[43]   [1977] I.R. 267 at 284 (Henchy J.)

[44]   [1977] I.R. 267 at 283.

[45]   See para.7–11 above.

8–14 There are two main rules of natural and constitutional justice:

- Tribunals must be impartial
- Tribunals must give a fair hearing to each party

Tribunals must be Impartial

8–15 A tribunal must be completely impartial, i.e. a neutral and unbiased body deciding the legal questions within its powers, applying the maxim *nemo iudex in causa sua*.[46] Barron J. has explained what constitutes bias in law as follows:

> "In law it is any relationship, interest or attitude which actually did influence or might be perceived to have influenced a decision or judgment already given or which might be perceived would influence a decision or judgment yet to be given. The general nature of the relationship, interest or attitude is not capable of precise definition. The relationship may be family, social or business. The interest may be financial or proprietary. The attitude may be one of good will or ill will."[47]

Impartiality is also required by art.5(4) of the ECHR, as it has been held that the reference to a "court" requires an impartial court or tribunal. In *D.N. v Switzerland*[48] the patient was examined by a psychiatrist who stated twice that he would not be recommending her release and then sat as one of five members of the relevant tribunal. The court stated that the fact that before the hearing the psychiatrist had already twice formulated his conclusion, namely that he would propose to the tribunal to dismiss the application, gave rise to a situation of legitimate fear by the applicant that her case would not be approached with due impartiality. These fears would be legitimately reinforced by the fact that the psychiatrist was the sole psychiatric expert among the judges.[49]

8–16 There are various consequences of the requirement of impartiality. For example, a Tribunal should not deal with a case if one of its members knows the patient personally. Tribunal members should also be careful to keep their distance from the approved centre staff, to reinforce their neutrality. It would be inappropriate for tribunal members to have any kind of meeting or communication, apart from brief polite conversations, with the medical personnel or the legal representative either before or after the hearing.

---

[46] See generally Hilary Delany, "Recent Developments in relation to the *Nemo Iudex in Causa Sua Principle*" (1999) 6 D.U.L.J. 66.

[47] *Orange Telecommunications Ltd. v Director of Telecommunications Regulation* [2000] 4 I.R. 159 at 221.

[48] (2003) 37 E.H.R.R. 21.

[49] (2003) 37 E.H.R.R. 21, paras 54–56. See further Peter Bartlett, Oliver Lewis and Oliver Thorold, *Mental Disability and the European Convention on Human Rights* (Leiden: Martinus

In addition, the tribunal must be not be biased in favour of the independent psychiatrist who examines the patient. The tribunal must not act as any kind of "rubber-stamp" for that psychiatrist's views.

8–17 The various psychiatrists, i.e. the admitting psychiatrist, the responsible psychiatrist, the independent psychiatrist and the psychiatrist member of the MHT, may be acquainted with each other. There are various precedents which provide guidance on such issues. If, for example, two of the psychiatrists were in the same class in university, that would not be problematic. Generally, courts have been sympathetic to the reality that in Ireland, specialised professions are usually small pools whose members often know each other.[50] However, if one of them is in a position of seniority over another (e.g. about to sit on an interview panel concerning them) then it would not be appropriate to proceed.

8–18 Members of the tribunal should not reveal the likely outcome of the case during the hearing, as this reveals pre-judgement and may cause the patient's lawyer to alter the presentation of the evidence. The patient might be able to challenge the tribunal's decision later on this basis (see *Kiely v Minister for Social Welfare (No.1)*,[51] para.8–12 above.)

8–19 The patient is the only party at the tribunal hearing and the tribunal itself may need to ask questions of the patients to probe any weakness in their account. If one asks questions of someone, one may be perceived as against them. If the questioning is intensive, there may be an argument that this is unconstitutional and any order made invalid. There is case law which warns tribunals not to "descend into the forensic arena":

> "It ill becomes an assessor who is an affiliate of the quasi-judicial officer, to descend into the forensic arena ... the taint of partiality will necessarily follow if [the appeals officer or assessor] intervenes to such an extent as to appear to be presenting or conducting the case against the claimant."[52]

Great care should be taken by tribunal members in preserving their neutrality while cross-examining witnesses. Tribunals may, in some more contested cases, need to engage a lawyer to ask questions on their behalf, as permitted by s.49(6)(f).[53] This would conform with the practice in tribunals of inquiry. If the

Nijhoff, 2006), pp.62–3, referring to *R. v MHRT, North and East London, ex p. H.* [2001] E.W.H.C. Civ. 415; [2002] Q.B. 1 and *Re Egglestone and Mousseau and Advisory Review Board* (1983) 150 D.L.R. (3d.) 86.

[50] *Dublin and County Broadcasting Ltd. v Independent Radio and Television Commission*, unreported, Murphy J., High Court, May 12, 1989.

[51] [1971] I.R. 21.

[52] *Kiely v Minister for Social Welfare (No.2)* [1977] I.R. 267 at 283.

[53] Section 49(6)(f) states that cross-examination may be "by or *on behalf of*" the tribunal, which is probably intended to mean that there may be counsel for the tribunal in some cases.

State argues that it does not have sufficient resources to fund such a lawyer, this resources argument will not justify a breach of constitutional justice.

8–20 When the tribunal is considering its decision privately after hearing the evidence, the discussion should concern only the evidence as presented, and speculation about other matters should not take place. Only members of the tribunal should be present for discussion of the decision. The importance of this point was emphasised in *Flanagan v U.C.D.*,[54] where the Registrar of University College Dublin acted as prosecutor in a hearing before a three-member committee of discipline concerning alleged plagiarism by a student. After the hearing, the student was asked to leave the room, but the registrar and his assistant remained for the discussion of the result, and this was held to be a clear breach of fair procedures.

8–21 One possible outcome of a judicial review is that the case will be sent back to the MHT for reconsideration. If that happens, the case should be heard by a new set of tribunal members, other than those who heard the case first time round, because they may be biased by virtue of being brought before the High Court: see the account of *Kiely v Minister for Social Welfare (No.2)*[55] at para.8–12 above.

Tribunals must give a fair hearing to any party

8–22 Tribunals must apply the *audi alteram partem* principle and ensure that they give a fair hearing to any party.

Article 5(4) of the ECHR provides that everyone deprived of liberty by detention is entitled to take proceedings by which the lawfulness of their detention shall be decided speedily by a court. The European Court has held in the vagrancy cases that the procedure followed by the "court" must have a judicial character and give to the individual concerned guarantees appropriate to the kind of deprivation of liberty in question.[56]

While *Winterwerp v the Netherlands*[57] is primarily cited for its statement of the three requirements for detention of patients with mental disorders,[58] it also contains important guidance regarding the right to a fair hearing. Mr Winterwerp was committed to a psychiatric hospital by the direction of a local *burgomaster* (mayor). His detention was renewed annually by the Regional Court but he was not allowed to be heard by the court, nor was he notified of its orders. He also

---

[54] [1988] I.R. 724.
[55] [1977] I.R. 267.
[56] *De Wilde, Ooms and Versyp v Belgium (No. 1)* (1979–80) 1 E.H.R.R. 373, para.76.
[57] *Winterwerp v The Netherlands* (1979–80) 2 E.H.R.R. 387.
[58] See para.1–23 above. The court held that the decision to detain must be supported by objective medical expertise, the mental disorder must be serious enough to warrant compulsory confinement, and the validity of confinement must be based on the persistence of the disorder.

objected to the fact that he had no legal assistance and that he had no opportunity of challenging the medical reports. The court held that art.5(4) of the Convention had been breached. The court said that the judicial proceedings referred to in art.5(4) need not always be attended by the same guarantees as those required under art.6(1) for civil or criminal litigation but it was essential that the person concerned should have access to a court and the opportunity to be heard either in person or, where necessary, through some form of representation, failing which, he would not have been afforded the fundamental guarantees of procedure applied in matters of deprivation of liberty. Mental illness might entail restricting or modifying the manner of exercise of such a right, but it could not justify impairing the very essence of the right. Indeed, special procedural safeguards might prove called for in order to protect the interests of persons who, on account of their mental disabilities, were not fully capable of acting for themselves.[59]

8–23 Seating arrangements should show equality of treatment for those appearing at the hearing. Kennedy suggests that the patient and clinician should not be placed at opposite ends of a row or separated by the patient's legal advocate in such a way as to polarise a "courtroom drama and turn an inquisition into an adversarial contest harmful to therapeutic relationships."[60]

The tribunal should allow adequate time for each witness to be examined and cross-examined, and not be tempted to try to speed proceedings along and cut any evidence short, except in extreme circumstances. Any document which is produced must be given to the patient or the patient's legal representative in time for them to examine it and prepare their response to it.

Normally in a tribunal there would be two obvious "sides", but in the case of MHTs, the patient and the approved centre should probably not be regarded as two "sides" (see para.8–19 above.) The approved centre's psychiatrist would need to be treated fairly and not have matters sprung on them out of the blue. Given that normally the patient is legally represented and the approved centre may not have such representation, the tribunal should try to avoid undue imbalance and unfairness which might result.

8–24 As was noted earlier, it is part of constitutional justice that points must be put to witnesses in cross-examination, to give them an opportunity to respond to them. Section 49(6)(d) would seem to contemplate that written statements are only admissible with the consent of the patient. The question of whether the independent psychiatrist should give oral evidence at the MHT hearing has been discussed in detail above at para.7–20. It seems that before a patient could insist that the psychiatrist be called for cross-examination, the patient would need to indicate specific and real grounds of inquiry that they would like to raise with the psychiatrist.

---

[59] *Winterwerp v The Netherlands* (1979–80) 2 E.H.R.R. 387, para.60.
[60] Harry Kennedy, *The Annotated Mental Health Acts* (Dublin: Blackhall, 2007), pp.124–5.

MHTs may not delegate their functions

8–25 There is a strong principle that a power must be exercised by the authority in which it has been vested by the legislature.[61] It cannot be transferred to another person or body. This is expressed in the Latin maxim, *Delegatus non potest delegare*: A person to whom power has been delegated cannot delegate that power to another. A straightforward example is *O'Neill v Beaumont Hospital Board*.[62] In this case, a certificate, stating that the plaintiff's services were unsatisfactory, with the consequence that he could not be confirmed in his post, was declared by Murphy J. to be invalid. The reason for this decision was that the certificate had been issued by the chief executive officer of the hospital rather than by the board in which the statutory instrument constituting the hospital had vested this function.

In principle, the maxim may apply to all types of decision. However, the nature of the decision is one of the factors conditioning whether the rule applies in any particular situation. The principle is at its strictest in the case of court proceedings but is also fairly stringently applied in the case of quasi-judicial tribunals, like MHTs. Courts may allow some latitude in the case of routine administrative matters, especially when these are being executed by the staff of the body in which the decision is vested, e.g. by the tribunal's clerk.

In addition, the non-delegation principle can be uprooted or qualified by express statutory provision. In the present field there are a number of functions related to the MHTs which are expressly vested in the Mental Health Commission, e.g. setting up the visit of the independent psychiatrist.

But where the no-delegation principle does apply, it means that the decision must be made by all three members of the tribunal and it cannot delegate its functions to one member; the clerk to the tribunal, much less the Commission's staff; or a member of staff of the approved centre. It is unlikely that tele-conferencing or e-mail could be used in substitution for a proper physical meeting of the tribunal members to make a decision.

CALLING THE PATIENT AS A WITNESS

8–26 Normally, the patient would be a witness on their own account and would be examined by their legal representative and cross-examined by the tribunal. If the patient did not appear as a witness, it might be open to the tribunal to call the patient as a witness instead. As this is not a criminal trial, there is no explicit legal principle stating that the patient need not give evidence. It is suggested, however, that tribunals should first request that the patient consent to giving

---

[61] See generally Gerard Hogan & David Gwynn Morgan, *Administrative Law in Ireland*, 3rd edn (Dublin: Round Hall, 1998), pp.481–492.

[62] [1990] I.L.R.M. 419 (This point was not taken in the Supreme Court.)

evidence (and note this in the record). If the patient does not consent, the tribunal should only rarely call the patient as a witness, preferably only in situations where the tribunal believes that it will actually work in the patient's favour to do so.

IS THE TRIBUNAL INQUISITORIAL OR ADVERSARIAL?

8–27 In legal terms, the term "adversarial" means that a court makes a decision having heard both sides of the case as presented by the opposing parties. By way of contrast, in "inquisitorial" procedures, the court is involved in establishing facts, collecting evidence and questioning witnesses. There are occasional calls for the legal system to adopt an inquisitorial approach, especially regarding family law matters.[63] Denham J. has also cautioned against "gamesmanship" in the adversarial system.[64] However, when the Law Reform Commission considered whether to replace the adversarial system in family law, it concluded that the best approach was to combine pragmatism with fair procedures and to maintain the adversarial system, while supplementing it with specific inquisitorial elements.[65] The Commission said that judicial proceedings, even though conducted with informality and sensitivity, are not therapeutic exercises and it is not possible to exclude from them some element of confrontation.[66] The Commission emphasised that court procedures must respect natural and constitutional justice.

8–28 There are a number of factors, which will be outlined shortly, which indicate that the MHT system is inquisitorial in nature. However, it must be recognised that the tribunals remain obliged to abide by the rules of natural and constitutional justice, and that elements of the adversarial system will therefore apply. It would be worrying if tribunals were to misunderstand their inquisitorial nature as an excuse to waive procedural protections. As the Law Reform Commission has stated:

> "There is an important distinction to be drawn between informality and laxity in procedures. The former is desirable and already pertains in many family proceedings; the latter is unacceptable and may result in the infringement of fundamental rights."[67]

---

[63] See for example Kieran McGrath, "Protecting Irish Children Better: The Case for an Inquisitorial Approach in Child Care Proceedings" (2005) 5(1) J.S.I.J. 136.

[64] *People (DPP) v Redmond* [2006] 3 I.R. 188 at 194. Denham J. was dissenting in the case.

[65] Law Reform Commission, *Family Courts* (L.R.C. 52, 1996), para.10.03.

[66] Law Reform Commission, *Family Courts* (L.R.C. 52, 1996), para.10.03, quoting from Law Reform Commission, *Consultation Paper on Family Courts* (1994), para.12.

[67] Law Reform Commission, *Family Courts* (L.R.C. 52, 1996), para.10.03, quoting from Law Reform Commission, *Consultation Paper on Family Courts* (1994), para.12.

In addition, legal representatives remain obliged to represent their clients' views to the tribunal, even if this may make the hearing more adversarial than it might have been otherwise. As was discussed at paras 7–49 to 7–52 above, the best interests principle is not addressed to legal representatives.

The main factor which points to the tribunal being inquisitorial in nature is the fact that there is only one party: the patient.[68] The approved centre is not a party to the hearing and is not entitled to examine or cross-examine witnesses. Questions are asked by the patient or their legal representative and the tribunal. In addition, the tribunal has the powers to direct witnesses to attend and give evidence and to direct any person to produce documents. Section 49(9) refers to the tribunal carrying out an "investigation" under the Act, but other references in the Act are to a "review".[69]

8–29 There are English authorities on this question. In *W. v Egdell*,[70] Scott J. stated that it was important to notice that the nature of a hearing before a Mental Health Review Tribunal (MHRT) was inquisitorial, not adversarial.[71] He referred to various tribunal rules which supported this point, including the power of the tribunal to subpoena witnesses and call for further information and reports.[72] Stanley Burton J. re-iterated this viewpoint in *R. (Ashworth Hospital Authority) v MHRT for West Midlands and North West Regions*,[73] saying that the procedure at MHRTs was "to a significant extent inquisitorial"[74] and citing the same tribunal rules.[75]

The Mental Health Commission emphasises in its Procedural Guidelines that MHTs should not be conducted in an adversarial manner.[76] The Commission also states that an inquisitorial approach which seeks to protect each patient's human rights and is governed by best interest principles is viewed by the Commission as the most effective manner in which to conduct an MHT. The Irish College of Psychiatrists was concerned that adversarial or contentious language would be used in tribunal hearings which would damage therapeutic relationships.[77] Lee has also stated that he sees the hearings as inquisitorial due to the paternalistic nature of Act.[78]

---

[68] See para.8–01 above.

[69] See, for example, Mental Health Act 2001—long title, s.18 and s.49(1).

[70] [1990] Ch. 359.

[71] [1990] Ch. 359 at 375.

[72] He also referred to aspects of the English tribunal system which do not apply in Ireland, e.g. the fact that the medical member examined the patient before the hearing.

[73] [2001] E.W.H.C. Admin. 901; [2002] M.H.L.R. 13.

[74] [2001] E.W.H.C. Admin. 901, para. 16; [2002] M.H.L.R. 13 at 18.

[75] Approved by Munby J. in *R (D.J.) v Mental Health Review Tribunal* [2005] E.W.H.C. 587 (Admin.) at paras 82 and 124; [2005] M.H.L.R. 56 at 73 and 80–81.

[76] Mental Health Commission, *Mental Health Tribunals: Procedural Guidance and Administrative Protocols* (2006), para.3.5.

[77] Irish College of Psychiatrists, *First Submission to the Mental Health Commission on the Code of Practice for the Mental Health Act 2001* (January 2003), p.25.

[78] Gary Lee, "Far From the Madding Crowd" (2008) 102(6) Gaz.L.S.I. 40 at 41.

8–30 Reference may also be made to some European case law on art.5(4). In *Sanchez-Reisse v Switzerland*,[79] a case concerning extradition proceedings, it was held that art.5(4) required an adversarial procedure and that the principle of equality of arms be applied.[80] Similarly, in a case concerning criminal proceedings for fraud, it was held that a court examining an appeal against detention must provide guarantees of a judicial procedure. The proceedings must be adversarial and must always ensure "equality of arms" between the parties, the prosecutor and the detained person.[81]

8–31 While tribunals must be careful to have regard to the therapeutic relationship which exists between the psychiatrist and the patient, they must also continue to observe natural and constitutional justice. Sarkar and Adshead argue that the English tribunal system is "not adversarial enough", as medical opinion is seldom challenged on cross-examination, even in cases where the clinical issues are central to the question of detention, and in many tribunal hearings subjective opinions disguised as medical facts are not uncommonly introduced.[82]

BURDEN OF PROOF

8–32 English and Welsh legislation formerly placed the burden of proof on patients by requiring those seeking discharge to demonstrate to the tribunal that they did not meet the standard for confinement.[83] This was referred to as a "Kafkaesque situation" by Bartlett and Sandland.[84]

The legislation was held to be incompatible with arts.5(1) and 5(4)[85] of the ECHR in *R v MHRT, North & East London, ex parte H*.[86] This case concerned the statutory provision concerning restricted patients, but would apply equally to non-restricted patients. Lord Phillips M.R. rejected an argument that the relevant statutory provision could be interpreted in a Convention-compliant fashion, saying:

---

[79] (1987) 9 E.H.R.R. 71.

[80] (1987) 9 E.H.R.R. 71, para.51.

[81] *Nikolova v Bulgaria* (2001) 31 E.H.R.R. 3, para.58.

[82] S.P. Sarkar & G. Adshead, "Black Robes and White Coats: Who Will Win the New Mental Health Tribunals?" (2005) 186 Br. J. Psychiatry 96 at 97.

[83] Section 72(1)(b) of the Mental Health Act 1983.

[84] Peter Bartlett and Ralph Sandland, *Mental Health Law: Policy and Practice*, 3rd edn (Oxford: Oxford University Press, 2007). p.434.

[85] Article 5(1) provides that everyone has the right to liberty except in certain exceptional cases, including the lawful detention of persons of unsound mind; art.5(4) states that everyone deprived of liberty is entitled to take proceedings by which the lawfulness of the detention shall be decided speedily by a court and release ordered if the detention is not lawful.

[86] [2001] E.W.C.A. Civ. 415; [2002] Q.B. 1. See Anselm Eldergill, "The Incompatible Burden of Proof at Mental Health Review Tribunals" (2001) J. Mental Health L. 75.

"It is of course the duty of the court to strive to interpret statutes in a manner compatible with the Convention and we are aware of instances where this has involved straining the meaning of statutory language. We do not consider however that such an approach enables us to interpret a requirement that a tribunal must act if satisfied that a state of affairs does not exist as meaning that it must act if not satisfied that a state of affairs does exist. The two are patently not the same."[87]

The Court of Appeal held that the reverse burden of proof violated art.5(1) because in *Winterwerp*[88] it had been held that a person must be "reliably shown" to be of unsound mind to be detained, and that the same approach had to be applied when considering whether to admit a patient as that which had to be applied when considering whether the continued detention of the patient was lawful.[89] Article 5(4) was also violated because, if the function of the tribunal was to consider whether the detention of the patient was lawful, it was required to apply the same test that the law required to be applied as a precondition to admission.[90]

The Court of Appeal, in issuing its declaration of incompatibility in March 2001, took a historic step, as it was the first occasion on which a British court had declared national legislation to be incompatible with the ECHR under the Human Rights Act 1998. Amending legislation was passed to remedy the situation.[91] The new provision states that it is for those opposing the discharge to prove, or the tribunal to be satisfied, that the patient is suffering from mental disorder. In *T.S. v Mental Health Tribunal*,[92] O'Keeffe J. agreed with submissions by the State respondents that *R. v MHRT, North East London, ex parte H.* related to a consideration of the compatibility with art.5(4) of a first instance review, i.e. the formal review conducted in Ireland pursuant to s.18 of the 2001 Act.[93]

8–33 Two years later, the European Court of Human Rights confirmed that reverse burdens of proof in civil mental health cases were incompatible with the Convention in *Reid v UK*.[94] Mr Reid was a restricted patient detained under Scottish mental health legislation, whose detention was reviewed periodically by a Sheriff. The burden of proof lay on the patient in these proceedings, and

---

[87] [2002] Q.B. 1 at 10.
[88] (1979–80) 2 E.H.R.R. 387.
[89] [2002] Q.B. 1 at 10–11.
[90] [2002] Q.B. 1 at 11.
[91] Mental Health Act 1983 (Remedial) Order 2001, S.I. 2001/3712. See now s.72 Mental Health Act 1983 as amended by Mental Health Act 2007; Richard Jones, *Mental Health Act Manual*, 11th edn. (London: Thomson Sweet and Maxwell, 2008), pp.359–362.
[92] High Court, unapproved, O'Keeffe J., October 24, 2008. See para.7–77 above.
[93] High Court, unapproved, O'Keeffe J., October 24, 2008, p.11.
[94] (2003) 37 E.H.R.R. 9.

Reid argued that this breached art.5(4) of the ECHR.[95] The court noted that there was no direct Convention case law governing the onus of proof in art.5(4) proceedings; however, it was implicit in the case law that it was for the authorities to prove that an individual satisfies the conditions for compulsory detention, rather than the converse.[96] The court referred to the requirement in the *Winterwerp* case that it be "reliably shown" that the person was of unsound mind. The United Kingdom had argued that, once evidence was before the Sheriff, issues of the burden of proof were largely irrelevant for the Sheriff in reaching his findings on the material before him. However, the European Court was not persuaded that the onus of proof placed on the applicant in the proceedings by the applicable legislation was irrelevant to the outcome. The court therefore found that in so far as the burden of proof was placed on the applicant in his "appeal"[97] to establish that his continued detention did not satisfy the conditions of lawfulness, it was not compatible with art.5(4) of the Convention.[98]

8–34 The Irish Act does not deal specifically with the question of the burden of proof; it is merely stated that the MHT must be satisfied of certain matters if it is to affirm the order. In light of the ECHR, it is unlikely that the burden of proof is on the patient. The approved centre is not a party to the proceedings in the traditional sense, and so there is no party to bear the burden of proof (which is the conventional legal arrangement). However, to affirm the Admission Order, the tribunal must be satisfied that there is more evidence for than against detention.

The issue of the burden of proof in Circuit Court appeals is considered above at paras 7–71 to 7–77.

STANDARD OF PROOF

8–35 As MHTs are adjudicating on civil matters, it is to be presumed that the standard of proof required is the balance of probabilities. In the English case of *R. (N.) v Mental Health Review Tribunal (Northern Region)*[99] it was held that the standard was the balance of probabilities. Richards L.J. said that while there is a single civil standard of proof on the balance of probabilities, it is flexible in its *application*. In particular, the more serious the allegation or the more serious

---

[95] His case had reached the House of Lords, on other issues, as *Reid v Secretary of State for Scotland* [1999] 2 A.C. 512.

[96] (2003) 37 E.H.R.R. 9, para.69–70.

[97] While the word "appeal" was used in the relevant legislation, the matter was akin to an application for a review under Irish law, rather than an appeal. This point was emphasised by O'Keeffe J. in *T.S. v Mental Health Tribunal*, unapproved, High Court, October 24, 2008—see para.7–77 above.

[98] (2003) 37 E.H.R.R. 9, para.73.

[99] [2005] E.W.C.A. Civ. 1605, [2006] Q.B. 468.

the consequences if the allegation is proved, the stronger the evidence must be before a court will find the allegation proved on the balance of probabilities.[100] In the context of MHRTs, cogent evidence will in practice be required in order to satisfy the tribunal, on the balance of probabilities, that the conditions for continuing detention are met.[101] In balancing the individual's interests and the interests of the public in such cases, tribunals should not demand an especially high evidential requirement in order to meet the standard of the balance of probabilities.[102] Richards L.J. also held that the balance of probabilities standard applies in matters of judgment as to appropriateness and necessity, even though there it had been argued that some issues are not susceptible to proof to a defined standard but are to be determined by a process of evaluation and judgment.[103]

8–36 The European Court of Human Rights has held that for a person to be detained on grounds of their mental health, they must be "reliably shown" to be of unsound mind.[104] The Court of Appeal held in *R. (N.) v Mental Health Review Tribunal* held that the application of the standard of proof on the balance of probabilities in the way the court had described it was capable of meeting the "reliably shown" standard.[105]

8–37 The 2001 Act requires the tribunal to be "satisfied" of certain matters before it confirms an Admission or Renewal Order.[106] Griffin J. suggested in *O'Dowd v North Western Health Board*[107] that the use of the word "satisfied" in the 1945 Act indicated that the Oireachtas had in mind a somewhat higher standard of proof than that which a plaintiff must ordinarily discharge in a civil case.[108] While this suggestion has not been repeated in subsequent cases, it is somewhat consistent with the statements in the *R. (N.) v MHRT* case to the effect that the more serious the allegation or the more serious the consequences if the allegation is proved, the stronger the evidence must be before a court will find the allegation proved on the balance of probabilities. In the *R. (N.) v MHRT* case[109] Richards L.J. approved of a statement in an earlier case that "is satisfied" is an expression with a range of meanings covering the criminal standard of proof ("satisfied so as to be sure"), through the civil standard ("satisfied on a balance of probabilities") to being a synonym for "concludes" or "determines" and therefore having an entirely neutral function.[110]

---

[100]   [2006] Q.B. 468 at 497–8.
[101]   [2006] Q.B. 468 at 500.
[102]   [2006] Q.B. 468 at 501.
[103]   [2006] Q.B. 468 at 508.
[104]   *Winterwerp v Netherlands* (1979–80) 2 E.H.R.R. 387, para.39.
[105]   [2006] Q.B. 468 at 503.
[106]   Mental Health Act 2001, s.18(1).
[107]   [1983] I.L.R.M. 186.
[108]   [1983] I.L.R.M. 186 at 194.
[109]   [2006] Q.B. 468 at 507.
[110]   *In Re H. (Minors) (Sexual Abuse: Standard of Proof)* [1996] A.C. 563, 576 *per* Lord Lloyd of Berwick.

8–38 It may be noted here that in discussing the meaning of "serious like-lihood" in s.3(1)(b) of the 2001 Act in *M.R. v Byrne and Flynn*[111] O'Neill J. stated that what the Act envisages is a standard of proof of a high level of probability. He continued:

> "This is beyond the normal standard of proof in civil actions of 'more likely to be true', but it falls short of the standard of proof that is required in a criminal prosecution namely beyond a reasonable doubt and what is required is proof to a standard of a high level of likelihood as distinct from simply being more likely to be true."[112]

LEVEL OF EVIDENCE REQUIRED BY A TRIBUNAL

8–39 A tribunal does not necessarily need to hear oral evidence on every point which arises. In *B. v Clinical Director of Our Lady's Hospital Navan*,[113] which was discussed at para.5–46 above, the patient's solicitor had raised the issue of compliance with ss.23 and 24 of the 2001 Act at an MHT hearing, but it appears that oral evidence on this point was not heard. In the application under Art.40, the patient's counsel contended that it was "simply not good enough for the tribunal to rely upon a ticked box as evidence of compliance and in view of the issue being raised, the said tribunal should not have proceeded to its deter-mination on this matter without hearing oral evidence on the issue."[114] However, Sheehan J. rejected this argument, stating that the tribunal was entitled to hold that there was corroboration of s.23 compliance in the note of Dr Lucey's registrar, as well as in the certificate of Dr McDonagh and in all the circum-stances of this case he held that the tribunal was entitled to be satisfied that s.23 had been complied with.[115]

8–40 According to the Mental Health Commission's Quality Assurance Directions, a best interests approach to client representation could properly incorporate a requirement to always test the evidence and a requirement to always request the best evidence available.[116]

---

[111] [2007] I.E.H.C. 73; [2007] 3 I.R. 211.
[112] [2007] 3 I.R. 211 at 222.
[113] [2007] I.E.H.C. 403; High Court, *ex tempore*, Sheehan J., 5 November 2007.
[114] [2007] I.E.H.C. 403, para.7.
[115] [2007] I.E.H.C. 403, para.8.
[116] Mental Health Commission, *Quality Assurance Directions: Legal Representatives* (2008), p.6.

CHAPTER 9

SCOPE OF MENTAL HEALTH TRIBUNAL REVIEWS

CRITERIA FOR MHT REVIEWS

9–01 The function of the standard Mental Health Tribunal (MHT) hearing is to review the patient's detention and decide whether to confirm or revoke the relevant Admission or Renewal Order. To affirm the order, the MHT must be satisfied that:

1. the patient is "suffering from a mental disorder" *and*
2. *certain procedures*[1] (summarised below) have been complied with, or, "if there has been a failure to comply with [these procedures], that the failure does not affect the substance of the order and does not cause an injustice."[2]

If the MHT is not satisfied that both of the above criteria are fulfilled, then it must revoke the order and direct that the patient be discharged.

These two criteria can usefully be labelled as the substantive criterion and the procedural criterion, respectively. In practice, the MHT may decide to consider the procedural criterion first as a preliminary issue, because if the patient succeeds on a procedural point, then they must be discharged regardless of whether the substantive criterion is satisfied.

9–02 As regards the substantive criterion, the question of whether the patient is "suffering from a mental disorder" involves both a consideration of the patient's diagnosis, the definition of "mental disorder",[3] and the necessity for their detention.[4] The question concerns the patient's *current* mental state at the time of the tribunal sitting ("*is* suffering") rather than their mental state at the time of detention (except where the order has already been revoked—see paras 7–60 to 7–63 above). As McCarthy J. observed in *P.G. v Branigan*[5]:

---

[1] The Tribunal must be satisfied "that the provisions of sections 9, 10, 12, 14, 15 and 16, where applicable, have been complied with."

[2] Mental Health Act 2001, s.18(1)(a).

[3] See Chapter 3 above.

[4] Detention may be based either on a serious likelihood of harm to self or others, or a finding that failure to admit will lead to deterioration of the patient's condition or prevent administration of appropriate treatment (s.3(1)).

[5] [2008] I.E.H.C. 450; High Court, McCarthy J., December 12, 2008.

"It seems to me that what the tribunal is called upon to do is to affirm an order or revoke it and "direct that the patient be discharged". It may take the first of those steps if (amongst other things) it is "satisfied that the person is suffering from a mental disorder" i.e. at the time when the review is being conducted since the present tense is used ("is"). Obviously the tribunal is not thereby called upon to decide whether or not, at some time in the past, a person was suffering from a mental disorder and, indeed, it has no power to do so."[6]

This substantive question involves considering all of the law reviewed earlier in Chapter 3 on the criteria for involuntary admission, as the criteria for admission are the reverse of the criteria for discharge. However, as noted in England, "the patient applying for discharge is *ex hypothesi* in a different situation from the person who is in the community". The patient is living in a controlled environment and may behave differently in the community.[7] In addition, tribunals will presumably take account of the availability of a place for the patient to reside, whether with family or in a community residence, as a factor in determining whether discharge is appropriate. But there must not be unreasonable delays in release due to unavailability of suitable accommodation.[8]

9–03 While the MHT focuses on the patient's mental state on the day of the tribunal hearing, it may consider the patient's past medical history. It would be inappropriate for MHTs to exclude relevant evidence concerning the patient's condition. Evidence of past medical history could, for example, assist the MHT in determining whether the patient is likely to continue to take their medication if discharged. Charleton J. has commented by way of analogy that "it is clear that if a person had a physical disease in the past, that this is a relevant consideration in attempting a diagnosis of a current condition."[9] Similarly, Eldergill has stated that "[t]he word ['then'][10] should not, however, be interpreted so literally as to mean that a tribunal must therefore disregard the history of the patient's condition or recent fluctuations in his mental state."[11]

9–04 In *M.R. v Byrne and Flynn*,[12] it was argued that a patient's detention was not lawful if the psychiatrist had renewed her detention with reference to

---

6   [2008] I.E.H.C. 450, pp.6–7.
7   *R v London South West Region MHRT ex parte Moyle* [1999] M.H.L.R. 195, para.34.
8   See discussion of *Johnson v UK* and *Kolanis v UK* at paras 9–07 to 9–09 below.
9   *Han v President of the Circuit Court* [2008] I.E.H.C. 160; High Court, Charleton J., May 30, 2008, para.9.
10 "Then" appears in the English legislation in the phrase "is then suffering" which is the equivalent of the phrase "is suffering" in the Irish legislation.
11 Anselm Eldergill, *Mental Health Review Tribunals: Law and Practice* (London: Sweet and Maxwell, 1997), p.466; cited in Peter Bartlett & Ralph Sandland, *Mental Health Law: Policy and Practice*, 3rd edn (Oxford: Oxford University Press, 2007), p.400. See further discussion in Bartlett and Sandland at pp.400–401.
12 [2007] I.E.H.C. 73; [2007] 3 I.R. 211.

s.3(1)(a), based on serious likelihood of harm, but the tribunal had on two occasions affirmed her detention with reference to s.3(1)(b), the need for treatment criterion. O'Neill J. rejected that argument, stating that in many cases of severe mental illness there was overlap between s.3(1)(a) and (b)[13] and that the condition of this applicant or any other applicant, perhaps in response to treatment, could change.[14] He analysed the tribunal's decision in great detail and concluded that its decision was entirely consistent with the evidence before it, all of the elements as provided for in s.3(1)(b) for a finding of "mental disorder" were considered and a determination made in respect of each of these essential elements and the record of the tribunal recorded all of this.[15]

9–05 Turning to the procedural criterion, the "certain procedures" referred to earlier which must be complied with, where applicable, are:

- Section 9: provisions regarding the application for recommendation for admission
- Section 10, on the recommendation for admission by a registered medical practitioner
- Section 12, on the power of a Garda to take a person into custody
- Section 14, on the Admission Order
- Section 15, on duration and renewal of Admission Orders
- Section 16, on provision of information to the patient

It is notable that the MHT has the power to consider procedural matters, as English tribunals do not have such power.[16] The English courts have held that tribunals have no power to consider the validity of the admission which gave rise to the liability to be detained, and tribunals cannot be used where it is sought to challenge the underlying validity of the admission. English tribunals do not have jurisdiction to entertain applications for decisions as to the vires of patients' admission.[17]

However, in granting tribunals power to consider procedural issues, the Act restricts the power to the consideration of only certain procedural sections, an issue which will be considered below at paras 9–15 to 9–23. In addition, the wording which allows tribunals to waive minor procedural irregularities because the failure does not affect the substance of the order and does not cause an injustice gives rise to further difficulties (see paras 9–24 to 9–38.)

---

[13] [2007] 3 I.R. 211 at 222.
[14] [2007] 3 I.R. 211 at 225.
[15] [2007] 3 I.R. 211 at 230.
[16] See, for example, s.72 Mental Health Act 1983 (England and Wales) as amended.
[17] *Ex Parte Waldron* [1986] Q.B. 824 at 846, *per* Ackner L.J.; *R. v East London & City MH NHS Trust ex p Von Brandenburg* [2003] U.K.H.L. 58 at para.9(3); [2004] 2 A.C. 280 at 293.

MHTS MAY NOT UNREASONABLY POSTPONE RELEASE WHILE SUITABLE
ACCOMMODATION IS SOUGHT

9–06 Tribunals will presumably take account of the availability of a place for
the patient to reside, whether with family or in a community residence, as a
factor in determining whether discharge is appropriate. European case law
permits this, and unless the Irish courts interpret the right to liberty differently
in some future case, the same reasoning will apply here. This line of case law
has been approved in *J.B. v Mental Health (Criminal Law) Review Board.*[18]

9–07 In *Johnson v UK*[19], the patient had been convicted of actual bodily harm
in 1984. While he was on remand, he had been diagnosed as having schizophrenia superimposed on a psychopathic personality. The court made a hospital
and restriction order and he was admitted to Rampton Special Hospital. In June
1989, a Mental Health Review Tribunal (MHRT) found that he no longer had a
mental illness and ordered his conditional discharge to hostel accommodation,
but deferred the order until suitable accommodation could be found. In May
1990 it was reported that a hostel had still not been found and in April 1991 the
tribunal made the same order again. In January 1993, the tribunal ordered Mr
Johnson's unconditional discharge. The European Court of Human Rights
found that art.5(1) had been breached and awarded £10,000 damages.

The court stated that it does not automatically follow from a finding by an
expert authority that the mental disorder which justified a patient's compulsory
confinement no longer persists, that the patient must be immediately and
unconditionally released. Such a rigid approach to the interpretation of that
condition would place an unacceptable degree of constraint on the responsible
authority's exercise of judgment to determine in particular cases, and on the
basis of all the relevant circumstances, whether the interests of the patient and
the community into which they were to be released would in fact be best served
by this course of action. A responsible authority is entitled to exercise discretion
in deciding whether in the light of all the relevant circumstances and the interests
at stake it would be appropriate to order the immediate and absolute discharge
of a person who is no longer suffering from the mental disorder which led to his
confinement.[20] That authority should be able to retain some measure of
supervision over the progress of the person once he is released into the
community and to that end make his discharge subject to conditions. It could
not be excluded either that the imposition of a particular condition might in
certain circumstances justify a deferral of discharge from detention having
regard to the nature of the condition and to the reasons for imposing it. However,
it was of paramount importance that appropriate safeguards were in place so as
to ensure that any deferral of discharge was consonant with the purpose of

---

[18]   [2008] I.E.H.C. 303. See discussion of this case at paras 18–31 to 18–33 below.
[19]   (1997) 27 E.H.R.R. 296.
[20]   (1997) 27 E.H.R.R. 296, para.63.

art.5(1) and with the aim of the restriction in sub-paragraph (e) and, in particular, that discharge was not unreasonably delayed.[21]

The court held, having regard to the situation which resulted from the decision taken by the tribunal and to the lack of adequate safeguards including provision for judicial review to ensure that the applicant's release from detention would not be unreasonably delayed, that his continued confinement after June 1989 could not be justified on the basis of art.5(1)(e) of the Convention.[22]

9–08 The *Johnson* case is distinguishable from cases under the Mental Health Act 2001 because it concerned a patient who had been convicted of a criminal offence, and the tribunal had power to order a conditional discharge. However, the principles it established are applicable to civil cases as well. The case establishes that even if a person has recovered from their mental disorder, a tribunal may decide to continue their detention if necessary while suitable accommodation is being sought. Bartlett and Sandland refer to this as "an extraordinarily conservative reading of the phrase 'person of unsound mind' in Art.5.1(e)."[23] They say that this case is an "extreme example" of how the European Court is strong on ensuring appropriate due process protections, but weak on substantive issues.[24]

9–09 In the later case of *Kolanis v UK*,[25] the patient had been convicted of causing grievous bodily harm with intent, had schizophrenia and was detained in a psychiatric hospital. She applied for discharge to an MHRT, which in August 1999 ordered conditional discharge, the conditions being that she should live at home with her parents, be supervised by a social worker and a psychiatrist and comply with her treatment. Importantly, she continued to have schizophrenia and require medication for the condition. The authorities did not find a psychiatrist in the area who was willing to supervise Ms Kolanis in the community.[26] In August 2000 another tribunal ordered that she be discharged, under medical supervision, into a hostel. She was not discharged to a hostel until December 2000. The court held that art.5(1) was *not* violated, as Ms Kolanis continued to have a mental illness which justified detention. Her case differed significantly from *Johnson* in that she continued to have schizophrenia. However, art.5(4) had been breached as, even where there are difficulties in fulfilling a conditional discharge, a patient is entitled to a review of their

---

[21]   (1997) 27 E.H.R.R. 296, para.63.

[22]   (1997) 27 E.H.R.R. 296 at 325.

[23]   Peter Bartlett and Ralph Sandland, *Mental Health Law: Policy and Practice*, 3rd edn (Oxford: Oxford University Press, 2007), p.29.

[24]   Peter Bartlett and Ralph Sandland, *Mental Health Law: Policy and Practice*, 3rd edn (Oxford: Oxford University Press, 2007), p.29.

[25]   (2006) 42 E.H.R.R. 12.

[26]   See also the patient's unsuccessful Judicial Review application: *R. (K.) v Camden & Islington Health Authority* [2000] E.W.H.C. Admin. 353; [2001] E.W.H.C. Civ. 240; [2002] Q.B. 198.

detention. For over a year, she had no access to a review of her detention and this did not conform with the requirement of speediness for such a review. The court noted that the domestic courts had acknowledged in a similar case that there had been a breach of art.5(4).[27] The court awarded €6,000 compensation.

9–10 The question of postponement of discharge of a patient while suitable accommodation is being sought arose indirectly in *S.M. v Mental Health Commission*.[28] This case is considered in detail at paras 6–20 to 6–29 above. There were some suggestions that the reason the judicial review was being sought in the first place was because the patient was being detained for so long in the hospital and not transferred out of the hospital because suitable accommodation was not available. Her psychiatrist was of the view that the patient's ongoing medical needs could only be met by her taking sustained and stabilising medication. Ideally, the more suitable regime for the applicant's care was by way of supported accommodation rather than involuntary admission in St. Patrick's Hospital, where necessary supports would ensure that her significant medication regime was adhered to. The psychiatrist had made persistent, systematic attempts to secure appropriate supported accommodation for the applicant and this approach was ongoing.[29] It was reported in the media that the psychiatrist had been seeking such accommodation from the Health Service Executive (HSE) for more than 10 months.[30]

MHTS MAY ONLY AFFIRM OR REVOKE ORDERS

9–11 If the MHT decides to revoke the Admission or Renewal Order, it must direct that the patient be discharged.[31] There is no statutory power to defer a discharge or make recommendations concerning leave of absence or transfer to another centre.[32] Nor do MHTs have the power to make a conditional discharge, even though such a power is available to the Mental Health (Criminal Law) Review Board.[33] The distinction between the civil and criminal tribunal systems in this regard mirrors a similar distinction in English law.[34]

It would be better if the MHTs had more extensive powers, e.g. to order conditional discharge, or defer discharge. The availability of a wider range of

---

[27] *R. (I.H.) v Secretary of State for the Home Department* [2002] E.W.C.A. Civ. 646; [2003] Q.B. 320. See also the subsequent decision at [2003] U.K.H.L. 59; [2004] 2 A.C. 253.

[28] [2008] I.E.H.C. 441; [2009] 2 I.L.R.M. 127; McMahon J., High Court, October 31, 2008.

[29] [2009] 2 I.L.R.M. 127 at 129–130.

[30] Mary Carolan, "Woman's Hospital Detention Ruled Unlawful by Court", *Irish Times*, November 1, 2008.

[31] Section 18(1)(b).

[32] Compare s.72(3) of the Mental Health Act 1983 (England and Wales).

[33] See paras 18–26 to 18–34 below.

[34] Section 73(2) of the Mental Health Act 1983 (England and Wales), which grants a power of conditional discharge, only applies to restricted patients.

orders would allow the MHTs to tailor their decisions to the exact circumstances of the patient in question.

9–12 In *S.M. v Mental Health Commission*,[35] the following arguments were made by counsel for the patient: First, it was submitted that if the tribunal's jurisdiction is limited under s.18 of the 2001 Act to affirming or revoking the psychiatrist's Renewal Order then it fails to provide a sufficient independent review mechanism for the purpose of art.5 of the ECHR, and accordingly the court should make a declaration that the statutory provision is incompatible with the State's obligations under the Convention provisions. Secondly, in the alternative, counsel submitted that s.18 may be read in a manner that is compatible with art.5 of the Convention, and should be so read as to enable the tribunal to *vary* the psychiatrist's order.[36] Because McMahon J. decided that the patient's detention was unlawful on other grounds, he did not make any findings regarding these submissions. See further paras 9–15 to 9–16 below.

TRIBUNALS MAY NOT REVIEW DETENTION IF CERTAIN PERIODS HAVE EXPIRED

9–13 The Act specifies in s.15 that Admission Orders and Renewal Orders remain in force for certain periods and "shall then expire." The law concerning the duration of Admission and Renewal Orders has been considered extensively above in Chapters 4 and 6.

If a patient's period of detention has expired, then the tribunal cannot affirm or revoke the relevant order. Peart J. stated in *A.M.C. v St. Luke's Hospital, Clonmel*[37]:

> "[T]he effect of renewing the order on the 4th December 2006 was that unless a review was completed by the 25th December 2006, it expired by virtue of the provisions of s.15(1) of the Act. Thereafter the applicant was not held in detention by virtue of any extant order, and the review and the affirmation of the expired order on the 29th December 2006 was of no effect in reviving it."[38]

9–14 Peart J. later made an analogous finding in *A.M. v Kennedy*[39]: a tribunal may not review a Renewal Order which was made when the previous period of detention had expired. He held that a Renewal Order for six months from August 18, 2006 under the 1945 Act did "what it says on the tin"[40] and the relevant order had expired on February 18, 2007. A Renewal Order under the 2001 Act had

---

[35] [2008] I.E.H.C. 441; [2009] 2 I.L.R.M. 127; High Court, McMahon J., October 31, 2008.
[36] [2009] 2 I.L.R.M. 127 at 133.
[37] [2007] I.E.H.C. 65; [2007] 2 I.R. 814.
[38] [2007] 2 I.R. 814 at 823.
[39] [2007] I.E.H.C. 136; [2007] 4 I.R. 667.
[40] [2007] 4 I.R. 667 at 676.

been made on February 19, 2007, but Peart J. held that the applicant was not lawfully detained on that date. Therefore, the Renewal Order was one which could not be lawfully made given the expiration of the previous order on the previous day, and the affirmation of that order by the tribunal on February 20, 2007, was of no effect.[41]

Returning to the *A.M.C.* case, Peart J. found that if the period for review of detention has expired, then the tribunal cannot affirm or revoke the order:

> "I am in no doubt that the effect of making the order of renewal on the 4th December 2006 was to require that any review by the Tribunal would occur not later than the 25th December 2006. ... [T]he Act is unforgiving in that respect, and the Court cannot invent a means of forgiveness from without the terms of the Act."[42]

Earlier in the same case, Peart J. had surmised that the tribunal, by ticking the third box[43] on Form 8 may have been of opinion that s.18(1)(a)(ii) enabled it to overlook the fact that a period greater than 21 days from the making of the order had passed, thereby enabling it to have jurisdiction to make the order affirming the order since in its view no injustice arose. He stated, however, that "given the very specific provision that upon the expiration of 21 days the order 'shall expire', such latitude as is suggested in s.18(1)(a)(ii) could not, I think, extend so far as to enable it to embrace that difficulty."[44]

TRIBUNALS MAY NOT CONSIDER COMPLIANCE WITH PROCEDURES OTHER THAN LISTED SECTIONS

9–15 To affirm the order, the MHT must be satisfied that the patient is suffering from a mental disorder and certain procedures have been complied with, or, if there has been a failure to comply with these procedures, that the failure does not affect the substance of the order and does not cause an injustice. A very specific list of procedures is provided, i.e. "sections 9, 10, 12, 14, 15 and 16."[45]

It has been specifically confirmed in various judgments, summarised below, that tribunals may not consider compliance with procedures other than those in the listed sections, although they may note their concern about the matter in their decisions. It is arguable that this breaches the ECHR, as it unduly limits the review which may be undertaken by the tribunal. As was noted earlier,

---

[41]   [2007] 4 I.R. 667 at 677.

[42]   [2007] 2 I.R. 814 at 823.

[43]   At the time, this was the box which allowed the tribunal to find that if there had been a failure to comply with certain provisions, the failure did not affect the substance of the order and did not cause an injustice.

[44]   [2007] 2 I.R. 814 at 820.

[45]   Section 18(1)(a)(i) of the Mental Health Act 2001.

[46]   See para.9–12 above.

arguments that the tribunals' limited powers were in breach of art.5 were raised in the *S.M.* case.[46] In the *Winterwerp* case, it was held that the term "lawful" in art.5(4) covers conformity with procedural as well as substantive rules.[47] In *Brogan v UK*,[48] a case concerning detention under the Prevention of Terrorism Act 1984, it was held that arrested or detained persons are entitled to a review hearing upon the procedural and substantive conditions which are essential for the "lawfulness", in the sense of the Convention, of their deprivation of liberty. This meant that the applicants should have had available to them a remedy allowing the competent court to examine not only compliance with the procedural requirements set out in s.12 of the 1984 Act but also the reasonableness of the suspicion grounding the arrest and the legitimacy of the purpose pursued by the arrest and the ensuing detention.[49] Thus, an art.5(4) "court" reviewing detention must be able to review both procedural and substantive grounds for a person's detention. This was confirmed in *Nikolova v Bulgaria*.[50]

9–16 One counter-argument which may be made is that patients who are prevented from raising certain points before tribunals may still make an application to the High Court under Art.40.4.2 of the Constitution. However, in *X. v UK*[51] it was held that a review by way of habeas corpus procedure was not sufficient for a continuing confinement. The court referred to the fact that in habeas corpus cases, the case is considered on the basis of affidavit evidence, and the focus is on enquiring into whether the detention is in compliance with the requirements stated in the relevant legislation and with the applicable principles of the common law.[52] As a result, the habeas corpus proceedings were not in compliance with art.5(4).

9–17 In *C.C. v Clinical Director of St. Patrick's Hospital (No.1)*,[53] it was argued that tribunals ought to have power to release a patient if s.13 of the 2001 Act, concerning removals to approved centres, were breached. The applicant relied on *Storck v Germany*[54] in which it was held that art.5(1) must be construed as laying down a positive obligation on the State to protect the liberty of its citizens, and that the State cannot absolve itself from responsibility by delegating its obligations in such matters to private bodies or institutions. McMahon J. rejected this argument as follows:

> "[T]he Tribunal is a statutory creation with limited powers given to it under the Mental Health Act 2001. It has no power to order the applicant's release

---

[47] (1979–80) 2 E.H.R.R. 387, para.39.
[48] (1989) 11 E.H.R.R. 117.
[49] (1989) 11 E.H.R.R. 117, para.65.
[50] (2001) 31 E.H.R.R. 3, para.58.
[51] (1981) 4 E.H.R.R. 188.
[52] (1981) 4 E.H.R.R. 188, para.56.
[53] [2009] I.E.H.C. 13; High Court, McMahon J., January 20, 2009.
[54] *Storck v Germany* (2006) 43 E.H.R.R. 6. See para.10–23 below.

under the Act no more than the applicant's solicitor who is also appointed under the legislation with limited functions. When the issue was first raised by the applicant's solicitor on 19th December before the Tribunal, the Tribunal considered the matter, and held that it did not have jurisdiction to make the order requested and offered the applicant an adjournment. Had the applicant availed of the adjournment it would have given the applicant's solicitor the opportunity of making the same request to those who had power of release including presumably the clinical director. If the applicant got no satisfaction from the clinical director then the applicant could have commenced proceedings against the clinical director's refusal under Art.40.4 of the Constitution. A claim, however, that the State failed under the Convention to protect the applicant's right to liberty, because the Tribunal did not have the power under the Act, is not sustainable for the simple reason that the applicant did not have the correct target for his complaint."[55]

McMahon J. went on to say that the positive obligation on the State to protect the applicant's liberty did not mean that any part of the State's apparatus must intervene to secure the release. The State had a mechanism which, if addressed, would have been obliged to consider such a request immediately. The protections under the Mental Health Act 2001, moreover, were continuous and adequate in this regard. To request someone in the State apparatus to make an order which it had no authority to make did not mean that the State was in breach of art.5(1). It was only if there was no authority in the State to make such a decision or if a person who had the authority wrongfully refused such a request that the State could be held to be in breach. Reading of the Mental Health Act 2001 in its entirety clearly established a procedure for continuous and regular assessment and supervision of the detention of a person under that legislation in a manner which wholly conformed to the requirements of art.5(1) as set out in the *Storck* case.[56]

9–18 It has been held that tribunals cannot consider issues of compliance with the Mental Treatment Act 1945 or the following sections of the Mental Health Act 2001: s.13 (removal of persons to approved centres), s.17 (referral of Admission Order or Renewal Order to tribunal) and s.22 (transfer of patient to hospital). It may also be noted here that ss.23 and 24, dealing with re-grading of voluntary patients who indicate a wish to leave, are not in the list of sections, although there has not yet been a decision explicitly stating that tribunals may not consider them.[57]

---

[55] [2009] I.E.H.C. 13, pp.26–27.
[56] [2009] I.E.H.C. 13, p.28.
[57] In *Q. v Governor of St Patrick's Hospital*, High Court, O'Higgins J., *ex tempore*, December 21, 2006, the tribunal appears to have acted as if it had power to consider compliance with ss. 23 and 24. Similarly, see *B. v Clinical Director of Our Lady's Hospital Navan and Others* [2007] I.E.H.C. 403, discussed at para.5–46 above; *T.O'D. v Kennedy* [2007] 3 I.R. 689, discussed at para.5–53 above and para.9–27 below.

9–19 The case of *J.H. v Russell*[58] has been reviewed above at paras 5–07 to 5–08. Mr H. had been detained on an involuntary basis for two years, followed by apparently voluntary status for six months and then, finally, further involuntary detention from September 2005 to January 2007. In the course of the High Court case, Clarke J. held that an MHT could not consider the validity of detention under the Mental Treatment Act 1945:

"It seems to me that the transitional provisions are clear as to their meaning. When setting out the procedural matters with which the tribunal has to satisfy itself, s.18 specifies, in its terms, the relevant procedural requirements of the Act of 2001, itself. It therefore requires the tribunal to be satisfied that the procedural requirements of the Act of 2001 were complied with. It does not (as it easily could have if it were so intended) set out an obligation on the tribunal to satisfy itself that the person concerned (in the case of a person formerly detained under the Act of 1945) was properly detained under the provisions of the Act of 1945.

There is, indeed, logic in the Oireachtas having adopted that position. The tribunal is established to deal with a new regime. The tribunal will be well capable of making decisions as to whether the procedures set up under that new regime have been complied with and to reach a determination on such issues, including a determination as to whether any lack of complete compliance might give rise to an injustice. It would be much more difficult for the tribunal to concern itself with the difficult and flawed regime under which persons were detained under the Act of 1945."[59]

Clarke J. went on to specifically find that an MHT "does not have a jurisdiction to consider the procedural validity of a person's previous detention under the Act of 1945".[60]

9–20 O'Neill J. reached the same conclusion in *W.Q. v Mental Health Commission*,[61] which was discussed above at paras 6–39 to 6–40. This was a case where it was found that it was not permissible for a Renewal Order to be signed by a psychiatrist from outside the approved centre, who was not involved in care and treatment, but was brought in for purposes of review. The patient had originally been detained under the 1945 Act and, as regards the powers of the MHT, O'Neill J. noted that the tribunal was confined to considering compliance with the numbered sections.[62] He approved of Clarke J.'s finding in *J.H. v Russell* that the tribunal could not consider the procedural validity of detention under the 1945 Act.[63] O'Neill J. said that the applicant's grievance in regard to

[58] [2007] I.E.H.C. 7; [2007] 4 I.R. 242.
[59] [2007] 4 I.R. 242 at 256.
[60] [2007] 4 I.R. 242 at 257.
[61] [2007] I.E.H.C. 154; [2007] 3 I.R. 755.
[62] [2007] 3 I.R. 755 at 768.
[63] Under s.184 of the 1945 Act, the authorised medical officer was required to certify that the

the 1945 Act, being readily apparent at the time, should have been brought to the attention of the High Court at the time by way of an application for an inquiry under Art.40.4 of the Constitution.[64] Another point raised in the *W.Q.* case was the failure to convene a tribunal to review the patient's detention before the Renewal Order was made in January 2007.[65] This point involved reference to s.17(1)(a) of the 2001 Act which requires that the Commission refer a case to a tribunal in certain circumstances. Again, O'Neill J. noted that this matter was also outside the scope of the tribunal's consideration because s.17 is not listed amongst the sections in respect of which an MHT is required to consider compliance.[66]

9–21 Feeney J.'s decision in *R.L. v Clinical Director of St. Brendan's Hospital*[67] was considered above at paras 4–36 to 4–37. His decision was that, even if there had been non-compliance with s.13 (regarding removals to approved centres), this would not vitiate a valid Admission Order made under s.14. Feeney J. said that this view was significantly reinforced having regard to s.18, where it is indicated that whether the provisions of ss.9, 10 12, 14, 15 and 16 have been complied with is a matter which requires consideration by the tribunal, but that is not so in relation to s.13.[68] He said that when one looks at the scheme of the Act, that was not surprising because s.13 relates to the manner in which somebody is brought to the institution and received and not detained. Section 14 is not dependent upon how a person arrived at an approved centre. He concluded that removal or means of removal was not and could not be read as a *sine qua non* to an Admission Order. An Admission Order is a separate and stand alone matter.[69] On appeal, the Supreme Court reached a similar conclusion to that reached by Feeney J.[70] Hardiman J. stated that the court could not see any authority for the proposition that s.14 cannot work at all, that it simply cannot be operated, if there is a defect in the execution of the removal under s.13.[71] He did not specifically refer to the fact that s.13 is not listed in the list of sections given in s.18(1)(a)(i).

---

person required not more than six months suitable treatment for his recovery. O'Neill J. found that "it simply could not have been envisaged that the applicant's recovery could have been achieved in the six-month prescribed period". ([2007] 3 I.R. 755 at 764). Therefore, the order made on July 3, 2006 under s.184 of the 1945 Act was invalid ab initio.

64   [2007] 3 I.R. 755 at 770.
65   As W.Q.'s situation was governed by the transitional provisions, s.72(4) of the 2001 Act required that his detention be referred to a tribunal before the expiration of his detention under the 1945 Act.
66   [2007] 3 I.R. 755 at 769.
67   [2008] I.E.H.C. 11; [2008] 3 I.R. 296; High Court, Feeney J., January 17, 2008.
68   [2008] 3 I.R. 296 at 299.
69   [2008] 3 I.R. 296 at 299.
70   *R.L. v Clinical Director of St. Brendan's Hospital & Ors.*, Supreme Court (*ex tempore*), February 15, 2008.
71   *R.L. v Clinical Director of St. Brendan's Hospital & Ors.*, Supreme Court (*ex tempore*), February 15, 2008, p.6.

9–22 The reasoning in the *R.L.* case was approved in *C.C. v Clinical Director of St. Patrick's Hospital (No.1)*,[72] discussed above at paras 4–38 to 4–41. McMahon J. acted on the assumption that the Gardaí had illegally detained the applicant, thus breaching s.13, but held that, even if this were the case, her admission was lawful. The applicant's solicitor had raised the possible non-compliance with s.13 as a preliminary issue at the MHT hearing. The MHT decided that an apparent breach of s.13 during the admission procedure did not render the Admission Order void. McMahon J. endorsed the MHT's decision as follows:

> "In view of these facts and also because whatever was alleged against the garda, had occurred before the applicant came to the hospital and was not authorised or known to the hospital until then, the decision of the Tribunal cannot be faulted. Indeed, the Tribunal might have been open to criticism had it acted otherwise, bearing in mind its obligations and powers under the Mental Health Act 2001."[73]

McMahon J. also rejected an argument that once the matter was brought to its attention, the MHT should have ordered the patient's release. He said that the Tribunal is a statutory creature and has only such powers as have been given to it under the Mental Health Act 2001. No statutory power has been given to it to make such an order and it would be wrong of the court to order a statutory body which has no powers under the legislation to have ordered the applicant's release.[74] Moreover, McMahon J. said it was somewhat anomalous for the applicant to argue that the Gardaí have no powers under the legislation to become involved in such matters, on the one hand, and that they should stand condemned for this ultra vires conduct, while at the same time suggesting that the court should recognise an obligation on the Tribunal to act in an ultra vires fashion by ordering the release of the applicant. McMahon J. continued:

> "The Tribunal has no more power to do so than the applicant's own solicitor who is not given any such power under the Act. Would it be logical to argue that the applicant's own solicitor, under the Act, should have taken it upon himself to walk the applicant out of the hospital on the grounds that she was being wrongfully detained? Where would such authority come from?"[75]

9–23 In *P.McG. v Medical Director of the Mater Hospital*[76], considered at para.4–108 above, it was held that a patient's detention was lawful, even though a requirement in s.22 of the 2001 Act that the clinical director "arrange" transfer out of the approved centre had not been complied with. When the case came

---

[72] [2009] I.E.H.C. 13; High Court, McMahon J., January 20, 2009
[73] [2009] I.E.H.C. 13, p.17.
[74] [2009] I.E.H.C. 13, p.21.
[75] [2009] I.E.H.C. 13, p.21.
[76] [2007] I.E.H.C. 401; [2008] 2 I.R. 332; Peart J., High Court, November 29, 2007.

before an MHT, the patient's solicitor argued that s.22(1) had not been complied with because the transfer must be arranged by the Clinical Director. However, the MHT affirmed the patient's detention, noting that it was concerned that s.22 had not been complied with. The MHT could not discharge the patient due to non-compliance with s.22, as this is not one of the procedural sections within its jurisdiction. Sheehan J. stated that the tribunal was correct in its view that any lack of compliance with s.22 of the Act "was not something which was within its jurisdiction to examine and make findings in relation to."[77] He noted that the tribunal had concerns about the failure to adhere to s.22 in this case and "correctly made a note of that concern in its decision."[78] Sheehan J. endorsed the approach of the patient's solicitor in choosing to make an application under Art.40.4 of the Constitution in light of the non-compliance with s.22. It is also of interest that counsel for the tribunal noted that s.18(1)(a) makes no reference to s.22 and he submitted that the Oireachtas could be seen therefore as not regarding s.22 as going to the legality of detention. While Sheehan J. did not specifically agree with this submission, it is one which may be made in future cases regarding this and other sections.

PROCEDURAL FAILURES WHICH DO NOT AFFECT THE SUBSTANCE OF THE ORDER AND DO NOT CAUSE AN INJUSTICE

9–24 Section 18(1)(a)(ii) of the 2001 Act states that the tribunal must be satisfied that certain procedures have been complied with or "if there has been a failure to comply with [these procedures], that the failure does not affect the substance of the order and does not cause an injustice." This provision only concerns the pre-tribunal-hearing phase; it is not a licence to the tribunal itself to breach procedures. Furthermore, the patient might still, in some cases, have other remedies concerning a breach of the 2001 Act (see Chapter 2 above.)

Under the Mental Treatment Act 1945, there was some case law which suggested that the procedures to detain patients had to be followed strictly and that some technical arguments might succeed, as patients are being deprived of their constitutional right to liberty. For example, in *Melly v Moran and North Western Health Board*,[79] the Supreme Court held that there was a prima facie lack of reasonable care where a doctor examined a patient but did not sign the relevant statutory form until three days later, when the Act required signature within 24 hours of examination.[80]

---

[77]   [2008] 2 I.R. 332 at 338.
[78]   [2008] 2 I.R. 332 at 338.
[79]   Supreme Court, unreported, May 28, 1998.
[80]   See further paras 2–51 to 2–57 above.

9–25 The question of which procedural failings may be excused by tribunals has arisen in a number of cases, and it is best to consider these in chronological order first, before summing up the approach of the courts. In the treatment of the cases which follow, there will be a need to refer to the debate on whether a purposive interpretation of the Act is required and the meaning of such interpretation, which is discussed in more detail above at paras 1–63 to 1–74.

9–26 *Q. v Governor of St. Patrick's Hospital*[81] concerned a voluntary patient who was re-graded under s.24 of the 2001 Act but s.23 had not been invoked, as she had not indicated an intention to leave. The MHT had relied on s.18(1) to affirm the order. However, O'Higgins J. found that while a purposive approach was to be adopted in interpreting the Act, one could not do violence to the section and he found that s.18(1) could be not used in these circumstances. He stated, "… it seems to me that that is not merely a procedural defect, that it is a *sine qua non* for the exercise of the jurisdiction in section 24 because it says 'where a person is detained pursuant to section 23' and that did not apply." He found Ms Q.'s detention to be unlawful and ordered her immediate release. It may be noted that a tribunal does not have jurisdiction to consider procedural issues concerning ss.23 and 24.

9–27 Charleton J. interpreted s.18 as permitting tribunals to cure virtually any procedural defect in *T.O'D. v Kennedy*.[82] The patient was classified as voluntary, indicated a desire to leave and was detained for 24 hours under s.23. He should then have been re-graded within the 24-hour period under s.24, but in fact this did not happen until six days after the expiry of the 24-hour period. The tribunal decided to affirm the order under s.18. Again, it may be noted that technically the tribunal did not have jurisdiction to consider compliance with ss.23 and 24. In finding the detention to be lawful, Charleton J. emphasised the best interests principle in s.4, and the fact that it infuses the entire Act, including the decisions made by tribunals. He interpreted s.18 as follows:

> "Section 18(1) of the Mental Health Act 2001 specifically mentions ss. 9, 10, 12, 14, 15 and 16 and then excuses a failure to comply with such provisions provided that failure does not affect the substance of an order detaining a patient and does not cause an injustice. … I have no doubt that in referring to these sections that concern the administration of involuntary detention, s.18(1) refers to the entirety of them and not simply to more minor matters as to typing, time or procedure. I would hold that the purpose of s.18(1) is to enable the mental health tribunal to consider afresh the detention of mental patients and to determine, notwithstanding that there may have been defects as to their

---

[81] O'Higgins J., *ex tempore*, 21 December 2006; noted in Gerry Cunningham & Orla Keane, "Summary of Art. 40.4 Judgments since the Commencement of the Mental Health Act 2001" (Dublin: Mental Health Commission, 2007).

[82] [2007] I.E.H.C. 129; [2007] 3 I.R. 689.

detention, whether the order of admission or renewal before it should now be affirmed. In doing so, the mental health tribunal looks at the substance of the order. This, in my judgment, means that it is concerned with whether the order made is technically valid, in terms of the statutory scheme set up by the Act of 2001 or, if it is not, whether the substance of the order is sufficiently well justified by the condition of the patient."[83]

He specifically held that the purpose of s.18(1) was to enable the tribunal to affirm the lawfulness of a detention which had become flawed due to a failure to comply with relevant time limits.[84] He said that an injustice can be caused by a reckless failure to fulfil the statutory scheme. If, for instance, a person were to be warehoused, without any proper review, and without any genuine attempt to comply with the statutory provisions of the Mental Health Act 2001, that would constitute an injustice, notwithstanding that the substance of the orders earlier made, but long elapsed, were valid. The ordinary remedy, however, where there is an issue as to the appropriateness of a time limit and compliance with the other statutory norms, is to bring the matter before the MHT. He expressly held that if, at a time when the High Court considers an application for habeas corpus, a period of unlawful detention has been cured validly by a decision of the MHT under s.18(1), the remedy is no longer available.[85] Charleton J. said that the applicant clearly had a mental disorder, he had never been subjected to reckless or inhumane treatment as to his detention and any further review should take place within the statutory scheme under the Act, as this was what the Oireachtas intended.[86]

9–28 A different approach was taken by O'Neill J. in *W.Q. v Mental Health Commission*,[87] which has already been discussed above at paras 6–39 to 6–40. Two tribunals had affirmed the patient's detention, the first held on January 22, 2007 and the second held on April 16, 2007. O'Neill J. found that there were three defects in the patient's detention when the first tribunal sat but the tribunal only had jurisdiction to consider one of these, the fact that the Renewal Order was signed by a psychiatrist who was not a psychiatrist responsible for the care and treatment of the patient concerned.[88] In considering the meaning of s.18, O'Neill J. stated:

---

[83]   [2007] 3 I.R. 689 at 704.
[84]   [2007] 3 I.R. 689 at 705.
[85]   [2007] 3 I.R. 689 at 705.
[86]   [2007] 3 I.R. 689 at 705–6.
[87]   [2007] I.E.H.C. 154; [2007] 3 I.R. 755.
[88]   The three defects were: (1) Under s.184 of the 1945 Act, the authorised medical officer was required to certify that the person required not more than six months' suitable treatment for his recovery. O'Neill J. found that "it simply could not have been envisaged that the applicant's recovery could have been achieved in the six month prescribed period" ([2007] 3 I.R. 755 at 764). (2) As W.Q.'s situation was governed by the transitional provisions, s.72(4) of the 2001 Act required that his detention be referred to a tribunal before the expiration of his detention

"In my opinion, the best interests of a person suffering from a mental disorder are secured by a faithful observance of and compliance with the statutory safeguards put into the Act of 2001 by the Oireachtas. That, together with the restriction in s.18(1)(a)(ii), means that only those failures of compliance which are of an insubstantial nature and do not cause injustice can be excused by a mental health tribunal. Therefore it necessarily follows that there must be in existence either an admission order or renewal order, where appropriate, which in substance is valid. An order which contains a flaw which undermines or disregards the statutory basis for lawful detention as provided for in this Act, could not be excused under s.18. Therefore the absence of the necessary valid preceding order or the making of an order by the wrong person are in my opinion defects which take the purported order outside or beyond the statutory scheme provided and cannot be cured under s.18. It is clear that what was envisaged by the Oireachtas, was that a mental health tribunal would have the power to excuse minor errors of an insubstantial nature but no more."[89]

As the Renewal Order had been made by "the wrong person", this could not have been excused by the tribunal. The tribunal's affirmation of the Renewal Order, having regard to the fundamental defect in it, by reason of it having been made by the wrong psychiatrist, was invalid.[90] However, as this defect was not raised at the tribunal hearing, and a new Renewal Order had been affirmed by the second tribunal, the patient's detention was now lawful. O'Neill J. said that "the defects were neither cured, excused nor ignored."[91] What had occurred was that, in the process of events, the applicant had lost competence to lay claim to, or place reliance on, these defects to challenge the validity of the Renewal Order.[92]

9–29 One point raised in *M.D. v Clinical Director of St. Brendan's Hospital*[93] (discussed above at paras 6–16 to 6–19) was that the psychiatrist had failed to tick the relevant box on the information notice to notify the patient whether he was being detained under an Admission Order or a Renewal Order, which was a breach of s.16 of the 2001 Act. The tribunal had affirmed the patient's detention on May 15, 2007. On one view, the tribunal was, strictly speaking, reviewing the Admission Order which had been made on April 26, and which seems to have been properly notified to the patient.[94] On another view, the

---

under the 1945 Act but this had not happened. (3) It was not permissible for a Renewal Order to be signed by a psychiatrist from outside the approved centre, who was not involved in care and treatment, but was brought in for purposes of review. The tribunal only had jurisdiction regarding the third defect, which concerned s.15 of the 2001 Act.

[89] [2007] 3 I.R. 755 at 768.
[90] [2007] 3 I.R. 755 at 768–9.
[91] [2007] 3 I.R. 755 at 771.
[92] [2007] 3 I.R. 755 at 771.
[93] [2008] 1 I.R. 632.
[94] It is not explicitly stated in the judgments that the patient had been properly notified of his detention within 24 hours of April 26, 2007.

tribunal was reviewing the patient's "detention" and so was entitled to take account of any procedural matter, including a Renewal Order which was made before the hearing. As the Renewal Order had been made on May 10, five days before the tribunal hearing regarding the Admission Order, the tribunal seems to have been made aware of the failure to tick the relevant box. It appears that neither the patient nor his solicitor had been notified of the making of the Renewal Order at all,[95] and, when the solicitor found the form on the file, the failure to tick the relevant box was noted.

9–30 In the High Court, Peart J. held that the psychiatrist's oversight did not result in any unlawfulness of detention.[96] By the time the case reached the Supreme Court, a second tribunal hearing had been held on May 29, which affirmed the patient's detention. While the Supreme Court found the detention to be lawful, Hardiman J. considered the question of the role of the tribunal in such a case in more detail. He expressed "some anxiety" about the procedures adopted in this case. The patient had an "absolute right" to be informed of the statutory provision under which he was being detained. If the psychiatrist herself was uncertain as to the power she was considering exercising, that was a matter which would cast doubt on the question of whether she should proceed to make an order at all.[97] He noted that, at the tribunal hearing on May 29, the psychiatrist purported to amend her order of May 10 by indicating that the power she had then been exercising was that conferred by s.15 of the 2001 Act. Hardiman J. stated this could not be regarded as a satisfactory amendment. There was an obligation on the doctor to give notice of the making of her order to the patient and to the Commission within 24 hours of its making. An amendment made 19 days after the original order was purportedly made could hardly be regarded as meeting such a requirement.[98] He said that neither the psychiatrist nor the tribunal could avoid or frustrate the review simply by the making of an inadequate or insufficient record of the exercise by them of the very considerable powers conferred upon them by statute.[99] Hardiman J. found that the psychiatrist's failure to tick the relevant box could not possibly operate to deprive a tribunal of the powers necessary to carry out its statutory obligations under s.18. "So to hold would be to compound the confusion which had arisen and to deprive the patient of his entitlement to a review of the s.14 detention."[100]

---

[95] The applicant submitted that "a renewal order pursuant to s.15 was made, without his knowledge, a few days before the mental health tribunal was due to sit ... He was not told of this nor was the lawyer whom the Mental Health Commission was obliged to appoint to look after his interests." (Per Hardiman J., Supreme Court–[2008] 1 I.R. 632 at 645.)

[96] [2008] 1 I.R. 632 at 640.

[97] [2008] 1 I.R. 632 at 648.

[98] [2008] 1 I.R. 632 at 648.

[99] [2008] 1 I.R. 632 at 644.

[100] [2008] 1 I.R. 632 at 649.

9–31 When the tribunal was filling in Form 8, which recorded its decision, it ticked both the box which indicated that the provisions of ss.9, 10, 12, 14, 15 and 16 had been complied with and the box indicating that if there had been a failure to comply with any such provisions, the failure did not affect the substance of the order and did not cause an injustice. Hardiman J. expressed concern that, the psychiatrist having omitted to comply with s.16(2)(a), the tribunal nevertheless certified that s.16 had been complied with when "it manifestly had not."[101] He does not discuss the fact that it is arguable that s.16 had been complied with as regards the Admission Order made on April 26 which the tribunal was reviewing at the time. On the other hand, as noted earlier, s.18 states that the tribunal reviews the patient's "detention" rather than the actual order.

Hardiman J. made the following additional comments regarding the tribunal's decision:

> "In my view it was illogical to reach both of these findings. If the first finding was correct, the second was otiose. If the proviso contained in s.18(1)(a)(ii) (that there has been a failure it did not affect the substance of the order or cause an injustice) requires to be invoked, as it did, then that situation will arise only if there has in fact been a failure to comply with some section of the Act of 2001. Moreover, I cannot see how it can be certified, as it was, that if there has been a failure to comply with any such provision then the failure did not affect the substance of the order and did not cause an injustice unless the precise failure in question is identified and its effect ascertained."[102]

He also stated that the tribunal consists of three persons, a lay representative, a lawyer and a psychiatrist. It was important that, if it is found that a particular section of the 2001 Act has not been complied with, that fact should be ascertained, recorded, and its effect discussed. Only in this way can the MHT hope to contribute to a situation of total compliance with the statutory provisions.[103]

9–32 In *J.B. v Director of Central Mental Hospital (No.2)*,[104] discussed above at paras 6–41 to 6–44, MacMenamin J. found the patient to be in lawful detention even though the Renewal Order had been signed by a psychiatrist who was not on the staff of the approved centre in which the patient was detained. The tribunal appears to have decided that it would affirm the Renewal Order and found that, under s.21(4) of the Act of 2001, the psychiatrist was authorised to sign the Renewal Order.[105] MacMenamin J. said that, as he had held that the

---

[101] [2008] 1 I.R. 632 at 649.
[102] [2008] 1 I.R. 632 at 649.
[103] [2008] 1 I.R. 632 at 649.
[104] [2007] I.E.H.C. 201; [2007] 4 I.R. 778.
[105] [2007] 4 I.R. 778 at 791. The tribunal appears to have made this decision on May 14, 2007, but adjourned the hearing to allow further evidence to be heard.

applicant's detention was lawful, it was unnecessary to consider the meaning and effect of s.18(1)(a)(ii). He would reserve for an appropriate case the question as to how, and in what manner, the requirements of the "substance of the order" and the term "injustice" are to be reconciled, particularly having regard to the jurisdiction of the superior courts to ensure that rights of patients are protected and safeguarded by way of inquiry under Art.40.4.[106] He stated that, "one could not disagree with the views of Ó Néill J. in *W.Q. v Mental Health Commission* that the best interests of a person suffering from a mental disorder are secured by a faithful observance of, and compliance with, the statutory safeguards put into the Act of 2001 by the Oireachtas and that only those failures of compliance which are of an insubstantial nature and do not cause injustice can be excused by such a tribunal."[107]

9–33 The tribunal in *J.H. v Lawlor*,[108] discussed above at paras 6–45 to 6–47, had affirmed the patient's detention, in spite of the fact that he had been detained for 20 minutes over the 24-hour period permitted by s.23. Rather than relying on its power to "cure" a procedural defect under s.18, the tribunal found that "the admission form was signed within the 24 hour period." No mention is made in the judgment of the fact that tribunals do not have the power to consider the question of compliance with s.23.

Peart J. commented that there was no reference to the power provided for in s.18 in the tribunal's decision; it was clear that the tribunal was of the view that the 24-hour period was not exceeded but it was not clear what the basis for that conclusion was.[109] Peart J. continued as follows:

> "But I would just comment that if the notice party [i.e. the tribunal] had in fact decided the matter by availing of s.18(1)(a)(ii) of the Act, it would appear to have been entitled to do so, and that the order affirming the admission order would then have 'cured' the fact that the admission order was signed outside the 24 hours from the making of the detention order. I state that in view of what counsel for the notice party has submitted. But I cannot see that in the present case the matter was dealt with in that way.
>
> Nevertheless, the provisions of s.18(1)(a)(ii) of the Act are helpful in arriving at a conclusion on the present application."[110]

9–34 Peart J. went on to quote extensively from Charleton J.'s decision in *T.O'D. v Kennedy*[111] and to approve of his reasoning, while noting that the instant case differed in that the tribunal had not relied on its power in s.18 to

---

[106]   [2007] 4 I.R. 778 at 794.
[107]   [2007] 4 I.R. 778 at 794.
[108]   [2007] I.E.H.C. 225; [2008] 1 I.R. 476.
[109]   [2008] 1 I.R. 476 at 485.
[110]   [2008] 1 I.R. 476 at 485.
[111]   [2007] I.E.H.C. 129; [2007] 3 I.R. 689.

cure a procedural irregularity. He found that no prejudice of any kind had been suffered by the applicant by the fact that the Admission Order was not signed until 20 minutes later than the statutory time limit. No fundamental right of the applicant had been breached in any way whatsoever. No protection intended by the Act to be afforded to the applicant had been denied to him as a result. The purpose intended by the Oireachtas to be fulfilled by this Act had been in all respects fulfilled by the events which occurred.[112] Peart J. continued:

> "To order the release of such a person onto the side of the street because of such slavish adherence to the time scale provided in this section would truly enable form to triumph over substance. That could not, in such circumstances, be the court's duty in my view.
>
> I should of course add that in the present case one is dealing at worst with a 20 minute period in excess of the 24 hour period mentioned in the section. Each case of delay, if it be such, will have to be considered in its own context and on its own facts. But the guiding principle in such applications for release pursuant to Art. 40.4.2° of the Constitution should be whether the protections intended to be afforded to the patient have been diluted by the events which have taken place to the point where the intention of the Oireachtas has been frustrated, albeit without *mala fides* on the part of the detainor or those personnel involved in the care of the patient and his/her detention."[113]

Peart J. said that his conclusion that the patient's detention was lawful was consistent with a situation where the Oireachtas has in s.18(1)(a)(ii) of the Act specifically empowered the tribunal to overlook a failure to comply with a provision where it does not affect the substance of the order or cause an injustice.[114]

9–35 In *E.H. v Clinical Director of St. Vincent's Hospital*[115] an incorrect date was inserted on a Renewal Form and the tribunal decided that it had no jurisdiction to affirm the order, as the documentation was false on the face of it. O'Neill J. noted that this was a "surprising feature of the case."[116] It is unclear whether the tribunal referred to s.18 in its decision, or the exact nature of the error regarding the date on the form.

9–36 *A.R. v Clinical Director of St. Brendan's Hospital*[117] concerned a failure on the part of a psychiatrist to tick a box on a renewal form indicating that the patient continued to suffer from a mental disorder. O'Keeffe J. stated that he found the reasoning of Charleton J. in *T.O'D. v Kennedy* more persuasive than

---

[112] [2008] 1 I.R. 476 at 488.
[113] [2008] 1 I.R. 476 at 489.
[114] [2008] 1 I.R. 476 at 490.
[115] [2009] I.E.H.C. 69; High Court, O'Neill J., February 6, 2009.
[116] [2009] I.E.H.C. 47 at p.10.
[117] [2009] I.E.H.C. 143; High Court, O'Keeffe J., March 24, 2009.

that of O'Neill J. in *W.Q. v Mental Health Commission* in relation to the interpretation and application of s.18(1). The failure to comply with s.15(4) in this limited respect did not affect the substance of the order. The tribunal acted lawfully and was entitled to apply s.18(1)(a)(ii) in the manner it did. For these reasons, he was satisfied that the applicant was detained in accordance with law, and he refused the application for his release.

9–37 This series of cases concerning the meaning of s.18 are mainly clustered in the period from April to July 2007. There are clearly two schools of thought: some cases hold that s.18 can only be used to excuse minor failures of an insubstantial nature, while others hold that tribunals can excuse virtually any procedural defect, unless it is in reckless disregard of the statutory scheme. Statistically speaking, there is more support for the first school. O'Neill J. has clearly held in *W.Q.* that only failures of an insubstantial nature which do not cause an injustice can be excused[118] and this approach was expressly followed by MacMenamin J. in *J.B. (No.2)*.[119] Similar reasoning was used by O'Higgins J. in *Q. v Governor of St. Patrick's Hospital*,[120] where he held that one cannot do violence to the section and a tribunal cannot excuse a failure to use ss.23 and 24 in sequence. This approach is also supported indirectly by Hardiman J. in *M.D.*[121] when he states that tribunals must contribute to a situation of total compliance with statutory provisions, although, admittedly, he was focusing on the necessity for the MHT to record its decision carefully rather than on the meaning of s.18. Charleton J. belongs to the second school; in the *T.O'D.* case[122] he stated that s.18 refers to the entirety of the relevant sections, not simply minor matters as to typing, time or procedure and he held that a tribunal could affirm a detention under s.23, which was six days longer than permitted. This reasoning was approved of by Peart J. in *J.H. v Lawlor*,[123] concerning a detention which was 20 minutes longer than permitted, although Peart J. did say that each case of delay will have to be considered in its own context and on its own facts. O'Keeffe J. also adopted the second school of thought in *A.R. v Clinical Director of St. Brendan's Hospital*.[124]

9–38 Unfortunately, it is not possible to state definitively what the current legal position is regarding the meaning of s.18(1)(a)(ii). There appears to be more support for the view that it can only be used to excuse minor failures of an insubstantial nature, but it is possible that the courts will swing again in the opposite direction. From the perspective of constitutional and human rights, the

---

[118]   [2007] I.E.H.C. 154; [2007] 3 I.R. 755 at 768.
[119]   [2007] I.E.H.C. 201; [2007] 4 I.R. 778 at 794.
[120]   High Court, O'Higgins J., ex tempore, December 21, 2006.
[121]   [2008] 1 I.R. 632 at 649.
[122]   [2007] I.E.H.C. 129; [2007] 3 I.R. 689 at 704.
[123]   [2007] I.E.H.C. 225; [2008] 1 I.R. 476 at 486.
[124]   [2009] I.E.H.C. 143; High Court, O'Keeffe J., March 24, 2009.

view that s.18 can only be used to excuse minor failures would be more appropriate, given that the patient's liberty is at stake.

Submissions Regarding Procedural Irregularities must be made at MHT

9–39 If there are procedural irregularities, it is important that the legal representative raise these at the MHT hearing, if the MHT has jurisdiction to consider them. In the *W.Q.* case,[125] considered above at paras 6–39 to 6–40, O'Neill J. noted that the fact that the Renewal Order had been signed by a psychiatrist not entitled to do so was apparent at all times. However, the issue had not been raised at the MHT hearing. He said that there is a need for good order in the care and treatment of patients and the management of that care and treatment. The rendering invalid of an otherwise valid Renewal Order by reason of a defect in a prior Renewal or Admission Order was inimical to good order in this process and ultimately not in the best interests of someone suffering from a mental disorder. There cannot be a reliance upon defects, even substantial defects in earlier Admission or Renewal Orders, where these defects could have been complained of in an MHT or brought to the attention of the High Court on an Art.40.4 inquiry, but were not, to challenge the validity of a Renewal Order which in itself is valid.[126]

O'Neill J. relied on the *dictum* of Henchy J. in *State (Byrne) v Frawley*[127], where he said, "What has been lost in the process of events is not the right guaranteed by the Constitution but the prisoner's competence to lay claim to it in the circumstances of this case." In this case the defects were "neither cured, excused nor ignored."[128] What had occurred was that, in the process of events, the applicant had lost competence to lay claim to, or place reliance on these defects to challenge the validity of the Renewal Order. He said that the principle that a legal or statutory provision which is subsequently found to be invalid may be sheltered from nullification and thus accorded the continuance of legal force and effect, where its invalidity is not asserted at the appropriate time, and where those affected by it and concerned with it, in good faith, have treated it as valid and acted accordingly, was now well established in our jurisprudence following the judgments of the Supreme Court in *A. v Governor of Arbour Hill Prison*.[129] In his view, the above conclusion was entirely consistent with that principle.

---

[125] [2007] I.E.H.C. 154; [2007] 3 I.R. 755.
[126] [2007] 3 I.R. 755 at 770.
[127] [1978] I.R. 326 at 350.
[128] [2007] 3 I.R. 755 at 770–771.
[129] [2006] I.E.S.C. 45, [2006] 4 I.R. 88.

Non-Application of Domino Effect

9–40 It does not automatically follow that, if a period of detention is invalid, any subsequent renewal of that detention is also unlawful, which would be a "domino effect." As was noted above at para.9–39, in the *W.Q.* case,[130] O'Neill J. stated that the rendering invalid of an otherwise valid Renewal Order by reason of a defect in a prior renewal or Admission Order was inimical to good order in the process and ultimately not in the best interests of someone suffering from a mental disorder. The statutory scheme was based on short periods of detention, each disconnected from each other. A patient who required long-term treatment for a mental disorder will have made in respect of him several Renewal Orders over many years. A finding of invalidity of a Renewal Order which in itself is valid in all respects, because of a defect in a previous Renewal Order or Admission Order was a "wholly undesirable eventuality and, in all probability, not in the best interests of persons suffering from a mental disorder."[131] He also said that the "domino effect" much feared by the respondents was avoided.[132]

Eldergill has commented on this aspect of the *W.Q.* case as follows, "The objection to this is that one cannot renew nothing. Once an Admission Order has expired for want of renewal, nothing then exists to be renewed subsequently."[133]

A different approach was taken by Clarke J. in *J.H. v Russell*[134] when he held that if a person's detention was not valid as of November 1, 2006, then the provisions of the 2001 Act concerning the transition of persons formerly detained under the 1945 Act could not apply. In a sense, this is a finding that invalidity of detention under the 1945 Act has a domino effect and renders subsequent detention under the 2001 Act unlawful.

The question of a "domino effect" as regards other aspects of the 2001 Act is considered above at paras 2–29 to 2–37.

Reasons for Decisions

9–41 The tribunal must make its decision within the statutory 21-day deadline, and a notice in writing containing the reasons for the decision must be given "as soon as may be after the decision" and within the 21-day period.[135] Lee has

---

[130]   [2007] 3 I.R. 755 at 770.
[131]   [2007] 3 I.R. 755 at 769.
[132]   [2007] 3 I.R. 755 at 771. The respondents had submitted that if the validity of a Renewal Order could be attacked because of a flaw in a prior Renewal Order made perhaps several years before, there would be a "domino effect" and a current Renewal Order could not confidently be relied upon because of the potential for its undoing, resulting from flaws effecting Renewal Orders made in the past.
[133]   Anselm Eldergill, "The Best is the Enemy of the Good: The Mental Health Act 2001" (2008) J. Mental Health L. 21 at 35.
[134]   [2007] I.E.H.C. 7; [2007] 4 I.R. 242 at para.5.1.
[135]   Section 18(5).

noted that the tribunal has a relatively short period of time in which to draft the decision; in practice, it is usually delivered within an hour or so following the hearing.[136]

9–42 In a number of English cases, the importance of proper, adequate reasons for their decisions being given by tribunals has been stressed. For example, in *R. v MHRT, ex parte Clatworthy*,[137] the tribunal reached a contrary decision to the opinions of two doctors and it was held that the tribunal should have explained why.

In *R. v Ashworth Hospital Authority, ex parte H.*,[138] H. had been detained at Ashworth Hospital. Five medical reports before the MHRT recommended his continued detention and only one psychiatrist, Dr Williams, recommended his release. The tribunal decided to discharge H. with immediate effect, recording its reasons as follows:

> "The Tribunal accepted the medical evidence that the patient suffers from a mental illness namely schizophrenia which manifested itself in the 1980s in assaultative behaviour, paranoid ideas and auditory hallucinations. This behaviour extended to the 1990 [*sic*]. Since 1997 there have been no further episodes of violence. The patient accepts that he has a mental illness and complies with medication—he states he will continue to do so. He presented well to the Tribunal and responded appropriately to questions. Dr Williams has known the patient for some years and we accept his evidence of:
> * an assurance of compliance
> * the recent three year non-violent history
> * the level of insight
> * a period of recent stability and the maintenance of a job."[139]

The hospital commenced a challenge by judicial review of the tribunal decision as irrational and inadequately reasoned. The tribunal decision was stayed pending the outcome of the proceedings; and an injunction was granted to prevent H. leaving hospital in reliance on the decision. The Court of Appeal said that the reasons given by a tribunal must deal with the substantive points in front of the tribunal. This must include explaining why disputed evidence is accepted or rejected. It is not sufficient simply to state that one expert view is accepted and another is rejected. Although it is not usually necessary for these reasons to be lengthy, the reasoning process must be set out. On the facts, there was powerful if not overwhelming expert evidence against discharge, with five witnesses favouring continued detention, and so cogent reasons were required

---

[136] Gary Lee, "Far From the Madding Crowd" (2008) 102(6) Gaz. L.S.I. 40 at 43.
[137] [1985] 3 All ER 699.
[138] [2002] E.W.C.A. Civ 923; [2003] 1 W.L.R. 127.
[138] [2002] E.W.C.A. Civ. 923 at para.19.

for its rejection, especially as previous attempts to discharge H. into the community had failed and he had been detained for a number of years. The tribunal reasons did not meet this test and therefore the court quashed the decision.

9–43 Hardiman J. stated in the *M.D.* case that the requirement that the MHT must give reasons for its decision "is an absolutely essential part of the Tribunal's functions and is necessary in law because of the Tribunal's very considerable powers directly to affect the rights of a patient, including his right to liberty."[140] He said that the requirement also arose from the terms of s.49(6)(j) of the 2001 Act, which obliges the MHT to attend to "the making of a sufficient record of proceedings of the tribunal". Hardiman J. said that the requirement to give reasons for an MHT's decision in his view arose both in natural justice and under statute. He added, "Neither the consultant psychiatrist nor the Tribunal can avoid or frustrate the review simply by the making of an inadequate or insufficient record of the exercise by them of the very considerable powers conferred upon them by statute."[141] As noted earlier, Hardiman J. found that it was illogical for an MHT to find that s.16 has been complied with and also to find that, if it has not been complied with, the failure does not affect the substance of the order and does not cause an injustice. He stated that it was only by properly ascertaining and discussing issues that the MHT could hope to contribute to a situation of total compliance with the statutory provisions.[142]

In *M.R. v Byrne and Flynn*, O'Neill J. commented that it is not appropriate to subject the MHT record to intensive dissection, analysis and construction. The record is not to be seen as, or treated as, a discursive judgment, but simply as the record of a decision made contemporaneously, on specific evidence or material, within a specific statutory framework.[143]

9–44 The tribunal makes a record of its proceedings on a form provided by the Commission. Reasons for the decision are recorded on this form. According to the procedural guidelines, the record of proceedings should include details as to majority or unanimous decisions, and the dissenting member if they request this to be recorded.[144] In giving reasons for decisions, the tribunal may note concerns about failures to comply with procedures, even if those failures are outside the MHT's jurisdiction.[145]

---

[140] *M.D. v Clinical Director of St Brendan's Hospital & Anor.* [2007] I.E.S.C. 37; [2008] 1 I.R. 632 at 644.
[141] [2008] 1 I.R. 632 at 644.
[142] [2008] 1 I.R. 632 at 649.
[143] [2007] I.E.H.C. 73; [2007] 3 I.R. 211 at 227.
[144] Mental Health Commission, *Mental Health Tribunals: Procedural Guidance and Administrative Protocols* (2006), para.4.3.
[145] *P.McG. v Medical Director of Mater Hospital* [2008] 2 I.R. 332 at 338.

In standard cases, the tribunal also completes Form 8, which records the MHT's decision. In the *M.R.* case, O'Neill J. suggested that Form 8 should be amended to allow the tribunal to express a separate decision on whether there has been compliance with the relevant procedures or not, and separately from that, if there has not been compliance, whether that non-compliance does not affect the substance of the order and does not cause an injustice.[146] These changes were implemented in a new version of Form 8 issued in November 2007.

---

[146] *M.R. v Byrne & Flynn* [2007] I.E.H.C. 73; [2007] 3 I.R. 211 at 230.

CHAPTER 10

TREATMENT FOR A MENTAL DISORDER

INTRODUCTION

10–01 It is likely that medical staff will wish to administer treatment of some sort to most people admitted to a psychiatric centre, whether they have been admitted on a voluntary or involuntary basis. As a general principle of law, treatment cannot be given without consent, otherwise the treatment may be battery or negligence.[1] This principle is underpinned by the constitutional rights to autonomy[2] and bodily integrity. However, if the patient lacks capacity to consent to treatment, such treatment may be administered if it is in their "best interests." A functional approach to capacity, i.e. a new assessment of capacity for each new decision or task, is to be recommended, but questions may be raised regarding the current status of the functional test in Irish law where a person has been involuntarily admitted under the Mental Health Act 2001 or has been admitted to wardship.[3] The functional approach may be contrasted with a status approach, which entails making a decision regarding capacity on the basis of their disability rather than evaluating the person's capacity to make a specific decision at a specific time.[4]

10–02 There are specific rules in the Mental Health Act 2001 concerning treatment of involuntarily detained patients, but, before turning to those, it is important to consider the general principles first.

It is also important to note at the outset that, while important principles have been laid down in case law over the years concerning consent to treatment, in practice many patients may not benefit from these precedents. In the case of voluntary patients, for example, the phenomenon of de facto detention may apply,[5] and may well extend to issues of treatment. As Bartlett and Sandland note concerning "informal patients" in England, the equivalent of voluntary patients in Ireland, "the status of informality means that a patient is always potentially vulnerable to pressure to conform to the wishes of his or her treatment

---

[1] Simon Mills, *Clinical Practice and the Law*, 2nd edn. (Haywards Heath: Tottel, 2007), p.77.

[2] Mary Donnelly, "The Right of Autonomy in Irish Law" (2008) 14(2) *Medico-Legal Journal of Ireland* 34.

[3] Mary Donnelly, "Assessing Legal Capacity: Process and the Operation of the Functional Test" (2007) 2 *Judicial Studies Institute Journal* 141 at 143.

[4] European Group of National Human Rights Institutions, Amicus Brief in the European Court of Human Rights, Application No. 13469/06, *D.D. v Lithuania*, April 2008, p.1.

[5] See above paras 5–26 to 5–30.

providers."[6] The Tipperary Inquiry reported that many long-stay residents appeared to have little information about their diagnosis or medication.[7] In addition, in some wards, long-term prescription of benzodiazepine appeared to be associated with a lack of needs-based therapeutic and recreational activities.[8] However, a study at St John of God's Hospital regarding involuntary patients found that 63 per cent of patients stated that their treatment was discussed with them and 73 per cent consented to taking medication.[9] The 2008 Report of the Inspector of Mental Health Services expresses concern about high levels of prescription of benzodiazepines. It appears that a significant number of people in approved centres are on both regular and PRN (pro re nata: as required) medication. The vast majority of PRN medication has no time limit for the prescription and has no review date written on the prescription.[10] Given such a context, in many cases it is unlikely that patients' theoretical right to refuse such drugs has any real meaning.

10–03 For discussion of Irish law on consent to treatment, reference may be made to the extensive literature available.[11] The leading cases in Ireland include *Re A Ward of Court*[12] and *Fitzpatrick & Ryan v F.K. & Attorney General*.[13] The Irish courts have also drawn on case law from England and elsewhere, as will be discussed below.

---

[6] Peter Bartlett & Ralph Sandland, *Mental Health Law: Policy and Practice*, 3rd edn (Oxford: Oxford University Press, 2007), p.293.

[7] Mental Health Commission, *Report of the Committee of Inquiry to Review Care and Treatment Practices in St. Michael's Unit, South Tipperary General Hospital, Clonmel and St. Luke's Hospital, Clonmel, Including the Quality and Planning of Care and the Use of Restraint and Seclusion and to Report to the Mental Health Commission* (2009), para.14.2.4.

[8] Mental Health Commission, *Report of the Committee of Inquiry to Review Care and Treatment Practices in St. Michael's Unit, South Tipperary General Hospital, Clonmel and St. Luke's Hospital, Clonmel, Including the Quality and Planning of Care and the Use of Restraint and Seclusion and to Report to the Mental Health Commission* (2009), p.6.

[9] Brian O'Donoghue, John Lyne, Michelle Hill, Conall Larkin & Larkin Feeney, "Involuntary Admission from the Patients' Perspective: A Study on Patients' Attitudes Towards Their Involuntary Admissions Under the MHA2001", abstract available at *http://www.irishpsychiatry.ie/pdf/Dr%20B%20O%20Donoghue%206.pdf* [Accessed September 25, 2009]

[10] *Annual Report of Mental Health Commission and Inspector of Mental Health Services 2008*, Book 1, p.86.

[11] See, for example, Mary Donnelly, "Treatment for a Mental Disorder: The Mental Health Act 2001, Consent and the Role of Rights" (2005) 40 *Irish Jurist* 220; Mary Donnelly, "The Right of Autonomy in Irish Law" (2008) 14(2) M.L.J.I. 34; Mary Donnelly, *Consent: Bridging the Gap between Doctor and Patient* (Cork University Press, 2002); Deirdre Madden, *Medicine, Ethics and the Law* (Dublin: Butterworths, 2002); Simon Mills, *Clinical Practice and the Law*, 2nd edn (Haywards Heath: Tottel, 2007); Vincent IO Agyapong & Margo Wrigley, "Mental Capacity: Legislation and Medical Treatment Decisions in Ireland" (2009) 26 *Irish Journal of Psychological Medicine* 37.

[12] *In Re A Ward of Court (withholding medical treatment) (No.2)* [1996] 2 I.R. 79; [1995] 2 I.L.R.M. 401.

[13] *Fitzpatrick & Ryan v F.K. & Attorney General (No.2)* [2008] I.E.H.C. 104; High Court, Laffoy J., April 25, 2008.

Irish law does not as yet provide for community treatment orders, even though such orders have been introduced in other jurisdictions.[14]

EXAMINATION OF PATIENT WITHOUT CONSENT

10–04 Various sections of the Mental Health Act 2001 and the Criminal Law (Insanity) Act 2006 refer to persons being examined. For example, the medical practitioner examines the person under s.10 of the 2001 Act before making a recommendation for admission, and a psychiatrist examines the patient before making an Admission or Renewal Order. The independent psychiatrist also examines the patient. Similarly, the court may order under the 2006 Act that a person be examined with a view to establishing if they have a mental disorder.[15]

Questions may arise as to whether the person has consented to the examination and, if not, whether the examination may proceed. In *Matter v Slovakia*[16] the applicant had been deprived of legal capacity for a number of years. He then requested that a court consider whether his legal capacity could be restored. He refused to be examined by any medical expert, so the court ordered that he be examined forcibly. The Strasbourg Court held that this breached his privacy rights under art.8(1) but was justified under art.8(2). The court noted that the interference complained of had a legal basis, in the Code of Civil Procedure. The court also found that it pursued the legitimate aim of protecting the applicant's own rights and health.[17] In determining whether an interference was "necessary in a democratic society", the court took into account that a margin of appreciation is left to the Contracting States. Having regard to the case as a whole, the court held that the interference in question was not disproportionate to the legitimate aims pursued. It was therefore "necessary in a democratic society" within the meaning of art.8(2).

Matter v Slovakia was followed in the Northern Ireland case of *Re B.S.*[18] where Stephens J. held that a forcible examination of a woman to establish whether she was incapable by reason of mental disorder of managing her property and affairs was justified under art.8(2). He said that on the facts of the case a medical examination would pursue two legitimate aims within art.8(2) of the Convention, namely the aim of protecting the health of B.S. and the aim of the protection of the rights of B.S. It was for the protection of her health in that

---

[14] See ss.17A–17G Mental Health Act 1983 (England and Wales), as inserted by Mental Health Act 2007; Richard Jones, *Mental Health Act Manual*, 11th edn (London: Thomson Sweet and Maxwell, 2008), pp.115–125; Brendan D. Kelly, "Community Treatment Orders under the Mental Health Act 2007 in England and Wales: What Are the Lessons for Irish Mental Health Legislation?" (2009) 15 M.L.J.I. 43; Mary Donnelly, "Community-Based Care and Compulsion: What Role for Human Rights?" (2008) 15 *Journal of Law and Medicine* 782.

[15] Criminal Law (Insanity) Act 2006, s.4(6) and s.5(3).

[16] (2001) 31 E.H.R.R. 32. See also *Varbanov v Bulgaria* [2000] M.H.L.R. 263, para.4–23 above.

[17] (2001) 31 E.H.R.R. 32, para.65.

[18] [2009] N.I. Fam. 5.

if she did suffer from a treatable condition then treatment could be provided and that she was not subjected to emotional harm. It was for the protection of her rights in that if she was incapable of managing her own affairs then her property rights should be protected.[19]

10–05 A court should take care to give the person a fair hearing before ordering that they be examined without their consent, as illustrated by *M.G. v Germany*.[20] That was a case heard by the UN Human Rights Committee concerning an alleged violation of the International Covenant on Civil and Political Rights. The Ellwangan Regional Court, without hearing or seeing Ms G. in person, ordered her to undergo a medical examination to assess her capacity to take part in proceedings. The Committee concluded that her rights under art.17, in conjunction with art.14(1), of the Covenant had been violated.[21]

If the person themselves has initiated the legal action, then it is more straight-forward for a court to hold that they must submit to a medical examination which may be necessary for the case. Thus, in *McGrory v Electricity Supply Board*,[22] the Supreme Court held that a plaintiff in a personal injuries action must submit to medical examination. Keane C.J. said that the plaintiff who sues for damages for personal injuries by implication necessarily waives the right of privacy which they would otherwise enjoy in relation to their medical condition. He added that the law must be in a position to ensure that a plaintiff does not unfairly and unreasonably impede the defendant in the preparation of their defence by refusing to consent to a medical examination.[23] He relied on Northern Irish, English and Canadian authority which supported this viewpoint.[24]

The *McGrory* principle has been applied to a complainant in a criminal case in *J.F. v D.P.P.*[25] In that case, a man had alleged that he had been indecently assaulted by Mr F. Mr F. was charged with indecent assault in 2001 regarding assaults alleged to have taken place in 1988. In 2002, Mr F. obtained leave from the High Court to apply, by way of judicial review, for an order restraining the respondent from proceeding with the prosecution, essentially on the ground of delay. In response, the Director of Public Prosecutions (DPP) argued that the delay had arisen as a consequence of the effect of his acts upon the complainant, and cited an affidavit from a psychologist at a Rape Crisis Centre. Mr F. then sought to have the complainant examined by another psychologist, but the complainant would not consent to this examination. The Supreme Court ordered that the psychologist's affidavit tendered on behalf of the DPP should be struck

[19] [2009] N.I. Fam. 5, para.43.
[20] (2009) 48 E.H.R.R. SE5.
[21] Article 14 concerns fair trial rights and art.17 concerns privacy rights.
[22] [2003] I.E.S.C. 45; [2003] 3 I.R. 407.
[23] [2003] 3 I.R. 407 at 414.
[24] *McDowell v Strannix* [1951] N.I. 57; *Ross v Towey Upholstery Ltd* [1962] N.I. 3; *Edmeades v Thames Board Mills* [1969] 2 Q.B. 67; *Dunn v British Coal Corporation* [1993] I.C.R. 591; *Hay v University of Alb Hosp* (1991) 2 Med. L.R. 204; *Shaw v Skeet* (1996) 7 Med. L.R. 371.
[25] [2005] I.E.S.C. 24; [2005] 2 I.R. 174.

out.[26] Hardiman J. issued a strongly worded judgment emphasising the need for equality of arms and rejecting the argument that the complainant in a criminal case should be treated differently than the plaintiff in a civil case. He relied heavily on European Court of Human Rights case law,[27] while noting that the constitutional right to fair procedures also applied.

10–06 In the context of an examination for the purposes of the Criminal Law (Insanity) Act 2006, Groarke J. of the Circuit Court recently queried whether a defendant had consented to medical evidence being given concerning an examination by a psychiatrist of the defendant.[28] When asked in court if he minded the psychiatrist giving evidence in court about the assessment, the defendant replied he "did not mind one way or the other". Groarke J. said he did not take this as a consent from somebody whose mental capacity was in question.

ENGLISH LAW

10–07 *Re T. (Adult: Refusal of Medical Treatment)*[29] concerned a pregnant woman admitted to hospital following a car accident. She was not a member of the Jehovah's Witness faith, but her mother was. After a conversation with her mother, she stated that she did not want a blood transfusion for religious reasons. She later signed a form to this effect. It had not been explained to her that it might be necessary to give her a blood transfusion to save her life. After an emergency caesarean, she was put on a ventilator. The Court of Appeal upheld a decision which had been made by the High Court authorising blood transfusions. The court found that Ms T. was not in a physical or mental condition which enabled her to reach a decision binding on the medical authorities and, even if she was, the influence of her mother was such as to vitiate the decision she expressed. Lord Donaldson stated that, prima facie, every adult has the right and capacity to decide whether or not they will accept medical treatment, even if a refusal may risk permanent injury to their health or even lead to premature death. He continued:

> "Furthermore, it matters not whether the reasons for the refusal were rational or irrational, unknown or even non-existent. This is so notwithstanding the very strong public interest in preserving the life and health of all citizens. However the presumption of capacity to decide, which stems from the fact that the patient is an adult, is rebuttable."[30]

---

[26] See reporter's note regarding form of order—[2005] 2 I.R. 174 at 188.

[27] Hardiman J. relied on *Steel and Morris v United Kingdom*, Application 68146/01, (2005) 41 E.H.R.R. 22 and *Bonisch v Austria* (1985) 9 E.H.R.R. 191.

[28] Tom Shiel and Ruadhán Mac Cormaic, "Charges Dropped After Man Fails to Get Assessment', *Irish Times*, June 20, 2009.

[29] [1992] 3 W.L.R. 782; [1992] 4 All E.R. 649.

[30] [1992] 3 W.L.R. 782 at 799.

Lord Donaldson stated that doctors faced with a refusal of consent have to give very careful and detailed consideration to what was the patient's capacity to decide at the time when the decision was made. It may not be a case of capacity or no capacity. It may be a case of reduced capacity. What matters is whether at that time the patient's capacity was reduced below the level needed in the case of a refusal of that importance, for refusals can vary in importance. Some may involve a risk to life or of irreparable damage to health. Others may not. He said that in some cases doctors will not only have to consider the capacity of the patient to refuse treatment but also whether the refusal has been vitiated because it resulted not from the patient's will, but from the will of others. In cases of doubt as to the effect of a purported refusal of treatment, where failure to treat threatens the patient's life or threatens irreparable damage to their health, doctors and health authorities should not hesitate to apply to the courts for assistance.[31] Lord Donaldson also said that doctors will need to consider what is the true scope and basis of the refusal:

> "Was it intended to apply in the circumstances which have arisen? Was it based upon assumptions which in the event have not been realised? A refusal is only effective within its true scope and is vitiated if it is based upon false assumptions. ... Forms of refusal should be redesigned to bring the consequences of a refusal forcibly to the attention of patients."[32]

10–08 In *Re C. (Adult: Refusal of Medical Treatment)*[33] the applicant had schizophrenia and was detained in a secure hospital. He had an ulcerated foot which had become gangrenous and he refused to consent to an amputation of his leg, which was recommended by the medical team.[34] Drawing on precedents such as In *Re T. (Adult: Refusal of Treatment)*[35] and *Airedale N.H.S. Trust v. Bland*,[36] Thorpe J.'s analysis included the following passage:

> "I think that the question to be decided is whether it has been established that C's capacity is so reduced by his chronic mental illness that he does not sufficiently understand the nature, purpose and effects of the proffered amputation.
>
> I consider helpful Dr. Eastman's analysis of the decision-making process into three stages: first, comprehending and retaining treatment information, second, believing it and, third, weighing it in the balance to arrive at choice."[37]

---

[31] [1992] 3 W.L.R. 782 at 799.
[32] [1992] 3 W.L.R. 782 at 799.
[33] [1994] 1 W.L.R. 290; [1994] 1 All E.R. 819.
[34] The medical advice stated that he only had a 15 per cent chance of survival without the amputation. However, it was also noted that amputation carried a 15 per cent mortality risk.
[35] [1993] Fam. 95.
[36] [1993] A.C. 789.
[37] [1994] 1 W.L.R. 290 at 295.

Applying that test to the facts, Thorpe J. found that Mr C. had capacity to refuse the treatment and granted an injunction against the amputation of his leg without his written consent.

10–09 *Re M.B. (An Adult: Medical Treatment)*[38] was one of a number of cases concerning refusal of a pregnant woman to consent to a caesarean section. In this case, the issue arose because the woman had a needle phobia and so would not consent to being injected. Butler-Sloss L.J. (as she then was) included the following in the analysis:

> "A person lacks capacity if some impairment or disturbance of mental functioning renders the person unable to make a decision whether to consent to or to refuse treatment. That inability to make a decision will occur when:
> (a) the patient is unable to comprehend and retain the information which is material to the decision, especially as to the likely consequences of having or not having the treatment in question;
> (b) the patient is unable to use the information and weigh it in the balance as part of the process of arriving at the decision."[39]

Applying this test to the facts, the Court of Appeal held that the medical intervention was in the patient's best interests and granted a declaration that it would be lawful for the consultant gynaecologist to operate on her, using reasonable force if necessary.

10–10 A graphic illustration of the issues which may arise is provided by *Re W. (Adult: Refusal of Treatment)*.[40] A prisoner with psychopathic disorder was aggrieved that he was not transferred to a hospital and he protested by cutting open his leg and inserting objects in it to ensure that it would become infected. He refused all treatment for the condition of his leg and threatened further acts of self-harm. He had also inserted two taps in his anus, although he later agreed to have them surgically removed. There were three psychiatric reports, all of which concluded that he had mental capacity to refuse treatment. Butler-Sloss P. therefore declared that W. had mental capacity to be able to choose to refuse treatment at present and for the foreseeable future.

Irish Case Law

10–11 *Re A Ward of Court*[41] concerned a woman who had been in a near persistent vegetative state for 23 years. A gastrostomy tube was surgically

---

[38] [1997] 2 F.L.R. 426; [1997] E.W.C.A. Civ. 3093.
[39] [1997] 2 F.L.R. 426 at 437.
[40] [2002] E.W.H.C. 901 Fam.; [2002] M.H.L.R. 411.
[41] *In Re A Ward of Court (Withholding Medical Treatment) (No.2)* [1996] 2 I.R. 79; [1995] 2 I.L.R.M. 401.

inserted into her stomach. She had a minimal capacity to recognise, for example, the long-established nursing staff and to react to strangers by showing distress. She also followed or tracked people with her eyes and reacted to noise. As she was a ward of court, the court was asked for a declaration as to whether this treatment should continue.

The Supreme Court ultimately decided that the gastrostomy tube could be removed. The court held that it must decide what is in the best interests of the ward, applying the *parens patriae* jurisdiction of the courts regarding wards of court. The constitutional right to life was of great importance and if there was an interaction of constitutional rights which could not be harmonised, the right to life would take precedence over any other rights. The ward had unenumerated rights to privacy, self-determination and bodily integrity, which meant that if she were mentally competent she could refuse to consent to further treatment. The ward had lost her mental capacity, but had a constitutional right to equality of treatment. Hamilton C.J. said that as the process of dying was part, and an ultimate, inevitable consequence, of life, the right to life necessarily implies the right to have nature take its course and to die a natural death and, unless the individual concerned so wishes, not to have life artificially maintained by the provision of nourishment by abnormal artificial means, which have no curative effect and which are intended merely to prolong life.[42] He approved of Lynch J.'s adoption of the standpoint of a prudent, good and loving parent in determining the ward's best interests. Denham J. said that a constituent of the right of privacy is the right to die naturally, with dignity and with minimum suffering. This right is not lost to a person if they become incapacitated or insentient.[43] Flaherty J. explicitly rejected a "substituted judgement" approach to this case.[44] In a short dissenting judgment, Egan J. stating that the removal of the tube would result in death within a short period of time and, given that the ward had limited cognitive function, a strong and cogent reason to justify the taking of a life had not been established.

In the course of her judgment, Denham J. provided a significant list of factors which the court took into account in making its decision. These factors included the ward's current condition, her current medical treatment and care, the degree of bodily invasion of the ward the medical treatment requires, the prognosis on medical treatment, any previous views that were expressed by the ward that are relevant, the family's view and the ward's constitutional rights to life, privacy, bodily integrity, autonomy, dignity in life and dignity in death.[45]

10–12 The *Ward of Court* case has been the subject of widespread analysis and commentary, much of which is beyond the scope of this book. For example, Tomkin and McAuley question whether the courts properly analysed the question of transfer of *parens patriae* jurisdiction from the Lord Chancellor to

[42]   [1996] 2 I.R. 79 at 124.
[43]   [1996] 2 I.R. 79 at 163.
[44]   [1996] 2 I.R. 79 at 133.
[45]   [1996] 2 I.R. 79 at 167 (the full list of factors is *not* set out in the text above).

the courts.[46] They also suggest that a policy decision be taken, and statutorily implemented, about what sort of tribunal should be established to address medico-legal issues of treatment withdrawal.[47]

10–13 In *J.M. v Board of Management of St. Vincent's Hospital*,[48] a woman was in a coma after refusing to consent to a blood transfusion. She had recently adopted her husband's religion and become a Jehovah's Witness. Before the coma began, she had alternated between a decision to refuse blood and a decision to accept it. Finnegan P. followed the principles stated in the *Ward of Court* case and decided to permit the giving of a blood transfusion. He said that because of her cultural background and her desire to please her husband and not offend his sensibilities, Ms M. elected to refuse treatment. She did not make a clear final decision to have, or not to have, the treatment. She was pre-occupied with her husband and his religion as a Jehovah's Witness rather than with whether to have the treatment and her own welfare. Finnegan P. was strongly of the opinion that if Ms M. was lucid and strong and aware of her husband's present decision, she would agree with a decision to have the treatment, as she would have a desire to live. She would also be comforted by her husband's attitude to the decision.[49]

10–14 Laffoy J. grappled with complex issues in the recent case of *Fitzpatrick & Ryan v F.K. & Attorney General (No.2)*.[50] Ms K. was a patient of the Coombe Hospital in 2006. She gave birth to a baby boy and shortly afterwards suffered a massive post-partum haemorrhage resulting in cardiovascular collapse. Ms K. refused to take blood because she was a Jehovah's Witness. However, she had originally registered at the hospital as a Roman Catholic and the hospital only learnt that she was a Jehovah's Witness after the haemorrhage began. There were also concerns that she may not have fully understood the seriousness of her condition. For example, she said that she might be given Coca Cola and tomatoes as an alternative to a blood transfusion. There were also some suggestions of communication difficulties, as she was speaking through a relative who was her interpreter. At an ex parte hearing held that afternoon, Abbott J. ordered that the transfusion should take place.[51] The legal issues were then litigated in detail after the fact, in a case initiated by plenary summons, the

---

[46] David Tomkin & Adam McAuley, *"Re A Ward of Court*: Legal Analysis" (1995) 1 *Medico-Legal Journal of Ireland* 45 at 46. Note the subsequent case of *In Re Wards of Court and Dolan* [2007] I.E.S.C. 26; [2008] 1 I.L.R.M. 19 in which Geoghegan J. reviewed the law concerning the jurisdiction of the High Court in wardship matters.

[47] David Tomkin & Adam McAuley, *"Re A Ward of Court*: Legal Analysis" (1995) 1 M.L.J.I. 45 at 50.

[48] [2003] 1 I.R. 321.

[49] [2003] 1 I.R. 321 at 325.

[50] [2008] I.E.H.C. 104; High Court, Laffoy J., April 25, 2008.

[51] Abbott J. held that Ms K. was competent to refuse treatment. He found that the welfare of the child, which was newly born into this State with no parent in sight other than Ms K., was paramount. Therefore, it was in the interests of the child that the wishes of his mother, which

plaintiffs being the Master and the Secretary/Manager of the hospital.[52] Clarke J. refused to add the Watch Tower Bible and Tract Society of Ireland as a co-defendant or notice-party.[53] Laffoy J. then presided over a 37-day hearing on the substantive issues before issuing her judgment in 2008. The core issue to be considered was whether Ms K. had capacity to refuse the blood transfusion at the time. Having reviewed the authorities, Laffoy J. summarised them as follows:

"[I]t seems to me that the relevant principles applicable to the determination of the capacity question are as follows:

(1) There is a presumption that an adult patient has the capacity, that is to say, the cognitive ability, to make a decision to refuse medical treatment, but that presumption can be rebutted.

(2) In determining whether a patient is deprived of capacity to make a decision to refuse medical treatment whether—

(a) by reason of permanent cognitive impairment, or

(b) temporary factors, for example, factors of the type referred to by Lord Donaldson in *In re T*,[54]

the test is whether the patient's cognitive ability has been impaired to the extent that he or she does not sufficiently understand the nature, purpose and effect of the proffered treatment and the consequences of accepting or rejecting it in the context of the choices available (including any alternative treatment) at the time the decision is made.

(3) The three-stage approach to the patient's decision-making process adopted in the *C*. case[55] is a helpful tool in applying that test. The patient's cognitive ability will have been impaired to the extent that he or she is incapable of making the decision to refuse the proffered treatment if the patient—

(a) has not comprehended and retained the treatment information and, in particular, has not assimilated the information as to the consequences likely to ensue from not accepting the treatment,

(b) has not believed the treatment information and, in particular, if it is the case that not accepting the treatment is likely to result in the patient's death, has not believed that outcome is likely, and

(c) has not weighed the treatment information, in particular, the alternative choices and the likely outcomes, in the balance in arriving at the decision.

(4) The treatment information by reference to which the patient's capacity is to be assessed is the information which the clinician is under a duty to

---

might result in her death, should be overridden. See commentary in Donnelly, "The Right of Autonomy in Irish Law" (2008) 14 (2) M.L.J.I. 34 at 36–7.

52   The original ex parte order granted by Abbott J. remained in existence.

53   *Fitzpatrick and Ryan v F.K. (No.1)* [2006] I.E.H.C. 392; [2007] 2 I.R. 406; [2008] I.L.R.M. 68; High Court, Clarke J. December 7, 2006.

54   *Re T. (Adult: Refusal of Medical Treatment)* [1992] 3 W.L.R. 782; [1992] 4 All E.R. 649.

55   *Re C. (Adult: Refusal of Medical Treatment)* [1994] 1 All E.R. 819.

impart—information as to what is the appropriate treatment, that is to say, what treatment is medically indicated, at the time of the decision and the risks and consequences likely to flow from the choices available to the patient in making the decision.

(5) In assessing capacity it is necessary to distinguish between misunderstanding or misperception of the treatment information in the decision-making process (which may sometimes be referred to colloquially as irrationality), on the one hand, and an irrational decision or a decision made for irrational reasons, on the other hand. The former may be evidence of lack of capacity. The latter is irrelevant to the assessment.

(6) In assessing capacity, whether at the bedside in a high dependency unit or in court, the assessment must have regard to the gravity of the decision, in terms of the consequences which are likely to ensue from the acceptance or rejection of the proffered treatment. In the private law context this means that, in applying the civil law standard of proof, the weight to be attached to the evidence should have regard to the gravity of the decision, whether that is characterised as the necessity for 'clear and convincing proof' or an enjoinder that the court 'should not draw its conclusions lightly'."[56]

10–15 Applying these principles to the facts, Laffoy J. said that Ms K. had misled the hospital about her religion and her reason for doing so was unconvincing. Ms K. had said that she had stated she was a Roman Catholic for consistency with her asylum application, but Laffoy J. said that Ms K. had ample opportunity on her numerous visits to the hospital to notify it that in an emergency she would not take a blood transfusion on religious grounds. Laffoy J. also noted that Ms K. had told the hospital that her husband was not in the country when in fact he was. She said, "this episode raises not only a serious question about Ms K.'s credibility, but also about her ability to understand the consequences of a decision to refuse a blood transfusion for her baby's future care."[57] Ms K.'s "excuse" for misrepresenting her husband's whereabouts to the hospital personnel was that she was afraid he would be arrested because he was in the State without a visa. Laffoy J. said that it was hardly a rational response to the enquiry regarding her husband's whereabouts to leave the hospital with no information on the basis of which the hospital could identify the baby's next of kin.[58] As regards Ms K.'s evidence given during the hearing, Laffoy J. said that it was difficult to determine whether she was being evasive or whether she genuinely did not understand what was being put to her. Her demeanour gave some insight as to why the hospital personnel who were treating her would have harboured doubts about her understanding of the gravity of her condition.[59]

---

[56]   [2008] I.E.H.C. 104, p.44.
[57]   [2008] I.E.H.C. 104, p.69.
[58]   [2008] I.E.H.C. 104, pp.68–9.
[59]   [2008] I.E.H.C. 104, pp.81–2.

Taking all of these factors into account, Laffoy J. concluded that the Master and the hospital personnel should have doubted, and genuinely did doubt, Ms K.'s capacity to give a valid refusal on the morning of the incident.[60] There was objective evidence that Ms K.'s capacity was impaired to the extent that she did not have the ability to make a valid refusal to accept the appropriate medical treatment which was proffered to her, a blood transfusion.[61] Laffoy J. added that "the situation in which Ms K. was transfused against her wishes unfortunately was of her own making"[62], as she had misrepresented her religion when she registered at the hospital.

10–16 Various procedural points arose about the nature of the ex parte application which had been made before Abbott J. on the day in question. Reference was made to *St. George's Healthcare and N.H.S. Trust v S.*[63] in which the Court of Appeal was highly critical of the conduct of an ex parte application and set it aside *ex debito justiciae*. Laffoy J. found that the process in the *F.K.* case had been fundamentally defective.[64] One of the most significant defects was that Ms K. was not told that the application was taking place. Laffoy J. accepted the Master's evidence that the omission to inform Ms K. was an oversight.[65] She said it would be unfair to find that failure to tell Ms K. of the intended application to court constituted a breach of her constitutional rights. Laffoy J. made various recommendations at the end of her judgment, including a suggestion that a practice direction be put in place in the High Court setting out the procedure to be followed in relation to urgent applications in case of medical emergencies for authority to administer blood transfusions and other medical procedures.[66]

10–17 The *F.K.* case establishes that the three-stage approach to the patient's decision-making process adopted in the *C.* case is a helpful tool in applying the test of capacity. It might have been helpful if psychiatric evidence were available concerning Ms K.'s capacity, but the absence of such evidence may be justified by the fact that the court was reviewing in hindsight the evidence available to the medical personnel on the day in question. It is arguable that a different conclusion on the facts could have been reached, and that the court is unduly critical of Ms K. for her misrepresentations, which she felt were required due to her asylum application. The statement that the situation was of Ms K.'s "own making" is questionable. There may also have been an over-emphasis on the "Coca-Cola and tomatoes" conversation as evidence of lack of capacity.

---

60 [2008] I.E.H.C. 104, p.103.
61 [2008] I.E.H.C. 104, p.132.
62 [2008] I.E.H.C. 104, p.106.
63 [1998] 3 W.L.R. 936.
64 [2008] I.E.H.C. 104, p.123.
65 [2008] I.E.H.C. 104, p.75.
66 [2008] I.E.H.C. 104, p.135.

10–18 It is sometimes suggested that a relative may consent to treatment for an incapable adult patient but this has no legal basis.[67] However, contact with the next of kin may reveal that the patient has made an anticipatory choice which might be taken into account.[68]

10–19 In summary, the position at common law is that consent to treatment is required, unless the patient lacks capacity or is subject to undue influence. The clinician is also under a duty to impart information as to what is the appropriate treatment at the time of the decision and the risks and consequences likely to flow from the choices available to the patient in making the decision.

THE EUROPEAN CONVENTION ON HUMAN RIGHTS

10–20 Treatment of persons with mental disorder also raises issues regarding the European Convention on Human Rights (ECHR). Treatment without consent may constitute a breach of either art.8 (privacy) or art.3 (torture) of the ECHR. While art.8 permits certain interferences with privacy rights, the prohibition in art.3 is absolute.

10–21 Article 8(1) states that everyone has the right to respect for their private and family life, their home and correspondence. Article 8(2) permits interference by a public authority with the exercise of this right if it is in accordance with law and is necessary in a democratic society in the interests of national security, public safety or the economic well-being of the country, for the prevention of disorder or crime, for the protection of health or morals, or for the protection of the rights and freedoms of others.

"Private life" includes a person's physical and psychological integrity and therefore a compulsory medical intervention, even if it is of minor importance, constitutes an interference with this right.[69] Such intervention must therefore, at the very least, be in accordance with law, which means that it is either authorised by statute or by common law. The law must be accessible and sufficiently precise so as to allow an individual to regulate his or her conduct. Detainees are in a particularly vulnerable position and must be protected against arbitrary interferences with their privacy.[70]

The intervention must also be necessary for the protection of health, for the prevention of crime or for the protection of others.

---

[67] Mary Donnelly, "Treatment for a Mental Disorder: The Mental Health Act 2001, Consent and the Role of Rights" (2005) 40 *Irish Jurist* 220 at 235, fn.74.

[68] *Re T. (Adult: Refusal of Medical Treatment)* [1992] 3 W.L.R. 782 at 787 (Lord Donaldson).

[69] *Y.F. v Turkey* (2004) 39 E.H.R.R. 34, para. 33; *Storck v Germany* (2006) 43 E.H.R.R. 6, para. 143.

[70] *Y.F. v Turkey* (2004) 39 E.H.R.R. 34, para.43.

10–22 The Strasbourg Court stated in *Pretty v United Kingdom*[71] that the notion of personal autonomy is an important principle underlying the interpretation of the guarantees in art.8.[72] In this case, the applicant had motor neurone disease and wanted her husband to assist her to die by suicide. The court said that in the sphere of medical treatment, the refusal to accept a particular treatment might, inevitably, lead to a fatal outcome, yet the imposition of medical treatment, without the consent of a mentally competent adult patient, would interfere with a person's physical integrity in a manner capable of engaging the rights protected under art.8(1) of the Convention. As recognised in domestic case law, a person might claim to exercise a choice to die by declining to consent to treatment which might have the effect of prolonging their life.[73] However, the national law criminalising assisted suicide did not breach art.8, as it was designed to safeguard life by protecting the weak and vulnerable, especially those not in a condition to take informed decisions against acts intended to end life or assist in ending life.[74] In *R. (Purdy) v DPP*[75] the House of Lords ordered the DPP to publish a policy which sets out the factors that will be taken into account in deciding whether or not to prosecute for the offence of assisted suicide under the Suicide Act 1961.[76]

10–23 In *Storck v Germany*,[77] the treatment given to the applicant was not lawful under domestic law and so the court did not have to consider whether it was medically necessary.[78] The applicant was placed in a locked ward of a private psychiatric clinic from 1977 to 1979 at her father's request, even though she had attained the legal age of majority. She had not been placed under guardianship and had never signed a declaration that she had consented to her placement in the institution. Neither had there had been a judicial decision authorising her detention in a psychiatric hospital. She was given strong medication without her consent during her time in the clinic. Whenever she had refused to take medicaments, these had been administered to her by force. The applicant repeatedly tried to flee from the clinic, and was brought back by force by the police in March 1979. The court found that, given that the applicant had not only constantly resisted her continued stay in the clinic, but had equally resisted her medical treatment, so that at times, she had to be administered medicaments by force, the medical treatment had been conducted on her against

---

[71] *Pretty v United Kingdom* (2002) 35 E.H.R.R. 1.

[72] *Pretty v United Kingdom* (2002) 35 E.H.R.R. 1, para.61.

[73] *Pretty v United Kingdom* (2002) 35 E.H.R.R. 1, para.63.

[74] *Pretty v United Kingdom* (2002) 35 E.H.R.R. 1, para.74.

[75] [2009] U.K.H.L. 45; [2009] 3 W.L.R. 403.

[76] Section 2(1) of the Suicide Act 1961 (England and Wales) states, "A person who aids, abets, counsels or procures the suicide of another, or an attempt by another to commit suicide, shall be liable on conviction on indictment to imprisonment for a term not exceeding fourteen years."

[77] (2006) 43 E.H.R.R. 6.

[78] Brenda Hale, "The Human Rights Act and Mental Health Law: Has it Helped?" (2007) J. Mental Health L. 7 at 16.

her will. The court further noted that the findings of at least one expert indicated that the medicaments the applicant had received in the clinic had been counter-indicated and had caused serious damage to her health. However, the court did not need to determine whether the applicant's treatment had been *lege artis*,[79] as, irrespective of this, it had been carried out against her will and already therefore constituted an interference with her right to respect for private life.[80]

The Court of Appeal in Germany, as confirmed by the superior courts, had not interpreted the provisions of civil law relating to the applicant's compensation claim in tort or contract in the spirit of art.8. It followed that there has been an interference with the applicant's right to respect to private life which was imputable to the respondent State.[81] The applicant's detention was not "in accordance with law" under art.8(2) because there was no court order, which was required by domestic law.[82] She was awarded €75,000 compensation as regards breaches of arts 5 and 8 which had occurred.

10–24 In *Shtukaturov v Russia*,[83] discussed below at para.13–19, the applicant had been declared legally incapable by a court on the application of his mother. Russian legislation did not provide for a "tailor-made response" and as a result, in the circumstances the applicant's rights under art.8 were limited more than strictly necessary. The court concluded that the interference with the applicant's private life was disproportionate to the legitimate aim pursued. There was, therefore, a breach of art.8 of the Convention on account of the applicant's full incapacitation.

10–25 Article 3 of the ECHR states that no one shall be subjected to torture or inhuman or degrading treatment or punishment. The behaviour complained of must reach a minimum level of severity to engage art.3.[84] While intention to degrade is relevant to the threshold, it is not determinative; ill-treatment may breach art.3 even if there is no intent to do so.[85]

10–26 In *Herczegfalvy v Austria*[86] the European Court of Human Rights considered that the position of inferiority and powerlessness which is typical of patients confined in psychiatric hospitals calls for increased vigilance in reviewing whether the Convention has been complied with. The court said that

---

[79]   According to the law of the art (medicine).
[80]   (2006) 43 E.H.R.R. 6, para.144.
[81]   (2006) 43 E.H.R.R. 6, para.148.
[82]   (2006) 43 E.H.R.R. 6, para.152.
[83]   [2008] M.H.L.R. 238.
[84]   Peter Bartlett, Oliver Lewis and Oliver Thorold, *Mental Disability and the European Convention on Human Rights* (Leiden: Martinus Nijhoff, 2006), p.77.
[85]   *Peers v Greece* (2001) 33 E.H.R.R. 51, para.74; *Price v U.K.* (2001) 34 E.H.R.R. 1285, para.30; Peter Bartlett, Oliver Lewis and Oliver Therold, *Mental Disability and the European Convention on Human Rights* (Leiden: Martinus Nijhoff, 2006), p.78.
[86]   (1992) 15 E.H.R.R. 437.

while it is for the medical authorities to decide, on the basis of the recognised rules of medical science, on the therapeutic methods to be used, if necessary by force, to preserve the physical and mental health of patients who are entirely incapable of deciding for themselves and for whom they are therefore responsible, such patients nevertheless remain under the protection of art.3, the requirements of which permit of no derogation.[87] The court added:

> "The established principles of medicine are admittedly in principle decisive in such cases; as a general rule, a measure which is a therapeutic necessity cannot be regarded as inhuman or degrading. The Court must nevertheless satisfy itself that the medical necessity has been convincingly shown to exist."[88]

The court found that the treatment which had been given to the patient in this case was not in breach of art.3. He had been diagnosed with paranoia querulans and was extremely aggressive. His treatment included being force-fed, handcuffed to a bed and forcibly injected. According to Lewis, the court "did not take a particularly progressive stance" in this case, and the court adopted a highly deferential "therapeutic necessity" test.[89]

10–27 However, in *Nevermerzhitsky v Ukraine*,[90] concerning a prisoner with capacity to refuse treatment, it was held that the manner in which he had been force-fed was "torture" under art.3. The court stated that a measure which is of therapeutic necessity from the point of view of established principles of medicine cannot in principle be regarded as inhumane and degrading. The same could be said about force-feeding that was aimed at saving the life of a particular detainee who consciously refuses to take food.[91] The medical necessity must have been convincingly shown to exist. Furthermore, the court must ascertain that the procedural guarantees for the decision to force-feed are complied with. Moreover, the manner in which the applicant is subjected to force-feeding during the hunger strike should not trespass the threshold of a minimum level of severity envisaged by the court's case law under art.3 of the Convention.[92] The court concluded that the Government had not demonstrated that there was a "medical necessity" established by the domestic authorities to force-feed the applicant. The restraints applied—handcuffs, a mouth-widener and a special

---

[87] (1992) 15 E.H.R.R. 437 at para.82.

[88] (1992) 15 E.H.R.R. 437 at para.82.

[89] Oliver Lewis, "Protecting the Rights of People with Mental Disabilities: the European Convention on Human Rights" (2002) 9 *European Journal of Health Law* 293 at 304. For further discussion of the application of art.3 in this area see Peter Bartlett, Oliver Lewis and Oliver Thorold, *Mental Disability and the European Convention on Human Rights* (Leiden: Martinus Nijhoff, 2006), pp.126–9.

[90] (2006) 43 E.H.R.R. 32.

[91] See *X. v Germany* (1984) 7 E.H.R.R. 152.

[92] (2006) 43 E.H.R.R. 32, para.94.

rubber tube inserted into the food channel—in the event of resistance, with the use of force, amounted to torture within the meaning of art.3 of the Convention, as there was no medical necessity.[93]

10–28 In the English case of *R. (Wilkinson) v Broadmoor Special Hospital Authority*[94] it was held that the requirement in *Herczegfalvy* that the medical necessity be "convincingly shown" to exist required a proper hearing on the merits about whether treatment could be administered against the patient's will, thus changing the question for the court from one of procedure to one of substance.[95] On the facts, the patient's later application to the Strasbourg Court was found to be inadmissible.[96]

TREATMENT AND CAPACITY IN THE MENTAL HEALTH ACT 2001

10–29 There was no mention of consent to treatment in the Mental Treatment Act 1945. It was presumed that once the patient was involuntary detained they were not competent to decide whether they should be given medical treatment and that treatment could be given without consent.[97] As Donnelly argues, it is difficult to see how this presumption could have withstood modern judicial scrutiny.[98] The presumption was not reflected in the Department of Health's *Guidelines on Good Practice and Quality Assurance in Mental Health Services*,[99] which stated that patients "should have informed consent and be aware of their rights in relation to the refusal of treatment".

Section 4 of the Health Act 1953 states that nothing in that Act requires any person to submit themselves to health examination or treatment.[100] This section did not affect the general presumption referred to above, as patients involuntarily detained under the 1945 Act would have been regarded as in a different category from other patients. The section remains in force and was not amended by the

---

[93]   (2006) 43 E.H.R.R. 32, paras 97–99.

[94]   [2001] E.W.C.A. Civ. 1545; [2002] 1 W.L.R. 419.

[95]   Peter Bartlett and Ralph Sandland, *Mental Health Law: Policy and Practice*, 3rd edn (Oxford: Oxford University Press, 2007), pp.309–312.

[96]   *Wilkinson v. United Kingdom* [2006] M.H.L.R. 144.

[97]   Department of Health, *Green Paper on Mental Health* (Dublin: Stationery Office, 1992), para.22.2; Mary Donnelly, "Treatment for a Mental Disorder: The Mental Health Act 2001, Consent and the Role of Rights" (2005) 40 Ir. Jur. 220 at 223.

[98]   Mary Donnelly, "Treatment for a Mental Disorder: The Mental Health Act 2001, Consent and the Role of Rights" (2005) 40 Ir. Jur. 220 at 223.

[99]   Department of Health and Children, *Guidelines on Good Practice and Quality Assurance in Mental Health Services* (1998), para.3.4.

[100] The full text is as follows: (1) Nothing in this Act or any instrument thereunder shall be construed as imposing an obligation on any person to avail himself of any service provided under this Act or to submit himself or any person for whom he is responsible to health examination or treatment. (2) Any person who avails himself of any service provided under this Act shall not be under any obligation to submit himself or any person for whom he is responsible to a health examination or treatment which is contrary to the teaching of his religion.

2001 Act. Its effect was discussed in *North Western Health Board v H.W. and C.W.*[101]

10–30 The Health (Mental Services) Act 1981, which was never commenced, stated that the Medical Council would make rules governing consent to therapeutic procedures for treatment of mental illness.[102] It seems that there was some criticism of this, including from the Medical Council itself.[103] The relevant section stated that it was "notwithstanding the provisions of" s.4 of the Health Act 1953 and Hardiman J. noted in the *North Western Health Board* case that, though this provision created an exception to the general rule constituted by s.4 of the 1953 Act, it appeared to him to evidence the legislature's acknowledgement, in 1981, that the general position of voluntarism continued unaltered in relation to psychiatric treatment, except in this respect.[104]

The Green Paper and White Paper of 1992 and 1995[105] included proposals for reform of the law concerning consent to treatment which were implemented by Pt 4 of the Mental Health Act 2001 (ss.56–61). These provisions also apply to any person detained in the Central Mental Hospital (CMH) under the Criminal Law (Insanity) Act 2006.[106]

10–31 In the case of civil patients, Pt 4 only applies to those adult patients who are involuntarily detained under the 2001 Act.[107] In 2007, the percentage of involuntary admissions and re-gradings combined was roughly 11.5 per cent.[108] 10.1 per cent of residents were involuntary, 2.1 per cent were wards of court and

---

[101] [2001] 3 I.R. 622 at 702–3, 749–50 and 752–3.

[102] Health (Mental Services) Act 1981, s.44. The full text was as follows: (1) The Medical Council may, with the consent of the Minister, make rules in accordance with accepted medical practice —(a) in regard to the application to any person of any specified therapeutic procedure for the treatment of mental illness, and (b) specifying the conditions to be complied with and the precautions to be taken to safeguard the rights and well-being of patients to whom the procedure is applied. (2) It shall not be lawful to apply or cause to be applied any procedure so specified unless the person has given his consent in the manner provided for in the rules or, notwithstanding the provisions of section 4 of the Health Act, 1953, where the person has not the mental capacity to give his consent, consent is given by a person specified in the rules.

[103] "The Medical Council and a number of other medical interests have been critical of section 44 of the Bill."—Minister Woods, 323 *Dáil Debates* 168, October 16, 1980.

[104] *North Western Health Board v H.W. & C.W.* [2003] 2 I.R. 622 at 749. Hardiman J. states at 750, "it appears to me that the principle of voluntarism in respect of medical treatment is plainly established in so far as public medical services are concerned".

[105] Department of Health, *Green Paper on Mental Health* (Dublin: Stationery Office, 1992), Chapter 22; Department of Health, *A New Mental Health Act: White Paper* (Dublin: Stationery Office, 1995) Chapter 6.

[106] Criminal Law (Insanity) Act 2006, s.3(3): "Part 4 of the Act of 2001 shall apply to any person who is detained in a designated centre under this Act." At present, the CMH is the only designated centre.

[107] This is because the term "patient" is used in Pt 4 and "patient" is defined by ss.2 and 14 as a person to whom an Admission (or Renewal) Order relates.

[108] See para.3–20 above.

2.4 per cent were subject to a court order, all of whom were in the CMH.[109] It is regrettable that voluntary patients, who comprise the vast majority of patients, remain governed by the common law concerning consent to treatment.[110] This means that they do not have the same protections as are granted by the Mental Health Act 2001 to involuntary patients, e.g. there is no statutory requirement of a second opinion for continued administration of medicine for longer than three months to voluntary patients.[111]

Sections 56 and 57 of the 2001 Act

10–32 The 2001 Act states in s.57 that the consent of a patient[112] shall be required for treatment except where, in the opinion of the responsible consultant psychiatrist (RCP), the treatment is necessary to safeguard the life of the patient, to restore their health, to alleviate their condition, or to relieve their suffering, and by reason of their mental disorder the patient concerned is incapable of giving such consent.[113] On the meaning of the RCP, see paras 6–37 to 6–50 above.

"Treatment" is defined in s.2 as including the administration of physical, psychological and other remedies relating to the care and rehabilitation of a patient under medical supervision, intended for the purposes of ameliorating a mental disorder. Reference may be made here to English case law concerning the meaning of "treatment", bearing in mind that a different definition applies in England and Wales.[114] For example, it has been held that the exercise of powers of control and discipline are implied when a patient is detained.[115] It is also possible for force-feeding to be considered as part of medical treatment.[116]

Section 8 states that nothing in s.8(1) shall be construed as authorising the involuntary admission of a person to an approved centre by reason only of the fact that the person is suffering from a personality disorder or is addicted to drugs or intoxicants. It is therefore unclear whether treatment for a personality disorder, for example, can be considered as failing within the definition of "treatment" in s.2. Again, some assistance may be provided by referring to the

---

[109] Mental Health Commission, *Annual Report 2007*, Book 1, p.58.

[110] See further discussion of voluntary patients, para.10–02 above.

[111] Compare paras 10–39 to 10–43 below regarding administration of medicine for longer than three months to *involuntary* patients.

[112] As stated earlier, this only applies to patients who are involuntarily detained.

[113] Mental Health Act 2001, s.57(1). Section 57(2) states that s.57 shall not apply to the treatment specified in ss.58, 59 or 60, i.e. psychosurgery, electro-convulsive therapy or administration of medicine for longer than three months.

[114] Up to 2007, "medical treatment" was defined as including nursing, and also included care, habilitation and rehabilitation under medical supervision–s.145(1) of the Mental Health Act 1983. See now amendments by Mental Health Act 2007; Richard Jones, *Mental Health Act Manual*, 11th edn (London: Thomson Sweet and Maxwell, 2008), pp.529–30.

[115] *Pountney v Griffiths* [1976] A.C. 314; the relevance of this case to the present day is noted by Peter Bartlett and Ralph Sandland, *Mental Health Law: Policy and Practice*, 3rd edn (Oxford, Oxford Universtiy Press, 2007), p.299.

[116] *B. v Croydon Health Authority* [1995] 1 All E.R. 683.

English position. In *R. v Ashworth Hospital, ex parte B.*[117] the applicant had both a mental illness (paranoid psychosis) and psychopathic disorder. The House of Lords held that he could be treated for both conditions, even though he had been detained on the basis of the illness. However, much of the reasoning in the case turns on the wording of the English legislation, which at the time expressly permitted detention based on psychopathic disorder. Baroness Hale's reasoning included the following:

> "It is not easy to disentangle which features of the patient's presentation stem from a disease of the mind and which stem from his underlying personality traits. The psychiatrist's aim should be to treat the whole patient. In this case, the patient's mental illness having been stabilised on medication, the aim was to address the underlying features of his personality which were getting in the way of his transfer back to a less restrictive setting. Once the state has taken away a person's liberty and detained him in a hospital with a view to medical treatment, the state should be able (some would say obliged) to provide him with the treatment which he needs. It would be absurd if a patient could be detained in hospital but had to be denied the treatment which his doctor thought he needed for an indefinite period while some largely irrelevant classification was rectified."[118]

10–33 Issues may also arise if the patient has a physical disorder as well as a mental disorder. In theory, the treatment for the physical disorder may not be covered in the meaning of "treatment". However, as English case law shows, there is "considerable ambiguity in how the line between mental disorder and physical disorder has been drawn."[119] In *Re C.*,[120] there was no reference to the Mental Health Act 1983 because the gangrene was regarded as entirely unconnected with the mental disorder.[121] However, in *Tameside and Glossop Acute Services Trust v C.H.*[122] it was held that a caesarean section on a pregnant woman who was detained under the Mental Health Act constituted "treatment" for her mental disorder as the delivery of a healthy baby would be clearly beneficial to her mental health.

10–34 The reference in s.57 to treatment which is "necessary to safeguard the life of the patient, to restore his or her health, to alleviate his or her condition, or to relieve his or her suffering, and by reason of his or her mental disorder the patient concerned is incapable of giving such consent" must be read in light of the meaning of "consent", which is defined in s.56:

---

[117] [2005] U.K.H.L. 20; [2005] 2 A.C. 278.
[118] [2005] 2 A.C. 278 at 293.
[119] Peter Bartlett and Ralph Sandland, *Mental Health Law: Policy and Practice*, 3rd edn (Oxford, Oxford University Press, 2007), p.303.
[120] [1994] 1 W.L.R. 290.
[121] *B. v Croydon Health Authority* [1995] 1 All E.R. 683 at 688.
[122] [1996] 1 F.L.R. 762.

In this Part "consent", in relation to a patient, means consent obtained freely without threats or inducements, where—

(a) the consultant psychiatrist responsible for the care and treatment of the patient is satisfied that the patient is capable of understanding the nature, purpose and likely effects of the proposed treatment; and

(b) the consultant psychiatrist has given the patient adequate information, in a form and language that the patient can understand, on the nature, purpose and likely effects of the proposed treatment.[123]

The reference to "without threats or inducements" means that the consent cannot be obtained by coercion. For example, in the English case of In *Re T. (Adult: Refusal of Treatment)*[124] it was held that the patient's refusal to give consent was not voluntary partly due to undue influence from her mother.[125]

10–35 By defining capacity as "capable of understanding the nature, purpose and likely effects of the proposed treatment", the Oireachtas has adopted a test which is narrower than the three-stage test in *Re C.*[126] (followed in *F.K.*[127]), i.e. capacity to comprehend and retain treatment information, believe it and weigh it in the balance to arrive at choice. Donnelly comments that there is no justification for setting the standard for capacity at a lower level for patients with a mental disorder than that which is applied to patients in other contexts.[128] The narrow test of capacity in s.56 is also in stark contrast with the more sophisticated test adopted in the Scheme of the Mental Capacity Bill 2008.[129]

10–36 The decision as to whether the patient is capable of consenting is made by the responsible consultant psychiatrist and there is no statutory review mechanism provided for this. As a result, it is quite possible that if a patient does not consent to treatment, some psychiatrists may be inclined to decide that the patient lacks capacity and therefore can be given treatment without consent. This is an example of the potential clash between "legalism" and "medicalism" in mental health law. Part 4 of the 2001 Act introduces legalistic principles which may be resisted by medical personnel who see them as unduly interfering with their professional discretion.[130] In addition, this legalism may conflict with the

---

[123] Mental Health Act 2001, s.56.

[124] [1992] 3 W.L.R. 782.

[125] [1992] 3 W.L.R. 782 at 803 (Butler-Sloss L.J.)

[126] [1994] 1 W.L.R. 290.

[127] *Fitzpatrick & Ryan v F.K. & Attorney General (No.2)* [2008] I.E.H.C. 104; High Court, Laffoy J., April 25, 2008.

[128] Mary Donnelly, "Treatment for a Mental Disorder: The Mental Health Act 2001, Consent and the Role of Rights" (2005) 40 Ir.Jur. 220 at 229.

[129] See Head 2 in Department of Justice, Equality and Law Reform, *Scheme of Mental Capacity Bill 2008*; para.13–31 below.

[130] In England, the Mental Health Act 1983 was seen as a "return to 'legalism', with its provisions relating to the medical treatment of detained patients being seen as a key expression of this

common law in some respects, as the common law has traditionally given control to the medical professionals.[131]

Donnelly goes so far as to say that the right to refuse treatment in the 2001 Act will be "illusory"[132] due to the lack of a realistic remedy available for its enforcement. She also suggests that the patient's own psychiatrist may, for a number of reasons, be an inappropriate person to carry out the function of assessing the patient's capacity.[133]

10–37 The final requirement of s.56 is that the psychiatrist must give the patient adequate information, in a form and language that the patient can understand, on the nature, purpose and likely effects of the proposed treatment. When Dunne surveyed service users, she found that side effects were not always discussed or taken seriously by the consultants/Non-Consultant Hospital Doctors (NCHDs).[34] She also found that many medical personnel had little or no interest in working with service users to reduce or otherwise modify the dose taken.[135]

The Minister of State noted that there had been some suggestions that the side effects of medicines were not explained to patients.[136] He pointed out that this was provided for in s.56 and had also been addressed in the Regulations for Approved Centres.[137]

The Approved Centres Regulations apply to all residents of approved centres, both voluntary and involuntary.[138] Regulation 20 provides, inter alia, that the registered proprietor shall ensure that the following information is provided to each resident in an understandable form and language: verbal and written information on the resident's diagnosis and suitable written information relevant to the resident's diagnosis unless, in the resident's psychiatrist's view, the provision of such information might be prejudicial to the resident's physical or mental health, well-being or emotional condition; and information on indications for use of all medications to be administered to the resident, including any possible side effects.[139] The registered proprietor must also ensure that an

---

shift."—Peter Bartlett and Ralph Sandland, *Mental Health Law: Policy and Practice*, 3rd edn (Oxford, Oxford University Press, 2007), p.296.

[131] Peter Bartlett and Ralph Sandland, *Mental Health Law: Policy and Practice*, 3rd edn (Oxford, Oxford University Press, 2007), p.296.

[132] Mary Donnelly, "Treatment for a Mental Disorder: The Mental Health Act 2001, Consent and the Role of Rights" (2005) 40 Ir. Jur. 220 at 233.

[133] Mary Donnelly, "Treatment for a Mental Disorder: The Mental Health Act 2001, Consent and the Role of Rights" (2005) 40 Ir. Jur. 220 at 231.

[134] Elizabeth Dunne, *The Views of Adult Users of the Public Sector Mental Health Services* (Dublin: Mental Health Commission, 2006), p.31.

[135] Dunne, *The Views of Adult Users of the Public Sector Mental Health Services* (Dublin: Mental Health Commission, 2006), p.31.

[136] Department of Health and Children, *Review of the Operation of the Mental Health Act 2001: Findings and Conclusions* (May 2007), p.26.

[137] Mental Health Act 2001(Approved Centres) Regulations 2006, S.I. No. 551 of 2006.

[138] Mental Health Act 2001(Approved Centres) Regulations 2006, S.I. No. 551 of 2006.

[139] Mental Health Act 2001(Approved Centres) Regulations 2006, S.I. No. 551 of 2006, Reg. 20(1)(c) and (e).

approved centre has written operational policies and procedures for the provision of information to residents.[140]

10–38 In interpreting ss.56 and 57 of the 2001 Act, reference may also be made to other sections of the Act. For example, the principles in s.4 have obvious relevance, i.e. the "principal consideration" of the best interests of the patient; the entitlement of the patient to make representations regarding treatment; and the person's rights to dignity, bodily integrity, privacy and autonomy. In addition, it is notable that when an Admission Order is made, it authorises the patient's reception, detention and treatment.[141] Section 66(1)(g) states that approved centre regulations may provide for individual care plans, as far as practicable in consultation with the resident. Individual Care Plans are regulated by Reg.15,[142] discussed at para.12–39 below. Finally, s.69 deals with bodily restraint and seclusion and will be discussed below at paras 12–20 to 12–29.

Medicine for longer than three months (Adults)

10–39 Section 60 of the 2001 Act provides that where medicine has been administered to a patient[143] for the purposes of ameliorating their mental disorder for a continuous period of three months, the administration of that medicine shall not be continued unless either (a) the patient gives their consent in writing to the continued administration of that medicine, or:

> (b) where the patient is unable or unwilling to give such consent—
>> (i) the continued administration of that medicine is approved by the consultant psychiatrist responsible for the care and treatment of the patient, and
>> (ii) the continued administration of that medicine is authorised (in a form specified by the Commission) by another consultant psychiatrist following referral of the matter to him or her by the first-mentioned psychiatrist.

The section also provides that the consent or approval and authorisation shall be valid for a period of three months and thereafter for periods of three months, if, in respect of each period, the like consent or approval and authorisation is obtained.

10–40 Section 61 provides that in the case of a child detained under s.25, medicine may only be given for longer than three months if "either" (a) it is

---

[140] Mental Health Act 2001 (Approved Centres) Regulations 2006, S.I. No. 551 of 2006, Reg. 20(2).
[141] Mental Health Act 2001, s.15(1).
[142] Mental Health Act 2001(Approved Centres) Regulations 2006, S.I. No. 551 of 2006, Reg. 15.
[143] This only applies to involuntarily detained patients.

approved by the RCP and (b) it is authorised by another consultant psychiatrist. Grammatically, the wording does not make sense and the Minister of State has acknowledged that there appears to be a drafting error.[144] The Mental Health Commission has also stated that the wording is inadequate.[145] Presumably, the intention is that both (a) and (b) should apply and the word "either" should be removed. The effect of s.61 is that in the case of a child, regardless of their capability of consent, medicine may be administered for longer than three months if authorised by a second psychiatrist. There is no reference to the parents in s.61.

10–41 It is important to note that s.60 does not by implication authorise the administration of medicine for *less than three months* without the patient's consent. The requirements of s.57 must be satisfied during the first three months of any administration of medicine, i.e. medicine may only be administered with the consent of the patient or, if the patient is incapable of giving consent, where the treatment is necessary to safeguard the life of the patient, to restore their health, to alleviate their condition, or to relieve their suffering.

The reference to "unable or unwilling to give consent" in s.60 does not fit with modern notions of autonomy of patients, as it provides that treatment may be given if the patient is capable of refusing consent, but is unwilling to consent. No such principle appears in the common law, and it would be inconsistent with constitutional and human rights. The Minister of State accepted the principle in 2007 that the reference to "unwilling" should be removed.[146]

The inclusion of "unwilling" in s.60 also means that if a capable patient consented to medicine for three months, they would then lose the right to refuse treatment after that, and the medicine could be continued provided a second psychiatrist authorised it. It is likely that this anomalous position is as a result of an error in drafting.[147]

10–42 The requirement of the authorisation of "another consultant psychiatrist" does not add very much to the general requirements of Part 4. There is no requirement that this psychiatrist come from outside the hospital, or be

---

[144] Department of Health and Children, *Review of the Operation of the Mental Health Act 2001: Findings and Conclusions* (May 2007), p.28.

[145] "The Commission's legal advice is that the reference in this Section to consent is not comprehensive and appears to be inadequate. In the absence of an amendment to this Section or clarification from the courts, the Commission advises that both the approval of the consultant psychiatrist responsible for the care and treatment of the child and authorisation from another consultant psychiatrist are sought."—Mental Health Commission, *Code of Practice Relating to Admission of Children Under the Mental Health Act 2001* (COP–S33 (3)/01/2006, 2006), para.3.5.

[146] Department of Health and Children, *Review of the Operation of the Mental Health Act 2001: Findings and Conclusions* (May 2007), p.28.

[147] Mary Donnelly, "Treatment for a Mental Disorder: The Mental Health Act 2001, Consent and the Role of Rights" (2005) 40 Ir. Jur. 220 at 237.

appointed by the Mental Health Commission. In practice, therefore, the psychiatrist will presumably be a member of staff of the same approved centre as the patient's RCP.

Kennedy has noted that consultant psychiatrists are autonomous practitioners and each is independently responsible for their actions under the Act. He also notes that, as a matter of practice, almost all consultant psychiatrists are employed by the Health Service Executive (HSE) but the common contract for consultants guarantees clinical independence.[148] The Health Services Executive Forum on the Provision of Second Opinions under the Mental Health Act 2001 recommended, and the HSE agreed, that the HSE would establish a demonstrably independent second-opinion system. The HSE Forum considered the term "demonstrably independent" and the following was the agreed definition as applicable to this project: "The consultant psychiatrist should be selected from a randomised panel; Service users need to be confident that a truly independent opinion is given. ... Only the consultant who referred the case is involved; Where possible there should be a level of choice for the service user; The consultant psychiatrist responsible for the care and treatment of the patient should not choose the consultant who will be asked to provide the second opinion."[149] Kennedy comments that the establishment and management of the panel would introduce sufficient randomisation to ensure that the second opinion was demonstrably independent, and that this is over and above the legal requirement, but considered best practice.[150]

In England and Wales, the second opinion must be given by an independent doctor appointed by the Mental Health Act Commission.[151] It has been held that the decision of the second opinion doctor on medication must be accompanied by clear written reasons, unless reasons would severely affect the mental or physical health of the patient.[152]

10–43 The relevant statutory form is Form 17.[153] The RCP completes p.1, stating that they examined the patient on a stated date and are of the opinion that it would be to the benefit of the patient to be administered medication without consent for stated reasons. Item 6 asks for details of the medication and how it will benefit the patient. The psychiatrist ticks a box stating whether the patient is unable or unwilling to give consent to the treatment. The psychiatrist also states whether they have given the patient adequate information, in a form and language that the patient can understand, on the nature, purpose and likely

---

[148] Harry Kennedy, *The Annotated Mental Health Acts* (Dublin: Blackhall, 2007), p.98.
[149] Harry Kennedy, *The Annotated Mental Health Acts* (Dublin: Blackhall, 2007), pp.98–9.
[150] Harry Kennedy, *The Annotated Mental Health Acts* (Dublin: Blackhall, 2007), p.99.
[151] Mental Health Act 1983 (England and Wales), s.58.
[152] *R. (Wooder) v Feggetter and M.H.A.C.* [2002] E.W.C.A. Civ. 554; [2003] Q.B. 219.
[153] Mental Health Commission, *Form 17, Treatment Without Consent: Administration of Medicine For More Than 3 Months, Involuntary Patient (Adult)*. At the time of writing, the current version of the form was issued in December 2007.

effects of the proposed treatment. Page 3 is completed by the second psychiatrist, and includes the same statements, e.g. the date of examination of the patient, whether the patient is unable or unwilling to give consent and how the treatment will benefit the patient.

Electro-Convulsive Therapy (Adults)

10–44 Electro-convulsive therapy (ECT) is one of the most controversial treatments in mental health. Some refer to it as "barbaric"[154] while others assert it is effective and safe.[155] The World Health Organisation Resource Book states that there should be no ECT without informed consent.[156]

The only statistics available on its usage in Ireland date from 2003, when it was reported that 745 people had received the treatment. The figure was 38.7 people per 100,000 in the Southern Health Board region, compared with 8.4 per 100,000 in the South-Eastern Health Board region.[157]

10–45 Section 59(1) of the 2001 Act provides that a programme of ECT shall not be administered to a patient[158] unless either (a) the patient gives their consent in writing or (b) where the patient is unable or unwilling to give such consent, the programme is approved by the RCP and authorised by another consultant psychiatrist. There is no requirement that ECT may not be given until a tribunal has affirmed the Admission Order. For example, this means that a patient could be admitted, given ECT 10 days after admission and then discharged on Day 18 by a tribunal.

The Act also provides that the Commission shall make rules providing for the use of ECT, and that a programme of ECT shall not be administered to a patient except in accordance with such rules.[159]

In the case of a child who has been detained, ECT may only be administered with the approval of the District Court.[160]

Again, the reference to "unwilling" in s.59 is problematic and the Minister of State has accepted the principle that the word should be removed.[161]

---

[154] Michael Corry, "Barbaric Age of Electric Shock 'Cure' Must Vanish", *Irish Times*, June 25, 2008.
[155] UK ECT Review Group, "Efficacy and Safety of Electroconvulsive Therapy in Depressive Disorders: a Systematic Review and Meta-Analysis" (2003) 361 *Lancet* 799.
[156] Melvyn Freeman & Soumitra Pathare, *WHO Resource Book on Mental Health, Human Rights and Legislation* (Geneva: World Health Organisation, 2005), p.64.
[157] Antoinette Daly, Dermot Walsh, Ros Moran, Yulia Kartalova O'Doherty, *Activities of Irish Psychiatric Services 2003* (Health Research Board, 2004), p.132.
[158] This only applies to detained patients.
[159] Mental Health Act 2001, s.59(2).
[160] Mental Health Act 2001, s.25(13).
[161] Department of Health and Children, *Review of the Operation of the Mental Health Act 2001: Findings and Conclusions* (May 2007), p.27.

10–46 The Mental Health Commission has issued Rules Governing the Use of ECT for Detained Patients[162] and a Code of Practice for Voluntary Patients.[163] Version 2 of the Rules and Code of Practice apply from January 1, 2010. The Rules provide that a programme of ECT refers to not more than 12 treatments. A patient must be considered capable of giving informed consent for ECT, including anaesthesia, unless there is evidence to the contrary.[164] The RCP must be satisfied that the patient has capacity to provide consent before they obtain consent for a programme of ECT, including anaethesia, from the patient.[165] Capacity to consent is defined as follows:

> Capacity to consent must ensure that the patient can:
> a) Understand the nature of ECT
> b) Understand why ECT is being proposed
> c) Understand the benefits, risks and alternatives to receiving ECT
> d) Understand and believe the broad consequences of not receiving ECT
> e) Retain the information long enough to make a decision to receive or not receive ECT
> f) Make a free choice to receive or refuse ECT
> g) Communicate the decision to consent to ECT[166]

A patient must be aware that they can refuse to give consent or withdraw consent for ECT at any time.[167] No relative, carer or guardian can give consent for ECT on behalf of the patient.[168] Consent must not be obtained through coercion or threats.[169] Where a patient is unable to give consent or is unwilling to give consent, s.59(1)(b) of the 2001 Act[170] applies and is reproduced in the Rules. There are detailed provisions as to the written and oral information which must be provided to the patient.[171] However, it is unfortunate that the Rules do not provide a statement of the exact written information which must be provided, rather than the general nature of the information. A consent form is provided as part of the Rules.[172] The ECT register must also be completed.

---

[162] Mental Health Commission, *Rules Governing the Use of Electro-Convulsive Therapy* (version 2, 2009). See also *Review of Rules Governing the use of Electroconvulsive Therapy* (Mental Health Commission, 2008).

[163] Mental Health Commission, *Code of Practice Governing the Use of Electro-Convulsive Therapy for Voluntary Patients* (version 2, 2009).

[164] *Rules Governing the Use of Electro-Convulsive Therapy*, Rule 2.1.

[165] *Rules Governing the Use of Electro-Convulsive Therapy*, Rule 2.2.

[166] *Rules Governing the Use of Electro-Convulsive Therapy*, Rule 2.3.

[167] *Rules Governing the Use of Electro-Convulsive Therapy*, Rule 2.6.

[168] *Rules Governing the Use of Electro-Convulsive Therapy*, Rule 2.7.

[169] *Rules Governing the Use of Electro-Convulsive Therapy*, Rule 2.8.

[170] See para.10–45 above.

[171] *Rules Governing the Use of Electro-Convulsive Therapy*, Rules 3.1–3.8.

[172] A consent form for ECT must include, as a minimum, all the particulars included in the "Consent Form for ECT Programme"—Rule 2.9.

[173] *Rules Governing the Use of Electro-Convulsive Therapy*, Rule 1.1. Contrast *Bolam v Friern*

The patient must be placed under general anaesthetic and given muscle relaxants.[173] Anaesthesia must be given by an anaesthetist who has experience in providing anaesthesia for ECT.[174] ECT must only be carried out in a dedicated ECT suite in an approved centre or, where deemed appropriate, in a specified location in a critical care area in a general hospital or maternity hospital. An ECT suite must have a private waiting area, an adequately equipped treatment room and an adequately equipped recovery room.[175] There must be a minimum number of two registered nursing staff in the ECT suite at all times to safely meet the needs of patients, one of whom must be trained in ECT and shall be known as "a designated ECT nurse".[176]

10–47 The Code of Practice regarding voluntary patients is basically in the same terms as the Rules regarding detained patients, except that the reference to obtaining authorisation from a second psychiatrist in s.59 is omitted, as it does not apply to voluntary patients. In addition, the code of practice is explicitly stated not to be legally binding, while it is also stated that best practice requires that it be followed to ensure the Act is implemented consistently by persons working in mental health services. A failure to implement or follow the Code could be referred to during the course of legal proceedings.[177]

10–48 If a patient who was initially admitted on a voluntary basis has lost capacity to consent, they may be re-graded as involuntary under ss.23 and 24, provided they indicate a wish to leave, or alternatively they may be discharged and re-admitted using the involuntary admission procedures. Dunne *et al* have argued, in the context of ECT treatment, that this is:

> "[N]either in the spirit of the Act nor in the best interests of the patient. It would constitute an 'involuntary discharge' in a patient incapable of consenting to discharge. This violates the treatment contract."[178]

10–49 The Act, Rules and Code of Practice do not contain a specific authorisation of physical or mechanical restraint of the patient in connection with ECT. As the other relevant rules[179] only allow physical and mechanical

---

H.M.C. [1957] 1 W.L.R. 582 where ECT was given in unmodified form, i.e. without the prior administration of a relaxant drug.

[174] *Rules Governing the Use of Electro-Convulsive Therapy*, Rule 7.1.

[175] *Rules Governing the Use of Electro-Convulsive Therapy*, Rule 9.2.

[176] *Rules Governing the Use of Electro-Convulsive Therapy*, Rule 11.6.

[177] *Code of Practice Governing the Use of Electro-Convulsive Therapy for Voluntary Patients*, para.1.2.

[178] Ross Dunne, Adam Kavanagh & Declan M McLoughlin, "Electroconvulsive Therapy, Capacity and the Law in Ireland" (2009) 26 *Irish Journal of Psychological Medicine* 3 at 4.

[179] Mental Health Commission, *Rules Governing the Use of Seclusion and Mechanical Means of Bodily Restraint* (version 2, 2009); Mental Health Commission, *Code of Practice on the Use of Physical Restraint in Approved Centres* (version 2, 2009).

restraint where the patient is an immediate threat of serious harm to themselves or others, it is arguable that a patient cannot be restrained in order to administer ECT. On the other hand, a court might well hold that it is implicit in the administration of ECT without consent that the patient may be restrained in order to administer the treatment.

Form 16[180] applies to the administration of ECT and is in similar terms to Form 17 regarding medicine for longer than three months (see para.10–43 above).

10–50 In June 2008, a Private Members' Bill was introduced to delete s.59 of the 2001 Act and replace it with the following wording: "A programme of electroconvulsive therapy shall not be administered to a patient unless the patient gives his or her informed consent in writing to the administration of the programme of therapy".[181] Senator De Búrca stated that there is a great deal of uncertainty as to why it is that the ECT procedure is effective at all, where it is effective in some patients. Given the scientific uncertainty surrounding it, the Green Party believed that its use without the consent of the patient must be prevented until we have the scientific knowledge that can explain how and why it works and on what patients it can be effective.[182] Minister of State Moloney responded that if the treating consultant psychiatrist is of the opinion that ECT is the most effective treatment in the circumstances, the law should make provision for the administration of that treatment to those who are not in a position to give their consent, within the necessary safeguards of the 2001 Act. He stated that it could be argued that to do otherwise would be in contravention of the State's duty of care to the involuntary patient.

Psychosurgery (Adults)

10–51 Psychosurgery is rarely performed and it has been said that it has not been performed in Ireland for 20 years.[183] It is possible that some Irish patients travel outside the State to avail of psychosurgery, but no figures are available. The 2001 Act requires both the consent of the patient and the authorisation of a Mental Health Tribunal (MHT).

Section 58 of the 2001 Act defines psychosurgery as any surgical operation that destroys brain tissue or the functioning of brain tissue and which is performed for the purposes of ameliorating a mental disorder.[184] In order for

---

[180] Mental Health Commission, *Form 16, Treatment Without Consent: Electroconvulsive Therapy, Involuntary Patient (Adult)*. At the time of writing, the current version of the form was issued in December 2007.

[181] Mental Health (Involuntary Procedures) (Amendment) Bill 2008, Bill No. 36 of 2008, sponsored by Senators Déirdre de Búrca, David Norris and Dan Boyle.

[182] 190 *Seanad Debates* 484 (June 25, 2008).

[183] Senator Déirdre de Búrca, 190(6) *Seanad Debates* 481 (June 25, 2008).

[184] Mental Health Act 2001, s.58(6).

psychosurgery to take place, the patient[185] must give their consent in writing to the psychosurgery and it must be authorised by an MHT.[186] The tribunal authorises the psychosurgery if it is satisfied that it is in the best interests of the health of the patient concerned.[187] The role of the MHT in cases concerning psychosurgery is considered above at para.7–70.

In the case of a detained child, psychosurgery may only take place if authorised by the District Court.[188]

10–52 Form 15[189] concerns psychosurgery. The RCP states that they are of the opinion that it would be to the benefit of the patient to have psychosurgery for stated reasons. They state that they have given the patient adequate information, in a form and language that the patient can understand, on the nature, purpose and likely effects of the proposed treatment and they are satisfied that the patient is capable of understanding this information and that the patient has consented in writing to undergo psychosurgery. Finally, the RCP requests that the Mental Health Commission refers the proposal to an MHT. If the MHT issues a decision concerning psychosurgery, Form 8 will be used.

10–53 The 2008 Private Members' Bill proposed that s.58 of the 2001 Act be repealed.[190] Minister of State Moloney responded that if the Bill were accepted, the administration of psychosurgery would not be prohibited; rather the legislative protection for the patient in terms of requiring their consent, and the authorisation of the procedure by an MHT, would be removed. He stated that the Bill in effect reduced the protection for persons suffering from mental illness and its acceptance would undermine achievements over recent years in securing better protection for such vulnerable people. In his view, it was important that provisions relating to psychosurgery should be retained in legislation in order to protect involuntary patients against the arbitrary use of the procedure in the future.[191]

TREATMENT OF CHILDREN

10–54 The law concerning children must be considered in light of the constitutional protection of the family in Arts 41 and 42. There is a constitutional presumption that the welfare of the child is to be found within the family.[192] The

---

[185] This only applies to detained patients.
[186] Mental Health Act 2001, s.58(1).
[187] Section 58(3).
[188] Section 25(12).
[189] Mental Health Commission, *Form 15, Proposal to Perform Psychosurgery, Involuntary Patient (Adult)*. At the time of writing, the current version of the form was issued in December 2007.
[190] Mental Health (Involuntary Procedures) (Amendment) Bill 2008, Bill No.36 of 2008.
[191] 190 *Seanad Debates* 490 (June 25, 2008).
[192] *Re J.H.* [1985] I.R. 375 at 395.

family has been interpreted as meaning the family based on marriage.[193] In exceptional cases, where parents fail in their duty towards their children, the State shall under Art.42.5 endeavour to supply the place of the parents, with due regard to children's rights. In some contexts, parents may include married and unmarried parents.[194] Children also have personal rights as citizens under Art.40.3.[195]

10–55 In *North Western Health Board v H.W. and C.W.*[196] the Supreme Court refused to order that a baby be given a "heel-prick" Phenylketonuria (PKU) test against the wishes of his married parents. The court applied the presumption that the welfare of the child is to be found within the family and held that this could only be displaced if there was a fundamental threat to the capacity of the child to function as a human person deriving from exceptional dereliction of duty on the part of parents.[197] Kilkelly has argued that insufficient consideration was given to the autonomous rights of the child in this case.[198]

As a result of various issues which have arisen with the constitutional status of children, the Government has proposed a constitutional amendment on children's rights.[199]

Reference may also be made to *Glass v U.K.*[200] in which a breach of art.8 of the ECHR was found where medical treatment was given to a 14-year-old boy against his mother's wishes.[201] In addition, art.12 of the Convention on the

---

[193] *The State (Nicolaou) v An Bord Uchtála* [1966] I.R. 567; Gerard Hogan & Gerry Whyte, *J.M. Kelly: The Irish Constitution*, 4th edn (Dublin: Butterworths, 2003), pp.1839–40.

[194] Walsh J. stated in *G. v An Bord Uchtála* [1980] I.R. 32 at 68, "One of the duties of a parent or parents, be they married or not, is to provide as best the parent or parents can the welfare of the child and to ward off dangers to the health of the child."

[195] See for example *F.N. & E.B. v C.O. & Ors. (Guardianship)* [2004] 4 I.R. 311 and cases discussed in Ursula Kilkelly, *Children's Rights in Ireland : Law, Policy and Practice* (Sussex: Tottel, 2008), pp.61–5.

[196] [2001] 3 I.R. 622.

[197] [2001] 3 I.R. 622 at 741 (Murray J.).

[198] Ursula Kilkelly, *Children's Rights in Ireland: Law, Policy and Practice* (Sussex: Tottel, 2008), pp.67–8. See also Keane C.J's dissenting judgment, emphasising the best interests of the child as the paramount consideration.

[199] See Twenty Eighth Amendment of the Constitution Bill 2007 and commentary in Ursula Kilkelly, *Children's Rights in Ireland: Law, Policy and Practice* (Sussex: Tottel, 2008), pp.74–83. The amendment was stalled pending the Lisbon Treaty referendum which took place in 2009.

[200] (2004) 39 E.H.R.R. 15.

[201] The boy was on a ventilator and was administered diamorphine without his mother's consent. In addition, the hospital had placed a Do Not Resuscitate (DNR) order on his file without her consent or knowledge. The court found that the administration of the diamorphine breached the boy's privacy rights and the hospital could have made an emergency High Court application. The court did not consider it necessary to examine separately the applicants' complaint regarding the inclusion of the DNR notice in the boy's case notes without his mother's consent and knowledge.

Rights of the Child states the child's rights to express an opinion in matters affecting the child and to have that opinion heard.[202]

10–56 Normally the parents and medical professionals will agree regarding the treatment of the child, but if they disagree, there may be a need for a court to intervene, often in cases concerning members of the Jehovah's Witness community who refuse to consent to blood transfusions for their children. The court proceedings may concern the inherent jurisdiction of the courts,[203] or may take the form of an application to take the child into care under the Child Care Act 1991[204] or to have the child made a ward of court.[205] Sometimes, the application concerns foetuses, where the court orders that once the child is born he or she may receive certain treatment.[206]

10–57 Section 23(1) of the Non-Fatal Offences against the Person Act 1997 (NFOAP Act) states that the consent of a minor who has attained the age of 16 years to any surgical, medical or dental treatment which, in the absence of consent, would constitute a trespass to their person, shall be as effective as it would be if they were of full age; and where a minor has by virtue of this section given an effective consent to any treatment, it shall not be necessary to obtain any consent for it from their parent or guardian. "Surgical, medical or dental treatment" includes any procedure undertaken for the purposes of diagnosis, and s.23 applies to any procedure (including, in particular, the administration of an anaesthetic) which is ancillary to any treatment as it applies to that treatment.[207] Nothing in s.23 shall be construed as making ineffective any consent which would have been effective if s.23 had not been enacted.[208]

---

[202] Article 12 is referred to in *N. v N. [Hearing a Child]* [2008] I.E.H.C. 382; High Court, Laffoy J., December 3, 2008. On art.12 generally, see Aisling Parkes, "Hearing the Voices of the Vulnerable: Children with Disabilities and the Right to be Heard Under International Law" (2008) 26 *Irish Law Times* 170.

[203] *Case Concerning Baby B.*, Birmingham J., reported in Ronan McGreevy, "Court Lets Hospital Give Blood to Baby if Necessary", *Irish Times*, December 29, 2007 (eight-day-old baby in National Maternity Hospital, Dublin).

[204] See Chris Dooley, "Gardaí Called as Parents Refuse Transfusion For Boy", *Irish Times*, March 3, 2000 (case involving a two-year-old boy in Waterford).

[205] *Case Concerning Baby Janice* (not her real name), Finnegan P., March 18, 2004 and Abbott J., August 5, 2004, reported in "Court Extends Order For Heart Surgery Baby", *Irish Times*, August 6, 2004 (five-month-old baby in Our Lady's Hospital for Sick Children, Dublin); *Case Concerning S.O'L.*, reported in Ali Bracken, "Bid to Stop Blood Transfusion Had 'No Role' in Girl's Death", *Irish Times*, February 8, 2007 (15-year-old girl, Wexford General Hospital, 2005).

[206] *Case Concerning Woman at Coombe Women's Hospital*, Finnegan P., reported in Padraig O'Morain, "Order on HIV Mother to Affect Religious Groups" *Irish Times*, July 20, 2002; note also correction in *Irish Times*, July 22, 2002 (Mother had H.I.V.; religious affiliation not clear); *Case Concerning Babies C. and D.*, Laffoy J., reported in Mary Carolan, "Court Allows Blood Treatments to Save Twin Babies' Lives", *Irish Times*, April 25, 2008 (twins due to be delivered at Cork University Hospital).

[207] Non-Fatal Offences Against the Person Act 1997, s.23(2).

[208] Non-Fatal Offences Against the Person Act 1997, s.23(3).

This section is generally regarded as setting the age of consent for medical treatment at 16. However, it is at least arguable that the section is facilitative of consent rather than requiring consent.[209] In addition, it is unclear whether s.23 covers refusal of treatment (as opposed to consent to treatment.)[210] The section leaves open the question whether a minor *under 16* may consent to treatment.[211] Case law concerning the English equivalent of this section[212] is of assistance. In the leading case of *Gillick v West Norfolk and Wisbech A.H.A.*[213] it was held that as regards children under 16, who are *not* covered by the equivalent English section, an individual assessment of the maturity of the patient must be carried out in each case, evaluating whether the patient understands the nature of the advice being given and whether the patient has sufficient maturity to understand what is involved. This is now referred to as "*Gillick* competence".

Treatment of Children: the Mental Health Act 2001

10–58 As a matter of statutory interpretation, it is very significant that the Non-Fatal Offences against the Person Act 1997 preceded the Mental Health Act 2001. In the case of detained children, it is arguable that the Mental Health Act 2001 is the applicable law, if there is a conflict between it and s.23 of the 1997 Act. However, if this is what the Oireachtas intended, a clause referring to the 1997 Act (e.g. "notwithstanding s.23 of the 1997 Act") should have been inserted in the 2001 Act. Donnelly is of the view that "there is nothing in the M.H.A. to exclude the application of the Non-Fatal Offences Against the Person Act 1997."[214] However, she does point out that the possibility of an involuntary minor patient being found to be capable of refusing treatment for a mental disorder would be slim.[215]

10–59 The 2001 Act contains three provisions concerning consent and detained children (up to age 18). Section 61 provides that in the case of a child detained under s.25, medicine may only be given for longer than three months if (a) it is approved by the RCP and (b) it is authorised by another consultant psychiatrist.[216]

209   See the argument and counter-argument in Mary Donnelly, "Treatment for a Mental Disorder: The Mental Health Act 2001, Consent and the Role of Rights" (2005) 40 Ir. Jur. 220 at 239.
210   Mary Donnelly, *Consent: Bridging the Gap Between Doctor and Patient* (Cork University Press, 2002), p.48.
211   See Bryan McMahon & William Binchy, *Law of Torts*, 3rd edn (Dublin: Butterworths, 2000), p.82; Law Reform Commission, *Bioethics: Advance Care Directives* (LRC Consultation Paper 51–2008), p.82.
212   Family Law Reform Act 1969, s.8 (England and Wales).
213   [1986] A.C. 112.
214   Mary Donnelly, "Treatment for a Mental Disorder: The Mental Health Act 2001, Consent and the Role of Rights" (2005) 40 Ir. Jur. 220 at 239.
215   Mary Donnelly, "Treatment for a Mental Disorder: The Mental Health Act 2001, Consent and the Role of Rights" (2005) 40 Ir. Jur. 220 at 239.
216   See further para.10–40 above.

The effect of s.61 is that in the case of a child, regardless of their capability of consent, medicine may be administered for longer than three months if authorised by a second psychiatrist. There is no reference to the parents in s.61. Section 25(12) and (13) require the approval of the District Court before ECT or psychosurgery may be performed on a detained child.

10–60 The Mental Health Commission has issued two documents containing guidance regarding consent and children. The *Reference Guide: Children*[217] stated that s.23 of the 1997 Act did not apply to psychiatric treatment and therefore, the consent of the parent/guardian or courts would be required for any psychiatric procedure or intervention where consent was required.[218] The Commission may have assumed that psychiatric treatment was not "medical" treatment but this view is difficult to justify.[219] The *Guide* also stated that a child admitted under s.25 of the 2001 Act could be administered medication with or without consent for the purposes of ameliorating their mental disorder for a period of three months.[220] Again, this position may not be as straightforward as the Commission suggests for various reasons, such as the 1997 Act and the *Gillick* case.[221]

The *Code of Practice on the Admission of Children*[222] states that if a child (under 18 and unmarried) is to receive voluntary in-patient treatment, consent of one or both parents must be obtained.[223] It states that the definition of "child" in the 2001 Act raises an issue in relation to children aged 16 and 17 years in the context of s.23 of 1997 Act and that there is a question as to whether s.23 of the 1997 Act enables children aged 16 and 17 years to admit themselves voluntarily to an approved centre for treatment. The Commission states that its legal advice is that attempts to reconcile s.23 of the 1997 Act with the provisions of the 2001 Act give rise to significant difficulty. While it may be that the definition of medical treatment under the Non-Fatal Offences Against the Person Act 1997 (NFOAP Act 1997) would include psychiatric treatment, and one commentator has interpreted it to be so, the Act does not appear to contemplate the giving of consent to treatment by a "child", a term which, because of the way

---

[217] *Reference Guide: Mental Health Act 2001–Part Two (Children)* (Dublin: Mental Health Commission, 2006).

[218] *Reference Guide: Mental Health Act 2001–Part Two (Children)* (Dublin: Mental Health Commission, 2006), para.3.3.

[219] Mary Donnelly, "Treatment for a Mental Disorder: The Mental Health Act 2001, Consent and the Role of Rights" (2005) 40 Ir. Jur. 220 at 239, fn.90.

[220] *Reference Guide: Mental Health Act 2001—Part Two (Children)* (Dublin: Mental Health Commission, 2006), para.4.8.1.

[221] Mary Donnelly, "Treatment for a Mental Disorder: The Mental Health Act 2001, Consent and the Role of Rights" (2005) 40 Ir. Jur. 220 at pp.238–9.

[222] Mental Health Commission, *Code of Practice Relating to Admission of Children under the Mental Health Act 2001* (COP–S33(3)/01/2006, 2006).

[223] Mental Health Commission, *Code of Practice Relating to Admission of Children under the Mental Health Act 2001* (COP–S33(3)/01/2006, 2006), para.2.8 and para.3.2.

it is defined in the 2001 Act, includes s.23 NFOAP Act 1997 minors.[224] The Commission states that it cannot advise mental health professionals to operate on the assumption that s.23 NFOAP Act 1997 means that the consent of children aged 16 and 17 is effective to permit treatment under the Act. The Code states that it appears that, as a matter of fundamental principle, the more extensive and/or far-reaching the intervention proposed, the more cautious the treating professional should be in relying exclusively on a child's consent. Such caution would be particularly indicated where the parent(s) of the child are opposed to the intervention. The Commission's legal advice is that, irrespective of whether children aged 16 and 17 years are capable as a matter of law or fact of providing an effective consent to treatment, the views of 16 and 17 year olds as to their treatment should be sought as a matter of course.[225] It will then be a matter for the treating health professional to judge the weight (if any) to be accorded to such views in all the circumstances.[226]

The Code also states that the existence of consent to treatment does not, of itself, impose an obligation to treat on a heath professional. Where there is disagreement as between child and parent(s), particularly in respect of some significant aspect of treatment, it is open to the professional involved to decline to give that treatment (where, for instance, the co-operation of the patient would be an important factor in whether the treatment is successful or not) or to seek guidance from the High Court as to how to proceed.[227] The Code also states that the issue of capacity to give a valid consent may arise in any given case. Just as an adult may not be competent to give a valid consent, a 16- or 17-year-old (assuming that s.23 NFOAP Act 1997 is applicable), may not be competent to give such consent.[228]

10–61 A legislative amendment clarifying the relationship between s.23 of the 1997 Act and the consent provisions in the 2001 Act would appear to be needed. The lack of clarity on this issue creates significant practical difficulties for mental health professionals.

---

[224] Mental Health Commission, *Code of Practice Relating to Admission of Children under the Mental Health Act 2001* (COP–S33(3)/01/2006, 2006), paras 2.10–11.

[225] Mental Health Commission, *Code of Practice Relating to Admission of Children under the Mental Health Act 2001* (COP–S33(3)/01/2006, 2006), para.2.12.

[226] Mental Health Commission, *Code of Practice Relating to Admission of Children under the Mental Health Act 2001* (COP–S33(3)/01/2006, 2006), para.3.3.

[227] Mental Health Commission, *Code of Practice Relating to Admission of Children under the Mental Health Act 2001* (COP–S33(3)/01/2006, 2006), para.2.13.

[228] Mental Health Commission, *Code of Practice Relating to Admission of Children under the Mental Health Act 2001* (COP–S33(3)/01/2006, 2006), para.2.14.

CONSENT TO CLINICAL TRIALS

10–62 While patients who have been detained on an involuntary basis under the Mental Health Act 2001 may not participate in clinical trials,[229] there is no such restriction on voluntary patients who are being treated at approved centres.

10–63 During the Dáil debates on the Mental Health Bill 1999, Dan Neville T.D. stated that the Minister had given him information that 53 clinical trials were conducted from 1998 to 2000 in "mental institutions."[230] Deputy Neville had also asked[231] for information on the statistics prior to 1997 but there had been a delay of at least five months in obtaining this information. According to the Irish Medicines Board, the numbers of clinical trials involving psychiatric patients which took place during the years 2000, 2001 and 2002 were seven, four and six respectively.[232] Deputy Neville was informed in 2006 that there were four clinical trials conducted on psychiatric patients in 2003, six in 2004 and one in 2005.[233]

There have been allegations that clinical trials on children in institutional settings in the 1960s and 1970s were conducted without proper consents being obtained, and these issues were referred to the Commission to Inquire into Child Abuse in 2001.[234] However, this referral was found to be ultra vires in 2003.[235]

The Inspector of Mental Hospitals stated in 1999 that while all drug trials in psychiatric hospitals were the subject of approval by local ethics committees and were in conformity with the Clinical Trials legislation, the Inspectorate was aware of the difficulties with the concept of consent in relation to such trials on the part of persons suffering from mental illness whether in in-patient care or in community care.[236] The Inspectorate was considering the advisability of setting up an obligatory register of drug trials involving psychiatric patients.

10–64 The law concerning consent in clinical trials is now governed by two separate pieces of legislation. Most trials are currently governed by the European Communities (Clinical Trials on Medicinal Products For Human Use)

---

[229] Section 70 of the Mental Health Act 2001 states: "Notwithstanding section 9(7) of the Control of Clinical Trials Act, 1987, a person suffering from a mental disorder who has been admitted to an approved centre under this Act shall not be a participant in a clinical trial."

[230] 536 *Dáil Debates* 1462 (May 23 2001).

[231] 528 *Dáil Debates*, Written Answers: Clinical Trials (December 12, 2000). See also 529 *Dáil Debates*, Written Answers: Clinical Trials (January 30, 2001).

[232] 561 *Dáil Debates*, Written Answers: Clinical Trials (February 11, 2003). See also 616 *Dáil Debates*, Written Answers: Clinical Trials (March 21, 2006)—The Minister promised to forward more recent statistics to Deputy Neville.

[233] *Dáil Debates*, Written Answers, Clinical Trials, 38088/06 (November 15, 2006).

[234] Commission to Inquire Into Child Abuse Act, 2000 (Additional Functions) Order 2001, S.I. No. 280 of 2001.

[235] *Hillary v Minister for Education and Science & Ors* [2004] I.E.H.C. 121; [2005] 4 I.R. 333. The judgment includes extracts from the relevant report of the Chief Medical Officer.

[236] *Report of Inspector of Mental Hospitals 1999*, pp.9–10.

Regulations, 2004.[237] However, if the trial is of a non-medicinal product, it is governed by the Control of Clinical Trials Acts 1987–2006.[238]

10–65 Assuming the trial comes within the terms of the 2004 Regulations, if the subject is "able to consent", then the subject must have an interview in which they are given the opportunity to understand the nature, objectives, risks and inconveniences of the trial, and the conditions under which it is to be conducted. The subject must give their informed consent to taking part in the trial and may, without being subject to any resulting detriment, withdraw from the clinical trial at any time by revoking their informed consent.[239] "Informed consent" is defined as consent given freely after the person is informed of the nature, significance, implications and risks of the trial. References to informed consent shall include references to informed consent given or refused by an adult unable by virtue of physical or mental incapacity to give informed consent, prior to the onset of that incapacity.[240]

If the subject is an "incapacitated adult", the following conditions and principles apply.[241] The subject's legal representative[242] must have an interview in which they are given the opportunity to understand the nature, objectives, risks and inconveniences of the trial and the conditions under which it is to be conducted. The legal representative must give their informed consent to the subject taking part in the trial. The legal representative's consent represents the subject's presumed will. The subject must receive information according to their capacity of understanding regarding the trial, its risks and its benefits. The explicit wish of a subject who is capable of forming an opinion and assessing information to refuse participation in, or to be withdrawn from, the clinical trial at any time must be considered by the investigator. There must be grounds for expecting that administering the medicinal product to be tested in the trial will

---

[237] S.I. No. 190 of 2004. These Regulations implement Directive 2001/20/EC on the implementation of good clinical practice in the conduct of clinical trials on medicinal products for human use. The Regulations have been amended by the European Communities (Clinical Trials on Medicinal Products for Human Use) (Amendment) Regulations 2004, S.I. No 878 of 2004 and the European Communities (Clinical Trials on Medicinal Products for Human Use) (Amendment No. 2) Regulations 2006, S.I. No. 374 of 2006.

[238] Control of Clinical Trials Act 1987; Control of Clinical Trials and Drugs Act 1990; Irish Medicines Board Act 1995; Irish Medicines Board (Miscellaneous Provisions) Act 2006; Irish Medicines Board, *Guide to Clinical Trials Applications* (2004).

[239] European Communities (Clinical Trials on Medicinal Products For Human Use) Regulations, 2004, Sch.1, Pt 3.

[240] European Communities (Clinical Trials on Medicinal Products For Human Use) Regulations, 2004, Sch.1, Pt 1, para.3.

[241] European Communities (Clinical Trials on Medicinal Products For Human Use) Regulations, 2004, Sch.1, Pt 5.

[242] "Legal representative" means a person who, by virtue of their family relationship with the adult, is suitable to act as the legal representative for the purposes of the trial and is available and willing to act for those purposes, or if there is no such person, a solicitor nominated by the relevant health care provider.

produce a benefit to the subject outweighing the risks or produce no risk at all. The clinical trial must be essential to validate data obtained in other clinical trials involving persons able to give informed consent, or by other research methods. The trial must relate directly to a life-threatening or debilitating clinical condition from which the subject suffers and it must be a situation where the clinical trial cannot be properly conducted without using subjects incapable of giving an informed consent. The trial must be designed to minimise pain, discomfort, fear and any other foreseeable risk in relation to the disease and the cognitive abilities of the patient. The interests of the patient always prevail over those of science and society.

10–66 A distinctive feature of this framework is the use of proxy consent from the patient's "legal representative" as defined by the Regulations.[243] Such proxy consent is not a feature of general law on consent. In addition, it is notable that there must be grounds for expecting that administering the product will produce a benefit to the subject outweighing the risks or produce no risk at all. The distinction between therapeutic and non-therapeutic research is difficult to define with precision, and there are also significant issues with the analysis of benefits to patients from trials.[244]

These conditions and principles were the subject of extensive debate in the negotiations for the Directive which they implement, and useful general literature on the Directive may be consulted for further analysis of the requirements.[245]

10–67 In the case of trials of non-medicinal products, the issue of consent is dealt with in s.9 of the Control of Clinical Trials Act 1987, which provides for proxy consent by a person or persons who, in the opinion of the relevant ethics committee, is or are competent to give a decision on such a participation.[246]

---

[243] See note 242 above.
[244] See generally Penney Lewis, "Procedures That Are Against the Medical Interests of Incompetent Adults" (2002) 22 *Oxford Journal of Legal Studies* 575.
[245] See, for example, Kathleen Liddell et al, "Medical Research Involving Incapacitated Adults: Implications of the EU Clinical Trials Directive 2001/20/EC" (2006) 14 Med. Law Rev 367; Pamela R. Ferguson, "Clinical Trials and Healthy Volunteers" (2008) 16 Med. L. Rev. 23.
[246] Control of Clinical Trials Act 1987, s.9(7)(b).

CHAPTER 11

COMMON LAW DUTIES: NEGLIGENCE AND CONFIDENTIALITY

NEGLIGENCE

11–01 It is not proposed in this chapter to provide a detailed analysis of the principles of the law of medical negligence, which is available elsewhere.[1] Instead, some issues of medical negligence which specifically concern mental health law will be considered.

A set of facts which gives rise to a possible negligence claim may also constitute another tort, such as false imprisonment, assault or battery.[2] It is important for legal practitioners to consider other causes of action rather than leaping instantly to an action for negligence.[3]

It must also be noted that a civil action concerning an act purportedly done in pursuance of the Mental Health Act 2001 requires the leave of the High Court under s.73 of the Act.[4]

The Existence of a Duty of Care

11–02 It is axiomatic that a medical professional owes a duty of care to a patient they are treating, and that the professional's employer will be vicariously liable for acts done in the course of employment.

11–03 If the patient has been convicted of a crime, the English courts have been slow to allow the patient to sue for negligent treatment before the crime. In *Clunis v Camden and Islington H.A.*[5] Mr Clunis had been discharged from hospital and was subject to after-care under s.117 of the Mental Health Act 1983. He failed to keep outpatient appointments arranged by his psychiatrist and then killed Jonathan Zito in an unprovoked attack at an underground station. He

---

[1] For example, Bryan McMahon & William Binchy, *Law of Torts*, 3rd edn (Dublin: Butterworths, 2000), Chapter 14; Ciarán Craven and William Binchy (eds.), *Medical Negligence Litigation: Emerging Issues* (Dublin: Firstlaw, 2008); Simon Mills, *Clinical Practice and the Law*, 2nd edn (Haywards Heath: Tottel, 2007), Chapter 6.

[2] See further paras 2–48 to 2–49 above.

[3] Peter Bartlett & Ralph Sandland, *Mental Health Law: Policy and Practice*, 3rd edn (Oxford: Oxford University Press, 2007), p.593.

[4] See paras 2–51 to 2–57 above.

[5] [1998] Q.B. 978.

pleaded guilty to manslaughter on the grounds of diminished responsibility and was ordered to be detained in a secure hospital. He claimed that the psychiatrist should have realised that he was in urgent need of treatment and was dangerous, and that, had he been given treatment, he would not have committed manslaughter and would not have been subject to the prolonged detention which he faced. The Court of Appeal struck out his claim.

Beldam L.J. applied the maxim *ex turpi causa non oritur actio* and found that Mr Clunis' action was therefore barred as a matter of public policy. Though his responsibility for killing Mr Zito was diminished, he must be taken to have known what he was doing and that it was wrong. He said that a plea of diminished responsibility accepts that the accused's mental responsibility is substantially impaired but it does not remove liability for their criminal act.[6] The court also found that s.117 concerning after-care did not create a private law cause of action for failure to carry out duties imposed by the statute, and Parliament could not be supposed to have intended to create such an extensive and wide-ranging liability for breaches of responsibility under s.117. The court found that the provision of after-care services under the Act was inconsistent with a coexisting common law duty of care.

11–04 The *Clunis* case has been criticised on a number of grounds. For example, it has been argued that Mr Clunis should have been able to sue for the adverse effects of failure to provide appropriate care *before* the killing.[7] In addition, the reasoning regarding the lack of a common law duty of care concerning after care has been questioned.[8]

Mr Clunis brought his case to Strasbourg and argued that art.8 of the European Convention on Human Rights (ECHR) had been breached due to the failure to protect his physical and psychological integrity.[9] The European Court of Human Rights found that in the instant case there was no direct link between the measures which, in the applicant's view, should have been taken by the Health Authority and the prejudice caused to his psychiatric well-being attendant on the realisation of the gravity of his act, his conviction and subsequent placement in a mental hospital without limit of time.[10] It could not be said that the Authority's failure to discharge its statutory duty under s.117 led inevitably to the fatal stabbing of Jonathan Zito. It was a matter of speculation as to

---

[6] [1998] Q.B. 978 at 989. See also the recent decision in *Gray v Thames Trains* [2009] U.K.H.L. 33 where it was ruled that a victim of a train crash who had post-traumatic stress disorder and later pleaded guilty to a manslaughter on grounds of diminished responsibility could not sue the train company for the loss of earnings suffered while in detention.

[7] Peter Bartlett and Ralph Sandland, *Mental Health Law; Policy and Practice*, 3rd edn (Oxford: Oxford University Press, 2007), p.599.

[8] Peter Bartlett and Ralph Sandland, *Mental Health Law; Policy and Practice*, 3rd edn (Oxford: Oxford University Press, 2007), pp.599–600.

[9] *Clunis v U.K.* [2001] M.H.L.R. 162.

[10] *Clunis v U.K.* [2001] M.H.L.R. 162, para.82.

whether the applicant would have consented to become an in-patient on a voluntary basis or followed a prescribed course of medication or co-operated in any other way with the authorities. The court found that the complaint of violation of art.8 was manifestly ill-founded.[11]

11–05 In New South Wales, Australia, it has been held by a two-to-one majority that even if a patient is later acquitted of murder on grounds of mental illness, it would be contrary to public policy to permit them to recover damages from the health authority for their time spent in hospital.[12]

11–06 There is some doubt in England as to whether a medical professional owes a duty of care to a person when exercising a statutory function under mental health legislation, such as certifying that a person has a mental disorder. Jones is of the view that a duty of care exists.[13] In *Everett v Griffiths*[14] it was assumed that a recommending doctor owed a duty of care to the patient but it was found that there was no negligence in the completion of the certificate. In some later cases, courts granted leave to sue doctors who had issued certificates.[15] However, in two other cases in the 1990s, it has been stated that the duty of care of such doctors remains an open question.[16]

In Ireland, there has been no explicit discussion of this issue in the reported cases, but it appears to be implicit in the cases decided concerning leave for legal proceedings under s.260 of the Mental Treatment Act 1945 that the relevant medical professionals owed a duty of care to the person in each case.[17]

11–07 Complex issues arise where a third party claims that the professional owed a duty of care to that party.

The case of *Tarasoff v Regents of the University of California*,[18] discussed below at para.11–21, demonstrates that, at least under Californian law, if the patient presents a serious danger of violence to another, the therapist may incur an obligation to use reasonable care to protect the intended victim against such danger.

---

[11] *Clunis v U.K.* [2001] M.H.L.R. 162, para.83.

[12] The patient killed a woman six hours after he had been discharged after a brief voluntary admission. *Hunter Area Health Service v Presland* [2005] N.S.W.C.A. 33; (2005) 63 N.S.W.L.R. 22; Russ Scott, "Hunter Area Health Services v. Presland: Liability of Mental Health Services for Failing to Admit or Detain a Patient with Mental Illness" (2006) 13 *Psychiatry, Psychology and Law* 49.

[13] Richard Jones, *Mental Health Act Manual*, 11th edn (London: Thomson Sweet & Maxwell, 2008), p.89. See also the analysis of this issue by Peter Bartlett and Ralph Sandland in *Mental Health Law: Policy and Practice*, 3rd edn (Oxford: Oxford University Press, 2007), at pp.595–8.

[14] [1921] 1 A.C. 631.

[15] *Winch v Jones* [1986] Q.B. 296; *Buxton v Jayne* [1960] 1 W.L.R. 783.

[16] *Clunis v Camden and Islington H.A.* [1998] Q.B. 978 at 993; *X. (Minors) v Bedfordshire County Council* [1995] 3 All E.R. 353 at 384.

[17] See references to cases under s.260 of 1945 Act at para.2–52 above.

[18] 17 Cal. 3d. 425, 131 Cal. Rptr. 14, 551 P. 2d. 334 (1976).

11–08 If the person in danger is not identified or identifiable, then a duty of care does not arise. In *Palmer v Tees H.A.*[19] the patient, Mr Armstrong, had had a number of admissions to hospital and was variously diagnosed or recorded as suffering from personality disorder or psychopathic personality. He killed a four-year-old child, the daughter of the plaintiff, Ms Palmer, at a time when he was an out-patient. The family lived on the same street as Mr Armstrong. Ms Palmer claimed that the hospital had been negligent in its treatment of her daughter and in discharging Mr Armstrong. She claimed damages for bereavement and for nervous shock arising from her daughter's death. Stuart-Smith L.J. held that there was insufficient proximity between the hospital and the four-year-old victim. He agreed with the court below that the potential victim must be identified or identifiable, though even then this may not be sufficient to establish proximity. He referred to the *Tarasoff* case and other US cases, noting that *Tarasoff* concerned an identified victim.[20] He made significant comments about the nature of proximity in cases such as this:

> "An additional reason why in my judgment in this case it is at least necessary for the victim to be identifiable (though as I have indicated it may not be sufficient) to establish proximity, is that it seems to me that the most effective way of providing protection would be to give warning to the victim, his or her parents or social services so that some protective measure can be made. ... It may be a somewhat novel approach to the question of proximity, but it seems to me to be a relevant consideration to ask what the defendant could have done to avoid the danger, if the suggested precautions, i.e. committal under s. 3 of the Mental Health Act or treatment, are likely to be of doubtful effectiveness, and the most effective precaution cannot be taken because the defendant does not know who to warn. This consideration suggests to me that the Court would be unwise to hold that there is sufficient proximity."[21]

11–09 In the Circuit Court case of *C. v North Western Health Board*,[22] it was decided that a health board owed a duty of care to a man who was attacked by a patient who had escaped from a psychiatric hospital, but on the facts it was held that the duty of care had not been breached. White J. found that if the patient was dangerous and this was known, "every step possible" would have to

---

[19] [1999] E.W.C.A. Civ. 1533; [1999] M.H.L.R. 106.
[20] [1999] E.W.C.A. Civ. 1533, paras 29–30. He also noted at para.28 the earlier English case of *Holgate v Lancashire Mental Hospital Board* [1937] 4 All E.R. 19, in which it was assumed that a hospital owed a duty to a victim of assault by a patient, but he said that that case occurred at a time when the essential elements of a duty of care were much less clearly defined and it could not be reconciled with *Hill v Chief Constable of West Yorkshire* [1989] A.C. 53 on the question of proximity.
[21] [1999] E.W.C.A. Civ. 1533, para.32.
[22] [1997] Irish Law Log Weekly 133 (Circuit Court, Judge White), summarised in Ciaran Craven, "Litigation Against Psychiatrists 1997–1999" (1999) 5 M.L.J.I. 70.

be taken to prevent him from doing damage. In so far as foreseeability of damage was concerned, the court noted, in reliance on *Condon v C.I.E.*,[23] that once damage of a type was reasonably foreseeable it was irrelevant that the extent of the damage or the precise manner in which it was brought about were actually foreseen.

Breaches of the Duty of Care

11–10 In Ireland, the test of medical negligence is stated in *Dunne (Infant) v National Maternity Hospital*[24] and states, for example, that the practitioner should normally follow general and approved practice, unless such practice has inherent defects which ought to be obvious to any person giving the matter due consideration. Deviations from general and approved practice may also occur unless no medical practitioner of like specialisation and skill would have followed the course had they been taking the ordinary care required from a person of their qualification.[25]

11–11 The English courts, in the 1957 case of *Bolam v Friern H.M.C.*[26] originally adopted a standard of care based on whether a responsible body of medical opinion would have behaved as the defendant did. As it happens, that was a mental health case where the court found that the hospital was not negligent in administering "unmodified" electro-convulsive therapy (ECT), i.e. without a muscle relaxant, as that was the normal practice at the time.[27] A limited caveat to the *Bolam* test was introduced by the *Bolitho* case in 1997: the exponents of the professional opinion relied upon must demonstrate that such opinion has a logical basis and that a defensible conclusion has been reached on comparative risks and benefits.[28]

11–12 In *Armstrong v Eastern Health Board*[29] the plaintiff had a long psychiatric history, including admissions to hospital. In May 1983 her husband brought her to a G.P. who wrote a referral letter noting that she had suicidal ideas. At the hospital, she was assessed by a psychiatrist and it was decided not to admit her. She and her husband left the hospital in anger. Later that day, she jumped from a balcony and sustained serious injuries. Egan J. said that it would

---

[23] High Court, Barrington J., November 16, 1984.
[24] [1989] I.R. 91.
[25] [1989] I.R. 91 at 109 (Finlay C.J.).
[26] [1957] 1 W.L.R. 582.
[27] The patient had sustained bilateral bone fractures of his acetabula due to the violent muscular contractions and spasms. There was no manual restraint used other than to support the patient's chin and hold his shoulders, nurses being present on either side of the couch in case the patient fell off.
[28] *Bolitho v City and Hackney H.A.* [1998] A.C. 232.
[29] High Court, Egan J., October 5, 1990.

seem that the psychiatrist's assessment was wrong but a doctor is not negligent because of the fact alone that their assessment is wrong.[30] The assessment was challenged, however, not on the allegation that it was wrong but that it was based on insufficient information. The psychiatrist had no documentary evidence for the assessment and had not dealt with Ms Armstrong before. Before the assessment, the psychiatrist had a conversation with a colleague who was familiar with Ms Armstrong's history. Egan J. noted that the notes in the "Log Book" referred to suicidal thoughts, including references to jumping from a balcony. It was also noted that on a previous occasion Ms Armstrong was given an injection and pacified before she left the hospital. Medical evidence was given in the case that many threats of suicide are not genuine but they must be taken more seriously when an actual method of suicide is mentioned (in this case of jumping off the balcony).[31] Mr Armstrong, the plaintiff's husband, gave evidence to the effect that the psychiatrist never read the referral letter from the G.P., which mentioned suicidal ideas, and Egan J. concluded that the psychiatrist did not read the letter.

The psychiatrist stated that even if she had not read the referral letter and allowing that she had not read the entries in the Log Book, her assessment would still have been the same. Egan J. found as a matter of probability that Mrs Armstrong would have ended up in hospital on the date in question if the psychiatrist had been in possession of the information referred to. Egan J. found that two psychiatrists were negligent in the duty they owed to the plaintiff. He made no finding of contributory negligence against Ms Armstrong, as he was satisfied that she was not really in control of her thoughts when she jumped from the balcony. Egan J. said:

> "I do not hold that clinical notes or entries in Log Books must always be read in all circumstances. There must be many occasions when there is simply not sufficient time and an emergency decision is required. Notes, however, are made for a purpose and should be read in the ordinary course. I imagine it was not unusual for one doctor to rely on a verbal summary given by another doctor who was well acquainted with the patient but this cannot always be excused."[32]

11–13 The family of a Sligo farmer with depression claimed that the hospital had been negligent in discharging him in *Healy v North Western Health Board*.[33] Mr Healy had drowned himself four days after discharge from a 10-day period in hospital. While there were notes of his assessment on admission and of an interview on Day 4, there was no note of a pre-discharge assessment. There were significant differences in the views of medical witnesses on either side,

---

[30] High Court, Egan J., October 5, 1990, p.8.
[31] High Court, Egan J., October 5, 1990, p.11.
[32] High Court, Egan J., October 5, 1990, pp.12–13.
[33] High Court, Flood J., January 31, 1996.

including, for example, a difference about the level of formality required in record keeping. However, the witnesses on both sides agreed that a patient with depression should be assessed for risk of suicide before being discharged. Flood J. said that as the pressures on release may be quite substantially greater than the pressures in hospital, it is therefore necessary that the person responsible for discharge should satisfy themselves that the patient was in a "firm remission". In his view there was no evidence of any assessment that Mr Healy had reached a status "of firm remission".[34] On the contrary, as a matter of probability, a person from firm remission would be unlikely to have killed themselves within four days. It had to be accepted that it could happen but, in his view, in the absence of specific evidence of deterioration, it would be an unlikely event. As a matter of probability, it was unlikely that such an assessment was ever carried out in relation to Mr Healy, or if it was carried out, it was an inadequate assessment or inadequately considered. Accordingly he found the defendants guilty of negligence in so discharging Mr Healy at a time when they knew or ought to have known that he was not in a firm remission.[35]

Webb and O'Leary have argued that if all depressed patients were to remain in hospital until firm remission was achieved, there would be a major policy dilemma for the psychiatric services. Their findings indicated that the median length of hospital stay for such patients would increase from 41 to 55 days. This would represent a profound reversal in the Government's policy of developing an increasingly community-orientated psychiatric service with less reliance on in-patient beds.[36] They say that suicide is a rare event, even within a psychiatric service, and is therefore very difficult to predict. They had not been able to show in their study that keeping all depressed patients in hospital until they had achieved full remission was likely to improve this record.[37]

11–14 In 1999 and 2005, there were media reports concerning the case of John Manweiler, who sued the Eastern Health Board for negligence, trespass to his person, assault, battery, false imprisonment and breach of constitutional rights in his treatment at St Brendan's psychiatric hospital.[38] It was reported that the jury found that he was unlawfully detained.[39] It was found that he had been unlawfully prescribed an anti-psychotic drug over 11 years.[40] A psychiatrist

---

34 High Court, Flood J., January 31, 1996, p.20.
35 High Court, Flood J., January 31, 1996, p.21.
36 Marcus Webb & Denis O'Leary, "What Is a 'Firm Remission'?" (1999) 5 M.L.J.I. 4.
37 Marcus Webb & Denis O'Leary, "What Is a 'Firm Remission'?" (1999) 5 M.L.J.I. 4 at 7.
38 "Patient Given the Wrong Drug Over 11-Year Period", *Irish Examiner*, February 20, 1999; "Man Alleges Wrongful Detention in Hospital", *Irish Times*, April 9, 2005; Carl O'Brien, "Vindication for a Solitary Man", *Irish Times*, May 21, 2005; Carl O'Brien, "€3m. Psychiatric Detention Award to be Appealed", *Irish Times*, June 13, 2005.
39 He was in hospital for a three-month period in 1984 and for a few weeks in 1991. While he entered the hospital voluntarily in 1984, it appears that his status was changed to involuntary after admission. The 1991 admission was voluntary.
40 The drug Clopixol was administered to him for 11 years on an out-patient basis.

threatened to have Mr Manweiler locked up in a unit at St Brendan's if he failed to continue on Clopixol and Mr Manweiler had submitted to the treatment solely because of the threat. The jury also found that health authorities had aggravated the injury to him by the manner in which they conducted their defence of the action. He was awarded €2.9 million damages and later, while an appeal was pending, accepted a settlement of €500,000.[41]

11–15 In *Madigan v Governor of St. Patrick's Hospital*,[42] Johnson J. dismissed a claim of negligence where a patient with depression was under a regime of observation which permitted her to leave the ward to go to occupational therapy. She then left the hospital and killed herself. Johnson J. said it was the decision of the medical profession and the nursing profession that this was the regime appropriate for the treatment of Ms Madigan at the time. The nurses at any given time during the day, if they had any apprehension or misgiving, or were in any way alerted to any alteration in mood or of the condition of the patient, could change the regime and impose a stricter regime on the patient. Quoting the *Dunne* principles, he found that the treatment provided by the defendants was not negligent.

11–16 There were various cases taken under s.260 of the Mental Treatment Act 1945 applying for leave of the High Court to sue.[43] In most of these cases, leave to institute proceedings was not granted. Where leave was granted, it was either because a time limit had been breached,[44] a doctor did not appear to have examined the plaintiff at all, or a relative who applied for a recommendation for admission had failed to notify the plaintiff of the nature of the medical certificate and the plaintiff's right to a second medical examination.[45]

Actions under art.2 of the ECHR

11–17 Article 2 of the ECHR states that everyone's right to life shall be protected by law. The ECHR has held that the State must take appropriate steps to safeguard the lives of those within its jurisdiction.[46] Article 2 is considered in this chapter, as a negligence action may be the means by which a plaintiff seeks a remedy against an organ of the State for failure to take appropriate steps to

---

[41] Carl O'Brien, "€3m. Psychiatric Award Cut to €500,000', *Irish Times*, August 24, 2005.

[42] [2006] I.E.H.C. 259; High Court, Johnson J., July 14, 2006.

[43] See further para.2–52 above.

[44] *Bailey v Gallagher* [1996] 2 I.L.R.M. 433 (more than seven days elapsed between the doctor's examination of the plaintiff and the plaintiff being detained); *Melly v Moran and North Western Health Board*, Supreme Court, May 28, 1998 (more than 24 hours elapsed between the examination by the doctor and his completion of recommendation for admission).

[45] The latter two circumstances applied in *Kiernan v Harris* [1998] I.E.H.C. 71; O'Higgins J., High Court, May 12, 1998.

[46] *Edwards v U.K.* (2002) 35 E.H.R.R. 19, para.54.

safeguard life. It may also be useful to plead breach of art.2 of the ECHR in appropriate cases.

11–18 In *Osman v U.K.*[47] the court stated that in certain well-defined circumstances art.2 may imply a positive obligation on the authorities to take preventative operational measures to protect an individual whose life is at risk from the criminal acts of another individual.[48] The court continued:

> "In the opinion of the court where there is an allegation that the authorities have violated their positive obligation to protect the right to life in the context of their above-mentioned duty to prevent and suppress offences against the person, it must be established to its satisfaction that the authorities knew or ought to have known at the time of the existence of a real and immediate risk to the life of an identified individual or individuals from the criminal acts of a third party and that they failed to take measures within the scope of their powers which, judged reasonably, might have been expected to avoid that risk. The Court does not accept the Government's view that the failure to perceive the risk to life in the circumstances known at the time or to take preventive measures to avoid that risk must be tantamount to gross negligence or wilful disregard of the duty to protect life. Such a rigid standard must be considered to be incompatible with the requirements of Article 1 of the Convention and the obligations of Contracting States under that Article to secure the practical and effective protection of the rights and freedoms laid down therein, including Article 2. For the Court, and having regard to the nature of the right protected by Article 2, a right fundamental in the scheme of the Convention, it is sufficient for an applicant to show that the authorities did not do all that could be reasonably expected of them to avoid a real and immediate risk to life of which they have or ought to have knowledge. This is a question which can only be answered in the light of all the circumstances of any particular case."[49]

In this case, a teacher, Mr Paget-Lewis, had killed Ali Osman, the father of a boy to whom Paget-Lewis had developed an attachment, and the son of a deputy head teacher, Mr Perkins. Paget-Lewis was later convicted of two charges of manslaughter having pleaded guilty on grounds of diminished responsibility. Mr Osman's widow sued the police for negligence, claiming that they failed to take appropriate action to protect her family. The Court of Appeal had dismissed her claim, holding that the police did not have liability to individuals for damage caused to them by criminals whom the police had failed to apprehend when it was possible to do so, as it would be against public policy.[50] The European Court held that art.2 had not been breached, as the applicants had failed to point to any

---

[47]   (2000) 29 E.H.R.R. 245.
[48]   (2000) 29 E.H.R.R. 245, para.115.
[49]   (2000) 29 E.H.R.R. 245, para.116.
[50]   *Osman and Another v Ferguson and Another* [1993] 4 All E.R. 344.

decisive stage in the sequence of events leading up to the tragic shooting when it could be said that the police knew or ought to have known that the lives of the Osman family were at real and immediate risk from Paget-Lewis.[51] However, the court found a breach of art.6 because the Court of Appeal's application of the exclusionary rule to protect the police from negligence actions in the context at issue, without further enquiry into the existence of competing public interest considerations, served to confer a blanket immunity on the police for their acts and omissions during the investigation and suppression of crime and amounted to an unjustifiable restriction on an applicant's right to have a determination on the merits of their claim against the police in deserving cases.[52]

11–19 In *Savage v South Essex Partnership NHS Foundation Trust*,[53] a patient had absconded from a psychiatric hospital and killed herself. Her daughter sued the NHS Trust, claiming damages for breach of the deceased's right to life under art.2 of the ECHR. On a preliminary issue, the proper test to establish a breach of the right under art.2 was laid down by the House of Lords. It was held that where members of staff knew or ought to have known that a particular detained mental patient presented a real and immediate risk of suicide, art.2 imposed an operational obligation on hospital authorities, distinct from and additional to their more general duties, which required the staff to do all that could reasonably be expected of them to prevent the patient taking his or her own life.[54]

MENTAL HEALTH RECORDS AND CONFIDENTIALITY

11–20 It is a general principle of medical law that medical and other professionals should preserve confidentiality regarding the patient.[55] This principle conforms with the constitutional right to privacy[56] and the protection of privacy in art.8 of the ECHR.

Under data protection legislation, personal data within the meaning of the legislation (which covers electronic data and certain non-electronic files) must be obtained and processed fairly, kept accurate and up to date and protected by adequate security measures.[57] The patient may request access to the data and this may only be refused if it would be likely to cause serious harm to their physical

---

[51] (2000) 29 E.H.R.R. 245, para.121.
[52] (2000) 29 E.H.R.R. 245, para.151.
[53] [2008] U.K.H.L. 74; [2009] 2 W.L.R. 115.
[54] [2009] 2 W.L.R. 115 at 137–8 (Lord Rodger).
[55] Simon Mills, *Clinical Practice and the Law*, 2nd edn (Haywards Heath: Tottel, 2007), Chapter 3, pp.51–72.
[56] *McGee v Attorney General* [1974] I.R. 284; *Kennedy v Ireland* [1987] I.R. 587.
[57] Data Protection Acts 1988 to 2003. See generally Denis Kelleher, *Privacy and Data Protection Law in Ireland* (Sussex: Tottel Publishing, 2006.)

or mental health. In addition, the data may only be communicated by, or after consultation with, an appropriate health professional.[58]

Freedom of information law may also apply, if information about an individual is held by a public body which is listed as governed by the legislation.[59] Access may be refused if it might be prejudicial to health, well-being or emotional condition, but the refusal must be accompanied by a statement that, if the requester wishes, the information will be made available for inspection by a health professional nominated by the requester.[60]

11–21 Confidentiality may be breached where the patient consents, assuming they have capacity to consent.[61] It may also be breached in limited circumstances even where the patient does not consent. In some cases, courts might uphold a breach of confidentiality where it is necessary to safeguard the welfare of a third party. In the well-known American case of *Tarasoff v Regents of the University of California*[62] a student (P.) had confided to his psychologist that he wished to kill Ms Tarasoff. While the psychologist ensured that P. was civilly committed, he did not notify Ms Tarasoff of the threat to her safety. P. was later released from hospital and killed Ms Tarasoff. The court held that when a therapist determines that their patient presents a serious danger of violence to another, they incur an obligation to use reasonable care to protect the intended victim against such danger. The discharge of this duty may require the therapist to take one or more of various steps. Thus, it may call for them to warn the intended victim, to notify the police, or to take whatever steps are reasonably necessary under the circumstances. *Tarasoff* has not been uniformly followed in the United States and the scope of the duty has been curtailed by legislative changes.[63]

There is no Irish decision considering the issues raised by *Tarasoff*. However, the Medical Council's Guide to Ethical Conduct and Behaviour states that confidentiality may be breached "when necessary to safeguard the welfare of another individual or patient."[64] The Guide also states that if the patient has a communicable infection which puts others at serious risk, those who might be at risk should be informed.[65] Similarly, the Data Protection Act 1988 permits disclosure to prevent injury or other damage to a person's health.[66]

---

[58] Data Protection (Access Modification) (Health) Regulations 1989, S.I. No. 82 of 1989.
[59] Freedom of Information Acts 1997 to 2003. See generally Maeve McDonagh, *Freedom of Information Law*, 2nd edn (Dublin: Thomson Round Hall, 2006).
[60] Freedom of Information Act 1997, s.28(3)–(4). See, for example, *Mr X. and the HSE (Midland Area)*, Case Number 040348, 2005; Letter Decision in Case 050330, *Ms X. and the HSE*, September 7, 2007.
[61] Note that a statement from the person that they "do not mind one way or the other" may not be sufficient—see above, para.10–06.
[62] 17 Cal. 3d. 425, 131 Cal. Rptr. 14, 551 P. 2d. 334 (1976); Kyle, "From Tarasoff to Bradley: Courts Struggle to Apply the Duty to Control Mental Patients" (1984) 14 Cumb. L. Rev. 165.
[63] Bernadette McSherry, "Confidential Communications Between Clients and Mental Health Care Professionals" (2002) 37 Ir. Jur. 269 at 272.
[64] Medical Council, *Guide to Ethical Conduct and Behaviour*, 6th edn (2004), para.16.3(4).
[65] Medical Council, *Guide to Ethical Conduct and Behaviour*, 6th edn (2004), para.16.8.
[66] Data Protection Act 1988, s.8(d).

11–22 Under the European Convention, breaches of confidentiality have been upheld where a psychiatrist had concerns regarding a patient's son's health[67] and in another case where prison staff were notified of the health status of a prisoner with HIV.[68]

11–23 In another category of cases, breaches of confidentiality have been upheld where it is necessary to protect the interests of society. For example, in *W. v Egdell*[69] a psychiatrist examined a prisoner on behalf the prisoner's solicitors. His report was not used in court, as the application being made at the time was withdrawn, but the psychiatrist was concerned about the risk to society posed by the prisoner. He therefore reported his concerns to the responsible medical officer at the prison, who passed them on to the Home Secretary. The court upheld the breach of confidentiality due to the very real threat to society posed by Mr W. Bingham L.J. said:

> "There is one consideration which in my judgment, as in that of the judge, weighs the balance of public interest decisively in favour of disclosure. It may be shortly put. Where a man has committed multiple killings under the disability of serious mental illness, decisions which may lead directly or indirectly to his release from hospital should not be made unless a responsible authority is properly able to make an informed judgment that the risk of repetition is so small as to be acceptable. A consultant psychiatrist who becomes aware, even in the course of a confidential relationship, of information which leads him, in the exercise of what the court considers a sound professional judgment, to fear that such decisions may be made on the basis of inadequate information and with a real risk of consequent danger to the public is entitled to take such steps as are reasonable in all the circumstances to communicate the grounds of his concern to the responsible authorities. I have no doubt that the judge's decision in favour of Dr. Egdell was right on the facts of this case.[70]

In *Stone v South East Strategic Health Authority*[71] it was held that publication of the report of an inquiry into two homicides carried out by Mr Stone was lawful, even though it included details of Mr Stone's medical records. Davis J. stated that there was a true public interest in the public at large knowing of the

---

[67] *Andersson v Sweden*, Application No. 20022/92; Judgment August 27, 1997. This case concerned art.6, the right to fair trial, as the applicant claimed that she could not appeal to a court against the psychiatrist's decision to disclose the information. At Commission stage, the Commission had found the applicant's complaint that art.8 was breached to be manifestly ill-founded, as the disclosure of the information pursued the legitimate aims of protecting "health or morals" and the "rights and freedoms of others."

[68] *T.V. v Finland* (1994) 18 E.H.R.R. CD179 (European Commission of Human Rights).

[69] [1990] Ch. 359. See similar reasoning in *R. v Crozier* (1990) 12 Cr. App. R. (S.) 206.

[70] [1990] Ch. 359 at 424.

[71] [2006] E.W.H.C. 1668 (Admin.); [2006] M.H.L.R. 288. See Nell Munro, "Privacy v. Publication: Homicide Inquiries in the Balance" (2007) 15 Med. L. Rev. 109.

actual care and treatment supplied (or, as the case may be, not supplied) to Mr Stone; and knowing, and being able to reach an informed assessment of, the failures identified and steps that may be recommended to be taken to address identified deficiencies.[72]

11–24 Courts have permitted breaches of confidentiality when it is in the interests of the patient. In *L.K. v Clinical Director of Lakeview Unit, Naas General Hospital*[73] there was doubt as to whether the applicant for an inquiry under Art.40 of the Constitution had capacity to consent to release of her records and a psychiatric examination. Clarke J. directed that a psychiatrist review her records and examine her, on the basis that the minimum entitlement of an applicant in her position was to a reasonable facility to enable her to put before the court an expert view on the material factual matters to the issues which arose.[74] This reasoning was followed by Peart J. in *E.J.W. v Watters*[75] which is discussed above at para.7–55.

11–25 Confidentiality may also be breached in the context of litigation, or preparation for litigation. In *C. v Íarnród Éireann*[76] Mr C. applied for a post with the respondent and attended two medical examinations. He initiated a claim under the Employment Equality Act 1998 and later objected to the fact that his medical records had been passed to the respondent's legal department without his authorisation. The Equality Officer referred to the *McGrory* case[77] and decided that by initiating his claim, Mr C. waived his right to privacy in relation to his medical records and the respondent did not require his authorisation to pass his medical records to its legal department for the purpose of defending the claim.[78]

11–26 In the English case of *C. v C.*[79] a doctor refused, in advance of the trial, to disclose medical information concerning the wife who was involved in divorce proceedings, even at her request. Lewis J. said:

> "It is, of course, of the greatest importance from every point of view that proper secrecy should be observed in connection with venereal disease clinics, and that nothing should be done to diminish their efficiency or to infringe the confidential relationship existing between doctor and patient. But, in my opinion, those considerations do not justify a doctor in refusing to divulge confidential information to a patient or to any named person or persons when

---

[72] [2006] M.H.L.R. 288 at 297.
[73] [2006] I.E.H.C. 196; [2007] 2 I.R. 465; High Court, Clarke J., May 17, 2006.
[74] [2007] 2 I.R. 465 at 471.
[75] Unapproved, High Court, Peart J., November 25, 2008.
[76] Decision E2003/054, Equality Tribunal, November 26, 2003.
[77] *McGrory v E.S.B.* [2003] I.E.S.C. 45; [2003] 3 I.R. 407. See above, para.10–05.
[78] Decision E2003/054, Equality Tribunal, November 26, 2003, pp.7–8.
[79] [1946] 1 All E.R. 562.

asked by the patient so to do. In the circumstances of this case the information should have been given, and in all cases where the circumstances are similar the doctor is not guilty of any breach of confidence in giving the information asked for."[80]

11–27 Courts and tribunals will also routinely order or direct that witnesses answer questions or produce documents which may be confidential. The breaches of confidentiality which result are not unlawful. No legal privilege attaches to the confidential clinical encounter.[81]

---

[80] [1946] 1 All E.R. 562 at 563.
[81] See discussion in Simon Mills, *Clinical Practice and the Law*, 2nd edn (Haywards Heath: Tottel, 2007), p.56. Contrast the privilege which attaches to consultations with a lawyer or sacerdotal privilege with a priest.

CHAPTER 12

REQUIREMENTS CONCERNING INSTITUTIONAL CARE

SECLUSION AND RESTRAINT

Seclusion and Restraint in Practice

12–01 Seclusion is the placing or leaving of a person in a room alone with the exit door locked, fastened or held in such a way as to prevent the person from leaving.[1] Restraint may either be physical or mechanical. Physical restraint is the use of physical force (by one or more persons) for the purpose of preventing the free movement of a resident's body when he or she poses an immediate threat of serious harm to self or others.[2] Mechanical restraint means the use of devices or bodily garments for the purpose of preventing or limiting the free movement of a patient's body.[3] Chemical restraint (use of medication to restrain patients) is not specifically covered by the rules and codes made by the Mental Health Commission.

12–02 It is difficult to assess the frequency of use of seclusion and restraint in mental health centres, intellectual disability services and prisons. Some references in reports published in recent years include the following: in 2003, the European Committee on the Prevention of Torture visited three establishments for people with intellectual disability: Grove House Intellectual Disability Service in Cork, St Joseph's Intellectual Disability Service in Portrane[4] and St Raphael's Centre in Youghal. The Committee noted[5] that soft restraints (ribbons) were on occasion used at St Raphael's and, at St Joseph's, one resident was regularly restrained in a soft straitjacket for 10 to 15 minutes at a time to prevent self-injury. All such episodes were authorised by a doctor and carefully noted. The delegation concluded that the information gathered did not give rise to concern as regards

---

[1] Mental Health Commission, *Rules Governing the Use of Seclusion and Mechanical Means of Bodily Restraint* (version 2, 2009), para.2.1.1.

[2] Mental Health Commission, *Code of Practice on the Use of Physical Restraint in Approved Centres* (version 2, 2009), para.4.1.

[3] Mental Health Commission, *Rules Governing the Use of Seclusion and Mechanical Means of Bodily Restraint* (version 2, 2009), para.2.3.1.

[4] St Joseph's was on the grounds of St Ita's Hospital, Portrane, Dublin.

[5] *Report to the Government of Ireland on the Visit to Ireland Carried out by the European Committee for the Prevention of Torture and Inhuman or Degrading Treatment or Punishment (CPT) from 20 to 28 May 2002*, CPT/Inf (2003) 36, p.40.

the use of seclusion and means of physical restraint in the three establishments visited.

12–03 The 2004 report of the Inspector of Mental Health Services noted as regards St Joseph's Intellectual Disability Service in Portrane that in 2003 there were 136 episodes of seclusion involving 15 patients.[6] There was evidence that some patients were locked in their bedrooms at night. Although this was not deemed to be seclusion under the Mental Treatment Act 1945, it resulted in patients being deprived of their liberty. The seclusion policy, dated May 1999, was in urgent need of review. Throughout the inspection, it was evident that numerous types of restraint were in use in the hospital. These included straitjackets, physically restraining chairs, cot sides, manual restraint and the use of psychotropic medication. There was a protocol on the use of restraint in the hospital. This protocol needed to be reviewed and a comprehensive policy on the use of restraint needed to be developed and implemented. The Inspectorate stated that it found the use of straitjackets unacceptable.[7] The Inspectorate recommended that there should be a review of the current seclusion and restraint policy/guidelines, new policies should be implemented that prohibit the use of straitjackets and a policy should be implemented to end the practice of locking people in their rooms at night.[8]

12–04 In the 2005 Inspectorate report, it was noted that mechanical restraint was used on one unit in St Joseph's[9] in the form of a straitjacket in the case of one patient.[10] This was recorded in the register and signed by the medical staff. The duration of use of this restraint was recorded as lasting from 30 to 40 minutes once or twice a day and was used to prevent serious self-injury. Due to the introduction of a behavioural programme, the frequency of use of this restraint had been reduced. However, the Inspectorate noted that it was unacceptable that this form of restraint continued to be used in a modern mental health and intellectual disability service. The Inspectorate was informed that efforts were being made to provide alternatives, which included psychological treatments, extra staffing and staff training.[11]

---

[6] Mental Health Commission, *Annual Report 2004 Including the Report of the Inspector of Mental Health Services 2004*, p.438.

[7] Mental Health Commission, *Annual Report 2004 Including the Report of the Inspector of Mental Health Services 2004*, p.438. See also Mary Raftery, "Asylum Nostalgia Misplaced", *Irish Times*, September 15, 2005.

[8] Mental Health Commission, *Annual Report 2004 Including the Report of the Inspector of Mental Health Services 2004*, p.440.

[9] Dún na Rí, Unit 11, St Joseph's Intellectual Disability Service, Portrane, Dublin.

[10] Mental Health Commission, *Annual Report 2005 Including the Report of the Inspector of Mental Health Services 2005*, Book 2, p.121.

[11] Mental Health Commission, *Annual Report 2005 Including the Report of the Inspector of Mental Health Services 2005*, Book 2, p.121.

12–05 The Central Mental Hospital (CMH) report[12] in 2006 noted that in Unit A, the women's service, seclusion appeared to be used regularly with little use of alternatives to seclusion.[13] Women's underwear was routinely removed during seclusion and they were not allowed appropriate choice of sanitary protection. Policy on the unit allowed male staff to be involved in the restraint of women patients. Involvement of male staff did not appear to be confined to exceptional situations.[14] It appeared from records that most patients admitted to Unit B were placed in seclusion independently of any risk assessment.[15] In Unit 4, rates of seclusion had dropped dramatically.[16] The evidence pointed to an excessive use of seclusion specifically within the two admission wards. This was supported by the seclusion records noting the number of episodes of seclusion and the total number of seclusion hours.[17] The documentation supporting the use of seclusion was variable, with at times no clear rationale for the use of seclusion detailed. There appeared to be limited alternatives considered to seclusion although the recent introduction of RAID training[18] did seem to be viewed as a positive move and appeared to be reducing the use of seclusion in Unit 4.[19] It appeared that many incidents where control and restraint were used were not recorded in the relevant case notes, nor on an Untoward Incident Form or on a Prevention and Management of Violence and Aggression Form. From those records that were reviewed by the Inquiry Committee, it appeared that the use of control and restraint was undertaken in a manner that was in keeping with current established practice.[20]

12–06 The 2006 Inspectorate report regarding another unit[21] at St Joseph's in Portrane stated that there was one patient who exhibited challenging behaviour. Previously he was managed in a straitjacket.[22] However, the episodes of him being placed in a straitjacket had dramatically decreased and alternatives had

12 Mental Health Commission, *Report of the Committee of Inquiry into Current Care and Treatment Practices in the Central Mental Hospital* (2006).
13 Mental Health Commission, *Report of the Committee of Inquiry into Current Care and Treatment Practices in the Central Mental Hospital* (2006), p.37.
14 Mental Health Commission, *Report of the Committee of Inquiry into Current Care and Treatment Practices in the Central Mental Hospital* (2006), p.37.
15 Mental Health Commission, *Report of the Committee of Inquiry into Current Care and Treatment Practices in the Central Mental Hospital* (2006), p.44.
16 Mental Health Commission, *Report of the Committee of Inquiry into Current Care and Treatment Practices in the Central Mental Hospital* (2006), p.65.
17 Mental Health Commission, *Report of the Committee of Inquiry into Current Care and Treatment Practices in the Central Mental Hospital* (2006), p.93.
18 Reinforce Appropriate Implode Disruptive training.
19 Mental Health Commission, *Report of the Committee of Inquiry into Current Care and Treatment Practices in the Central Mental Hospital* (2006), p.94.
20 Mental Health Commission, *Report of the Committee of Inquiry into Current Care and Treatment Practices in the Central Mental Hospital* (2006), p.94.
21 St Claire's Unit, St Joseph's Intellectual Disability Service, Portrane, Dublin.
22 Mental Health Commission, *Annual Report 2006 Including the Report of the Inspector of Mental Health Services 2006*, Book 2, p.99.

been looked at to assist the staff in managing this patient's challenging behaviour. The Inspectorate stated that the staff should be commended for undertaking an alternative approach to managing this person's challenging behaviour and they should continue to use alternatives to the straitjacket. It was suggested to the team that they chart the amount of times the patient was placed in a mechanical restraint. A record was kept in the register. Another form of mechanical restraint in this unit was a Posey belt, which prevented people from slipping out of chairs.[23]

12–07 The report on certain services in Tipperary in 2009,[24] concerning visits made in 2007, contains a number of references to seclusion and restraint. The report stated that seclusion is a safety measure, not a treatment, and should only be used as a last resort, when there is an immediate threat to the individual or others.[25] The report stated:

> "Seclusion was not always used as a last resort. Poor ward design, low staffing levels and a lack of activities to occupy residents contributed to more frequent use. An audit of the need for seclusion would assist in substantially reducing its use. A note of the consideration of alternative management, the finishing time of seclusion and the name of the member of staff were often missing from seclusion records. The use of physical restraint generally complied with legal requirements."[26]

An audit covering 2005 noted that 9 per cent of seclusions took place because of staff shortages. It also identified that the recording of the starting time of the episode of seclusion was unclear in some cases and some signatures were not legible. The average length of time of seclusion was higher in St Michael's Unit and in St Luke's Hospital than that in UK and French data.[27]

---

[23] Mental Health Commission, *Annual Report 2006 Including the Report of the Inspector of Mental Health Services 2006*, Book 2, p.99.

[24] Mental Health Commission, *Report of the Committee of Inquiry to Review Care and Treatment Practices in St. Michael's Unit, South Tipperary General Hospital, Clonmel and St. Luke's Hospital, Clonmel, Including the Quality and Planning of Care and the Use of Restraint and Seclusion and to Report to the Mental Health Commission* (2009).

[25] Mental Health Commission, *Report of the Committee of Inquiry to Review Care and Treatment Practices in St. Michael's Unit, South Tipperary General Hospital, Clonmel and St. Luke's Hospital, Clonmel, Including the Quality and Planning of Care and the Use of Restraint and Seclusion and to Report to the Mental Health Commission* (2009), p.6.

[26] Mental Health Commission, *Report of the Committee of Inquiry to Review Care and Treatment Practices in St. Michael's Unit, South Tipperary General Hospital, Clonmel and St. Luke's Hospital, Clonmel, Including the Quality and Planning of Care and the Use of Restraint and Seclusion and to Report to the Mental Health Commission* (2009), p.6.

[27] Mental Health Commission, *Report of the Committee of Inquiry to Review Care and Treatment Practices in St. Michael's Unit, South Tipperary General Hospital, Clonmel and St. Luke's Hospital, Clonmel, Including the Quality and Planning of Care and the Use of Restraint and Seclusion and to Report to the Mental Health Commission* (2009), p.104.

Many of the entries in one of the seclusion registers made no reference to the threat of serious harm. Many entries recorded no consideration of alternatives to seclusion and those that did gave cursory descriptions that did not indicate serious consideration of alternative interventions.[28] One example of this was an entry which stated that the resident had been secluded because he was, "interfering with other patients' property and pulling out bedclothes causing some to be frightened". The alternative intervention to seclusion was recorded as, "Attempted to persuade … to remain in bed but to no avail".[29]

The inquiry team stated that lack of activities for residents, staff shortages and inadequate ward layout made the use of seclusion more likely. The end of periods of seclusion was not recorded consistently on St Michael's Unit. There had been no audit of the need for the use of seclusion. Ward doors were locked in St Luke's Hospital without careful consideration of each resident's needs, and without full consideration of all alternatives, resulting in unnecessary restriction of freedom. There was a culture of risk avoidance, leading to blanket restrictions, rather than specific responses being based on individual risk assessments.[30]

12–08 In nursing homes for the elderly, restraints may also be used. The Leas Cross report in 2006[31] noted that an alarming number of the residents were noted as being nursed in Buxton chairs, and although there was a written policy on restraints, there was only evidence of one relatively cursory attempt at surveying restraints and consent.[32] The documentation as supplied gave no sense of the application of an informed policy on restraints which reflected the reality that restraints pose a very great hazard to frail older people in nursing homes.[33] Nursing homes with a high use of restraints were associated with low performance on a number of key quality-of-care indices.[34] There was almost no documentation on the use of bedails.[35]

---

[28] Mental Health Commission, *Report of the Committee of Inquiry to Review Care and Treatment Practices in St. Michael's Unit, South Tipperary General Hospital, Clonmel and St. Luke's Hospital, Clonmel, Including the Quality and Planning of Care and the Use of Restraint and Seclusion and to Report to the Mental Health Commission* (2009), p.105.

[29] Mental Health Commission, *Report of the Committee of Inquiry to Review Care and Treatment Practices in St. Michael's Unit, South Tipperary General Hospital, Clonmel and St. Luke's Hospital, Clonmel, Including the Quality and Planning of Care and the Use of Restraint and Seclusion and to Report to the Mental Health Commission* (2009), p.105.

[30] Mental Health Commission, *Report of the Committee of Inquiry to Review Care and Treatment Practices in St. Michael's Unit, South Tipperary General Hospital, Clonmel and St. Luke's Hospital, Clonmel, Including the Quality and Planning of Care and the Use of Restraint and Seclusion and to Report to the Mental Health Commission* (2009), pp.108–9.

[31] Health Service Executive (HSE), *Leas Cross Review* (2006).

[32] HSE, *Leas Cross Review* (2006), p.34. See also *Commission of Investigation (Leas Cross Nursing Home) Final Report* (2009).

[33] The Report cited O'Keeffe, S.T., "Down with Bedrails?" *Lancet* 2004; 363 (9406): 343–4.

[34] The Report cited Schnelle J.F., et al. "The Minimum Data Set Prevalence of Restraint Quality Indicator: Does It Reflect Differences in Care?' *Gerontologist* 2004; 44(2):245–55.

[35] *Leas Cross Review* (2006), p.34.

Constitutional and Human Rights

12–09 The unenumerated constitutional right to bodily integrity might be raised by a patient who was unduly secluded or restrained. This argument was raised concerning a prisoner in solitary confinement in 1976 in *State (C.) v Frawley.*[36] Mr C. was serving sentences in Mountjoy Prison for breaking and entering and robbery with violence. There was psychiatric evidence that he had a personality trait disturbance of a sociopathic type. Finlay P. said that at some periods at least, the disturbance of his personality had been so acute that it rendered him for some time of legally unsound mind. He had had an "almost unbelievably cruel" upbringing in an institution to which he was sent after the breakdown of his parents' marriage.[37] His condition manifested itself in an aggressive and continuous hostility to authority and to the features of society which represent authority. He had repeatedly climbed over the walls and on to the roofs of prisons and hospitals. He had also repeatedly swallowed metal objects, such as bed springs and handles of spoons, and had inserted wire and sharp objects into his body. He had been certified as insane on a number of occasions and had been transferred to the CMH, Dundrum, usually for short periods of a month or less. For most of the time he had been in prison, he had been kept in solitary confinement with the interruption of varying but short periods of exercise and association with other prisoners. Whilst out of solitary confinement he was usually kept handcuffed for some period.

Finlay P. said that when the Executive imprisons an individual in pursuance of a lawful warrant of a court, then it seemed to him to be a logical extension of the principle laid down in the *Ryan case*[38] on bodily integrity that it may not, without justification or necessity, expose the health of that person to risk or danger.[39] The restraints of which Mr C. most vehemently complained had been designed and implemented to eliminate or diminish, so far as was reasonably practical, the possibility of him harming himself by swallowing foreign bodies, by self injury or by injury arising from his climbing and escaping activities.[40]

It had also been argued that the court should have regard to art.3 of the European Convention on Human Rights (ECHR) regarding freedom from torture and inhuman and degrading treatment. Finlay P. dealt with this argument as follows:

> "If the unspecified personal rights guaranteed by Article 40 follow in part or in whole from the Christian and democratic nature of the State, it is surely

---

[36] [1976] I.R. 365.
[37] The brief reference to his cruel institutional upbringing was three decades before the Ryan Commission report–*Report of the Commission to Inquire into Child Abuse* (Chair: Mr Justice Sean Ryan) (2009).
[38] *Ryan v Attorney General* [1965] I.R. 294 (the water fluoridation case which established the right to bodily integrity as an unspecified constitutional right).
[39] [1976] I.R. 365 at 372.
[40] [1976] I.R. 365 at 372.

beyond argument that they include freedom from torture, and from inhuman or degrading treatment and punishment. Such a conclusion would appear to me to be inescapable even if there had never been a European Convention on Human Rights, or if Ireland had never been a party to it."[41]

Finlay P. said that the question of whether the conditions of detention in this case constituted a failure to protect Mr C. from torture or inhuman or degrading treatment or punishment had caused him trouble, but notwithstanding the "harshness of the privations" which Mr C. had undergone, he found that the conditions did not constitute such a failure.[42] He was satisfied that the purpose and intention of the restrictions and privations surrounding Mr C.'s detention were neither punitive nor malicious. He concluded:

> "I must construe the entire concept of torture, inhuman and degrading treatment and punishment as being not only evil in its consequences but evil in its purpose as well. It is most commonly inspired by revenge, retaliation, the creation of fear or improper interrogation. It is to me inconceivable to associate it with the necessary discharge of a duty to prevent self-injury or self-destruction."[43]

Bearing in mind that at the time the ECHR was only rarely referred to in the Irish courts, and that the jurisprudence of the Strasbourg Court was only beginning to develop at this stage, it is not surprising that Finlay P. interpreted torture and inhuman or degrading treatment or punishment in such a narrow fashion. However, the case established the principle that freedom from torture and inhuman or degrading treatment or punishment could be raised as part of an argument concerning bodily integrity.

12–10 The European case law on art.3 of the ECHR is now more well developed, although the court has tended not to find breaches of the article in cases concerning patients. The behaviour complained of must reach a minimum level of severity to engage art.3.[44] While intention to degrade is relevant to the threshold, it is not determinative; ill-treatment may breach art.3 even if there is no intent to do so.[45]

In *Herczegfalvy v Austria*,[46] discussed above at para.10–26, no breach of art.3 was found where the patient was force-fed, handcuffed to a bed and forcibly

---

[41]   [1976] I.R. 365 at 374.

[42]   [1976] I.R. 365 at 374.

[43]   [1976] I.R. 365 at 374.

[44]   Peter Bartlett, Oliver Lewis and Oliver Thorold, *Mental Disability and the European Convention on Human Rights* (Leiden: Martinus Nijhoff, 2006), p.77.

[45]   *Peers v Greece* (2001) 33 E.H.R.R. 51, para.74; *Price v U.K.* (2001) 34 E.H.R.R. 1285, para.30; Bartlett, Lewis & Thorold, *Mental Disability and the European Convention on Human Rights* (Leiden: Martinus Nijhoff, 2006), p.78.

[46]   (1992) 15 E.H.R.R. 437.

injected. The court stated, however, that the position of inferiority and power-lessness which is typical of patients confined in psychiatric hospitals calls for increased vigilance in reviewing whether the Convention has been complied with.[47] The court applied a test of "therapeutic necessity" regarding the methods which could be used to treat the patient "if necessary by force."[48]

12–11 It is possible to argue that seclusion engages art.5 as a breach of "residual liberty". In *Miller v The Queen*[49] the Canadian Supreme Court held that a prisoner unlawfully subject to solitary confinement suffered a breach of his residual liberty. This reasoning was held to be inapplicable to art.5 of the ECHR by the majority of the House of Lords in *R. (Munjaz) v Mersey Care N.H.S. Trust*.[50] Lord Bingham referred to the *Ashingdane case*[51] where it was held that art.5 cannot found a complaint directed to the category of institution within an appropriate system.[52] However, Lord Steyn delivered a strong dissent on this point and the concept of residual liberty may prove capable of further development.[53]

12–12 Article 8 concerning privacy rights has more potential for patients wishing to challenge seclusion and restraint. In *R. (Munjaz) v Mersey Care N.H.S. Trust*[54] a patient challenged the seclusion policy at Ashworth Hospital under various Convention articles, including art.8. The House of Lords focussed mainly on art.8. Lord Bingham said that it was obvious that seclusion, improperly used, may violate a patient's art.8 right in a serious and damaging way and may found a claim for relief.[55] It must then be considered whether it is justified under art.8(2). He said that seclusion under Ashworth's policy was plainly necessary for the prevention of disorder or crime, for the protection of health or morals, or for the protection of the rights and freedoms of others. Properly used, the seclusion would not be disproportionate because it would match the necessity giving rise to it.[56] Lord Hope cited Recommendation Rec (2004) 10 of the Committee of Ministers[57] to demonstrate that seclusion may be resorted to in appropriate circumstances.[58] Applying art.8 to the facts in the case, the House of Lords split 3:2 on the result, the majority reversing a unanimous

---

[47] (1992) 15 E.H.R.R. 437, para.82.
[48] (1992) 15 E.H.R.R. 437, para.82.
[49] (1985) 24 D.L.R. (4th) 9.
[50] [2005] U.K.H.L. 58; [2006] 2 A.C. 148.
[51] *Ashingdane v United Kingdom* (1985) 7 E.H.R.R. 528.
[52] [2006] 2 A.C. 148 at 192.
[53] Peter Bartlett & Ralph Sandland, *Mental Health Law: Policy and Practice*, 3rd edn (Oxford: Oxford University Press, 2007), p.343.
[54] [2005] U.K.H.L. 58; [2006] 2 A.C. 148.
[55] [2006] 2 A.C. 148 at 192.
[56] [2006] 2 A.C. 148 at 192.
[57] See below, para.12–14.
[58] [2006] 2 A.C. 148 at 210.

Court of Appeal decision and finding that, even though Ashworth's policy departed from the Code of Practice,[59] art.8(2) had not been violated because "the law" in art.8(2) was not limited to statutory enactment or to measures such as the Code having their base in statute. Bartlett and Sandland have argued that *Munjaz* means that neither domestic law nor the Convention offers any real protection to those subject to long-term seclusion, if that seclusion is in accordance with the policy of the hospital in question.[60] Foster noted that the decision was likely to alarm patients' representatives, who had relied upon the Code as a basis for challenging practices they regarded as oppressive.[61]

Interestingly, at Court of Appeal stage in the *Munjaz* case,[62] the case of another patient, S., was considered,[63] and it was found that his seclusion for 12 days in unsuitable conditions was unjustified and disproportionate.[64] For procedural reasons, the court declared that his seclusion was unlawful, without specifying which Convention articles had been breached.[65]

12–13 Principle 11 of the UN *Principles for the Protection of Persons with Mental Illness and the Improvement of Mental Health Care*[66] states that physical restraint or involuntary seclusion of a patient shall not be employed except in accordance with the officially approved procedures of the mental health facility and only when it is the only means available to prevent immediate or imminent harm to the patient and others. It also states that restraint or seclusion shall not be prolonged beyond the period which is strictly necessary for this purpose.

12–14 Article 27 of Committee of Ministers Rec (2004) 10[67] states:

1. Seclusion or restraint should only be used in appropriate facilities, and in compliance with the principle of least restriction, to prevent imminent harm to the person concerned or others, and in proportion to the risks entailed.
2. Such measures should only be used under medical supervision, and should be appropriately documented.

---

[59] Department of Health & Welsh Office, *Mental Health Act 1983 Code of Practice*, 3rd edn (London: HMSO, 1999)

[60] Peter Bartlett and Ralph Sandland, *Mental Health Law: Policy and Practice*, 3rd edn (Oxford: Oxford University Press, 2007), pp.343–4.

[61] Simon Foster, "One Code to Rule Them All, One Code to Bind Them: The Seclusion of Detained Patients", Case note on *R v Ashworth Hospital Authority, ex parte Munjaz* (2006) J. Mental Health L. 76 at 87.

[62] *R. (Munjaz) v Mersey Care N.H.S. Trust* [2003] E.W.C.A. Civ. 1036; [2004] Q.B. 395.

[63] Note that S's case concerned Airedale NHS Trust.

[64] [2004] Q.B. 395 at 438.

[65] See further commentary in Peter Bartlett and Ralph Sandland, *Mental Health Law: Policy and Practice*, 3rd edn (Oxford: Oxford University Press, 2007), p.344.

[66] United Nations, *Principles for the Protection of Persons with Mental Illness and the Improvement of Mental Health Care*, adopted by General Assembly resolution 46/119 of 17 December 1991.

3. In addition:
   (i) the person subject to seclusion or restraint should be regularly monitored;
   (ii) the reasons for, and duration of, such measures should be recorded in the person's medical records and in a register.
4. This Article does not apply to momentary restraint.

Restraint

Common Law Position

12–15 As a matter of general principle, the tort of battery occurs where a person directly and intentionally (or possibly negligently) causes some physical contact with the person of another without consent.[68] It appears that reasonable restraint of detained patients is permitted at common law. In *Pountney v Griffiths*[69] a nurse physically restrained a patient when the patient would not return to his ward at the end of a visit from relatives. The House of Lords stated that a hospital has powers of control over all mentally disordered patients, whether admitted voluntarily or compulsorily, though the nature and duration of the control varies with the category to which the patient belongs.[70] Lord Edmund-Davies agreed with the argument of counsel for the nurse that the English 1959 Act contained frequent provision for the detention of patients, or for their detention and treatment, for example, ss.25(1), 26(1), 43, 63(1)(b) and 65(3)(a). Where a person ordered to be kept in custody during Her Majesty's pleasure (such as the patient in this case) was directed by the Secretary of State to be removed to a special hospital, s.71(4) provided that the direction was to have the like effect as a hospital order made under s.60. Section 60 orders were made where the mental disorder of the named person "warrants the detention of the patient in a hospital for medical treatment" (s.60 (1)(a)(ii)), and that necessarily involved the exercise of control and discipline. Suitable arrangements for visits to patients by family and friends were an obvious part of a patient's treatment. Such visits inevitably involved the ushering of him back to his quarters when the permitted visiting time was ended.[71] The issue in the case was whether the leave of the High Court was required before the patient could initiate a criminal prosecution for assault against the nurse.[72] The House of Lords held that such leave was

---

[67] Committee of Ministers, Recommendation Rec (2004)10 of the Committee of Ministers to member states concerning the protection of the human rights and dignity of persons with mental disorder (Council of Europe, 2004).

[68] See generally Eoin Quill, *Torts in Ireland*, 2nd edn (Dublin, Gill and Macmillan, 2004), pp.181–4.

[69] [1976] A.C. 314.

[70] [1976] A.C. 314 at 334 (Lord Edmund-Davies).

[71] [1976] A.C. 314 at 335 (Lord Edmund-Davies).

[72] The English legislation requiring leave before proceedings are brought applies both to criminal and civil proceedings, whereas the Irish legislation only applies to civil proceedings. See further paras 2–51 to 2–57 above.

required, as the nurse was purportedly acting in pursuance of the Act when he restrained the patient.[73]

12–16 Reasonable restraint may also be justified in situations where a court orders medical treatment for a patient who lacks capacity. In *Trust A and Trust B v H. (An Adult Patient)*[74] Sir Mark Potter P. authorised a hysterectomy of a detained patient who lacked capacity and had an ovarian cyst. He stated that, in the case of a patient who lacks capacity to consent, it is lawful to impose treatment despite the absence of consent and even to overcome non-co-operation of a resisting patient by sedation and a moderate and reasonable use of restraint in order to achieve it, if the treatment is in the patient's best interests. The lawfulness of such restraint had to be carefully considered when assessing the balance of benefit and disadvantage in the giving of the proposed medical treatment and where the best interest of the patient truly lies, and a patient such as H. had the right not to be subjected to degrading treatment under art.3 of the ECHR.[75]

12–17 As regards voluntary patients, various common law justifications may be relied upon to justify restraint, such as self-defence (which includes defence of others), preventing the patient harming themselves, or safety.[76] However, the exact scope of each of these justifications is debatable.

12–18 In some cases, a criminal prosecution might be brought for assault, now governed by the Non-Fatal Offences Against the Person Act 1997, in which case the accused may raise a defence of self-defence, again including defence of others. There have been two reports of criminal prosecutions for assaults on patients in recent years, one in a mental hospital[77] and one in a general hospital.[78]

The 1945 and 2001 Acts

12–19 The Mental Treatment Act 1945 stated that no person could apply mechanical means of bodily restraint to a person of unsound mind unless the restraint was necessary for the purposes of medical or surgical treatment or to

---

[73]   The patient alleged that the nurse had punched him on the shoulder, but the nurse claimed that he had only lightly brushed against him.

[74]   [2006] E.W.H.C. 1230 (Fam.).

[75]   [2006] E.W.H.C. 1230 (Fam.), para.27.

[76]   Brenda Hoggett, *Mental Health Law*, 4th edn (London: Sweet & Maxwell, 1996), pp.140–3; Peter Bartlett and Ralph Sandland, *Mental Health Law: Policy and Practice*, 3rd edn (Oxford: Oxford University Press, 2007), p.339.

[77]   "Nurse Jailed for Attack on Patient Who Later Died", *Irish Times*, June 24, 2006; "Jailed Ex-Nurse Wins Appeal", *Irish Independent*, March 28, 2007. See also "Beating by Care Officer Was Not 'Direct' Cause of Man's Death", *Irish Independent*, October 4, 2007.

[78]   Eithne Donnellan and Sonya McLean, "'Sentence Later for Nurse Who Poisoned Patient", *Irish*

prevent the person of unsound mind injuring themselves or others.[79] Strictly speaking, this applied only to *mechanical* restraint of "persons of unsound mind".[80] Where any person applied mechanical means of bodily restraint to a person of unsound mind, they were required to proceed in accordance with regulations made by the Minister.[81] Where mechanical means of bodily restraint were applied in a mental institution to a patient, the Act required that full particulars of the application be entered forthwith in a book to be kept for that purpose.[82] This latter requirement appeared to apply to all patients, not only "persons of unsound mind". The relevant Regulations were made in 1961.[83] These Regulations were obviously extremely out-dated, e.g. they included a provision that the regulations on restraint did not apply to "any restraint which is necessary for the sole purpose of giving electrical or other special treatment to a patient, or for the purpose of feeding a patient."[84]

12–20 Section 69(1) of the Mental Health Act 2001 states that a person shall not apply mechanical means of bodily restraint to a patient unless such restraint is determined, in accordance with rules made by the Commission under s.69(2), to be necessary for the purposes of treatment or to prevent the patient from injuring themselves or others and unless the restraint complies with such rules. For the purposes of the section, "patient" includes detained and voluntary patients.[85] A person who contravenes this section or a rule made under it shall be guilty of an offence.[86]

As with the 1945 Act, this section is limited to mechanical restraint. As a result, while the Commission has made *rules* governing mechanical restraint,[87] it has issued a *code of practice* regarding physical (non-mechanical) restraint.[88] Version 2 of the rules and code of practice apply from January 1, 2010.

Times, December 5, 2006; "Suspended Term for Assaults on Patients", *Irish Times*, December 19, 2006.

[79] Mental Treatment Act 1945, s.263(1).

[80] In recent years, there were far fewer "persons of unsound mind" detained under the 1945 Act than temporary patients.

[81] Mental Treatment Act 1945, s.263(2).

[82] Mental Treatment Act 1945, s.264.

[83] Mental Treatment Regulations 1961, S.I. No. 261 of 1961.

[84] Mental Treatment Regulations 1961, S.I. No. 261 of 1961, Reg.6(4)(e)(iv).

[85] Mental Health Act 2001, s.69(3). This includes a child detained under s.25.

[86] Mental Health Act 2001, s.69(2).

[87] Mental Health Commission, *Rules Governing the Use of Seclusion and Mechanical Means of Bodily Restraint* (version 2, 2009). See also *Review of Rules Governing the use of Seclusion and Mechanical Means of Bodily Restraint and Review of Code of Practice on the Use of Physical Restraint in Approved Centres* (Mental Health Commission, 2008).

[88] Mental Health Commission, *Code of Practice on the Use of Physical Restraint in Approved Centres* (version 2, 2009).

Rules on Mechanical Restraint

12–21 For the purposes of the Rules, mechanical means of bodily restraint is defined as "the use of devices or bodily garments for the purpose of preventing or limiting the free movement of a patient's body".[89] "Device" is defined as "an item/object made or adapted for the purpose of restraining a patient's movement or access to his/her body".[90] It does not include the use of cot sides or bed rails, which are not regarded as a use of mechanical means of bodily restraint. Restraint is therefore defined in a functional manner, focussing on the function of the devices rather than the type of device. It is unclear whether medication injected to restrain a patient would come within this definition, although it is unlikely.

The Rules state that mechanical means of bodily restraint must only be used either when a patient poses an immediate threat of serious harm to themselves or others or on an ongoing basis for enduring risk of harm to self or others.[91] As regards "immediate threat", etc., reference may be made to the judgment of O'Neill J. in *M.R. v Byrne and Flynn*,[92] discussed above at paras 3–13 to 3–16.

12–22 The use of mechanical means of bodily restraint for immediate threat of serious harm may be initiated by registered medical practitioners and/or registered nurses.[93] Where the use of mechanical means of bodily restraint has been initiated by a registered nurse, there must be a medical review within four hours.[94]

The mechanical means of bodily restraint register must also be completed.[95]

The patient's next of kin or representative[96] must be notified, with the patient's consent, of the mechanical restraint, as soon as practicable. If the patient lacks capacity and cannot consent, the notification should still occur.[97] A child's parent or guardian must be notified as soon as possible.[98]

[89] *Rules Governing the Use of Seclusion and Mechanical Means of Bodily Restraint*, para.2.3.1.
[90] *Rules Governing the Use of Seclusion and Mechanical Means of Bodily Restraint*, p.10.
[91] *Rules Governing the Use of Seclusion and Mechanical Means of Bodily Restraint*, Pts 4 and 5.
[92] [2007] I.E.H.C. 73; [2007] 3 I.R. 211.
[93] *Rules Governing the Use of Seclusion and Mechanical Means of Bodily Restraint*, para.14.1.
[94] *Rules Governing the Use of Seclusion and Mechanical Means of Bodily Restraint*, para.14.3.
[95] *Rules Governing the Use of Seclusion and Mechanical Means of Bodily Restraint*, paras 14.3–14.5.
[96] *Rules Governing the Use of Seclusion and Mechanical Means of Bodily Restraint*, p.12: "Representative" means a person of the patient's choosing or a legal professional or guardian *ad litem* appointed by the patient, statutory organisation or court to represent the best interests of the patient.
[97] *Rules Governing the Use of Seclusion and Mechanical Means of Bodily Restraint*, para.14.7.
[98] *Rules Governing the Use of Seclusion and Mechanical Means of Bodily Restraint*, para.20.1.

12–23 Each approved centre must have a written policy in relation to the use of mechanical means of bodily restraint, including the provision of information to the patient.[99] Approved centres must also have a policy and procedures for training staff in relation to mechanical means of bodily restraint.[100]

The application of mechanical means of bodily restraint on the patient for enduring risk of harm to self or others must be ordered by a registered medical practitioner under the supervision of the consultant psychiatrist responsible for the care and treatment of the patient or the duty consultant psychiatrist acting on their behalf.[101]

Code of Practice on Physical Restraint

12–24 As explained above, as s.69 only applies to mechanical restraint, the Commission does not have the statutory power to make rules regarding non-mechanical restraint. It has therefore issued a code of practice on physical (non-mechanical) restraint.[102] As noted in the Code, the Act does not impose a legal duty on persons working in the mental health services to comply with codes of practice, but best practice requires that they be followed to ensure the Act is implemented consistently by persons working in the mental health services. A failure to implement or follow the Code could be referred to during the course of legal proceedings.[103]

For the purpose of the Code, physical restraint is defined as "the use of physical force (by one or more persons) for the purpose of preventing the free movement of a resident's body when he or she poses an immediate threat of serious harm to self or others".[104] This is a functional definition; it focuses on the function of the physical force rather than the type of force used. It does not seem to include the use of drugs to prevent free movement.

The code provides that physical restraint should only be used in the best interests of the resident and only when a resident poses an immediate threat of serious harm to themselves or others and all alternative interventions to manage the resident's unsafe behaviour have been considered.[105]

---

[99] *Rules Governing the Use of Seclusion and Mechanical Means of Bodily Restraint*, para.18.2.

[100] *Rules Governing the Use of Seclusion and Mechanical Means of Bodily Restraint*, para.19.1.

[101] *Rules Governing the Use of Seclusion and Mechanical Means of Bodily Restraint*, paras 21.1 to 21.5.

[102] Mental Health Commission, *Code of Practice on the Use of Physical Restraint in Approved Centres* (version 2, 2009).

[103] Mental Health Commission, *Code of Practice on the Use of Physical Restraint in Approved Centres* (2009), para.2.2.

[104] Mental Health Commission, *Code of Practice on the Use of Physical Restraint in Approved Centres* (2009), para.4.1.

[105] Mental Health Commission, *Code of Practice on the Use of Physical Restraint in Approved Centres* (2009), paras 1.1–1.2.

12–25 The use of physical restraint may be initiated by registered medical practitioners, registered nurses or other members of the care team.[106] An order for physical restraint shall last a maximum of 30 minutes.[107]

As soon as is practicable, and *no later than three hours* after the episode of physical restraint, the medical practitioner should examine the resident and complete the relevant section of the Clinical Practice Form for Physical Restraint. The Clinical Practice Form for Physical Restraint should also be signed by the consultant psychiatrist responsible for the care and treatment of the resident or the duty consultant psychiatrist as soon as is practicable and in any event *within 24 hours*.[108]

Neck holds and the application of heavy weight to the resident's chest or back should be avoided.[109] Limited use of physical restraint involving the resident in the "prone", face-down position is permitted in exceptional circumstances by staff who have received appropriate training. A record of the use of prone restraint should be entered into the resident's clinical file.[110]

Each approved centre should have a written policy in relation to the use of physical restraint, including the provision of information to the resident.[111] Approved centres should also have a policy and procedures for training staff in relation to physical restraint.[112]

Seclusion

12–26 The 1945 Act did not contain a specific reference to seclusion, other than requiring the Inspector to report on seclusion in each institution.[113] However, the 1961 Regulations contained requirements concerning seclusion.[114] The Regulations did not apply to locking of doors "during the hours fixed generally for the patients in the institution to retire for sleep".[115]

Section 69(1) of the Mental Health Act 2001 states that a person shall not place a patient in seclusion unless such seclusion is determined, in accordance

[106] Mental Health Commission, *Code of Practice on the Use of Physical Restraint in Approved Centres* (2009), para.5.1.
[107] *Code of Practice on the Use of Physical Restraint in Approved Centres* (2009), para.5.5.
[108] Mental Health Commission, *Code of Practice on the Use of Physical Restraint in Approved Centres*, para.5.7.
[109] Mental Health Commission, *Code of Practice on the Use of Physical Restraint in Approved Centres*, para.6.6.
[110] Mental Health Commission, *Code of Practice on the Use of Physical Restraint in Approved Centres*, para.6.7.
[111] Mental Health Commission, *Code of Practice on the Use of Physical Restraint in Approved Centres*, para.9.2.
[112] Mental Health Commission, *Code of Practice on the Use of Physical Restraint in Approved Centres*, para.10.1.
[113] Mental Treatment Act 1945, s.237 as amended by Mental Treatment Act 1961, s.33.
[114] Mental Treatment Regulations 1961, S.I. No. 261 of 1961, Reg.6.
[115] Mental Treatment Regulations 1961, S.I. No. 261 of 1961, Reg.6(1)(a).

with rules made by the Commission under s.69(2), to be necessary for the purposes of treatment or to prevent the patient from injuring themselves or others and unless the seclusion complies with such rules. For the purposes of the section, "patient" includes detained and voluntary patients.[116] A person who contravenes this section or a rule made under it shall be guilty of an offence.[117]

As the Irish Act elevates regulation of seclusion to the status of rules rather than a code of practice, much of the debate about departure from the English code of practice in the *Munjaz* case, discussed above at paras 12–11 to 12–12, does not apply directly here. In strict legal terms, there is no facility to depart from the statutory rules in Ireland.

12–27 The rules[118] define seclusion as "the placing or leaving of a person in any room alone, at any time, day or night, with the exit door locked or fastened or held in such a way as to prevent the person from leaving."[119] However, the locking of a patient in their bedroom at night in the National Forensic Service (CMH) as part of their individual risk assessment and management plan for the purposes of enhanced security, does not constitute seclusion under the rules.[120]

Seclusion must only be used in the best interest of the patient and only when a patient poses an immediate threat of serious harm to themselves or others.[121] The Commission appears to have relied upon UN Principle 11, quoted above at para.12–13, to provide a narrower scope for seclusion than in the Act. Rec (2004) 10 of the Committee of Ministers[122] provides a similarly narrow scope for seclusion. As regards "immediate threat", etc. reference may be made to the judgment of O'Neill J. in *M.R. v Byrne and Flynn*,[123] discussed above at paras 3–13 to 3–16.

Seclusion may be initiated by registered medical practitioners and/or registered nurses, and must be recorded in the seclusion register. There must be a medical review within four hours, if the seclusion was initiated by a nurse.[124]

12–28 A seclusion order shall remain in force for a maximum period of *8 hours* from the commencement of the seclusion episode.[125] This period may be

---

[116] Mental Health Act 2001, s.69(3). This includes a child detained under s.25.

[117] Mental Health Act 2001, s.69(2).

[118] Mental Health Commission, *Rules Governing the Use of Seclusion and Mechanical Means of Bodily Restraint* (version 2, 2009). These rules apply from January 1, 2010.

[119] Mental Health Commission, *Rules Governing the Use of Seclusion and Mechanical Means of Bodily Restraint* (2009), para.2.11.

[120] Mental Health Commission, *Rules Governing the Use of Seclusion and Mechanical Means of Bodily Restraint* (2009), para.2.2.1.

[121] Mental Health Commission, *Rules Governing the Use of Seclusion and Mechanical Means of Bodily Restraint* (2009), para.1.1.

[122] See above, para.12–14.

[123] [2007] I.E.H.C. 73; [2007] 3 I.R. 211.

[124] Mental Health Commission, *Rules Governing the Use of Seclusion and Mechanical Means of Bodily Restraint* (version 2, 2009), paras 3.1 to 3.5.

[125] Mental Health Commission, *Rules Governing the Use of Seclusion and Mechanical Mean of Bodily Restraint* (2009), para.3.3.

extended by an order made by the registered medical practitioner under the supervision of the consultant psychiatrist responsible for the care and treatment of the patient or duty consultant psychiatrist following an examination, for a further period not exceeding eight hours to a maximum of two renewals (24 hours) of continuous seclusion.[126]

The patient's next of kin or representative[127] must be notified, with the patient's consent, of the seclusion, as soon as practicable. If the patient lacks capacity and cannot consent, the notification should still occur.[128] A child's parent or guardian must be notified as soon as possible.[129]

12–29 If a patient's seclusion order is to be renewed after 24 hours' continuous seclusion, the consultant psychiatrist responsible for the care and treatment of the patient or the duty consultant psychiatrist must examine the patient.[130] If a decision is made by the consultant psychiatrist responsible for the care and treatment of the patient concerned, or the duty consultant psychiatrist acting on their behalf, to continue to seclude a patient for a total period exceeding 72 hours, the Inspector of Mental Health Services must be notified in writing.[131]

Bodily searches must respect the right of the patient to dignity, bodily integrity and privacy.[132] Seclusion facilities must not be used as bedrooms.[133] There are special requirements regarding continuous observation, nursing reviews and medical reviews during seclusion.[134] Use of CCTV is regulated, e.g. CCTV must be incapable of recording and be incapable of storing a patient's image on a tape, disc, hard drive or in any other form.[135] Each approved centre must have a written policy in relation to the use of seclusion, including the

---

[126] Mental Health Commission, *Rules Governing the Use of Seclusion and Mechanical Mean of Bodily Restraint* (2009), para.6.1.

[127] Mental Health Commission, *Rules Governing the Use of Seclusion and Mechanical Mean of Bodily Restraint* (2009), p.12: "Representative" means a person of the patient's choosing or a legal professional or guardian *ad litem* appointed by the patient, statutory organisation or court to represent the best interests of the patient.

[128] Mental Health Commission, *Rules Governing the Use of Seclusion and Mechanical Mean of Bodily Restraint* (2009), para.3.7.

[129] Mental Health Commission, *Rules Governing the Use of Seclusion and Mechanical Mean of Bodily Restraint* (2009), para.13.1.

[130] Mental Health Commission, *Rules Governing the Use of Seclusion and Mechanical Mean of Bodily Restraint* (2009), para.6.2.

[131] Mental Health Commission, *Rules Governing the Use of Seclusion and Mechanical Mean of Bodily Restraint* (2009), para.6.3.

[132] Mental Health Commission, *Rules Governing the Use of Seclusion and Mechanical Mean of Bodily Restraint* (2009), para.4.4.

[133] Mental Health Commission, *Rules Governing the Use of Seclusion and Mechanical Mean of Bodily Restraint* (2009), para.8.4.

[134] Mental Health Commission, *Rules Governing the Use of Seclusion and Mechanical Mean of Bodily Restraint* (2009), para.5.1.

[135] Mental Health Commission, *Rules Governing the Use of Seclusion and Mechanical Mean of Bodily Restraint* (2009), para.12.2.

provision of information to the patient.[136] Approved centres must also have a policy and procedures for training staff in relation to seclusion.[137]

APPROVED CENTRES

12–30 While much of the focus of mental health law is on whether a person's involuntary admission is justified, the law can also play a role in regulating conditions in which patients, both voluntary and involuntary, are treated. As has been noted earlier,[138] Mental Health Tribunals (MHTs) do not review conditions of detention. The 1945 Act contained rudimentary provisions for inspection of mental hospitals, but these were inadequate for various reasons.[139] For example, the Inspector was not independent of the Department of Health and did not have any power to recommend that an institution be closed.[140]

12–31 The 2001 Act has radically changed the nature of regulation of conditions of treatment by establishing an independent Commission and Inspectorate,[141] and permitting the Commission to attach conditions to the registration of approved centres, or even to remove a centre from the register. However, the Regulations regarding standards in approved centres are made by the Minister, after consultation with the Commission.

The Register of Approved Centres

12–32 Registration of approved centres is dealt with in Pt 5 of the Mental Health Act 2001, ss.62-68. It is a criminal offence under s.63 to "carry on a centre" unless the centre is registered and a centre which is so registered is referred to as an "approved centre".[142] A "centre" means a hospital or other in-patient facility for the care and treatment of persons suffering from mental illness or mental disorder.[143] It applies both to voluntary and involuntary

---

[136] Mental Health Commission, *Rules Governing the Use of Seclusion and Mechanical Mean of Bodily Restraint* (2009), para.10.2.
[137] Mental Health Commission, *Rules Governing the Use of Seclusion and Mechanical Mean of Bodily Restraint* (2009), para.11.1.
[138] See above, Chapter 9.
[139] See above, para.2–75.
[140] Note that the 1945 Act included a register of private institutions and a register of private charitable institutions and the Minister could remove an institution from the relevant register (s.121 and s.143). There were less stringent requirements concerning other "mental institutions", chiefly district mental hospitals or other institutions maintained by Health Boards (referred to as mental hospital authorities in the Act). While there was a register of "approved institutions" (s.158) there was no provision for removal of an institution from the register.
[141] See paras 2–67 to 2–78 above.
[142] Mental Health Act 2001, s.63.
[143] Mental Health Act 2001, s.62.

treatment. It is clear that this covers psychiatric hospitals and psychiatric wards in general hospitals. But the question of how far this definition extends could be quite difficult in some situations. The centre must be a "hospital or in-patient facility", which narrows the scope of the definition, but while "mental disorder" is given a narrow definition in s.3,[144] "mental illness" is defined relatively broadly (see para.3–04 above). It is at least possible that there are some patients with mental illness being cared for and treated on a voluntary basis in centres which are not approved centres. Questions arise as to whether the mix of patients in a centre has an effect on whether it should be on the register. If, for example, a centre had 50 patients with physical illnesses and 10 patients with mental illness, should it then be on the register? Matters may also be further complicated by patients who have a dual diagnosis of an intellectual disability and a mental illness.

Some assistance is provided by the fact that elsewhere in the Act the term "mental health services" is used frequently, and this is limited to care and treatment "under the clinical direction of a consultant psychiatrist".[145] For example, the functions of the Commission concern "the delivery of mental health services".[146] However, as a matter of statutory interpretation, s.63 is not confined to "mental health services". This is probably to prevent a situation where a centre which is quite obviously primarily meant to treat those with mental disorders could avoid s.63 by not appointing a psychiatrist as clinical director, but nevertheless the net result is that the definition of "centre" contains potential pitfalls for the unwary. Note also that s.71 states that the governing body of each approved centre must appoint in writing a consultant psychiatrist to be the clinical director of the centre.

12–33 Presumably, prosecutions are unlikely in situations where a facility is technically in breach of the Act but is unaware of its breach.[147] If the Commission became aware of such a centre, it could request it to apply for registration to rectify the matter. The Commission has noted that the definition of "centre" is broad and therefore caution should be exercised when interpreting the term "approved centre", as the term does not solely refer to centres that are admission units.[148] To maintain awareness of the legal requirement for facilities that meet the definition of "centre" to register with the Commission, advertisements were placed in three national newspapers in March and September 2008.[149]

---

[144]   See Chapter 3 above.
[145]   Mental Health Act 2001, s.2(1).
[146]   Mental Health Act 2001, s.33(1).
[147]   Note that the Mental Health Commission may prosecute offences summarily—s.74(1) of 2001 Act.
[148]   Mental Health Commission, *Annual Report 2008 Including the Report of the Inspector of Mental Health Services 2008*, Book 1, p.24.
[149]   Mental Health Commission, *Annual Report 2008*, Book 1, p.24.
[150]   Mental Health Act 2001, s.67. This expressly made subject to s.12 (power of a Garda to take

12–34 It is also an offence under s.67 to detain a person suffering from a mental disorder in any place other than an approved centre.[150] In other words, involuntary admissions under the Act may only be made to approved centres. In 2007 47 centres of the 61 registered were actively involved in admitting patients subject to Involuntary Admission Orders.[151] If it were argued that s.67 is breached where a prisoner has a mental disorder and is being kept in prison rather than treated in an approved centre, the response would probably be that the prisoner is held under criminal justice legislation and this authorises their detention in prison.

12–35 The Mental Health Commission maintains the register of approved centres and persons may apply for registration of approved centres.[152] The period of a registration is three years. Conditions may be attached to a registration, e.g. requiring refurbishment or maintenance, requiring review of policies and procedures relating to patients, or specifying the minimum number of staff to be employed in the centre.[153] The Commission must notify the proprietor in advance of attaching conditions to a registration, and give the proprietor the opportunity of making representations.[154] Following the Tipperary Inquiry report, the Mental Health Commission proposed to attach conditions to the continued operation of the two approved centres requiring the Health Service Executive (HSE) to produce a plan with precise timescales to address breaches in Regulations, Rules and Codes of Practice found by the Inspectorate of Mental Health Services during its inspection. The Commission stated it would require a quarterly report on the achievement of targets set in the plan.[155]

The Commission may remove a centre from the register if the premises do not comply with the Approved Centre Regulations, the carrying on of the centre is not in compliance with the Regulations, the proprietor has been convicted of an offence under Pt 5, the proprietor has furnished false or misleading information or the proprietor has, not more than one year beforehand, contravened a condition of a conditional registration.[156] Again, there is provision for advance notice and an opportunity to make representations.[157]

Appeals against decisions concerning registration may be brought to the District Court within 21 days.[158] The court may either confirm or vary the Commission's decision.

---

a person believed to be suffering from a mental disorder into custody) and s.22 (transfer of patient to hospital, e.g. transfer of a patient to a surgical ward for surgery).

[151] Mental Health Commission, *Report on the Operation of Part 2 of the Mental Health Act 2001* (2008), p.33.
[152] Mental Health Act 2001, s.64.
[153] Mental Health Act 2001, s.64(6).
[154] Mental Health Act 2001, s.64(11).
[155] Mental Health Commission press release dated April 3, 2009.
[156] Section 64(5).
[157] Section 64(11).
[158] Section 65.

12–36 The transitional provisions of the Act originally stated that during the period of three years from the commencement of Part 2 (i.e. three years from November 1, 2006), a hospital or other in-patient facility for the care and treatment of persons with a mental disorder which, immediately before such commencement, was providing such care and treatment would be deemed to be an approved centre.[159] During this period, certain provisions of the 1945 Act would apply to some of these centres.[160] The section specifically allowed for a shorter period to be prescribed, and this occurred by means of Regulations made in 2008[161] which shortened the period to one of one year and four months, which expired on March 1, 2008. The effect of this was that all "deemed" approved centres had to apply for registration as approved centres by March 1, 2008.

12–37 There are currently 65 centres on the register of approved centres.[162] 40 of these had originally been deemed approved under the transitional provisions.[163] Fifteen of them are Victorian (and older) buildings.[164] The "registered proprietor" may either be a named person or a body corporate. If it is a body corporate, the Act provides that in some circumstances a director, manager, secretary or other officer may, as well as the body corporate, be guilty of an offence.[165] The Tipperary Inquiry stated that at the time of the inquiry the Local Health Manager was the registered proprietor, but in February 2008 the HSE indicated it would be the registered proprietor.[166] It was suggested to the 2007 review of operation of the Act that the registered proprietor should be authorised to direct the clinical director and other members of the management of an approved centre as appropriate to adhere to regulations prescribed by the Minister and rules specified by the Commission. The Minister considered this proposal and believed that providing for such powers under the Act was unnecessary. The report stated that it is the responsibility of all service providers to ensure that all members of staff of the approved centres are aware of and adhere to their obligations and responsibilities arising from the Act.[167]

---

[159] Section 72(6).
[160] Section 72(7)–(9).
[161] Mental Health Act 2001 (Period Prescribed Under Section 72(6)) Regulations 2008, S.I. 44 of 2008.
[162] A list of centres on the register may be found on the Commission's website at *http://www.mhcirl.ie.* [Accessed September 27, 2009]. The actual register must be available for public inspection—s.64(2)(b).
[163] Mental Health Commission, *Annual Report 2008 Including the Report of the Inspector of Mental Health Services 2008*, Book 1, p.24.
[164] Mental Health Commission, *Annual Report 2008*, Book 1, p.60.
[165] Mental Health Act 2001, s.74(3) and (4).
[166] Mental Health Commission, *Report of the Committee of Inquiry to Review Care and Treatment Practices in St. Michael's Unit, South Tipperary General Hospital, Clonmel and St. Luke's Hospital, Clonmel, Including the Quality and Planning of Care and the Use of Restraint and Seclusion and to Report to the Mental Health Commission* (2009), p.19.
[167] Department of Health and Children, *Review of the Operation of the Mental Health Act 2001: Findings and Conclusions* (2007), p.30.

Approved centre status may either apply to an entire hospital (e.g. St Ita's Hospital or St Otteran's Hospital) or to a clinic or unit within a hospital (e.g. St Michael's Unit in the Mercy Hospital or the Lakeview Unit in Naas General Hospital). If patients subject to involuntary Admission Orders were accommodated outside the clinic or unit which has approved centre status, an offence would occur.[168] Similarly, it would be an offence to "carry on a centre" (i.e. an in-patient facility for care and treatment of persons suffering from mental illness or mental disorder) outside the approved centre.[169] If a detained patient is in the approved centre but requires transfer to another place for treatment, then the procedure in s.22 must be followed. The transfer must be arranged by the clinical director of the approved centre.[170]

The CMH is one of the approved centres, which means that it is regulated both under the 2001 Act and the Criminal Law (Insanity) Act 2006, under which it is a "designated centre".

The Approved Centre Regulations

12–38 The Approved Centre Regulations are made by the Minister, after consultation with the Commission.[171] The Act lists topics which may be covered in the Regulations, including accommodation, care and welfare of residents, record-keeping, individual care plans, cleaning and cleanliness, etc.[172] It is an offence for a registered proprietor or any person to fail or refuse to comply with the regulations.[173] It is also an offence to obstruct the Inspector in performance of functions under the regulations, or to fail to comply with a requirement of the Inspector under the regulations.[174] The Commission may also apply to have a person convicted of non-compliance disqualified from carrying on an approved centre.[175]

It is notable that the Regulations are made by the Minister rather than the Commission. This contrasts with other powers in the Act, e.g. the power to make regulations concerning electro-convulsive therapy (ECT), where the Commission makes the regulations on its own.[176] However, the Act and Regulations both state that the Regulations will be enforced by the Commission.[177]

---

[168] See Mental Health Act 2001, s.67.
[169] See Mental Health Act 2001, s.63.
[170] See further paras 4–105 to 4–108 above.
[171] Mental Health Act 2001, s.66(1).
[172] Mental Health Act 2001, s.66(2).
[173] Mental Health Act 2001, s.66(3).
[174] Mental Health Act 2001, s.66(5).
[175] Mental Health Act 2001, s.66(4).
[176] Mental Health Act 2001, s.59(2).
[177] Mental Health Act 2001, s.66(2)(i) and Mental Health Act 2001 (Approved Centres) Regulations 2006, S.I. No. 551 of 2006, Reg.35.

12–39 The Approved Centre Regulations were made in 2006[178] and cover areas such as the following: Food, Clothing, Personal Property, Recreation, Visits, Communication, Searches, Care of Dying, Individual Care Plans, Therapeutic Services, Children's Education, Transfers, General Health, Information, Privacy, Premises, Medicines, Health and Safety, CCTV, Staffing, Records, Tribunals, Complaints and Insurance. For example, the registered proprietor must ensure that each resident has an individual care plan.[179] An "individual care plan" means a documented set of goals developed, regularly reviewed and updated by the resident's multi-disciplinary team, so far as practicable in consultation with each resident. The individual care plan must specify the treatment and care required, which shall be in accordance with best practice; must identify necessary resources; and must specify appropriate goals for the resident. For a resident who is a child, their individual care plan must include education requirements. The individual care plan must be recorded in the one composite set of documentation.[180]

12–40 There are ongoing issues of non-compliance with the regulations, even though it is an offence not to comply. In the 2007 Annual Report, approved centres provided self-assessments of compliance with the Regulations. For example, as regards Individual Care Plans, 82.8 per cent of centres reported that they complied with the regulations, 15.5 per cent said that they partially complied and 1.7 per cent either replied "not applicable" or did not respond to this question. Moreover, 48.3 per cent complied fully with the standards concerning visits and 55.2 per cent complied fully with the standards regarding premises.[181] The report stated that caution should be exerted when interpreting the self-assessment results. In reviewing the self-assessment forms, it became apparent that although some centres indicated "fully in compliance" for a given regulation, the evidence provided on how the centre demonstrated compliance suggested only partial compliance or non-compliance with that regulation.[182] The Inspectorate found only an 18 per cent compliance rate regarding individual care plans in 2007.[183]

The 2008 report stated that when viewed as a whole, compliance with the regulations was disappointing. The main areas of poor compliance related to

---

[178] Mental Health Act 2001 (Approved Centres) Regulations 2006, S.I. No. 551 of 2006.

[179] Mental Health Act 2001 (Approved Centres) Regulations 2006, S.I. No. 551 of 2006, Reg.15.

[180] Mental Health Act 2001 (Approved Centres) Regulations 2006, S.I. No. 551 of 2006, Reg.2.

[181] Mental Health Commission, *Annual Report 2007 Including the Report of the Inspector of Mental Health Services 2007*, Book 1, p.25. Note these are sample figures from a table which covers 34 different standards.

[182] Mental Health Commission, *Annual Report 2007 Including the Report of the Inspector of Mental Health Services 2007*, Book 1, p.26.

[183] This figure concerning 2007 is contained in Mental Health Commission, *Annual Report 2008*, Book 1, p.25.

buildings/premises, staffing and individual care plans.[184] The Inspectorate commented as follows:

> "We concluded that, similar to national attitudes in previous years to drink-driving legislation, a cultural shift had not yet taken place among the clinicians. Consultants, in particular, had a tendency to view the documentary requirements as "mere technicalities" in many cases. Some consultants failed to understand the legal nature of the requirements, while others were unaware of the basis of these requirements in the State's human rights commitments. A number failed to view the matter from the perspective of the service users, who have a right to involvement in their treatment and to an integrated treatment plan. In many cases, it was a matter of 'we've always done it this way'."[185]

12–41 The Inspectorate also made some other notable comments in the 2008 report. It stated that the Victorian (and older) asylums comprised 15 of the 63 approved centres inspected. Despite valiant efforts by local staff, these buildings were inadequate for the purpose of providing treatment to vulnerable individuals with serious mental illness according to human rights standards.[186] There was an uneven distribution of resources throughout the country. Territoriality or "wearing the county jersey" appeared to take precedence over genuine needs in terms of acquisition of resources, funding and staffing. The Inspectorate found examples of several inequitable discrepancies whose origins lay in the current or former existence of an asylum in the locality with associated staffing resources. It noted wide variations in the use of ECT as well as the use of seclusion and restraint and prescribing patterns. Variations appeared to be more a feature of local custom and preference than of evidence-based practice.[187]

12–42 The Commission's general approach to non-compliance with the Regulations was explained by the Chief Executive in the 2007 report. She stated that current evidence on the impact of interventions designed to improve performance and quality of care favoured the adoption of a responsive regulatory approach. Such an approach, responding to the context, conduct and culture of those regulated, provides for a graduated response from the regulator, ranging from persuasion and use of rewards to licence refusal or revocation. She said that the Mental Health Commission was monitoring the implementation of

---

[184] Mental Health Commission, *Annual Report 2008 including the Report of the Inspector of Mental Health Services 2008*, Book 1, p.61.

[185] Mental Health Commission, *Annual Report 2008 including the Report of the Inspector of Mental Health Services 2008*, Book 1, p.61.

[186] Mental Health Commission, *Annual Report 2008 including the Report of the Inspector of Mental Health Services 2008*, Book 1, p.60.

[187] Mental Health Commission, *Annual Report 2008 including the Report of the Inspector of Mental Health Services 2008*, Book 1, p.62.

detailed action plans submitted by the mental health service providers as part of the regulatory process.[188]

However, a tougher approach was taken in 2009 when the Commission issued its press release following the Tipperary Inquiry.[189] The Tipperary report[190] made findings which included the following: A high number of residents had sustained fractures; wards were unnecessarily locked; seclusion was being used too often; patients were forced to wear nightclothes during the day; there were no comprehensive needs assessments or care plans for residents. The report also highlighted the over-use of locked wards. For example: "Although very few residents were detained under the Mental Health Act 2001 several ward doors were locked and staff referred to residents being 'allowed out' or given 'parole', when they should have been free to come and go as they wished."[191]

Quality Framework

12–43 In addition to the Regulations, the Commission has also produced a Quality Framework for Mental Health Services in 2007.[192] From a legal point of view, this has not been designated as a statutory code of practice and so is very much in the "soft law" category. The Commission has stated that The Quality Framework is much broader and more challenging than the regulations, as it aims to deliver the highest standards and best practices across all mental health services.[193]

The Quality Framework comprises of 8 themes, 24 standards and 163 criteria. The themes include provision of a holistic, seamless service and the full continuum of care provided by a multi-disciplinary team; respectful, empathetic relationships between people using the mental health service and those providing them; an empowering approach to service delivery; a quality physical environment that promotes good health and upholds the security and safety of service users; access to services; family/chosen advocate involvement and support; staff skills, expertise and morale; and systematic evaluation and review of mental health services underpinned by best practice.

---

[188] *Annual Report 2007*, Book 1, p.8.

[189] See above, para.12–35.

[190] Mental Health Commission, *Report of the Committee of Inquiry to Review Care and Treatment Practices in St. Michael's Unit, South Tipperary General Hospital, Clonmel and St. Luke's Hospital, Clonmel, Including the Quality and Panning of Care and the Use of Restraint and Seclusion and to report to the Mental Health Commission* (2009).

[191] *Report of the Committee of Inquiry to Review Care and Treatment Practices in St. Michael's Unit, South Tipperary General Hospital, Clonmel and St. Luke's Hospital, Clonmel, Including the Quality and Panning of Care and the Use of Restraint and Seclusion and to report to the Mental Health Commission* (2009), para.13.1.3. This applied to St. Luke's Hospital.

[192] Mental Health Commission, *Quality Framework: Mental Health Services in Ireland* (2007).

[193] Mental Health Commission, *Report on the Operation of Part 2 of the Mental Health Act 2001* (2008), p.64.

For example, Standard 2.2 states that "Service user rights are respected and upheld". Five criteria are then provided under this standard. For example, the mental health service should comply with relevant legislation, regulations, professional standards and codes of ethics protecting and respecting the rights of the service user (and a list of these is provided). Information should be communicated in a way that is easily understood by the service user, and repeated as required, being aware that explanations may be necessary on more than one occasion. Supportive written material should be made available in a variety of languages, formats and media to meet communication needs at all levels in the mental health service. The service user should have access to responsive and fair formal complaints procedures. The mental health service should have a policy in place regarding the implementation of this standard and it should monitor its performance in relation to this standard as part of a quality improvement process.[194]

Code of Practice on Patient Deaths and Incident Reporting

12–44 The Commission has issued a Statutory Code of Practice on patient deaths and incident reporting.[195] The Code of Practice is applicable to approved centres, day hospitals, day centres and 24-hour staffed residences. An "incident" is defined as an event or circumstance which could have resulted, or did result, in unnecessary harm to a service user.

The Code re-states the requirement in the Approved Centres Regulations 2006 for all deaths of any resident of an approved centre to be notified to the Commission within 48 hours of the death occurring.[196] In addition, all sudden, unexplained deaths of persons attending a day hospital, day centre or currently living in a 24-hour staffed community residence should be notified to the Commission as soon as possible and in any event within seven days.[197]

Approved centres should provide a six-monthly summary report of all incidents occurring in approved centres to the Commission, which includes details of how such incidents were managed.[198] This requirement also applies to day hospitals, day centres and 24-hour staffed residences.[199]

The Commission intends to identify any trends or patterns occurring in services. Information provided in the six-monthly incident summary reports to the Commission should be anonymous at resident/service user level. The Commission will produce annual reports on deaths in approved centres and

---

[194] Mental Health Commission, *Quality Framework: Mental Health Services in Ireland* (2007), p.27.

[195] Mental Health Commission, *Code of Practice for Mental Health Services on Notification of Deaths and Incident Reporting* (COP–S33–01–2008, 2008).

[196] Reg. 14(4) of the Approved Centre Regulations 2006.

[197] *Code of Practice on Notification of Deaths and Incident Reporting*, para.2.5.

[198] *Code of Practice on Notification of Deaths and Incident Reporting*, para.3.5.

[199] *Code of Practice on Notification of Deaths and Incident Reporting*, para.3.8.

sudden, unexplained deaths in day hospitals, day centres and 24-hour staffed community residences.[200]

Inquiries under Section 55

12–45 Section 55(1) of the 2001 Act states that the Commission may, and shall if so requested by the Minister, cause the Inspector or such other person as may be specified by the Commission, to inquire into (a) the carrying on of any approved centre or other premises in the State where mental health services are provided, (b) the care and treatment provided to a specified patient or a specified voluntary patient by the Commission, (c) any other matter in respect of which an inquiry is appropriate having regard to the provisions of the Act or any regulations or rules made thereunder or any other enactment. A report of such an inquiry shall be absolutely privileged.[201]

Inquiries have been set up on two occasions—into the CMH[202] and elements of the Tipperary mental health services.[203]

Examples of Recommendations in the CMH report included that the locking of bedrooms should be determined primarily on an individual basis and should be determined by the risk posed by the individual patient; those patients who have their bedrooms locked should have call buttons in their rooms to be able to communicate with staff when they require assistance; all units in the CMH should be self staffing to ensure continuity of care and to enhance the unit-based staff's role and responsibilities within the Multi-Disciplinary Team (MDT); a keyworker system should be introduced ensuring that each patient has a keyworker from the most appropriate profession; all patients should be involved in their care plan and should receive a copy; and a consistent model of care should be implemented on all units.[204] See also para.12–05 above.

The findings of the Tipperary Inquiry have been summarised earlier at para.12–07. This report led to a proposal by the Commission to attach conditions to the registration of the two approved centres.[205]

---

[200] *Code of Practice on Notification of Deaths and Incident Reporting*, paras 5.1–5.3.

[201] Mental Health Act 2001, s.55(3).

[202] Mental Health Commission, *Report of the Committee of Inquiry into Current Care and Treatment Practices in the Central Mental Hospital* (2006).

[203] Mental Health Commission, *Report of the Committee of Inquiry to Review Care and Treatment Practices in St. Michael's Unit, South Tipperary General Hospital, Clonmel and St. Luke's Hospital, Clonmel, Including the Quality and Planning of Care and the Use of Restraint and Seclusion and to Report to the Mental Health Commission* (2009).

[204] Mental Health Commission, *Report of the Committee of Inquiry to Review Care and Treatment Practices in St. Michael's Unit, South Tipperary General Hospital, Clonmel and St. Luke's Hospital, Clonmel, Including the Quality and Planning of Care and the Use of Restraint and Seclusion and to Report to the Mental Health Commission* (2009), pp.192–3.

[205] See para.12–35 above.

Chapter 13

MENTAL CAPACITY

13–01 This chapter reviews the law concerning mental capacity, focusing mainly on the existing law concerning wards of court and enduring powers of attorney. There are recent proposals for major reform in these areas, in the form of the scheme of the Mental Capacity Bill 2008, considered at paras 13–30 to 13–39. Capacity to marry, make wills and make contracts is also considered.

Wards of Court

13–02 Ireland's law concerning wards of court is widely acknowledged to be woefully out-dated and is due to be replaced in the near future by new legislation on mental capacity. Pending reform of the law, this chapter will outline the current legal position.[1]

In 2008, the Office of the General Solicitor for Minors and Wards of Court dealt with 473 wardship cases.[2] In addition, the Office of Wards of Court dealt with 2,310 wardship cases.[3] The total number of wards is currently estimated at 2,200, of whom 10 per cent are minors.[4] There were 70 wards of court resident in approved centres in November 2007.[5]

The wards of court procedure is primarily used when a person is of "unsound mind" and incapable of managing their affairs, and significant decisions need to be made concerning their property. However, it has also been used in cases where the welfare, rather than the property, of the person requires protection. The main legislation governing this area is the Lunacy Regulation (Ireland) Act 1871[6] as amended. The courts also have powers under their inherent jurisdiction and

---

[1] For detailed treatment of the law, see Anne-Marie O'Neill, *Wards of Court in Ireland* (Dublin: FirstLaw, 2004); Law Reform Commission, *Consultation Paper on Law and the Elderly* (CP23–2003); Law Reform Commission, *Consultation Paper on Vulnerable Adults and the Law: Capacity* (CP37–2005); Law Reform Commission, *Report on Vulnerable Adults and the Law* (Report 83, 2006).

[2] Courts Service, *Annual Report 2008*, p.74.

[3] Courts Service, *Annual Report 2008*, p.74.

[4] Noel Doherty, Office of Wards of Court, quoted in Carol Coulter, "Bill Will Create Role of Personal Guardian", *Irish Times*, February 6, 2009. In 2003, the estimated total number of wards was 2,600—Law Reform Commission, *Consultation Paper on Law and the Elderly* (CP23, 2003), para.4.03.

[5] Mental Health Commission, *Annual Report 2007 Including the Report of the Inspector of Mental Health Services 2007*, Book 1, p.58. The 2008 annual report does not include a census of patients.

[6] 34 & 35 Vic., c.22. See also Ord.67, Rules of the Superior Courts 1986, S.I. No. 15 of 1986, as amended.

the *parens patriae* prerogative.[7] Powers concerning wards of court are primarily exercised by the President of the High Court and the Registrar of Wards of Court.

The Wardship Procedure

13–03 In order for an adult to be admitted to wardship under the 1871 Act, a person must be both of "unsound mind" and incapable of managing their person or property.[8] In the case of *Re Catherine Keogh*[9] Finnegan P. emphasised the necessity of both criteria being fulfilled. As the jury had only found that one criterion was satisfied (incapability of managing person or property), Ms Keogh was not admitted to wardship. While there was authority that in some cases that "and" in a statute should be read disjunctively rather than conjunctively,[10] Finnegan P. said that the very long-established practice in relation to wards of court has been to treat the word "and" as conjunctive and to make orders only where both the requirements, unsoundness of mind and incapacity of managing one's person or affairs, are satisfied. He said it was inappropriate for the court to review at this late stage the interpretation of the 1871 Act, which has for so long been adopted.[11]

13–04 In the *Dolan* case in 2004, Kelly J. at High Court stage appeared to suggest that the term "of unsound mind" meant "no more than that the person is incapable of managing their affairs."[12] The Law Reform Commission states that this needs to be understood in the context of the facts of the case, where the parents were seeking to avoid their son being made a ward of court on the basis that they were unhappy to have the stigmatising label "of unsound mind" applied to their son. Nevertheless, the Commission stated that it sits uneasily with the *Re Keogh* case.[13] The Supreme Court appears to have approved of Kelly J.'s interpretation of the meaning of the term "of unsound mind".[14] The court also stated that the case law has given a special meaning to "unsound mind" in the

---

[7]   This is a matter of some controversy; see, for example, the summary of the issues in the *Consultation Paper on Law and the Elderly* at paras 4.04–4.13, and more recent consideration of this issue by the Supreme Court in *In Re Wards of Court and Dolan* [2007] I.E.S.C. 26; [2008] 1 I.L.R.M. 19 at 27–29.

[8]   Prior to the 1871 Act, Jonathan Swift was declared to be insane in 1742 by means of a writ *de Lunatico Inquirendo*—see J. Banks, "The Writ 'de Lunatico Inquirendo' (Swift)" (1861) 31 Dublin Q. J. Med. Sci. 83; James C. Harris, "Gulliver's Travels: The Struldbruggs" (2005) 62 Arch. Gen. Psychiatry 243.

[9]   High Court, Finnegan P., October 15, 1992.

[10] *Maxwell on Statutes*, 12th edn, 1969, p.232.

[11] High Court, Finnegan P., October 15, 1992, p.4.

[12] *F.D. (Infant) v. Registrar of Wards of Court* [2004] I.E.H.C. 126; [2004] 3 I.R. 95 at 105.

[13] *Consultation Paper on Vulnerable Adults and the Law: Capacity*, para.4.20.

[14] See *In Re Wards of Court and Dolan* [2007] I.E.S.C. 26; [2008] 1 I.L.R.M. 19 at 26, where Geoghegan J. stated that, in the High Court, Kelly J. "went on to explain that the expression 'person of unsound mind' had a special meaning and not the perceived offensive meaning which

wards of court context to get round the legal difficulties arising from the terminology in the Lunacy (Regulation) statute.[15] Donnelly comments that the linguistic gymnastics required create further difficulties in this problematic area:

> "While the term 'unsound mind' has long been abandoned in other juris-dictions as lacking specificity it is rather more difficult to justify assimilating the term into the clearly different requirement that the individual must be 'incapable of handling his affairs.' This requires not just that the language of the 1871 Act be entirely disregarded but it also expands the ambit of the ward-ship jurisdiction by effectively removing one of the criteria for admission."[16]

13–05 There is no definition[17] of "unsound mind" and, from a human rights perspective, a narrow definition would reduce the risk of inappropriate detentions.[18] In practice, the wards of court office expects that practitioners will state whether the person is "of unsound mind" even though this creates difficulties: As Ní Chúlacháin notes:

> "[I]t creates a difficult practical obstacle—a petition in lunacy must be supported by two medical affidavits attesting to a person's "unsoundness of mind" and this poses a difficulty where the proposed ward is mentally ill, disabled or is in a permanent vegetative state (PVS). Many medical practitioners are unwilling to equate such mental states with unsoundness of mind. Moreover, some medical practitioners have a problem with the term *per se*, seeing it as a term of art which connotes some risk of causing harm to others."[19]

Even where the criteria for wardship are satisfied, the court has a discretion as to whether or not to make a Wardship Order.[20]

13–06 Generally, a petition to have a person admitted to wardship is brought to the High Court[21] by a family member of the proposed ward. The petition must be supported by supporting affidavits of two registered medical practitioners.

---

was being attributed to it by the parents. It meant no more than that the appellant was incapable of managing his affairs."

[15] [2008] 1 I.L.R.M. 19 at 21.

[16] Mary Donnelly, "Legislating for Incapacity: Developing a Rights-Based Framework" (2008) 30 D.U.L.J. 395 at 399.

[17] The poet Nuala Ní Dhómhnaill was made a ward of court in the 1980s due to her relationship with a Turkish man—see Emmanuel Kehoe, "TV Review: Political Satire in a Bit of a State", *Sunday Business Post*, April 29, 2007; RTÉ *Arts Lives* documentary, "Taibhsí i mBéal na Gaoithe" (Director: Pat Collins), April 2007.

[18] Interestingly, the term "persons of unsound mind" is used in art.5(1)(e) of the ECHR.

[19] Siobhán Ní Chúlacháin, "Wardship: Time for Reform?" (2000) 5 *Bar Review* 239 at 240.

[20] *In Re D.* [1987] I.R. 449 at 456 per Finlay C.J.; *In Re Wards of Court and Dolan* [2007] I.E.S.C. 26; [2008] 1 I.L.R.M. 19 at 25 *per* Geoghegan J.

[21] The Circuit Court has concurrent jurisdiction where the property does not exceed €6,349 in value or the income therefrom does not exceed €381 per annum—s.22(2) of the Courts (Supplemental Provisions) Act 1961, as amended by s.2(3) of the Courts Act 1971.

After the petition is submitted, if the President is satisfied with the medical evidence, he or she makes an "inquiry order" which requires that a medical visitor[22] examines the person and reports to the President. This is then followed by a hearing at which the President (or jury) decides whether to admit the person to wardship. There are significant omissions in the procedural rights of the proposed ward. For example, they are not automatically furnished with the medical affidavits and the report of the medical visitor. In addition, there is no provision for support, whether legal or advocacy services, to be made available to the respondent once they have been notified of the impending wardship inquiry. In *Eastern Health Board v M.K.*[23] Denham J. stated that wardship proceedings must be fair and in accordance with constitutional justice. The Law Reform Commission has raised questions about the compliance of these procedures with constitutional justice, the *Winterwerp* case[24] and art.6 of the European Convention on Human Rights (ECHR).[25]

13–07 If the petition for wardship of a child is brought by a health authority, it was held in *Stevenson v Landy and Others*[26] that the child's parent would ordinarily be entitled to legal aid. Lardner J. said that in cases where the applicant for legal aid is a parent and the issues are concerned with the future custody, residence, maintenance or education of a child or the general welfare of the child, and a case is made which warrants the conclusion that such case is likely to be of assistance to the court in determining such issues, in his opinion a Certificate of Legal Aid should be granted.[27] The Supreme Court recently stated in *Magee v Farrell and Others*[28] that the decision in *Stevenson v Landy* was based on the construction of the relevant clause of the Legal Aid Scheme and insofar as Lardner J. based his judgment on *The State (Healy) v O'Donoghue*[29] he was incorrect to do so.[30] Finnegan J. said in *Magee v Farrell* that there is no true analogy between custody proceedings and criminal proceedings to justify the extension of the principle in *The State (Healy) v Donoghue* to wardship proceedings.

[22] The "medical visitor" is a consultant psychiatrist on a panel for this purpose.
[23] [1999] 2 I.R. 99 at 111.
[24] *Winterwerp v The Netherlands* (1979–80) 2 E.H.R.R. 387.
[25] Law Reform Commission, *Consultation Paper on Vulnerable Adults and the Law: Capacity* (CP37, 2005), paras 4.10–4.14.
[26] High Court, Lardner J., February 10, 1993.
[27] High Court, Lardner J., February 10, 1993, p.8. Lardner J. quashed the refusal of the Certifying Committee and the Appeals Committee to grant a Certificate. He directed that the application be remitted to the Certifying Committee to reconsider it in the light of the views he had expressed on the meaning of paragraph 3.2.3.(4) of the Scheme after obtaining such additional information (if any) as they considered necessary from the applicant as to the specific case she wished to make to the court.
[28] [2009] I.E.S.C. 60; Supreme Court, July 28, 2009.
[29] [1976] I.R. 325. In this case it was held that Art.38 of the Constitution requires the provision by the State of legal aid in criminal trials.
[30] [2009] I.E.S.C. 60, *per* Finnegan J.

13–08 In some cases, the person's family may object to the proposed wardship and instead propose that an alternative trust be established for the person's benefit. The Supreme Court recently decided in *In Re Wards of Court and Dolan*[31] that a preliminary issue should be tried by the High Court as to whether it was open to the President or whatever judge might be delegated by them to protect the relevant moneys by means other than making Mr Dolan a ward of court and if so whether such a course of action would be desirable in this case. Geoghegan J. stated that he had in mind the creation of a trust or some formal scheme between the court and the parents involving suitable undertakings and suitable reporting arrangements.[32] He believed that from time to time, ever since the presidency of Finlay P. and possibly earlier, various Presidents had secured appropriate arrangements through obviously caring parents so as to avoid the necessity of formal wardship. At least one other member of the court had a similar recollection.[33]

When the preliminary issue was later tried by Sheehan J., however, he held that the court did not have power to create such a trust.[34] Sheehan J. acknowledged that the jurisdiction of the High Court is broader than the Act of 1871, as a result of the *parens patriae* jurisdiction formerly exercised by the Lord Chancellor and now exercised by the President of the High Court. However, he found that the full and original jurisdiction of the High Court is to deal with justiciable controversies and that the creation of a trust is not a justiciable controversy. An examination of previous cases had been conducted, but in none of those cases was the High Court the settlor of a trust. As a result of this case, it is not possible for a family to argue against the proposed wardship and instead propose that an alternative trust be established for the person's benefit. Wardship is the only mechanism available.

13–09 Most cases are heard by the President alone without a jury.[35] If the criteria for wardship are satisfied, a Declaration is made that the person is of unsound mind and is incapable of managing their person or property. The inquiry appears to be inquisitorial rather than adversarial, and the rules of evidence are relaxed.[36] However, this again raises questions of compliance with art.6.[37]

13–10 The most commonly used procedure for admission to wardship is s.15 of the 1871 Act, and it is this procedure which has been summarised in the

---

[31] [2007] I.E.S.C. 26; [2008] 1 I.L.R.M. 19.

[32] [2008] 1 I.L.R.M. 19 at 29.

[33] [2008] 1 I.L.R.M. 19 at 30.

[34] *Re Francis Dolan* [2008] I.E.H.C. 264; [2009] 1 I.L.R.M. 173; High Court, Sheehan J., July 29, 2008.

[35] Under s.18 of the 1871 Act, if a respondent is resident outside the jurisdiction the inquiry must be held before a jury.

[36] However, see guidelines from Supreme Court regarding fair procedures and hearsay evidence in *Eastern Health Board v. M.K. and M.K.* [1999] 2 I.R. 99; [1999] 2 I.L.R.M. 321.

[37] Law Reform Commission, *Consultation Paper on Vunerable Adults and the Law: Capacity* (CP37, 2005), para.4.15.

previous paragraphs. However, it is possible to use alternative procedures in some circumstances. The procedure under s.12 of the 1871 Act may be used where the standard s.15 procedure is not feasible, e.g. in cases of urgency or where a person considers that somebody needs to be taken into wardship but does not wish to start the proceedings themselves. The procedure is triggered when a case is brought to the attention of the Registrar of Wards of Court, who may then inquire into the matter and request one of the medical visitors to examine the proposed ward. There is no petition and two medical affidavits are not supplied. The report of the medical visitor is then treated as a petition for inquiry and the process continues as described above.[38] Under s.68 of the 1871 Act, a simplified procedure is provided for persons with little property.[39] The President of the High Court may make an order without directing an inquiry where a person's property/income is below a prescribed level. The statutory threshold level is €6,349.[40]

13–11 Section 103 of the 1871 Act provides a rarely used procedure for temporary wardship.[41] This can be used where it is established that a person is "of weak mind and temporarily incapable of managing his affairs." Orders made under s.103 may appoint a guardian to act for a defined time which may not exceed six months and may not be renewed more than once. Section 70 of the 1871 Act lays down a procedure for the taking into wardship of a person who has been "acquitted on the ground of insanity, or found to be insane".[42] This might technically continue to apply today, even since the enactment of the Criminal Law (Insanity) Act 2006.

13–12 There is also a practice in the wards of court office of informally dealing with bank accounts where the funds are less than €30,000.[43] In a document headed "Receipt of funds on behalf of persons lacking mental capacity", it is provided that where a person lacking the mental capacity to deal with their affairs is entitled to funds less than €30,000 held by a bank, building society or other financial institution, the President of the High Court will, in certain circumstances, allow that the funds be paid to a family member of such person rather than requiring that a wardship application be brought. The solicitor acting in the matter should write to the Registrar of Wards of Court setting out the circumstances of the case and furnishing a medical report as to the mental condition of the person entitled to the funds. If the President is satisfied that there is a suitable member of the beneficiary's family recommended by the

---

[38] *Consultation Paper on Law and the Elderly*, paras 4.28–9.
[39] *Consultation Paper on Law and the Elderly*, para.4.30.
[40] Courts Act 1971, s.4, amending s.68 of 1871 Act—Where the property is valued at less than €6,349 or where the income from the property is less than €381 per annum.
[41] *Consultation Paper on Law and the Elderly*, paras 4.31–2.
[42] See Anne-Marie O'Neill, *Wards of Court in Ireland* (Dublin: First Law, 2004), pp.80–83.
[43] See references to a Practice Direction in *Re Francis Dolan* [2008] I.E.H.C. 264; [2009] 1 I.L.R.M. 173.

solicitor. they may allow that family member to receive the funds and give a valid discharge for the same. The Registrar will then write to the solicitor seeking an undertaking in writing from the proposed recipient that they will apply the funds solely for the maintenance and benefit of the person entitled to the same and will account to the Registrar for sums so applied. Upon receipt of the undertaking, the Registrar will confirm in writing the directions of the President and, if they so allow, the funds may then be released.[44]

The Impact of Wardship

13–13 The court normally appoints a person, usually a family member, as Committee of the ward.[45] The court usually gives the Committee power to collect the ward's income and use it for the maintenance of the ward and of the ward's dependants and to deal with the ward's property. Once a person is declared a ward of court, they effectively lose the right to make most decisions about their person and property. So, they may not enter binding contracts or institute or defend legal proceedings[46] and they may not sell or buy property or have a bank account.[47] The ward may not travel outside the country (unless the court consents) and may not marry.[48] The committee is prohibited from changing the ward's residence, except by leave of the Judge or Registrar. A ward of court may, however, make a will, as a functional test of capacity applies to testamentary capacity.[49]

13–14 The Law Reform Commission states that it seems that, in Ireland, the High Court has exclusive jurisdiction to grant or withhold consent to the treatment of a ward of court, subject to the principle that, in the case of an emergency, a doctor is entitled to take urgent action which is considered necessary to preserve the life and health of a patient.[50] The Commission describes the practice as follows:

---

[44] Document headed "Receipt of Funds on Behalf of Persons Lacking Mental Capacity", provided by Registrar of Wards of Court in personal communication to author, July 16, 2009.

[45] Both a Committee of the Person and a Committee of the Estate may be appointed but usually the same person is appointed to both roles. For an example of separate appointment see *Re K. (Ward of Court)* [2001] 1 I.R. 338 (Supreme Court, January 19, 2001).

[46] The question of issuing legal proceedings was litigated in *Re K. (Ward of Court)* [2001] 1 I.R. 338.

[47] *Consultation Paper on Law and the Elderly*, para.4.45.

[48] Marriage of Lunatics Act 1811; Mary Donnelly, "Assessing Legal Capacity: Process and the Operation of the Functional Test" (2007) 2 *Judicial Studies Institute Journal* 141 at 150. As Donnelly notes, it is arguable that the 1811 Act is unconstitutional.

[49] See paras 13–57 to 13–65 below. For the procedure which applies if a ward wishes to make a will, see Anne-Marie O'Neill, *Wards of Court in Ireland* (Dublin: First Law, 2004), p.175.

[50] *Consultation Paper on Law and the Elderly*, para.4.50.

"In practice, a request for consent—for example, to carry out an elective surgical procedure or administer an anaesthetic—is normally made by the clinical director of the hospital, or the surgeon concerned, to the Office of Wards of Court. The Registrar of Wards of Court has explained to the Commission that he is authorised by the President of the High Court to issue, in the latter's name, consents to the carrying out of procedures that may be considered 'non-controversial', for example, routine investigative procedures, or treatment of fractures or other injuries. Other procedures, however, are considered to be 'controversial', and these are considered personally by the President of the High Court. These latter categories of procedures are those which may be regarded as non-routine, or which carry a more substantial risk to the patient, (examples given are the insertion of gastrostomy tubes or amputation of limbs). The second category also includes procedures to which the ward, if capable of indicating agreement, did not agree; or to which the next-of-kin did not agree, if the ward was personally incapable of indicating agreement. In such cases the President of the High Court seeks the advice of one of the members of his panel of Medical Visitors as to whether it would be appropriate to give the consent of the Court to the treatment."[51]

Donnelly argues that if, following a separate assessment of capacity to make healthcare decisions, the ward is found to be capable, their right to make their own decision in this respect should subsist and should not be determined by the fact that they are a ward.[52] The *Re A Ward of Court (No.2)* case,[53] and the *J.M.* case,[54] considered above at paras 10–10 to 10–13, contain detailed consideration of consent issues concerning wards of court. At common law, once a person was made a ward of court, there was a "presumption of continuance", i.e. it was presumed that they lacked capacity unless the contrary were proven.[55] However, it is unclear whether this presumption continues to apply, and it has been found not to apply in England and Wales.[56]

13–15 The extensive loss of legal power which arises as a result of being declared a ward of court constitutes a status approach to capacity. The status of a person as a ward triggers a number of legal consequences. While some of the people concerned may have the legal capacity to make specific decisions, their

---

[51] *Consultation Paper on Law and the Elderly*, para.4.50. In a footnote, the Commission states that the practice of the Office of Wards of Court in relation to these matters is outlined in *The Application of Wardship to the Health Sector*, a lecture delivered by G.N. Rubotham, former Registrar of Wards of Court.

[52] Mary Donnelly, "Assessing Legal Capacity: Process and the Operation of the Functional Test" (2007) 2 *Judicial Studies Institute Journal* 141 at 151.

[53] [1996] 2 I.R. 79.

[54] [2003] 1 I.R. 321.

[55] Mary Donnelly, "Assessing Legal Capacity: Process and the Operation of the Functional Test" (2007) 2 *Judicial Studies Institute Journal* 141 at 146.

[56] *Masterman-Lister v Brutton & Co.* [2002] E.W.C.A. Civ. 1889; Mary Donnelly, "Assessing Legal Capacity: Process and the Operation of the Functional Test" (2007) 2 *Judicial Studies Institute Journal* 141 at 155–6.

general decision-making capacity has been removed by their status.[57] As discussed above in Chapter 10, a functional approach to capacity is now generally preferred.

13–16 Often, when individuals who are brought into wardship are living in a psychiatric hospital or care facility, an order is made that they should be detained there until further order.[58] This detention is not subject to the protections granted by the Mental Health Act 2001, as there was a saver in the 1945 Act which was not repealed by the 2001 Act.[59] As Keys states, "wards of court in mental health care … are effectively deprived of their liberty, but have no rights under the 2001 Act, due to the saving clauses in the Act."[60] This means, for example, that they do not have periodic reviews of their detention by a Mental Health Tribunal (MHT) and are not governed by the requirements of ss.56–60 of the 2001 Act concerning treatment.

It is unclear whether it is possible to have a person who is a ward of court involuntarily admitted under the 2001 Act. There is no express prohibition on this in the legislation, but it might be argued that it is inappropriate to order a person's detention under one Act (the 2001 Act) when they have already been detained by the High Court under another Act (the 1871 Act).

13–17 The wardship order is of indefinite duration and is not subject to automatic periodic review. There are some possibilities for review in the legislation, but these tend to arise only if a complaint is made.[61] The lack of periodic review appears to conflict with the *Winterwerp* principles,[62] at least where the ward is deprived of their liberty.[63] If the patient is in de facto detention, this would conflict with the decision in *H.L. v United Kingdom*.[64] On the other hand, as Baroness Hale has noted, "[t]here is no Strasbourg case which implies into article 5(4) the requirement of a judicial review in every case where the patient is unable to make her own application."[65]

---

[57] *Consultation Paper on Law and the Elderly*, para.1.20.

[58] *Consultation Paper on Law and the Elderly*, para.4.47.

[59] Section 283 of the Mental Treatment Act 1945 states, inter alia, "(1) Nothing in this Act shall affect any power exercisable immediately before the commencement of this section by a Judge of the High Court or a Judge of the Circuit Court in connection with the care and commitment of the persons and estates of persons found to be idiots or of unsound mind; (2) No power, restriction, or prohibition contained in this Act shall apply in relation to a person of unsound mind under the care of a Judge of the High Court or of a Judge of the Circuit Court." Section 283 remains in force–see s.6 Mental Health Act 2001 and Schedule.

[60] Mary Keys, "Capacity: Whose Decision is it Anyway?", Conference Paper, NUI Galway, November 2007, p.8.

[61] *Consultation Paper on Vulnerable Adults and the Law: Capacity*, para.4.25–6.

[62] (1979–80) 2 E.H.R.R. 387; see above para.1–23. See also Claire Murray, "Safeguarding the Right to Liberty of Incapable Compliant Patients with a Mental Disorder In Ireland" (2007) 14 D.U.L.J. 279.

[63] *Consultation Paper on Vulnerable Adults and the Law: Capacity*, paras 4.28–9.

[64] (2005) 40 E.H.R.R. 32; see above paras 5–28 to 5–29.

[65] *R. (M.H.) v Secretary of State for Health* [2005] U.K.H.L. 60, para.24; [2006] 1 A.C. 441 at

If the ward is detained in a public psychiatric unit, then they must be visited by a medical visitor at least once a year.[66] If detained in a private hospital, the visits must occur at least four times a year.[67] The distinction between public and private hospitals is difficult to justify.[68]

13–18 An application may be made to have a person discharged from wardship, provided appropriate medical evidence is produced.[69] The ward may apply informally to the High Court to be remitted to management of their own affairs. A medical report should be sent to the Registrar of Wards of Court indicating that the ward has recovered and the Registrar will then submit the matter to the President of the High Court who may discharge the matter out of wardship, or an order could be made directing a medical visitor's examination of the ward and the submission of a report.

13–19 In *Shtukaturov v Russia*[70] the applicant had been declared legally incapable by a court on the application of his mother. He was not present or represented at the hearing, which lasted 10 minutes. The decision deprived the applicant of his capacity to act independently in almost all areas of life: he was no longer able to sell or buy any property on his own, to work, to travel, to choose his place of residence, to join associations, to marry, etc. He was detained in a hospital and on several occasions the applicant requested his discharge from hospital. He contacted the hospital administration and a lawyer with a view to obtaining his release, and once he attempted to escape from the hospital.

The European Court of Human Rights noted that the interference with the applicant's private life was very serious. As a result of his incapacitation the applicant became fully dependant on his official guardian in almost all areas of life. The court found that the proceedings before the domestic court were procedurally flawed. Thus, the applicant did not take part in the court proceedings and was not even examined by the judge in person. The domestic court relied solely on the findings of a medical report which did not explain what kind of actions the applicant was unable to understand or control. The incidence of the applicant's illness was unclear, as were the possible consequences of the applicant's illness for his social life, health, pecuniary interests, etc.[71]

The court accepted that the applicant was seriously ill. However, "the existence of a mental disorder, even a serious one, cannot be the sole reason to justify full incapacitation."[72] By analogy with the cases concerning deprivation

---

455. See critical commentary in Peter Bartlett & Ralph Sandland, *Mental Health Law: Policy and Practice*, 3rd edn (Oxford: Oxford University Press, 2007) at pp.573–4.

[66] The Visitor reports on the ward's mental and physical condition to the President of the High Court.

[67] Lunacy Regulation (Ireland) Act, 1871, s.57; Anne-Marie O'Neill, *Wards of Court in Ireland* (Dublin: First Law, 2004).

[68] *Consultation Paper on Vulnerable Adults and the Law: Capacity*, para.4.27.

[69] See Anne-Marie O'Neill, *Wards of Court in Ireland* (Dublin: First Law, 2004), p.180.

[70] [2008] M.H.L.R. 238.

[71] [2008] M.H.L.R. 238, paras 90–93.

[72] [2008] M.H.L.R. 238, para.94.

of liberty, in order to justify full incapacitation the mental disorder must be "of a kind or degree" warranting such a measure.[73] However, the questions to the doctors, as formulated by the judge, did not concern "the kind and degree" of the applicant's mental illness. As a result, the medical report did not analyse the degree of the applicant's incapacity in sufficient detail. The national law did not leave the judge another choice. The Russian Civil Code distinguished between full capacity and full incapacity, but it did not provide for any "borderline" situation other than for drug or alcohol addicts. The court referred in this respect to the principles formulated by Recommendation No. R (99) 4 of the Committee of Ministers of the Council of Europe.[74] Although these principles have no force of law for the court, the court stated that they may define a common European standard in this area.[75] Contrary to these principles, Russian legislation did not provide for a "tailor-made response". As a result, in the circumstances the applicant's rights under art.8 were limited more than strictly necessary. The court concluded that the interference with the applicant's private life was disproportionate to the legitimate aim pursued. There was, therefore, a breach of art.8 of the Convention on account of the applicant's full incapacitation.

It has been suggested that the court demonstrated the trend away from the status approach in this case by stating that the existence of a mental disorder, even a serious one, cannot be the sole reason to justify full incapacitation.[76] In addition, the court may be seen as in effect endorsing the functional approach by concluding that there was a lack of proportionality in the legal response to the applicant's capacity in that case.[77]

Enduring Powers of Attorney

13–20 A power of attorney is a document which appoints a person, called the donee or attorney, and invests them with power to act either generally or in a manner specified on behalf of a person who gives the power, called the donor. A power of attorney could be used, for example, where the donor is going abroad and wishes another person to be able to sign documents in their absence. Powers of attorney were regarded as a branch of the law of agency, and at common law an agency was revoked automatically on the principal's insanity.[78]

In order to allow a power of attorney to continue after a person lost mental capacity, the concept of an enduring power of attorney (EPA) was introduced in

---

[73] The Court cited *Winterwerp v Netherlands* (1979–80) 2 E.H.R.R. 387.

[74] Committee of Ministers, *Principles Concerning the Legal Protection of Incapable Adults*, Recommendation No. R(99)4 (Council of Europe, 1999).

[75] [2008] M.H.L.R. 238, para.95.

[76] European Group of National Human Rights Institutions, *Amicus Brief in the European Court of Human Rights, Application No. 13469/06, D.D. v Lithuania*, April 2008, p.2.

[77] European Group of National Human Rights Institutions, *Amicus Brief in the European Court of Human Rights, Application No. 13469/06, D.D. v Lithuania*, April 2008, p.2.

[78] *Drew v Nunn* (1879) 4 Q.B.D. 661; *Yonge v Toynbee* [1910] 1 K.B. 215.

the Powers of Attorney Act 1996.[79] The EPA contains a statement by the donor to the effect that the donor intends the power to be effective during any subsequent mental incapacity of the donor.[80] "Mental incapacity", in relation to an individual, means incapacity by reason of a mental condition to manage and administer their own property and affairs.[81] It is important to note that when the EPA is executed it has no real legal effect, but it will come into effect when it is registered. An application to register may only be made when the attorney has reason to believe that the donor of the EPA becomes or is becoming mentally incapacitated.[82]

13–21 The detailed requirements for an EPA may be found in the Act, the Regulations,[83] the Law Society Guidelines[84] and commentary by O'Neill, Gallagher and the Law Reform Commission.[85] The document creating the EPA must include a statement by a registered medical practitioner verifying that the donor had the mental capacity, with the assistance of such explanations as may have been given to the donor, to understand the effect of creating the power.[86] Notice of the execution of the EPA must be given to specified persons.[87]

13–22 An application to register an EPA must be made to the Registrar of Wards of Court, on notice to defined persons. There were 241 EPAs registered in 2008.[88] The attorney must produce a certificate from a registered medical practitioner that the donor is, or is becoming, incapable by reason of a mental condition of managing and administering their own property and affairs.[89] Objections to registration may be made, although this rarely occurs. In *Application of Hamilton and Williams*[90] it was argued by the donor's son that the proposed attorneys were unsuitable due to alleged lack of management skills. Morris P. did not uphold the objection, stating that one of the proposed attorneys was the donor's daughter and it was perfectly normal for a donor to choose a member of their family or somebody sympathetic to them to act as an attorney.[91]

---

[79] The Act followed the Law Reform Commission's proposals in its *Report on Land Law and Conveyancing Law (2) Enduring Powers of Attorney* (Report 21, 1989).

[80] Powers of Attorney Act 1996, s.5(1).

[81] Powers of Attorney Act 1996, s.4(1).

[82] Powers of Attorney Act 1996, s.9.

[83] Enduring Powers of Attorney Regulations 1996, S.I. No. 196 of 1996; Enduring Powers of Attorney (Personal Care Decisions) Regulations 1996, S.I. No. 287 of 1996.

[84] Law Society, *Enduring Powers of Attorney: Guidelines for Solicitors* (2004).

[85] Anne Marie O'Neill, *Wards of Court in Ireland* (Dublin: FirstLaw, 2004), Chapter 8; Brian Gallagher, *Powers of Attorney Act 1996* (Dublin: Round Hall Sweet & Maxwell, 1998); Law Reform Commission, *Consultation Paper on Law and the Elderly* (CP23, 2003), Chapter 3.

[86] Enduring Powers of Attorney Regulations 1996, S.I. No. 196 of 1996, prescribed forms in Schedules 1 and 2.

[87] Reg. 7, Enduring Powers of Attorney Regulations 1996, S.I. No. 196 of 1996.

[88] Courts Service, *Annual Report 2008*, p.74.

[89] Powers of Attorney Act 1996, s.9(4).

[90] [1999] 3 I.R. 310; [1999] 2 I.L.R.M. 509.

[91] [1999] 3 I.R. 310 at 314.

He said that lack of business skill is not a valid objection to registration of an EPA under the 1996 Act.[92]

13–23 The court may, notwithstanding that an instrument may not comply with the provisions of the Act or regulations, register the instrument as an enduring power if it is satisfied that certain requirements have been met.[93] Where an instrument has been registered, the court has various functions if an application is made to it, e.g. it may determine any question as to the meaning or effect of the instrument, give directions with respect to the management or disposal by the attorney of the property and affairs of the donor or give directions regarding a personal care decision made or to be made by the attorney.[94] An EPA is not automatically invalidated if the donor becomes a ward of court but the court has power to invalidate an EPA in these circumstances.[95]

13–24 The attorney may have power over the property, financial and business affairs and personal care decisions of the donor.[96] A personal care decision means a decision on where the donor should live, with whom the donor should live, whom the donor should see and not see, what training or rehabilitation the donor should get, the donor's diet and dress, inspection of the donor's personal papers, or housing, social welfare and other benefits for the donor.[97] Personal care decisions made by the attorney must be made in the donor's best interests and the Act sets out what the attorney must take into account when making such decisions.[98]

The scope of "personal care decisions" does not extend to decisions on medical treatment or surgery. Minister Taylor stated in the Dáil when the Bill was being debated that provisions to deal with those aspects would need to incorporate safeguards for the various circumstances that could arise and would necessarily have to be elaborate.[99]

Donnelly suggests that the low take-up of EPAs may be due to lack of knowledge of EPAs among the public and legal practitioners or to the fact that healthcare decisions are not covered. She states that it is also possible that, under the current scheme, EPAs are not a sufficiently attractive legal mechanism to

---

[92] [1999] 3 I.R. 310 at 314.
[93] Powers of Attorney Act 1996, s.10(5).
[94] Powers of Attorney Act 1996, s.12.
[95] Powers of Attorney Act 1996, s.5(9).
[96] The scope of the attorney's power will be stated in the document.
[97] Powers of Attorney Act 1996, s.4(1). The EPA may specify which personal decisions may be made by the attorney.
[98] Powers of Attorney Act 1996, s.6(7). Matters to be taken into account include the past and present wishes and feelings of the donor and the factors which the donor would consider if they were able to do so; the need to permit and encourage the donor to participate, or to improve the donor's ability to participate, as fully as possible in any decision affecting the donor; and the views of certain persons (e.g. anyone engaged in caring for the donor) as to the donor's wishes and feelings and as to what would be in the donor's best interests.
[99] 461 *Dáil Debates* 2029–30 (February 20, 1996). See also 465 *Dáil Debates* 1126 (May 15, 1996).

encourage people to take active steps to ensure that their wishes and rights are respected after their incapacity.[100]

Proposed Reforms

13–25 In its more recent Consultation Papers and Report on Vulnerable Adults, the Law Reform Commission proposed various reforms to the Powers of Attorney legislation.[101] One of the most significant proposals was that EPAs would extend to some medical decisions.[102] These proposals have led to publication of Pt 3 of the Scheme of the Mental Capacity Bill 2008.[103] Part 3 would replace the 1996 Act.[104] For discussion of the other parts of the 2008 Bill, see paras 13–30 to 13–39 below.

The Guiding Principles in Head 1 of the Bill would apply and "capacity" and "best interests" would now have the same meaning as in Heads 2 and 3 of the Bill.[105] A personal welfare decision would include a decision on healthcare but would not authorise the refusing of consent to the carrying out of life-sustaining treatment.[106] It would extend to giving or refusing consent to the carrying out or continuation of treatment by a person providing healthcare for the donor. It would not extend to making such decisions in circumstances other than those where the donor lacks, or the attorney reasonably believes that the donor lacks, capacity.[107] The High Court would have exclusive jurisdiction concerning non-therapeutic sterilisation, withdrawal of artificial life-sustaining treatment and organ donation.[108]

Part 3 contains similar provisions on restraint of the donor by an attorney, as are provided concerning restraint by a personal guardian.[109] It would be a criminal offence for a donee of an EPA to ill-treat or wilfully neglect the donor.[110]

Applications for registration of EPAs would be made to the Public Guardian. A revocation could be made by or on behalf of a donor at any time, whether the instrument has been registered or not, provided the donor has capacity to do

---

[100] Mary Donnelly, "Legislating for Incapacity: Developing a Rights-Based Framework" (2008) 30 D.U.L.J. 395 at 428.

[101] Law Reform Commission, *Consultation Paper on Law and the Elderly* (CP23, 2003); Law Reform Commission, *Consultation Paper on Vulnerable Adults and the Law: Capacity* (CP37, 2005); Law Reform Commission, *Report on Vulnerable Adults and the Law* (Report 83, 2006).

[102] Law Reform Commission, *Report on Vulnerable Adults and the Law* (Report 83, 2006), paras 4.29–4.32.

[103] Department of Justice, Equality and Law Reform, *Scheme of Mental Capacity Bill 2008.*

[104] Part 3 would not repeal the 1996 Act; instead it would have effect only as respects an enduring power of attorney drawn up after the coming into force of the Part—see Head 57.

[105] See para.13–31 below.

[106] Scheme of Mental Capacity Bill 2008, Head 48.

[107] Scheme of Mental Capacity Bill 2008, Head 48.

[108] Scheme of Mental Capacity Bill 2008, Head 21.

[109] Scheme of Mental Capacity Bill 2008, Head 48(5)–(7). See para.13–34 below.

[110] Scheme of Mental Capacity Bill 2008, Head 27.

so.[111] The functions of the Public Guardian would include supervision of donees of powers of attorney.[112] The Public Guardian could appoint a Special or General Visitor to report on a donee, and must make codes of practice for the guidance of donees.[113]

13–26 The Law Society has recommended that a donor of an EPA should have to specifically opt in to include authority in relation to healthcare decisions and it should be possible to appoint different attorneys in relation to different authorities.[114] The Society disagrees with the reservation of certain issues such as non-therapeutic sterilisation to the High Court. It states that the courts have consistently stated that regard should be had to the wishes of a person with regard to healthcare decisions. It therefore appears to the Society to be inconsistent with the human rights principles of privacy and autonomy as expressed in the guiding principles of the scheme to provide for a court decision in such circumstances.[115]

The Society recommends that the list of matters covered by regulation[116] should be expanded to include the requirement by donees of enduring powers of attorney to file accounts and report on the welfare of a person who lacks capacity, as this would assist in preventing abuse. The Society recommends that different levels of supervision should be provided for, based on a risk analysis.[117] It also suggests that there be special protection for whistleblowers in the legislation.

REFORM OF MENTAL CAPACITY LAW

13–27 Reform of mental capacity law has become topical in a number of jurisdictions in recent years. For example, an Adults with Incapacity Act was enacted in Scotland in 2000,[118] a Mental Capacity Act was enacted in England and Wales in 2005,[119] and the Bamford Review in Northern Ireland has proposed changes in mental capacity law.[120] The recent adoption of the Convention on the

---

[111] Scheme of Mental Capacity Bill 2008, Head 54(5)(a).
[112] Scheme of Mental Capacity Bill 2008, Head 32(2)(c).
[113] Scheme of Mental Capacity Bill 2008, Head 39.
[114] Law Society, *Submission on Scheme of Mental Capacity Bill 2008* (2009), p.8.
[115] Law Society, *Submission on Scheme of Mental Capacity Bill 2008* (2009), pp.8–9.
[116] Scheme of Mental Capacity Bill 2008, Head 32(5).
[117] Law Society, *Submission on Scheme of Mental Capacity Bill 2008* (2009), p.7. See also p.9.
[118] Adults With Incapacity (Scotland) Act 2000, as amended. See generally Hilary Patrick, *Mental Health, Incapacity and the Law in Scotland*, 2nd edn (Sussex: Tottel Publishing, 2006); Adrian Ward, *Adults With Incapacity Legislation* (London: Thomson W. Green, 2007).
[119] See generally Peter Bartlett, *Blackstone's Guide to the Mental Capacity Act 2005*, 2nd edn (Oxford University Press, 2008); Richard Jones, *Mental Capacity Act Manual*, 3rd edn (London: Sweet & Maxwell, 2008).
[120] Bamford Review of Mental Health and Learning Disability, *A Comprehensive Legal Framework for Mental Health and Learning Disability* (2007).

Rights of Persons with Disabilities[121] has also raised awareness of mental capacity law.

In 1995, the White Paper on Mental Health proposed the introduction of Adult Care Orders for people with mental disorder who are abused, exploited or neglected, or at risk of abuse or exploitation.[122] This proposal was not implemented in the Mental Health Act 2001 and is not discussed in the Law Reform Commission's consultation papers and report.[123]

The Law Reform Commission's consideration of issues of mental capacity began with its Consultation Paper on *Law and the Elderly* in 2003.[124] The Commission stated that while the majority of elderly people do not need any special legal support or protection, there is a significant minority who, because of illness or disability, impaired mental capacity or social and economic dependency, do need protection. They may require protection from physical or mental abuse, they may need protection from misuse of their money or property, at some stage they may need help with making decisions and, ultimately, may need a substitute decision maker.[125] The Commission reviewed the law concerning legal capacity, capacity to make a will, enduring powers of attorney, wards of court and protection against abuse. It proposed that the wards of court system should be abolished and replaced by a new system for protecting vulnerable adults.[126] It proposed a substitute decision-making system which it proposed to call Guardianship. This would provide for the making of Guardianship orders in the case of people who do not have legal capacity and who are in need of guardianship and the appointment of Personal Guardians who would make some of the required substitute decisions. A Guardianship Tribunal chaired by a judge would make the decision about the general legal capacity of an individual. There would also be an intervention and personal protection system which would provide for specific orders–Services Orders, Intervention Orders and Adult Care Orders. The system would be supervised by a new independent Office of the Public Guardian.

13–28 The Commission issued a second consultation paper on *Vulnerable Adults and the Law: Capacity* in 2005.[127] This paper considered legal capacity issues relevant to all adults with limited decision making, not just older adults. The Commission recommended that the proposed capacity legislation should

---

121 Convention on the Rights of Persons with Disabilities, 2006 [A/RES/61/106].
122 Department of Health, *A New Mental Health Act: White Paper* (Dublin: Stationery Office, 1995), Chapter 8.
123 See Anne Marie O'Neill, *Wards of Court in Ireland* (Dublin: FirstLaw, 2004), pp.186–191. The Commission cites the White Paper briefly for other purposes in its *Consultation Paper on Law and the Elderly* (2003) at paras 6.62–3.
124 Law Reform Commission, *Consultation Paper on Law and the Elderly* (CP23, 2003).
125 Law Reform Commission, *Consultation Paper on Law and the Elderly* (CP23, 2003), para.1.
126 Contrast Anne-Marie O'Neill, *Wards of Court in Ireland* (Dublin: First Law, 2004), pp.206–8, who recommends reform of the wards of court system rather than its abolition.
127 Law Reform Commission, *Consultation Paper on Vulnerable Adults and the Law: Capacity* (CP37, 2005).

contain a functional definition of capacity which focuses on an adult's cognitive ability to understand the nature and consequences of a decision in the context of available choices. It also recommended that where it has been determined that a person lacks capacity in a particular area which has an ongoing impact on their decision-making ability, the proposed capacity legislation should make provision for a system of automatic periodic review of that determination, with appropriate procedural safeguards to protect the rights of the person concerned. The Commission recommended that capacity to make healthcare decisions should be assessed on the basis of the statutory functional test of capacity proposed in the Consultation Paper, and that the code of practice for healthcare professionals should provide guidelines on the assessment of capacity to make a healthcare decision.

13–29 These consultation papers were followed by a report on *Vulnerable Adults and the Law*[128] in 2006, which included a draft Scheme of a Mental Capacity and Guardianship Bill as an Appendix. The Commission noted that it had changed its recommendations to some extent in light of developments since publication of the earlier papers, and in light of submissions received. Thus, for example, it concluded that the wide-ranging role envisaged for the Office of Public Guardian in 2003, particularly as regards the making of Service Orders and Adult Care Orders, would not be appropriate given the developments within the Health Service Executive (HSE).[129] The Commission also recommended that a "common sense" approach should be applied in determining when a separate functional assessment of capacity is merited. It said that in certain situations a person is unlikely to recover lost capacity.Therefore, in individual situations, where an adult profoundly lacks or has lost decision-making capacity in a particular sphere, or generally, and is unlikely to regain it, the need to carry out a capacity assessment every time a decision requires to be made may be reduced.[130] The Commission made a number of references to the Mental Capacity Act 2005, which had recently been passed in England and Wales. Donnelly has argued that the Commission's Report should have recommended the appointment of personal advocates, thus recognising that special efforts have to be made to provide meaningful protection for the rights of people lacking capacity.[131]

A Private Members' Bill on mental capacity and guardianship,[132] based on the Law Reform Commission's scheme, was presented in 2007 by Senators Henry and O'Toole and debated briefly in the Seanad.[133]

---

[128] Law Reform Commission, *Report on Vulnerable Adults and the Law* (Report 83, 2006).

[129] Law Reform Commission, *Report on Vulnerable Adults and the Law* (Report 83, 2006), para.1.53.

[130] Law Reform Commission, *Report on Vulnerable Adults and the Law* (Report 83, 2006), para.2.69. See commentary in Mary Donnelly, "Assessing Legal Capacity: Process and the Operation of the Functional Test" (2007) 2 *Judicial Studies Institute Journal* 141 at 148–9.

[131] Mary Donnelly, "Legislating for Incapacity: Developing a Rights-Based Framework" (2008) 30 D.U.L.J. 395 at 436.

[132] Mental Capacity and Guardianship Bill 2007.

[133] 186 *Seanad Debates* 425–450 (February 21, 2007).

The Scheme of the Mental Capacity Bill

13–30 The Department of Justice, Equality and Law Reform published the Heads of a Mental Capacity Bill in September 2008.[134] This Bill would repeal the Lunacy (Regulation) Ireland Act 1871[135] and set up a scheme broadly similar to the one suggested in the Law Reform Commission's report. The Bill also makes proposals regarding powers of attorney, which are discussed above at paras 13–25 to 13–26. The Bill does not close the *"Bournewood* gap", discussed above in Chapter 5.

13–31 The Bill commences with a set of guiding principles in Head 1 which include a presumption of capacity, the least restrictive principle and the need to take account of the person's past and present wishes, where ascertainable. Acts and decisions must be made in the person's best interests. In determining best interests, regard must be had to the criteria in Head 3. For example, the person making the determination must permit and encourage the person to participate as fully as possible in any act or decision.[136] They must take into account the views of any carer or other relevant person. However, there is sufficient compliance with Head 3 if a person reasonably believes that what they do or decide is in the best interests of the person concerned.[137]

Capacity to make a decision is defined in Head 2 as the ability to understand the nature and consequences of a decision in the context of available choices at the time the decision is to be made. A person lacks capacity if they are unable to understand the information relevant to the decision, to retain that information, to use or weigh that information as part of the process of making the decision, or to communicate their decision.

13–32 The Bill adopts a tiered approach to decision making. At the lowest level, Head 16 deals with "informal decision-making". If a person does an act in connection with the personal care, healthcare or treatment of another person whose decision-making capacity is in doubt and if that person complies with Head 16(2), the person will not incur liability. Head 16(2) requires that it is in the other person's best interests that the act be done, the person took reasonable steps to establish whether the other person lacked capacity regarding the matter and the person reasonably believed when doing the act that the other person lacked capacity in relation to the matter. However, this does not exclude liability (civil or criminal) for negligence in doing the act.

---

[134] Department of Justice, Equality and Law Reform, *Scheme of Mental Capacity Bill 2008*. For ease of reference, the Scheme of the Bill will be referred to as "the Bill" in the text.

[135] *Scheme of Mental Capacity Bill*, Head 23.

[136] The Law Reform Commission's scheme did not contain a best interests section, and the Commission expressed reservations about the best interests principle at paras 2.94–6 of its 2006 report. See counter arguments in Mary Donnelly, "Legislating for Incapacity: Developing a Rights-Based Framework" (2008) 30 D.U.L.J. 395 at 424.

[137] Scheme of Mental Capacity Bill 2008, Head 3(2).

The second and third tiers in the Bill are the Personal Guardian and the court. The Bill does not establish a tribunal; instead it gives jurisdiction to the Circuit Court and to the High Court.[138] Where the rateable valuation of any land to which an application relates exceeds €254, the Circuit Court must, if an application is made to it, transfer the proceedings to the High Court.[139] The courts may make declarations as to whether a person has or lacks capacity to make a certain decision (or decisions on certain matters) and as to the lawfulness or otherwise of any act done, or yet to be done, in relation to the person.[140] If the court has declared that a person lacks capacity to make a decision concerning welfare, or property and affairs, the court may make the decision on the person's behalf[141] or appoint a Personal Guardian to make the decision or decisions on the person's behalf.[142] The court may make such further orders or give such directions, and confer on a Personal Guardian such powers or impose on them such duties, as it thinks necessary or expedient for giving effect to, or otherwise in connection with, an order or appointment made by it.[143] Lists of powers which may be conferred on Personal Guardians are provided, such as where the person should live, giving or refusing consent to healthcare treatment, management of property and sale or acquisition of property.[144] The High Court would have exclusive jurisdiction concerning non-therapeutic sterilisation, withdrawal of artificial life-sustaining treatment and organ donation.[145]

13–33 Applications would normally, with the permission of the court, be made on notice to the person to whom the application relates. Interim orders could be made.[146] The court could appoint a suitable person (who may be a legal representative) to act in the name of, or on behalf of, or to represent the person to whom the proceedings relate.[147] The Minister must draw up a scheme for legal advice and, where warranted, legal representation.[148] Rules of Court must make provision for various matters, including the manner in which proceedings are commenced and enabling the court to proceed with a hearing in the absence of

---

[138] The courts when exercising jurisdiction under the Bill would be known as the High Court for Care and Protection and the Circuit Court of Care and Protection. The Law Society has recommended the creation of a specialist tribunal or court—Law Society, *Submission on Scheme of Mental Capacity Bill 2008* (2009), p.2.

[139] Scheme of Mental Capacity Bill 2008, Head 4. The Law Society has suggested that court jurisdiction should not be linked to valuation of property—Law Society, *Submission on Scheme of Mental Capacity Bill 2008* (2009), p.2.

[140] Scheme of Mental Capacity Bill 2008, Head 5.

[141] Where the court is satisfied that the matter is urgent or it is otherwise expedient for it to do so.

[142] Scheme of Mental Capacity Bill 2008, Head 6.

[143] Scheme of Mental Capacity Bill 2008, Head 6(4).

[144] Scheme of Mental Capacity Bill 2008, Heads 7 and 8.

[145] Scheme of Mental Capacity Bill 2008, Head 21.

[146] Scheme of Mental Capacity Bill 2008, Head 12.

[147] Scheme of Mental Capacity Bill 2008, Head 9(5).

[148] Scheme of Mental Capacity Bill 2008, Head 15.

the person to whom the proceedings relate.[149] The Rules would also permit the application to court to be disposed of without a hearing.[150]

13–34 Head 11 contains restrictions on the powers of Personal Guardians. The Personal Guardian may not refuse consent to the carrying out or continuation of life-sustaining treatment. They may not do an act that is intended to restrain the person unless acting within the scope of an authority expressly conferred by the court, the person lacks capacity in relation to the matter (or the Personal Guardian reasonably believes this), the Personal Guardian reasonably believes that it is necessary to do the act to prevent harm, or the act is a proportionate response to the likelihood of the person suffering harm or the seriousness of that harm.[151] Restraint is defined as using, or threatening to use, force to secure the doing of an act which the person resists; or restricting the person's liberty of movement, whether or not the person resists; or authorising another person to do any of these things.[152] However, a Personal Guardian does more than merely restrain a person if they deprive that person of their liberty within the meaning of art.5(1) of the ECHR (whether or not the Personal Guardian is a public authority).[153]

13–35 The person who has been found to lack capacity may apply, with the court's permission, at any time for a review of the decision regarding their capacity.[154] In any event, the court must review the decision at intervals of such length, not being more than 36 months, as the court considers appropriate.

It would be a criminal offence for a Personal Guardian (or other person caring for a person lacking capacity) to ill-treat or wilfully neglect the person.[155] The Bill also gives effect in the State to the Hague Convention on the International Protection of Adults 2000.[156]

13–36 The Public Guardian would be appointed by the Government on the nomination of the Minister.[157] They would hold office for six years, and could be re-appointed for a second or subsequent term.[158] The objectives and functions of the Public Guardian are set out in Head 32. These include supervising

---

[149]   Scheme of Mental Capacity Bill 2008, Head 9(6).
[150]   The Irish Human Rights Commission has recommended that Head 9(6)(c) should be amended to specifically provide that an application to court can only be disposed of without a hearing in the limited circumstances where a provisional measure is needed in a case of emergency.
[151]   Scheme of Mental Capacity Bill 2008, Head 11(7). See similar provision in s.6 Mental Capacity Act 2005 (E.&W.).
[152]   Scheme of Mental Capacity Bill 2008, Head 11(8).
[153]   Scheme of Mental Capacity Bill 2008, Head 11(9).
[154]   Scheme of Mental Capacity Bill 2008, Head 14(1). Applications may also be brought by a Personal Guardian–Head 9(1).
[155]   Scheme of Mental Capacity Bill 2008, Head 27.
[156]   Scheme of Mental Capacity Bill 2008, Head 58 and Schedule 4.
[157]   Scheme of Mental Capacity Bill 2008, Head 29.
[158]   Scheme of Mental Capacity Bill 2008, Head 30.

Personal Guardians, receiving reports from Personal Guardians, dealing with complaints and providing information and advice to Personal Guardians. They could direct a Special or General Visitor to visit a Personal Guardian and make a report on such matters as they may direct.[159] The Law Society has recommended the use of the title "reviewer" rather than "visitor".[160] It also recommends inclusion of protection for whistleblowers.[161]

The Public Guardian must also issue codes of practice governing assessment of capacity, informal decision making, guidance of Personal Guardians and urgent treatment.[162] All codes of practice must be approved by the Minister for Justice, Equality and Law Reform.[163] It has been suggested that the Office of Public Guardian should be established on an interim basis (as, for example, happened with the National Consumer Agency) to enable the process of drawing up codes to begin while the Bill is being discussed, to inform the development of an appropriate legislative framework.[164]

Responses to the Scheme of the Bill

13–37 The Irish Human Rights Commission (IHRC) has made a number of observations on the scheme of the Bill.[165] The Commission recommends that there should be access to legal representation and legal aid at all applications concerning determination of whether a person lacks capacity.[166] The Commission bases this recommendation on the Strasbourg cases, *Airey v Ireland*[167] and *Steel and Morris v United Kingdom*[168] and the Irish cases *State (Healy) v O'Donoghue*[169] and *Stevenson v Landy*.[170] It may be added that the lack of automatic access to legal representation and legal aid is a major omission in the Bill. This is in stark contrast with the Mental Health Act 2001, which provides automatic legal aid for involuntarily admitted patients.

The Commission expresses dissatisfaction with the Bill's provisions concerning periodic review of capacity, including the reference to 36 months in

---

[159] Scheme of Mental Capacity Bill 2008, Head 32(2)(e). See also Head 32(6) and Head 38.

[160] Law Society, *Submission on Scheme of Mental Capacity Bill 2008* (2009), pp.7–8.

[161] Law Society, *Submission on Scheme of Mental Capacity Bill 2008* (2009), p.8.

[162] Scheme of Mental Capacity Bill 2008, Head 39.

[163] In the case of healthcare matters, the approval by the Minister for Justice will occur following consultation with the Minister for Health and Children.

[164] Mary Donnelly, "Legislating for Incapacity: Developing a Rights-Based Framework" (2008) 30 D.U.L.J. 395 at 437–8.

[165] Irish Human Rights Commission, *Observations on the Scheme of the Mental Capacity Bill 2008*.

[166] Irish Human Rights Commission, *Observations on the Scheme of the Mental Capacity Bill 2008*, pp.8–11.

[167] (1979) 2 E.H.R.R. 305.

[168] (2005) 41 E.H.R.R. 22.

[169] [1976] I.R. 325.

[170] High Court, Lardner J., February 10, 1993. See para.13–07 above.

Head 14. It recommends that there should be a standalone provision requiring the court, at the time a declaration is made, to set a time frame for a review of its decisions based on the individual circumstances of the case. There should also be a provision setting out a reasonable time limit for automatic periodic review of the court's decisions.[171] The Law Society made a similar suggestion.[172]

In order to protect the right to a fair hearing, the Commission recommends that the subject of incapacity proceedings should have the opportunity to challenge the evidence presented to the court and to present their own independent evidence, medical or otherwise.[173] The court should only be able to proceed with a hearing in the absence of the person if, in the opinion of the court, such attendance might be prejudicial to the person's mental health, well-being or emotional condition.

The Commission recommends that the Bill should expressly provide that court orders should specify the necessary supervision required of the Personal Guardian, including their obligation to report at regular intervals, as determined by the court based on the individual circumstances of the case.[174]

13–38 Existing wards of court, including those detained in approved centres, would still remain under the old system unless they successfully apply for a review of their wardship. The Irish Human Rights Commission recommends that no person should be admitted to detention under the 2008 Scheme without the safeguards contained in the 2001 Act in relation to the permissible grounds for detention and the procedure by which a person may be received and detained in an approved centre. It states that any person who lacks legal capacity to make healthcare decisions and is admitted to an approved centre should be admitted as an involuntary patient under the 2001 Act with all the ensuing safeguards necessary to ensure their lawful detention under art.5 of the ECHR. Alternatively, the 2008 Scheme could be amended to ensure that equivalent safeguards, as contained in the 2001 Act, are applied to persons detained for treatment under that Act.[175] The Commission points out that there might be constitutional difficulties were an MHT to be reviewing a decision of a superior court to detain a person, even if the tribunal were reviewing the need for ongoing detention of that person within the meaning of the 2001 Act. The IHRC considers that it is preferable to ensure that persons admitted under the 2008 Scheme are deemed to be involuntary patients under the 2001 Act. This would ensure that their admission would require the decision of a consultant psychiatrist, whose decision might then be reviewed by a tribunal without any difficulties, and would also ensure the other safeguards under the 2001 Act.[176]

---

[171] *Observations on the Scheme of the Mental Capacity Bill 2008*, p.16.
[172] Law Society, *Submission on Scheme of Mental Capacity Bill 2008* (2009), p.5.
[173] *Observations on the Scheme of the Mental Capacity Bill 2008*, p.13.
[174] *Observations on the Scheme of the Mental Capacity Bill 2008*, pp.7–8.
[175] *Observations on the Scheme of the Mental Capacity Bill 2008*, pp.19–20.
[176] *Observations on the Scheme of the Mental Capacity Bill 2008*, p.25.

Relationship between the Scheme of the Bill and the Mental Health Act 2001

13–39 It is important that the relationship between the Mental Health Act 2001 and the Scheme of the 2008 Bill be clarified and the rights of persons who lack capacity be strengthened. The IHRC's proposal that any person admitted to an approved centre under the 2008 Scheme should be admitted on an involuntary basis under the 2001 Act is a possible way forward, although it may not be appropriate in all cases and may need further development.

More importantly, the Scheme of the 2008 Bill does not comprehensively address the problem of the "Bournewood gap", discussed above in Chapter 5. The problem of compliant incapacitated patients who are classified as "voluntary" but in reality are in de facto detention raises serious human rights concerns which need to be addressed as a matter of urgency.

ADVANCE CARE DIRECTIVES

13–40 An Advance Care Directive is where a person consciously sets out their wishes about what should happen to them in the event of an accident or illness that makes it impossible for them to communicate their wishes directly.[177] Advance Care Directives are relevant to mental health law, given that the person's illness which makes it impossible to communicate their wishes may be a mental disorder. They are sometimes also referred to as a "living will".[178] The right to prepare an Advance Care Directive stems from a person's right to self-determination and their related rights to bodily integrity, privacy and dignity.[179] There are various types of Advance Care Directive. One key distinction is that in some directives, a healthcare proxy will be nominated, whereas in others there will be no such nomination. If a healthcare proxy is named, they will ensure that the wishes as expressed by the author of the Advance Care Directive are followed and consult with the medical professional if there is any ambiguity in the Advance Care Directive.[180]

There has been legislation concerning Advance Care Directives in all states of the United States, beginning in 1976[181], and more recently in England and Wales.[182]

---

[177] Law Reform Commission, *Bioethics: Advance Care Directives* (LRC Consultation Paper 51–2008), p.2.

[178] See discussion of terminology in LRC, *Bioethics: Advance Care Directives*, paras 1.12–1.18.

[179] Irish Council for Bioethics, *Is It Time For Advance Healthcare Directives? Opinion* (2007), p.15.

[180] *Bioethics: Advance Care Directives,* paras 1.63–1.65.

[181] See for example Bretton J. Horttor, "A Survey of Living Will and Advanced Health Care Directives" (1998) 74 *North Dakota Law Review* 233.

[182] Sections 24–26 of the Mental Capacity Act 2005.

There is no formal legal mechanism for Advance Care Directives in Ireland at present, but there is no law prohibiting them, which means that in practice medical personnel will attempt to take into account such directives.

13–41 The recent Law Reform Commission Consultation Paper follows previous reports by the Medical Council[183] and the Irish Council for Bioethics.[184] It does not deal with psychiatric Advance Care Directives[185] or psychiatric Ulysses Directives. A Ulysses Directive is where a person binds themselves to psychiatric treatment and overrides, in advance, their refusals during acute episodes of their illness. The Commission also does not deal with euthanasia or assisted suicide.

Given that patients have a constitutional right to refuse treatment,[186] the Commission recommends that the law on Advance Care Directives should cover negative directives to refuse treatment only, not positive directives requesting a particular type of treatment.[187] A similar approach was taken by the Court of Appeal in *R. (Burke) v General Medical Council*.[188] The Commission provisionally recommends that a refusal to consent to treatment on religious grounds will in general (subject to constitutional considerations) constitute a valid Advance Care Directive.[189] The Commission provisionally recommends that the capacity to refuse healthcare decisions should be assessed on the functional test of capacity. The Commission also provisionally recommends that the statutory codes of practice be formulated to guide healthcare professionals when assessing the capacity of an individual.[190] It recommends that makers of Advance Care Directives should be encouraged to consult with a medical professional when making an Advance Care Directive. In the case of Advance Care Directives refusing life-sustaining medical treatment, it recommends that medical advice must be obtained for the Advance Care Directive to be valid.[191]

The Commission provisionally recommends that both oral and written Advance Care Directives would be valid, while noting that a practitioner or a court will be hesitant to rely on a refusal without clear evidence that it was meant to be taken seriously.[192] In the case of life-sustaining treatment, the Commission provisionally recommends that only written Advance Care Directives would be valid, and these would need to be witnessed. A competent

---

[183]　Medical Council of Ireland, *Discussion Document on Advance Directives* (2006).
[184]　Irish Council for Bioethics, *Is It Time For Advance Healthcare Directives? Opinion* (2007).
[185]　Where a person expresses their treatment preferences regarding a mental disorder in writing.
[186]　*Re A Ward of Court (No.2)* [1996] 2 I.R. 79.
[187]　This does not mean that such requests cannot be made, only that they will not be binding.
[188]　[2005] E.W.C.A. Civ. 1003; [2005] 2 F.L.R. 1223. See also *Burke v United Kingdom*, Application No. 19807/06.
[189]　*Bioethics: Advance Care Directives*, paras 2.49–2.64.
[190]　*Bioethics: Advance Care Directives*, para.3.35.
[191]　*Bioethics: Advance Care Directives*, paras 4.22–4.23.
[192]　*Bioethics: Advance Care Directives*, para.4.09, citing Peter Bartlett, *Blackstone's Guide to the Mental Capacity Act 2005*, 2nd edn (Oxford, 2008), para.3.116.

person should be permitted to verbally revoke their Advance Care Directive regardless of whether it was a verbal or written Advance Care Directive.[193] As Campbell notes, although limiting revocation to the competent author of the directive only may seem unduly strict, its benefit lies in the fact that it may prevent hasty drafting of living wills.[194]

13–42 The Consultation Paper includes detailed discussion of possible legal liability of medical professionals who give treatment which is contrary to an Advance Care Directive.[195] This potential liability includes criminal charges, torts such as negligence and battery and professional misconduct proceedings. The Commission provisionally recommends that a healthcare professional would not be liable if they follow an Advance Care Directive which they believe to be valid and applicable.[196] Due to the ethical issues involved in following an Advance Care Directive, the Commission invites submissions on whether consequences and sanctions should follow if a medical professional fails to follow a valid and applicable Advance Care Directive.[197]

As this book went to press, the Law Reform Commission issued its report on Advance Care Directives.[198]

13–43 As stated earlier, the Law Reform Commission chose not to deal with psychiatric Advance Care Directives or Ulysses contracts. The introduction of these directives and contracts would lead to further complex issues which may be discussed in the future. There is a growing literature available which considers some of the issues which would arise.[199] For example, Exworthy argues that the enactment of the Mental Capacity Act 2005 in England and Wales was a missed opportunity to introduce psychiatric Advance Care Directives. He says:

> "Advance decisions in favour of specified psychiatric treatments offer the prospect of more than just a ready reference to a person's legally competent choices after he has lost capacity. The process of formulating an appropriate and relevant advance decision demands a dialogue between the individual concerned and the mental health professionals. This can be beneficial in its

---

[193] *Bioethics: Advance Care Directives,* para.4.78.
[194] Elizabeth Campbell, "The Case for Living Wills in Ireland" (2006) 12 *Medico-Legal Journal of Ireland* 5 at 15.
[195] *Bioethics: Advance Care Directives*, Chapter 5.
[196] *Bioethics: Advance Care Directives*, para.5.51.
[197] *Bioethics: Advance Care Directives*, para.5.64.
[198] Law Reform Commission, *Bioethics: Advance Care Directives* (Report 94, 2009).
[199] Tim Exworthy "Psychiatric Advance Decisions: an Opportunity Missed" (2004) *Journal of Mental Health Law* 129; Elizabeth Gallagher, "Advance Directives for Psychiatric Care: A Theoretical and Practical Overview for Legal Professionals" (1998) *Psychology, Public Policy and Law* 746; George Szmukler & John Dawson, "Commentary: Towards Resolving Some Dilemmas Concerning Psychiatric Advance Directives" (2006) 34 *Journal of the American Academy of Psychiatry and the Law* 398.

own right and can also have a more pervasive effect on the therapeutic relationship and the person's subsequent psychiatric career."[200]

Since Exworthy's article was published, there has been limited introduction of psychiatric Advance Care Directives in England and Wales through the Mental Health Act 2007. The 2007 Act amended the Mental Health Act 1983 to allow for some recognition of advance directives concerning electro-convulsive therapy (ECT).[201]

MARRIAGE

Capacity to Marry

13–44 In *Durham v Durham*[202] it was said that the contract of marriage is a very simple one, which does not require a high degree of intelligence to comprehend. Hannen P. said that it is an engagement between a man and woman to live together, and love one another as husband and wife, to the exclusion of all others.[203] The free consent of both parties is a prerequisite to a valid marriage. As well as requiring an exercise of independent will, "informed consent" means that each party must have an understanding of the nature and responsibilities of marriage.[204] Munby J. has said that we must be careful not to set the test of capacity to marry too high, "lest it operate as an unfair, unnecessary and indeed discriminatory bar against the mentally disabled."[205] The relatively low threshold of understanding required is illustrated by *Re Park*[206] where a man was held to have capacity to marry at 11am on a particular day, but not to have the capacity to make a will at 2.45pm on the same day.

The Marriage of Lunatics Act 1811[207] renders void a marriage contracted by a person found to be a "lunatic" by inquisition. The modern effect of this is that it appears that any marriage by a ward of court will be void even if conducted during a lucid interval.[208] The 1811 Act has been continued in force in 2004 and 2007.[209] Donnelly notes that it is arguable that the 1811 Act is unconstitutional.[210]

---

[200] Tim Exworthy, "Psychiatric Advance Decisions: An Opportunity Missed" (2004) J. Mental Health L. 129 at 141.

[201] See s.58A of the Mental Health Act 1983, as inserted by s.27 of the Mental Health Act 2007; commentary in Richard Jones, *Mental Health Act Manual*, 11th edn (London: Thomson Sweet and Maxwell, 2008), pp.315–7.

[202] (1885) 10 P.D. 80.

[203] (1885) 10 P.D. 80 at 82.

[204] *Consultation Paper on Vulnerable Adults and the Law: Capacity*, para.6.31.

[205] *Sheffield City Council v E.* [2004] E.W.H.C. 2808 (Fam); [2005] Fam. 326, para.144.

[206] [1954] P. 112; [1953] 3 W.L.R. 1012.

[207] 51 Geo.3, c.37.

[208] Law Reform Commission, *Consultation Paper on Vulnerable Adults and the Law: Capacity* (CP 37, 2005), para.6.48, citing *Turner v Myers* (1808) 1 Hag. Con. 414.

[209] Civil Registration Act 2004; Statute Law Revision Act 2007.

[210] Mary Donnelly, "Assessing Legal Capacity: Process and the Operation of the Functional Test" (2007) 2 *Judicial Studies Institute Journal* 141 at 150.

The Law Reform Commission stated in 2005 that it regarded the 1811 Act as anachronistic and out of step with modern views of mental disability and a functional approach to capacity issues. It said that the 1811 Act may breach the right to marry under art.12 of the ECHR.[211] The Commission's view was that the Act serves no useful purpose and on balance it considered that it should be repealed.[212]

The scheme of the Mental Capacity Bill 2008[213] states that the Bill would not affect the law concerning capacity and consent to marriage or civil partnership.[214] It also proposes to repeal the Marriage of Lunatics Act 1811.[215]

Nullity

13–45 There have been numerous cases concerning annulment of marriage based on mental incapacity.[216] It is sometimes stated that there is a presumption that a marriage is valid unless the opposite is proven, but some doubt has been expressed about this.[217] The court will consider whether the person had capacity to enter the marriage and also to sustain a normal, caring relationship.

13–46 In *R.S.J. v J.S.J.*,[218] the husband was seeking the annulment based on his own mental incapacity. Barrington J. said that if it could be shown that at the date of the marriage, the petitioner, through illness, lacked the capacity to form a considerate or caring relationship with his wife, this would be a ground on which a decree of nullity might be granted.[219] He relied on a comment by Kenny J. in

---

[211] *Hamer v UK* (1982) 4 E.H.R.R. 139.
[212] *Consultation Paper on Vulnerable Adults and the Law: Capacity*, para.6.50. See also Law Reform Commission, *Report on Vulnerable Adults and the Law* (Report 83, 2006), paras 3.15–3.19.
[213] Department of Justice, Equality and Law Reform, *Scheme of Mental Capacity Bill 2008.*
[214] Scheme of Mental Capacity Bill 2008, Head 20(1).
[215] Scheme of Mental Capacity Bill 2008, Head 20(2).
[216] See *Consultation Paper on Vulnerable Adults and the Law: Capacity*, paras 6.41–6.47; Simon Mills, *Clinical Practice and the Law*, 2nd edn (Haywards Heath: Tottel, 2007), pp.185–190.
[217] See, for example, doubts expressed by McCarthy J. in *U.F. v J.C.* [1991] 2 I.R. 330 at 358–9: "If the observations of Kenny J. in *S. v. S.* [1976–77] I.L.R.M. 156 mean, as apparently in the instant case Keane J. thought, that there is a greater onus imposed upon a petitioner, then, in my view, this was an incorrect statement of the law applicable in this jurisdiction. There may have been a misunderstanding of the reference to the Constitution contained in *N. (orse. K.) v. K.* [1985] I.R. 733; the guarantee protects the institution of marriage but it does not presuppose the existence of a valid marriage in any given case so as to increase the burden of proof where a petitioner calls in aid s.13 of the Act of 1870. It begs the question to say that the constitutional guarantee endorses, for instance, the citation from Lord Birkenhead in *C. (orse. H.) v. C.* [1921] P. 399. The burden of proof point only arises where there is an issue of fact. There was no such issue here. The point is irrelevant to the issue as to what constitutes incapacity."
[218] [1982] I.L.R.M. 263.
[219] [1982] I.L.R.M. 263 at 265.

S. v S.[220] that the courts should recognise the great advances made in psychological medicine since 1870[221] and should frame new rules to reflect them. Barrington J. accepted that the petitioner, both before and after his marriage, suffered from some form of personality defect or illness similar to schizophrenia. However, he found the petitioner's own evidence in many respects unsatisfactory, and he was not satisfied that he had proved that on the date of his wedding he was so incapacitated as to make the marriage void or voidable. Even if the marriage in this case were a voidable marriage, it would be a marriage voidable at the instance of the wife and not of the husband. It would be necessary for the husband to show that the wife had repudiated the marriage.

13–47 The marriage in *D. v C.*[222] was found to be voidable due to the husband's manic depression (bipolar disorder) before, during and after the marriage, which had severely impaired his capacity to form and sustain a normal marriage. The nullity order was granted, as it was sought by the wife and she had not approbated the marriage.[223] Costello J. rejected the argument that she was estopped from petitioning for nullity due to earlier court proceedings concerning a barring order. He said that the previous court acted on the assumption that the plaintiff in those proceedings was the "spouse" of the defendant in them but the court was not asked to determine the validity of the marriage and he concluded therefore that no estoppel of any sort arose by virtue of those proceedings.

13–48 In *D.C. (Orse. D.W.) v D.W.*[224] there was clear evidence that the wife had schizophrenia at the time of the marriage and that she incapable, because of the schizophrenia, of entering into and forming a normal marriage relationship with her husband. Blayney J. held that the marriage was voidable and that the husband had repudiated and avoided the marriage by his earlier seeking and obtaining a decree of nullity from the ecclesiastical courts. In later cases, it was held that the other spouse need not have repudiated the marriage.[225]

13–49 The husband's paranoid schizophrenia in *M.E. v A.E.*[226] was held to have prevented him from giving full, free and informed consent to the marriage, as a

---

[220]   [1976–77] I.L.R.M. 156; Supreme Court, July 1, 1976.
[221]   The origins of the law of nullity as it applies in Ireland lie in the provisions of the Matrimonial Causes and Marriage Law (Ireland) Amendment Act 1870.
[222]   [1984] I.L.R.M. 173.
[223]   The wife did not know that her husband had a psychiatric illness at the time of their marriage until several years after the ceremony had taken place and, until she obtained legal advice shortly before the institution of the nullity proceedings, she was unaware that her husband's illness entitled her to a nullity decree.
[224]   [1987] I.L.R.M. 58.
[225]   *P.C. v V.C.* [1990] 2 I.R. 91; *P.McG. v. A.F.* [2003] I.E.H.C. 19; High Court, Quirke J., May 7, 2003; *O'K. v O'K.* [2005] I.E.H.C. 384; High Court, O'Higgins J., July 29, 2005
[226]   [1987] I.R. 147. For a case involving paranoid psychosis, see *P.K. v M.B.N. (Orse. K.)*, Supreme Court, April 3, 1995.

result of which the marriage was void. O'Hanlon J. said that as the absence of the necessary capacity to understand the nature of the duties and responsibilities which marriage creates rendered the marriage void and not merely voidable, it was unnecessary to deal with the question of the possible approbation by the petitioner of a voidable marriage. A similar result was reached in *J.S. v M.J.*[227] where the wife had depression occurring as part of a schizo-affective illness which pre-dated the marriage.

13–50 In *O'K. v O'K.*,[228] O'Higgins J. stated that it is important to note that the existence of bipolar illness does not indicate that a person has not the capacity to enter and sustain a marital relationship. Very many people subject to this illness are capable of contracting and sustaining rich, enduring marital relationships. The question in the case was as to whether the petitioner, by reason of his illness and his personality, was incapable of sustaining such a relationship. His illness had manifested itself in the mid-1980s and had caused him to be hospitalised on several occasions, on one of which he was an involuntary patient in a psychiatric hospital. The illness had had devastating effects on his professional life and led to huge disruption and unhappiness in his private life. Unfortunately, despite medical treatment the petitioner continued to suffer from his illness and there had been some impairment to his cognitive function. In addition to his serious illness the petitioner had a great difficulty or inability to appreciate the feelings of others. In those circumstances, a decree of nullity was granted.

13–51 A personality disorder may be a sufficient ground for annulment, as illustrated by *W. (Orse. C.) v C.*[229] Barron J. accepted psychiatric evidence that the husband suffered from a gross personality disorder which had been present all his life and predated his marriage. He had a complete contempt for authority and saw others only as puppets to be manipulated. He was unable to see any fault in himself and was incapable of changing. The husband was unable to form a meaningful relationship with any marriage partner. Barron J. also held that the wife's decision in the circumstances to marry him could only be regarded as one brought about by the strain of her circumstances and the "lack of ability for normal thought" which she was manifesting at that time.[230]

13–52 However, an "inadequate" or "immature" personality was held not to be sufficient on the facts in *P.C. v D.O'B.*[231] Carroll J. found that the wife at the

---

[227] [1997] I.E.H.C. 183; High Court, Lavan J., December 10, 1997.
[228] [2005] I.E.H.C. 384; High Court, O'Higgins J., July 29, 2005.
[229] [1989] I.R. 696.
[230] The wife, a school teacher, was pregnant as a result of forced intercourse and had been told by her school that she would lose her job if she did not marry the father of the child. She felt that she was dirty and dishonoured and that she was no longer an ordinary member of society. She said that she went around "like a zombie" during this time.
[231] High Court, Carroll J., October 2, 1985.

time of the marriage had an inadequate or immature personality.[232] She said this was a mental condition, not a mental illness. On one view, anyone who is immature is unsuited for marriage, but it could not be a ground for nullity unless it existed to an abnormal degree. The wife's immaturity was not of a sufficient degree to warrant holding that her consent to marriage was vitiated. The wife, notwithstanding her immaturity, was capable of contracting and did contract a valid marriage.

13–53 McCracken J. said in *S.C. v P.D.*[233] that what must be considered is the situation at the time of the marriage, and the law had not been extended so far as to say that a decree of nullity may be granted where a person suffered from a latent illness which did not affect their ability to enter into a marriage, but which might subsequently affect the ability to sustain that marriage. The wife suffered from a manic-depressive illness, a latent illness which, at the time of the marriage, had never manifested itself. At the time of the marriage, while she suffered from a latent illness, that illness did not render her incapable of forming and sustaining a normal life-long marital relationship, and thus the court did not grant the decree of nullity.[234]

13–54 Budd J. noted in *J.S. v C.S.*[235] that it may well be that a party who was incapable at the time of the marriage of forming a meaningful marital relationship, may, with medical help, stand a realistic prospect of being cured so that the capacity to form the required relationship may be restored or acquired. He also said that it may be that in an appropriate case, much consideration will have to be given to the prospect of curative treatment.[236] For this reason, he observed that there seems to be much to be said for the courts having the assistance of an independent psychiatric assessor. He rejected arguments that this appointment of an independent assessor would breach the wife's rights to bodily integrity and privacy, stating that she could refuse to attend if she wished.[237]

13–55 The question of homosexuality of a spouse as a possible ground for nullity has led to much litigation. Obviously, homosexuality is no longer

---

[232] The medical evidence was that she presented originally with a variety of behavioural problems, drug abuse, impulse control with men, and impulse control in coping with stress. Dr P. said that the diagnostic label for her was an immature personality or, in other, words an inadequate personality. He said she reacted impulsively to situations. Her two periods as an in-patient in hospital were relatively brief admissions during crisis periods.

[233] High Court, McCracken J., March 14, 1996.

[234] McCracken J. also noted that had she been treated with lithium at a much earlier stage, she would have been perfectly capable of sustaining the marriage, and indeed it might well have survived.

[235] [1997] 2 I.R. 506.

[236] [1997] 2 I.R. 506 at 511.

[237] [1997] 2 I.R. 506 at 521.

classified as a mental disorder, which meant that the courts had to consider whether it might in some cases lead to an incapacity to form and sustain a marriage relationship. Keane J. in the High Court in *U.F. v J.C.*[238] held that a petitioner who has contracted a marriage with someone of strongly homosexual inclinations but whose marriage is in all other respects valid could not obtain from the court an annulment of that marriage when the petitioner was unaware at the time of the marriage of those inclinations on the part of their intended spouse. However, the Supreme Court took the opposite view, holding that it was not necessary that the grounds of relief "should be confined to advances and knowledge which can be placed before the court, as strictly coming within the definition of psychiatric medicine".[239] It was sufficient to show that the relevant incapacity "arose from some other inherent quality or characteristic which could not be said to be voluntary or self-induced".[240] Recognition by psychiatrists of the existence of a homosexual nature and inclination, which is not susceptible to being changed, made it, in the court's view, a necessary and permissible development of the law of nullity that it should recognise that in certain circumstances the existence in one party to a marriage of an inherent and unalterable homosexual nature may form a proper legal ground for annulling the marriage at the instance of the other party to the marriage in the case, at least, where that party has no knowledge of the existence of the homosexual nature.[241]

13–56 Another source of litigation has been the question of emotional immaturity. In *B.D. v M.C. (orse. M.D.)*[242] it was held that the wife, at the time of the marriage and at all times material to the case, was suffering from such a degree of emotional immaturity as to preclude the formation of a normal marriage relationship. Barrington J. did not know if her condition could be described as an illness. It was apparently a "disorder" which required and might be susceptible to psychotherapy. But whether it was an illness or a disorder, he found that it was equally incapacitating so far as the formation of a marital relationship was concerned. This reasoning was followed by O'Hanlon J. in *P.C. v V.C.*,[243] where he held on the facts that there were elements of emotional immaturity and psychological disorder on both sides which prevented the formation of a normal, viable relationship with each other. Similarly, in *O'R. v B.*[244] Kinlen J. found that the husband at the time of entering into the marriage was so emotionally immature that he was unable to enter into and sustain a normal marital relationship. It was also clear that the wife came into the marriage with a baggage of various traumas and therefore both parties entered into an immature relationship.

---

[238] [1991] 2 I.R. 330.
[239] [1991] 2 I.R. 330 at 357 (Finlay C.J.).
[240] [1991] 2 I.R. 330 at 357 (Finlay C.J.).
[241] [1991] 2 I.R. 330 at 357 (Finlay C.J.).
[242] High Court, Barrington J., March 27, 1987.
[243] [1990] 2 I.R. 91.
[244] [1995] 2 I.L.R.M. 57.

O'Higgins J. in *J.W.H. v G.W.*[245] accepted it as being well-settled law that the court may grant a decree of nullity on the basis of incapacity to enter into a marital relationship by virtue of lack of emotional maturity as well as an incapacity by virtue of various psychological factors. He said he was of the view, however, that the emotional immaturity "has to be such as would render the person quite incapable of forming and sustaining marriage relationship."[246] On the facts in this case, there was no evidence of any psychological abnormality or lack of intelligence and he was not satisfied that the emotional immaturity, which was undoubtedly present, was such as would preclude the petitioner from contracting a valid marriage.

WILLS

13–57 According to the Succession Act, to be valid a will shall be made by a person who "is of sound disposing mind."[247] This is regarded as the legislative adoption of a judicial term of art, and therefore the requirement that the testator should know and approve the contents of the will also applies.[248] The combined effect is that "a testator should know and approve of the contents of the will and, at the time of execution of the will, be of sound mind, memory and understanding."[249]

A test of what constitutes "sound disposing mind" was set out by Cockburn C.J. in *Banks v Goodfellow*[250]:

> "It is essential … that a testator shall understand the nature of the act and its effects; shall understand the extent of the property of which he is disposing; shall be able to comprehend and appreciate the claims to which he ought to give effect; and with a view to the latter object that no disorder of the mind shall poison his affections, pervert his sense of right, or prevent the exercise of his natural faculties; that no insane delusion shall influence his will on disposing of his property, and bring about a disposal of it which would not have been made otherwise."[251]

Kelly J. approved of the *Banks v Goodfellow* test in *In Re O'Donnell.*[252]

---

[245] [1998] I.E.H.C. 33; High Court, O'Higgins J., February 25, 1998.
[246] [1998] I.E.H.C. 33; High Court, O'Higgins J., February 25, 1998, pp.6–7.
[247] Succession Act 1965, s.77. See generally Albert Keating, *Probate Causes and Related Matters* (Dublin: Round Hall Sweet & Maxwell, 2000), pp.46–49.
[248] *In the Goods of Glynn* [1990] 2 I.R. 326 at 337 (McCarthy J.); *In the Estate of Blackall*, Unreported, Supreme Court, April 1, 1998, p.13 (Lynch J.) For an example of a case where the testator was of sound mind but did not know and approve of the will's contents, see *In re Begley: Begley v. McHugh* [1939] I.R. 479.
[249] *In the Goods of Glynn* [1990] 2 I.R. 326 at 337 (McCarthy J.).
[250] (1870) L.R. 5 Q.B. 549; [1861–73] All E.R. Rep. 47.
[251] [1861–73] All E.R. Rep. 47 at 56.
[252] *In Re Andrew O'Donnell Deceased*, High Court, Kelly J., March 24, 1999.

The test for capacity to make a will is different than for other purposes, as illustrated by the case of *Re Park*[253] where a man was held to have capacity to marry at 11am on a particular day, but not to have the capacity to make a will at 2.45pm on the same day. Singleton L.J. disapproved of statements to the effect that a higher degree of capacity was required to make a will than for other purposes,[254] but nevertheless it is difficult to avoid this conclusion.

13–58 Normally, it would be expected that a person would have appropriate mental capacity both at the time they give instructions as regards the content of the will and also at the later stage when they sign the will. Difficulties can arise if their level of capacity changes between those two times. In *Re Glynn*[255] Mr Glynn gave instructions regarding his will to a priest and afterwards suffered a stroke which left him unable to speak. Fifteen days after the stroke, he executed the will in hospital by signifying his assent by means of nodding his head as the will was read to him, and then marking an "X" on the will. There was medical evidence that he would have been disorientated at the time. The Supreme Court split two to one, the majority holding that there was ample evidence that Mr Glynn fully appreciated what was going on and that the terms of the document upon which he placed his mark fully represented what he wanted done with regard to his property.[256] Walsh J., dissenting, said that the High Court decision had been based only on the opinion formed by the priest and his friend, who, having no medical expertise whatever, based their opinion on their previous acquaintance with the deceased, though they had never seen him in that condition before, as against the expert medical testimony of the medical practitioners attending the deceased. In Walsh J.'s view that was a finding which could not be upheld.[257]

13–59 It is a well-established common law principle that a duly executed will carries both a presumption of due execution and a presumption of testamentary capacity.[258] However, in a case where, for example, a person suffers a stroke which may affect their capacity, the onus shifts and lies on the party pro-pounding the will.[259] In *In Bonis Corboy*[260] arteriosclerosis of the cerebral vessels and convulsions had caused deterioration of the testator's brain and he was confined to bed. Budd J. said that the High Court should have had regard to important considerations concerning the onus of proof, and "nothing less than firm medical evidence by a doctor in a position to assess the testator's mental capacity could suffice to discharge the onus of proving him to have been a

---

[253]   [1954] P. 112; [1953] 3 W.L.R. 1012.
[254]   [1954] P. 112 at 120–122.
[255]   [1990] 2 I.R. 326.
[256]   [1990] 2 I.R. 326 at 341 (McCarthy J.).
[257]   [1990] 2 I.R. 326 at 337.
[258]   [1990] 2 I.R. 326 at 340 (McCarthy J.).
[259]   [1990] 2 I.R. 326 at 330 (Hamilton P.).
[260]   [1969] I.R. 148.

capable testator."[261] However, the issue of the onus of proof in this case was not decided solely on the basis that the testator had reduced mental capacity; instead a key additional factor was that one of the defendants had been instrumental in obtaining this codicil benefiting her and therefore this ought to have "excited the suspicion of the court", placing a heavy onus of proof on her.[262] On the facts, the Supreme Court held that the codicil was invalid.[263]

13–60 If a testator has a mental illness, a court may still find that the will was valid if the condition is well-controlled by medication. In *Re O'Donnell*[264] the testator had paranoid schizophrenia and the court heard extensive evidence from medical and other witnesses over a number of days. Kelly J. found that, as a matter of probability, at the time when the deceased made his will, he was not manifesting any of the florid symptoms of schizophrenia and his condition was well controlled by medication. From his dealings with the solicitor, he clearly understood the extent of the property of which he was disposing. In making provision for his brother and sisters he had an appreciation and comprehension of the claims to which he ought to give effect. Kelly J. did not believe that any disorder of his mind "poisoned his affections or perverted his sense of right or prevented the exercise of his natural faculties." Neither was he of the view that any "insane delusion" was present which influenced his will or brought about a disposal of property which, if the mind had been sound, would not have been made. Kelly J. said that while some members of the family might be disappointed as a result of the way in which the deceased's property was disposed of, it was up to him to make the decision.[265]

13–61 Old age may have some relevance as part of the overall facts of the case concerning whether the testator had capacity and whether they were the subject of undue influence. Brady states that old age is not, without more, proof of testamentary incapacity but it may be invoked in support of a plea that the

---

[261] [1969] I.R. 148 at 167.

[262] [1969] I.R. 148 at 164.

[263] See further commentary in Mary Donnelly, "Assessing Legal Capacity: Process and the Operation of the Functional Test" (2007) 2 *Judicial Studies Institute Journal* 141 at 156. Similarly, in *In the Goods of O'Connor* [1978] I.L.R.M. 247 D'Arcy J. held that the evidence of the plaintiff under whose "protection" the deceased lived must be approached with suspicion and the court must be vigilant and zealous in examining it.

[264] *In Re Andrew O' Donnell Deceased*, High Court, Kelly J., March 24, 1999. Note that in this case Kelly J. did not have to make a decision on the onus of proof, as counsel for the plaintiff had accepted that if the onus of proof lay on him in relation to question No. 3 (whether the deceased was of sound disposing mind and testamentary capacity), he had discharged it. Kelly J. was prepared to approach the case on that basis and so he began his consideration of the evidence on the assumption (though without deciding the issue) that the burden of proof was on the plaintiff in respect of all of the questions which had to be decided.

[265] See also Michael Hourican, "Testamentary Capacity" (2000) 5(4) C.P.L.J. 95.

testator did not know and approve of the contents of their will, or that the will was procured as the result of undue influence.[266]

The Law Reform Commission has described and commented on the practice of the Probate Office:

> "The Probate Office staff work on the basic assumption that a testator had capacity to make a valid will. They do not require proof of the testator's legal capacity unless doubts are raised about it. Age alone does not give rise to doubts. There are various circumstances in which doubts may be raised, for example, if the Death Certificate states the cause of death as 'senile dementia' or 'Alzheimer's disease', if it is asserted that the will was executed during a 'lucid interval' or if the testator was a patient in a psychiatric hospital or resident in a residential care unit for people with mental disabilities. If the Death Certificate states the cause of death as dementia or Alzheimer's disease, then in the view of the Probate Office doubt is cast on the testator's capacity even if the will was made many years before the death. This seems to be unnecessary and the doubt should only arise if the will was made within a few years of the death."[267]

If the testator was a patient in a psychiatric hospital or a resident in a residential care unit for people with mental disabilities, it is the standard practice of the Probate Office to request an affidavit from a doctor who attended the deceased at the relevant time.[268] If the testator is a ward of court but has sufficient capacity to make a will, procedures must be followed which include the involvement of the office of wards of court.[269]

13–62 The issue of costs of court proceedings concerning validity of a will is an important one, as the cost of the proceedings may be paid from the estate, thus diminishing the value of the inheritances. In *In bonis Morelli: Vella v Morelli*[270] the will was unsuccessfully challenged on the basis it was not validly executed. The Supreme Court held that there had been reasonable grounds for the litigation, which had been conducted bona fide and, therefore, that the plaintiff should be allowed her costs out of the estate of the deceased. The effect

---

[266] James Brady, *Succession Law in Ireland*, 2nd edn (Dublin: Butterworths, 1995), p.78. Compare Barron J. (dissenting) in *In Re Blackall*, Supreme Court, April 1, 1998, p.41: "Since want of intelligence may be brought about by supervening physical infirmity or the decay of advancing age, it is essential to determine whether there is sufficient intelligence to understand and appreciate the testamentary act in its different bearings. In the instant case the age of the testatrix alone imposed the onus of his establishing that the power to make a will remained. The fact that she also suffered a stroke added to that onus."

[267] Law Reform Commission, *Consultation Paper on Law and the Elderly* (CP23, 2003), para.2.25.

[268] Law Reform Commission, *Consultation Paper on Law and the Elderly* (CP23, 2003), para.2.27.

[269] Anne-Marie O'Neill, *Wards of Court in Ireland* (Dublin: First Law, 2004), p.175.

[270] [1968] I.R. 11.

was that both sides' costs were paid out of the estate. According to Budd J., an investigation of the circumstances under which a will is made should be held, where the circumstances reasonably call for it, and it is something required in the public interest.[271] This reasoning was recently followed in *Elliot v Stamp*.[272]

13–63 In England, a "Golden Rule" has evolved that a solicitor, when drawing up a will for an elderly person or someone who is seriously ill, should ensure that the will is witnessed or approved by a medical practitioner.[273] The medical practitioner should record their examination and findings and, where there is an earlier will, it should be examined and any proposed alterations should be discussed with the testator.

13–64 The Law Reform Commission considered the question of testamentary capacity and concluded that legislative reform was not necessary. However, it noted that the contemporaneous certification of capacity by a medical practitioner is desirable as a prudent precaution in cases of doubtful capacity and where a later challenge to a will appears likely. The Commission considered that guidelines on the assessment of testamentary capacity should be drawn up by the Law Society and the Medical Council for the assistance of both solicitors and medical practitioners.[274] The Commission considered the possibility of "statutory wills" where a person has lost mental capacity, but rejected it on the basis that there was a strong possibility that assisting decision makers may be inclined to unfairly favour their own interests in making applications under a statutory will procedure.[275] However, it recommended that in exceptional circumstances, the High Court should be given the discretionary power to order the alteration of a will of an adult who lacks testamentary capacity. This might apply, for example, where there has been a considerable change in circumstances since the execution of the will, which ought to be reflected.[276]

This recommendation of the Commission is reflected in the Scheme of the Mental Capacity Bill 2008, which provides that where a person who has made a valid will loses testamentary capacity, the High Court may, acting on its own initiative or on application to it by the Office of Public Guardian, alter the will

---

271 [1968] I.R. 11 at 31.

272 [2008] I.E.S.C. 10; [2008] 2 I.L.R.M. 283.

273 See *Elliot v Stamp* [2008] I.E.S.C. 10; [2008] 2 I.L.R.M. 283, paras 2.33–2.34, citing *Re Simpson (Deceased); Schaniel v Simpson* (1977) 121 Sol.J. LB 224 and *Re Morris (Deceased): Special Trustees for Great Ormond Street Hospital for Children v Rushin* [2001] W.T.L.R. 1137. See also *Kenward v Adams, The Times*, Nov. 29, 1975.

274 *Consultation Paper on Law and the Elderly*, paras 2.36–2.37.

275 Law Reform Commission, *Report on Vulnerable Adults and the Law* (Report 83, 2006), paras 3.52–3.58.

276 Law Reform Commission, *Report on Vulnerable Adults and the Law* (Report 83, 2006), paras 3.59–3.60.

where exceptional circumstances have arisen since the loss of testamentary capacity and the interests of justice demand it.[277]

13–65 The Law Society has provided a set of guidelines on drafting wills for elderly clients in 2009 which contains useful guidance for solicitors.[278] The guidelines note, for example, the importance of the testator being seen alone, without the benefit of third-party assistance, in either communicating or formulating their wishes. Assistance in assessing capacity, referring to case law, is given. Solicitors are advised to obtain corroborative information where necessary, including a diagnostic assessment of the client, i.e. medical evidence. Mental illness does not preclude testamentary capacity. Where a client with a known mental illness presents themselves and indicates a wish to make a will, a solicitor must clearly establish the presence or absence of testamentary capacity. If in doubt, medical opinion should be sought before proceeding. If the client is under the care of a consultant, their opinion may be the more relevant one, rather than the testator's general practitioner. Solicitors are also advised to act expeditiously, as otherwise they may be sued by disappointed beneficiaries.[279] They are also advised that while taking instructions from an elderly client concerning the completion of a will, they should take the opportunity to explain the concept of, and the advantages and risks involved in, completing an enduring power of attorney.

CONTRACTUAL CAPACITY

13–66 The law concerning contractual capacity was reviewed in detail by the Law Reform Commission in 2005.[280] A person must be capable of understanding the nature and effect of the specific contract into which they are entering. The degree of understanding required will vary according to the complexity of transaction. If a person is so affected by mental illness as not to have any idea what they are signing, they may seek to repudiate the obligations created by the document by pleading non est factum ("this is not my deed"). A successful plea of non est factum renders a contract void ab initio whereas lack of capacity to understand renders it voidable.[281]

---

[277] Department of Justice, Equality and Law Reform, *Scheme of Mental Capacity Bill 2008,* Head 19(2).

[278] Law Society, "Drafting Wills for the Elderly Client: Guidelines For Solicitors" (2009) 103(1) Gaz.L.S.I. 48.

[279] The guidelines cite *Hooper v Fynmores* (2002) Lloyds Ref.P.N.18.

[280] Law Reform Commission, *Consultation Paper on Vulnerable Adults and the Law: Capacity* (CP37, 2005), Chapter 5.

[281] Law Reform Commission, *Consultation Paper on Vulnerable Adults and the Law: Capacity* (CP37, 2005), paras 5.06–5.08 and cases cited therein.

"Unsoundness of mind" is a good defence to an action for breach of contract if it can be shown that the other party was aware of it. Alternatively, the circumstances may be such that any reasonable person would be aware of the person's lack of capacity.[282]

13–67 At common law, a person who sells and delivers "necessaries" to an adult without mental capacity to contract is entitled to recover a reasonable price for such necessaries. Section 2 of the Sale of Goods Act 1893 encapsulated the position at common law in respect of the sale of goods.[283]

It would appear that any purported attempt by a ward of court to enter into a contract will be void irrespective of the other party's knowledge of their status as a ward of court.[284]

13–68 The Commission recommended in 2005 that a presumption of capacity to contract should form part of a statutory presumption of capacity.[285] The proposed Public Guardian should be given power to declare a contract purportedly entered into by an adult whom it is alleged lacked contractual capacity binding on both parties, or to declare the contract void for lack of capacity, and to make any adjustment to the rights of the parties considered just in the circumstances.[286] These two recommendations were not repeated in the 2006 Report.[287]

The Commission also recommended that the proposed capacity legislation should provide that an adult who lacks the capacity to enter into a particular contract is nonetheless obliged to pay the supplier a reasonable amount for necessaries supplied. "Necessaries" should be statutorily defined as goods *and services* supplied which are suitable to the person's reasonable living requirements but excluding goods and services which could be classed as luxury in nature.[288] Head 18 of the scheme of the Mental Capacity Bill proposes to implement the Commission's recommendation concerning contracts for necessaries.[289]

---

[282] Law Reform Commission, *Consultation Paper on Vulnerable Adults and the Law: Capacity* (CP37, 2005), paras 5.10–5.11.

[283] *Consultation Paper on Vulnerable Adults and the Law: Capacity,* para.5.23. Section 2 of the Sale of Goods Act 1893 states: "… where necessaries are sold and delivered to an infant, minor, or to a person who by reason of mental incapacity or drunkenness is not competent to contract, he must pay a reasonable price therefor. Necessaries in this section means goods suitable to the condition in life of such infant or minor or other person, and to his actual requirements at the time of the sale and delivery."

[284] *Re Walker* [1905] 1 Ch. 160.

[285] *Consultation Paper on Vulnerable Adults and the Law: Capacity,* para.5.37.

[286] *Consultation Paper on Vulnerable Adults and the Law: Capacity,* para.5.40.

[287] Law Reform Commission, *Report on Vulnerable Adults and the Law* (Report 83, 2006), paras 3.02–3.07.

[288] *Consultation Paper on Vulnerable Adults and the Law: Capacity,* paras 5.43–4; Recommendation repeated in 2006 Report at paras 3.06–3.07.

[289] Department of Justice, Equality and Law Reform, *Scheme of Mental Capacity Bill 2008*, Head 18.

CHAPTER 14

MENTAL HEALTH AND OTHER ASPECTS OF CIVIL LAW

EMPLOYMENT EQUALITY ACT 1998

14–01 The Employment Equality Act 1998, as amended by the Equality Act 2004, outlaws direct and indirect discrimination in employment on nine grounds, including disability.[1] The amended Act implements the Framework Directive[2] in Ireland, and thus EU case law is of relevance.

"Disability" is broadly defined to include, inter alia:

(d) a condition or malfunction which results in a person learning differently from a person without the condition or malfunction, or

(e) a condition, illness or disease which affects a person's thought processes, perception of reality, emotions or judgement or which results in disturbed behaviour.[3]

14–02 An employer is obliged to take appropriate measures (also known as reasonable accommodation)[4] to enable a person who has a disability to have access to employment, to participate or advance in employment, or to undergo training, unless this would impose a disproportionate burden on the employer.[5] In determining whether measures would impose such a burden, account shall be taken of the financial and other costs entailed, the scale and financial resources of the employer's business, and the possibility of obtaining public funding or other assistance.[6]

---

[1] See generally Shivaun Quinlivan, "Disability Discrimination", Chapter 8 in Anne Marie Mooney-Cotter & Jane Moffatt (eds.), *Discrimination Law*, Law Society of Ireland Professional Practice Guide (London: Cavendish, 2005); Olivia Smith, "Disability, Discrimination and Employment: A Never-Ending Legal Story?" (2001) 23 D.U.L.J. 148; Frances Meenan, *Working Within the Law—A Practical Guide for Employers and Employees*, 2nd edn (Dublin: Oak Tree Press, 1999)

[2] Directive 2000/78/EC Establishing a General Framework for Equal Treatment in Employment and Occupation (the Framework Directive).

[3] Employment Equality Act 1998, s.2(1).

[4] Employment Equality Act 1998, s.16(3)(a), as amended by s.9, Equality Act 2004: "reasonable accommodation (in this subsection referred to as 'appropriate measures')".

[5] Employment Equality Act 1998, s.16(3), as amended by s.9, Equality Act 2004. The 1998 Act originally stated that a refusal or failure to provide for special treatment or facilities would not be deemed reasonable unless such provision would give rise to a cost, other than a nominal cost, to the employer.

[6] Employment Equality Act 1998, s.16(3)(c), as amended.

14–03 It has been held that the definition of disability covers schizophrenia,[7] anxiety and depression,[8] a depressive illness,[9] anorexia and bulimia[10] and obsessive compulsive disorder.[11] A parent, guardian or other person acting in place of a parent can be the complainant where a person is unable by reason of an intellectual or psychological disability to pursue a claim effectively.[12] In addition, a family member may be able to claim "discrimination by association" if they are discriminated against due to their association with a person with a disability.[13]

14–04 In *A Government Department (Minister for Justice, Equality and Law Reform) v A Worker (Prison Officer)*[14] there was conflicting medical evidence as to whether the employee had a psychiatric illness (depressive illness) or an adjustment disorder, which was described as a position mid–way between normal distress or unhappiness and clinical depression, effectively "an exaggerated form of unhappiness". The Labour Court stated that if the Act were to be construed so as to blur the distinction between emotional upset, unhappiness or the ordinary human reaction to stressful situations or the vicissitudes of life on the one hand, and recognised psychiatric illness on the other, it could be fairly described as an absurdity. The court accepted that no statute can be construed so as to produce an absurd result or one that is repugnant to common sense, and that this common law rule of construction has now been given statutory effect by s.5(1) of the Interpretation Act 2005. On the facts, the court found that the employee had a psychiatric illness and the court did not have to decide whether an adjustment disorder came within the Act, but it left open the possibility that it might not.

14–05 The question of "appropriate measures" (also known as "reasonable accommodation") for a person with a mental disorder can be a difficult one, as illustrated by *C. v Iarnród Éireann*.[15] Mr C. applied for the position of gate

---

[7] *A Complainant v Civil Service Commissioners*, DEC–E2002–015, para.5.7.

[8] *Mr. O. v A Named Company*, Equality Tribunal, DEC–E2003/052; *An Employer v A Worker (Mr.O.)(No.1)* ADE/04/2, Labour Court, January 5, 2005; *An Employer v A Worker (Mr.O.) (No.2)*, Determination No. EED0410, Labour Court, January 5, 2005.

[9] *A Government Department (Minister for Justice, Equality and Law Reform) v A Worker (Prison Officer)*, ADE/07/23, Labour Court, March 25, 2009.

[10] *A Health and Fitness Club v A Worker* ED/02/59, Labour Court, February 18, 2003.

[11] *A Company v A Worker*, ED/04/13, Labour Court, February 9, 2005.

[12] Employment Equality Act 1998, s.77(4)(a), as amended by Equality Act 2004, s.32. Note the position before the 2004 Act: In *A Complainant v FÁS* (DEC–E2003/029) an attempt by a father to bring a claim under the 1998 Act on behalf of his son who had a learning disability was rejected. The Equality Officer said she had no jurisdiction to investigate the claim.

[13] Employment Equality Act 1998, s.6(1)(b) as amended by Equality Act 2004, s.4. See *Coleman v Attridge Law*, Case C–303/06, [2008] 3 C.M.L.R. 27. This case concerns the mother of a child with a physical disability.

[14] ADE/07/23, Labour Court, March 25, 2009.

[15] DEC–E2003/054, Equality Tribunal.

keeper with Iarnród Éireann and at his second medical examination he told the medical examiner that he had a history of depression. He was not offered the job as a result, and claimed discrimination on the disability ground. The Equality Officer appears to have accepted the evidence of the Chief Medical Officer, who said that Mr C. had manic-depressive psychosis and outlined three aspects of the condition:

(a) Periods of low moods.
(b) Periods of elation when a patient loses contact with reality and has a feeling of grandeur and indestructibility. During these periods a patient is unaware that anything is wrong and consequently is not in a position to seek help. Patients tend to be a danger to themselves and others, but mostly themselves. It is a common cause for admission to a psychiatric hospital.
(c) Medication which was prescribed for the complainant acts on their central nervous system and can cause side effects including impairment to vigilance.[16]

The Chief Medical Officer believed that it was a life-long condition which was likely to flare up again. Mr C. submitted that he had never been admitted to hospital for his condition and that he was, now, in control if it. He believed that he would not be a risk due to his condition. He said that there were gatekeepers working for Iarnród Éireann who had depression. He also expressed his dissatisfaction that his medical records had been passed to Iarnród Éireann's legal department and he indicated that he had given no authorisation for what he alleged was a breach of confidentiality.

Iarnród Éireann (IE) argued that it would have been unsafe to appoint Mr C. to the position, as it is "safety critical." It said that Mr C. had admitted that he only took medication for his condition "when he felt that there was exacerbation" of his depression and that he discontinued taking medication when he felt that his condition had "stabilised". IE stated that this admission caused it considerable concern, as employing Mr C. as a gatekeeper would entail giving him responsibility for hundreds of lives and he would not be able to employ his full faculties as a result of his untreated condition. IE believed that Mr C. was a danger to himself and others and that no reasonable accommodation could be made to allow him to carry out the job, apart from having someone with him at all times, which would not be practicable or affordable.[17]

The Equality Officer held that Mr C. had not been discriminated against under the Employment Equality Act 1998. She stressed that the job was a safety critical one, and found that IE could not have provided special treatment or facilities to enable Mr C. to do the job without having to incur a cost other than

---

[16] *C. v Iarnród Éireann* (2003), Equality Tribunal, E2003/054, para.5.5.
[17] *C. v Iarnród Éireann* (2003), Equality Tribunal, E2003/054, para.5.6.

nominal cost.[18] She did not engage in detailed analysis of the reasonable accommodation which might be required. Referring to *McGrory v Electricity Supply Board*,[19] she also decided that, by making the complaint, Mr C. waived his right to privacy in relation to his medical records and IE did not require his authorisation to pass his medical records to its legal department for the purpose of defending the claim.[20]

EQUAL STATUS ACT 2000

14–06 The Equal Status Act 2000, as amended by the Equality Act 2004, prohibits discrimination, harassment and related behaviour in connection with the provision of services, property and other opportunities to which the public generally or a section of the public has access. The same nine grounds, including disability, apply as under employment equality. "Disability" is defined as in employment equality and therefore the case law on the meaning of disability applies. In *Mr X. v A Town Council*[21] severe depression was held to be a "disability" within the meaning of the Act.

Providers of goods or services[22] must normally make reasonable accommodation for people with disabilities, unless this would give rise to a cost other than nominal cost.[23] Unlike the employment equality legislation, the reference to "nominal cost" was not changed with the amendments made in 2004 and there is now a significant divergence between the protections offered under the separate Acts.[24]

14–07 There are various exceptions in the Act, e.g. where a person has a disability that, in the circumstances, could cause harm to the person or to others, treating the person differently to the extent reasonably necessary to prevent such harm does not constitute discrimination.[25]

14–08 The Act does not prohibit the taking of any action that is required by or under any enactment.[26] Certain preferential treatment and positive measures are

---

[18] *C. v Iarnród Éireann* (2003), Equality Tribunal, E2003/054, para.5.8. Note that the definition of reasonable accommodation has changed since this case was decided. It now reads that the employer shall take appropriate measures, where needed in a particular case, unless the measures would impose a disproportionate burden on the employer—s.16(3)(b) of the 1998 Act, as amended by s.9 of the 2004 Act.

[19] [2003] I.E.S.C. 45; [2003] 3 I.R. 407.

[20] *C. v Iarnród Éireann*, E2003/054, para.5.9.

[21] DEC–S2008–042, Equality Tribunal.

[22] A broad definition of provision of goods and services is adopted–s.4(6) Equal Status Act 2000.

[23] Equal Status Act 2000, ss.4(1)–(2).

[24] Shivann Quinlivan, "Disability Discrimination", Chapter 8 in Anne Marie Mooney-Cotter & Jane Moffatt (eds.), *Discrimination Law* (London: Cavendish, 2005), p.126. See also pp.130–131.

[25] Equal Status Act 2000, s.4(4).

[26] Equal Status Act 2000, s.14(a). See *Kane and Kane v Eirjet (in liquidation)*, DEC–S2008–026,

permitted.[27] In addition, treating a person differently does not constitute discrimination where the person is incapable of entering into an enforceable contract or of giving an informed consent and, for that reason, the treatment is reasonable in the particular case.[28] The Law Reform Commission has suggested that it may not be considered reasonable to refuse to enter into a contract for necessaries because the supplier would be entitled to recover a reasonable price for the goods despite the person's lack of capacity.[29]

14–09 In *Ms. D. (a Tenant) v A Local Authority*[30] the complainant had a diagnosis of claustrophobia and agoraphobia, which led to severe anxiety and panic attacks, confining her to home. She had been in the care of a multidisciplinary psychiatric team, led by a consultant psychiatrist, for a number of years and treatment was ongoing. It was the local authority's intention to re-house her in the longer term in a new apartment built to a specification set out in the programme of urban renewal for the housing of single occupancy households. This comprises an apartment of 50m² area. Ms D. stated that this was not sufficient space for her due to her condition and applied for an allocation of a larger apartment in the region of 60m² which she believed would enable her to live as independently as possible within the neighbourhood. Representatives of the local authority did not meet with Ms D.'s medical team, despite their making themselves available for consultation. The authority made a selection of apartments available to Ms D. and was prepared at all times to adapt an apartment to facilitate her needs but it refused to consider the allocation of a larger apartment than that warranted by her status as a single person.

The medical evidence presented at the hearing satisfied the Equality Officer that Ms D. has a phobic disorder. The World Health Organisation has classified phobic disorders in the mental and behavioural disorder category. The Equality Officer was satisfied that Ms D.'s condition fell under s.2(1)(e) of the Equal Status Act 2000.[31] In failing to take into account the complainant's specific need for larger space in her apartment, and by ignoring the recommendations forwarded by her medical team, the Equality Officer found that Ms D. was discriminated against on the disability ground. She ordered that the prioritisation and assessment criteria for housing provision be broadened to take into account the specific requirements of disabled persons; that Ms D. be facilitated with a larger apartment within six months; and that the Local Authority pay Ms D. €2,500 as redress for the effects of the discrimination suffered.

---

concerning safety legislation requirements and "mental handicap" on aircraft.
[27] Equal Status Act 2000, s.14(b).
[28] Equal Status Act 2000, s.16(2)(b).
[29] Law Reform Commission, *Consultation Paper on Vulnerable Adults and the Law: Capacity* (CP 37, 2005), para.5.30.
[30] DEC–S2007–057, Equality Tribunal.
[31] DEC–S2007–057, para.3.3.

14–10 The complainant in *Mr X. v Health Services Executive*[32] was diagnosed as having schizophrenia and claimed that he was discriminated against on the grounds of his disability when the Health Service Executive (HSE) failed to do all that was reasonable to accommodate his needs by providing special facilities that would enable him to access the services of a psychologist as part of his treatment for schizophrenia. The complainant claimed that he was being denied the most effective means of treatment for his illness and he contended that if he had been suffering from any illness other than a mental illness he would have received the appropriate treatment. The complainant also claimed that he requested that the treatment of a psychologist be made available to him under the National Treatment Purchase Fund. This request was also denied on the basis that mental illnesses were not covered by this scheme. The HSE claimed that the complainant was under the supervision of Dr X., whose initial prognosis was that the complainant's illness should be treated by way of medication. The HSE accepted that the medical team which was treating the complainant did not have access to the services of a psychologist (as a result of budgetary constraints) at that juncture; however, it submitted that the complainant's treatment was being administered in accordance with the instructions and prognosis of his medical team. The HSE also submitted that the National Treatment Purchase Fund was an independent statutory agency so it did not have any role or authority in terms of the manner in which treatment was administered under this scheme.

Having regard to the evidence of Dr X., the Equality Officer said that it was not until March 2005 that the doctor formed the view that the complainant could benefit from the treatment of a psychologist, but the HSE did not have access to the services of a psychologist as a result of budgetary constraints until nine months later. However, the Equality Officer was satisfied that the inability of the HSE to obtain the services of a psychologist was an administrative issue and did not amount to less favourable treatment of the complainant. He was also satisfied that the complainant was referred to a psychologist on the instructions of his medical team as soon as one became available, although he could not start the treatment until June 2006 as a result of a deterioration in his medical condition. The Equality Officer was satisfied that the medical treatment administered was carried out in accordance with the clinical judgement of the medical team. Accordingly, he found that the complainant had failed to establish a prima facie case of discrimination on the disability ground. He was also satisfied that the HSE did not have any role in the manner in which treatment was administered under the National Treatment Purchase Fund.

Disability Act 2005

14–11 The Disability Act 2005 provides that an application may be made for an independent assessment of need, without regard to cost or capacity to provide

---

[32] DEC–S2008–112, Equality Tribunal.

any services identified in the assessment.[33] The assessment is undertaken by assessment officers, appointed by the HSE, who will be independent in carrying out their statutory functions. The assessment report indicates whether a person has a disability; the nature and extent of the disability; the health and education needs arising from the disability; the services considered appropriate to meet those needs and the timescale ideally required for their delivery; and when a review of the assessment should be undertaken.[34] "Disability" means "a substantial restriction in the capacity of the person to carry on a profession, business or occupation in the State or to participate in social or cultural life in the State by reason of an enduring physical, sensory, mental health or intellectual impairment."[35] The disability threshold is quite high, and mild disabilities that do not need continuous services may not qualify.[36] The Health Information and Quality Authority (HIQA) sets appropriate standards for carrying out the assessment process.[37]

Currently, the Act is only in force as regards children under five.[38] The Minister has stated that she aims to have Part 2 apply to all persons with a disability by 2011.[39]

14–12 The needs assessment is followed by a service statement, produced by a liaison officer.[40] A person may make a complaint to the HSE about various matters, e.g. the failure of a health or education service provider to provide or to fully provide a service set out in the service statement.[41] Complaints are heard by a complaints officer, appointed by the HSE. Appeals regarding complaints are investigated by an independent appeals officer. The appeals officer's determination is final and may only be appealed on a point of law to the High Court. A clause in an earlier version of the Bill, to the effect that the process is "non-justiciable" has been removed.[42] However, Clissmann argues that the Act is effectively non-justiciable:

> "For those who lobbied long and hard to have a 'rights-based' Disability Act, the legislation that was finally enacted came as a disappointment because of the discretionary and resource-bound nature of the services to be available to

---

[33] Disability Act 2005, ss.8–10. See generally Alma Clissmann, "Assessments Start Under the Disability Act 2005 (Part 2)" (2007) 101(6) Gaz. L.S.I. 18.

[34] Disability Act 2005, s.8(7).

[35] Disability Act 2005, s.2(1).

[36] See generally Alma Clissmann, "Assessments Start Under the Disability Act 2005 (Part 2)" (2007) 101(6) Gaz. L.S.I. 18, p.19.

[37] See Health Information and Quality Authority, *Standards for the Assessment of Need* (2007).

[38] Disability Act 2005 (Commencement) Order 2007, S.I. No. 234 of 2007.

[39] Press Release: "Minister Harney Welcomes Commencement of Part 2 of the Disability Act", June 1, 2007.

[40] Disability Act 2005, s.11.

[41] Disability Act 2005, s.14.

[42] See s.47 Disability Bill, 2001 and commentary in Law Reform Commission, *Report on Vulnerable Adults and the Law* (Report 83, 2006), para.1.36.

disabled children and adults. Part 2 sets out a detailed procedure, involving five different types of officers, and it makes it clear that, while an assessment may identify everything a person should ideally have, what will be available will be subject to the constraints of budgets and availability. Furthermore, the entitlements are not justiciable. Only appeals on a point of law lie to the High Court from determinations of the appeals officers."[43]

14–13 The Act obliges six Government Departments[44] to prepare Sectoral Plans, which set out information on the services, facilities and activities which come within the remit of each of the six departments. The plans highlight how the functions of the departments, and the key bodies which they oversee, serve the needs of people with disabilities and set out a programme for future development.

14–14 The Law Reform Commission has stated that the 2005 Act provides an important legislative context against which the interaction between the State and persons with limited decision-making capacity can be considered. The Commission noted that the 2005 Act provides for a novel structure by which these matters are determined, in particular through the direct involvement of State bodies, such as the HSE and Government Departments, together with appropriate independent complaints machinery.[45]

---

[43] See generally Alma Clissmann, "Assessments Start Under the Disability Act 2005 (Part 2)" (2007) 101(6) Gaz. L.S.I. 18, p.18.

[44] The Minister for Health and Children; the Minister for Social and Family Affairs; the Minister for Transport; the Minister for the Environment, Heritage and Local Government; the Minister for Communications, Energy and Natural Resources; and the Minister for Enterprise, Trade and Employment.

[45] Law Reform Commission, *Report on Vulnerable Adults and the Law* (Report 83, 2006), para.1.44.

PART 3
CRIMINAL MATTERS

CHAPTER 15

THE INSANITY DEFENCE

INTRODUCTION

15–01 It is generally agreed that a person with mental illness or disorder should not be dealt with in the ordinary way by the criminal law.[1] One rationale for this is that the person's mental condition interferes with their ability to act autonomously and "rationally."[2] Others are that such a person cannot be "deterred" by punishment[3] or that punishing such a person would not be consistent with the concept of retribution or "just desserts".[4]

15–02 Enormous difficulties arise in seeking to define mental illness or disorder for the purposes of the criminal law.[5] The debates in this area have been wide-ranging and heated. As a very general summary, it can be said that there has been a general movement away from purely cognitive definitions of mental illness and mental disorder to broader definitions which encompass volitional or emotional factors.

A key factor in criminal law and mental health is the dichotomy between legal and other (e.g. psychiatric, psychological or sociological) perspectives. McAuley describes how the law proceeds on the basis that individuals are moral agents who are responsible for their actions, while psychiatry is concerned with the clinical problem of diagnosing and treating mental disorders.[6] Casey and

---

[1] This is accepted even by those who argue in favour of determinism as opposed to free will—see Michael Moore, *Law and Psychiatry: Rethinking the Relationship* (Cambridge University Press, 1984), pp.351–365; R.D. Mackay, *Mental Condition Defences in the Criminal Law* (Oxford: Clarendon Press, 1995), p.76. For a summary of "hard" determinism, see Lawrie Reznek, *Evil or Ill?: Justifying the Insanity Defence* (London: Routledge, London, 1997), pp.7–10.

[2] R.J. Lipkin, "Free Will, Responsibility and the Promise of Forensic Psychiatry" (1990) 13 Int. J. L. & Psych. 331 at 331–2 and 355–6.

[3] Glanville Williams, *Criminal Law: The General Part*, 2nd edn (London: Stevens, 1961), p.428. Hart has pointed out that this view is open to criticism—H.L.A. Hart, *Punishment and Responsibility* (Oxford University Press, 1968), p.19.

[4] S.J. Morse, "Excusing the Crazy: The Insanity Defense Reconsidered" (1985) Sou. Cal. L. Rev. 777 at 783.

[5] These difficulties have led some to call for the abolition of the insanity defence. Barbara Wootton in *Crime and the Criminal Law: Reflections of a Magistrate and Social Scientist*, 2nd edn (London: Stevens, 1981) believed that the law was attempting the impossible in deciding between those who were mentally disordered or criminally responsible. See also Norval Morris, *Madness and the Criminal Law* (University of Chicago Press, 1982).

[6] Finbarr McAuley, *Insanity, Psychiatry and Criminal Responsibility* (Dublin: Round Hall Press, 1993), p.4 and p.15. McAuley believes it is a serious mistake to suppose that psychiatric

Craven say that lawyers use concepts of disease and causation that do not accurately reflect complex clinical constructs, while psychiatrists are primarily concerned with the well-being of the individual patient.[7] The contrast between legal and other perspectives is not confined to definitional issues but also applies to the entire approach to dealing with mental health: Gostin[8] has contrasted "legalism" and "welfarism" by saying that the former wraps the patient in a network of substantive and procedural protections against unjustified loss of liberty and compulsory treatment while the latter replaces legal safeguards with professional discretion which is seen as allowing speedy access to treatment and care, unencumbered by a panoply of bureaucracy and procedures.

15–03 There was a general consensus for decades that Ireland's criminal law concerning mental health was in need of reform. In 1978, the Henchy committee[9] drafted a report outlining major changes which were necessary. Successive Ministers for Justice promised changes in the law, and Fianna Fáil published a Bill while in Opposition.[10] The Government finally published a Bill in December 2002. After intermittent debates in the Oireachtas spread over a three-year period, during which Minister McDowell apologised to Mr Justice Henchy for the delay in reforming the law,[11] the result was the Criminal Law (Insanity) Act 2006,[12] which was enacted on April 12, 2006 and came into force on June 1, 2006.[13]

---

explanation implies a form of behavioural determinism that leaves no room for purposive action, p.15.

[7] Patricia Casey & Ciaran Craven, *Psychiatry and the Law* (Dublin: Oak Tree Press, 1999), p.xxiii. They also state on the same page that the concerns of the lawyer are more diverse, ranging from issues of property rights to individual safety and the public interest.

[8] Larry Gostin, *Mental Health Services: Law and Practice* (London: Shaw and Sons, 1986: looseleaf with updates), p.v.

[9] *Third Interim Report of the Interdepartmental Committee on Mentally Ill and Maladjusted Persons. Treatment and Care of Persons Suffering from Mental Disorder Who Appear Before the Courts on Criminal Charges* [Chair: Henchy J.] (Dublin, 1978).

[10] Criminal Justice (Mental Disorder) Bill 1996.

[11] 171 *Seanad Debates* Col.794 (February 19, 2003).

[12] For general reviews of the Act see Whelan, "The Criminal Law (Insanity) Act 2006" in: T.J. McIntyre, Keith Spencer and Darius Whelan, *Criminal Legislation Annotated 2006–2007* (Dublin: Thomson Round Hall, 2008); Tony McGillicuddy, "The Criminal Law (Insanity) Act 2006" (2006) 11 *Bar Review* 95; Harry Kennedy, *The Annotated Mental Health Acts* (Dublin: Blackhall, 2007). For commentary on earlier versions of the Bill, see Gerard Conway, "Fitness to Plead in Light of the Criminal Law (Insanity) Bill 2002" (2003) 13(4) Ir.Crim.L.J. 2; Anne Marie O'Neill, *Irish Mental Health Law* (Dublin: First Law, 2005); Simon Mills, "Criminal Law (Insanity) Bill 2002: Putting the Sanity Back into Insanity" (2003) 8 Bar Rev. 101; Dara Robinson, "Crazy Situation" (2003) 97(1) Gaz.L.S.I. 12.

[13] Criminal Law (Insanity) Act 2006 (Commencement) Order 2006, S.I. No. 273 of 2006. The establishment day for the Mental Health (Criminal Law) Review Board was September 27, 2006–Mental Health (Criminal Law) Review Board (Establishment Day) Order 2006, S.I. No. 499 of 2006.

There are a number of useful sources which may be consulted for description and analysis of the law prior to the enactment of the 2006 Act.[14] As will be discussed below, the Act did not change the common law definitions of insanity and unfitness to plead, but instead the changes it introduced concentrated on important procedural questions such as the introduction of automatic periodic reviews of detention by the new Mental Health (Criminal Law) Review Board and provision for appeals from insanity verdicts. The main substantive change was the introduction of the concept of diminished responsibility into Irish law.

MENTAL DISORDER UNDER THE 2006 ACT

15–04 The 2006 Act states that mental disorder includes mental illness, mental disability, dementia or any disease of the mind but does not include intoxication.[15] This definition is primarily relevant to decisions by criminal courts as to whether a person is not guilty by reason of insanity, unfit for trial or guilty of manslaughter on grounds of diminished responsibility. The presence of a mental disorder is only one part of such decisions; the additional criteria in the relevant sections, discussed below, must also be satisfied. Once a decision that a person is not guilty by reason of insanity or is unfit for trial has been made, the Act then generally permits detention of the person if they have a "mental disorder within the meaning of the Act of 2001", i.e. the Mental Health Act 2001. The two separate definitions of mental disorder are used at different stages, and care must be taken in reading the Act to avoid confusion between their meanings.

Note that "mental disorder" is said to "include" the listed conditions, which means that arguments may be made that conditions which are not listed may come within the Act.

15–05 During the Oireachtas debates, there was detailed debate concerning the definition of mental disorder. Some senators proposed that the definition in this Act should be aligned with that in the Mental Health Act 2001. However, Minister McDowell opposed this on the grounds that the 2001 Act has a particular purpose, which is to govern the circumstances in which people can or

---

[14] See, for example, Finbarr McAuley, *Insanity, Psychiatry and Criminal Responsibility* (Dublin: Round Hall Press, 1993); Finbarr McAuley and J. Paul McCutcheon, *Criminal Liability: A Grammar* (Dublin: Round Hall Sweet and Maxwell, 2000); Anne Marie O'Neill, *Irish Mental Health Law* (Dublin: First Law, 2005); Patricia Casey & Ciaran Craven, *Psychiatry and the Law* (Dublin: Oak Tree Press, 1999); Peter Charleton, Paul McDermott & Marguerite Bolger, *Criminal Law* (Dublin: Butterworths, 1999); Conor Hanly, *An Introduction to Irish Criminal Law*, 2nd edn (Dublin: Gill and Macmillan, 2006); T.J. McIntyre & Sinéad McMullan, *Criminal Law*, 2nd edn (Dublin: Thomson Round Hall, 2005); Darius Whelan, "Some Procedural Aspects of Insanity Cases" (2001) 11(3) Ir. Crim. L.J. 3; Darius Whelan, "Fitness to Plead and Insanity in the District Court" (2001) 11(2) Ir. Crim. L.J. 2.

[15] Criminal Law (Insanity) Act 2006, s.1.

cannot be admitted to psychiatric institutions against their wishes, and the Criminal Law (Insanity) legislation has a different purpose: to establish a workable template for decisions by courts that people are to be excused criminal responsibility in certain circumstances and to deal with other issues, such as inability to plead. He went on to say:

> "I do not believe—this is a particularly important point—that decisions in terms of involuntary admissions to hospitals and judicial decisions about the impropriety in that regard should have necessary spillover effects into the law of criminal responsibility. Likewise, I do not believe decisions in the criminal courts as to the meaning of a particular matter should have a spillover effect on the treatment of patients who have nothing to do with the criminal law."[16]

Minister McDowell later stated that the Mental Health Commission had told him in correspondence that it now accepted the need for variation in definitions of mental disorder between the 2001 Act and this Act. He said that the Commission examined the issue following the Seanad debate and came to the conclusion that the arguments the Minister made were valid.[17] Senator Henry, who had initially argued for alignment of the definitions, later stated that she understood the need for the two definitions. She said, "It is good that throughout the rest of the Bill 'mental disorder' is described as being within the meaning of the Act of 2001 because these people will have the protection of Part 4 of that Act when detained in a designated centre under this legislation."[18]

Minister McDowell also refused to accept an amendment to delete "disease" and substitute "other disease or medical condition". He said that this would be "far too vague and would allow arguments to be made which would have the effect of widening the scope of the defence".[19]

15–06 Common law concerning "disease of the mind" holds that the question is not whether the accused had a recognised mental illness, nor whether the brain is diseased; the issue is whether the accused's mental faculties were impaired by illness. This means that, for example, arteriosclerosis and hyperglycaemia caused by diabetes have been held to be "diseases of the mind". In *R. v Kemp*[20] the accused made a motiveless and irrational attack on his wife with a hammer. He was charged with grievous bodily harm with intent to murder. He had arteriosclerosis which caused congestion of the blood on his brain, causing a temporary lapse of consciousness. Devlin J. stated:

> "The law is not concerned with the brain but with the mind, in the sense that 'mind' is ordinarily used, the mental faculties of reason, memory and under-

---

[16] 176 *Seanad Debates* Col.255 (April 7, 2004).
[17] 616 *Dáil Debates* Col.2045 (March 23, 2006).
[18] 183 *Seanad Debates* Col.621 (April 6, 2006).
[19] Select Committee on Justice, Equality, Defence and Women's Rights, January 18, 2006.
[20] [1957] 1 Q.B. 399.

standing. If one read for 'disease of the mind' 'disease of the brain,' it would follow that in many cases pleas of insanity would not be established because it could not be proved that the brain had been affected in any way, either by degeneration of the cells or in any other way. In my judgment the condition of the brain is irrelevant and so is the question of whether the condition of the mind is curable or incurable, transitory or permanent. There is no warranty for introducing those considerations into the definition in the McNaghten Rules. Temporary insanity is sufficient to satisfy them. It does not matter whether it is incurable and permanent or not."[21]

Devlin J.'s judgment was in the form of a ruling on legal submissions which had been made. He later charged the jury accordingly, and the jury returned an insanity verdict.[22]

15–07 Even though there is no specific reference to automatism in the *Kemp* case, it is often referred to as an example of "insane automatism", in the sense that the accused was found to be insane where he had a lapse of consciousness caused by an *internal* condition (arteriosclerosis). By way of contrast, in a case of "sane automatism" (or "non-insane automatism"), discussed below at paras 19–23 to 19–24, the lapse of consciousness is caused by an *external* factor, e.g. insulin injections, and may lead to a full acquittal.

Diabetes is another example of a physical condition which may constitute a "disease of the mind". In *R. v Hennessy*,[23] diabetes caused hyperglycaemia (excessive blood sugar) and was held to be insanity as it was an internal factor. There have also been cases where epilepsy has been held to be a disease of the mind.[24]

15–08 It is unclear whether personality disorders come within the reference to "disease of the mind". Minister McDowell contrasted the Bill with the Mental Health Act 2001 and said, "we have crafted this legislation so as not to close the door and slam it in the face of personality disorder".[25] At a later stage, however, in rejecting an amendment to define mental illness, he said he was concerned that if this amendment was adopted, it could open the prospect of personality disorders being brought within the definition. He said, "We are not in the business of excusing people from criminal liability because of their character or propensities. It must be much more fundamental than that."[26] Personality disorders are considered further below at paras 15–29 to 15–33.

---

[21] [1957] 1 Q.B. 399 at 407.

[22] At the time, the verdict was "guilty but insane" under the Trial of Lunatics Act 1883.

[23] [1989] 1 W.L.R. 287; [1989] 2 All E.R. 9.

[24] *Bratty v A.G. for Northern Ireland* [1963] A.C. 386; *Sullivan v D.P.P.* [1984] A.C. 156; *Ellis* case, Central Criminal Court, 1987, summarised in Finbarr McAuley, *Insanity, Psychiatry and Criminal Responsibility* (Dublin: Round Hall, 1993), pp.118–119.

[25] 176 *Seanad Debates* Col.259 (April 7, 2004).

[26] 616 *Dáil Debates* Col.2038 (March 23, 2006).

15–09 The original Bill referred to "mental handicap" but the Minister eventually accepted an amendment that this be changed to "mental disability".[27] However, he did not accept an amendment to change this to "intellectual disability", as he said there were lobby groups which were seeking to expand the meaning of that term. Technical arguments might be made about whether "mental disability" includes a learning disability, but it is likely that courts would recognise that a broad definition is to be adopted.

15–10 The Act states that "intoxication" (which is excluded from the definition of mental disorder) means being under the intoxicating influence of any alcoholic drink, drug, solvent or any other substance or combination of substances.[28] The original Bill did not define "intoxication" and Minister McDowell initially opposed the insertion of a definition. However, he later agreed to insert a definition based on s.4 of the Public Order Act 1994, for the sake of clarity. He cited the Law Reform Commission's report on Intoxication,[29] which states that the definition of intoxication or intoxicant, in the sense that either term involves the consumption of drugs as well as alcohol, does not appear to have given rise to any difficulty in any jurisdiction and in practice, intoxication is not accepted as a defence in Irish courts, but if anything, intoxication was found to be an aggravating factor.[30] The exclusion of intoxication from the definition of mental disorder may give rise to difficulties in cases where a person is intoxicated and has a mental illness.[31] See further paras 16–10 to 16–14 below.

THE INSANITY DEFENCE

15–11 While the insanity defence tends to be the best-known aspect of criminal law concerning mental disorder, it is important to place it in the context of the other aspects. As an alternative to an insanity verdict, mental disorder in a person charged with a crime may lead to their being diverted from the criminal justice system,[32] a decision not to prosecute being taken, their being found unfit for trial,[33] a reduction in sentence if found guilty,[34] a diminished responsibility verdict,[35] or a transfer from prison to a psychiatric centre for treatment.[36]

According to Hutchinson & O'Connor, Central Mental Hospital (CMH) case registers show that 50 patients were acquitted on grounds of insanity from 1937

---

[27] 616 *Dáil Debates* Col.2045 (March 23, 2006).
[28] Criminal Law (Insanity) Act 2006, s.1.
[29] Law Reform Commission, *Report on Intoxication* (LRC 51, 1995).
[30] 616 *Dáil Debates* Col.2036 (March 23, 2006).
[31] Tony McGillinddy, "The Criminal Law (Insanity) Act 2006" (2006) 11 *Bar Review* 95 at 95.
[32] See paras 19–01 to 19–08 below.
[33] See Chapter 17 below.
[34] See paras 19–17 to 19–22 below.
[35] See Chapter 16 below.
[36] See paras 19–31 to 19–38 below.

to 1995.[37] The insanity defence is most likely to be raised in cases where a person is charged with murder, although it is not confined to such cases. Dooley studied 610 homicides between 1972–1991 and found that in 12.2 per cent of cases (n=74), there was a clear history of previous psychiatric involvement.[38] A psychiatric outcome (unfit to plead or guilty but insane) was reached in 5.1 per cent of cases (n=31). He also studied homicides from 1992 to 1996 and found past psychiatric history in 11.7 per cent of cases and a psychiatric outcome in 2 per cent of cases.

15–12 The current statutory provision concerning the insanity defence is s.5(1) of the Criminal Law (Insanity) Act 2006:

> Where an accused person is tried for an offence and, in the case of the District Court or Special Criminal Court, the court or, in any other case, the jury finds that the accused person committed the act[39] alleged against him or her and, having heard evidence relating to the mental condition of the accused given by a consultant psychiatrist, finds that—
> (a) the accused person was suffering at the time from a mental disorder, and
> (b) the mental disorder was such that the accused person ought not to be held responsible for the act alleged by reason of the fact that he or she—
>> (i) did not know the nature and quality of the act, or
>> (ii) did not know that what he or she was doing was wrong, or
>> (iii) was unable to refrain from committing the act,
> the court or the jury, as the case may be, shall return a special verdict to the effect that the accused person is not guilty by reason of insanity.

15–13 During the Oireachtas debates, Minister McDowell refused to accept amendments which would have removed the reference to "Insanity" in the title of the Act, and replaced it with "Mental Disorder". Such a change had been supported by the Mental Health Commission. He argued that if the term "mental disorder" were used, juries would be more likely to find that the mental disorder defence applied: "To change the word 'insanity' to 'mental disorder' would send a signal that thresholds were being significantly lowered."[40] The Minister did not agree with the Irish Human Rights Commission on this point.[41] It is surprising that the opportunity was not taken to replace the word "insanity" with a more modern term such as "mental disorder", as the "insane" label stigmatises

---

[37] Lynn Hutchinson & Art O'Connor, "Unfit to Plead in Ireland" (1995) 12 Ir. Jnl. Psychol. Med. 112 at 114.

[38] Enda Dooley, *Homicide in Ireland 1972–1991* (Dublin: Stationery Office, 1995). See also Enda Dooley, *Homicide in Ireland, 1992–1996* (Dublin: Stationery Office, 2001).

[39] "Act" includes omission, and references to committing an act include references to making an omission—s.1, 2006 Act.

[40] 176 *Seanad Debates* Col.261 (April 7, 2004).

[41] Irish Human Rights Commission, *Observations on the Criminal Law (Insanity) Bill 2002*, September 2003, p.5.

the defendant more severely than other terms. However, the verdict is now "not guilty by reason of insanity" (NGRI) rather than "guilty but insane" and this at least removes the pejorative classification of the person as "guilty" of a criminal act.

15–14 The decision on insanity is normally made by a jury.[42] Evidence from a consultant psychiatrist must be heard before the verdict can be returned, a new statutory requirement introduced by the 2006 Act. In addition, the defence must have notified the prosecution, within 10 days of the accused being asked how they wish to plead, that it intends to adduce evidence of the accused's mental condition.[43] Section 5(4) of the 2006 Act lays down a special rule regarding murder cases: If the accused contends insanity, the court must allow the prosecution to adduce evidence to prove diminished responsibility.

15–15 If the criteria in the Act are satisfied, the accused is found NGRI. Up to 2006, the verdict was "guilty but insane" under the Trial of Lunatics Act 1883, but it was regarded as an acquittal, albeit a special type of acquittal which resulted in detention. The new verdict is also a special type of acquittal in that the judge will normally go on to consider whether the person requires detention. In the majority of cases the person will probably be detained.

15–16 The Act requires that the mental disorder be "such that the accused person ought not to be held responsible for the act alleged". Therefore, it must be shown that the accused had a mental disorder and that due to the mental disorder they are not responsible for the act or omission. The three alternative limbs which may apply are that the accused (i) did not know the nature and quality of the act, (ii) did not know that what they were doing was wrong, or (iii) was unable to refrain from committing the act. The first two limbs may be taken together and are sometimes referred to as "cognitive insanity". The third limb may be classified as "irresistible impulse".

The First and Second Limbs

15–17 The definition of insanity in the 2006 Act is effectively a restatement of the common law position, although without the reference to "defect of reason". The first and second limbs are sometimes referred to as "cognitive insanity" because they focus on what the person knew, namely that the person did not know the nature and quality of the act, or did not know that what they were doing was wrong. These limbs derive from the McNaghten Rules of 1843.[44]

---

[42] The exceptions are where an insanity verdict is reached by the Special Criminal Court or the District Court.

[43] Section 19, Criminal Law (Insanity) Act 2006.

[44] *R. v McNaghten* (1843) 10 Cl. & F. 200; 8 E.R. 718; [1843–60] All E.R. Rep. 229. For the

15–18 McNaghten killed the Prime Minister's Secretary, mistaking him for the Prime Minister, as McNaghten had the "insane" belief that he was being persecuted by the Tory Party and that his life had been endangered as a result. Tindal C.J. told the jury McNaghten should be acquitted unless they were satisfied he was capable of distinguishing right from wrong with respect to the act of which he stood charged. The jury's acquittal caused controversy and the House of Lords in its legislative capacity put questions to the Law Lords regarding the proper scope of the insanity defence. The Law Lords laid down a series of guidelines for the courts, now referred to as the McNaghten Rules.[45] Rule 1[46] stated that persons who labour under partial delusions only, and are not in other respects insane, and who act under the influence of an insane delusion, of redressing or avenging some supposed grievance or injury, or producing some public benefit, are nevertheless punishable if they knew at the time of committing the crime that they were acting contrary to the law of the land. Rule 2 stated that every man is presumed to be sane and to possess a sufficient degree of reason to be responsible for his crimes until the contrary be proved. Rule 3, the core rule referred to as the first and second limbs of the insanity defence, stated:

> "To establish a defence on the ground of insanity, it must be clearly proved that, at the time of the committing of the act, the party accused was labouring under such a defect of reason, from disease of the mind, as not to know the nature and quality of the act he was doing, or, if he did know it, that he did not know he was doing what was wrong."[47]

Rule 4 stated that a person labouring under a partial delusion only, and not in other respects insane, must be considered in the same situation as to responsibility as if the facts with respect to which the delusion exists were real. For example, if under the influence of his delusion a man supposes another man to be in the act of attempting to take away his life and he kills that man, as he supposes, in self-defence, he would be exempt from punishment. If his delusion was that the deceased had inflicted a serious injury to his character and fortune and he killed him in revenge for such supposed injury, he would be liable for punishment.

The rules were stricter than previous case law, and McNaghten probably could not have relied on them, as he knew he was killing a human being and if his delusion about persecution were true he probably would not have been able to rely on a defence such as self-defence.

---

historical background, see Nigel Walker, *Crime and Insanity in England*, vol.1 (Edinburgh University Press, 1968).

[45] The Rules did not apply to McNaghten himself, who had already been acquitted.

[46] The numbering of the rules does not appear in the report of the case and has been added by subsequent commentators.

[47] Rule 3 continues: "The mode of putting the latter part of the question to the jury on these occasions has generally been, whether the accused at the time of doing the act knew the difference between right and wrong: which mode, though rarely, if ever, leading to any mistake

15–19 When the McNaghten Rules state that the person "did not know he was doing what was wrong", the English courts have held that "wrong" means contrary to law. In *R. v Windle*[48] W. killed his wife by administration of 100 aspirins. The evidence was that both the accused and his wife had mental disorders and the defence stated that W. had a form of communicated insanity known as "folie à deux". Windle had given himself up to the police and said "I suppose they'll hang me for this?" Doctors on both sides agreed he knew he was doing an act forbidden by law. The issue of insanity did not go to the jury. W. was convicted and the Court of Criminal Appeal upheld this. Lord Goddard C.J. said:

> "Courts of law can only distinguish between that which is in accordance with law and that which is contrary to law. There are many acts which, to use an expression which is to be found in some of the old cases, are contrary to the law of God and man. For instance, in the Decalogue will be found the laws 'Thou shalt not kill' and 'Thou shalt not steal.' Those acts are contrary to the law of man and also to the law of God. If the seventh commandment is taken, 'Thou shalt not commit adultery,' although that is contrary to the law of God, so far as the criminal law is concerned it is not contrary to the law of man. That does not mean that the law encourages adultery; I only say that it is not a criminal offence. The law cannot embark on the question, and it would be an unfortunate thing if it were left to juries to consider whether some particular act was morally right or wrong. The test must be whether it is contrary to law."[49]

15–20 Strictly speaking, the *ratio* of the *Windle* case holds it was correct to tell the jury that the accused could not rely on the defence if he knew that his act was legally wrong. It does not necessarily preclude it also being held that if the accused knows either that their act is morally wrong or that it is legally wrong then it cannot be said that they do not know they were doing what was wrong.[50]

However, there are strong arguments that the accused ought to be able to avail of the insanity defence if they know that the act is unlawful but they believe that their act is not morally wrong. As Mackay points out, an example might occur where an accused does not know that what he is doing is wrong, as he believes that by killing his victim he will bring him back to life, as a consequence of his

---

with the jury, is not, as we conceive, so accurate when put generally and in the abstract, as when put with reference to the party's knowledge of right and wrong in respect to the very act with which he is charged. If the question were to be put as to the knowledge of the accused solely and exclusively with reference to the law of the land, it might tend to confound the jury, by inducing them to believe that an actual knowledge of the law of the land was essential in order to lead to a conviction; whereas the law is administered upon the principle that every one must be taken conclusively to know it, without proof that he does know it."

48 [1952] 2 Q.B. 826; [1952] 2 All E.R. 1.
49 [1952] 2 Q.B. 826 at 833.
50 See *Blackstone's Criminal Practice* (2007), at A3–18, quoted with approval in *R. v Johnson (Dean)* [2007] M.H.L.R. 310 at 313.

delusional system, centred around his belief that he himself is a god and that the victim is also a god possessed by demons.[51] Mackay argues that to convict such a person with mental disorder on the basis that they may have retained some abstract awareness that it was against the law to do what they did when their sense of reality was distorted just seems plain "wrong".[52]

15–21 In the Australian case of *Stapleton v R*.[53] it was held that, in applying the test of insanity, the question was whether the accused knew that his act was wrong according to the ordinary principles of reasonable men, not whether he knew it was wrong being contrary to the law. The Australian Criminal Code now re-formulates the test as "the person did not know that the conduct was wrong (that is, the person could not reason with a moderate degree of sense and composure about whether the conduct, as perceived by reasonable people, was wrong)".[54] The Canadian courts have reached similar conclusions.[55]

15–22 Mackay has stated that in practice in the English courts, the *Windle* case is often ignored and the accused may be found NGRI if they knew that the act was contrary to law but did not know it was morally wrong.[56] In its answer to a case stated in *Doyle v Wicklow County Council*,[57] the Supreme Court stated that in a case where, on an issue of insanity in criminal damage, "it appears that although the person who committed the damage knew the nature and quality of his and understood its wrongfulness, *morally and legally*, the judge may consider whether such person was debarred from refraining from committing the damage because of a defect of reason due to his mental illness."[58] O'Neill has stated that in practice Irish juries are told that "wrong" in the context of the McNaghten Rules means morally wrong.[59]

The debate was re-ignited in 2007 with the English case of *R. v Johnson (Dean)*.[60] The Court of Appeal was asked to consider whether lack of knowledge

---

[51] R.D. Mackay, "Righting the Wrong? Some Observations on the Second Limb of the M'Naghten Rules" [2009] Crim. L.R. 80. This is one of three examples given by Mackay of extracts from psychiatric reports studied as part of empirical research.

[52] R.D. Mackay, "Righting the Wrong? Some Observations on the Second Limb of the M'Naghten Rules" [2009] Crim. L.R. 80 at 84.

[53] (1952) 86 C.L.R. 358.

[54] Australian Criminal Code 1995, s.7.3(1)(b). See generally Bernadette McSherry, "The Reformulated Defence of Insanity in the Australian Criminal Code Act of 1995" (1997) 20 Int.J. L. & Psych. 183. See also s.23(2) of the Crimes Act 1961 (New Zealand).

[55] See *R. v Chaulk* [1990] 2 C.R. (4th) 1; [1990] 3 S.C.R.1303 and *R. v Oommen* [1994] 2 S.C.R. 507.

[56] R.D. Mackay, *Mental Condition Defences in the Criminal Law* (Oxford: Clarendon Press, 1995), pp.102–108.

[57] [1974] I.R. 55.

[58] [1974] I.R. 55 at 60 (emphasis added). Griffin J. noted, at 70, the difference between the *Windle* and *Stapleton* cases.

[59] Anne-Marie O'Neill, *Irish Mental Health Law* (Dublin: First Law, 2005), p.486, citing direction of Lavan J. in the *O'Donnell* case, unreported, Central Criminal Court, January–April 1996.

[60] *R. v Johnson (Dean)* [2007] E.W.C.A. Crim. 1978; [2007] M.H.L.R. 310. See R.D. Mackay,

of moral wrongness would be sufficient to raise the insanity defence. The court stated that the *Windle* case was settled law (subject to perhaps restricting the *ratio* as mentioned above). Latham L.J. acknowledged the different approach taken in Australia, and Mackay's reports as to what occurred in practice in England. Nevertheless, he held that it was not appropriate to disturb the settled case law at Court of Appeal level and instead the matter might be re-considered in the House of Lords.[61]

Inability to Refrain

15–23 The third limb, that the person was unable to refrain from committing the act, is referred to as "irresistible impulse" or volitional insanity, in the sense that it affects the person's will.[62] The main authority for this is the 1974 Supreme Court case of *Doyle v Wicklow County Council*.[63] The possibility of an irresistible impulse limb being added to the defence of insanity had been raised in earlier cases such as *Attorney General v O'Brien*[64] and, more significantly, in *People (A.G.) v Hayes*.[65]

15–24 In *Doyle v Wicklow County Council*[66] Raymond O'Toole had deliberately burned down Doyle's abattoir. He believed that his love of animals entitled him to burn down the abattoir and he would not be liable to criminal punishment. There was psychiatric evidence that O'Toole's judgment was distorted and he was emotionally disturbed. It was said that he could not be called sane and he needed psychiatric treatment and detention. Mr Doyle applied to Wicklow County Council for compensation for criminal damage. If O'Toole was insane, no compensation would be awarded, as there no "malice". The Circuit Court judge submitted certain questions of law for determination by way of case stated to the Supreme Court. The Supreme Court adopted the approach which had

"Righting the Wrong? Some Observations on the Second Limb of the M'Naghten Rules" [2009] Crim. L.R. 80.

[61] At the time of writing, no House of Lords (or Supreme Court) decision has been issued.

[62] See discussion in Finbarr McAuley, *Insanity, Psychiatry and Criminal Responsibility* (Dublin: Round Hall, 1993), Chapter 3. McAuley believes that "volitional insanity" is the accurate term to use. However, since his book was written, the Court of Criminal Appeal has approved of the label "irresistible impulse" in *People (DPP) v Courtney*, Court of Criminal Appeal, July 21, 1994.

[63] [1974] I.R. 55.

[64] [1936] I.R. 263. See also *A.G. v Boylan* [1937] I.R. 449; *People (A.G.) v Manning* (1955) 89 I.L.T.R 155; *People (A.G.) v McGrath* (1960) 1 Frewen 192; *People (A.G.) v Coughlan* (June 1968) cited in Roderick O'Hanlon, "Not Guilty Because of Insanity" (1968) 3 Ir. Jur. (n.s.) 61. Note the raising of another possible re-formulation of the insanity defence, based on US case law, in *People (A.G.) v McGlynn* [1967] I.R. 232.

[65] Central Criminal Court, Henchy J., November 30, 1967, cited in Roderick O'Hanlon, "Not Guilty Because of Insanity" (1968) 3 Ir. Jur. (n.s.) 61 and followed in *Doyle v Wicklow County Council* [1974] I.R. 55.

[66] [1974] I.R. 55. See Niall Osborough, "McNaghten Revisited" (1974) 9 Ir. Jur. (n.s.) 76.

earlier been adopted in *People (A.G.) v Hayes*.[67] Griffin J. stated that in his opinion, the McNaghten Rules did not provide the sole or exclusive test for determining the sanity or insanity of an accused. He adopted the reasoning of Henchy J. in *Hayes* to the effect that "it is open to the jury to say, as say they must, on the evidence, that this man understood the nature and quality of his act, and understood its wrongfulness, morally and legally, but that nevertheless he was debarred from refraining from assaulting his wife fatally because of a defect of reason, due to his mental illness".[68] This was then rephrased in the answer to the case stated as follows:

(i) the judge in determining such issue of insanity should apply the standards or rules appropriate to a criminal trial;

(ii) the rules in McNaghten's Case do not provide the sole or exclusive test for determining such issue and the opinions of the judges in that case must be read as being specifically limited to the effect of insane delusions;

(iii) in a case where, on such issue, it appears that although the person who committed the damage knew the nature and quality of his act and understood its wrongfulness, morally and legally, the judge may consider whether such person was debarred from refraining from committing the damage because of a defect of reason due to his mental illness.[69]

The eventual result in the case was that it was found that O'Toole was insane and therefore compensation for criminal damage was not payable.[70]

15–25 The *Doyle* case has the advantage of moving the McNaghten Rules beyond mere consideration of what the accused person "knew" to consideration of issues of impairment of volition caused by mental disorder. Griffin J. approved of statements by Henchy J. in *Hayes* that this was one of the limitations of the McNaghten rules, that they focused on knowledge. Even though the *Doyle* formulation may be unsatisfactory in its terminology, it opens the possibility of a broader consideration of the accused's mental disorder and its effect on the accused's actions. Ultimately, the jury must decide whether the mental disorder was such that the accused ought not to be held responsible for the act. The addition of a third limb merely enables more cases to go to juries, but juries remain the ultimate arbiters on the issue of responsibility.

15–26 It is notable that the introduction of an irresistible impulse limb has been rejected by the English courts and by the Privy Council. Lord Hewart L.C.J. was

---

[67] Central Criminal Court, Henchy J., November 30, 1967, cited in Roderick O'Hanlon, "Not Guilty Because of Insanity" (1968) 3 Ir. Jur. (n.s.) 61 and followed in *Doyle v Wicklow County Council* [1974] I.R. 55.

[68] Extract from *Hayes* case quoted [1974] I.R. 55 at 71.

[69] [1974] I.R. 55 at 60.

[70] [1974] I.R. 55 at 74: The High Court (Henchy J.) found that the youth who had set fire to the premises had not been criminally responsible for his act, and allowed the appeal.

in no doubt that uncontrollable impulse was a fantastic, subversive theory and was not part of the law in *R. v Kopsch*:

> "[T]he complaint against the judge is that he did not tell the jury that something was the law which was not the law. The argument of counsel for the defence began with the proposition that the law was as he represented, but, as it proceeded, drifted into the different position that the law ought to become, or ought to have become, what he represented. It is the fantastic theory of uncontrollable impulse which, if it were to become part of our criminal law, would be merely subversive. It is not yet part of the criminal law, and it is to be hoped that the time is far distant when it will be made so. The jury may well have thought that the defence of insanity in this case, as in so many cases, was the merest nonsense."[71]

Similarly, the Privy Council rejected attempts to introduce an irresistible impulse limb in *A.G. for South Australia v Brown*.[72] One factor referred to was that a diminished responsibility verdict might be more appropriate in such a case.[73]

15–27 In *People (DPP) v Courtney*,[74] the Court of Criminal Appeal approved of the following statement of the law in Lynch J.'s charge to the jury:

> "This is a limited form of insanity recognised by our law, commonly called irresistible impulse. That means in this case an irresistible impulse caused by a defect of reason due to mental illness. Merely because an impulse is not in fact resisted does not mean that it is an irresistible impulse. If so, no one could ever be convicted of a crime—they would only have to say, I found the impulse irresistible. It must be an irresistible impulse, not an unresisted impulse, to constitute that form of insanity.
>
> Diminished self control or weakened resistance to impulse is not necessarily the same as irresistible impulse. Diminished self control makes the resistance to an impulse more difficult but does not necessarily make it irresistible. This must arise from a defect of reason due to mental illness, and in this case this defect of reason due to mental illness is mainly attributed to events on the second tour in Lebanon, which was completed approximately three years before the events with which you are concerned. Dr O'Connor and the two psychologists all say that the accused's self control was significantly diminished but not lost. Did the accused act because he did not resist the impulses rather than because he could not? That is for you to decide, bearing in mind all the evidence and the facts as found by you on the basis of such evidence."

---

[71] (1927) 19 Cr. App. R. 50 at 51–2.
[72] [1960] A.C. 432.
[73] [1960] A.C. 432 at 459.
[74] Court of Criminal Appeal, July 21, 1994.

O'Flaherty J. said that the court was of the opinion that this was a very full description of what was involved in this defence.[75]

15–28 During the debates on the Bill which became the 2006 Act, Senator Henry proposed that the third limb be deleted, as everyone would be claiming they had an irresistible impulse to do something, including those who sexually abuse children. Minister McDowell referred to the rejection of such a defence in England, but stated that he had decided not to "close it off" in Ireland, as it was part of the Irish common law and had been confirmed on two occasions, in *Doyle* and in *Courtney*.[76]

Personality Disorders

15–29 The issue of how personality disorders should be dealt with by the law is one which has led to a great deal of debate. As was noted above at para.3–04, s.8 of the Mental Health Act 2001 states that a person may not be detained under that Act solely on the grounds of a personality disorder. Psychopathy is one example of a personality disorder which may arise in criminal cases, and it is important not to confuse it with psychosis. In *People (A.G.) v Messitt*,[77] which will be considered below at para.15–37, a doctor had stated that the accused was a psychopath, prone to violence. The court stated that if the accused or his advisers are not prepared to make the case that he is insane, the duty of putting such evidence as is available on the topic before the jury rests on the People, if the Attorney General is of opinion that the evidence is such that the jury might reasonably conclude that the accused was insane. In this case there was evidence available, but not given to the jury, which established that the accused was an aggressive psychopath who was prone to episodes of uncontrollable violence. Kenny J. stated that the doctor should have been called as a witness and he should have been asked to elaborate on his remark that the accused was a psychopath. The jury should also have received assistance on the nature of the insanity which would justify a verdict of guilty but insane, and on the onus of proof on that issue.[78]

15–30 In *R. v Byrne*[79] it was held that sexual psychopathy could be an "abnormality of mind" under s.2 of the Homicide Act 1957 (England and Wales), concerning diminished responsibility. Lord Parker C.J. said that "abnormality of mind" was wide enough to cover the mind's activities in all its aspects, not only the perception of physical acts and matters and the ability to form a rational

---

[75] Court of Criminal Appeal, July 21, 1994.
[76] 176 *Seanad Debates* Col.389 (April 8, 2004).
[77] [1972] I.R. 204.
[78] [1972] I.R. 204 at 213.
[79] [1960] 2 Q.B. 396.

judgment whether an act is right or wrong, but also the ability to exercise will power to control physical acts in accordance with that rational judgment.[80]

15–31 The finding in *Byrne* was apparently extended to the insanity defence in Ireland by an obiter dictum of Finlay C.J. in *People (DPP) v O'Mahony*:

> "Having regard to the definition of the defence of insanity laid down by this Court in *Doyle v Wicklow County Council*, it is quite clear that the appellant in *R. v Byrne*, if tried in accordance with the law of this country on the same facts, would have been properly found to be not guilty by reason of insanity."[81]

While this comment was not part of the *ratio* of the case, it remains of importance and will, of course, be relevant to legal arguments about psychopathy in Irish law. The comment must be read in context. Finlay C.J. was explaining that *Doyle v Wicklow County Council* established the irresistible impulse limb of the insanity defence in Ireland, and how this differed from the English position, where irresistible impulse might be relevant to diminished responsibility but not insanity. He did not address directly the thorny issue of whether psychopathy is a "disease of the mind" for the purposes of the insanity defence. Finlay C.J. twice noted that there was medical evidence that O'Mahony had a psychotic condition[82] and it is possible that there was some confusion between psychopathy and psychosis in the case.

15–32 In two high-profile cases in the 1990s, *Gallagher*[83] and *O'Donnell*,[84] the question of whether the accused had a personality disorder or a mental disorder was central to the conflicting psychiatric evidence given at each trial. It is difficult to summarise the evidence based on media reports alone, but in essence it appears that medical witnesses who stated that Gallagher or O'Donnell had a personality disorder tended also to be of the opinion that the man in question was not entitled to avail of the insanity defence. In the end, an insanity verdict was returned for Gallagher but a verdict of guilty of murder was returned for O'Donnell.

15–33 It is unclear whether people with personality disorders who have committed crimes are primarily prisoners or patients, and as a result they end up

---

[80] [1960] 2 Q.B. 396 at 403.

[81] [1985] I.R. 517 at 522. See commentary by Finbarr McAuley, *Insanity, Psychiatry and Criminal Responsibility* (Dublin: Round Hall, 1993), p.52.

[82] [1985] I.R. 517 at 520 and 522.

[83] *Irish Times* reports of Gallagher trial, summarised in Finbarr McAuley, *Insanity, Psychiatry and Criminal Responsibility* (Dublin: Round Hall, 1993), p.123.

[84] *Irish Times* reports of O'Donnell trial, January to April 1996, especially the four weeks of evidence from psychiatrists and psychologists. *Irish Times*, March 8, 9, 12, 13, 14, 15, 16, 20, 21, 22, 23, 26, 27, 28 and 29, 1996; see also judge's charge to jury and reports following verdict—*Irish Times*, April 2 and 3, 1996.

falling between two stools. The former Inspector of Prisons, Kinlen J., commented as follows:

> "The Government must address the problem of how to cope with people (including prisoners) who have personality problems but now have no asylums. They should not be put into prison. They should be under the Department of Health rather than Justice. They are presently treated unjustly and despite individual efforts to cope they are placed in an impossible and disgraceful situation which is unfair to them, to Governors and staff, and fellow prisoners by incarcerating them in a prison."[85]

Sleep Disorders

15–34 In *R. v Burgess*[86] B. attacked and injured his neighbour while sleepwalking. They had each had one glass of martini. He claimed non-insane automatism, but the trial judge ruled that he was precluded from raising a defence of automatism without involving an issue of insanity. It was held that as his sleep disorder was a pathological (disease-like) condition which was likely to recur, it was therefore a disease of the mind, and he was found not guilty by reason of insanity.

However, in *People (DPP) v Reilly (John)*,[87] sleep disorder was raised as a ground for an automatism defence, but the judge did not require that insanity be considered. There is no consideration of the *Burgess* case in the judgment, and instead the emphasis is on the fact that the accused had consumed a great deal of alcohol. The Court of Criminal Appeal held that voluntary intoxication was not a defence to a crime of manslaughter. However, Dillon argues that there should have been a more detailed consideration by the court of the sleep disorder in this case:

> "The jury was inadequately charged because of both the excessive emphasis placed on the role of alcohol in 'bringing about' the automatism and the failure to direct the jury that sleep could be a cause or a partial cause of the automatism. Indeed, the charge to the jury gave the impression that they could not acquit if they had a reasonable doubt that the applicant was in a state of confusional arousal or sleep-related automatism."[88]

---

[85] *Third Annual Report of Inspector of Prisons and Places of Detention 2004–2005*, para.22.11.
[86] [1991] 2 Q.B. 92. See generally William Wilson, Irshaad Ebrahim, Peter Fenwick & Richard Marks, "Violence, Sleepwalking and the Criminal Law: Part 2: the Legal Aspects" [2005] Crim. L.R. 614
[87] [2004] I.E.C.C.A. 9; [2005] 3 I.R. 111.
[88] Michael Dillon, "Intoxicated Automatism is no Defence: Majewski is Law in Ireland" (2004) 14(3) Ir. Crim. L.J. 7 at 13.

THE ROLE OF PSYCHIATRIC AND PSYCHOLOGICAL EVIDENCE

15–35 Psychiatric and psychological evidence is important in assisting the jury to decide whether the accused person had a psychiatric condition or "disease of the mind".[89] In *DPP v Abdi*,[90] the appellant argued that a psychiatrist's evidence on the appellant's motivation in the killing should be inadmissible. However, the Court of Criminal Appeal rejected this argument as follows:

> "Dr McCaffrey said only a person in an acute psychotic state could perform the crime; Dr Bourke said that only a person who is psychiatrically ill or in the grip of a very considerable degree of malice could perform the act. These things having been said and relied on, Dr Mohan gave evidence to the contrary. He opined as to the existence of a sane if perverted attitude on the part of the accused, capable of constituting malice of the sort Dr Bourke referred to, as a causation other than insanity, and in Dr Mohan's view more probable than insanity, for the crime. We will therefore consider that Dr Mohan's evidence was in principle admissible."[91]

The court went on to emphasise that the jury continues to have a central role in insanity cases. Hardiman J. said that the role of the expert witness is not to supplant the tribunal of fact, be it judge or jury, but to inform the tribunal so that it may come to its own decision. Where there is a conflict of expert evidence, it is to be resolved by the jury or by the judge, if sitting without a jury, having regard to the onus of proof and the standard of proof applicable in the particular circumstances. He said that expert opinion should not be expressed in a form which suggests that the expert is trying to subvert the role of the finder of fact.[92]

15–36 In the recent case of *DPP v Mulder*,[93] various grounds of appeal were submitted based on the manner in which psychiatric evidence had been admitted at a murder trial in which the accused was raising insanity. For example, one of the psychiatrists had commented in his evidence that the applicant was "cunning, deceitful, manipulative and plausible". The applicant's counsel submitted that this evidence was prejudicial, had no probative value and was not true psychiatric evidence. The Court of Criminal Appeal was satisfied that the comments in question arose necessarily from the obligation on the part of the psychiatrist to give a frank opinion as to whether the applicant was in fact suffering from depression at the time of the offence and to offer an opinion having regard to his assessment and the materials and notes which he examined.

---

[89]   See generally Harry Kennedy, "Limits of Psychiatric Evidence in Criminal Courts: Morals and Madness" (2005) 11(1) M.L.J.I. 13.
[90]   [2004] I.E.C.C.A. 47; [2005] 1 I.L.R.M. 382.
[91]   [2005] 1 I.L.R.M. 382 at 389–90.
[92]   [2005] 1 I.L.R.M. 382 at 393.
[93]   [2009] I.E.C.C.A. 45; Court of Criminal Appeal, April 27, 2009.

He was, in the opinion of the court, offering this view in part explanation for his conclusion that the applicant was not suffering from depression. He gave his reasons for that conclusion and was fully cross-examined in respect thereof. The court therefore dismissed this ground of appeal.

RAISING THE DEFENCE

15–37 In *People (AG) v Messitt*,[94] the Court of Criminal Appeal held that in certain cases evidence should be heard on the defendant's insanity at the time of the alleged offence, even if they do not raise the issue themselves. Kenny J. said:

> "If the accused or his advisors are not prepared to make the case that he is insane, the duty of putting such evidence as is available on the topic before the jury rests on the People, if the Attorney General is of opinion that the evidence is such that the jury might reasonably conclude that the accused was insane."[95]

15–38 The Supreme Court of Canada has held in *R v Swain*[96] that the common law rule permitting the Crown to adduce evidence of insanity against the defendant's wishes violates s.7 of the Canadian Charter. The court went on to fashion a new common law rule that allowed the Crown to raise insanity only in two situations: first, after the trier of fact had concluded that the defendant was otherwise guilty of the charge, and secondly, after the defendant's own defence has (in the view of the trial judge) put the defendant's capacity for criminal intent in issue.[97] There is also some Australian authority that the Crown may not raise the issue of insanity when the defendant has not raised any issue relating to their mental condition.[98]

15–39 The Canadian and Australian approach is to be preferred to *Messitt*, as it is an essential principle of an adversarial system that the defendant chooses how to conduct their own defence. Assuming the defendant is fit for trial (and

---

[94] [1972] I.R. 204.

[95] [1972] I.R. 204 at 213. This was not a straightforward case, as the defendant was representing himself, a doctor had said in the jury's presence that the defendant was a psychopath, the jury had asked for assistance on the mental condition of the defendant at the time of the crime, and the jury had added a rider about the defendant's mental condition to its verdict. It has been noted that there is "no restriction at all" in *Messitt* on the duties of prosecuting counsel to raise the insanity defence–Niall Osborough, "The Answerability of the Offender: The Indicia of Responsibility", Society of Young Solicitors, Lecture 78, 1974, p.12.

[96] (1991) 63 C.C.C. (3d.) 481; 5 C.R. (4th) 253; [1991] S.C.R. 933.

[97] See Part XX.1 of the Canadian Criminal Code dealing with 'Mental Disorder' added by S.C. 1991, c.43, s.4; A.J.C. O'Marra, "Hadfield to Swain: The Criminal Code Amendments Dealing with the Mentally Disordered Accused" (1993) 36 Crim.L.Q. 49.

[98] *R. v Joyce* [1970] S.A.S.R. 184; *R. v Jeffrey* [1967] V.R. 467.

ideally the criteria for unfitness should be broadened),[99] then the defendant is fit to make decisions about whether to raise the insanity defence or not.[100] If the State is concerned that the defendant will not receive treatment for a mental condition, or that the defendant has a mental disorder and is dangerous, there are other mechanisms for dealing with this.

15–40 The 2006 Act is silent on the issue of whether the court may raise the insanity defence, but it does state that once one mental condition defence (insanity or diminished responsibility) has been raised by the accused in a murder case, the prosecution may give evidence to prove the other defence.[101]

15–41 If an accused pleads guilty and is fit to plead at the time, the Supreme Court held in *People (DPP) v Redmond*[102] that the court should normally accept that plea, even if there is evidence which might point towards an insanity defence. The accused had been charged with causing serious harm contrary to s.4(1) of the Non-Fatal Offences Against the Person Act 1997. He had stabbed a patient in an unprovoked attack in the vicinity of a psychiatric hospital. There were psychiatric reports produced at sentencing stage and the Judge of the Circuit Court said in the Case Stated that there were substantial grounds for believing that the accused may have been insane in law at the time of the commission of the alleged offence.

Geoghegan J. stated that the accused had decided to plead guilty in the ordinary way. Nobody was suggesting that he was not fit to plead nor was there any certainty or even near certainty that if the facts emerging from the book of evidence were true he would have been insane at the time of the offences in the legal sense. In these circumstances, he found it difficult to see how the accused could be forced to alter his plea. The only conceivable basis would be the fact that the judge, apparently as a consequence of questioning, elicited from counsel for the accused that the plea was tactical, in that the accused did not want to be sent to a mental hospital indefinitely, rather than have a fixed short-term prison sentence at most. On this point, Geoghegan J. said:

> "I have never heard of the motive of an accused for pleading in a particular way being investigated and it would be against all the principles of the criminal law if it could be done unless of course an issue of duress had arisen. But that issue would be raised by the accused himself. ... An accused is entitled to have tactical reasons as to whether, for instance, he pleads guilty

---

[99] See paras 17–07 to 17–11.
[100] Contrast Kenny J., "It is not an answer to this to say that the accused does not wish this evidence to be given. One of the questions in issue is his sanity: his fitness to plead does not involve the conclusion that he is the only person to make a decision as to whether the issue of his insanity is to be considered by the jury"—[1972] I.R. 204 at 213–214.
[101] Criminal Law (Insanity) Act 2006, s.5(4).
[102] [2006] I.E.S.C. 25; [2006] 3 I.R. 188; [2006] 2 I.L.R.M. 182.

rather than not guilty and I do not think his motive should ever be examined. From the accused's point of view the reason that he pleaded was a perfectly good one and I think that it would be harsh to accuse him of abusing the process of the court by doing so nor do I think that it in any way was an abuse of the process of the court."[103]

Kearns J. stated that an intervention by the trial judge to reject the accused's plea of not guilty would run counter to an accused person's right in the ordinary way to select their preferred line of defence. This seemed to him to be an integral part of the right to a fair trial which is guaranteed by Art.38 of the Constitution. He saw nothing wrong or objectionable in a course of action whereby an accused person, adopting a pragmatic approach to an upcoming trial in consultation with his legal and medical advisers and on their advice, would weigh up the advantages of getting a reduced but finite sentence by pleading guilty instead of opting for a fully contested trial where the prosecution or the court might introduce an issue of insanity with its concomitant risk of indefinite confinement in a prison for the "criminally insane" in the wake of any jury finding of insanity. He said that this "balancing approach" in most instances will be a practical, common sense course which, in his opinion, had much to commend it under the current legal regime and was an approach with which practitioners in this area of law would be familiar.[104]

Fennelly J., concurring, said that if an accused appears not to be fit to plead (unlike in this case), the prosecution has the right to raise the issue of insanity, in which case it appeared that it would have to be proven beyond reasonable doubt. This fact is a corrective to the fear that a grossly insane person could avoid the detention that is the consequence of a finding of insanity by pleading guilty.[105]

15–42 Denham J. dissented, saying that the judge was being asked to collude in a situation where he had substantial grounds for believing that there was no crime. The judge was "being asked to support a sham".[106] She said that a judge has duties, not only to an accused, but also in relation to the people of the State, the common good and the prosecution. An important right is the right to have a fair trial, to have a trial in due course of law. It was important that the people have confidence that the courts conduct trials in a fair and just manner. She concluded:

> "It is open to the trial judge to vacate the plea of guilty by the accused and have a jury determine whether at the time of the commission of the actions alleged the accused was sane or not. This approach best serves the interests of

[103] [2006] 3 I.R. 188 at 205.
[104] [2006] 3 I.R. 188 at 216.
[105] [2006] 3 I.R. 188 at 210–211.
[106] [2006] 3 I.R. 188 at 197.

justice and the integrity of the judicial system. I do accept that there is a likely consequence that the accused will be detained in a medical institution for whatever period of time is necessary to treat a dangerous psychiatric condition and that such detention may be indefinite.

However, it appears to me that there is a balance of rights to be achieved— the right to enter a plea does not cap the right to a fair trial, the right to due process, the community's right to fair administration of justice, and the people's right to the protection of the integrity of the judicial system."[107]

15–43 While there are strong arguments on both sides in this case, on balance the majority decision appears to be correct. The majority rightly emphasise that the accused person is presumed to be sane and if they are fit to plead, the court should normally accept that plea. While the word "autonomy" does not appear in the decision, it would appear to be consistent with the autonomy of the accused in this case to respect his decision to plead guilty for tactical reasons.

BURDEN OF PROOF

15–44 At common law it is presumed that a person is sane and according to *Woolmington v DPP*,[108] the onus is definitely and exceptionally placed upon the accused to establish the defence of insanity. It was said in one Irish case that insanity must be proven beyond a reasonable doubt, but this would be unlikely to be followed today.[109]

The modern view is that the defence must be established by the accused on the balance of probabilities. In *People (DPP) v O'Mahony*, Finlay C.J. stated that if it were established, as a matter of probability, that due to an abnormality of mind consisting of a psychotic condition the appellant had been unable to control himself, he would have also been entitled to a finding of not guilty by reason of insanity.[110] Kearns J. said in *People (DPP) v Redmond* that it was agreed by counsel for the accused, the prosecution and the Attorney General that an accused person enjoys a presumption of sanity under the McNaghten Rules and that the onus of proof of establishing insanity when it rests on the defence is to the standard of the balance of probabilities.[111]

---

[107]   [2006] 3 I.R. 188 at 199.
[108]   [1935] A.C. 462 at 475, per Viscount Sankey L.C. See generally T.H. Jones, "Insanity, Automatism and the Burden of Proof on the Accused" (1995) 111 L.Q.R. 475.
[109]   *People (A.G.) v Fennell (No.1)* [1940] I.R. 445; See Finbarr McAuley, *Insanity, Psychiatry and Criminal Responsibility* (Dublin: Round Hall, 1993), p.94; Úna Ní Raifeartaigh, "Reversing the Burden of Proof in a Criminal Trial: Canadian and Irish Perspectives on the Presumption of Innocence" (1995) 5 Ir.Crim.L.J. 135 at 136, fn.5.
[110]   [1985] I.R. 517 at 522.
[111]   [2006] 3 I.R. 188 at 213.

15–45 The Canadian Supreme Court has held that the burden of proof in insanity cases violated s.11(d) of the Charter, which provides that there is a presumption of innocence.[112] However, the court went on to hold that the burden of proof was a reasonable limit under s.1 of the Charter and therefore valid.[113]

15–46 The Scottish Law Commission considered the question of the burden of proof in its 2004 Report and concluded that the current legal position should be retained. The Commission noted that it would be difficult for the prosecution to prove that the accused was not insane, e.g. it could not force the accused to undergo a psychiatric examination. In addition, mental state is an internal matter and events do not show mental state. Finally, there is a risk of false claims of mental disorder.[114]

15–47 In *H. v United Kingdom*,[115] the applicant submitted that the law of insanity imposed an unjustifiable burden on him to show that he was suffering from such a defect of reason owing to a disease of the mind as not to know the nature and quality of his act, and that this was contrary to the presumption of innocence in art.6(2) of the European Convention on Human Rights (ECHR). However, the Commission noted that the McNaghten Rules did not concern the presumption of innocence, as such, but the presumption of sanity. The Commission quoted from the *Salabiaku* case:

> "Presumptions of fact or of law operate in every legal system. Clearly, the Convention does not prohibit such presumptions in principle. It does, however, require the Contracting States to remain within certain limits in this respect as regards criminal law. … Article 6(2) does not … regard presumptions of fact or of law provided for in the criminal law with indifference. It requires States to confine them within reasonable limits which take into account the importance of what is at stake and maintain the rights of the defence."[116]

The Commission observed that in English law the burden of proof remains with the prosecution to prove beyond reasonable doubt that the accused did the act or made the omission charged. It did not consider that requiring the defence to present evidence concerning the accused's mental health at the time of the

---

[112] *R. v Chaulk* (1990) 2 C.R. (4th) 1; [1990] 3 S.C.R. 1303. See Patrick Healy, "*R v Chaulk*: Some Answers and Some Questions on Insanity" (1991) 2 C.R. (4th) 95; Don Stuart, "Will Section 1 Now Save Any Charter Violation? The *Chaulk* Effectiveness Test is Improper" (1991) 2 C.R. (4th) 107.

[113] Section 1 states, "The Canadian Charter of Rights and Freedoms guarantees the rights and freedoms set out in it subject only to such reasonable limits prescribed by law as can be demonstrably justified in a free and democratic society."

[114] Scottish Law Commission, *Report on Insanity and Diminished Responsibility*, Report 195, 2004, paras 5.1–5.28.

[115] European Commission of Human Rights, Application No. 15023/89, April 4, 1990.

[116] *Salabiaku v France* (1991) 13 E.H.R.R. 379, para.28.

alleged offence constituted in the present case an infringement of the presumption of innocence. Such a requirement could not be said to be unreasonable or arbitrary. It found, therefore, no appearance of a violation of art.6(2) in the present case.

NOTICE OF EVIDENCE AS TO MENTAL CONDITION

15–48 Section 19 of the 2006 Act provides that if the defence intends to adduce evidence regarding the accused's mental condition, it must give notice to the prosecution within 10 days of the accused being asked how he or she wishes to plead to the charge. The notice must be in such form as rules of court provide. If such notice has not been given, evidence of this nature shall not be adduced by the defence without leave of the court.

There is a difference in the wording of subss.(1) and (2). Subsection (1) requires that the relevant notice be given regarding evidence of mental condition "in any proceedings for an offence", whereas subs.(2) requires leave of the court for such evidence "during the course of the trial for the offence concerned." It is arguable that subs.(2) should be construed narrowly, and would not require leave of the court to be sought for evidence of mental condition during preliminary stages of a case, during a hearing on fitness for trial, during a "trial of the facts" under s.4(8), or at sentencing stage.

15–49 The original Bill stated that evidence could not, without leave of the court, be adduced by the defence during the course of a trial as to the mental condition of the accused unless notice of intention to do so was given to the prosecution in such form and within such period as rules of court would provide. Senator Terry proposed an amendment which was more specific, referring to notice "within 10 days of arraignment for the principal charge". The Government accepted the principle of the amendment, and later changed the wording to "within 10 days of the accused being asked how he or she wishes to plead to the charge". Minister McDowell stated that the applicability of the word "arraignment" to the District Court was doubtful and so the new wording would apply to indictment procedures in the District Court.[117]

Minister McDowell pointed out that the use of the term "mental condition" rather than "mental disorder" in this section is deliberate, as the question of whether a person is suffering from a mental disorder as defined in the Act would not have been addressed at that point. In addition, the Henchy report had similarly used "mental state" for the equivalent section of its draft Bill.[118]

15–50 This section refers to the notice being given "within 10 days of the accused being asked how he or she wishes to plead to the charge", and it is

[117] Select Committee on Justice, Equality, Defence and Women's Rights, January 18, 2006.
[118] Select Committee on Justice, Equality, Defence and Women's Rights, January 18, 2006.

arguable that time runs for up to 10 days *before or after* the person is asked how they plead. Dictionaries state that "within" means "inside" or "not beyond a period of time". In most statutes, the use of the phrase "within x days of" appears to indicate a period of time after an event. See also "within 48 hours of" in s.14(8)(b) of the 2006 Act. However, McGillicuddy suggests[119] that the notice period is 10 days before the date on which the accused is asked to plead to the offence. There may be an error in the drafting here, as the phrase "not less than 10 days before" should have been used if that was what was intended. More specific wording is used in the analogous section concerning notice of alibi, s.20 of the Criminal Justice Act 1984, as amended, including reference to "before the end of the prescribed period" and a definition of "prescribed period" which includes the period of 14 days after the date the accused is served with the book of evidence.

The relevant rules of court appear to envisage the notice being given after the accused has been asked how they wish to plead.[120]

INSANITY IN THE DISTRICT COURT

15–51 The procedure regarding the insanity defence in Ireland was, until 2006, governed by s.2 of the Trial of Lunatics Act 1883. The 1883 Act remained in force in England and there was detailed discussion in that jurisdiction of the question whether the insanity defence was available at Magistrates' Court level.[121] Analogies could clearly have been drawn between that question and the question of the availability of the insanity defence in our District Court.[122] The debate in England was then resolved by the Court of Appeal decision in *R. v Horseferry Road Magistrates' Court ex parte K*.[123] where it was held that the common law defence of insanity remained available to a defendant in a summary trial before magistrates. The decision relied heavily on White's detailed analysis of the common law situation and the historical impact of statutory changes.[124] The thrust of his analysis was that at common law insanity had been

---

[119] Tony McGillicuddy, "The Criminal Law (Insanity) Act 2006" (2006) 11 *Bar Review 95* at 99.
[120] District Court (Insanity) Rules 2007, S.I. No. 727 of 2007, Circuit Court Rules (Criminal Law (Insanity) Act 2006) 2007, S.I. No. 596 of 2007 and Rules of the Superior Courts (Criminal Law (Insanity) Act 2006) 2007, S.I. No. 597 of 2007.
[121] "Practical Point 2" (1979) 143 J.P.N. 469; Michael Crosta, "Sullivan's Choice" (1984) 148 J.P.N. 245; Stephen White letter (1984) 148 J.P.N. 318; White, "Insanity in a Magistrates' Court" (1984) 148 J.P.N. 419 (continued at 435 and 452); Crosta letter (1984) 148 J.P.N. 557; White, "Insanity Defences and Magistrates' Courts" [1991] Crim. L.R. 501.
[122] See Darius Whelan, "Fitness to Plead and Insanity in the District Court" (2001) 11(2) *Irish Criminal Law Journal* 2.
[123] [1997] Q.B. 23. The implications of the case are reviewed in Stephen White & Paul Bowen, "Insanity Defences in Summary Trials" (1997) 61 J.Crim.L. 198.
[124] White, "Insanity in a Magistrates' Court", (1984) 148 J.P.N. 419 (continued at 435 and 452). The Divisional Court in *Ex parte K*. did not expressly refer to White's article, but the judgment

a defence to any charge and the legislative history showed that Parliament had legislated merely to provide a special verdict procedure in relation to trials on indictment. The reference to "any indictment or information" in the Trial of Lunatics Act 1883 was inserted to accommodate criminal informations, which could be filed in the High Court at the time. The Divisional Court later held in *DPP v H*.[125] that the insanity defence was not available where a strict liability offence was triable summarily, although this decision was criticised.[126]

15–52 There was no detailed consideration in Ireland of the question of insanity defences in District Court summary trials, but in 1967 Walsh J. stated obiter in *State (C.) v Minister for Justice* that, since there was no statutory verdict set out regarding such trials, the court was governed by the common law rule that the form of verdict was one of acquittal.[127] The Henchy Committee appears to have overlooked Walsh J.'s statement in the *C.* case completely and stated that "at present the District Court has no jurisdiction to give such a verdict".[128] The District Court's lack of jurisdiction was later referred to as "a lacuna which could perhaps be challenged on constitutional grounds, although there is some judicial authority on a related issue which suggests that the challenge might not be successful".[129] The Henchy Committee proposed that the District Court should have a specific statutory power to deal with insanity defences.[130]

15–53 The Criminal Law (Insanity) Act 2006 now states that the District Court may return a verdict of not guilty by reason of insanity if the criteria in the Act apply.[131] The court makes the decision on its own, without the involvement of a jury. If the NGRI verdict is returned, the District Court also has the same powers as other courts concerning committal to a designated centre for assessment and

---

follows the sequence of White's argument very closely and White has stated that a copy of the article was handed to the court–see White's letter at [1997] Crim. LR 243.

[125] [1997] 1 W.L.R. 1406.

[126] See Tony Ward, "Magistrates, Insanity and the Common Law" [1997] Crim. LR 796. Ward argues at p.802, for example, that McCowan L.J. used a fallacious argument when he stated that H.'s defence was based on absence of mens rea and since no mens rea was required for the offence of drunken driving, the insanity defence was irrelevant. Ward points out that the basis of H.'s argument was that he did not know that drunken driving was either morally or legally wrong and that such knowledge is not part of the mens rea of any offence.

[127] *State (C.) v Minister for Justice* [1967] I.R. 106 at 121. Walsh J. does not, however, explicitly state that the person must be released after such an acquittal. Contrast Patricia Casey and Ciaran Craven, *Psychiatry and the Law* (Dublin: Oak Tree Press, 1999) at p.387, fn.78, who believe that the 1883 Act applies to misdemeanours.

[128] *Third Interim Report of the Interdepartmental Committee on Mentally Ill and Maladjusted Persons. Treatment and Care of Persons Suffering from Mental Disorder Who Appear Before the Courts on Criminal Charges* [Chair: Henchy J.] (Dublin, 1978). para.6.

[129] William Binchy, "Mental Retardation and the Criminal Law" (1984) 2 I.L.T. (n.s.) 111 at 111.

[130] *Third Interim Report of the Interdepartmental Committee on Mentally Ill and Maladjusted Persons. Treatment and Care of Persons Suffering from Mental Disorder Who Appear Before the Courts on Criminal Charges* [Chair: Henchy J.] (Dublin, 1978), draft Bill, s.13.

[131] Criminal Law (Insanity) Act 2006, s.5(1).

committal to such a centre for in-patient care and treatment.[132] As detention in the Central Mental Hospital (CMH) is no longer automatic, it is possible that the insanity defence will be raised more frequently than it was before at District Court level, particularly if there is clear medical evidence that the defendant had a temporary mental disorder at the time of the offence which no longer exists at the time of the trial.

CONSEQUENCES OF INSANITY VERDICT

15–54 Under the Trial of Lunatics Act 1883, if a jury found the accused "guilty but insane", they were automatically detained in the CMH, Dundrum, until the executive decided to release them. In *Application of Gallagher (No.1)*,[133] the Supreme Court held that it was not unconstitutional for such persons to be detained at the pleasure of the government. It was arguable, however, that the lack of a requirement that the accused be found by the court to have a mental disorder warranting detention breached the Constitution or the European Convention on Human Rights (ECHR). In *Winterwerp v the Netherlands*[134] it had been held that the decision to detain must be supported by objective medical expertise, the mental disorder must be serious enough to warrant compulsory confinement and the validity of confinement must be based on the persistence of the disorder. To take an extreme example, a person might have robbed a bank in 1985 while they had a mental disorder. If tried in 2005 and found "guilty but insane" they would automatically have been sent to the CMH, even though they might no longer have had a mental disorder.

15–55 Under the 2006 Act, detention of a person found not guilty by reason of insanity is no longer automatic. If the court does not believe that the person has a mental disorder and may require detention, the court will not order their detention. The Act does not specifically state this, but it is implicit in the wording of ss.5(2) and (3).

However, if the court considers the person found not guilty by reason of insanity has a mental disorder within the meaning of the Mental Health Act 2001 and may be in need of in-patient care or treatment the court may commit the person to a designated centre[135] for up to 14 days to be examined by an approved medical officer.[136] This period of committal may be extended by the court for up to six months.[137] An extension may be applied for by any party and the court may only grant it after consultation with an approved medical officer.

---

[132] Criminal Law (Insanity) Act 2006, s.5(2) and (3).
[133] [1991] 1 I.R. 31.
[134] (1979–80) 2 E.H.R.R. 387.
[135] At present, the CMH is the only designated centre.
[136] Criminal Law (Insanity) Act 2006, s.5(3)(a).
[137] Criminal Law (Insanity) Act 2006, s.5(3)(b). An "approved medical officer" means a consultant

In the original Bill, an initial period of 28 days was allowed for such examinations, but this period was later reduced to 14 days. When this amendment was being discussed, Senator Henry asked whether it meant that the person could be an out-patient for 14 days and Minister Lenihan replied "yes".[138] However, the Act does not appear to envisage out-patient treatment at this stage, as it states that the court may "commit" the person to the centre for examination.

The Mental Health Commission recommended that the Bill should be amended to facilitate remand of the person on bail in order to attend for assessment on an out-patient basis.[139]

Keys has argued that the power of the court to refer for assessment based on its own view and without a medical assessment may be contrary to the principle in *Winterwerp v the Netherlands*[140] that detention in a psychiatric care centre must be based on objective medical expertise.[141]

15–56 The approved medical officer reports on whether the person is suffering from a mental disorder and is in need of in-patient care or treatment.[142] If the court, having considered the report and any other evidence adduced before it, is satisfied that the person has a mental disorder within the meaning of the Mental Health Act 2001, the court shall commit the person to a centre until an order is made under s.13.[143] An order under s.13 is an order by the Mental Health (Criminal Law) Review Board making such order as it thinks proper in relation to the patient, e.g. further care, conditional discharge, unconditional discharge, out-patient treatment or supervision.[144]

There is no specific possibility of the court finding that out-patient treatment is the most appropriate outcome, whereas such a possibility is provided for in the case of unfitness for trial cases.[145] The possibility of out-patient treatment in unfitness for trial cases was added as a late amendment, as Minister McDowell believed that "no one with a mental disorder should be inappropriately held in police custody or in prison".[146] He also referred to the Henchy report and the submission of the Mental Health Commission as reasons to introduce the

psychiatrist within the meaning of the Mental Health Act 2001. The 2001 Act as amended by the Health Act 2004 defines a consultant psychiatrist as a consultant psychiatrist who is employed by the Health Service Executive (HSE) or by an approved centre or a person whose name is entered on the division of psychiatry or the division of child and adolescent psychiatry of the Register of Medical Specialists maintained by the Medical Council in Ireland.

[138] 180 *Seanad Debates* Col.37 (April 19, 2005).
[139] Mental Health Commission, Second Submission on Criminal Law (Insanity) Bill, January 2006.
[140] (1979–80) 2 E.H.R.R. 387.
[141] Mary Keys, Unpublished paper on Criminal Law (Insanity) Bill 2002.
[142] Criminal Law (Insanity) Act 2006, s.5(3)(c).
[143] Criminal Law (Insanity) Act 2006, s.5(2).
[144] See further Chapter 18 below.
[145] Criminal Law (Insanity) Act 2006, s.4(3)(b) and s.4(5)(c).
[146] 616 *Dáil Debates* Col.2059 (March 23, 2006).

possibility of out-patient treatment. The Minister did not explain why these reasons did not apply equally to those found not guilty by reason of insanity, and the point was not raised by other Deputies or Senators.

15–57 The person can only be detained if they have a mental disorder within the meaning of the Mental Health Act 2001. Under s.3(1) of that Act, "mental disorder" means mental illness, severe dementia or significant intellectual disability as defined, together with the "harm ground" or the "need for treatment ground". These criteria have been discussed in detail in Chapter 3 above.

15–58 The effect of all of this is that once a person is found to be insane in the criminal law sense, he or she can only be detained if he/she has a mental disorder in the civil law sense. While there is a great deal of logic in this approach, it gives rise to certain issues. The position for persons with personality disorders is unclear. Section 8 of the Mental Health Act 2001 states that a person cannot be detained under that Act solely because of a personality disorder. The 2006 Act specifically states that a person found not guilty by reason of insanity may only be detained if they have a mental disorder within the meaning of the 2001 Act, but it is unclear whether the section of that Act prohibiting detention based on personality disorder alone has an impact on "a mental disorder within the meaning of the 2001 Act". Minister McDowell referred to s.8 of the Mental Health Act 2001 and said:

> "It may or may not be that this is a tacit admission that mental disorder could include a personality disorder and, therefore, s.8 was necessary to take it out of that realm. Alternatively, the whole Act could be read as stating mental disorder under the 2001 Act was not intended to cover personality disorder."[147]

The lack of clarity regarding the criteria for detention under the 2006 Act (by way of cross-reference to the 2001 Act) may breach the requirement in art.5 of the ECHR that detention be "in accordance with a procedure prescribed by law". The Strasbourg Court has held that domestic law concerning deprivation of liberty must be sufficiently accessible to the individual and sufficiently precise to enable the individual to foresee the consequences of the restriction.[148] If this point were litigated, reference could be made to the *Gallagher (No.2)* case,[149] in which it was held that the detention of a person with a personality disorder could be continued under the pre-2006 regime. However, this was a decision about continuation of detention a number of years after the special verdict had been returned, and did not address the question of initiation of detention.

---

[147] 176 *Seanad Debates* Col.259 (April 7, 2004).
[148] *Steel v United Kingdom* (1999) 28 E.H.R.R. 603, para.54; Richard Jones, *Mental Health Act Manual*, 11th edn (London: Thomson Sweet and Maxwell, 2008), p.921.
[149] *Application of Gallagher (No.2)* [1996] 3 I.R. 10.

15–59 While the person is detained using the civil criteria, they do not have the same rights as patients detained under the Mental Health Act 2001, apart from the specific statement in s.3(3) of the 2006 Act that Part 4 of the Mental Health Act 2001 (on consent to treatment) applies to any person detained in a designated centre under the 2006 Act. For example, the civil patient is detained for an initial period of 21 days, within which there must be a review by a Mental Health Tribunal (MHT), while the case of a person found not guilty by reason of insanity need only be reviewed every six months by the Mental Health (Criminal Law) Review Board.

When the person is detained, there is no statutory right to written information regarding the grounds for their detention.[150] Information on detention is required by art.5(2) of the ECHR.[151]

APPEALS

15–60 The previous legal position was that as an insanity verdict was an acquittal, there could be no appeal against it.[152] Section 8 of the 2006 Act now provides that the person found not guilty by reason of insanity may appeal the verdict on any or all of three possible grounds: (a) that it was not proved that they had committed the act in question; (b) that they were not, at the time when the act was committed, suffering from any mental disorder of the nature referred to in s.5(1)(b); and (c) that the court ought to have made a determination in respect of this person that they were unfit to be tried.

Depending on the grounds of appeal and whether it is a murder case, the appeal court[153] may either acquit the person, find them guilty of the offence, find them unfit to be tried, substitute a diminished responsibility verdict or dismiss the appeal. The appeal court may also substitute a verdict of guilty of another offence of which it is satisfied that the person could (by virtue of the charge) and ought to have been convicted.[154] If an appeal court finds that a person is unfit for trial, it will have the same powers to deal with the person as the court of trial would have had under s.4 if it had come to the same conclusion.[155]

15–61 The Government refused to accept amendments removing the power of appeal courts to substitute a verdict of guilty of another offence of which they

---

[150] Compare s.16(2), Mental Health Act 2001.
[151] See further, para.1–24 above.
[152] *Felstead v The King* [1914] A.C. 534; *R. v Taylor* [1915] 2 K.B. 709.
[153] The Circuit Court or the Court of Criminal Appeal.
[154] Criminal Law (Insanity) Act 2006, s.8(3), s.8(8). This option only applies when the appeal is on the ground that the person was not, at the time when the act was committed, suffering from a mental disorder and the appeal court finds that the appellant committed the act but was not suffering from a mental disorder of the nature referred to in s.5(1)(b).
[155] Criminal Law (Insanity) Act 2006, s.9(2).

are satisfied that the person could (by virtue of the charge) and ought to have been convicted. Some Senators argued that this power was "quite remarkable".[156] However, Minister Lenihan said that the bracketed words "(by virtue of the charge)" were important, and that this option thus only applies where there is a choice open on the charge, not to additional or other charges. It would apply, for example, where an appeal court wished to substitute a verdict of manslaughter on grounds of diminished responsibility for a NGRI verdict in a murder trial.

15–62 Section 9 provides that an appeal regarding the decision to make or not to make an order of committal of a person found not guilty by reason of insanity may be taken by either the defence or the prosecution. The appeal court may make any order which it was open to the court of trial to make.

---

[156] Senator Cummins, 180 *Seanad Debates* Col.38 (April 19, 2005).

CHAPTER 16

DIMINISHED RESPONSIBLITY AND INFANTICIDE

DIMINISHED RESPONSIBILITY

16–01 One of the problems with the insanity defence has been that it has an "all or nothing" quality—the accused person is either "insane" or not insane. There has been an increasing recognition that in some cases the accused falls into a grey area where they are half-way between full responsibility for the act and lack of responsibility due to a mental disorder.

The concept of diminished responsibility originated in Scotland and has become well-established in many common law jurisdictions.[1] Mr Justice Hugh O'Flaherty, addressing a conference in 1997, called for the introduction of a diminished responsibility verdict:

> "I believe there is still a serious defect in our law in that we do not have a defence of diminished responsibility. It is either guilty of murder or being insane within the M'Naghten rules.
>
> As I say there is an absurdity in the law here, but the remedy is within easy reach of the legislature: introduce a defence of diminished responsibility."[2]

The diminished responsibility verdict was introduced in England and Wales in s.2 of the Homicide Act 1957. In 1985, the Irish Supreme Court held in *People (DPP) v O'Mahony*[3] that the defence did not exist in common law.

16–02 Section 6 of the Criminal Law (Insanity) Act 2006 now provides that where a person is tried for murder and the jury[4] finds that the person who did the act alleged, was at the time suffering from a mental disorder, and the mental disorder was not such as to justify finding them not guilty by reason of insanity, but was such as to diminish substantially their responsibility for the act, the jury

---

[1] See generally R.D. Mackay, *Mental Condition Defences in the Criminal Law* (Oxford: Clarendon Press, 1995), Chapter 4; Finbarr McAuley, *Insanity, Psychiatry and Criminal Responsibility* (Dublin: Round Hall Press, 1993); Scottish Law Commission, *Report on Insanity and Diminished Responsibility* (Report 195, 2004); Edward E. Tennant, *The Future of the Diminished Responsibility Defence to Murder* (Chichester: Barry Rose, 2001).

[2] Hugh O'Flaherty, "The Expert Witness and the Courts" (1997) 3 M.L.J.I. 3 at 5.

[3] [1985] I.R. 517. See Faye Boland, "Diminished Responsibility as a Defence in Irish Law", Part I (1995) 5 Ir.Crim.LJ 173, Part II (1996) 6 Ir.Crim.LJ 19.

[4] In the case of the Special Criminal Court, the court makes the decision.

[5] Criminal Law (Insanity) Act 2006, s.1.

shall find the person not guilty of murder but guilty of manslaughter on the ground of diminished responsibility.

"Mental disorder" includes mental illness, mental disability, dementia or any disease of the mind, but does not include intoxication.[5] The partial defence is only available in murder cases, and the effect is to reduce the conviction from murder to manslaughter.

Section 19 requires that the defence must have notified the prosecution, within 10 days of the accused being asked how they wish to plead, that it intends to adduce evidence of the accused's mental condition. See further paras 15–48 to 15–50 above.

16–03 There is no specific statutory requirement that the court must have heard evidence relating to the person's mental condition from a consultant psychiatrist, in contrast to s.5(1) of the 2006 Act concerning the insanity defence. In practice, psychiatric evidence will normally be adduced.

The burden of proof is on the defence to show that the accused is, by virtue of s.6, not liable to be convicted of murder (see further paras 16–15 to 16–17 below). If the accused contends diminished responsibility, the court must allow the prosecution to adduce evidence to prove insanity.[6]

16–04 The Act states that the diminished responsibility verdict is returned by the jury (except for trials in the Special Criminal Court). After the Act came into force, it was initially thought that it was not possible for the accused to plead guilty of manslaughter on the grounds of diminished responsibility. They could raise the defence, and if the prosecution was broadly in agreement with it, then the trial would probably be shortened as a result. However, in the transcript of the *O'Dwyer* case in 2007, defence counsel stated that the offer of a plea[7] had been made and that it seemed to be possible legally but could not be taken because the psychiatrist who was giving evidence for the State had taken a contrary view.[8] Later in 2007, a plea of guilty to manslaughter on the grounds of diminished responsibility was accepted in *People (DPP) v Crowe*.[9] The fact of the plea is mentioned by the Court of Criminal Appeal in its decision concerning the sentence in the *Crowe* case in 2009.[10]

By way of comparison, the English Act[11] does not refer to the verdict being returned by the jury, and therefore it has been easier for the courts to rule that a

---

[6] Criminal Law (Insanity) Act, s.5(4).

[7] From the context, this appears to refer to a plea of guilty to manslaughter on the grounds of diminished responsibility.

[8] Transcript of *DPP v O'Dwyer*, Central Criminal Court, June 18, 2007, p.22.

[9] The plea of guilty to manslaughter is reported in "Father of Two Jailed for Life for Shotgun Killing', *Irish Times*, October 9, 2007. The fact that this plea was on the grounds of diminished responsibility is recorded in *People (DPP) v Crowe* [2009] I.E.C.C.A. 57; [2009] 2 I.L.R.M. 225; Court of Criminal Appeal, May 27, 2009.

[10] *People (DPP) v Crowe* [2009] I.E.C.C.A. 57; [2009] 2 I.L.R.M. 225; Court of Criminal Appeal, May 27, 2009. See further paras 16–21 to 16–23 below.

[11] Homicide Act 1957, s.2.

guilty plea may be accepted. In *R. v Cox*, Winn L.J. stated in the Court of Appeal:

> "It is, the court thinks, worthy of remark that from the very outset of the trial it was quite clear not only that the defendant was prepared to plead guilty to manslaughter on the grounds of diminished responsibility but that the medical evidence available, in the possession of the prosecution as well as the defence, showed perfectly plainly that that plea was a plea which it would have been proper to accept. However, the matter proceeded to be tried by the jury, as a result of which time and money was spent and the defendant was no doubt kept in some anxiety and uncertainty whilst the trial went on. The court desires to say yet again, not at all for the first time in the experience of every member of the court, that there are cases where, on an indictment for murder, it is perfectly proper, where the medical evidence is plainly to this effect, to treat the case as one of substantially diminished responsibility and accept, if it be tendered, a plea to manslaughter on that ground, and avoid a trial for murder."[12]

The Act does not provide for an appeal from a diminished responsibility verdict, therefore presumably the normal rules on appeals of all manslaughter verdicts apply.

16–05 While diminished responsibility may not be raised in cases other than murder, the courts often give reduced sentences in non-murder cases where the accused's responsibility was reduced by their mental condition.[13] Geoghegan J. said, obiter, in the Supreme Court in *People (DPP) v Redmond* that he rejected the proposition that, given that there is no defence in Irish law of diminished responsibility, the sentencing judge on the plea of guilty cannot take into account diminished responsibility. He stated that a sentencing judge can take into account any factor at all, whether physical or mental, which might tend reasonably to either mitigate or aggravate a sentence.[14]

English Case Law

16–06 References to the English experience regarding diminished responsibility must be made with caution. In England, the courts did not add the third "irresistible impulse" limb to the insanity defence, as our Supreme Court did in the *Doyle* case.[15] As a result, in England, a person who was unable to refrain from committing the act could not raise an insanity defence and would be forced

---

[12] [1968] 1 W.L.R. 308 at 310. See also Law Commission, *Partial Defences to Murder*, Consultation Paper No 173 (London, 2003), paras 7.17–7.18.

[13] Thomas O'Malley, *Sentencing Law and Practice*, 2nd edn (Dublin: Thomson Round Hall, 2006), pp.401–408. See further paras 19–17 to 19–22 below.

[14] [2006] 3 I.R. 188 at 205–6.

[15] *Doyle v Wicklow County Council* [1974] I.R. 55.

to plead diminished responsibility. In addition, the English definition of diminished responsibility is very different from ours, including problematic references to "abnormality of mind", "arrested or retarded development of mind" and "inherent causes".[16] A 2009 Bill proposes to re-formulate the diminished responsibility defence in England.[17]

A wide variety of mental conditions have been held to constitute "abnormality of mind" for the purposes of the English Act. It must always be borne in mind that the Act requires that the abnormality "substantially impaired" the person's mental responsibility[18] and this issue will vary depending on the factual situation and the medical evidence. In general terms, the scope of the partial defence is much wider than the complete defence of insanity. Whereas insanity in England is confined to certain cognitive disorders, diminished responsibility covers volitional disorders, for example uncontrollable urges and extreme emotional states, as well as states of cognitive disorder which fall outside the terms of the McNaghten Rules.[19]

Reported English cases in which a diminished responsibility verdict have been returned include *R. v Ahluwalia*,[20] a case concerning a battered woman who killed her husband, and *R. v Seers*,[21] a case of reactive depression.

16–07 In English cases some personality disorders, including psychopathy, have led to diminished responsibility verdicts, e.g. *R. v Byrne*,[22] *R. v Turnbull*[23] and *R. v Martin (Anthony)*.[24]

The Law Reform Commission has expressed the view, however, that the scope of the definition of diminished responsibility in the Criminal Law (Insanity) Act 2006 is narrower than the English test, closer to the Scottish test and that "[p]robably therefore, psychopathy will not come within the ambit of the definition".[25]

16–08 Mackay conducted a comprehensive empirical study of the diminished responsibility plea in operation and found that between 1997 and 2001 there had

---

[16] See R.D. Mackay, *Mental Condition Defences in the Criminal Law* (Oxford: Clarendon Press, 1995), Chapter 4.

[17] Coroners and Criminal Justice Bill 2009. See below, para.16–09.

[18] Homicide Act 1957, s.2.

[19] Law Commission, *Partial Defences to Murder*, Consultation Paper No 173 (London, 2003), para.7.6.

[20] [1992] 4 All E.R. 889.

[21] (1984) 79 Cr. App. R. 261.

[22] [1960] 2 Q.B. 396.

[23] (1977) 65 Cr. App. R. 242

[24] [2001] E.W.C.A. Crim. 2245; [2003] Q.B. 1.

[25] Irish Law Reform Commission, "Synopsis of Irish Law Relating to the Defence of Diminished Responsibility" in: Law Commission, *Partial Defences to Murder—Overseas Studies*, Appendices to Consultation Paper 173, London, 2003, 111 at 116.

been around 171 successful diminished responsibility pleas.[26] In his study, the total number of cases accessed was 157, including 21 unsuccessful pleas. In 80.3 per cent of the cases (n=126), the finding was one of diminished responsibility, of which 6.3 per cent (n=8) were contested. Moreover, 22 of the contested cases resulted in murder convictions, 21 of which were failed diminished responsibility pleas. This means that out of a total of 36 contested cases, diminished responsibility pleas were successful in 22.2 per cent (n=8) of these cases. Of the 126 diminished responsibility verdicts, 49.2 per cent (n=62) resulted in a restriction order, 4.8 per cent (n=6) in a hospital order and 46 per cent (n=58) were punished in the normal way. Of this third group, 10 were given discretionary life penalties, while 16 received probation orders and 2 were given suspended prison sentences. The study includes summaries of all the cases involved, two of which are as follows:

> Case 1
> D., a male aged 34, stabbed V., a black stranger aged 56, in the back at a railway station. D. was following command hallucinations to kill a black man. In 1996 D. received a hospital order for robbery and wounding after he had heard voices telling him to stab a black man. After the alleged offence he was detained in Broadmoor under s. 48 MHA. 3 of the 4 psychiatric reports on file favoured Diminished Responsiblity [DR] on the basis of schizophrenia. D.'s plea of DR was accepted and he received a restriction order.

> Case 59
> D., a female aged 51, poisoned her two sons, aged 20 and 23, both of whom suffered from cerebral palsy. Looking after them became too much for her. 2 reports favoured DR on the basis of depression. D.'s DR plea was accepted and she was given a three year probation order which was later discharged on the grounds of good progress.

16–09 It is notable that a Bill has been published in England which proposes to change the wording of the statutory provision concerning diminished responsibility. Section 46 of the Coroners and Justice Bill 2009 proposes the following new wording:

> (1) A person ("D") who kills or is a party to the killing of another is not to be convicted of murder if D was suffering from an abnormality of mental functioning which—
>   (a) arose from a recognised medical condition,
>   (b) substantially impaired D's ability to do one or more of the things mentioned in subsection (1A), and

---

[26] R.D. Mackay, "The Diminished Responsibility Plea in Operation–An Empirical Study" in Law Commission, *Partial Defences to Murder: Final Report* (Report No. 290, London, 2004), Appendix B.

      (c) provides an explanation for D's acts and omissions in doing or being a party to the killing.

(1A) Those things are—
      (a) to understand the nature of D's conduct;
      (b) to form a rational judgment;
      (c) to exercise self-control.

(1B) For the purposes of subsection (1)(c), an abnormality of mental functioning provides an explanation for D's conduct if it causes, or is a significant contributory factor in causing, D to carry out that conduct.

The main effect of this proposal would be to narrow the defence so that it only applies to "recognised medical conditions".

See also recent proposals for change in Scotland.[27]

Alcohol and Drugs

16–10 The situation regarding alcohol, drugs and diminished responsibility is complex. While the Irish Act excludes intoxication from the definition of "mental disorder", this does not necessarily mean that anybody who was intoxicated due to alcohol or drugs could not raise the partial defence of diminished responsibility. In some cases, a person might have an underlying mental disorder and happen to be intoxicated at the time of the offence. If the jury found that the mental disorder substantially diminished the person's responsibility, it could return a diminished responsibility verdict. Another possible scenario is that a person might have alcohol dependency syndrome or some other mental disorder, which a court might find not to be included in the meaning of "intoxication"[28] and therefore not excluded from the meaning of mental disorders.

The relationship between intoxication and diminished responsibility has been the subject of much discussion in England.[29] It is instructive to refer briefly to the case law, bearing in mind that there is no specific exclusion of intoxication in the English Act.

16–11 In *R. v Tandy*[30] Ms Tandy, who was an alcoholic, had killed her 11-year-old daughter after consuming 90 per cent of a bottle of vodka and had been convicted of murder. Watkins L.J. stated as follows:

---

[27] Section 117, Criminal Justice and Licensing (Scotland) Bill 2009.

[28] Section 1 of the 2006 Act defines "intoxication" as "being under the intoxicating influence of any alcoholic drink, drug, solvent or any other substance or combination of substances".

[29] See the discussion of "drink, drugs and diminished responsibility" in R.D. Mackay, *Mental Condition Defences in the Criminal Law* (Oxford: Clarendon Press, 1995), pp.194–197.

[30] (1988) 87 Cr. App R. 45; [1989] 1 W.L.R. 350.

"The principles involved in seeking answers to these questions are, in our view, as follows. The appellant would not establish the second element of the defence [that that abnormality of mind was induced by disease, namely, the disease of alcoholism] unless the evidence showed that the abnormality of mind at the time of the killing was due to the fact that she was a chronic alcoholic. If the alcoholism had reached the level at which her brain had been injured by the repeated insult from intoxicants so that there was gross impairment of her judgment and emotional responses, then the defence of diminished responsibility was available to her, provided that she satisfied the jury that the third element of the defence [that the abnormality of mind induced by the disease of alcoholism was such as substantially impaired her mental responsibility for her act] existed. Further, if the appellant were able to establish that the alcoholism had reached the level where although the brain had not been damaged to the extent just stated, the appellant's drinking had become involuntary, that is to say she was no longer able to resist the impulse to drink, then the defence of diminished responsibility would be available to her, subject to her establishing the first and third elements, because if her drinking was involuntary, then her abnormality of mind at the time of the act of strangulation was induced by her condition of alcoholism.

On the other hand, if the appellant had simply not resisted an impulse to drink and it was the drink taken on the Wednesday which brought about the impairment of judgment and emotional response, then the defence of diminished responsibility was not available to the appellant."[31]

16–12 In the House of Lords case of *R. v Dietschmann*[32] the appellant was heavily intoxicated and also suffering from a mental abnormality which the medical witnesses described as an adjustment disorder, which was a depressed grief reaction to the death of his aunt, with whom he had had a close emotional and physical relationship. Lord Hutton said that in referring to substantial impairment of mental responsibility s.2(1) of the Homicide Act 1957 does not require the abnormality of mind to be the sole cause of the defendant's acts in doing the killing. In his opinion, even if the defendant would not have killed if he had not taken drink, the causative effect of the drink did not necessarily prevent an abnormality of mind suffered by the defendant from substantially impairing his mental responsibility for his fatal acts.[33] Lord Hutton went on to suggest that the jury be instructed as follows:

"Drink cannot be taken into account as something which contributed to his mental abnormality and to any impairment of mental responsibility arising from that abnormality. But you may take the view that both the defendant's mental abnormality and drink played a part in impairing his mental responsibility for the killing and that he might not have killed if he had not taken

---

[31] [1989] 1 W.L.R. 350 at 356.
[32] [2003] U.K.H.L. 10; [2003] 1 A.C. 1209.
[33] [2003] 1 A.C. 1209 at 1217.

drink. If you take that view, then the question for you to decide is this: has the defendant satisfied you that, despite the drink, his mental abnormality substantially impaired his mental responsibility for his fatal acts, or has he failed to satisfy you of that? If he has satisfied you of that, you will find him not guilty of murder but you may find him guilty of manslaughter. If he has not satisfied you of that, the defence of diminished responsibility is not available to him."[34]

16–13 The Court of Appeal recently held in *R. v Wood (Clive) (No.1)*[35] that *Dietschmann* requires a reassessment of the way in which *Tandy* is applied in the context of alcohol dependency syndrome where observable brain damage has not occurred. Assuming that the jury has decided that the person's alcohol dependence syndrome constitutes an abnormality of mind induced by disease or illness, its possible impact and significance in the individual case must be addressed. The resolution of this issue embraces questions such as whether the defendant's craving for alcohol was or was not irresistible, and whether his consumption of alcohol in the period leading up to the killing was voluntary (and if so, to what extent) or was not voluntary, and leads to the ultimate decision, which is whether the defendant's mental responsibility for his actions when killing the deceased was substantially impaired as a result of the alcohol consumed under the baneful influence of the syndrome.[36]

16–14 The Court of Appeal provided more detailed guidance on instructing juries in such cases in *R. v Stewart (James)*.[37] For example, Lord Judge C.J. stated that the issues likely to arise in this kind of case and on which the members of the jury should be invited to form their own judgment will include:

   (a) the extent and seriousness of the defendant's dependency, if any, on alcohol
   (b) the extent to which his ability to control his drinking or to choose whether to drink or not, was reduced,
   (c) whether he was capable of abstinence from alcohol, and if so,
   (d) for how long, and
   (e) whether he was choosing for some particular reason, such as a birthday celebration, to decide to get drunk, or to drink even more than usual.[38]

Burden of Proof

16–15 The burden of proof is on the defence to show that the accused is, by virtue of s.6, not liable to be convicted of murder.[39]

---

[34] [2003] 1 A.C. 1209 at 1227.
[35] [2008] E.W.C.A. Crim. 1305; [2009] 1 W.L.R. 496.
[36] [2009] 1 W.L.R. 496 at 508.
[37] [2009] E.W.C.A. Crim. 593.
[38] [2009] E.W.C.A. Crim. 593, para.34.
[39] Criminal Law (Insanity) Act 2006, s.5(2).

Compatibility of s.2 of the 1957 Act with art.6(2) of the European Convention on Human Rights (ECHR) (the presumption of innocence) was considered in *Robinson v UK*.[40] The Commission cited the previous decision concerning the insanity defence, *H. v UK*[41] and noted the similarities with this case. The Commission found the complaint to be manifestly ill-founded, stating:

"The Commission observes that in English law the burden of proof remains with the prosecution to prove beyond reasonable doubt that the accused did act as charged. The Commission does not consider that requiring the defence to present evidence concerning the accused's mental state at the time of the alleged offence, constitutes in the present case an infringement of the presumption of innocence. Such a requirement cannot be said to be unreasonable or arbitrary. It finds, therefore, no appearance of a violation of art 6, para 2 (art 6(2)) of the Convention in the present case."[42]

16–16 The Court of Appeal considered the same argument in *R. v Lambert, Ali and Jordan*[43] and held that the imposition of the burden of proof on the defendant in diminished responsibility cases was compatible with art.6(2) of the ECHR. The court noted that art.6(2) referred to a presumption of innocence as regards "a criminal offence" but that the diminished responsibility defence was not an ingredient of an offence as such, and was not in the indictment. Instead, if the defendant does not seek to rely on the defence, they will not be required to prove anything. Lord Woolf C.J. noted that there could be situations where there is an unco-operative defendant, and then it would be very difficult for the prosecution to satisfy a jury of the negative. He said that a defendant is not required to submit to an examination by a doctor and it would not be desirable to change the law to require him to submit to an examination. The change in the law brought about by s.2 of the Homicide Act 1957 was of benefit to defendants who were in a position to take advantage of it. It did not matter whether it is treated as creating a defence to a charge to murder or an exception or as dealing with the capacity to commit the offence of murder, s.2 still did not contravene art.6.[44] The court found ample support for its view in the judgments of the Supreme Court of Canada in *R. v Chaulk*[45] and in the decisions of the European Commission of Human Rights in *H. v UK*[46] and *Robinson v UK*.[47]

---

[40] Application No. 20858/92, European Commission of Human Rights, May 5, 1993.

[41] Application No. 15023/89, European Commission of Human Rights, April 4, 1990. See above, para.15–47.

[42] Application No. 20858/92, European Commission of Human Rights, May 5, 1993,

[43] [2002] Q.B. 1112. Affirmed in House of Lords: [2001] UKHL 37, [2002] 2 A.C. 545. At House of Lords stage, the focus was on the law concerning drugs offences rather than diminished responsibility.

[44] [2002] Q.B. 1112 at 1124–5.

[45] (1990) 62 C.C.C. (3d.) 193; [1990] 3 S.C.R. 1303.

[46] Application No. 15023/89, European Commission of Human Rights, April 4, 1990.

[47] Application No. 20858/92, European Commission of Human Rights, May 5, 1993.

16–17 This reasoning was also applied in the Northern Ireland case of *R. v McQuade*.[48] Kerr L.C.J. said:

> "The presumption does no more than assume that a defendant has normal mental capacity. Although the defendant who claims to suffer from mental abnormality may not be able from his own resources to produce evidence of this, such a condition is unquestionably personal to him and is one to which the prosecuting authorities will not normally be privy. It is reasonable that the defendant be required to prove that he suffers from the condition since it lies within his power to provide to medical experts the information necessary to establish its existence. The standard of proof that he is required to produce is such as will establish the proposition on the balance of probabilities, whereas if the burden were cast on the prosecution it would not only have to prove a negative (that the condition was not present) but would have to do so beyond reasonable doubt."[49]

Consequences of a Diminished Responsiblity Verdict

16–18 The Act does not state any specific consequence which flows from a verdict of manslaughter on the grounds of diminished responsibility. This means that the general law concerning manslaughter applies, i.e. the court may apply any sentence up to a maximum of life imprisonment and/or a fine.[50] It is not possible for the court to order that the person be sent to a psychiatric centre.[51] There are no reviews of detention by the Mental Health (Criminal Law) Review Board, as these are only relevant to cases where the accused is found not guilty by reason of insanity or unfit for trial. However, if the person receives a prison sentence and is then transferred from the prison to the Central Mental Hospital (CMH) or another designated centre, their case must be reviewed by the Review Board every six months.[52] When the person is detained, there is no statutory right to written information regarding the grounds for their detention.[53] Information on detention is required by art.5(2) of the ECHR.[54]

---

[48] [2005] N.I.C.A. 2; [2005] N.I. 331. See Emily Finch, "Diminished Responsibility: Psychological Injury" (2007) 71 *Journal of Criminal Law* 16.

[49] [2005] N.I.C.A. 2, para.28.

[50] See Thomas O'Malley, *Sentencing Law and Practice*, 2nd edn (Dublin: Thomson Round Hall, 2006), pp.248–256.

[51] Contrast the English law concerning "hospital orders" and "hospital and restriction orders". See Mental Health Act 1983, s.37 and s.41, as amended; Richard Jones, *Mental Health Act Manual*, 11th edn. (London: Thomson Sweet and Maxwell, 2008), pp.209–225 and 234–244.

[52] Criminal Law (Insanity) Act 2006, ss.15 to 18. See para. 18–12 below.

[53] Compare s.16(2), Mental Health Act 2001.

[54] See further, para.1–24 above.

16–19 In England, it has been noted that "diminished responsibility means exactly what it says; it reduces your responsibility, it does not extinguish it".[55] The leading guideline judgment on sentencing in diminished responsibility cases is *R. v Chambers*.[56] The Sentencing Guidelines Council has tabulated the guidelines as follows[57]:

Sentencing options	Circumstances
1. Hospital order	where recommended by psychiatric report
2. Life imprisonment	where hospital order not recommended and the offender constitutes a danger to the public for an unpredictable period
3. Determinate sentence	where no basis for hospital order but responsibility not minimal. Length determined by assessment of degree of responsibility and of time the accused will remain a danger to the public.
4. Release and suspension	no danger of repetition of violence. Responsibility grossly impaired and degree of responsibility minimal

16–20 Mackay's empirical research shows that the Hospital Order or Hospital and Restriction Order are widely used. Of the 126 diminished responsibility verdicts, 49.2 per cent (n=62) resulted in a restriction order,[58] 4.8 per cent (n=6) in a Hospital Order and 46 per cent (n=58) were punished in the normal way. Of this third group, 10 were given discretionary life penalties, while 16 received probation orders and 2 were given suspended prison sentences.[59]

---

[55]   *R. v Staines (Paula)* [2006] E.W.C.A. Crim. 15, [2006] M.H.L.R. 184, [2006] 2 Cr. App. R. (S.) 61, para.9.

[56]   (1983) 5 Cr.App.R (S) 190.

[57]   Sentencing Guidelines Council, *Current Sentencing Practice*, Reference B1–1, Last updated: 2007. See also Sentencing Guidelines Council, *Guideline Judgments Case Compendium* (2005, with updates).

[58]   A Restriction Order may also be referred to as a "Hospital and Restriction Order". The court orders that the person be sent to hospital for treatment and restricts the person's discharge, transfer or leave of absence from hospital for an unlimited period without the consent of the Secretary of State for Justice.

[59]   R.D. Mackay, "The Diminished Responsibility Plea in Operation–An Empirical Study" in Law Commission, *Partial Defences to Murder: Final Report* (Report No. 290, London, 2004), Appendix B.

16–21 The Irish Court of Criminal Appeal has issued one important judgment regarding sentencing in a diminished responsibility case since the 2006 Act came into force: *People (DPP) v Crowe*.[60] The applicant, together with another man, arrived at a party with shotguns and shot two victims at close range, one of whom died.[61] The applicant had pleaded guilty to manslaughter on the grounds of diminished responsibility[62] and the trial judge imposed a sentence of imprisonment for life on this charge. One psychiatrist had given evidence that Mr Crowe had a history of alcohol and drug abuse and some paranoid ideation. Another psychiatrist stated that, even if a mental disorder (post–traumatic stress disorder) was present at the material time, there was insufficient evidence that this mental disorder, would have of itself compromised Mr Crowe's capacity for the act. In his opinion, the effect of the variety of intoxicants being used by the appellant, in the particular context of being supported by his associates at the time, were determining factors in the act, overriding consideration of a mental disorder. The psychiatrist noted that the Criminal Law Insanity Act 2006 excludes intoxication from a consideration of diminished responsibility. In imposing a life sentence, the trial judge (Carney J.) said, "Most of the matters which have been urged on me in mitigation rest on a foundation of the accused having had a history of self-induced alcohol and drug taking. It seems to me that if people develop lifestyles revolving around the taking of drink and drugs they should not in my view come into this court and set up that as a mitigating factor for their consequent actions."[63]

16–22 In the Court of Criminal Appeal, Kearns J. quoted s.6 of the Criminal Law (Insanity) Act 2006 and said that notwithstanding the acceptance of the plea to manslaughter by reason of diminished responsibility in this case, the sentencing judge did not impose sentence on that basis. On the contrary, he had specifically rejected any contention that the applicant had substantially reduced responsibility because in his view the applicant had a history of self-induced alcohol and drug taking and could not rely upon those factors to mitigate his consequent actions. Kearns J. said, "In short, the sentencing judge rejected the defence which had been accepted on behalf of the Director of Public Prosecutions and this rejection formed the basis for the imposition of a life sentence." Kearns J. said that the life sentence, which was the maximum sentence available in law, did not reflect the fact that the prosecution accepted that the applicant had substantially diminished responsibility for the shooting by reason of mental disorder. He quoted the following statement from Walsh J. in *People (Attorney General) v O'Callaghan*, "In this country it would be quite contrary to the concept of personal liberty enshrined in the Constitution that any person should be punished in respect of any matter upon which he has not been convicted."[64]

[60]   [2009] I.E.C.C.A. 57; [2009] 2 I.L.R.M. 225; Court of Criminal Appeal, May 27, 2009.
[61]   The applicant did not fire the shot which killed the victim who died.
[62]   He also pleaded guilty to attempted murder and assault causing harm.
[63]   Quoted in [2009] 2 I.L.R.M. 225 at 230.
[64]   [1966] I.R. 501 at 516.

16–23 The Court of Criminal Appeal ruled that a sentence of 20 years was appropriate on the manslaughter charge, stating that the proper approach to sentencing in this case was one which would involve the imposition of a substantial but finite sentence, being one which recognised that the offence was at the absolute upper end of the scale, but recognising also that some measure of mitigation necessarily had to be incorporated in the sentence by reason of the early plea, the psychiatric history and the other factors relied upon by the applicant in advancing his submissions in this case. Kearns J. stated:

> "[I]mplicit in the acceptance of a plea to manslaughter by reason of diminished responsibility due to mental disorder is the recognition that the applicant can not and should not be treated in precisely the same manner as a person fully responsible for his own actions. It would be utterly destructive of s.6 of the Criminal Law (Insanity) Act, 2006, to hold otherwise. At the very least, the applicant is, in the view of the Court, entitled to expect the imposition of some sentence short of life imprisonment, with all the associated stigma attached to that sentence, where a manslaughter plea is accepted in this way."[65]

INFANTICIDE

16–24 The Infanticide Act 1949 may apply in cases when a mother is charged with the murder of her child who is aged under 12 months. The mother may be convicted of infanticide (which is the equivalent of manslaughter) if the balance of her mind is disturbed by reason of her not having fully recovered from the effect of giving birth to the child.[66] The 1949 Act also provided that an infanticide verdict could be returned if the balance of her mind was disturbed by reason of "the effect of lactation consequent upon the birth of the child." This outdated formulation has now been amended by s.22 of the 2006 Act to read as follows:

> [A]t the time of the act or omission the balance of her mind was disturbed by reason of her not having fully recovered from the effect of giving birth to the child or by reason of a mental disorder (within the meaning of the Criminal Law (Insanity) Act 2006) consequent upon the birth of the child.

In such cases, the mother will be dealt with under s.6(3) of the 2006 Act as if found guilty of manslaughter on grounds of diminished responsibility.

16–25 Minister McDowell explained that there had been some academic and legal criticism of the perceived narrow, medical, psychiatric basis for infanticide

---

[65] [2009] 2 I.L.R.M. 225 at 234.

[66] Infanticide Act 1949, s.1(3)(c). See generally Karen Brennan, "Beyond the Medical Model: a Rationale for Infanticide Legislation" (2007) 58 N.I.L.Q. 505; R.D. Mackay, *Mental Condition Defences in the Criminal Law* (Oxford: Clarendon Press, 1995), pp.207–213.

as set out in the current law, and accordingly, he had decided to remove the reference to lactation, which is dubious, and to replace it with a reference to mental disorder within the meaning of this new Act. The new definition could cover conditions such as post-puerperal depression.[67] It is interesting to note that the English and Welsh Law Commission recently decided not to recommend removal of the reference to lactation, as there is some evidence to support the theory.[68]

16–26 A significant procedural point is that a woman may be charged with infanticide in the first instance, whereas it is not possible to charge a person with manslaughter on the grounds of diminished responsibility; instead the person is prosecuted for murder and raises the partial defence of diminished responsibility. Minister McDowell explained that the procedure regarding infanticide was being retained "on humane grounds", as had been suggested by the Henchy committee.[69]

---

[67] 616 *Dáil Debates* Col.2035 (March 23, 2006).
[68] Law Commission, *Report on Murder, Manslaughter and Infanticide* (London, 2006), para.8.26.
[69] 616 *Dáil Debates* Col.2034 (March 23, 2006).

CHAPTER 17

FITNESS FOR TRIAL

THE CRITERIA FOR UNFITNESS FOR TRIAL

17–01 There has been a notable lack of discussion in case law of the criteria for fitness for trial in Ireland.[1] Since unfitness for trial is narrowly defined, a larger number of defendants are found fit for trial and may then go on to seek an insanity acquittal or a diminished responsibility verdict if appropriate. While the Irish courts have been willing to extend the insanity defence to include volitional insanity, there has been no corresponding broadening of the definition of unfitness for trial, perhaps due to the lack of cases in the area.

17–02 The classic criteria for determination of fitness for trial are laid down by Baron Alderson in *R v Pritchard*[2]:

[a] [W]hether he can plead to the indictment or not; …
   whether he is of sufficient intellect
[b] to comprehend the course of the proceedings on the trial,
[c] so as to make a proper defence—
[d] to know that he might challenge any of you [sc. the jury] to whom he may object—and
[e] to comprehend the details of the evidence.[3]

The test is a cognitive one, being based essentially on knowing and understanding. While five criteria are given (letters [a] to [e] above), if the person does

---

[1] On the law regarding fitness for trial generally, see Finbarr McAuley, *Insanity, Psychiatry and Criminal Responsibility* (Dublin: Round Hall, 1993), Chapter 7; Marie O'Neill, *Irish Mental Health Law* (Dublin: First Law, 2005), pp.439–467.

[2] (1836) 7 Car. & P. 303; 173 E.R. 135. See also the earlier case of *R v Dyson* (1831) 7 Car. & P. 305n; 173 E.R. 135n. Donald Grubin, in "What Constitutes Fitness to Plead?" [1993] Crim.L.R. 748 at 753, has lamented the fact that because Pritchard (and Dyson) were "deaf mutes", the focus in the criteria is on "mental deficiency" rather than mental illness. Previous authorities distinguished between mental deficiency and mental illness—M. Hale, *The History of the Pleas of the Crown*, vol.1, p.34 and Kenyon L.C.J. in *Proceedings in the Case of John Frith* (1790) 22 Howell's State Trials 308. See also Donald Grubin, *Fitness to Plead in England and Wales* (Sussex: Psychology Press, 1996.)

[3] (1836) 7 Car. & P. 303 at 304; 173 ER 135 at 135 (Letters [a] to [e] added.) Alderson B. said that there were three questions to be inquired into: "First, whether the prisoner is mute of malice or not; secondly whether he can plead to the indictment or not; thirdly, whether he is of sufficient intellect …"

not satisfy any one of them, they are unfit for trial.[4] In *R v Davies*[5], the question of the person's capability of properly instructing their counsel for their defence due to their "madness" was added as a criterion.[6]

17–03 It has been held in *R. v Podola*[7] that amnesia at the time of the trial does not constitute unfitness to plead.

In *R. v Robertson*,[8] only a rudimentary understanding on the part of the accused was required for him to be classified as fit for trial. Thereafter, he was said to be free to make decisions, even if they were not in his own best interests.

The Butler Committee recommended that there should be statutory criteria. The Committee believed that the reference to challenging jurors should be omitted and the ability to give adequate instructions to legal advisers and to plead with understanding to the indictment should be included.[9]

17–04 A low-level test of fitness for trial, described as the "limited cognitive capacity" test, was adopted in Canada in *R. v Taylor*.[10] The test involved an acceptance by the court of the following statements made by amicus curiae counsel:

> "… [T]he presence of delusions does not vitiate the accused's fitness to stand trial unless the delusion distorts the accused's rudimentary understanding of the judicial process … under this test, a court's assessment of an accused's ability to conduct a defence and to communicate with and instruct counsel is limited to an inquiry into whether an accused can recount to his/her counsel the necessary facts relating to the offence in such a way that counsel can then properly present a defence. It is not relevant to the fitness determination to

---

[4] R.D. Mackay, *Mental Condition Defences in the Criminal Law* (Oxford: Clarendon Press, 1995), p.224.

[5] (1853) 6 Cox C.C. 326.

[6] In *Davies* no reference was made to cognitive ability or intelligence; what was most important was whether the "madness" was genuine. *Pritchard* tends to be cited as if it includes the criterion in *Davies* (see Finbarr McAuley, *Insanity, Psychiatry and Criminal Responsibility*, Dublin: Round Hall Press, 1993, p.139; R.D. Mackay, *Mental Condition Defences in the Criminal Law* (Oxford: Clarendon Press, 1995), p.224), whereas in fact the cases are quite differently reasoned–Donald Grubin, "What Constitutes Fitness to Plead?" [1993] Crim. L.R. 748 at 753. Mackay refers to five criteria for unfitness—four of the *Pritchard* criteria, omitting (c)—making a proper defence, and the *Davies* criterion (although without citing *Davies*).

[7] [1960] 1 Q.B. 325. See Rupert Furneaux, *Guenther Podola* (London: Stevens, 1960). The Court of Criminal Appeal followed the previous Scottish case of *Russell v H.M. Advocate* 1946 S.C.(J.) 37.

[8] (1968) 52 Cr.App.R. 690; [1968] 3 All E.R. 557

[9] Home Office & Department of Health and Social Security, *Report of the Committee on Mentally Abnormal Offenders* [Chair: Lord Butler] (Cmnd.6244, London, 1975) (1974–5) 16 Parl. Papers 221, para. 10.3

[10] (1992) 77 C.C.C. (3d.) 551, 17 C.R. (4th) 371, 11 O.R. (3d.) 323. See Richard D. Schneider & Hy Bloom, "R v Taylor: A Decision Not in the Best Interests of Some Mentally Ill Accused" (1995) 38 Crim. L.Q. 183.

consider whether the accused and counsel have an amicable and trusting relationship, whether the accused has been co-operating with counsel or whether the accused ultimately makes decisions that are in his/her best interests."[11]

The Canadian Criminal Code defines fitness to stand trial as follows:

'[U]nfit to stand trial' means unable on account of mental disorder[12] to conduct a defence at any stage of the proceedings before a verdict is rendered or to instruct counsel to do so, and, in particular, unable on account of mental disorder to:
(a) understand the nature or object of the proceedings;
(b) understand the possible consequences of the proceedings, or
(c) communicate with counsel.[13]

This section appears to apply a cognitive standard only, even though s.16 of the same Code, in dealing with the test for criminal responsibility (formerly insanity) uses the word "appreciating" rather than "knowing."[14]

17–05 A higher-threshold test of competency to stand trial was adopted in *Dusky v United States*:

"We agree with the suggestion of the Solicitor General that it is not enough … to find that the 'defendant [is] oriented to time and place and [has] some recollection of events', but that the 'test must be whether he has sufficient present ability to consult with his lawyer with a reasonable degree of rational understanding—and whether he has a rational as well as a factual understanding of the proceedings against him.'"[15]

17–06 There has been no detailed consideration in the Irish courts of the criteria governing unfitness for trial, but there have been a few statements to the effect that a *Pritchard*-type test applies.[16]

The Criminal Law (Insanity) Act 2006 restates the common law definition of unfitness for trial in s.4(2) as follows:

---

[11] (1992) 77 C.C.C. (3d.) 551 at 564.
[12] Section 2 of the Code defines "mental disorder" as a "disease of the mind", which may not include mental handicap–see Denise Hitchen, "Fitness to Stand Trial and Mentally Challenged Defendants: A View from Canada" (1993) 4 Int.Bull. L. & Ment.H. 5.
[13] Section 2, Criminal Code of Canada, inserted by S.C. 1991, c.43.
[14] Section 16(1), Criminal Code of Canada.
[15] 362 US 402 at 402 (1960). The court did not require proof that the defendant had a mental illness or defect; but most US states require this.
[16] See *State (C.) v Minister for Justice* [1967] I.R. 106 at 115 (Ó Dálaigh C.J.); extract from affidavit of District Justice Ó hUadhaigh in *Re Dolphin: State (Egan) v Governor CMH*, High Court, Kenny J., January 27, 1972, p.3; *O'C. v Judges of Dublin Metropolitan District* [1994] 3 I.R. 246 at 252; *DPP (Murphy) v P.T.* [1998] 1 I.L.R.M. 344 at 363–4. See also the earlier

An accused person shall be deemed unfit to be tried if he or she is unable by reason of mental disorder to understand the nature or course of the proceedings so as to—

(a) plead to the charge,

(b) instruct a legal representative,

(c) in the case of an indictable offence which may be tried summarily, elect for a trial by jury,

(d) make a proper defence,

(e) in the case of a trial by jury, challenge a juror to whom he or she might wish to object, or

(f) understand the evidence.

"Mental disorder", as defined in s.1, includes mental illness, mental disability, dementia or any disease of the mind, but does not include intoxication.

The definition does not appear to cover a person with a physical disability, such as a deaf person who cannot understand sign language interpretation. McGillicuddy has suggested that the common law rules regarding fitness to plead of people with physical disabilities will continue to apply.[17]

17–07 The question whether the criteria for fitness for trial should be extended beyond the traditional cognitive criteria is a difficult one. The Ontario Court of Appeal has referred to the need to balance the need for people to be able to defend themselves properly against their right to choose their own defence, their autonomy and their right to have a trial within a reasonable time. Lacourcière J.A., writing for that court in *R. v Taylor*, referred to the need to balance these various factors and concluded as follows:

> "The 'limited cognitive capacity test' strikes an effective balance between the objectives of the fitness rules and the constitutional right of the accused to choose his own defence and to have a trial within a reasonable time … . In my opinion, the learned trial judge erred in adopting the 'analytic capacity' test which establishes too high a threshold for finding the accused fit to stand trial by requiring that the accused be capable of making rational decisions beneficial to him."[18]

17–08 Schneider and Bloom have argued convincingly for the wider "analytic capacity" type test, on the basis that mental illness affects not just a person's cognitive processes, but also their judgement, motivation, insight, emotional status and volition.[19] They refer to three different types of patient[20] who would

---

Irish case of *R. v Flynn* (1838) 1 Craw. & D. 283, where the person was under the influence of "intense nervous excitement" and incapable of understanding the proceedings.

[17] Tony McGillicuddy, "The Criminal Law (Insanity) Act 2006" (2006) 11 *Bar Review* 95 at 96.

[18] (1992) 77 C.C.C. (3d.) 551 at 566–7.

[19] Richard D. Schneider & Hy Bloom, "R v Taylor: A Decision Not in the Best Interests of Some Mentally Ill Accused" (1995) 38 Crim L.Q. 183 at 199.

[20] The punishment seeking, the paranoid and the grandiose accused.

pass the "limited cognitive capacity" test but ought to be unfit for trial. They believe that while the law may rightfully be indifferent to whether an accused makes decisions in their own best interests, the courts must care about whether a person has the *ability* to make decisions in their own best interests.[21] And in their view:

> "[W]here the accused is not capable of rational understanding of his legal predicament, it is possible but unlikely that his actions will be in his best interests. ... The 'right to choose' implies an informed, rational choice. Otherwise it is not choice at all so much as chance."[22]

17–09 While at least one writer has proposed the abolition of unfitness for trial findings,[23] others have called for various modifications of the criteria to expand the definition of fitness for trial beyond the traditional cognitive criteria.[24] One of the most interesting approaches has been the suggestion that the focus should be on the person's "decisional competence", considering whether the person can choose between alternative courses of action.[25] Mackay[26] favours such an approach and points out that this notion is beginning to achieve prominence in civil law, citing the Law Commission's Report on Mental Incapacity:

> "A person is without capacity if at the material time he or she is
> (1) unable by reason of mental disability to make a decision on the matter in question"[27]

Mental disability is defined as:

---

[21] Richard D. Schneider & Hy Bloom, "R v Taylor: A Decision Not in the Best Interests of Some Mentally Ill Accused" (1995) 38 Crim L.Q. 183 at 201.

[22] Richard D. Schneider & Hy Bloom, "R v Taylor: A Decision Not in the Best Interests of Some Mentally Ill Accused" (1995) 38 Crim L.Q. 183 at 205.

[23] Norval Morris, *Madness and the Criminal Law* (London, 1969), p.48. Morris proposes that fitness for trial findings be replaced by rules of court which would enable trial continuances.

[24] For example, in *Trials and Punishments* (Cambridge University Press, 1986), p.120, R.A. Duff states his belief that the accused should have the ability "to understand the moral dimensions of the law and of his own actions." See also R.A. Duff, "Fitness to Plead and Fair Trials: (1) A Challenge" [1994] Crim.L.R. 419. Grubin suggests that it should be left to "the trial judge to decide, in the light of the facts of the case, whether a mentally disordered defendant is fit to be tried" with a view to deciding whether the defendant can still have a fair trial—"What Constitutes Fitness to Plead?" [1993] Crim. L.R. 748 at 757–8.

[25] Richard J. Bonnie, "The Competence of Criminal Defendants: Beyond *Dusky* and *Drope*" (1993) 47 U. Miami L.Rev. 539 at 556.

[26] R.D. Mackay, *Mental Condition Defences in the Criminal Law* (Oxford: Clarendon Press, 1995), pp. 244–5.

[27] Law Commission, *Mental Incapacity* (Law Com. 231, HMSO, London, 1995), para 3.14. See generally Alan Parkin, "Where Now on Mental Incapacity?" [1996] 2 Web J.C.L.I.

"[A]ny disability or disorder of the mind or brain, whether permanent or temporary, which results in an impairment or disturbance of mental functioning."[28]

In addition, the Scottish Law Commission has proposed[29] that the test for unfitness for trial should be based on the person's ability to participate effectively in the proceedings, based partly on European Convention on Human Rights (ECHR) case law such as *Stanford v UK*[30] and *T. and V. v UK*.[31] A Bill has been prepared to give effect to this proposal.[32] Such a widening of the scope of unfitness for trial would be more protective of the person's constitutional right to a fair trial. Conway notes, however, that it is possible to argue that the inclusion of the general ground of ability to make a proper defence in the criteria for unfitness for trial allows the criteria to be widened beyond the traditional cognitive ones.[33]

17–10 The question of extending the criteria to include amnesia at the time of the trial (thus overruling *Podola*) was debated in the Butler Committee report[34] and the majority decided not to recommend a change of this nature. The majority believed that the law on unfitness was a concession to notions of justice but could not be extended too far and that amnesia could readily be feigned. In response, the minority[35] argued that the loss of memory might prevent the defendant from giving important evidence on the facts in issue or on the issue of mens rea. Walker subsequently added that it was no easier to feign amnesia than other disorders.[36]

17–11 The right to a fair trial requires a broad definition of unfitness for trial, not based on cognitive criteria alone. The current narrow definition means that

---

[28] Law Commission, *Mental Incapacity* (Law Com. 231, HMSO, London, 1995), para.3.12.
[29] Scottish Law Commission, *Discussion Paper on Insanity and Diminished Responsibility* (2003) and *Report on Insanity and Diminished Responsibility* (2004).
[30] Series A, No.282, January 25, 1994.
[31] (2000) 30 E.H.R.R. 121.
[32] See s.119, Criminal Justice and Licensing (Scotland) Bill 2009.
[33] Gerard Conway, "Fitness to Plead in Light of the Criminal Law (Insanity) Bill 2002" (2003) 13(4) Ir.Crim.L.J. 2 at 3–4.
[34] Home Office & Department of Health and Social Security, *Report of the Committee on Mentally Abnormal Offenders* (London, 1975), paras 10.4–10.11.
[35] Prof. Nigel Walker and Prof. Sir Denis Hill
[36] Nigel Walker, "Butler v The CLRC and Others" [1981] Crim.L.R. 596 at 600. See also Walker, *Crime and Insanity in England*, vol.1, (Edinburgh University Press, 1968), pp.235–7. Note that McAuley admits that *Podola* is open to criticism but states that it is preferable to jeopardising the prosecution of offences where the defendant's loss of memory was caused by drunkenness or concussion resulting from dangerous or reckless driving (Finbarr McAuley, *Insanity, Psychiatry and Criminal Responsibility* (Dublin: Round Hall, 1993, p.139.) The issue of motoring offences also crops up in the Butler Report and Walker has commented that "the real anxiety of the majority ... was chiefly concerned with motoring offences"—[1981] Crim.L.R. 596 at 600.

defendants may be tried who cannot make informed, rational decisions about the conduct of their defence. Alternatively, they may plead guilty because they do not have the capacity to decide otherwise. It is unwise to "balance" the right to a fair trial against other rights, as was done in the *Taylor* decision.[37] The right to a fair trial is such a fundamental norm that it ought to be rigorously protected. It follows that the definition of unfitness should also, in appropriate cases, cover personality disorders[38] and amnesia at time of trial.

DETERMINATION OF THE ISSUE OF FITNESS FOR TRIAL

17–12 The question of fitness for trial may arise at the instance of the defence, the prosecution or the court.[39] Section 19 of the 2006 Act states that the defence must have notified the prosecution, within 10 days of the accused being asked how they wish to plead, that it intends to adduce evidence of the accused's mental condition.[40]

Since it is part of the constitutional concept of a fair trial that the defendant must be fit for trial, the question inevitably arises whether the defendant may waive their right to a fair trial and choose not to raise the issue of fitness for trial. Courts in common law jurisdictions have held that they may find the defendant unfit for trial in spite of their objections. Although the rationale has not often been articulated, this approach appears to be based on a fundamental concern for the imbalance and injustice which would result in conducting a trial where the defendant was unfit for trial.[41] The approach is based on a fundamental principle and is to be preferred to the prospect of holding a trial where the defendant might have mental disorder and insist on the trial going ahead. In any event, since unfitness for trial is narrowly defined at present, courts use the power of raising the issue of fitness on their own initiative sparingly. In fact, it is arguable that more frequent use of this function is required, for example in a case where a person representing themselves appears to be acting extremely irrationally.

---

[37] See Ashworth's criticism of the notion of balance as a rhetorical device of which one must be extremely wary—*The Criminal Process: An Evaluative Study*, 2nd edn (Oxford University Press, 1998), p.30.

[38] Note that in a review of patients found unfit to plead and detained in the Central Mental Hospital (CMH) from 1937 to 1995, 3 of the 24 cases had a primary diagnosis of personality disorder–Lynn Hutchinson & Art O'Connor, "Unfit to Plead in Ireland" (1995) 12 Ir. Jnl. Psychol. Med. 112.

[39] Criminal Law (Insanity) Act 2006, s.4(1).

[40] Criminal Law (Insanity) Act 2006, s.19, discussed above at paras 15–48 to 15–50.

[41] See for example Finlay C.J. in *O'C. v Judges of Dublin Metropolitan District* [1994] 3 I.R. 246, where he stated that a preliminary examination was a judicial exercise and it would be constitutionally impermissible that it could go forward in circumstances where a person was incapable of following the proceedings and of instructing lawyers.

17–13 In *State (C.) v Minister for Justice*, both Ó Dálaigh C.J. and Walsh J. stated that a judge of the District Court must stop short if they are satisfied that the accused is unfit for trial[42] and implied that the judge would do this of their own initiative, even if the question had not been raised by either side. In *O'C. v Judges of Dublin Metropolitan District*, the Supreme Court allowed the District Court to inquire into the applicant's fitness for trial in spite of his objections.[43] Similarly, in *DPP (Murphy) v P.T.*,[44] McGuinness J. said that a judge was under a duty to inquire into fitness to plead of their own initiative if presented with psychiatric reports which implicitly raised questions of fitness. See also *Leonard v Garavan & DPP*, para.17–16 below.

17–14 In the case of Patrick Messitt,[45] a retrial was ordered partly on the grounds that the trial judge had failed to investigate the defendant's complaints that he was physically ill (due to administration of drugs by a doctor who believed he was a psychopath) and also failed to establish "that his violent conduct [during the trial] was not caused by mental illness".[46] The defendant had behaved in a disruptive manner[47] during the trial, he had been removed from the courtroom on three occasions and his counsel and solicitor had left the trial due to his insistence on making certain statements to the court. There had earlier been ambiguous medical evidence to the effect that he was fit to plead "as far as his physical condition is concerned", but that he was essentially a psychopath.[48] Kenny J., delivering the judgment of the Court of Criminal Appeal, appeared to believe that if the defendant was either physically or mentally incapable of conducting his defence and had been removed from the court, the jury ought to be discharged and he might be tried before another jury when he recovered.[49] For present purposes, what is significant is that there had been no specific request by the defendant for an inquiry as to his *mental* state (apart from an interruption in the presence of the jury telling them that a doctor had said he was a psychopath), but that the Court of Criminal Appeal nevertheless ruled that the trial judge should have investigated whether his "violent conduct" was caused by mental illness.[50]

---

[42] [1967] I.R. 106 at 115 (Ó Dálaigh C.J.) and 120 (Walsh J.).

[43] [1994] 3 I.R. 246.

[44] [1999] 3 I.R. 254 at 261.

[45] *People (AG) v Messitt* [1972] I.R. 204.

[46] [1972] I.R. 204 at 212.

[47] [1972] I.R. 204. It is not clear what "violence" had occurred, but violence is mentioned in the report a number of times.

[48] [1972] I.R. 204 at 207.

[49] See [1972] I.R. 204 at 210–11, where he cited *R. v Stevenson* (1791) 2 Leach 546, *R. v Streek* (1826) 2 C. & P. 413 and *R. v Flynn* (1838) 1 Craw. & D. 293.

[50] Later in the judgment, the court also ordered a retrial on the basis that evidence should have been heard on the defendant's insanity at the time of the alleged offence, even if he did not raise the issue himself. See para.15–37 above.

17–15 The English position is that the question of fitness for trial may be raised "at the instance of the defence or otherwise."[51] US courts regard the requirement that the defendant be competent as part of due process, and so the defendant's failure to raise the issue does not waive their right to due process.[52] In Canada, the prosecution may raise the issue of fitness for trial against the wishes of the defence[53] and concern has been expressed that this may occur in the absence of a strong prosecution case.[54] A possible solution to these concerns is a proper, mandatory, trial of the facts procedure,[55] together with the introduction of flexible disposal options so that if the defendant is found unfit for trial, they do not inevitably face unjustified lengthy detention in a mental hospital.

17–16 The duty of the District Court to consider the issue of fitness for trial arose in *Leonard v Garavan & DPP*.[56] The applicant, Ms Leonard, had been convicted in the District Court of public order offences and assault. A garda gave evidence that she was "roaring about God and the Devil and was calling down curses upon all those present". In the witness box, she made a 15-minute speech about her crusade against drug dealers. She had no legal representation during the trial. She had been asked about representation and said she would represent herself. She continuously shouted and interrupted the judge. Once convicted, she was transferred from Mountjoy to the Central Mental Hospital (CMH). She applied to the High Court for certiorari of the convictions and there was medical evidence to the effect that she was in a manic state and had bipolar affective disorder. McKechnie J. quashed the convictions, saying that the applicant did not have any appreciation of what was going on and she was effectively "unfit to plead". The case should not have proceeded, or alternatively, there was sufficient evidence before the judge to warrant an inquiry into her mental state, which should have taken place. He also held that she should have been offered legal representation again at sentencing stage.

---

[51] Criminal Procedure (Insanity) Act 1964, s.4(1); substance on this point is not affected by replacement of this section by s.2 of Criminal Procedure (Insanity and Unfitness to Plead) Act 1991.

[52] *Pate v Robinson* 383 U.S. 375 (1966).

[53] Simon Davis, "Fitness to Stand Trial in Canada in Light of the Recent Criminal Code Amendments" (1994) 17 Int. J.L.& Psych. 319 at 320.

[54] S. Verdun-Jones, "The Doctrine of Fitness to Stand Trial in Canada" (1981) 4 Int.J.L.& Psych. 363.

[55] See paras 17–28 to 17–30 below.

[56] [2003] 4 I.R. 60. See also the earlier case of *DPP (Murphy) v P.T.* [1999] 3 I.R. 254, where a 15-year-old boy was charged in the District Court with larceny of a sports jacket. The boy was placed in the care of the Eastern Health Board and the judge adjourned the proceedings to chambers to consider his medical and psychiatric condition. Documents appear to have shown a preliminary diagnosis of Asperger's Syndrome. The judge later decided to inquire into his fitness to plead of his (the judge's) own initiative. McGuinness J. in the High Court confirmed that the District Court was under a duty to enquire into P.T.'s fitness to plead.

17–17 The decision on fitness for trial is made under the 2006 Act by a judge rather than a jury, even for offences triable on indictment. This contrasts with the previous rule in s.17 of the Lunacy (Ireland) Act 1821, which was that the decision was made by a jury. In the case of an indictable offence to be tried by a jury, the District Court must send the matter forward to the court to which the person would have been sent forward if they were fit for trial.[57]

There appears to be a drafting error in the repeals listed in sch.2 of the 2006 Act. At item 10, the reference to s.4A(1)(c) of the Criminal Justice Act 1999 is erroneous. The Criminal Justice Act 1999 does not include a s.4A . The correct reference should be to s.4A of the Criminal Procedure Act 1967, which was inserted by s.9 of the 1999 Act. It is clear from the reference to s.4A of the Criminal Procedure Act 1967 at s.4(4)(c) of the 2006 Act that this s.4A is the one which should been amended.[58] If a technical argument were to be raised that s.4A(1)(c) of the Criminal Procedure Act 1967 was still in force, the court might have regard to the context and hold that in fact the paragraph is no longer of legal effect. Alternatively, if the court found that the paragraph was still in force, this would mean that there are two conflicting statutory provisions: On the one hand, s.4A(1)(c) states that where an accused person is before the District Court charged with an indictable offence, the court shall send the accused forward for trial to the court before which the person is to stand trial unless the accused is unfit to plead. On the other hand, s.4(4) of the 2006 Act lays down a new procedure which is to be followed if a person is charged with an indictable offence which is not being tried summarily, which involves sending the person forward to the higher court. A court might decide that the only sensible interpretation is to apply the new procedure laid down in the 2006 Act.

17–18 In the case of an indictable offence "which is being or is to be tried summarily", the judge of the District Court will decide on fitness for trial.[59] McGillicuddy has raised questions about the interpretation of this provision.[60] In cases where the accused can elect for summary trial, e.g. a minor theft offence, the charge cannot be tried summarily without the accused person's consent, which the person may be unable to give at that point. The court may be unable to deal with the issue of fitness to be tried in such a case. However, the question of the accused's ability to elect for a jury trial is one of the questions relevant to fitness to be tried (s.4(2)(c)), which may trigger the inquiry about fitness for trial being carried out in the District Court.[61]

---

[57] Criminal Law (Insanity) Act 2006, s.4(4)(a).
[58] See also the debate on amendment number 14, Select Committee on Justice, Equality, Defence and Women's Rights, January 18, 2006.
[59] Criminal Law (Insanity) Act 2006, s.4(3)(a).
[60] Tony McGilliuddy, "The Criminal Law (Insanity) Act 2006" (2006) 11 *Bar Review* 95 at 96.
[61] See also Tony McGillicuddy, "The Criminal Law (Insanity) Bill 2002", April 2, 2006, p.5, *http://www.lawlibrary.ie*, [Accessed September 28, 2009]

17–19 Where the question arises as to whether or not the accused is fit to be tried and the court considers that it is expedient and in the interests of the accused so to do, it may defer consideration of the question until any time before the opening of the case for the defence.[62] There is a similar statutory provision in England,[63] and it has been held in *R. v Burles*[64] that deferral may be used where the prosecution case is thin. It is unfortunate that this section has been included in the 2006 Act. When it is applied, the court permits the trial to go ahead in spite of serious doubts about the defendant's fitness for trial. It is quite possible that the defendant's conduct of their defence will be hampered by their mental condition and this fundamentally conflicts with the right to a fair trial. In addition, the supposed necessity to have postponements of this type virtually disappears if a proper, mandatory "trial of the facts" type procedure is introduced, as has happened in various jurisdictions.

17–20 There is no requirement of a committal and/or medical evidence of any particular kind for a court to find a person unfit to be tried. However, medical evidence is required *following* the finding of unfitness for trial if the person is to be detained.[65]

If issues arise about the applicability of art.6 of the ECHR to determinations of fitness for trial, reference may be made to the English cases in which it was held that such determinations are not part of criminal proceedings: *R. v M., K. and H.*,[66] *R. v Grant*[67] and *R. v H.*[68]

17–21 The 2006 Act does not repeal s.28 of the Juries Act 1976, which states that, "[w]henever a person charged with an offence to be tried with a jury stands mute when called upon to plead, the issue whether he is mute of malice or by the visitation of God shall be decided by the judge and, if the judge is not satisfied that he is mute by the visitation of God, the judge shall direct a plea of not guilty to be entered for him".[69]

PROCEDURE FOLLOWING DETERMINATION OF THE ISSUE OF
FITNESS FOR TRIAL

17–22 If the court determines that an accused person is unfit to be tried, the court must adjourn the proceedings until further order.[70] If the court determines

---

[62] Criminal Law (Insanity) Act 2006, s.4(7).
[63] Criminal Procedure (Insanity) Act 1964, s.4.
[64] [1970] 2 Q.B. 191. See also *R. v Webb* [1969] 2 Q.B. 178.
[65] See para.17–22 below.
[66] [2001] E.W.C.A. Crim. 2024; [2002] 1 W.L.R. 824.
[67] [2001] E.W.C.A. Crim. 2611; [2002] 1 Q.B. 1030.
[68] [2003] U.K.H.L. 1; [2003] 1 W.L.R. 411.
[69] See Edward Ryan & Philip Magee, *The Irish Criminal Process* (Dublin and Cork: Mercier Press, 1983), p.268.
[70] Section 4(3)(b) of the 2006 Act regarding the District Court; s.4(5)(c) regarding other courts.

that the person is fit to be tried, the case continues.[71] If the accused pleads guilty, having been found fit for trial, the court should ordinarily accept the plea, even if the guilty plea is for tactical reasons.[72]

Committal for examination and medical report are obligatory if the court wishes to detain a person found unfit for trial or order out-patient treatment for them. In order to determine the nature of the person's mental condition, the court commits them to a designated centre[73] for up to 14 days under s.4(6) and directs a report from an approved medical officer.[74] This 14-day period for examination cannot be extended.[75]

Keys has argued that the power of the court to refer for assessment based on its own view and without a medical assessment may be contrary to the principle in *Winterwerp v The Netherlands*[76] that detention in a psychiatric care centre must be based on objective medical expertise.[77] Ní Raifeartaigh suggests that the courts should interpret the Act in a Convention-compliant fashion on this issue.[78]

17–23 There have been media reports of problems with shortages of beds in the CMH in cases where assessments have been ordered by the District Court.[79] Professor Kennedy, who is Clinical Director of the CMH, is extremely critical of s.4(6) of the 2006 Act:

> "Another example concerns the omission of a 'diagnostic' stage in the definition of mental disorder in s.4(6) of the Criminal Law (Insanity) Act 2006, which has led to numerous inappropriate committals by district court judges, unassisted by psychiatric evidence or certification. Cases inappropriately committed have been on the grounds of intoxication, angry protests in court, youth, or pragmatic legal advocacy to avoid the imprisonment of their clients, to avoid acquiring a criminal record or to avoid deportation. These flaws appear to be examples of the belief that if a law works in theory but not in practice, reality must be wrong."[80]

---

[71] Section 4(3)(c), s.4(4)(c) and s.4(5)(d) of the 2006 Act.

[72] See discussion of *People (DPP) v Redmond* [2006] 3 I.R. 188, above, paras 15–41 to 15–43.

[73] At present, the CMH is the only designated centre.

[74] Section 4(6)(a). An "approved medical officer" means a consultant psychiatrist within the meaning of the Mental Health Act 2001. The 2001 Act as amended by the Health Act 2004 defines a consultant psychiatrist as a consultant psychiatrist who is employed by the Health Service Executive (HSE) or by an approved centre or a person whose name is entered on the division of psychiatry or the division of child and adolescent psychiatry of the Register of Medical Specialists maintained by the Medical Council in Ireland.

[75] Contrast insanity cases–s.5(3)(b) of the 2006 Act.

[76] (1979) 2 E.H.R.R. 397.

[77] Mary Keys, Unpublished paper on Criminal Law (Insanity) Bill 2002, p.5.

[78] Úna Ní Raifeartaigh, "The ECHR and the Criminal Justice System" (2007) 2 *Judicial Studies Institute Journal* 18 at 29–30.

[79] "Inquiry Ordered into Man's Mental Hospital Detention"; *Irish Times*, January 27, 2007; "Lawyers Urged to Sue State Over Rights"; *Irish Times*, January 26, 2008.

[80] Harry Kennedy, "A General Theory of Mental Disorder and Consolidated Mental Disability Legislation" (2008) 14 M.L.J.I. 51 at 55.

In the original Bill, a period of 28 days was allowed for such examinations, but this period was later reduced to 14 days, partly due to concern expressed by the Irish Human Rights Commission.[81] The Mental Health Commission recommended that the Bill should be amended to facilitate remand of the person on bail in order to attend for assessment on an out-patient basis.[82]

17–24 The Government has circulated the Heads of a Bill to amend the 2006 Act to address the problems which have arisen with s.4(6). While the Heads of the Bill have not been made public, the Irish Human Rights Commission's observations on them have.[83] It would appear that the Bill proposes a new requirement of medical evidence before a court orders 14-day detention for psychiatric examination under s.4(6)(a). The Irish Human Rights Commission has recommended that the wording of the Bill be changed to require the evidence to be that of a consultant psychiatrist. It also recommended that the 2006 Act should be amended to make some provision for out-patient assessments of persons under the 2006 Act in relation to whether they are fit to be tried where it is possible given the personal circumstances and mental health of the person to be assessed.[84]

17–25 Returning to the existing law, the court may, if it is satisfied, having considered the evidence of the approved medical officer and any other evidence, that the person is suffering from a mental disorder (within the meaning of the Mental Health Act 2001) and is in need of in-patient care or treatment, commit the person to a designated centre until an order is made under s.13.[85] Alternatively, the court may order out-patient treatment, in which case mental disorder as defined either in the 2001 Act or the 2006 Act may be involved.[86] As the CMH, currently the only designated centre, is located in Dublin, the option of out-patient treatment in the CMH is not practical for people residing outside the Dublin region.

17–26 The possibility of out-patient treatment was added as a late amendment, as Minister McDowell believed that "no one with a mental disorder should be

---

[81] Irish Human Rights Commission, *Observations on the Criminal Law (Insanity) Bill 2002*, September 2003.
[82] Mental Health Commission, *Second Submission on Criminal Law (Insanity) Bill 2002*, January 2006.
[83] Irish Human Rights Commission, *Observations on the Scheme of the Criminal Law (Insanity) Act 2006 (Amendment) Bill 2008* (November 2008).
[84] Irish Human Rights Commission, *Observations on the Scheme of the Criminal Law (Insanity) Act 2006 (Amendment) Bill 2008* (November 2008), pp.6–7.
[85] Section 4(3)(b)(i) and s.4(5)(c)(i) of 2006 Act. An order under s.13 is an order by the Mental Health (Criminal Law) Review Board making such order as it thinks proper in relation to the patient, e.g. further care, conditional discharge, unconditional discharge, out-patient treatment or supervision.
[86] Section 4(3)(b)(ii) and s.4(5)(c)(ii) of the 2006 Act.

inappropriately held in police custody or in prison".[87] He also referred to the Henchy report and the submission of the Mental Health Commission as reasons to introduce the possibility of out-patient treatment. Note, however, that out-patient treatment was not introduced as an option for those found not guilty by reason of insanity. The possibility of out-patient treatment contrasts with the regime concerning involuntary civil admission under the Mental Health Act 2001, where Mental Health Tribunals (MHTs) may only confirm or revoke an Admission Order, and cannot order out-patient treatment.

17–27 The person may only be detained if they have a mental disorder within the meaning of the Mental Health Act 2001. Therefore, once a person is found to be unfit for trial in the criminal law sense, they may only be detained if they have a mental disorder in the civil law sense. The position for persons with personality disorders is unclear. Section 8 of the Mental Health Act 2001 states that a person may not be detained under that Act solely because of a personality disorder. The 2006 Act states that a person found unfit for trial may only be detained if they have a mental disorder within the meaning of the 2001 Act, but it is unclear whether the section of that Act prohibiting detention based on personality disorder alone has an impact on "a mental disorder within the meaning of the 2001 Act". The lack of clarity regarding the criteria for detention under the 2006 Act (by way of cross-reference to the 2001 Act) may breach the requirement in art.5 of the ECHR that detention be "in accordance with a procedure prescribed by law".[88]

Note also that while a person is detained under s.4 of the 2006 Act using civil criteria from the 2001 Act, they do not have the same rights as a patient detained under the 2001 Act.

When the person is detained, there is no statutory right to written information regarding the grounds for their detention.[89] Information on detention is required by art.5(2) of the ECHR.[90]

Optional Trial of the Facts

17–28 There is no mandatory "trial of the facts" before a committal order is made. Instead, s.4(8) of the 2006 Act provides for an optional trial of the facts: Upon a determination having been made by the court that an accused person is unfit to be tried, it may, on application to it in that behalf, allow evidence to be adduced before it as to whether or not the accused person did the act alleged and if the court is satisfied that there is a reasonable doubt as to whether the accused did the act alleged, it shall order the accused to be discharged.

---

[87] 616 *Dáil Debates* Col.2059 (March 23, 2006).
[88] See further the discussion of the same issue regarding insanity cases at para.15–58 above.
[89] Compare s.16(2), Mental Health Act 2001.
[90] See further, para.1–24 above.

The original Bill referred to evidence as to whether the accused person "committed" the act alleged, but this was later changed to "did" the act alleged. Minister Lenihan said that the word "committed" carries a connotation that people might have known what they were doing when they committed the act and that it could be argued the word "did" is more neutral in that regard.[91]

If a trial of the facts takes place, there are restrictions on media reporting of the case in s.4(9). These restrictions were introduced as a result of amendments originally suggested by Senator Tuffy, and later accepted and redrafted by the Government. The restrictions were introduced because if a court concludes that there is not reasonable doubt that an accused did the act alleged, such a conclusion could be prejudicial to the interests and good name of the accused thereafter or at any future trial.[92]

17–29 If the court is satisfied that there is a reasonable doubt as to whether the accused did the act, they are "discharged" and the word "acquitted" is not used. However, Minister McDowell stated:

> "In effect, these provisions provide that where, despite the fact that the accused is unfit to be tried, the court is satisfied that there is a reasonable doubt that he or she committed the alleged act, it will acquit him or her. Accused persons may be unfit to be tried but if the court is, nonetheless, in a position to acquit them and say they are innocent, they should not be denied the benefit of having their innocence established merely by virtue of the fact that they have had some intervening mental illness."[93]

Note that in courts martial the word "acquit" is used in the relevant section.[94]

17–30 In England and Wales, a person who is found unfit to plead cannot be detained by a criminal court unless it has first been found that they did the alleged act.[95] It is regrettable that the 2006 Act does not require a mandatory trial of the facts before a person who has been found unfit for trial can be detained. If a trial of the facts is being introduced, it is difficult to see why it ought to be optional.[96] The trial of the facts system serves the very useful purpose of ensuring that the strength of the prosecution's case is tested before it is possible to detain the person. While the defendant's mental disorder may well restrict their ability to contradict the prosecution's case, at least the defendant is given an opportunity to attempt to do so. If the defendant's efforts fail, the result is not

---

[91]   180 *Seanad Debates* Col.32 (April 19, 2005).
[92]   180 *Seanad Debates* Col.33 (April 19, 2005).
[93]   171 *Seanad Debates* Col.771 (February 19, 2003).
[94]   Section 202(4) of the Defence Act 1954 as amended by s.21, Criminal Law (Insanity) Act 2006.
[95]   Section 4A of the Criminal Procedure (Insanity) Act 1964 as inserted by s.4 of the Criminal Procedure (Insanity and Unfitness to Plead) Act 1991.
[96]   Similarly, see Faye Boland, "The Criminal Justice (Mental Disorder) Bill 1996" [1997] 4 Web J.C.L.I. in "unfitness to plead" section.

a finding of guilt, it is a finding that they did the act or made the omission charged. Restrictions on media reporting of the trial of the facts (as in s.4(9) of the 2006 Act) protect defendants' reputations, and ensure a fair trial if they become fit for trial at a later stage.[97] If the defendant successfully contradicts the prosecution's case, then the defendant is discharged and cannot be detained. The trial of the facts is also consistent with the right to a speedy trial under the Irish Constitution and art.6(1) of the ECHR.

17–31 It appears that the trial of the facts is adjudicated upon by the judge alone, without a jury. McGillicuddy has questioned whether the judge or a jury would make such a decision where trials on indictment are involved.[98]

17–32 In *R. v Egan (Michael)*,[99] Ognall J. said that the prosecution, in a case of a trial of the facts on a bag-snatching theft charge, must prove that the defendant's conduct satisfied to the requisite extent all the ingredients of what otherwise, were it not for the disability, would be properly characterised as an offence. He said that although the words "the act" are used in the relevant legislation, the phrase means neither more nor less than proof of all the necessary ingredients of what otherwise would be an offence, in this case theft.[100] If the defendant had raised the question, for example, of whether he had the capacity to form an intention to permanently deprive the owner of the goods, then the jury would have to consider that issue.[101] However, in this case, the defence had instead argued that the defendant was not the "bag-snatcher" and so it was unnecessary for the judge to instruct the jury on the issue of whether the accused had the capacity to form the relevant intent.

17–33 In *R. v Antoine*[102] the House of Lords held that on a charge of murder, a trial of the facts is only concerned with the actus reus of the offence, not the mens rea. The Law Lords held that the defence of diminished responsibility is not available on a trial of the facts. Defences such as mistake, accident or self-defence may be considered if there is objective evidence concerning them. Lord Hutton stated that *Egan* should no longer be followed,[103] as it was inconsistent with *Attorney General's Reference (No.3 of 1998)*.[104]

---

[97] Clare Connelly, "Insanity and Unfitness to Plead" [1996] Jur.Rev. 253 at 211.
[98] Tony McGillicuddy, "The Criminal Law (Insanity) Act 2006" (2006) 11 *Bar Review* 95 at 97.
[98] (1998) 1 Cr.App.Rep. 121.
[100] (1998) 1 Cr.App.Rep. 121 at 124–5.
[101] The intention to permanently deprive the owner of the goods is no longer required in Ireland, since the Criminal Justice (Theft and Fraud Offences) Act 2001, s.4. However, the person must still intend to deprive the owner of the property.
[102] [2001] 1 A.C. 340.
[103] [2001] 1 A.C. 340 at 372.
[104] [2000] Q.B. 401.

It has been held in *R. v Grant (Heather)*[105] that provocation may not be considered. Richards J., delivering the judgment of the Court of Appeal, reasoned as follows:

"[T]he defence of provocation is intimately bound up with the defendant's state of mind. Any consideration of provocation inevitably requires examination of the defendant's state of mind, in determining whether there has been a sudden and temporary loss of self-control and whether that loss of self-control was caused by the conduct of the deceased. ... It would be unrealistic and contradictory, in relation to a person unfit to be tried, that a jury should have to consider what effect the conduct of the deceased had on the mind of that person. Parliament cannot have intended that question to be included within the determination of whether the person 'did the act' charged. The distinction applied in *R. v Antoine* between *actus reus* and *mens rea* is not clear-cut, but in our judgment provocation falls clearly on the *mens rea* side of the dividing line."[106]

It has recently been held in England that in the case of a trial involving multiple defendants, some of whom are fit for trial and some of whom are unfit for trial, the same jury may determine the criminal liability of those defendants who are fit for trial as well as whether those defendants who are unfit for trial "did" the acts.[107]

17–34 It may be argued that the trial of the facts engages art.6 of the ECHR and therefore that the protections in art.6 must be present, including the presumption of innocence However, the House of Lords held in *R. v H. (Fitness to Plead)*[108] that art.6 did not apply to a trial of the facts, as it was not a determination of a criminal charge. It was even possible for the person who had been the subject of the trial of the facts to be placed on the sex offenders register, as this was not a punishment.

17–35 The relevance of art.6 to trials of the facts was also litigated in Strasbourg in *Antoine v UK*.[109] The European Court of Human Rights stated that the trial of the facts procedure may be regarded as a mechanism protecting an applicant, wrongly accused of participation in a purported offence, from the making of any preventative orders. The lack of a possibility of a conviction and the absence of any punitive sanctions were key features. Though Hospital Orders might be imposed on defendants in criminal trials and involve the loss of liberty, it could

---

[105] [2001] E.W.C.A. Crim 2611; [2002] 1 Q.B. 1030.
[106] [2002] 1 Q.B. 1030 at 1048.
[107] *R. v B. and Others* [2008] E.W.C.A. Crim. 1997; [2009] 1 W.L.R. 1545.
[108] [2003] U.K.H.L. 1; [2003] 1 W.L.R. 411.
[109] Application No.62960/00, [2003] M.H.L.R. 292.

not be argued that such an order is a measure of retribution or deterrence in the sense of the imposition of a sentence of imprisonment.[110]

The court said that while the trial of the facts had strong similarities with procedures at a criminal trial, the proceedings were principally concerned with the actus reus. This served the purpose of striking a fair balance between the need to protect a person who had, in fact, done nothing wrong and was unfit to plead at their trial and the need to protect the public from a person who had committed an injurious act which would have been a crime if carried out with the appropriate mens rea. The court was satisfied that the essential purpose of the proceedings was to consider whether the applicant had committed an act the dangerousness of which would require a Hospital Order in the interests of the protection of the public. It concluded that the proceedings did not involve the determination of a criminal charge and therefore the question as to whether they were compatible with art.6(1) of the Convention, in that the applicant was unable to participate effectively due to his mental state, did not arise.[111]

The applicant also argued that his right to a fair trial within a reasonable time was being interfered with. However, the court stated that the criminal proceedings against the applicant were for practical purposes terminated when he was found unfit to stand trial. While it remained theoretically possible that at some later date the Secretary of State might decide that the applicant had become fit to plead, it could not be considered that the charge nonetheless remained pending. The Secretary of State might never in fact re-institute proceedings against the applicant. If he did, the question of whether the applicant was tried within a reasonable time would depend on an examination of the period between the first concrete step taken to institute another trial and the conclusion of those proceedings. There was accordingly no problem of delay arising in the determination of the criminal charge in the present circumstances.[112]

Procedure Following Detention

17–36 If the court orders the person's detention for in-patient treatment in a designated centre following a finding of unfitness for trial, the detention lasts "until an order is made under s.13".[113] The Mental Health (Criminal Law) Review Board must review the person's detention at least every six months.[114] If the review board finds that the person is no longer unfit to be tried, it shall order that the person be brought before the court which committed them to be dealt with as the court thinks proper.[115] If the board finds that the patient, although still unfit to be tried, is no longer in need of in-patient care or treatment,

---

[110]   [2003] M.H.L.R. 292, para.35.
[111]   [2003] M.H.L.R. 292, paras 36–7.
[112]   [2003] M.H.L.R. 292, para.39.
[113]   Criminal Law (Insanity) Act 2006, s.4(3)(b)(i) and s.4(5)(c)(i).
[114]   Criminal Law (Insanity) Act 2006, s.13(2). See Chapter 18 below.
[115]   Criminal Law (Insanity) Act 2006, s.13(8)(a).

the board may make such order as it thinks proper for the patient, whether for further detention in a designated centre or for their discharge, whether unconditionally or subject to conditions.[116]

If the clinical director of a designated centre forms the opinion that the patient is no longer unfit to be tried, they shall forthwith notify the court and the court shall order that the person be brought before it to be dealt with as the court thinks proper.[117] If the clinical director forms the opinion that the person, although still unfit to be tried, is no longer in need of in-patient care or treatment at a designated centre, they shall forthwith notify the board.[118] The board then reviews the case and makes such order as it thinks proper, whether for further detention, unconditional or conditional discharge.[119]

While it is not specifically mentioned in the Act, the Gardaí or the DPP may decide at any stage not to proceed with the prosecution. In the case of the DPP, this would take the form of a *nolle prosequi*.

PROCEDURE PRIOR TO DETERMINATION OF ISSUE IN DISTRICT COURT

17–37 Having considered the general law concerning fitness for trial in all courts, the particular position of the District Court will now be considered.[120]

The 2006 Act does not require that medical evidence be heard before a finding of unfitness for trial is made. Nor does it require that the person be committed to a hospital at this stage for assessment of their mental condition. Even though medical evidence is not required by the Act at this stage, it would obviously be desirable to hear such evidence where appropriate. For that purpose, the court may wish to allow time for medical evidence to be obtained.

There are two main choices open to the District Court if the question of fitness for trial arises and the parties are not ready to proceed with the issue on the day, or if reports need to be prepared prior to determining the issue: remand to a prison[121] or remand on bail. In the case of remand on bail, possibilities such as attachment of conditions may be considered.

If the court remands the person on bail, the question of fitness to enter into a recognisance would arise. In *R. v Green-Emmott*,[122] it was held that a person who has been certified as insane cannot enter into a binding recognisance. Walsh J.

---

[116]   See further Chapter 18 below.
[117]   Criminal Law (Insanity) Act 2006, s.13(3)(a).
[118]   Criminal Law (Insanity) Act 2006, s.13(4).
[119]   Criminal Law (Insanity) Act 2006, s.13(5).
[120]   See generally Darius Whelan, "Fitness for Trial in the District Court: The Legal Perspective" (2007) 2 *Judicial Studies Institute Journal* 124.
[121]   If the person is remanded to prison, it is possible for them to be transferred to the CMH under s.15 of the 2006 Act. The transfer is directed by the Governor of the prison, on receipt of appropriate psychiatric certification, and no court appearance is required. See further paras 19–31 to 19–37 below.
[122]   (1931) 22 Cr. App. R. 183; 29 Cox C.C. 280

referred to this precedent in *State (C.) v Minister for Justice*[123] and concluded that if the District Court decided that the person was unfit for trial, the court would have no alternative but to remand the person in custody, as they would not be able to enter into a recognisance.[124] It is unfortunate that the 2006 Act did not address this problem, for example by abolishing the mandatory recognisance in cases where the defendant is mentally unfit.[125]

If the person is fit to enter into a recognisance, the court might consider attaching conditions to the recognisance, relating to the person's mental disorder. The Bail Act 1997 states that the recognisance may be subject to such conditions as the court considers appropriate having regard to the circumstances of the case.[126] The conditions might include a requirement that the person attend a particular psychiatric centre on an out-patient basis.[127] Alternatively, conditions could require that the person permit themselves to be admitted to a psychiatric centre.[128]

17–38 The court does not have a statutory power to remand the person in custody to a local hospital. However, the court might in some cases comment on the possible need for treatment of the person. If the court is satisfied that the person will seek treatment on a voluntary basis, then that may be sufficient. Otherwise, if there is a serious likelihood of the person causing immediate and serious harm to themselves or others, the court could inquire of the Gardaí whether they have considered using their power to take a person believed to have a mental disorder into custody under s.12 of the Mental Health Act 2001.[129] This taking into custody must be followed forthwith by an application to a doctor for a recommendation for admission to an approved centre under the 2001 Act. Alternatively, the Gardaí may make an application under s.9 of the 2001 Act, without taking the person into custody. There is also the possibility of contacting the Health Service Executive (HSE) and requesting an "authorised officer" to consider applying for involuntary civil admission of the person.[130]

---

[123] [1967] I.R. 106.

[124] [1967] I.R. 106 at 126.

[125] The Henchy committee proposed adjournments of up to six months if a person was unable by reason of mental disorder to enter into a recognisance—*Third Interim Report of the Interdepartmental Committee on Mentally Ill and Maladjusted Persons: Treatment and Care of Persons Suffering from Mental Disorder Who Appear Before the Courts on Criminal Charges* [Chair: Henchy J.] (Prl. 8275, J85/1, Stationery Office, Dublin, 1978), draft Bill, s.37.

[126] Section 6(1)(b) of the Bail Act 1997.

[127] See discussion of the English equivalent in Peter Bartlett & Ralph Sandland, *Mental Health Law: Policy and Practice*, 3rd edn (Oxford: Oxford University Press, 2007), p.215.

[128] See Conor O'Neill, "Diverting the Mentally Ill from District Courts: Consequential Options", Annual District Court Conference, Adare, 2007, slide 24, where an example of conditional bail is given: The prison governor and a general practitioner complete forms in advance for admission under the Mental Health Act 2001; the bail conditions are that the accused permits himself to be brought to hospital, will remain there until discharged if he is admitted, will afterwards reside with his sister, accept appropriate treatment and abstain from illicit drugs.

[129] See above, paras 4–69 to 4–82.

[130] See above, paras 4–08 to 4–09.

17–39 As was noted above at paras 2–39 to 2–44, it has been recognised in some cases that if a person with a mental disorder is released from detention due to a breach of a statutory requirement, courts may take account of the person's mental disorder and need for treatment and ensure that arrangements are put in place for a fresh application for detention to be made. By analogy, an argument could be made that the District Court may in appropriate criminal cases facilitate involuntary civil detention of a person under the Mental Health Act 2001.

McInerney and O'Neill have reported that in practice, in the case of a seriously ill person requiring involuntary psychiatric treatment, the relevant paperwork for an involuntary civil admission will be prepared in advance of the court appearance and that the assistance of the Gardaí in transfer to hospital is sometimes requested.[131]

17–40 The Criminal Procedure Act 1967, as amended, provides that if the District Court is satisfied that any person who has been remanded is unable by reason of illness or accident to appear or to be brought before the court at the expiration of the period of remand, the court may, in their absence, remand the person on bail or in custody for an extended period.[132] There are authorities which support the use of this power in cases of mental disorders.[133] Care must be taken to comply with all the requirements of the section, e.g. it may only be used when the person has already been remanded at least once, and the person must be "unable" to appear in court.

17–41 An argument might be made that s.4(6) of the 2006 Act allows the District Court to commit the person to the CMH for up to 14 days before determining the question of fitness for trial, however it seems unlikely that s.4(6) allows committal *before* determining fitness for trial. The contents of the psychiatric report which must be produced by the approved medical officer as specified in s.4(6)(b), are relevant to the question of making an appropriate order in relation to the person *after* they have been found unfit for trial. If the psychiatric report were to assist the court in determining fitness for trial, then the sub-section would require that the report address the person's ability to understand the nature and course of the proceedings.[134] In addition, s.4(6) refers to the "exercise" of a "power" under subsections (3) or (5), and this seems to apply to making an appropriate order after the person has been found unfit for trial[135] rather than the subsection which refers to the "question" of fitness for

---

[131] Clare McInerney & Conor O'Neill, "Prison Psychiatric Inreach and Court Liaison Services in Ireland (2008) 2 J.S.I.J. 147 at 153.

[132] Section 24(5) of the Criminal Procedure Act 1967, as substituted by s.4 of the Criminal Justice (Miscellaneous Provisions) Act 1997. See also Ord.19(4) of District Court Rules 1997, S.I. No.93 of 1997.

[133] *In Re Dolphin: State (Egan) v Governor of Central Mental Hospital*, High Court, Kenny J., January 27, 1972; *State (Caseley) v Daly & O'Sullivan*, High Court, Gannon J., February 19, 1979.

[134] Section 4(2) of the Criminal Law (Insanity) Act 2006.

[135] Section 4(3)(b).

trial being "determined" by the court.[136] Finally, it is only in the sub-section concerning making an order after a finding of unfitness for trial[137] that reference is made to the court considering the psychiatric report adduced under s.4(6).

APPEALS

17–42 Section 7 of the 2006 Act provides that findings of unfitness to be tried may be appealed. If the relevant court allows the appeal, it may either order that the person be tried or retried, as the case may be. If the lower court postponed consideration of fitness for trial under s.4(7), the appeal court may acquit the person if it is of the opinion that they ought to have been found not guilty before fitness for trial was considered. If the appeal court sends the person back for trial or retrial, the accused may be tried or retried for a different offence, provided it is an offence of which they might be found guilty on a charge for the original offence.

A finding that the accused is fit (as opposed to unfit) for trial may not be appealed as such, although of course if the accused is convicted of the offence, an appeal lies against the conviction. Appeals to the Supreme Court are excluded by s.7(5); therefore, in the case of trials at Central Criminal Court level, the appeal must go to the Court of Criminal Appeal only.[138]

17–43 Section 9 of the 2006 Act provides that an appeal regarding the decision to make or not to make an order of committal of a person found unfit for trial may be taken by either the defence or the prosecution. The appeal court may make any order which it was open to the court of trial to make. If an appeal court finds that a person is not guilty by reason of insanity, it will have the same powers to deal with the person as the court of trial would have had under s.5 if it had come to the same conclusion.

PROHIBITION OF TRIAL WHERE PERSON CANNOT HAVE FAIR TRIAL DUE TO MENTAL CONDITION

17–44 It may be possible in some cases to apply for an order of prohibition by way of judicial review restraining the DPP from further prosecuting an offence where the applicant has a medical condition which is of such a nature and degree as to prevent the applicant from properly and adequately instructing their legal team for their defence to serious charges, and to such a degree that there is a real and substantial risk that, were they to face trial on these charges, they could not be said to have a fair trial.

---

[136] Section 4(3)(a).
[137] Section 4(3)(b).
[138] Criminal Law (Insanity) Act 2006, s.7(3).

In *J.O'C. v DPP*,[139] the applicant was charged with sexual offences which were alleged to have been committed between 1974 and 1978. There was clear medical evidence, both for the prosecution and the defence, that he had early onset Alzheimer's disease and that this would affect his ability to recollect events from that period. Peart J. granted the order of prohibition sought, emphasising that this was not a case of unfitness for trial:

> "However, as submitted by counsel for the applicant, the applicant is not making the case that he is 'unfit to plead' in the manner contemplated by [s.2 of the Criminal Lunatics Act 1800] ... . What is alleged here is not that the applicant is unable to say whether he is guilty or not guilty, or that he could not decide to make a challenge to a particular juror, or to understand the evidence. It is that, through the onset of Alzheimer's disease, he cannot sufficiently recollect events which are alleged to have happened some 28 years ago, and that he cannot for that reason properly defend himself against the charges which he denies."[140]

If this were a case of unfitness for trial, judicial review might have been refused on the basis of availability of an alternative remedy.[141]

In recent cases, the courts have tended to state that the applicant's medical condition is more a matter for the trial judge, to be decided under the fitness for trial procedure.[142]

---

[139]   High Court, Peart J., October 8, 2002. See generally Sinead Ring, "Justice Denied? An Analysis of the Difficulties Facing Applicants for Prohibition in Delayed Prosecutions for Child Sexual Abuse" (2009) *Criminal Law Online* (First Law).

[140]   High Court, Peart J., October 8, 2002, p.8. See further the analysis of this case in Gerard Conway, "Fitness to Plead in Light of the Criminal Law (Insanity) Bill 2002" (2003) 13(4) Ir. Crim. L.J. 2.

[141]   See Gerard Conway, "Fitness to Plead in Light of the Criminal Law (Insanity) Bill 2002" (2003) 13(4) Ir. Crim. L.J. 2 at 4.

[142]   See, for example, *J.B. v DPP* [2006] I.E.S.C. 66; Supreme Court, November 29, 2006; *D.T. v DPP* [2007] I.E.S.C. 2; Supreme Court, January 25, 2007.

CHAPTER 18

REVIEWS BY THE MENTAL HEALTH
(CRIMINAL LAW) REVIEW BOARD

THE LAW PRIOR TO 2006

18–01 Prior to 2006, persons who had been found to be "guilty but insane" were detained "at the pleasure of the executive". In a series of cases in the 1990s, the constitutional and other aspects of this were litigated in detail.[1] At one stage, Keane J. ruled in *Application of Neilan*[2] that the Trial of Lunatics Act 1883 was unconstitutional, as it interfered with the judicial power. However, the final decision on the matter was issued by the Supreme Court in *Application of Gallagher (No.1)*,[3] in which the Supreme Court upheld the constitutionality of the 1883 Act.

McCarthy J. said that detained people could apply to the executive for their release and fair and constitutional procedures would need to be used by the executive in inquiring into the matter. In a key passage towards the end of his judgment, he stated as follows:

"When the special verdict is returned, the court has no function of inquiry into the mental state of the former accused; that role is given to the executive. Pursuant to sub-s.2, the only order that could lawfully be made was an order that the accused be kept in custody as a criminal lunatic in such place and in such manner as the court should direct; immediately after the making of the order, or 'thereupon' as stated in the sub-section, the role of the executive arose—to provide an appropriate place for the safe custody of the accused in such place and in such manner as the executive thought appropriate, until such time as the executive was satisfied that having regard to the *mental health* of the accused it was, for both public and private considerations, safe to release him. In that sense, the role of the executive, on the making of the judicial order, became like unto the role of the executive in s.165 of the Mental Treatment Act, 1945. When the constitutional validity of that section was challenged in *In Re Philip Clarke* [1950] I.R. 235, as permitting detention without the intervention of the judicial power, the challenge was rejected. No

---

[1] See Darius Whelan, *Criminal Procedure and Mental Health*, Ph.D. thesis, Trinity College Dublin, 2000, Chapter 4; Cases considered below; *Application of Ellis* [1990] 2 I.R. 291; *Gallagher v Director of Central Mental Hospital*, High Court, Barron J., December 16, 1994.
[2] [1990] 2 I.R. 267; [1991] I.L.R.M. 184.
[3] [1991] 1 I.R. 31.

criticism has been levied against the Supreme Court of Justice in *Clarke*'s case.

If and when a person detained pursuant to s.2, sub-s.2 of the Act of 1883 seeks to secure his release from detention, as in the instant case, he may apply to the executive, as has been done in the instant case, for his release on the grounds that he is not suffering from any *mental disorder* warranting his continued detention in the public and private interests; then the executive, in the person of the Government or the Minister for Justice, as may be, must inquire into all of the relevant circumstances. In doing so, it must use fair and constitutional procedures. Such an inquiry and its consequence may be the subject of judicial review so as to ensure compliance with such procedures".[4]

This passage influenced the terms of reference of the advisory committees which were set up to advise the Minister on applications for release. It is also important that McCarthy J. refers to "mental health" in the first paragraph and "mental disorder" in the second paragraph.

18–02 The executive established three-person committees, consisting of a senior counsel, a general practitioner and a psychiatrist, to consider applications for release by patients who had been found "guilty but insane". The committees advised the Minister for Justice, who made the decisions on release. In *Kirwan v Minister for Justice*[5] it was held that legal aid must be granted to patients applying to a committee for their release.

In *Application of Gallagher (No.2)*,[6] the applicant brought an application under Art.40.4 of the Constitution, arguing that he was no longer in lawful detention, as he now had a personality disorder rather than a mental disorder and this was not sufficient to justify his continued detention. He also challenged a nine-month delay in implementation by the Minister of a recommendation by an advisory committee. Mr Maguire, who was the uncle and brother-in-law of the two people who had been killed by Mr Gallagher, sought to be represented at the Art.40.4 hearing, but this application was denied.[7]

The Divisional Court of the High Court, in *Gallagher (No.2)*, refused the application for release under Art.40.4. As part of its reasoning, the court focused on the reference to *mental health* in *Gallagher (No.1)* and held that it was lawful to continue the detention of a person in the Central Mental Hospital (CMH) if they had a personality disorder, as was the case with Mr Gallagher. Laffoy J. stated that the task was to determine whether by reason of mental ill-health the person currently constituted such a risk to public or to self that they should be detained. She said that mental ill-health in this context encompasses all forms of mental illness and disorder recognised by psychiatry: major illnesses, such as

---

4   [1991] 1 I.R. 31 at 38. Emphasis added.
5   [1994] 2 I.R. 417; [1994] 1 I.L.R.M. 444.
6   [1996] 3 I.R. 10.
7   *Application of Maguire* [1996] 3 I.R. 1.

schizophrenia and manic depression; lesser mental illnesses or neuroses; and personality disorders.[8]

The court also held that the Trial of Lunatics Act 1883 did not permit detention while a person was dangerous but did not have a mental disorder or personality disorder, saying that this would be preventative detention, which is unconstitutional.[9]

18–03 In the later case of *Reid v UK*,[10] a case concerning an applicant with anti-social personality disorder or psychopathic disorder, the European Court of Human Rights ruled that a patient need not be "treatable" in order to be detained under art.5(1)(e).[11]

18–04 The advisory committee procedure was open to challenge under the European Convention on Human Rights (ECHR), as it was not sufficiently independent of the executive. Article 5(4) requires that everyone who is deprived of their liberty by arrest or detention should be entitled to take proceedings by which the lawfulness of their detention will be decided speedily by a court and their release ordered if the detention is not lawful. The "court" must be independent of the executive,[12] but under the advisory committee procedure, the Minister, rather than the committee, made the decision on release.

18–05 One of the major changes introduced by the Criminal Law (Insanity) Act 2006 was the establishment of the Mental Health (Criminal Law) Review Board, which has the function of reviewing periodically the detention of persons found not guilty by reason of insanity, found unfit for trial or transferred from prison to the CMH for treatment.

COMPOSITION OF THE REVIEW BOARD

18–06 Schedule 1 provides that the Mental Health (Criminal Law) Review Board consists of a chairperson and members. The number of members is set by the Minister for Justice, Equality and Law Reform, having consulted the Minister for Health and Children. The chairperson must be a practising solicitor or barrister of 10 years' standing or a current or former judge of the Circuit Court, High Court or Supreme Court. The ordinary members must include at least one consultant psychiatrist. The members hold office for terms of five

---

[8]　*Application of Gallagher (No.2)* [1996] 3 I.R. 10 at 34.
[9]　[1996] 3 I.R. 10 at 18–19 (Geoghegan J.) and 34 (Laffoy J.) On preventative detention see *People (Attorney General) v O'Callaghan* [1966] I.R. 501; *Ryan v DPP* [1989] I.R. 399; *People (DPP) v Jackson*, Court of Criminal Appeal, April 26, 1993.
[10]　(2003) 37 E.H.R.R. 9.
[11]　See further para.3–11 above.
[12]　*X. v UK* (1981) 4 E.H.R.R. 188.

years, which are renewable. Staff may be appointed to assist the review board, and it establishes its own rules of procedure. The first members of the Mental Health (Criminal Law) Review Board, appointed in 2006, were Mr Justice Brian McCracken as Chairperson, Dr Michael Mulcahy, a Consultant Psychiatrist and Mr Tim Dalton, a former Secretary General of the Department of Justice, Equality and Law Reform. The board's website is at *http://www.mhclrb.ie* [Accessed October 20, 2009].

18–07 The Minister for Justice, Equality and Law Reform appoints the members of the review board. The Minister may also remove them for stated reasons, after consultation with the Minister for Health and Children.[13] Senator Henry commented during the Oireachtas debates on the Bill which became the 2006 Act:

> "[T]he Minister has the power to choose the members of the review boards envisaged in this legislation. Worse still, he has the power to remove them. As we always say, we are not worried about the present Minister but that we may not always have as reasonable and rational a Minister in the future. Such a Minister might not be so careful and cautious in appointing individuals to the review boards and in removing them if they act in a way he does not consider desirable. I am therefore sorry the review boards are not more like those envisaged in the mental health legislation".[14]

18–08 The National Disability Authority was concerned that the provision for the Minister to appoint the membership of the review board did not meet the requirements of the ECHR for the review system to be independent of the executive.[15] However, if a challenge were brought on that basis, strong arguments could be made that the members of the review board are independent of the Minister in their decision making, even though they are appointed by the Minister, just as judges are independent of the Government which appoints them. Reference would also be made to the statutory requirement of independence in s.11(2) of the 2006 Act.

18–09 The Mental Health Commission believed that the composition of the review board should be standardised and that it could be deemed fundamentally unfair that the composition of such boards would vary and questions about its independence could also be raised. The Commission also stated that the board

---

[13] Criminal Law (Insanity) Act 2006, Sch.1.

[14] 183 *Seanad Debates* Col.623 (April 6, 2006).

[15] National Disability Authority, *Submission to the Department of Justice, Equality and Law Reform on the Criminal Law (Insanity) Bill 2002*, May 2003. Similarly, the Irish Human Rights Commission recommended a more transparent appointments process: Irish Human Rights Commission, *Observations on the Criminal Law (Insanity) Bill 2002*, September 2003.

membership should include two consultant psychiatrists and two people from a senior mental health background, in addition to the chairperson.[16]

18–10 Section 11 provides that the Mental Health (Criminal Law) Review Board must be independent, have regard to patients' welfare and safety and have regard to the public interest. Minister McDowell refused to accept an amendment which would state that the patient's best interests were the principal consideration.[17]

Minister McDowell insisted that this review board needed to be separate from the Mental Health Tribunals (MHTs) established by the Mental Health Act 2001. He argued that the function of the review board would be a much more public one than that of the civil tribunals and "it will be subject to absolutely searing media scrutiny if anything goes wrong".[18]

FUNCTIONS OF THE REVIEW BOARD

18–11 Section 13 of the 2006 Act requires the review board to review the detention of a person found not guilty by reason of insanity or unfit for trial at least every six months. The board also reviews the cases of prisoners transferred from prison to a designated centre[19] and the cases of all patients detained in the CMH under the pre-2006 law.[20]

18–12 It is possible to amalgamate the main categories of case provided for in ss.13 and 17 into nine categories as follows:

- Section 13(3)[21] concerns unfitness for trial cases where the clinical director forms the view that the patient is no longer unfit to be tried, in which case the matter goes back before the court. In such cases, the review board does not become involved.
- Sections 13(4)–(5): This is where the clinical director forms the opinion that the patient, although still unfit to be tried, is no longer in need of in-patient care or treatment. The review board must review the case.

---

[16] Mental Health Commission, *Second Submission on the Criminal Law (Insanity) Bill 2002*, May 2003.
[17] 616 *Dáil Debates* Col.2064 (March 23, 2006).
[18] 176 *Seanad Debates* Col.366 (April 8, 2004).
[19] Criminal Law (Insanity) Act 2006, s.17. As the CMH is currently the only designated centre, references to a designated centre and the CMH will be used interchangeably.
[20] Criminal Law (Insanity) Act 2006, s.20 and s.17(5).
[21] References to subsection numbers of s.13 are to the subsections as originally enacted. Note that s.13(1) of the 2006 Act was repealed by s.197 of the Criminal Justice Act 2006 and this amendment took effect on August 1, 2006. As consequential amendments, subss.(2)–(10) were renumbered as subss.(1)–(9) .

- Sections 13(6)–(7): Here, the clinical director believes that a patient found not guilty by reason of insanity is no longer in need of in-patient care or treatment. The board must review the case.
- Sections 13(8)–(9): This is where a patient who has been found unfit to be tried applies to the board for a review of their case.
- Section 13(9): A patient found not guilty by reason of insanity seeks to initiate a review by the board.
- Section 13(10): The board may on its own initiative review detention of a patient found unfit to be tried or not guilty by reason of insanity.
- Section 17(1) permits the Minister to direct a review of the detention of a prisoner transferred to the CMH from a prison where the Minister is satisfied that it is in the interests of justice to do so. This only applies to detentions under s.15(2) or s.15(5)(a), i.e. cases where the prisoner did not consent to the transfer, or refused to receive care or treatment there for mental disorder.
- Under s.17(3), a prisoner who has been transferred to the CMH may apply for a review.
- Section 17(4) permits the review board itself to initiate a review of the detention of a prisoner who has been transferred to the CMH.

18–13 The review board must review each patient's detention at such intervals, not more than six months, as it considers appropriate. During 2008, the Board held 150 hearings (including second and subsequent hearings).[22] As can be seen from the list of categories above, depending on the category of case, a review may be initiated if the patient applies for it, if the clinical director or the Minister notifies the board, or of the board's own initiative.

18–14 For each category of case, the powers of the review board are laid down in the relevant subsection. The powers of the review board are extensive, e.g. under s.13(9), if it reviews the case of a patient found not guilty by reason of insanity, it can make such order as it thinks proper, whether for further detention, care or treatment, or for discharge whether unconditionally or subject to conditions for out-patient treatment or supervision, or both.

By way of contrast, the MHTs which review the cases of patients detained under civil legislation do not have powers to discharge patients with conditions; their primary function is either to affirm or revoke the Admission Order or Renewal Order.[23]

18–15 In one respect, the powers of the review board are narrower than the MHTs. The review board may only review the substance of the patient's detention (e.g. whether they continue to require in-patient care and treatment); it may not consider any procedural matters, such as whether there has been compliance with the statutory provisions concerning detention of a person found

---

[22] Statistics on Mental Health (Criminal Law) Review Board website.
[23] Mental Health Act 2001, s.18. See para.9–11 above.

unfit for trial. It is arguable under the ECHR that the review board should have the power to review both procedural and substantive matters, because it was held in the *Winterwerp* case that the term "lawful" in art.5(4) covers conformity with procedural as well as substantive rules.[24]

18–16 Before the board's hearing on the matter, there is no statutory requirement of a report of an independent psychiatrist concerning the patient's mental condition, unlike the situation under the civil legislation.[25]

18–17 There are two statutory provisions concerning the board's procedures. Schedule 1, para.13 states that the review board will establish its own rules of procedure. Section 12(6) states that the procedure *for reviews* must be such as is determined by the board with the consent of the Minister for Justice, Equality and Law Reform. Reading these two provisions together, it appears that the more important rules of the board, concerning reviews under the Act, must be set with the consent of the Minister. It is only as regards matters other than reviews that the Board sets its own rules without Ministerial consent. This might cover, for example, procedures concerning administrative meetings of the Board, as opposed to reviews.

The Irish Human Rights Commission referred to s.12(6) as a ministerial "veto" which should have been removed.[26] In response, Minister Fahey said, "Section [12(6)] requires the Review Board to make specific provision in its review procedures for the matters listed. The inclusion of the requirement for the Minister's consent to the procedures is merely to ensure that these matters are specifically addressed. The Review Board will be fully independent in how it undertakes its review functions".[27] Minister McDowell refused to accept an amendment which would have required the board to lay down its procedures by regulations.[28]

18–18 Section 12 provides that the review board holds sittings at which it may receive submissions and such evidence as it thinks fit. The sittings are held in private. A patient will not be required to attend if such attendance might be prejudicial to their mental health, well-being or emotional condition. The board must take account of the court record (if any) and assign a legal representative to the patient. It may direct arrangement of the attendance of the patient, direct witnesses to attend and produce documents, and give any other reasonable and just directions. Expenses of witnesses called by the board will be paid by the

---

[24] *Winterwerp v The Netherlands* (1979) 2 E.H.R.R. 387, para.39. See further paras 9–15 to 9–16 above.

[25] See Mental Health Act 2001, s.17, discussed at paras 7–16 to 7–20 above.

[26] Irish Human Rights Commission, *Observations on the Criminal Law (Insanity) Bill 2002* (2003), p.9.

[27] 610 *Dáil Debates* Col.76 (November 15, 2005).

[28] 616 *Dáil Debates* Col.2068 (March 23, 2006).

board. Various offences are created by s.12(4), e.g. refusal to answer a question to which the board may legally require an answer, or failure to produce a document legally required by the board to be produced.

The board must make provision for notifying the treating psychiatrist and the patient of the review, giving the patient a copy of relevant documents, enabling the patient and their legal representative to be present, enabling the Minister, the DPP and, where appropriate, the Minister for Defence to be heard, enabling written statements to be admissible with the patient's consent and examination of witnesses on oath or otherwise.[29]

18–19 The board has made rules of procedure which are available on its website. The rules of procedure provide, for example, that the review board shall notify the consultant psychiatrist responsible for the care or treatment of the patient who is the subject of the review, and the patient and their legal representative, of the date, time and place of the relevant sitting of the board at least 14 days before the date scheduled. The review board shall give the patient the subject of the review and their legal representative a copy of any document furnished to the board and an indication in writing of the nature and source of any information relating to the matter which shall have come to notice in the course of the review. The Minister for Justice, Equality and Law Reform, the DPP and, where appropriate, the Minister for Defence, shall be entitled to be heard or represented at all sittings of the review board. For this purpose, a notification of the date, time and place of the relevant sitting of the review oard shall issued at least 14 days before the date scheduled for the review.

Written statements shall be admissable as evidence by the review board with the consent of the patient who is the subject of the review or their legal representative. If a patient or their legal representatives intend to submit evidence from a medical practitioner at a hearing, a report in writing from such medical practitioner shall be furnished to the board at least five working days prior to the date of the hearing. Where emergency situations arise during the course of a review hearing, such as a patient becoming physically ill or emotionally distressed, the review board shall ensure that appropriate measures are put in place to deal with such situations.

Decisions of the board and the reasons therefore shall, whenever reasonably possible, be given on the day of the review hearing or, if not possible, within 14 working days. Such decisions shall be conveyed to the patient who is the subject of the review, their legal representative, the Director of the CMH, the DPP and the Minister for Justice, Equality and Law Reform or the Minister for Defence as appropriate. The review board may delegate to the Chief Executive Officer such administrative functions as it considers appropriate. The expenses of witnesses directed to attend before the review board shall be paid by the board out of moneys at its disposal. The expenses payable will be equivalent to the expenses payable to witnesses summoned to attend before the High Court.

---

[29] Criminal Law (Insanity) Act 2006, s.12(6).

18–20 Minister Fahey commented on the provision in s.14(6) permitting the Minister to be heard: "Provision is made in section [12(6)] for the Minister for Justice, Equality and Law Reform, the Director of Public Prosecutions and the Minister for Defence to be heard or represented at sittings of the review board. In the Minister's view, these provisions will ensure that issues relating to the protection of the public will always be kept very much to the fore when the review board is required to consider the possible release of such persons."[30] However, the Irish Human Rights Commission suggested that s.12(6)(e), allowing the Minister or DPP to be represented at sittings of the Mental Health (Criminal Law) Review Board, be removed.[31]

18–21 The board must also make provision for a scheme for legal aid to patients and the Terms and Conditions of the Legal Aid Scheme are available on the board's website. There are currently 29 solicitors on the legal representatives panel, as listed on the board's website. Automatic representation by lawyers is a positive feature of the Act in human rights terms.

18–22 It appears that only the review board and the patient may call witnesses and examine and cross-examine them.[32] This implies that the patient is the only party at the hearing, a situation which also occurs with the MHTs established for civil cases by the Mental Health Act 2001.[33]

18–23 The Act is silent on the question of the burden of proof in review board hearings, but ECHR case law would require that the burden of proof should not be placed on the patient.[34]

Every question at a sitting of the review board is to be determined by a majority vote, with the chairperson having a casting vote.[35]

There is no statutory appeal from the board's decisions. By way of contrast, a decision of a civil MHT may be appealed to the Circuit Court on the grounds that the person is not suffering from a mental disorder.[36]

The review board does not publish summaries of its decisions in its annual report or on its website, and it is arguable that selected decisions need to be made available to assist legal representatives in preparing cases.[37]

---

[30] 610 *Dáil Debates* Col.77 (November 15, 2005).
[31] Irish Human Rights Commission, *Observations on the Criminal Law (Insanity) Bill 2002* (2003), p.13.
[32] Criminal Law (Insanity) Act 2006, s.12(6)(h) and (i).
[33] See paras 8–01 and 8–19 above.
[34] See paras 8–32 to 8–34 above.
[35] Criminal Law (Insanity) Act 2006, Sch.1, para.12.
[36] Mental Health Act 2001, s.19, discussed at paras 7–71 to 7–76 above.
[37] See discussion at para.7–14 above of *P.P.A. v. Refugee Appeals Tribunal* [2006] I.E.S.C. 53; [2007] 4 I.R. 94.

18–24 As a public body, the Mental Health (Criminal Law) Review Board is subject to judicial review. As a result, it needs to comply carefully with principles of natural and constitutional justice such as *nemo iudex in causa sua, audi alteram partem* and the duty to give adequate reasons for decisions.[38]

Minister McDowell refused to accept an amendment stating that the review board would be covered by the Freedom of Information Acts 1997–2003, stating that this could be done by order (of the Minister for Finance) after the Act was passed. He said that the question as to whether documents of the board should be the subject of Freedom of Information (FOI) accessibility was one on which he would have to think long and hard, and he would like to take into account actual experience before making them such. He said that he would bring it to the attention of the appropriate Minister.[39]

TIMING OF REVIEWS

18–25 The review board must review all cases at intervals of such length, not being more than six months, as it considers appropriate.[40] The Irish Human Rights Commission criticised the six-month period as too lengthy and recommended that it be shortened to three months.[41]

If the patient requests a review, the board must hold a hearing "as soon as may be", unless it is satisfied that the review is not necessary due to a review already undertaken.[42]

European case law on "speediness" of reviews has been considered above at paras 7–25 to 7–26. However, it should be noted that the Strasbourg court is more tolerant of longer intervals between reviews in the case of persons charged with criminal offences who have been detained based on a court order.

The court has held that where a court initially orders detention, judicial review for the purposes of art.5(4) is incorporated in that decision, and the right to further judicial review arises later. In *Rocha v Portugal*,[43] the court said that the initial court order lasts only for a period of time that is proportional to the gravity of the offence. It was held that a person found not guilty by reason of insanity on a charge of intentional homicide could be detained under art.5(1)(a) for three years given the seriousness of the offence and the risk to the public, but the applicant then had the right to further judicial review.

---

[38] See discussion regarding MHTs at paras 8–09 to 8–25 above.
[39] Select Committee on Justice, Equality, Defence and Women's Rights, January 18, 2006.
[40] Criminal Law (Insanity) Act 2006, s.13(2).
[41] Irish Human Rights Commission, *Observations on the Criminal Law (Insanity) Bill 2002* (2003), p.10.
[42] Criminal Law (Insanity) Act 2006, s.13(8) and s.13(9).
[43] (2001) 32 E.H.R.R. 16.

However, in *Kolanis v UK*[44] a breach of art.5(4) was found where the applicant, who had been convicted of serious assault, did not have access to review of her detention for over a year.

There is no statutory requirement that the review board be informed that a person has been detained at a designated centre under the Act. McGillicuddy has commented that this is an omission from the Act, as such a provision would have assisted the board in ensuring that it reviewed all relevant cases every six months.[45]

CONDITIONAL DISCHARGE

18–26 A key difference between the civil MHTs and the Mental Health (Criminal Law) Review Board is that the civil MHTs may only affirm or revoke the detention order, whereas the review board has a number of options available to it, including conditional discharge. The precise wording of the Act refers to a discharge "subject to conditions for out-patient treatment or supervision or both".[46]

18–27 In England, the power of conditional discharge has been the subject of a number of cases.[47] For example, in *R. (S.H.) v Mental Health Review Tribunal*,[48] a tribunal had ordered the patient's conditional discharge, with one of the conditions being that he comply with medication prescribed by a specific doctor. The patient argued that the condition ought to be quashed because it interfered with his common law right of autonomy as regards whether he accepted or refused medical treatment. He also argued that it interfered with his right to privacy under art.8 of the ECHR. Holman J. stated that a person with mental capacity had the absolute right to choose whether to accept medical treatment, as did S.H. when he presented himself for medical treatment. In deciding whether to consent, the patient would be liable to take into account the imperative of the condition, just as he would take into account strong advice from a relative or a doctor in any such decision. The tribunal would not impose such a condition unless it had anticipated that the patient did consent to taking the treatment in question. It was the continuing conditional nature of the

---

[44] (2006) 42 E.H.R.R. 12.
[45] Tony McGillicuddy, "The Criminal Law (Insanity) Bill 2002", document dated April 2, 2006 available on Bar Council website, at *http://www.lawlibrary.ie/documents/legal%20commentary/ insanity.doc* [last accessed October 21, 2009], pp.12–13.
[46] For example, under s.13(9) the board may "make such order as it thinks proper in relation to the patient whether for further detention, care or treatment in a designated centre or for his or her discharge whether unconditionally or subject to conditions for out-patient treatment or supervision or both".
[47] See generally Richard Jones, *Mental Health Act Manual*, 11th edn (London: Thomson Sweet and Maxwell, 2008), pp.372–385.
[48] [2007] E.W.H.C. Admin. 884; [2007] M.H.L.R. 234.

patient's discharge which might pressurise him into consenting, rather than the condition itself. S.H. had made clear from first to last that he did wish to take the medication, was indeed eager to do so, and did consent to it on every occasion. Further, there was no discrete challenge at all in 2005–2006 to a continuation of the condition if his discharge was to remain conditional. In those circumstances, there was no infringement at all of his absolute right to choose. It was eminently justifiable to attach the condition, or continue to attach it, and the decisions of the tribunal were not unlawful or in violation of the rights of S.H. under art 8(1). If the condition did breach art.8(1), it was justifiable and proportionate within art.8(2), and adequate procedural rights were provided in the form of the tribunal hearing before the condition was imposed, and the right to a further hearing if there was a recall merely for a breach of the condition. Holman J. ended his judgment by stating that in his view it would be preferable for a tribunal, when imposing a condition similar to the one in this case, to add some words such as "subject always to his right to give or withhold consent to treatment or medication on any given occasion".[49]

18–28 If the review board orders the discharge of the patient subject to conditions under s.13 of the 2006 Act, there is no statutory power for any person or body to recall the patient to the designated centre if they breach those conditions. As a result, the board appears to have decided not to release any patient subject to conditions, until amending legislation is passed.[50] Naturally, this raises serious issues of constitutional rights and human rights, as it would appear to interfere with patients' right to liberty. On a practical level, it also "blocks" beds in the CMH which could otherwise be occupied by other patients in need of treatment.

However, it is possible for the clinical director, with the consent of the Minister, to direct the temporary release of a patient under s.14 on such conditions and for such periods as the clinical director deems appropriate.[51] Section 14 states that a patient must comply with any conditions to which their release is made subject[52] and if they break the conditions, they are deemed unlawfully at large and may be arrested.[53]

18–29 There have been two notable European Court of Human Rights cases concerning conditional discharge. In *Johnson v UK*[54] Mr Johnson was convicted

---

[49] [2007] M.H.L.R. 234, para.42.
[50] See "Flaw in Law Traps Patients", *Sunday Times*, January 27, 2008; "Department Warned of Flaw in Law on Releases", *Irish Examiner*, January 29, 2008; 645 *Dáil Debates* 693, January 31, 2008; "Legislative Error Denies Release to Mental Patients", *Sunday Business Post*, April 6, 2008.
[51] Criminal Law (Insanity) Act 2006, s.14(1).
[52] Criminal Law (Insanity) Act 2006, s.14(4).
[53] Criminal Law (Insanity) Act 2006, s.14(5)–(7).
[54] (1997) 27 E.H.R.R. 296.

of actual bodily harm in 1984. While he was on remand, a diagnosis of schizophrenia superimposed on psychopathic personality was made. Following the conviction, the court made a hospital and restriction order. In June 1989, a tribunal ordered his conditional discharge to hostel accommodation, as he was no longer suffering from a mental disorder, but deferred this until accommodation was found. There were great difficulties in finding a suitable hostel place for Mr Johnson. In April 1991, the tribunal made the same order again. Eventually, in January 1993 a tribunal ordered his unconditional discharge. The European Court of Human Rights found a breach of art.5(1) and awarded £10,000 damages plus £25,000 legal costs.

The court said that a responsible authority is entitled to exercise discretion in deciding whether in the light of all the relevant circumstances and the interests at stake it would be appropriate to order the immediate and absolute discharge of a person who is no longer suffering from the mental disorder which led to their confinement. That authority should be able to retain some measure of supervision over the progress of the person once they are released into the community and to that end make their discharge subject to conditions. It could not be excluded either that the imposition of a particular condition might in certain circumstances justify a deferral of discharge from detention having regard to the nature of the condition and to the reasons for imposing it.[55] The court continued:

> "It is, however, of paramount importance that appropriate safeguards are in place so as to ensure that any deferral of discharge is consonant with the purpose of Article 5(1) and with the aim of the restriction in sub-paragraph (e) and, in particular, that discharge is not unreasonably delayed."[56]

Bartlett and Sandland have commented that the *Johnson* case illustrates how the court is strong on due process rights but weak on substantive issues. They believe that the case gives "an extraordinarily conservative reading of the phrase 'person of unsound mind' in Article 5.1(e)".[57] In a sense, their comment echoes the Irish position in *Gallagher (No.2)* that a person cannot be detained if they no longer have a mental disorder.[58]

18–30 The applicant in *Kolanis v UK*[59] was convicted of serious assault, had a mental illness and was detained in a psychiatric hospital. She applied for discharge to a Mental Health Review Tribunal (MHRT), which decided on conditional discharge, the conditions being that she should live at home with her

---

[55] (1997) 27 E.H.R.R. 296, para.63.
[56] (1997) 27 E.H.R.R. 296, para.63.
[57] Peter Bartlett & Ralph Sandland, *Mental Health Law: Policy and Practice*, 3rd edn (Oxford: Oxford University Press, 2007), p.29.
[58] See above, para.18–02.
[59] (2006) 42 E.H.R.R. 12.

parents, be supervised by a social worker and a psychiatrist and comply with her treatment. The authorities did not find a psychiatrist in the area who was willing to supervise Ms Kolanis in the community. The court held that art.5(1) was not violated, as Ms Kolanis continued to have a mental illness which justified detention. However, there was a breach of art.5(4) as, even where there are difficulties in fulfilling a conditional discharge, the applicant was entitled to a review of the detention. For over a year, she had no access to a review of her detention.

18–31 An opportunity to consider the law concerning conditional discharge under the 2006 Act arose in *J.B. v Mental Health (Criminal Law) Review Board and Others*.[60] J.B. killed his five-year-old daughter in 2000 while he had severe mental illness. In 2002, he was found guilty but insane. His case had been reviewed a number of times by the Mental Health (Criminal Law) Review Board. Following assessment by his doctors, he was on temporary release under s.14 and lived with his family four nights a week, spending the remaining three in a low-security hostel on the grounds of the CMH. He was employed as a warehouse operative. In 2007, the review board found that he "[did] not currently suffer from a mental disorder".[61]

The review board and the medical team treating him would only release him with conditions attached, and he said he would be happy to abide by such conditions. The psychiatrists agreed that the conditions under which the applicant should be released included residing with his family, abstaining from excess drugs or alcohol, attending for regular appointments, complying with medication, accepting random visits, limiting his working week to 39 hours and not having sole responsibility for children. The board submitted it was entitled to refuse to discharge him on the grounds that the conditions could not be imposed by it and could not be enforced. J.B. sought various reliefs by way of judicial review, e.g. a declaration that he was entitled to be discharged subject to such conditions as might be deemed appropriate by the board.

18–32 Hanna J. said that it was clearly the intention of the Oireachtas that, although conditions might well be imposed on a discharge order, no means were to be available to enforce these conditions. While he had been invited to interpret the Act purposefully in order to infer some sort of enforcement regime into the Act, that would amount to legislating and would offend the principle of separation of powers.[62] Hanna J. believed that J.B. was at liberty to a degree commensurate with his medical needs and the public interest.[63]

---

[60] [2008] I.E.H.C. 303; Hanna J., High Court, July 25, 2008.
[61] [2008] I.E.H.C. 303, p.4.
[62] [2008] I.E.H.C. 303, p.22.
[63] [2008] I.E.H.C. 303, p.23.

In considering the Irish law on the issues in the case, Hanna J. does not refer to preventative detention issues, or the fact that in *Gallagher (No.2)*[64] it had been held that detention may only be continued on the grounds of mental ill-health and risk. The decision in *J.B.* seems inconsistent with the principles established in *Gallagher (No.2)* and a more detailed comparison of the principles of Irish law applicable would have been helpful.[65] There is emphasis in *J.B.* on the fact that the applicant was on temporary release four nights a week, but that does not change the fact that he was being detained three nights a week, even if it was in the low-security hostel in the grounds of the CMH. On the principles in *Gallagher (No.2)*, it is not permissible to detain a person on grounds of risk alone, but J.B.'s detention may be regarded as such, as the board had found that he was no longer suffering from a mental disorder.

18–33 Turning to the European Convention arguments, Hanna J. followed the *Johnson* case closely and found that the applicant's current state did not offend against the ECHR. He noted that this case differed from *Johnson*, in that the applicant here was living under very different conditions, spending the majority of his time with his family, and he said that the applicant had been afforded a significant measure of liberty.[66]

However, Hanna J. does not address the issue of delay as considered in the *Johnson* case. It will be recalled that, even though the court in *Johnson* held that a person's release may be delayed while suitable accommodation is sought, the court also held that there must not be an unreasonable delay in this. Mr Johnson was awarded compensation due to the delay in his release. The court did not give long-term licence for detention of people who no longer have a mental disorder. In J.B.'s case, if he continued to be detained three days a week for a number of months or years, this would appear to conflict with *Johnson* and ought to have been considered in the *J.B.* case. Hanna J. did say at one stage that he hoped the matter would evolve to a situation where J.B. could be released on informal conditions and then progress to full release.[67]

18–34 The Government has circulated the Heads of a Bill to amend the Criminal Law (Insanity) Act 2006 to address the gap in the Act concerning conditional discharge. While the Heads of the Bill have not been made public, the Human Rights Commission's observations on them have.[68] It would appear that the Bill proposes that if a person breaches the conditions in their conditional discharge as ordered by the review board, the person will be regarded as unlawfully at large and may be arrested.

---

[64] [1996] 3 I.R. 10.

[65] While there are some references to *Gallagher (No.2)*, they are on other points, not the question of preventative detention.

[66] [2008] I.E.H.C. 303, p.29.

[67] [2008] I.E.H.C. 303, p.29.

[68] Irish Human Rights Commission, *Observations on the Scheme of the Criminal Law (Insanity) Act 2006 (Amendment) Bill 2008* (November 2008).

The Irish Human Rights Commission has suggested that the Bill should state that the conditions should be reasonable, proportionate and within the power of the person to fulfil. In addition, the Bill should state that the review board should be able to review the conditions on the above grounds.[69]

---

[69]   Irish Human Rights Commission, *Observations on the Scheme of the Criminal Law (Insanity) Act 2006 (Amendment) Bill 2008* (November 2008), p.10.

CHAPTER 19

MENTAL HEALTH AND OTHER ASPECTS OF CRIMINAL LAW

DIVERSION FROM THE CRIMINAL JUSTICE SYSTEM

19–01 In Ireland, there has been very little discussion of the complex issue of diversion from the criminal justice system for those with mental disorders. The basic aim of diversion as a concept is to identify persons with mental disorders who come into contact with the criminal justice system and, where appropriate, ensure that they are treated in a psychiatric setting, whether residential or non-residential, rather than prosecuted for the alleged offence. Diversion can occur in a number of ways. A Garda might decide to have a person who has been arrested for a minor offence assessed by a psychiatrist and, on receiving the assessment, decide not to proceed with charges. A Garda who has exercised the power of detention under s.12 of the 2001 Act[1] might make a similar decision. If a file were sent to the DPP's office, charges might also be dropped at that stage. Once the person appears in court, the judge might facilitate diversion in some way as well. Even if the person is convicted of a crime, a non-custodial sentence may operate as de facto diversion.

19–02 As a matter of policy, the question of whether to divert or not is a difficult one and "[e]ach such individual represents, in microcosm, the dilemma of policy: treatment or punishment?"[2] On a medicalised view of mental disorder, the tendency would be towards treatment, but on a criminalised model, the tendency would be towards punishment. Matters are complicated by the difficulty of balancing the offender's need for treatment and right to liberty against society's need for protection from the risk of harm (even though only a small minority of people with mental disorder pose a risk to society).

19–03 The World Health Organisation's Resource Book on Mental Health, Human Rights and Legislation recommends that legislation should allow for diversion from the criminal justice system to the mental health system at all stages—from the time a person is first arrested and detained by the police,

---

[1] See paras 4–69 to 4–82 above. See also Mental Health Commission and An Garda Síochána, *Report of Joint Working Group on Mental Health Services and the Police* (2009).

[2] Peter Bartlett & Ralph Sandland, *Mental Health Law: Policy and Practice*, 3rd edn (Oxford: Oxford University Press, 2007), p.202.

throughout the course of the criminal investigations and proceedings and even after the person has begun serving a sentence for a criminal offence.[3]

19–04 The *Vision for Change* report in 2006 recommended that every person with serious mental health problems coming into contact with the forensic system should be accorded the right of mental health care in the non-forensic mental health services unless there are cogent and legal reasons why this should not be done.[4] The report discussed the role of the Gardaí and the structure of the forensic mental health services. It also proposed that the forensic mental health services should be expanded and reconfigured so as to provide court diversion services, and that legislation should be devised to allow this to take place.[5]

19–05 At present, there is a Prison Inreach and Court Liaison Service (PICLS) in operation at Cloverhill Prison in Dublin, which helps identify prisoners with severe mental illness, assists the courts in diverting them towards appropriate treatment options and offers treatment services to remand prisoners with less severe forms of mental illness.[6] In 2008, 91 patients were diverted to more appropriate community settings (67 to a community mental health facility, 24 to general psychiatric hospitals).[7]

19–06 Minister of State Fahy stated in the Oireachtas debates on the Criminal Law (Insanity) Bill that while the Minister for Justice, Equality and Law Reform generally favoured moves to ensure the more appropriate placement of persons suffering from mental illness as defined in criminal law and elsewhere, the proposal to establish a mental health court involved major policy and resource issues for the Department of Justice, the Prison Service, the Courts Service and, especially, the Department of Health and Children. In the circumstances, the immediate priority was the early enactment of the Criminal Law (Insanity) Bill.[8]

19–07 In a 2006 discussion paper on forensic mental health services, the Mental Health Commission stated that legislation must provide for options, other than certification, whereby mentally disordered persons who present before the courts can be detained for assessment or treatment and that this should include mechanisms for facilitating treatment in the community.[9] The Commission recommended that mental health professionals, Gardaí, lawyers and the courts

---

[3]   Melvyn Freeman & Soumitra Pathare, *WHO Resource Book on Mental Health, Human Rights and Legislation* (Geneva: World Health Organization, 2005), p.75.
[4]   Expert Group on Mental Health Policy, *A Vision for Change* (Dublin, 2006), p.137.
[5]   Expert Group on Mental Health Policy, *A Vision for Change* (Dublin, 2006), p.140.
[6]   See Clare McInerney & Conor O'Neill, "Prison Psychiatric Inreach and Court Liaison Services in Ireland" (2008) 2 J.S.I.J. 147. See also Conor O'Neill, "Liaison Between Criminal Justice and Psychiatric Systems: Diversion Services" (2006) 23(3) *Irish Journal of Psychological Medicine* 87.
[7]   Irish Prison Service, *Annual Report 2008*, p.40.
[8]   610 *Dáil Debates* Col.81 (November 15, 2005).
[9]   Mental Health Commission, *Forensic Mental Health Services for Adults in Ireland*, Discussion Paper, 2006, p.50.

should have a comprehensive range of legislative and service options available to them in relation to mentally disordered people involved in criminal proceedings. It stated that services should be based on a nationally funded policy of diversion towards treatment and recovery options and away from punitive measures. The Commission outlined the potential scope of court diversion schemes and stated that the development of court diversion schemes would require further legislative change.[10]

19–08 A court diversion scheme does not necessarily need to involve the establishment of a "mental health court" as such, but such courts have been established in a number of jurisdictions and have been the subject of a great deal of commentary.[11] A mental health court would have some similarities to the Drug Court which has been operating in Dublin.[12] The Irish Penal Reform Trust (IPRT) recommended that the Government consider the idea of the establishment of a mental health court in 2001.[13] The National Crime Council has proposed the establishment of community courts, which would be able to refer persons to mental health services where appropriate.[14] More recently, a Working Group of the Mental Health Commission and An Garda Síochána has recommended that the introduction of a mental health court be examined. The group proposes that a mental health court or community court be introduced on a pilot basis initially, while noting that mental health courts are not a panacea, a comprehensive strategy is required and mental health courts are just one element of the overall strategy.[15]

CUSTODY REGULATIONS

19–09 If a person is arrested and is in Garda custody, the provisions of the 1987 Custody Regulations apply.[16] These include certain rights concerning consultation of a solicitor, interviews and information for arrested persons.

---

[10] Mental Health Commission, *Forensic Mental Health Services for Adults in Ireland*, Discussion Paper, 2006, pp.28–9 and p.50.

[11] Steven Erickson et al, "Variations in Mental Health Courts: Challenges, Opportunities, and a Call for Caution" (2006) 42 *Community Mental Health Journal* 335; Richard D. Schneider, Hy Bloom & Mark Heerema, *Mental Health Courts: Decriminalizing the Mentally Ill* (Toronto: Irwin Law, 2007); Allison D. Redlich et al, "Patterns of Practice in Mental Health Courts: A National Survey" (2006) 30 *Law and Human Behavior* 347

[12] Working Group on a Courts Commission, *Fifth Report: Drug Courts*, 1998; Farrell Grant Sparks, *Final Evaluation of the Pilot Drug Court* (Courts Service, 2002).

[13] Irish Penal Reform Trust, *Community Solutions to the Criminalisation of the Mentally Ill in Ireland* (2001).

[14] National Crime Council, *Problem Solving Justice: The Case for Community Courts in Ireland* (2007).

[15] Mental Health Commission & An Garda Síochána, *Report of Joint Working Group on Mental Health Services and the Police* (2009), p.21. See also literature review, pp.80–83.

[16] Criminal Justice Act 1984 (Treatment of Persons in Custody in Garda Síochána Stations)

The Regulations provide that if a person in custody appears to the member in charge to be suffering from a mental illness, the member in charge shall summon a doctor or cause them to be summoned, unless the person's condition appears to the member in charge to be such as to necessitate immediate removal to a hospital or other suitable place. The member in charge shall ensure that any instructions given by a doctor in relation to the medical care of a person in custody are complied with.[17]

19–10 Regulation 22 states that the provisions of the Regulations relating to persons under the age of 18[18] shall apply in relation to a person in custody not below that age "whom the member in charge suspects or knows to be mentally handicapped". There is no definition of "mentally handicapped".

The Regulations regarding persons under 18 state that in general an arrested person under 18 shall not be questioned in relation to an offence or asked to make a written statement unless a parent, spouse[19] or guardian is present.[20] The member in charge may give authority for the person to be questioned in the absence of a parent, spouse or guardian in certain circumstances, e.g. where no parent, spouse or guardian has attended at the station within a reasonable time. The member in charge should in those circumstances arrange for the presence of the other parent, another guardian, an adult relative or some other responsible adult other than a garda.[21] In the application of this regulation to a person suspected or known to be "mentally handicapped", the responsible adult shall, where practicable, be a person who has experience in dealing with "the mentally handicapped".[22]

Regulations 1987, S.I. No. 119 of 1987, as amended by Criminal Justice Act 1984 (Treatment of Persons in Custody in Garda Síochána Stations) (Amendment) Regulations 2006, S.I. No. 641 of 2006. See commentary in Anne Marie O'Neill, *Irish Mental Health Law* (Dublin: First Law, 2005), pp.427–8.

[17] Criminal Justice Act 1984 (Treatment of Persons in Custody in Garda Síochána Stations) Regulations 1987, S.I. No. 119 of 1987, Reg.21.

[18] The original version of the Regulations specified the age of 17, but this was raised to 18 by the Criminal Justice Act 1984 (Treatment of Persons in Custody in Garda Síochána Stations) (Amendment) Regulations 2006, S.I. No. 641 of 2006.

[19] Criminal Justice Act 1984 (Treatment of Persons in Custody in Garda Síochána Stations) Regulations 1987, S.I. No. 119 of 1987, Reg.13(5)(b), as amended, provides as follows: "This Regulation (other than paragraph (3)), in its application to a person under the age of [eighteen] years who is married to an adult, shall have effect with the substitution of references to the person's spouse for the references (other than those in subparagraphs (a), (b) and (c) of paragraph (2)) to a parent or guardian and as if 'a parent or guardian' were substituted for 'the other parent or another guardian' in each place where it occurs in those subparagraphs".

[20] Criminal Justice Act 1984 (Treatment of Persons in Custody in Garda Síochána Stations) Regulations 1987, S.I. No. 119 of 1987, Reg.13.

[21] Criminal Justice Act 1984 (Treatment of Persons in Custody in Garda Síochána Stations) Regulations 1987, S.I. No. 119 of 1987, Reg.13(2).

[22] Criminal Justice Act 1984 (Treatment of Persons in Custody in Garda Síochána Stations) Regulations 1987, S.I. No. 119 of 1987, Reg.22(2).

FITNESS TO BE INTERVIEWED

19–11 Following concerns raised about the confession by Dean Lyons to two murders he did not commit, a Commission of Investigation was established.[23] The sole member of the Commission was George Bermingham, S.C., who found that Mr Lyons was borderline mentally handicapped and had a history of having attended a special school. Psychological testing established that he was abnormally and exceptionally suggestible and that he had an abnormal tendency to give in to leading questions. He had a long track record of making up stories that were wholly false and being able to tell these stories in a convincing manner. One issue which arose was whether the Custody Regulations[24] were followed correctly, and whether a responsible adult should have been present during the questioning of Mr Lyons. The Commission concluded that it would be wholly unreal now, with the benefit of hindsight, to expect that the member in charge could have identified a problem during the course of the very few minutes that he would have had with Mr Lyons as he processed him at the hatch.[25] The Minister for Justice said that an Expert Group would consider, inter alia, the adequacy of Garda training, protocols, regulations and procedures, in assessing the fitness of persons to be interviewed.[26] In April 2009, it was reported that the Expert Group would issue its report in the near future.[27]

19–12 In *People (DPP) v Bukoshi*,[28] the court emphasised that the onus is on the prosecution to establish that statements made to Gardaí were given of free will. There was evidence regarding the mental health of the accused but the trial judge had chosen to reject this. The Court of Criminal Appeal set aside the conviction, holding that the trial judge was in error in admitting in evidence the statements, as the video evidence could not counterbalance the full strength of the medical evidence that was before the trial judge.

19–13 Dunne J. commented in *S.C. v Clinical Director, St Brigid's Hospital, Ardee, Co Louth*[29] that it had been unwise to allow Mr C. to be interviewed by the Gardaí when the doctor had serious concerns in relation to Mr C.'s mental

---

[23] *Report of the Commission of Investigation (Dean Lyons case): Set Up Pursuant to the Commissions of Investigation Act 2004; Sole Member George Birmingham, SC* (Dublin: Stationery Office, 2006).

[24] See above, paras 19–09 to 19–10.

[25] *Report of the Commission of Investigation (Dean Lyons case): Set Up Pursuant to the Commissions of Investigation Act 2004; Sole Member George Birmingham, SC* (Dublin: Stationery Office, 2006), pp.83–4. Note also similar concerns raised about the case of Nora Wall and Paul McCabe–Breda O'Brien, "Miscarriage of Justice: Paul McCabe and Nora Wall" (2006) 95 *Studies* 355.

[26] Press Release: "Minister McDowell Publishes Dean Lyons Case Report", Department of Justice, Equality and Law Reform, September 1, 2006.

[27] Dáil Éireann, Written Answer 14397/09, April 22, 2009.

[28] [2008] I.E.C.C.A. 31; Court of Criminal Appeal, February 25, 2008.

[29] [2009] I.E.H.C. 100; High Court, Dunne J., February 26, 2009.

state at the time. She noted that there was no evidence before her to indicate if Mr C. was in a fit state to be questioned by the Gardaí when the doctor examined him. See further paras 4–80 to 4–82 above.

THE ROLE OF A LAWYER IN ADVISING A CLIENT WITH MENTAL DISORDER

19–14 The Law Society has recently published a Practice Note on Advising Clients with Mental Disorders.[30] The Note states that the question of mental disorder and similar disabilities has monumental significance early in the criminal justice process. The likely first point of contact between a solicitor and a client with mental disorder is at the Garda station. Although the Custody Regulations made pursuant to the Criminal Justice Act 1984[31] make express reference to the requirement for medical treatment for detainees appearing to be suffering from a mental illness, the detection of mental illness risks becoming a random event. Bearing in mind their lack of formal training in medicine, solicitors should be alert to symptoms exhibited in thought, speech or action of the detained person. If concerns arise, instructions should be taken from the detainee as to whether they are currently under medical care or on medication.

19–15 The Note also states that it might be useful for the solicitor to be present during any medical consultation, to ensure that the history/examination by the doctor is confined to a "mental state" examination, rather than intruding upon the alleged or suspected offence. A solicitor in this situation is there only for the client, and to assist them in what may very well be a difficult and stressful time. Maintaining that stance may be difficult in the teeth of many conflicting and varied imperatives, but often in such a pressurised situation, the only source of solid support available to the client is their legal advisor. Only in the rarest of cases is the personal safety of the solicitor likely to be at issue. Practitioners should recognise that a remand in custody, ostensibly for reasons of mental ill health, signifies, at least prima facie, a committal to the prison system—an outcome that will have only by chance a beneficial result for the client, and which accordingly should be, subject of course to instructions, resisted.

19–16 In conclusion, the Note states that the critical factor is that the interests of the client are paramount. In only a tiny minority of cases is a solicitor entitled to withdraw from the case, not to follow instructions, or to divulge instructions. That minority of cases relate primarily to highly disturbed people who pose a threat of serious physical harm or worse to themselves or third parties. The Note states that there is a useful discussion of the applicable principles in the *Tarasoff*

---

[30] Law Society Practice Note, "Advising a Mentally Disordered Client" (2009) 103(6) Gaz.L.S.I. 44.

[31] See above, paras 19–09 to 19–10.

case[32]. Although that case refers to the duty/entitlement of a therapist to disclose alleged threats to a third party, such an entitlement, which is unlikely to arise in the lifetime of a practising solicitor, is fully endorsed by the Law Society.

MENTAL HEALTH IN SENTENCING

19–17 There is a general willingness on the part of the courts to reduce sentences for persons who have a mental disorder which impacted on their level of responsibility for what they did, even though the disorder may not have been severe enough to warrant an insanity verdict. As O'Malley indicates, it is difficult to reconcile the principle of justice (that the offender's reduced culpability is a mitigating factor) with that of incapacitation of the offender for the purposes of public protection. He suggests that a possible solution is to select punishment based on culpability, while leaving open the possibility of protective restraint during or after the sentence.[33]

19–18 In *People (DPP) v M.C.*[34] Mr C., who had manic depressive psychosis, pleaded guilty to charges of buggery and gross indecency. Flood J. imposed a sentence of six years, with the final four suspended. He made some important observations about the principles applicable in such a case. He said that the fact that an accused person suffers from a mental disorder does not permit a court to impose a sentence upon them greater than that which would have been imposed had the offender not been suffering from that condition. The concept of preventative detention is repugnant to our system of constitutional justice. Flood J. stated that the sentencing principle of general deterrence has little or no application where the court is sentencing a mentally disordered accused. He continued:

> "In my view, the question to be determined by the Court in sentencing a mentally disordered offender is whether the existence of this condition requires that the sentence to be imposed should be reduced from what would otherwise be appropriate. The existence of a mental disorder in an accused person frequently incorporates a potential for recovery, and in exceptional cases a cure. In my view, if it can be established, by expert medical evidence, that the rehabilitation of a mentally disordered accused can be facilitated by the imposition of a less restrictive sanction then the Court, in a proper case, is justified in imposing a lesser sentence, or canvassing the range of non custodial sentencing options provided by law. The taking into account of these considerations in respect of a mentally disordered offender is but a particular example of the general constitutional duty of a trial judge to impose a sentence

---

[32] *Tarasoff v University of California* (1976) 17 Cal. 3d. 425. See above, para.11–21.
[33] Thomas O'Malley, *Sentencing Law and Practice*, 2nd edn (Dublin: Thomson Round Hall, 2006), p.407.

that strikes a balance between the particular circumstances of the commission of the relevant offence and the relevant personal circumstances of the person accused."[35]

19–19 In *DPP v Moore (Paul)*,[36] an application by the DPP for a review of a sentence on the grounds of undue leniency, the respondent claimed that he had organic personality disorder which reduced his moral responsibility for the crime. The Court of Criminal Appeal engaged in a detailed analysis of the available medical evidence and ultimately increased the sentence from 6 years to 10 years, as it concluded that the respondent had not established the proposition for which he contended. The court operated on the assumption that, if the respondent had proven the proposition, then his sentence would be reduced as a result. It also stated that it had been agreed that the onus of establishing the matters said to constitute mitigation lay on the respondent.[37]

19–20 Geoghegan J. noted in *People (DPP) v Redmond*[38] that it had been suggested that, given that there was no defence of diminished responsibility at the time, the sentencing judge on the plea of guilty could not take into account diminished responsibility. He said that he would wholly reject this proposition. If, for instance, a person who suffered from a psychiatric condition of some kind but did not qualify to come within the McNaghten Rules was found guilty, it could not be the case that the sentencing judge could not take into account whatever lessening of responsibility there may have been. Geoghegan J. said that a sentencing judge can take into account any factor at all, whether physical or mental, which might tend reasonably to either mitigate or aggravate a sentence.[39]

19–21 At present, courts cannot order that a sentenced person receive treatment in a psychiatric centre, which contrasts with the availability of the Hospital Order in England and Wales. One possibility is to make psychiatric treatment a condition of probation, but this will only be appropriate in some cases.[40] In 1978, the Henchy committee was of the view that "[t]he inability or restricted ability of the courts to order that convicted persons receive appropriate treatment is a grave defect in the present state of the criminal law".[41] The White Paper of 1995 stated that the absence of legal powers for courts to organise a medical report or

[34] High Court (Central Criminal Court), Flood J., June 16, 1995.
[35] High Court (Central Criminal Court), Flood J., June 16, 1995, p.17.
[36] [2005] I.E.C.C.A. 141; Court of Criminal Appeal, December 20, 2005.
[37] [2005] I.E.C.C.A. 141, p.5.
[38] [2006] I.E.S.C. 25; [2006] 3 I.R. 188; [2006] 2 I.L.R.M. 182.
[39] [2006] 3 I.R. 188 at 206.
[40] Thomas O'Malley, *Sentencing Law and Practice*, 2nd edn (Dublin: Thomson Round Hall, 2006), pp.406–7.
[41] *Third Interim Report of the Interdepartmental Committee on Mentally Ill and Maladjusted Persons. Treatment and Care of Persons Suffering from Mental Disorder Who Appear Before the Courts on Criminal Charges* [Chair: Henchy J.] (Dublin, 1978).

arrange treatment at sentencing stage was a major gap. The White Paper recommended that a sentencing court should be able to refer a convicted person to a psychiatric hospital for assessment and/or treatment.[42] The former Inspector of Prisons, Kinlen J., later quoted Professor Kennedy as recommending that the law allow judges to obtain opinions and to organise a psychiatric disposal when it is obvious to everyone that is the right thing to do. Kinlen J. said that he would welcome the implementation of the proposals on this issue which had been made in the White Paper.[43]

19–22 The introduction of a Hospital Order would be an appropriate means of ensuring that the courts reach the suitable conclusion for the case which is before them. The current system ties the hands of judges and vests an improper degree of control in the executive, after sentence, to decide which persons require treatment and which do not.

AUTOMATISM (CRIMINAL)

19–23 The automatism defence is available where a person acted in an involuntary manner due to an external factor such as concussion, anaesthetic or hypnosis. If the person is found to have been in an automatous state at the time of the crime, they are acquitted.[44] The question of detention in a psychiatric centre does not arise, as automatism is not dealt with in the Criminal Law (Insanity) Act 2006. Automatism of this type, which leads to a full acquittal, is sometimes referred to as "sane automatism" to indicate that the person is not availing of the insanity defence. The distinction between sane and insane automatism was discussed earlier at paras 15–07 and 15–34.

In *R. v Quick*,[45] Mr Quick was a nurse charged with assaulting a patient. It was found that his insulin injections had caused hyperglycaemia (too little blood sugar) and that this was automatism, as it was caused by an external factor.

In *People (DPP) v Reilly*[46], Mr Reilly raised a defence of automatism, claiming that he was in an automatous state due to a sleep disorder. However, the defence did not succeed, mainly due to the effect of intoxication at the time of the act (see further para.15–34 above).

19–24 It may even be possible in some cases to argue that post-traumatic stress disorder brought about by an external factor is automatism rather than insanity.

---

[42] Department of Health, *A New Mental Health Act: White Paper* (Dublin: Stationery Office, 1995), para.7.37.

[43] *First Annual Report by the Inspector of Prisons for the Year 2002–2003*, p.77.

[44] See also, on automatism in civil matters, *O'Brien v Parker* [1997] 2 I.L.R.M. 170.

[45] [1973] Q.B. 910.

[46] [2005] 3 I.R. 111. See Michael Dillon, "Intoxicated Automatism is No Defence: Majewski is Law in Ireland" (2004) 14(3) Ir. Crim. L.J. 7.

In *R. v T.*,[47] Ms T. was charged with robbery and assault. She successfully claimed that she had post-traumatic stress disorder, as she had been raped three days previously. Southan J. classified this as automatism as it was not a "disease of the mind", being caused by the external factor of the rape.[48] This is also referred to as "psychological blow automatism".

PRISONERS AND MENTAL HEALTH

19–25 There are high rates of mental illness in prisoners. For example, the six-month prevalence of psychosis is 7.6 per cent of male prisoners on remand and 2.7 per cent of male sentenced prisoners.[49] In principle, these prisoners should be treated in a psychiatric centre rather than detained in prison. However, for resourcing reasons, and perhaps also because prisoners are regarded as "second class citizens", many prisoners are not transferred to psychiatric centres or, if they are, it is only for a short period. The law concerning transfers from prisons to psychiatric centres will be considered below at paras 19–31 to 19–38.

There have been various attempts by prisoners to bring legal actions challenging their lack of access to appropriate mental health care.[50]

19–26 In *State (C.) v Frawley*,[51] discussed above at para.12–09, Mr C. was serving sentences in Mountjoy Prison for breaking and entering and robbery with violence. There was psychiatric evidence that he had a personality trait disturbance of a sociopathic type. His condition manifested itself in an aggressive and continuous hostility to authority and to the features of society which represent authority. He had repeatedly climbed over the walls and on to the roofs of prisons and hospitals. He had also repeatedly swallowed metal objects such as bed springs and handles of spoons and had inserted wire and sharp objects into his body. He had been certified as insane on a number of occasions and had been transferred to the Central Mental Hospital (CMH), usually for short periods of a month or less. For most of the time he had been in prison he had been kept in solitary confinement. Whilst out of solitary confinement he was usually kept handcuffed for some period. Finlay P. said that

---

[47] [1990] Crim. L.R. 256.

[48] See generally the detailed analysis of the automatism defence in R.D. Mackay, *Mental Condition Defences in the Criminal Law* (Oxford: Clarendon Press, 1995), pp.36–72.

[49] S. Linehan et al, "Psychiatric Morbidity in a Cross-Sectional Sample of Male Remanded Prisoners (42% of Remanded Men in Irish Prisons)" (2005) 22 *Irish Journal of Psychological Medicine* 128; Dearbhla Duffy, Sally Linehan, Harry G Kennedy, "Psychiatric Morbidity in the Male Sentenced Irish Prisons Population' (2006) 23(2) *Irish Journal of Psychological Medicine* 54.

[50] See generally Liam Herrick, "Prisoners' Rights" in Ursula Kilkelly (ed.), *ECHR and Irish Law*, 2nd edn (Bristol: Jordan, 2009), Chapter 11; Claire Hamilton & Ursula Kilkelly, "Human Rights in Irish Prisons" (2008) 2 J.S.I.J. 58.

[51] [1976] I.R. 365.

when the Executive imprisons an individual in pursuance of a lawful warrant of a court, then it may not, without justification or necessity, expose the health of that person to risk or danger.[52] The restraints had been designed and implemented to eliminate or diminish the possibility of him harming himself by swallowing foreign bodies, by self injury or by injury arising from his climbing and escaping activities.[53] Finlay P. said that the question of whether the conditions of detention in this case constituted a failure to protect Mr C. from torture or inhuman or degrading treatment or punishment had caused him trouble, but he found that the conditions did not constitute such a failure.[54]

19–27 The European Court of Human Rights found a violation of art.3 in *Keenan v UK*.[55] The lack of effective monitoring of Mr Keenan's condition and the lack of informed psychiatric input into his assessment and treatment disclosed significant defects in the medical care provided to a mentally ill person known to be a suicide risk. The belated imposition on him in those circumstances of a serious disciplinary punishment which might well have threatened his physical and moral resistance, was not compatible with the standard of treatment required in respect of a mentally ill person. It constituted inhuman and degrading treatment and punishment within the meaning of art.3.[56]

19–28 The IPRT and two named prisoners have commenced an action seeking various declaratory reliefs upon the basis that the defendants have failed in their constitutional obligation to provide adequate psychiatric treatment and/or facilities and/or services for prisoners in Mountjoy Men's Prison and Mountjoy Women's Prison, and further a declaration that the treatment of the named prisoners in Mountjoy Prison was a breach of their constitutional rights. One of the prisoners was placed in a padded cell in Mountjoy Prison for two weeks pending the availability of a bed in the CMH. The other was detained in a cell for several days, naked and covered in his own excrement. Both claimed that they were not adequately monitored by psychiatric professionals and argued that such conditions were both unconstitutional and contrary to art.3 of the ECHR.[57]

The IPRT was found to have locus standi to bring the claim in 2005.[58] Gilligan J. took into account the nature of the IPRT and the extent of its interest in the issues raised and the remedies which it seeks to achieve and the nature of the relief as sought. He was satisfied that if he were to deny standing to the

---

[52] [1976] I.R. 365 at 372.
[53] [1976] I.R. 365 at 372.
[54] [1976] I.R. 365 at 374.
[55] (2001) 33 E.H.R.R. 38.
[56] (2001) 33 E.H.R.R. 38, para.115.
[57] Liam Herrick, "Prisoners' Rights" in Ursula Kilkelly (ed.), *ECHR and Irish Law*, 2nd edn (Bristol: Jordan, 2009), pp.346–7.
[58] *Irish Penal Reform Trust Ltd. and Ors. v Governor of Mountjoy Prison* [2005] I.E.H.C. 305; High Court, Gilligan J., 2 September 2005.

IPRT, those whose interests it represents might not have an effective way of bringing the issues that are involved in the proceedings before the court. It was unlikely that individual psychiatrically ill prisoners would be able to command the expertise which is at the disposal of the IPRT and in these circumstances, were the court to refuse the IPRT locus standi, it appeared unlikely that justice would be done between the parties.[59]

In a brief judgment in 2008, the Supreme Court decided that the question of locus standi could not, in the circumstances of the case, be wholly separated from the issues of the justiciability of all or at least some of the matters in issue and in turn from the merits of the claims, the nature and substance of which might affect any decision on either the question of locus standi or justiciability. The court did not consider that the issue of locus standi could properly be determined in isolation as a preliminary issue and therefore it set aside the order and judgment of the High Court. In doing so, the court expressed no view on these issues and it stated that it would be a matter for the High Court to give such directions as it sees fit concerning the case management of the matter.[60]

19–29 The Strasbourg Court has drawn important distinctions between detentions under art.5(1)(a) ("the lawful detention of persons after conviction by a competent court") and detentions under art.5(1)(e) (persons of unsound mind). For example, persons detained under art.5(1)(e) must be detained in an appropriate therapeutic environment, whereas this does not apply to those detained under art.5(1)(a).[61] Also, the European Court of Human Rights accepts that deprivation of liberty under art.5(1)(a) is by its nature punitive, while this is not the case with detentions under art.5(1)(e).

In *Aerts v Belgium*,[62] Mr Aerts had allegedly committed a serious assault and, as he had borderline personality disorder and was found not to be criminally responsible, was detained under social protection legislation. He was not convicted of the offence. He was detained in a prison and not given appropriate treatment. He successfully claimed that the conditions of his confinement breached art.5(1).

However, in *Bizzotto v Greece*[63] a conviction for drug trafficking was given to the applicant. He was given a six-year sentence with the condition that he be given treatment for his drug addiction. He was detained in prison and not given the appropriate treatment. When he claimed a breach of art.5(1), his action failed because the court held that art.5(1)(a) was the main ground of his detention and therefore it would not insist that he be given the treatment.

---

[59] *Irish Penal Reform Trust Ltd and Ors. v Governor of Mountjoy Prison* [2005] I.E.H.C. 305; High Court, Gilligan J., September 2, 2005, p.23.

[60] *Irish Penal Reform Trust Ltd v Governor of Mountjoy Prison*, Supreme Court, April 2, 2008.

[61] See Peter Bartlett, Oliver Lewis and Oliver Thorold, *Mental Disability and the European Convention on Human Rights* (Leiden: Martinus Nijhoff, 2006), pp.39–41.

[62] (1998) 29 E.H.R.R. 50.

[63] Application No.22126/93, Judgment 15 November 1996, Reports of Judgments and Decisions 1996–V, p.1738.

Bartlett et al have commented that the difference between the two cases appears to be a nuance by the respective domestic courts, and that rights under the ECHR may depend to a considerable degree on divergence in domestic practice. In their view, this "provides cause for concern".[64]

TEMPORARY RELEASE AND PATIENT TRANSFERS

Temporary Release

19–30 A clinical director of a designated centre may direct a patient's temporary release with the consent of the Minister for Justice, Equality and Law Reform.[65] A practical example of this is seen in the *J.B. v Mental Health (Criminal Law) Review Board* case, where the patient was on temporary release four nights a week.[66]

A patient is deemed to be unlawfully at large if the period of temporary release has expired or one of the conditions of the temporary release is broken.[67] A Garda shall arrest, or an officer or servant of the designated centre may arrest, a person suspected to be unlawfully at large.[68] Minister McDowell refused to accept an amendment removing the power of officers or servants of designated centres to arrest, stating that there might be circumstances in which it would be dangerous to say that someone who was in a position to act could not do so.[69] However, officers or servants "may" arrest while gardaí "shall" do so.[70]

Senator Henry commented that under s.27(2) of the Mental Health Act 2001, Gardaí were granted a specific power to enter dwellings or other premises in order to detain patients but no such power was being granted by the criminal insanity legislation. Minister Lenihan replied that such a power existed under common law in any event.[71]

Under the pre-2006 law, problems arose when an advisory committee, considering a case of a patient found guilty but insane, recommended that the patient be transferred from the CMH to an ordinary mental hospital. At the conclusion of the litigation, Geoghegan J. recommended that the Executive

---

[64] Peter Bartlett, Oliver Lewis and Oliver Thorold, *Mental Disability and the European Convention on Human Rights* (Leiden: Martinus Nijhoff, 2006), p.41.

[65] Criminal Law (Insanity) Act 2006, s.14(1). Section 14(2) states that the clinical director may also order transfer from one designated centre to another with the consent of both the Minister for Justice and the Minister for Health and Children. This provision is currently not relevant, as there is only one designated centre.

[66] [2008] I.E.H.C. 303; High Court, Hanna J., July 25, 2008. See above, paras 18–31 to 18–33.

[67] Criminal Law (Insanity) Act 2006, s.14(5).

[68] Criminal Law (Insanity) Act 2006, s.14(7).

[69] 176 *Seanad Debates* Col.399 (April 8, 2004).

[70] 180 *Seanad Debates* Col.48 (April 19, 2005).

[71] 180 *Seanad Debates* Col.49 (April 19, 2005).

sanction the patient's temporary release on conditions, including a condition that he be accepted in a mental hospital of the Southern Health Board.[72]

Transfers from Prison to the CMH

19–31 If a prisoner has a mental disorder which cannot be treated in prison, they can be transferred to the CMH,[73] either with or without their consent. The transfer is directed by the governor of the prison. If the prisoner consents to the transfer, then it need only be supported by one "relevant officer" (psychiatrist or other doctor).[74] If the prisoner does not consent, then two relevant officers must support the transfer.[75] Under the previous legislation, transfers were made by the Minister for Justice, Equality and Law Reform[76] but under the new Act the transfer is directed by the governor of the prison and the Minister's involvement is confined to a requirement that they be notified of each direction.[77] Presumably, governors will only direct a transfer of a prisoner if a place is available in a designated centre, which depends on adequate resourcing of designated centres by the Department of Health and Children.

Once the prisoner arrives in the centre, if they refuse to receive care or treatment there, they will continue to remain there, provided two doctors certify that they need to remain there.[78] As regards consent to treatment while in the designated centre, the provisions of Part 4 of the Mental Health Act 2001 will apply.[79]

19–32 The provisions on transfer of prisoners to the CMH did not appear in the original Bill, but were added during the Oireachtas debates. Minister Lenihan explained that the existing procedures were "Byzantine and confusing in their operation to say the least" and that they had been criticised by the European Committee for the Prevention of Torture.[80]

The CMH, the only existing designated centre, can currently only take 95 patients, only a portion of the places can be occupied by people transferred from prison and demand for places exceeds supply. Many prisoners with severe mental health conditions cannot access the services they require. The annual reports of the Inspector of Prisons and Places of Detention contain repeated criticisms of the lack of spaces in the CMH.[81]

---

[72] *O'Halloran v Minister for Justice* [1999] 4 I.R. 287.
[73] The Act refers to a designated centre. At present, the CMH is the only designated centre.
[74] Criminal Law (Insanity) Act 2006, s.15(1).
[75] Criminal Law (Insanity) Act 2006, s.15(2).
[76] See Darius Whelan, "Criminal Procedure and Mental Health", Ph.D. thesis, Trinity College Dublin, 2000, Chapter 5.
[77] Criminal Law (Insanity) Act 2006, s.15(3)(c).
[78] Criminal Law (Insanity) Act 2006, s.15(5).
[79] Criminal Law (Insanity) Act 2006, s.3(3).
[80] 180 *Seanad Debates* Cols 46–47 (April 19, 2005).
[81] See, for example, *Third Annual Report of the Inspector of Prisons and Places of Detention 2004–2005*, pp.18–24.

19–33 If a prisoner is transferred from a designated centre to a prison under s.15, the prison governor must inform the clinical director of the designated centre, as soon as practicable, of the date, if known, on which the prisoner will cease to be a prisoner.[82] Once the prisoner ceases to be a prisoner, nothing in the 2006 Act is to be construed as prohibiting their voluntary or involuntary admission to any place under the Mental Health Act 2001 or any other Act.[83]

19–34 While the governor of the prison notifies the clinical director of the designated centre of the date on which the prisoner will cease to be a prisoner, it is not explicitly stated either in s.16 or s.18 that the person must be discharged once they cease to be a prisoner. Senator Henry raised this concern, "While amendment No. 44 is also good, I have a slight concern. After a person had finished his or her sentence, perhaps having been in the Central Mental Hospital for some time, is the clinical director in the Central Mental Hospital or another designated centre required to send him or her back to prison or can the person be discharged? The Bill does not seem to make provision for such people to be discharged if they have finished their sentence. At that stage they are patients".[84] Minister Lenihan's response was as follows, "When the sentence expires the person is then free. There is no question of needing to be re-conveyed to a prison in some kind of formal act of delivery. The person is at liberty once his or her sentence has expired. Of course, the provisions of the 2001 Act can apply to a person in that position."[85]

19–35 Section 17 provides that the cases of all prisoners transferred to the CMH must be reviewed by the Mental Health (Criminal Law) Review Board at such intervals, not longer than six months, as it considers appropriate.

There are three categories of review:

1. Section 17(1) permits the Minister to direct a review where the Minister is satisfied that it is in the interests of justice to do so. This only applies to detentions under s.15(2) or s.15(5)(a) , i.e. cases where the prisoner did not consent to the transfer, or refused to receive care or treatment there for mental disorder.
2. Under s.17(3), the patient may apply for a review.
3. Section 17(4) permits the review board to initiate a review itself.

Periodic reviews must also be made of the cases of prisoners detained in the CMH before June 1, 2006.[86]

---

[82] Criminal Law (Insanity) Act 2006, s.16(1).
[83] Criminal Law (Insanity) Act 2006, s.16(2).
[84] 183 *Seanad Debates* Col.625 (April 6, 2006).
[85] 183 *Seanad Debates* Col.626 (April 6, 2006).
[86] Criminal Law (Insanity) Act 2006, s.17(5).

The board has the power either to make no order (which means that the patient remains in the CMH), order the prisoner to be transferred back to the original prison, or order the prisoner to be transferred to another prison which the Minister considers appropriate. If ordering transfer to prison, the board must consult the Minister before making its order.

19–36 If a prisoner has been transferred to the CMH under s.15, and the clinical director believes that they are no longer in need of in-patient care or treatment, the clinical director shall direct the prisoner's transfer back to prison.[87] The clinical director must consult with the Minister before making the direction, and may either direct that the prisoner be transferred back to the original prison or to another prison which the Minister considers appropriate. Minister McDowell stated that consultation with the Minister is required before a transfer back to a prison in order to ensure that the prison from which the prisoner was originally transferred is the most suitable location for them to be sent at the time of transfer. In other words, if the prisoner came from Mountjoy Prison, the Minister might say he should be sent to Loughan House as it was more suitable, or vice versa.[88] The review board does not consider cases under this section (s.18) and McGillicuddy has described this as "anomalous".[89]

19–37 While most of the old legislation on transfers of prisoners to mental hospitals has been repealed by the 2006 Act,[90] two of those sections still remain. Section 12 of the Lunatic Asylums (Ireland) Act 1875[91] deals with the situation where a person is confined in the CMH, has not been certified to be of sound mind, and their prison sentence has expired. The Minister can order that the person be removed to another psychiatric centre. Section 17(6) of the Criminal Justice Administration Act 1914 applies to prisoners in cases of "disease" which cannot be treated in prison or who require a surgical operation which cannot properly be performed in prison. In such cases, the Minister can order that the prisoner be taken to a hospital or other suitable place for the purpose of treatment or the operation. This power was widely used in the 1980s.[92]

---

[87] Criminal Law (Insanity) Act 2006, s.18(1).
[88] 616 *Dáil Debates* Col.2070 (March 23, 2006).
[89] Tony McGillicuddy, "The Criminal Law (Insanity) Bill 2002", document dated 2 April 2006 available on Bar Council website, at *http://www.lawlibrary.ie/documents/legal%20commentary/ insanity.doc* [last accessed October 21, 2009], p.14.
[90] See 2006 Act, s.25 and Sch.2.
[91] 38 & 39 Vict., c.67.
[92] Art O'Connor & Helen O'Neill, "Male Prison Transfers to the Central Mental Hospital, a Special Hospital, 1983–1988" (1990) 7 Ir. J. Psychol. Med. 118 and "Female Prison Transfers to the Central Mental Hospital, a Special Hospital, 1983–1988" (1991) 8 Ir. J. Psychol. Med. 122.

Other Transfers

19–38 The issue of transfers from approved centres to the CMH has been considered above at paras 7–66 to 7–69.

A patient may be removed from a designated centre to a hospital to receive medical attention, and the Minister for Justice must be informed within 48 hours.[93]

The Minister may also authorise the removal of a patient from a designated centre to a specified place "where he or she is satisfied that it is in the interests of justice to do so".[94]

---

[93] Criminal Law (Insanity) Act 2006, s.14(8).
[94] Criminal Law (Insanity) Act 2006, s.14(9).

INDEX